STOCHASTIC WATER RESOURCES TECHNOLOGY

Titles of related interest

B. Henderson-Sellers: *Reservoirs*
D. M. McDowell and B. A. O'Connor: *Hydraulic Behaviour of Estuaries*
E. M. Wilson: *Engineering Hydrology*, Second Edition

Stochastic Water Resources Technology

N. T. Kottegoda

Department of Civil Engineering
University of Birmingham

First published 1980 by
THE MACMILLAN PRESS LTD
London and Basingstoke
Associated companies in Delhi Dublin
Hong Kong Johannesburg Lagos Melbourne
New York Singapore and Tokyo

Printed in Hong Kong

British Library Cataloguing in Publication Data

Kottegoda, N T
  Stochastic water resources technology.
  1. Hydraulic engineering—Mathematical
models
  2. Stochastic processes
  I. Title
  627′.01′84   TC153

ISBN 0–333–22346–2

Contents

Preface

In preparing this book the aim has been to provide an understanding of the theory and application of mathematical and statistical methods in hydrology and water resources engineering. The past few decades have seen vast developments in time series analysis, stochastic processes, probabilistic methods, systems engineering and decision analysis. New techniques have been developed and propounded in books and an increasing number of journals in the pure and applied sciences, but the complexity of the subject matter has encouraged authors to adopt styles which do not aid assimilation by the majority of potential users.

At the present time, there is a necessity for improved techniques to tackle the uncertainties and random effects which pervade water resources design and planning. Hitherto, restrictive assumptions and the problems of model choice have hampered progress in the application of classical statistical methods. The bayesian approach also has shortcomings, some of which are discussed herein. Knowledge about the mechanics of atmospheric processes, oceanic temperatures and other factors influencing climate is often inadequate. The same may be said about the land phase of the hydrological cycle. The practitioner cannot wait until mathematicians, climatologists and physicists solve the problems of engineering relevance, for the need to plan and implement schemes to meet the requirements of expanding populations requires that existing theories and mathematical methods are utilised and that their assumptions and limitations are appreciated. This book is designed to bridge the gulf that exists between the academic and the technologist and serves to introduce some useful techniques that may aid the design of water resources systems.

It is thought that the treatment will be valuable to advanced students and practising engineers. Prior requirements are an understanding of basic statistical theory and methods, and a background of elementary calculus and matrix algebra. Researchers, in particular, should benefit from the comprehensive reviews given here. It is hoped that the wide range of subjects taken up, the numerous citations and the extensive bibliography will make this a useful source of reference. It should also appeal to statisticians interested in practical applications.

Appreciation must be expressed here for the many who, by their encouragement, constructive criticisms and advice, have helped in the preparation of this book. T. A. Buishand, R. L. Holder and A. J. Lawrance read the original manuscript, or most of it, and offered numerous suggestions. Valuable assistance and comments were provided on the entire text by A. Anastassiou, I. D. Cluckie and J. Elgy; some ideas of A. Anastassiou have enhanced the introduction to chapter 8. Climatological sections were reviewed by E. T. Stringer and J. Williams. V. Yevjevich sent comprehensive appraisals on three of the chapters and J. Kelman was also particularly helpful. Parts of the contents were discussed with B. B. Mandelbrot and R. G. Quimpo. J. B. White gave his views on the engineering aspects of chapter 7, and N. J. Kavanagh considered chapters 8 and 9 from an economist's viewpoint. The author accepts full responsibility for any omissions, shortcomings or mistakes that may remain.

Serious notice has been taken of the opinions of graduate students; in recent years they have had to cope with original sections of the text in the form of lecture notes. Gratitude is also extended to several others who contributed in different ways. Special mention must be made of Sue Raybone who undertook nearly all of the typing. Thanks are due to those who provided the data. The author is indebted to the original writers who have inspired him. The greatest debt is owed to his family without whose patience and tolerance this book could not have been completed.

Birmingham, 1980   N. T. K.

1 Introduction and climate

Water is one of man's basic and precious resources. It is the first requirement for the survival of all forms of life, but, unlike oil, coal and other natural resources, water is renewable. Besides serving personal needs, it plays a vital role in agriculture, industry, navigation and the production of energy. The management and conservation of water is therefore essential in order to maximise social benefits, within various technological, economic, environmental and other constraints.

The twentieth century has seen a significant uptrend in demand for water throughout the world. This sharp increase in man's unquenchable thirst is partly due to the phenomenal growth in civilisation.

For domestic consumption alone several hundred litres per day are required, *per capita*, in western countries; in New York city, for instance, this rate is in excess of 1000 litres per head per day. In the poorer nations, on the other hand, the general lack of amenities has meant much lower averages; this may be about 10 litres per head per day or even less, and close to survival rates, in parts of Africa. However, as current development programmes continue and as living standards are raised, these consumption rates will inevitably rise.

More than 75 % of water utilised goes to satisfy agriculture; without irrigation the total food production in the world would be reduced by about a third. In fact, many of the great civilisations of the past arose in some of the largest river basins of the Earth when people mastered the art of using river water. The life-giving waters of the Nile, the rivers of Mesopotamia, the historic irrigation system of the Indus and China's Yellow River are notable examples; ancient Sri Lanka was replete with irrigation schemes some 2000 years ago. As climates become drier, some civilisations declined. This important subject of climate will be dealt with separately in the following sections.

In present times the world's population has been doubling over periods of decades in contrast with the slow growth over earlier centuries. According to the 1976 figures it is estimated that there are some 4000 million inhabitants; by the end of this century, forecasters are speaking of a total population of around 7000 million, in spite of the current decrease in growth rates in some populous nations. It follows inevitably that there will be increasing needs for more extensive water supply systems to meet agricultural, domestic and industrial demands; for instance, India needs to double its irrigation facilities by the year 2000 to avoid mass starvation by its population, currently estimated at over 600 million.

Unfortunately, only a minute proportion of available water could, in its existing condition or location, serve mankind. This is primarily because about 97.2 % of the estimated 326 million cubic miles of water on this planet are contained in the oceans. Of the remainder, polar ice caps and glaciers take up another 2.15 %. The rest consists of ground water including soil moisture, surface water in lakes and rivers and a part that lies in the atmosphere, the ground water being largely in excess of the others[1].

It is not, therefore, a lack of water on Earth that causes droughts and hardships. The main problem is that water is not often found when and where it is needed, and also it may not be of a good quality. Moreover, requirements vary; types of demand, rates and standards differ from the advanced to the developing countries and according to geographic situations. All of this highlights the importance of careful planning of water resources systems so that the greatest benefit can be obtained.

1.1 Hydrological uncertainties

This book is an introduction to the mathematical and statistical treatment of hydrology and water resource systems. It deals throughout with surface flow aspects. River flow is treated here as a random process; the appropriate word for this is stochastic, as will be explained in chapter 2. The justification is that river flow is a function of precipitation and other processes which, at the present level of knowledge, seem to evolve randomly in time and space. Even if the underlying phenomena and their interactions were thoroughly understood, it would not be possible to describe mathematically the rate of discharge in a natural water course without involving unsystematic or unknown effects. A brief examination of the processes in hydrology will validate this argument and will bring out the limitations of pure cause–effect types of relationships.

Firstly, the flow in a river at a particular time and place is principally caused by rainfall over an antecedent period. The functional relationship between the two variables is dependent on the physiographical characteristics of the river basin as well as on the temporal and spatial distribution of the contributory rainfall. In addition, there are numerous other factors. Catchment retention, diurnally and seasonally varying evaporation losses, transpiration from plants and infiltration which depends on soil characteristics, vegetation and ante-cedent rainfall are important constituents in any rainfall equation. River flows are also supplemented to varying extents by ground water that fluctuates

---

[1] See Leopold and Davis (1972) and van der Leeden (1975).

sporadically; lake overflows and the melting of snow may also contribute. Furthermore, the conveyance properties of water courses are affected by natural erosion and siltation. Again, it may be necessary to take account of changes in land use and vegetation, water resource developments and other forms of intervention. All these factors in combination make river flow a highly complex process within the hydrological cycle.

Any attempt to measure or estimate the variables involved will introduce errors which are themselves random. A common example of how erroneous deductions arise is the engineer's rating curve. This purports to relate, in a fully deterministic sense, the level in a river to its rate of flow; however, random effects such as changes in channel configuration, sediment movement and weed growth cause inaccuracies which may be severe, particularly after heavy floods. Again, the T-hour, say, unit hydrograph is taken to be a unique time graph of direct run-off at a particular river site due to unit input of effective rainfall, uniformly distributed in time and area over the entire river catchment above the site. However, in application it is found that, because of wide variations in antecedent rainfall, temperatures, surface roughness, presence of snow and so on, the unit graph itself seems to vary randomly from one storm to the next on the time scales of practical significance. Likewise a description of the configuration of ground-water aquifers is incomplete without considering the random processes involved. Here, for analytical purposes, flow and storage characteristics are assumed to be fixed spatially and temporally, whereas experience shows that the common assumptions pertaining to ground-water flows are generally unrealistic.

Indeed, the real world defies exact description. The best that can be achieved in solving the problem is an abstract picture through a so-called mathematical model. Furthermore, all the foregoing facts justify the pursuance of time series methods and the probabilistic notions that will be introduced in the following chapters. At the same time, processes need to be identified and modelled as far as practicable. This involves the scrutiny of inputs and outputs to a system. Depending on the problem, certain factors provide the basic framework and the potential or deterministic elements, whereas other factors provide the fluctuating or random elements.

Mathematical model building is obviously of little avail without taking into account the empirical evidence. It is not only the measured observations that are relevant but also the numerous technological, sociological, legal and economic factors and constraints. This multiobjective methodology then is the general systems approach[2]. It should play a major role in the development of modern water resources technology.

The above discussion of the nature of hydrological processes is incomplete

---

[2] Klir (1969) and Iserman (1975) give the systems theoretic background of phenomena identification; Yevjevich (1974) stresses the indeterminate aspects of hydrological processes.

without considering the important role of climate. The fact that climate has undergone changes and will continue to do so is, of course, indisputable; indeed, substantial differences occur over periods of decades, centuries and so on. The subject is none the less highly controversial. Arguments are mainly about the causes and significance of climatic variations over different time scales. At present some climatologists are speculating about climate in future periods of, say, 50 or 100 years; in the planning and management of water supply systems such periods are regarded as the economic horizons.

With regard to the impact of climate on future river flows, abstraction rates and the occurrences of floods, droughts and associated water shortages, there is great uncertainty. There is some repetitiveness in climatic patterns. For instance, the prolonged drought in the Sahel region of central Africa (on the southern periphery of the Sahara) during this decade has caused widespread starvation and deaths; however, as shown in figure 1.1, there have been similar spells in the past. It should be borne in mind that a drought is a subjective concept for which there is no common definition; they do, however, tend to cause greater hardships now than in historical times.

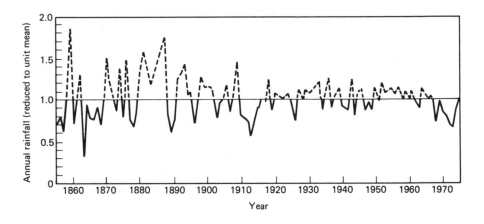

Figure 1.1   Mean annual rainfall in the Sahel region of central Africa: broken lines represent mean flows

Recent dry periods in the eastern United States, western Europe and Russia and delays in India's monsoons, have had severe economic consequences. Nevertheless, there are many who share the opinion that climatic variations will not necessitate radically different plans for the future[3]. The period 1931 to

---

[3] Matalas and Fiering (1977) discuss the need for robustness and resilience in planning and design; Bryson and Murray (1977) refer to the relationship between food production and climate.

1960 which forms part of many historical hydrometeorological records is said to have been an abnormal 30-year period over the past ten centuries[4]. In fact, the first half of the twentieth century is often referred to as a climatic optimum, and the unusual run of wet years therein is exemplified by figure 1.2; the

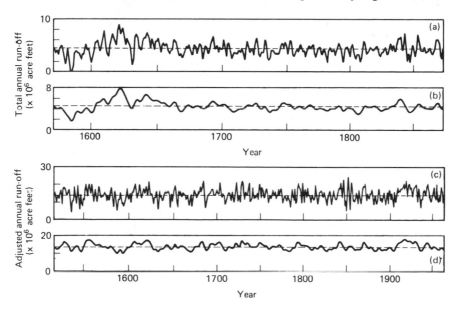

Figure 1.2 Hydrographs of annual flows reconstructed from tree ring data from information is given Smirnov (1969): (a) Green River at Green River, Utah, U.S.A., unfiltered; (b) Green River at Green River, Utah, U.S.A., filtered; (c) Colorado River at Lee Ferry, Arizona, U.S.A., unfiltered; (d) Colorado River at Lee Ferry, Arizona, U.S.A., filtered. (From Stockton (1977), by courtesy of the author)

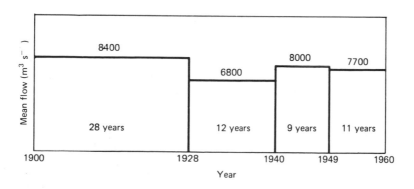

Figure 1.3 Changes in mean flow in the Volga at Volgograd, U.S.S.R.

[4] See Mason (1976, p. 478).

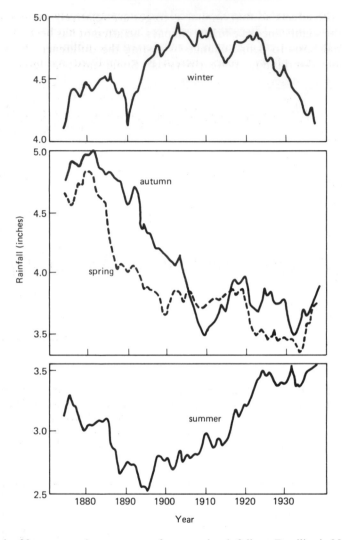

Figure 1.4 30-year moving average of seasonal rainfall at Deniliqui, New South Wales, Australia. (From Kraus (1954), by courtesy of the Royal Meteorological Society)

advancement of the Sahara and other deserts is perhaps a sign of the resumption of slow cooling since the 1960s. Climatic fluctuations in other parts of the world are also on record[5]. An example is given by the changes in the mean flow of the Volga in figure 1.3, which have been attributed to different atmospheric systems arising in the North Atlantic. However, there are cases such as that shown in figure 1.4 in which oscillations in seasonal rainfalls may

[5] Morris and Ratcliff (1976) speculate that Europe's drought in the mid-1970s has a recurrence interval of 250 years.

have opposite effects so that annual averages are relatively unaltered. With regard to the significance of climatic changes, an attempt has been made on an international basis to define change by testing the differences between the means of non-overlapping 10-year periods[6]. Some statistical tests suited for this purpose are described in the literature[7].

These examples emphasise the relevance of climate to the planning and management of water resources. It will be informative and beneficial, therefore, to take a closer look at the subject. Alternatively, readers solely interested in methodologies may proceed to subsection 1.2.4.

1.2 Climate and climatic change

According to Greek mythology, drastic changes in weather were the acts of the gods. For example, Homer writes in the Odyssey of Poseidon who in his fury produced storms against Odysseus. In more recent times, advances in astronomy might have been inhibited for other reasons, even because of charges of heresy; for instance, it is said that the Italian Bruno was burned alive about 400 years ago, because he postulated that the Earth goes round the Sun, contrary to what was then believed.

Modern forecasting technology and scientific reasoning have fortunately outstripped ancient cultural habits and the traditional sign-reading methods of sailors and farmers. It has long been established in meteorology that weather is primarily caused by radiation from the Sun and by the Earth's rotation. There is unequal heating of the Earth from the tropical regions with their vast forests and deserts to the polar regions and between land and oceanic surfaces. This gives rise to a global system of high- and low-pressure zones. Consequently atmospheric circulatory systems are produced. These are largely influenced by the rotation of the Earth on an axis that is inclined relative to the ecliptic plane and by the presence of mountainous areas.

Such complexities notwithstanding, sophisticated instruments and satellites coupled with advanced knowledge have brought short-term forecasting, over a few days (rather than over weeks or months), almost to within the realms of credibility[8]. There is success here because these forecasts generally deal with systems already in existence; even better results would be obtained if adequate world-wide data were available, particularly from oceanic surfaces in the southern hemisphere and if, in addition, all the physical factors were incorporated. Short-term weather forecasting is based quite considerably on the numerical integration of the Navier–Stokes and thermodynamic equations involving transfers of energy together with hypothetical sources and sinks. Over longer periods, on the other hand, forecasts are based on unborn systems,

[6] The idea is found in the work of Curry (1962, p. 22).
[7] The Welch or Fisher–Behrens test, as given by Kendall and Stuart (1973, pp. 153–7) may be applied here.
[8] See Namias (1965).

and therefore failure rates are high. It tends to become a statistical operation where even a gambler's intuition could be as fruitful as a climatologist's deduction. Man's knowledge of how the weather system works is incomplete, and for this reason long-term forecasts are subject to serious errors.

1.2.1 Climatic fluctuations

The totality or time average of meteorological conditions over a particular place or region is termed climate. By this definition, climate is not as unpredictable as the weather; nevertheless, it pulsates globally and locally in a highly complicated manner. Over the past million years or so climate is known to have had many types of fluctuations, and the ice ages are symptomatic of the longest of them. During these periods of deep freezing which seem to recur every 10^5 years on average, the polar ice caps advanced in the northern hemisphere up to latitudes close to those of New York and London. Such increases in the ice cover result in a higher albedo, which means the reflection of more heat from the Earth. At the same time atmospheric pressure systems are influenced by changes in the zigzagging circumpolar winds called the polar jetstream. This flows from west to east and is known locally as the westerlies; they vary continuously in strength and direction. Shifts in the position of the jetstream and changes in the number of its loops effect precipitation from the Sahara to the Middle East, India and America, bringing about at the same time changes in continental climate. (Incidentally, it is of topical interest to note that these effects have been evidenced even in the 1970s, and a major upheaval is not a prerequisite.) In between, over periods of about 1000 years or so, the world experiences 'minor ice ages' (such as that which prevailed a few centuries ago) which lead to secondary upheavals in global climate.

There are, in addition, oscillations of shorter duration. For instance, it is thought that complete reversals occur over periods of about 200 years[9]. Again, going back to the last century, the Austrian geographer E. Bruckner postulated after gathering all observational evidence up to 1885 (such as glacial records, temperature and rainfall readings and levels of lakes and rivers) that there is a cycle of 35 years; the credibility of this has, however, greatly diminished since then. Amongst many other such quasiperiodicities are the much-publicised sunspot rhythm which will be taken up later and the biennial atmospheric pulse[10]. Even the most significant of them tend to appear as mere humps in the variance spectrum[11]. It is useful none the less to examine the causes of climatic variations and their significance.

[9] This belief is held by Lamb (1972, 1977).
[10] See Landsberg et al. (1963) for evidence of the 2-year pulse; Joseph's 'seven years of feast and seven years of famine' in the book of Genesis, which is supposedly an allusion to a 14-year fluctuation in the Nile flows, is another example.
[11] The intricacies of the variance spectrum will be explained in chapter 2.

1.2.2   *Main causes of climatic change*

One particular line of thought in climatology is to attribute the long rhythmic changes of the past to gravitational effects of the Sun, the Moon and the other planets. Some of these cosmic geophysical effects have been investigated in Soviet research which has been prolific since the 1950s; the effects on the flows in the Volga and other rivers have also been described[12]. A pioneering advocate of such theories was the Yugoslav geophysicist Milankovitch (1930) who theorised that the ice age advances and retreat pulsations, which recur at intervals of around 100 000 years, are caused by variations in the ellipticity of the Earth's orbit around the Sun. In addition it was suggested, as shown in figure 1.5, that the tilted axis of rotation of the Earth rolls and wobbles over

[12] See Smirnov (1969).

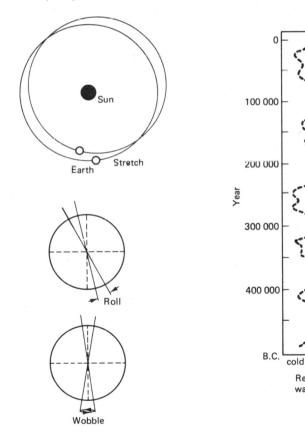

Figure 1.5   Milankovitch theory of prehistorical climatic fluctuations which are caused by the stretching, rolling and wobbling of the Earth's axis and have periods of approximately 100 000 years, 40 000 years and 20 000 years respectively. Net effects are shown on the right. Opposing theories deal with changes in solar energy and with planetary alignments

periods of 40 000 and 21 000 years respectively. Such astronomical gyrations will affect the amounts of radiation received on various parts of the Earth and can hence lead to profound shifts in terrestrial climate. On the other hand, according to some climatologists, the ice ages are due to long-term changes of solar energy. Also with reference to such long-term glaciations, the processes of mountain building, termed orogenesis, and the Köppen–Wegener theory of continential drift may be important factors. Furthermore, reversals in the Earth's magnetic field of which there is further evidence is perhaps relevant in this context[13].

In contrast with the ice ages and the like, climatic fluctuations over epochs such as decades and centuries are obviously of greater significance to the hydrologist. A well-known example of these is that associated with sunspots. In the Sun, which is in effect a detonating hydrogen bomb initiated about 2×10^9 years ago, the nucleii of hydrogen atoms, which have lost their electrons through high temperatures of up to $10^7 °C$, fuse to form helium, and hence large amounts of energy are released. The spots on the Sun which recur at intervals of about 11 years are thought to be accompanied by the eruption of flares of very hot gases. These can cause changes in atmospheric circulation, on the one hand, and could lead to increased ionisation and could hence produce additional nucleii for raindrops, on the other hand. It has also been theorised that tides are produced on the Sun and that the heights of these depend on the relative alignment of the planets, the influential planets being Venus, the Earth, Jupiter and Mars. However, the apparent relationship between such alignments and sunspots has been contradicted by others[14].

It has often been suggested, without firm evidence though, that subtle variations in solar energy are the root cause of climatic change; symptomatic sunspot effects are only part of these[15]. An associated causative factor is the areal change in polar ice caps which effects the Earth's albedo, as already mentioned. The absorptivities of different types of rock, soil and surface cover, as well as the reflectivities, are also highly significant; radiation of absorbed solar energy is a very important component of heat balance at all stages. Perhaps the greatest influence on future weather is thought to be exerted by temperatures and convection currents in the oceans, which act as gigantic reservoirs of heat; attempts have been made, for instance, to link the dates of the start of India's monsoons with conditions in the Indian Ocean and elsewhere. Of greater local interest are the intricate relationships between the processes of atmospheric circulation and climate. Unfortunately, knowledge about this is as yet rather limited.

Another important point about the atmosphere is that, while permitting at

[13] King (1974) has associated these magnetic field reversals with climatic changes. See Munk and MacDonald (1960) about the wobble of the Earth.
[14] Arguments for and against are given by Wood (1972) and Gribbin (1976, p. 47) respectively. As a separate issue, Berry (1974, pp. 169–86) prophesies interestingly on the future of man and the Universe.
[15] See Hughes (1977). Both the quantity and quality of radiation can vary.

least 80 % of solar radiation to pass through during the day, it traps up to 90 % of the Earth's radiation at night[16]. This is known as the greenhouse effect. It is in fact the atmospheric water vapour which, together with carbon dioxide and ozone, trap the terrestrial radiation; indeed, if there are no clouds, then almost all of the Earth's radiation at night is lost to space. On the other hand, water vapour can reflect part of the Sun's radiation. In addition, dust particles which are mainly due to volcanic eruptions float around the stratosphere; this could possibly make the Earth cooler: a reverse greenhouse effect. Variations in all these constituents can cause climatic change. Man's activities such as the release of carbon dioxide, which warms the air and is mainly caused by the burning of fossil fuels, and dust particles could also change atmospheric conditions and the absorption or reflection of radiation; some climatologists think that such effects may become quite substantial by the year 2000. Here, we must also take into account agricultural developments, deforestation, urbanisation and the overgrazing of pasture lands[17]. Moreover, there are other factors which may be far reaching such as the planned diversion of the Siberian rivers.

All of the foregoing discussion makes climate a highly complicated phenomenon. Furthermore, it is noted that changes in some parts of the world often have a different effect elsewhere; for instance, floods in some countries can be associated with droughts elsewhere. These may occur simultaneously or as delayed actions. Besides, the longer a fluctuation lasts, the more widespread is its impact. In summary, the variability of climate in space and time and the long-lasting influence of some of the causative factors must be borne in mind.

1.2.3 Records of climate

Ingenious methods of measuring climatic changes have been devised. For instance, records of climate extending back by about 110 000 years have been established during the past decade by scientists from Copenhagen University through the Greenland Ice Sheet Program[18]. The ice cap which is 2 miles deep here consists of layers of annual snowfalls that are naturally compressed and frozen; a 4-inch sample core about 4500 feet in length drilled into it has revealed temperature changes from prehistoric times, when analysed through a mass spectrometer. The procedure is to measure the proportion of rare oxygen atoms (oxygen 18) by probing small pieces of core. It is reasoned that the snow in Greenland is due to water evaporated from the Atlantic, and deductions of climatic change are based on the fact that, during colder epochs, molecules containing this heavier type of oxygen have little chance of travelling far north. On the contrary, those consisting of the common type (oxygen 16), which contain two fewer neutrons in each nucleus, have a faster rate of evaporation and remain much longer in the form of vapour. Figure 1.6 shows part of a

---

[16] See Lamb (1972).
[17] See Landsberg (1970).
[18] See Dansgaard et al. (1975).

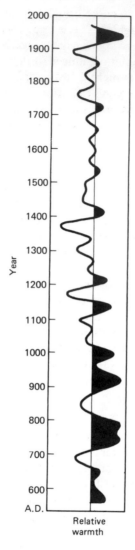

Figure 1.6 Graph of year against warmth at Crete, central Greenland: horizontal axis represents increments of oxygen 18 values; dark areas denote relatively warm periods. (From Dansgaard *et al.* (1975), by courtesy of W. Dansgaard)

historical temperature record established on this basis. A similar procedure is adopted when examining deep ocean cores. Samples taken from beneath the Carribbean, for example, have been used to estimate the lengths of cold spells over the past 100 000 years.

Sediments from old lake beds from Sweden and elsewhere provide another guide to climatic changes over thousands of years. The most valuable of these are the annually deposited layers called varves; the thicker ones are indicative of heavy rains or of rapid thaws accompanied by high temperatures. In this way an index of annual precipitation is formed, based on the relative thicknesses of the sediment layers[19].

Biological data too can be useful guides to prehistorical climate. The remains of plants and the bones of animals at unexpected latitudes are examples of these. In the same way, pollen deposited in sediments show the types of plant which had grown in a particular area. Again, the annual dates of the start of the wine harvests, in France and elsewhere, provide clues to the average weather conditions in historical times. Other indications of climatic change are found in the dates when Japanese cherry trees blossomed in the past.

Evidence of historical changes in climate that are of greater practical usefulness is found through tree ring dating[20]. This has been mainly based on trees from forests of pine, such as the giant *Sequoia* trees which have lived for centuries on the mountains of California and on the northern plateau of Arizona. The rate of growth of these trees is highly dependent on precipitation and is restricted during the winter because of a thick snow cover. In such cases, changes in the annual growth rings of trees are related to precipitation, provided that ground permeabilities are high and annual amounts of rainfall are not excessive so that water logging does not occur. Some tree ring records have been extended by more than 5000 years by using the wood from dead trees, but there are drawbacks on account of prolonged droughts or the presence of two separate rainy seasons in a year. The process of ageing itself may complicate the relationships. Another point is that growth may also be dependent on temperature and other climatic factors. For this reason European trees, with a few exceptions such as the spruce firs in northern Finland, are unsuitable as indicators of climatic change. Elsewhere, it is desirable for the information from tree rings to be averaged over a region and to be used in conjunction with data from other sources. Where precipitation is the predominant factor affecting growth, tree ring data have been used to extend annual flow records backwards, as shown in figure 1.2.

An indication of variations in solar energy dating back to at least about 5000 B.C. is again found in radio carbon data. This is based on the fact that, when carbon dioxide is absorbed by trees, a small proportion of the radioactive isotope of carbon, carbon 14, is retained; also, it is known that during cold epochs the production of radio carbon is intensified. Research in this area suggests that there is evidence of cold periods around 1000 B.C. and 3300 B.C. which are similar to the little ice age which affected Europe from the sixteenth to the eighteenth centuries[21]. The overall time scale provided by radio carbon dating is said to be most reliable for periods of about 20 000 years.

[19] Of similar interest are the siltation phases of the Nile which have lasted perhaps 10 000 years and longer; see also Vita-Finzi (1973, p. 85).
[20] See Fritts (1976) and Stockton (1977). Huntington (1914) was a pioneer.
[21] During the latter period the Thames froze several times and a frost fair is said to have been held on the frozen river in London for nearly 3 continuous months.

The phenomenon which seemed to have received most attention from researchers is sunspots, the possible causes of which were mentioned earlier. Although the ancient Greeks were aware of them, sunspots were first seen through a telescope by Galileo. Then in 1848 an index of sunspot relative numbers was formed by Rudolf Wolf, the Swiss astronomer. Figure 1.7 shows the annual means of these numbers. Sunspot activities vary in an approximately cyclic manner; the periods range from 13 years to 8 years with a mean of 11.1 years during the past four centuries of recorded observation[22].

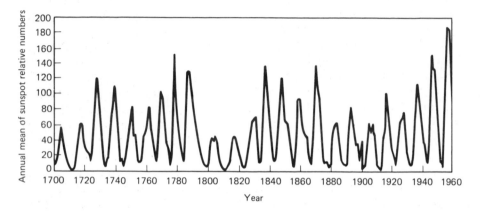

Figure 1.7   Annual means of sunspot relative numbers

Among the few apparently meaningful correlations with sunspot numbers are the levels in Lake Victoria and in other east African lakes (as, for example, in the work of Dixey (1964) and of Lamb (1972)) during the period 1893 to 1927 but not thereafter. Elsewhere, Smirnov (1969) found a correlation between sunspots and the mean flows in the Volga; also Indian scientists in Poona have recently correlated changes in the monsoons with sunspot activity. On the contrary, Rodríguez and Yevjevich (1967) investigated the relationships of 88 series of monthly precipitation, 174 series of annual precipitation in western U.S.A. and 16 series of annual run-off from several parts of the world with sunspot numbers, and they could not find any significant correlations. This generally confirms the views expressed several decades previously by Yule (1927) and by Walker (1936) after attempting to relate meteorological phenomena to sunspots. It seems reasonable to assume here that random influences on the hydrological cycle outweigh any deterministic effects due to the sunspot phenomenon. Also, it should be noted that possible changes in solar energy could take a variety of other forms.

[22] See Waldmeir (1961, 1968).

1.2.4 *Climate and water resource planning*

This extended commentary on climate will enable us to visualise the different types of fluctuations in their correct perspective[23]. It is emphasised here that climate is dependent on a highly complicated interplay between the effects of the atmosphere with its constituents, oceanic temperatures, polar ice caps, reflectivity and absorptivity, all of which are sensitive to even slight changes in solar radiation. The combination of these factors has not led to any deterministic patterns in the climatic history of the past few centuries (as borne out by modern methods of research using available records) which can be used for predictive purposes; from the statistical viewpoint, Gani (1975) has warned about reaching conclusions from scanty data and visual comparisons. The main task, of course, is to find practical solutions to the associated problems in water resources planning.

The point of view taken here is that the type of variations likely to occur over planning horizons does not warrant specific models of climatic change. Uncertainties in forecasts of populations and water demands could outweigh those of climate. The aim is therefore to accommodate the effects of climate within the specification of the time series models to be introduced in the following chapters.

Climatic variation can be viewed as a random process, though some climatologists would think the idea rather naive[24]. For instance, solar energy as filtered by the atmosphere and clouds might be thought of as a random phenomenon. So too may be the Earth's albedo and absorptivity, oceanic currents, atmospheric systems, humidity and other fluctuations. The concept of random processes cannot, of course, completely explain all these and precipitation. Indeed, the use of such techniques (for tackling the uncertainties) constitute only one approach to the problem. However, with the current state of knowledge, this seems to be the most feasible solution.

1.3 Scope of book

By way of initiating the procedure suggested above, we can do no better than to study the history of movement in time of the variables involved. This methodology is called time series analysis and is the subject of the next chapter. Prerequisites for application are observed data sequences. The analysis proceeds with the various components of a time series. This involves diagnostic tools such as the correlogram and the spectrum; after this we discuss the properties of multiple time series.

[23] For further reading, the National Academy of Sciences (1975) and the World Meteorological Organisation (1966) are recommended. Basic explanations of weather and climate are provided by Calder (1974).
[24] Curry (1962) relates climatic effects to random variations in energy and heat storages. Lorenz (1970) deals with mathematical models in general.

Now the random component in a time series, which represents the characteristics that are purely probabilistic, needs special attention. Chapter 3 deals with the distributions of random variables which are of practical importance in hydrology. The Pearson family and numerous other types are described here and in the complementary sixth chapter. Methods of estimation, goodness-of-fit tests and procedures for generating random variates are given.

Various methods of modelling time series constitute the next chapter. Basically, these concern linear models of the Box–Jenkins type and multisite models, including their choice and estimation of parameters. Data generated through these models are used for simulating complex water resource systems. Another important purpose is short-term forecasting as described at the end of this chapter; an example of this is Kalman filtering.

Chapter 5 concerns properties that are of practical significance in hydrology, whereas the preceding three chapters generally pertain to classical methods which are also used in other disciplines. Runs, range and reservoir storage problems are discussed here. Also included are special models such as the fractional gaussian noise types that are devised to maintain postulated long-term effects.

Extremely high flows, known as floods, deserve special attention mainly because of their importance in the design of civil engineering structures such as dams and bridges. Flood events too lend themselves to statistical treatment on account of the aforementioned random influences which control their magnitudes, times of occurrence and other properties. Extreme value distributions, lognormal and certain discrete types are described in chapter 6. The underlying assumptions are given and their limitations are pointed out. This includes the annual maximum and partial duration series; also, the probable maximum precipitation method, which engineers find refuge in when designing spillways of large dams, is outlined.

In retrospect, the simulation methods described in chapters 3 and 4 play an important role in the design and planning of water resource systems. However, in the case of a single reservoir, a more direct approach can be adopted, under certain conditions. The basis for this is Moran's theory of reservoirs which is the subject of chapter 7. This also includes the Gould method for dealing with reservoir failures over shorter time intervals and procedures for dealing with sequential dependence and seasonality in inflow data.

The last two chapters deal with operational and decision problems, as well as those of design and planning in water resources engineering. Chapter 8 begins with an introduction to the systems approach. A major part of this chapter is on linear and dynamic programming and on how these can be applied to reservoir design and other problems. The emphasis therein is on probabilistic methods. Applications of decision theory are taken up in the final chapter. The aim here is to guide the practitioner in some of the situations in which terminal decisions need to be taken. Elementary bayesian theory and other methods are explained; several practical examples are given.

To conclude, the structure of the book as outlined above is shown in figure

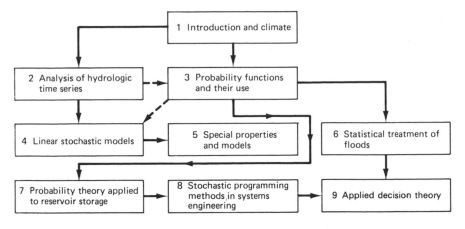

Figure 1.8   Structure of book and suggested lines for reading; the numbers given are the chapter numbers

1.8. Also given in the figure are suggested lines for study, research and application, depending on the objectives and main interests of the reader.

References

Berry, A. (1974). *The Next Ten Thousand Years*, Jonathan Cape, London

Bryson, R. A., and Murray, T. J. (1977). *Climates of Hunger: Mankind and the World's Changing Weather*, University of Wisconsin Press, Wisconsin

Calder, N. (1974). *The Weather Machine and the Threat of Ice*, British Broadcasting Corporation, London

Curry, L. (1962). Climatic change as a random series. *Ann. Assoc. Am. Geophys.*, **52**, 21–31

Dansgaard, W., Johnsen, S. J., Reeh, N., Gundestrup, N., Clausen, H. B., and Hammer, C. U. (1975). Climatic changes, Norsemen and modern man. *Nature (London)*, **255**, 24–8

Dixey, F. (1964). Cyclic phenomena in hydrology and solar activity. *J. Hydrol.*, **2**, 15–18

Fritts, H. C. (1976). *Tree Rings and Climate*, Academic Press, London

Gani, J. (1975). The use of statistics in climatological research. *Search*, **6**, 504–8

Gribbin, J. (1976). *Forecasts, Famines and Freezes*, Wildwood House, London

Hughes, D. W. (1977). The inconstant sun. *Nature (London)*, **266**, 405–6

Huntington, E. (1914). *The Climatic Factor*, Carnegie Institute of Washington, Washington, D.C.

Iserman, R. (1975). Modelling and identification of dynamic processes. *Computer Simulation of Water Resources Systems* (ed. G. C. Vansteenkiste), North-Holland, Amsterdam

Kendall, M. G., and Stuart, A. (1973). *The Advanced Theory of Statistics*, vol. 2, 3rd edn, Griffin, London

King, J. W. (1974). Weather and the earth's magnetic field. *Nature (London)*, **247**, 131–4

Klir, G. J. (1969). *An Approach to General Systems Theory*, Van Nostrand Reinhold, New York

Kraus, E. B. (1954). Secular changes in the rainfall regime of S. E. Australia. *Q.J.R. Meteorol. Soc.*, **80**, 591–601

Lamb, H. H. (1972), *Climate—Present, Past and Future*, vol. 1, *Fundamentals and Climate Now*, Methuen, London

——(1977). *Climate—Present, Past and Future*, vol. 2, *Climatic History and the Future*, Methuen, London

Landsberg, H. E. (1970). Man-made climatic changes. *Science*, **170**, 1265–74

Landsberg, H. E., Mitchell, J. M., Jr., Crutcher, H. L., and Quinlan, F. T. (1963). Surface signs of the biennial atmospheric pulse. *Mon. Weath. Rev.*, **91**, 549–56

van der Leeden, F. (ed.) (1975). *Water Resources of the World*, Water Information Center, Port Washington, New York

Leopold, L. B., and Davis, K. S. (1972). *Life Sciences Library: Water*, Time Life International, Nederland

Lorenz, E. N. (1970). Climatic change as a mathematical problem. *J. Appl. Meteorol.*, **9**, 325–9

Mason, B. J. (1976). Towards the understanding and prediction of climatic variations. *Q. J. R. Meteorol. Soc.*, **102**, 473–98

Matalas, N. C., and Fiering, M. B. (1977). Water resource system planning. *Climate, Climatic Change and Water Supply*, National Academy of Sciences, Washington, D.C., chapter 6

Milankovitch, M. (1930). *Handbuch der Klimatologie* I, Teil A (eds Koppen and Geiger), Berlin

Morris, R. M., and Ratcliff, P. A. S. (1976). Europe's drought (1): under the weather. *Nature (London)*, **264**, 4, 5

Munk, W. H., and MacDonald, G. J. F. (1960). *The Rotation of the Earth*, Cambridge University Press, Cambridge

Namias, J. (1965). Short-period climatic fluctuations. *Science*, **147**, 696–706

National Academy of Sciences (1975). *Understanding Climatic Change, A Program for Action*, National Academy of Sciences, Washington, D.C.

Rodríguez, I., and Yevjevich, V. (1967). Sunspots and hydrologic time series. *Proceedings of the International Hydrology Symposium, Fort Collins, Colorado*, vol. 1, pp. 397–405

Smirnov, N. P. (1969). Causes of long-period streamflow fluctuations. *Soviet Hydrology, Selected Papers*, vol. 3, American Geophysical Union, Washington, D.C., pp. 308–14

Stockton, C. W. (1977). Interpretation of past climatic variability from paleoenvironmental indicators. *Climate, Climatic Change and Water Supply*, National Academy of Sciences, Washington, D.C., chapter 2

Vita-Finzi, C. (1973). *Recent Earth History*, Macmillan, London

Waldmeier, M. (1961). *The Sunspot Activity in the Years* 1610–1960, Swiss Federal Observatory, Zurich

——(1968). Sonnenfleckenkurven und die Methode der Sonnenaktivitätsprognose. *Astronomische Mitteilungen der Eidgenoessischen Sternwarte, Zurich*, No. 286

Walker, G. T. (1936). The variations of level in lakes; their relations with each other and with sunspot numbers. *Q. J. R. Meteorol. Soc.*, **62,** 451–4

Wood, K. D. (1972). Sunspots and planets. *Nature (London)*, **240,** 91–3

World Meteorological Organisation (1966). Climatic change. *World Meteorol. Organ., Geneva, Tech. Note*, No. 79

Yevjevich, V. (1974). Determinism and stochasticity in hydrology. *J. Hydrol.*, **22,** 225–38

Yule, G. U. (1927). On a method of investigating periodicities in disturbed series with special reference to Wolfer's sunspot numbers. *Philos. Trans. A*, **226,** 267–98

2 Analysis of hydrologic time series

The principal aim of time series analysis is to describe the history of movement in time of some variable such as the rate of flow in a river at a particular site. River flow and other hydrological sequences are characterised by variability and oscillatory behaviour. This highlights the importance of studying time series, the properties of which are of great significance in the planning, designing and operation of water resource systems. The subject is a prerequisite to the stochastic models described in chapters 4 and 5.

Time-based characteristics of hydrological data are examined in this chapter, by using the correlogram, spectrum and other classical methods of analysis applicable to single and multiple series. The components of a time series and methods of analysis are explained here. A major part of the chapter deals with the diagnosis and estimation of trend, periodicity and other forms of dependence. Simplified definitions of the statistical terms used precede the analysis. Complementary properties such as range and runs are examined in chapter 5, whereas chapter 3 is concerned with probability distributions for modelling the random component and chapter 6 pertains to extreme (flood) events.

2.1 General definitions of time series and stochastic processes

A set of observations that measure the variation in time of some aspect of a phenomenon, such as the rate of flow in a river, the water level in a lake or well, the dissolved oxygen in a stream, or the sediment load in a channel, is termed a *time series*. The values taken in time by the set are called states; both state and time can be specified in discrete or continuous units. In general, a time series pertains to the category *continuous state and discrete time* in which observations are made of continuously changing phenomena at intervals of time (usually equal) or an average or total value is taken for each time interval. Examples of these are the temperatures recorded in a city at noon each day or the mean monthly barometric pressure at a station. Alternatively, we can visualise a *continuous time series* formed, say, on the chart of an automatic flow gauge on a river. Continuous data have one practical disadvantage, however; they cannot be easily handled on a digital computer. This has led to the widespread use of *discrete series* which comprise samples of continuous series except, of course, when dealing with numbers of occurrences (such as those of sunspots) in time.

Time series can also be studied collectively as multiple time series formed, for example, from flows in two or more rivers. The approach is adopted when investigating common time phenomena. Applications will be taken up in sections 2.8, 2.9 and 4.8.

The information contained in a discrete series is affected to a great extent by the choice of sampling interval. In practice, the choice depends on the purpose to be served. For example, when monitoring water quality data in a stream, daily or hourly time units may be necessary, whereas, for studying probabilities of storage levels in large reservoirs, monthly data may suffice. Precision of measurement is another important consideration. Again, the type of oscillatory behaviour in a time series, including its periodicities, and other properties could also point to an optimum sampling interval.

A characteristic property of natural time series is that there is usually time (that is, serial) dependence between observations. It follows, therefore, that the order of occurrence of observations is important. Another point is that the effect of this dependence increases as the sampling interval in a discrete series decreases; for example, there is more dependence between successive values of daily rainfall than between annual totals.

Events that can be quantified are termed random or stochastic variables when the outcomes or occurrences of the events are uncertain; here, events mean that the phenomena which are studied (for example, the 12 monthly river flows in a year) and the outcomes are the actual values taken[1]. A collection of outcomes of all events is called a process; if the outcomes are uncertain, it is called a stochastic process[2]. Thus, formally a stochastic process is a family of random variables $\{X(t), t \varepsilon T\}$ in which the parameter t usually denotes time. Also, the random variable $X(t)$ measures the state of the process (such as river flow) at time t, and the notation $t \varepsilon T$ signifies that the parameter t is some real number in the so-called index set or range T of all possible real numbers in the process. Furthermore, the set of random variables $X(t)$ constitutes a time series if arranged chronologically; it is, in fact, one realisation (that is, one from several other possible series) of the stochastic process. Again with regard to notation, an

---

[1] However, random in this sense does not mean that the current value of a process is completely independent of past values.

[2] According to Doob (1953), a stochastic process is the 'mathematical abstraction of an empirical process whose development is governed by probabilistic laws'. The word stochastic (which was apparently suggested 300 years ago by Jacob Bernoulli of Switzerland) means, according to its Greek origin, to contemplate or to conjecture. Roughly speaking, it can be regarded as synonymous with chance, random or probabilistic, but, more precisely, the interdependence of the random variables should be accounted for.

observed value of the variable $X(t)$ will be denoted by $x(t)$; when time is discrete, these will be X_t and x_t respectively.

Stochastic processes, therefore, deal with continuous or discrete state and time parameters. A specific example is the Poisson process, used in chapter 6 to model flood exceedances. Another example is the first-order Markov process explained in chapter 4 and used in chapter 7 for modelling reservoir storages, in which the antecedent value is sufficient to describe the current value. Amongst other types are the shot noise process applied to generate daily flows (see subsection 4.7.4) and the fundamental brownian motion process explained in section 5.4. A further generalisation in a stochastic process is that the time variable can be replaced by another such as length or space[3].

Now the main objective in studying time series is to understand the mechanism that generates the data and also, but not necessarily, to produce likely future sequences or to forecast events over a short period of time. These are attempted by making inferences regarding the underlying laws of the stochastic process from one or more sequences of recorded observations and then by postulating a model that fits the data, which are again used for estimation purposes. At first it is necessary to identify and analyse the different components of time series.

2.2   Components and main properties of time series

In general, a time series can be divided into a *deterministic component* which is one that can be determined for predictive purposes and a *stochastic component* consisting of chance and chance-dependent effects (which will be explained in section 2.5). The deterministic component may consist of types of non-periodic behaviour, the most common example being *trend* which is, in effect, a long smooth movement lasting over the span of the observations. The two practical cases of trend are a rising trend in which, as a general rule, values tend to increase with time and a falling trend to which the reverse situation applies. This may be due to changes in catchment characteristics consequent on urbanisation, deforestation and the like, or, on the other hand, some long-range climatic shifts may be the cause. Apart from trend there could be sudden changes called jumps, which are non-homogeneities of a particular type, resulting from man-made diversion works and other developments or from natural causes such as earthquakes and landslides.

The other main type of deterministic behaviour can be classified as *periodic* (or cyclical). This concerns an oscillatory movement which is repetitive over

---

[3] Cliff and Ord (1973), for instance, study spatial variation. Time series or stochastic processes are treated by Anderson (1971), Bartlett (1978), Doob (1953), Grenander and Rosenblatt (1966), Hannan (1970), Parzen (1962), Wold (1954) and Yaglom (1962) among others. The books by Bailey (1964), Bartholomew (1973), Brown (1963), Chatfield (1975), Davis (1941), Karlin and Taylor (1975), Kendall (1976) and Papoulis (1965) are less sophisticated; a review of hydrologic time series is given by Kisiel (1969).

fixed intervals of time. For example, if $X(t + \omega) = X(t)$ in a time series for all t, then the series is strictly periodic with period ω. This term should be applied only to well-established periodicities such as the annual or daily cycles, though even these do not fully conform with the definition. On the contrary, oscillatory movements associated, for instance, with the sunspot cycle explained in chapter 1, which are not proved beyond doubt, should not be included here[4].

The stochastic component, however, is constituted by irregular oscillations and random effects which cannot strictly be accounted for physically and which require probabilistic concepts for description[5]. An important characteristic that a discrete time series, say, X_t, $t = 1, 2, 3, \ldots$, may possess is *stationarity*. To define the property mathematically, let the estimated joint probability density functions for observations taken at times $1, 2, 3, \ldots, N$ and again at times $t + 1$, $t + 2$, $t + 3, \ldots, t + N$ be denoted by $f(x_1, x_2, x_3, \ldots, x_N)$ and $f(x_{1+t}, x_{2+t}, x_{3+t}, \ldots, x_{N+t})$ respectively[6]. Then, for a stationary stochastic process, the two sets of N-dimensional probability density functions are statistically identical for all values of N and t.

This could also be explained in a simpler manner. For instance, a set of annual river flows, which is not affected by significant climatic or environmental changes, is a stationary time series provided also that any varying effects of human activities or in catchment characteristics are negligible or can be accounted for. It means that statistical properties when computed from different parts of a stationary time series do not change except owing to sampling variations. Stationarity is, however, only applicable in a relative sense, because in practice there cannot be true stationarity. For instance, note the five concurrent sequences of annual data shown in figure 2.1; here, the Rhine annual flows (figure 2.1c) give the impression of being more stationary when compared with the flows in the Colorado River (figure 2.1a).

In a non-stationary time series, on the other hand, statistical properties differ from one segment to another and are therefore time dependent. Examples of these are daily river flow and other series in which seasonal changes are reflected as shown in figure 2.2.

Because a strictly stationary process is a mathematical concept, it is often necessary for practical and analytical purposes to restrict the conditions of stationarity to the mean and variance only. Such a series is referred to as a weakly stationary or second-order stationary series or one which is stationary in the wide sense. Another term which is commonly used for this type of series is covariance stationarity; an explanation of the covariance property is given in section 2.5. It will be clear that for gaussian processes, explained in chapter 3, the distinction between the two types of stationarity is irrelevant.

Stationary processes can be subdivided into *ergodic* and *non-ergodic* classes.

---

[4] The famous climatologist C. E. P. Brooks once said that 'cycles are rotten reeds from which to fashion pens for writing of future weather'.
[5] An excellent discussion of determinism and stochasticity in hydrology is given by Yevjevich (1974).
[6] Probability density and distribution functions are explained in chapter 3.

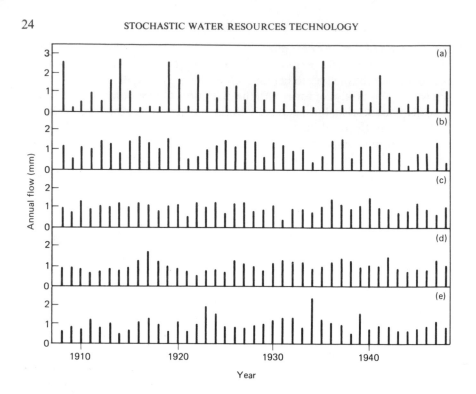

Figure 2.1   Annual flows in five rivers for the period 1907 to 1947, in which the data are reduced to unit mean: (a) Colorado River near Bellinger, Texas, U.S.A.; (b) Thames, near Teddington, Middlesex, England; (c) Rhine, near Basle, Switzerland; (d) Lake Victoria outflows, Africa; (e) Bungyip River, Bungyip, Australia

In a stationary stochastic process ergodicity is the property by which each realisation, that is, an occurrence (or observed sequence, though not in a strict mathematical sense) of the process, is a complete and independent representative of possible realisations of the process. Such realisations constitute an ensemble (a French word meaning together) which is theoretically an infinite number of possible sets of observations obtained, for example, through different recording instruments or through various personnel. Note here that the theoretical consideration of an ensemble of time series rather than a single one is analogous to the situation of the population and sample in statistics. To explain further, a process is said to be ergodic if time-averaged properties, such as the mean, over a single realisation are identical with the ensemble or spatial averages over all realisations of the process. It also means that (as explained in chapter 7 with reference to reservoir theory) by virtue of the property of ergodicity, a process will, regardless of its initial state, tend in probability to a limiting state[7]. For practical time series analysis, however, only one finite sample is available, and therefore stationary stochastic processes are often assumed to be ergodic.

[7] Fourier coefficients defined in section 2.6 are an exception to the rule.

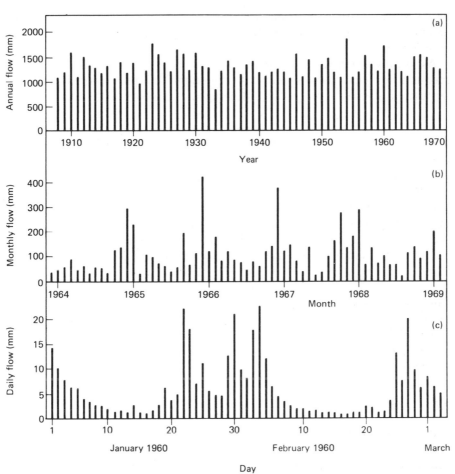

Figure 2.2 (a) Annual, (b) monthly and (c) daily inflow data at Caban Coch Reservoir, Wales

If we proceed further, stationary ergodic processes can be classified into dependent or independent types. If Pr denotes probability and $X_1, X_2, X_3, \ldots,$ X_n are random variables in a series, which take values $x_1, x_2, x_3, \ldots, x_n$ respectively, *then, for an independent sequence,* $\Pr(x_1 \leqslant a_1, x_2 \leqslant a_2, x_3 \leqslant a_3, \ldots, x_n \leqslant a_n) = \Pr(x_1 \leqslant a_1)\Pr(x_2 \leqslant a_2)\Pr(x_3 \leqslant a_3) \ldots \Pr(x_n \leqslant a_n)$ where $a_1, a_2, a_3, \ldots, a_n$ are some quantities. Dependent processes, explained in the following sections, are the contrary.

The first step in data analysis is to construct a sequence or segment of a time series, from the known observations, called a trace or time plot. This trace would give a visual indication of the significance and the relative strengths of the inherent behavioural patterns. It could also help in postulating a mathematical model, which is a device or formulation capable of reproducing the series, not in identical values or sequences, but so that pertinent characteristics are maintained.

As already noted, a stochastic model must have a probabilistic part that accounts for chance fluctuations. A commonly adopted procedure is to represent a stochastic process by a decomposition model of the type

$$X_t = T_t + P_t + \xi_t \tag{2.1}$$

where T_t and P_t denote the trend and periodic parts (which are the main constituents of the deterministic component) and ξ_t is the stochastic component. Note also that, in the stochastic component of equation 2.1, values are usually interdependent[8]. Such a model may not always be realistic because T_t and P_t may include random effects, or, on the other hand, deterministic effects may be passed on to the ξ_t component. This may be attributed to incorrect specification and to lack of complete understanding of natural processes. Moreover, the different parts may in effect act in a multiplicative manner, so that

$$X_t = T_t P_t \xi_t \tag{2.2}$$

This can be easily transformed into a linear model by taking logarithms. However, equation 2.1 is thought to provide a reasonable model in most cases.

The different components of a time series are shown in figure 2.3. Detailed examination of these is now taken up; also diagnostic and estimation procedures are given.

2.3   Trend

A steady and regular movement in a time series through which the values are, on average, either increasing or decreasing is termed a trend. This type of behaviour can be local, in which case the nature of the trend is subject to change over short intervals of time, or, on the other hand, we can visualise a global trend that is long lasting. Long-term trends are more appropriate to the steady growth rates in economics[9]. By contrast, if a trend in a hydrological time series appears, it is, in effect, part of a low-frequency oscillatory movement induced by climatic factors or through changes in land use and catchment characteristics.

An approximate model for describing trend is the polynomial type

$$X_t = x_0 + \alpha_1 t + \alpha_2 t^2 + \ldots + \alpha_n t^n + \xi_t \tag{2.3}$$

[8] The serially correlated residual which comprises this component may be subdivided into a sequentially dependent part and a completely random part denoted by, say, δ_t and η_t respectively.
[9] As a matter of general interest, stock market time series differ significantly from those in hydrology. Here, turning points and local trends are common features, apart from global trends; these reflect the influence of economic regulators and other factors, and they are also due to the establishment over shorter periods of speculative positions. However, there could also be sharp reversals in longer trends as evidenced by the débâcles of 1929 to 1932 and of 1973 to 1974.

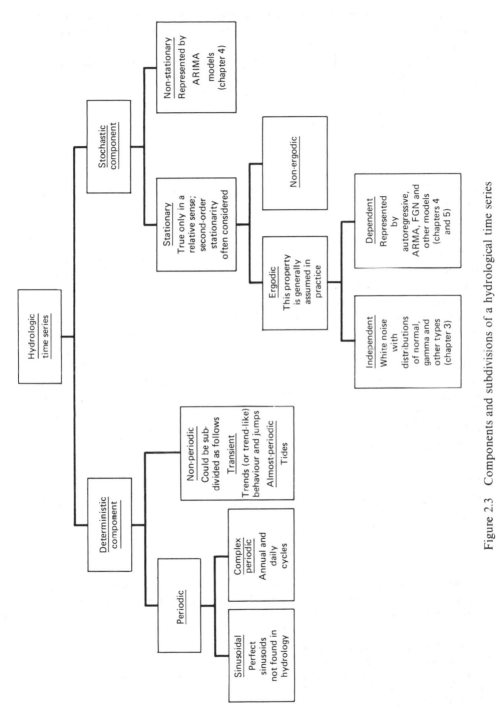

Figure 2.3 Components and subdivisions of a hydrological time series

in which ξ_t is a residual term. This can be fitted by least squares if we use the methods of multiple regression[10]. (For convenience the periodic component P_t of equation 2.1 is omitted here.)

It is advisable to use only annual data for the analysis of trend. In this way the periodic component P_t of equation 2.1 is suppressed. Furthermore, there will be no need then to worry about whether ξ_t has a highly non-normal distribution (to be explained in chapter 3).

Amongst other approximations is the exponential type

$$X_t = x_0 \exp(\alpha_1 t + \alpha_2 t^2 + \ldots + \alpha_n t^n + \xi_t) \qquad (2.4)$$

Such models are, however, too complicated to fit with sufficient confidence to a short series of data. In practice we attempt initially to fit a simpler type such as the linear model

$$X_t = x_0 + \alpha t + \xi_t \qquad (2.5)$$

Equations 2.5 or 2.3 (or 2.4) can be used to detrend a series (subject to prior testing as explained in subsection 2.3.2) and hence to analyse the residuals further. However, partly because of problems of estimation and prediction, filtering methods are sometimes used to change the time history[11].

The basic idea is to study one or a few characteristics at a time whilst eliminating or reducing the effect of others. By this type of smoothing, a more meaningful picture of the process is obtained. Notably, communication engineers (to whom a filter is a set of capacitors, resistors and the like) have developed procedures in their attempts to separate signals from noise; dealing with natural time series, on the other hand, can be rather involved. In general, filtering methods can be subdivided into moving-average and variate difference types. A practical approach which is often adopted is to subtract a lower-order polynomial from the observed data[12].

2.3.1 *Filtering methods*

Of the various methods of filtering short-term effects, the linear moving average given by

$$Y_t = (2k+1)^{-1} \sum_{j=-k}^{k} X_{t+j} \qquad (2.6)$$

in which the trend is calculated over a limited range of $2k+1$ values to transform an X series seems to be the most commonly used type. Initially, an optimum value of k is chosen to suit a particular series so that small oscillations are

[10] See, for example, Kendall (1976, p. 30).
[11] Note that the word filtering is in this context synonymous with smoothing, which enables us to study systematic behaviour more effectively in the frequency domain. It can also be used in a forecasting sense and in the time domain; a specific case of this is Kalman filtering, as explained in chapter 4.
[12] Durbin (1962) gives a mathematical analysis.

averaged out and smoothing is adequate but not excessive. When the average period of the oscillation is $2k + 1$, then a centred type of moving average is adopted. If the period is of extent $2k$ which is an even number, then the moving average is still taken over $2k + 1$ terms, but double weights are given to all but the first and last terms so that the transformation takes the form

$$Y_t = (X_{t-k} + 2X_{t-k+1} + 2X_{t-k+2} + \ldots + 2X_{t+k-2} + 2X_{t+k-1}$$
$$+ X_{t+k})/4k \qquad (2.7)$$

The moving-average type of trend fitting was first suggested by Beveridge (1921) more than 50 years ago when analysing 370 years of wheat prices in western Europe. He used the following moving average.

$$Y_t = 31X_t \bigg/ \sum_{j=-15}^{15} X_{t+j}$$

through which the trend in both the mean and the variance of the original series is removed[13].

Example 2.1   Annual flows of the Derwent at Yorkshire Bridge for the period 1938 to 1967 are tabulated below in millimetres of equivalent rainfall over the catchment area. Plot these values and smooth the series by taking an appropriate moving average.

Annual flows (mm)

946	1074	867	1058	838	837	1133	815	1138	869
910	868	927	1193	969	742	1386	737	1113	955
1143	665	1187	947	955	891	763	1288	1302	1029

The $30(=N)$ values are plotted in figure 2.4. By inspection there seems to be some type of irregular oscillation which occurs once every 2, 3 or 4 years, as seen from the spacing of the underlined values. Therefore, a $3(=m)$-year centred moving average $(x_{t-1} + x_t + x_{t+1})/3$ is taken to give the following $28(=N - m + 1)$ values.

Annual flows (*after moving average*)

		962	1000	921	911	936	928	1029	941
972	882	902	996	1030	968	1032	955	1079	935
1070	921	998	933	1030	931	870	981	1118	1206

---

[13] Kendall and Stuart (1976, p. 426) give details.

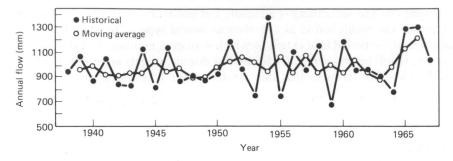

Figure 2.4   Three-point moving average applied to annual flows in the Derwent at Yorkshire Bridge, England, for the period 1938 to 1967

Note how the range between the maximum and minimum values is now reduced from 721(= 1386 − 665) to 324(= 1206 − 882); the number of meaningful oscillations is also much less. Another obvious point is that the short-term up-and-down movements, called high-frequency effects, are radically changed by detrending.

Longer moving averages will reduce the range further, and there will be fewer oscillations. The method is particularly useful for eliminating periodicities by averaging over sufficiently long periods; for example, a 12-month moving average should be taken in order to average out effectively the annual cycle in hydrological data.

An undesirable consequence of this type of trend removal is that artificial cycles can be induced in the data. This is known as the Slutzky–Yule effect, but it only becomes a serious problem when trend removal is done repetitively. To circumvent this problem, harmonic and other weighted types of trend removal have been applied in meteorology[14]. Spencer's fifteen-point formula which can remove up to cubic trend (if we refer to the other model given by equation 2.3, this includes terms up to t^3) is another method in this category which is termed low-pass filtering by electrical engineers.

For removing or reducing low-frequency oscillations, on the other hand, we require high-pass filtering methods through which high-frequency effects are basically maintained. Perhaps the best known are the variate difference methods of the first order given by $Y_t = X_t - X_{t-1}$, $t = 2, 3, 4, \ldots$, and of the second order which takes the form $Y_t = X_t - 2X_{t-1} + X_{t-2}$, $t = 3, 4, 5, \ldots$. There are also other types such as the quasidifferences $Y_t = X_t - \alpha X_{t-1}$ and $Y_t = (1 - \alpha)X_{t-1} - \alpha Y_{t-1}$, $0 < \alpha < 1$. The purpose of the last-named procedures is to reduce the distortion in the lower frequencies.

---

[14] Studies by Holloway (1958), who gives simple explanations of some of the procedures, by Craddock (1957) and by Brier (1961) are of particular interest. On the Slutzky–Yule effect, Slutzky (1937) and Yule (1921) explain various aspects, and a proof is also given by Granger and Hatanaka (1964, pp. 41, 42).

In all these methods, however, applications require considerable care and judgement to avoid misinterpretation. Generally speaking, they should be used in conjunction with spectral analysis explained in this chapter[15]. On the other hand, there may not be a real need for these filtering methods in many practical cases.

2.3.2 Tests for randomness and trend

In certain cases the presence of trend or seasonality is quite obvious, but often there is doubt whether any suspected systematic effects are significant or not. For this reason, a number of statistical tests for randomness has been devised. Some of these are specifically adopted for detecting trend. On the other hand, in order to ascertain whether seasonal effects are significant, a different test is called for. Again, when randomness is the hypothesis to be tested against some type of sequential dependence another type of test is required[16]. One example is the turning point test in which the number of high and low values, relative to adjacent ones, are examined. Unfortunately, this test is not efficient for detecting trend; it is, however, useful as a preliminary test for randomness.

(i) *Turning point test* In an observed sequence x_t, $t = 1, 2, 3, \ldots, N$, a turning point p occurs at time $t = i$ if x_i is either greater than x_{i-1} *and* x_{i+1} or less than the two adjacent values. If we consider three unequal observations (and ignore the trivial cases when two or more are equal), the six possible orders of magnitudes of these are (1) $x_{i-1} > x_i > x_{i+1}$, (2) $x_{i-1} > x_{i+1} > x_i$, (3) $x_i > x_{i-1} > x_{i+1}$, (4) $x_i > x_{i+1} > x_{i-1}$, (5) $x_{i+1} > x_{i-1} > x_i$ and (6) $x_{i+1} > x_i > x_{i-1}$. In a random series the six cases have equal probabilities of occurrence, and turning points occur in all except cases 1 and 6, which means that the chance of having a turning point is 2/3. It should be noted, however, that a turning point cannot occur at times $t = 1$ and $t = N$. Therefore, the expected number of turning points in a random series is $E(p) = 2(N - 2)/3$. Also, it can be shown that $\text{var}(p) = (16N - 29)/90$; consequently, p can be expressed as a standard measure, $z = \{p - E(p)\}/\{\text{var}(p)\}^{1/2}$, which is treated approximately as a standard normal deviate[17]. Because too few or too many turning points indicate non-randomness, a two-tailed test of significance is used as explained in the following example.

Example 2.2 Test the data in example 2.1 for randomness at the 5% level of significance. There are $23 (= p)$ turning points in the sequence which correspond to the 12 underlined observations (peaks) and 11 intermediate ones (troughs);

[15] Details of filtering methods are given by Kendall and Stuart (1976, chapter 46) and by Otnes and Enochson (1972, chapters 2, 3); see also Brown (1963, sections III, V).
[16] See, for example, Kendall and Stuart (1976, pp. 364–75). Also several tests with numerical examples are given by the Natural Environmental Research Council (1975, pp. 125–32); see also Keeping (1967) and Wallis and Matalas (1971).
[17] See Kendall (1976, pp. 22, 23) or Kendall and Stuart (1976, pp. 365, 366). The normal distribution and levels of significance are explained in chapter 3. The probabilities associated with standard normal deviates are given in the second column of table 6.9.

also $N = 30$. Therefore, $E(p) = 2 \times 28/3 = 18.67$, $\text{var}(p) = (16 \times 30 - 29)/90$ $= 5.01$ and $z = (23 - 18.67)/(5.01)^{1/2} = 1.93$. Because $-1.96 < z < 1.96$, the (null) hypothesis of no dependence in the series is not rejected at the 5% level of significance.

If a series is thought to have a trend component, Kendall's rank correlation test can be used to test the significance. This measures the 'disarray' in the data; it is particularly effective if the underlying trend is of a linear type as given by equation 2.5 or of a type which is approximately linear in form.

(ii) *Kendall's rank correlation test*   This test, which is also referred to as the τ test, is based on the proportionate number of subsequent observations which exceed a particular value. For a sequence $x_1, x_2, \ldots, x_N$, the standard procedure is to determine the number of times, say, p, in all pairs of observations $(x_i, x_j; j > i)$ that x_j is greater than x_i; the ordered (i, j) subsets are $(i = 1, j = 2, 3, 4, \ldots, N)$, $(i = 2, j = 3, 4, 5, \ldots, N)$, $\ldots$, $(i = N - 1, j = N)$. The maximum possible number of such pairs occurs for a continuously increasing sequence. This is a rising trend where succeeding values are throughout greater than preceding ones and p is given by $(N - 1) + (N - 2) + \ldots + 1$ which is the sum of an arithmetic progression and is given by $(N - 1)N/2$. If the observations are totally reversed, $p = 0$ and, hence it follows that, for a trend-free series, $E(p) = N(N - 1)/4$. Note therefore that, if p is close to $N(N - 1)/2$ or 0, it indicates the presence of a rising or falling trend, respectively.

The test is based on the statistic $\tau = 4p/N(N - 1) - 1$, which as shown above is such that for a random sequence $E(\tau) = 0$. It can also be shown that $\text{var}(\tau) = 2(2N + 5)/9N(N - 1)$ and that $\tau/\{\text{var}(\tau)\}^{1/2}$ converges rapidly to a standard normal distribution as N increases[18]. The test procedure is further clarified in the following example.

Example 2.3   From the data given in example 2.1, test whether the sequence from 1938 to 1947 is trend free. The data set is as follows: 946, 1074, 867, 1058, 838, 837, 1133, 815, 1138, 869. If we start with 946 as the first base number, that is, the one with suffix i in the above notation, the numbers on its right are examined, and a score of $+1$ is made each time the base number is exceeded. This is repeated eight times, for each of the other base numbers from 1074 to 1138; the results are as follows: 946, 4; 1074, 2; 867, 4; 1058, 2; 838, 3; 837, 3; 1133, 1; 815, 2; 1138, 0. Hence $p = 21$; $\tau = 4 \times 21/90 - 1 = -0.067$; $\text{var}(\tau) = 2 \times 25/810$ $= 0.0617$; the standard test statistic is $-0.067/(0.0618)^{1/2} = -0.268$. Because this is within the limits ± 1.96, the (null) hypothesis of no trend in the series is not rejected at the 5% level of significance using a two-tailed test.

(iii) *Regression test for linear trend*   There is also another alternative type of test to be used if it is thought that the trend is approximately linear. Standard methods of linear regression are used for the purpose[19]. If we refer to equation 2.5, the hypothesis to be tested in this case is $\alpha \neq 0$. The first step is to estimate α and its variance which are denoted by $\hat{\alpha}$ and $s_{\hat{\alpha}}^2$ respectively; the statistic t

[18] See Kendall and Stuart (1973, pp. 494–8).
[19] See, for example, Draper and Smith (1966, pp. 18–21).

$= \hat{\alpha}/s_{\hat{\alpha}}$ is then tested by using Student's t test. It is assumed here, as in other types of regression analysis, that the residuals ξ_t are stationary, sequentially independent and normally distributed.

Example 2.4 For the data given in example 2.3, test whether there is a significant linear trend. Assume that the values in the sequence can be represented by $x_t = x_0 + \alpha u_t + \xi_t$.

Year u_t	1	2	3	4	5	6	7	8	9	10
Annual flow x_t	946	1074	867	1058	838	837	1133	815	1138	869

Let $\sum$ denote $\sum\limits_{t=1}^{10}$. Then $\sum u_t = 55$, $\sum x_t = 9575$, $\sum u_t x_t = 52\,522$, $\sum u_t^2$ $= 385$ and $\sum x_t^2 = 9\,320\,377$; the mean values of the u and x items are respectively

$$\bar{u} = N^{-1} \sum u_t = 5.5$$

and

$$\bar{x} = N^{-1} \sum x_t = 957.5$$

Therefore,

$$\sum (u_t - \bar{u})(x_t - \bar{x}) = \sum u_t x_t - N^{-1} \sum u_t \sum x_t = -140.5$$

We also have

$$\sum (u_t - \bar{u})^2 = \sum u_t^2 - N^{-1} \left(\sum u_t \right)^2 = 82.5$$

and

$$\sum (x_t - \bar{x})^2 = \sum x_t^2 - N^{-1} \left(\sum x_t \right)^2 = 152\,314.5$$

Hence, we obtain the estimated values

$$\hat{\alpha} = \sum (u_t - \bar{u})(x_t - \bar{x}) \Big/ \sum (u_t - \bar{u})^2 = -1.70$$

$$\hat{x}_0 = \bar{x} - \hat{\alpha}\bar{u} = 966.9$$

Also, the estimated sum of squared errors is

$$\sum \xi_t^2 = \sum (x_t - \bar{x})^2 - \hat{\alpha}^2 \sum (u_t - \bar{u})^2 = 152\,076$$

which gives the standard error of regression

$$s = \left\{ \sum \xi_t^2 / (N - 2) \right\}^{1/2}$$

$$= 137.87$$

Hence the estimate of the variance of $\hat{\alpha}$ is

$$s_{\hat{\alpha}}^2 = s^2 \bigg/ \left\{ \sum (u_t - \bar{u})^2 \right\}$$
$$= (15.18)^2$$

and Student's t statistic

$$\hat{\alpha}/s_{\hat{\alpha}} = -0.11$$

Because this is not significant at the 1 % level of significance, the null hypothesis $\alpha = 0$ is not rejected.

It should be noted that linearity in trend is mainly a theoretical concept used to describe a general pattern, for, almost surely, trends in natural time series are non-linear. However, the approximation is justifiable (if we consider also the likely errors in polynomial models) for the purpose of studying the other components, after removing a trend, if it is significant[20].

On the other hand, hydrologic sequences are not subject to long-term movements, generally speaking, over observed time spans. Most of the exceptional cases appear to be caused by local changes in physical conditions. For example, catchment deforestation or other types of changes in urbanisation and land use cause alterations in erosional processes and evapotranspiration that lead to changes in the relationships between precipitation and river flows. Over a few years such changes may be undetected because of the higher significance of random factors, but their effects may be felt over a longer time scale[21].

From the practical viewpoint the local trend-producing factors should be identified in such cases, and projections to the future should take account of the likelihood of changes in them. This being so, it would be rational to expect a limiting state which is followed by a change in trend. However, if the cause is climatic change, which is not usually effective over periods of less than 50 or 100 years, confirmation should be sought by examining sequences of observations recorded in neighbouring areas. For this purpose, correlation with longer sequences of meteorological or climatic data is advantageous. In all cases, it is important to bear in mind the danger of extrapolating with no physical explanation.

2.4 Periodicity

Whereas observed trends are virtually part of long-term irregular fluctuations, periodic effects in hydrological time series are deterministic in nature with regard to their frequency of occurrence, because they are imposed on the series

---

[20] The tests given here are not suitable when non-homogeneities consist of jumps. If the times at which changes occur are known, jumps can be tested by means of a one-way analysis of variance; if not, it is best to use von Neumann's ratio (Buishand, 1977, p. 45).
[21] The work of Christiansen (1967) on hydrologic studies in northern Utah is one example.

by a cyclic phenomenon, that is, by one with a fixed period. The predominant periodic component is caused when the Earth revolves around the Sun in an elliptical orbit, whilst rotating on an axis inclined to the orbital plane. This is known as the seasonal effect and is clearly evidenced in closely spaced data such as those from monthly river-flow series as shown, for example, in figure 2.2(b). Another type of periodic behaviour is the diurnal one caused by the Earth's rotation and evidenced during a 24-hour period, in temperature, evapotranspiration and water quality data. In addition, the revolution of the Moon around the Earth results in a lunar cycle; this is shown, for instance, by the oscillations in tides and is termed almost-periodic behaviour.

In general, the periodic component in a time series can be represented through a system of sine functions after the trend component, if it exists, has been estimated and removed. The procedure used is termed harmonic analysis. This term originally arose in acoustics wherein musical instruments are identified by the harmonics which have frequencies that are multiples of the basic frequency produced. Subsequently, the French mathematician Fourier showed that a continuous function $\{X(t), t\varepsilon T\}$ (where T is an index set) can, in general, be equated to the sum of an infinite number of harmonics with frequencies of $1/T, 2/T, 3/T, \ldots$, where T is a number; the great advantage of these sinusoids is their ability to accommodate changes in natural time series. Hence, this type of representation is given the more general term Fourier series. For a discrete series, however, the number of possible harmonics is finite which, together with the amplitude and phase differences, can be estimated from an observed sequence.

Consider a trend-free set $X_1, X_2, X_3, \ldots, X_N$ of variables equispaced at time intervals Δt, which is known to have a periodic component. The harmonic representation of the sequence is

$$x_t = \mu + \sum_{i=1}^{L} \lambda_i \sin\left(\frac{2\pi t}{T}i + \phi_i\right) + \xi_t \qquad (2.8)$$

in which ξ_t is the stochastic component and $\mu = E(X)$ is the population mean. Also, i/T and T/i denote the frequencies of occurrence and wavelengths (which are the fixed times between, say, consecutive peaks in each case) respectively of the harmonics $i = 1, 2, 3, \ldots, L$; λ_i and ϕ_i are the amplitudes (that is, half the total height of the sine curve of each harmonic) and phases, which signify the horizontal alignments of the sine curves with respect to the origin respectively. It should be noted that, because at least three points are needed to draw a curve, the shortest wavelength a harmonic could have is $2\Delta t$. This means that L in equation 2.8 is equal to $N/2$ (or $N/2 - 0.5$ if N is odd). Figure 2.5 shows how a periodic signal can be decomposed into harmonic functions with varying frequencies (or wavelengths) and phases.

A case will now be studied in which the cycle has, without loss of generality, a wavelength of 1 year; this will be the fundamental frequency corresponding to $i = 1$ in equation 2.8. If the points $\tau = 1, 2, 3, \ldots, p$ specify the time span of the

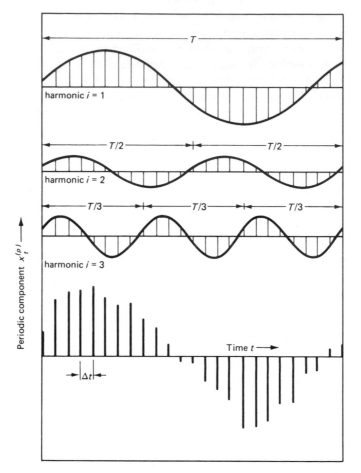

Figure 2.5   Harmonic decomposition of a periodic signal over a time span. The L harmonics (of which the first three are shown above) have frequencies $1/T$, $2/T$, $3/T$, $4/T, \ldots$, L/T and wavelengths T, $T/2$, $T/3$, $T/4, \ldots$, T/L, where $T/L \geq 2\Delta t$ and Δt is the sampling interval. Their ordinates are summed algebraically to give the periodic component $x_t^{(p)}$ of the sequence x_t

periodicity, the periodic means estimated from the sequence of observations x_1, $x_2, x_3, \ldots, x_N$ are given by

$$m_\tau = n^{-1} \sum_{i=1}^{n} x_{\tau + p(i-1)} \tag{2.9}$$

where $n = N/p$ is the number of years of data; the objective here is to represent the p values of m_τ by using equation 2.8[22]. Let μ_τ denote the harmonic fitted

[22] Buys-Ballot (1847) originated equation 2.9 for his meteorological investigations. Here, p can be 12 or 365, for instance, depending on whether Δt is 1 month or 1 day respectively.

means, for each value of τ in the annual cycle. In order to estimate the μ_τ values it is necessary to replace t, X_t and T in equation 2.8 by τ, m_τ and p. Then by writing $p/2$ for L and expanding the sine term of equation 2.8 with the use of the coefficients α_i and β_i,

$$\mu_\tau = \mu + \sum_{i=1}^{p/2} \alpha_i \sin(2\pi i\tau/p) + \sum_{i=1}^{p/2} \beta_i \cos(2\pi i\tau/p) \tag{2.10}$$

for $\tau = 1, 2, \ldots, p$, where p is even.

Strictly speaking, the analysis which follows is inapplicable if autocorrelations are significantly different from zero or if the variances σ_τ^2, $\tau = 1, 2, \ldots, p$, are periodic[23]. We assume therefore that these conditions are approximately satisfied.

In order to estimate μ, α_i and β_i, $i = 1, 2, 3, \ldots, p/2$, we minimise the sum S of squares of the differences between the p values of m_τ and μ_τ as given by

$$S = \sum_{\tau=1}^{p} \left\{ m_\tau - \mu - \sum_{i=1}^{p/2} \alpha_i \sin(2\pi i\tau/p) - \sum_{i=1}^{p/2} \beta_i \cos(2\pi i\tau/p) \right\}^2 \tag{2.11}$$

Partial derivates are now taken and, in this analysis, $\hat{\mu}$, $\hat{\alpha}_i$ and $\hat{\beta}_i$ denote estimates of μ, α_i and β_i. Initially, for the condition $\partial S/\partial \mu = 0$ in equation 2.11, it follows that $\hat{\mu} = p^{-1} \sum_{\tau=1}^{p} m_\tau$. Then $\partial S/\partial \alpha_i$ and $\partial S/\partial \beta_i$ are equated to zero for each i where $i = 1, 2, 3, \ldots, p/2$. From these, $p/2$ equations of the type

$$\sum_{\tau=1}^{p} \left[\sin(2\pi i\tau/p) \left\{ m_\tau - \hat{\mu} - \sum_{k=1}^{p/2} \hat{\alpha}_k \sin(2\pi k\tau/p) \right. \right.$$
$$\left. \left. - \sum_{k=1}^{p/2} \hat{\beta}_k \cos(2\pi k\tau/p) \right\} \right] = 0$$

and $p/2$ equations of the type

$$\sum_{\tau=1}^{p} \left[\cos(2\pi i\tau/p) \left\{ m_\tau - \hat{\mu} - \sum_{k=1}^{p/2} \hat{\alpha}_k \sin(2\pi k\tau/p) \right. \right.$$
$$\left. \left. - \sum_{k=1}^{p/2} \hat{\beta}_k \cos(2\pi k\tau/p) \right\} \right] = 0$$

are obtained for $i = 1, 2, 3, \ldots, p/2$.

Now, from the orthogonal properties of the sine and cosine functions,

$$\sum_{\tau=1}^{p} \sin(2\pi i\tau/p) = \sum_{\tau=1}^{p} \cos(2\pi i\tau/p)$$

$$= \sum_{\tau=1}^{p} \{ \sin(2\pi i\tau/p) \cos(2\pi k\tau/p) \}$$

$$= 0, \qquad i, k = 1, 2, \ldots, p/2$$

[23] See, for example, Avara (1975).

Also,

$$\sum_{\tau=1}^{p} \{\sin(2\pi i\tau/p)\sin(2\pi k\tau/p)\} = \sum_{\tau=1}^{p} \{\cos(2\pi i\tau/p)\cos(2\pi k\tau/p)\}$$

$$= 0, \qquad i, k = 1, 2, \ldots, p/2, i \neq k$$

Again,

$$\sum_{\tau=1}^{p} \sin^2(2\pi i\tau/p) = \sum_{\tau=1}^{p} \cos^2(2\pi i\tau/p) = p/2, \qquad i = 1, 2, \ldots, p/2-1$$

In addition,

$$\sum_{\tau=1}^{p} \sin^2(2\pi i\tau/p) = 0$$

$$\sum_{\tau=1}^{p} \cos^2(2\pi i\tau/p) = p, \qquad i = p/2$$

After substituting these properties in the partial differential equations, estimates $\hat{\alpha}_i$, $\hat{\beta}_i$, $i = 1, 2, \ldots, p/2$, of the parameters are obtained as follows.

$$\hat{\alpha}_i = (2/p) \sum_{\tau=1}^{p} m_\tau \sin(2\pi i\tau/p), \qquad i = 1, 2, \ldots, p/2-1, \hat{\alpha}_{p/2} = 0 \quad (2.12)$$

$$\hat{\beta}_i = (2/p) \sum_{\tau=1}^{p} m_\tau \cos(2\pi i\tau/p), \qquad i = 1, 2, \ldots, p/2-1$$

$$\hat{\beta}_{p/2} = (1/p) \sum_{\tau=1}^{p} m_\tau(-1)^\tau \tag{2.13}$$

In practice we often find that periodicities can be represented by one or two harmonics in monthly series and by four to six harmonics in daily series; in such cases the other harmonics are treated as noise and are passed on to the stochastic component. Objectively, the actual number to be fitted in each case can be found through an analysis of variance as shown in example 2.5[24].

Example 2.5   Monthly flows in the Teme at Tenbury Wells in millimetres of equivalent rainfall over the catchment area are tabulated below for the period 1957 to 1964.

---

[24] Most elementary statistical books deal with the analysis of variance, the F distribution and degrees of freedom; the degrees of freedom are also explained in subsection 3.5.1.

Year	Monthly flow (mm)											
	Jan.	Feb.	Mar.	Apr.	May	June	Jul.	Aug.	Sep.	Oct.	Nov.	Dec.
1957	37	64	42	15	8	5	4	39	57	27	60	35
1958	56	89	34	17	10	19	16	19	68	85	31	50
1959	84	22	27	39	21	8	5	4	2	3	19	90
1960	122	80	50	36	11	6	4	5	24	102	114	99
1961	61	46	18	38	36	8	6	4	3	20	16	46
1962	84	31	21	48	21	10	7	14	36	19	36	36
1963	23	19	106	49	20	10	13	6	6	5	56	24
1964	15	21	48	24	17	12	8	4	3	4	7	39

Estimate the number and coefficients of the harmonics to be fitted to model the periodicity in the mean monthly flows in the Teme. Hence, evaluate the harmonic fitted means for the 12 months (on the assumption that autocorrelation and periodicity in the standard deviations are negligible).

Initially, values of m_τ, $\tau = 1$ (January), 2, . . ., 12, are estimated. These are as follows: 60.25, 46.50, 43.25, 33.25, 18.00, 9.75, 7.88, 11.88, 24.88, 33.13, 42.38, 52.38. The 8-year sequence and the monthly means m_τ are shown in figure 2.6. Then, by using equations 2.12 and 2.13, the coefficients α_i, β_i are estimated for $i = 1, 2, . . . , p/2$ as follows.

i	$\hat{\alpha}_i$	$\hat{\beta}_i$
1	10.41	21.06
2	− 0.04	− 0.69
3	1.60	1.35
4	2.27	0.60
5	0.38	− 1.10
6	0	− 0.81

Therefore, the total number N of observations (x_t) equals 96 and the estimated mean $\bar{x}$ is 31.96.

The analysis of variance is given in table 2.1. Here, the null hypothesis is that the variance explained by a harmonic i, which is $(N/2)(\hat{\alpha}_i^2 + \hat{\beta}_i^2)$, where N is the total sample size, is zero. We proceed to test the $(\hat{\alpha}_i, \hat{\beta}_i)$ values for $i = 6, 5, 4, 3, 2, 1$, in order; to obtain the F ratios shown in the last column, the mean squared values are divided by the unexplained variances. If the null hypothesis is not rejected, the sum of squares is added to the residual sum of squares.

The total variance in the sequence is $78\,844/95 = 830$, which is the mean squared value obtained from the sum of squares and degrees of freedom given in the fourth row. The sum of squares and degrees of freedom for harmonics $i = 6$,

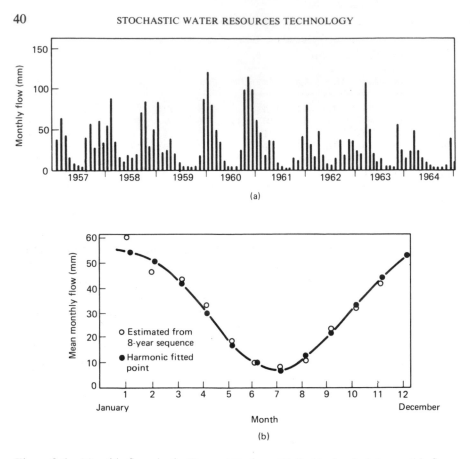

Figure 2.6   Monthly flows in the Teme at Tenbury Wells, England: (a) monthly flows for the period 1957 to 1964; (b) monthly mean estimated from the 8-year period with the harmonic fitted points joined by a smooth curve (see example 2.5)

Table 2.1   Analysis of variance

Variation	Sum of squares	Degrees of freedom	F ratio
(1) α_i, β_i, $i = 2, 3, 4, 5, 6$	$\sum_{i=2}^{6} (N/2)(\hat{\alpha}_i^2 + \hat{\beta}_i^2) = 597$	9	$(597/9)/(51\,761/84)$ $= 0.11$
(2) α_1, β_1	$(N/2)(\hat{\alpha}_1^2 + \hat{\beta}_1^2)\quad = 26\,486$	2	$(26\,486/2)/(52\,358/93)$ $= 23.52$
(3) Residuals		51 761	84
(4) Total	$\sum_{t=1}^{96} (x_t - \bar{x})^2\quad = 78\,844$	$N - 1$ $= 95$	

5, 4, 3 and 2 are given in the first row and those for the first harmonic are in the next row; the residual sum of squares shown in the third row is obtained by subtracting the sums of squares in the first two rows from that in the last row. From the tables of the F distribution, $F_{(2, 93)} = 7.5$ at the 0.001 level of significance. This means that the first harmonic is highly significant, but the other harmonics are not significant and are therefore ignored.

By substituting $\mu = \bar{x} = 31.96$, $\hat{\alpha}_1 = 10.41$ and $\hat{\beta}_1 = 21.06$ in equation 2.10 (with $\alpha_i, \beta_i = 0$ for $i = 2, 3, \ldots, 6$) the harmonic fitted values $\mu_\tau, \tau = 1, 2, \ldots, 12$ of the periodic means m_τ are estimated as follows: 55.40, 51.50, 42.37, 30.45, 18.93, 10.90, 8.52, 12.41, 21.55, 33.47, 44.99, 53.02. The sequence of monthly data is shown in figure 2.6 together with the sample estimated and harmonic means.

The objective in the above approach is to fit harmonic functions to the p statistics, within an established cycle, through a least-squares fit (in preference to, say, a moving average or even a free-hand curve as used by economists at the beginning of this century) and so to attempt to estimate the parameters of the parent process. This is justified by Yevjevich (1972a) because it leads to fewer parameters and the type of behaviour within the solar system indicates that the harmonic approach is appropriate; although the method is advantageous, there could be bias in the estimates[25]. The primary importance in harmonic analysis, however, is in its application to the periodogram (which is explained in section 2.6).

2.5 Autocorrelation

In one of the first methods of river-flow synthesis, Sudler (1927) transferred discrete values of trend-free annual flows from a 50-year historical sequence onto a pack of 50 cards; then the pack was shuffled, cards were drawn one at a time and their values were noted sequentially. In this way a synthetic set of data is obtained; each new shuffle and deal of the pack produces a different sequence of data. One serious drawback in this approach is that individual events are identical with those in the historical sequence so that statistics such as the mean and variance are invariable. Another major weakness in the method is that an important characteristic in the original time series is destroyed. This is the property of sequential dependence in a natural series by which low flows tend to follow low flows and high flows to follow high flows not consistently but just sufficiently so that, if the experiment is satisfactory, artificial sequences have the same appearance as the observed sequence with respect to the types of oscillatory behaviour therein.

The degree of linear dependence between events ℓ time units apart is measured by the autocovariance function, which, if positive, is directly related to

---

[25] A possible refinement is through *weighted* least squares (which Gauss wrote about 180 years ago); the justification is that the statistics for some months are less biased than others. This and other aspects are discussed by Bullard *et al.* (1977); see also Dawdy (1972).

the strength of storage processes in the atmosphere and within the catchment. From the theory of Wiener (1930), it is defined for a stationary continuous series $\{X(t), t\varepsilon T\}$ with zero mean, by the time average

$$C_\ell = \lim_{T \to \infty} \left\{ \frac{1}{2T} \int_{-T}^{T} X(t+\ell)X(t)\,dt \right\} \tag{2.14}$$

The variable ℓ is referred to as the lag. In a second-order or weakly stationary process, the autocovariance function is defined by the ensemble average

$$C_\ell = E\{X(t+\ell)X(t)\} \tag{2.15}$$

where E denotes the expected value. For a strictly stationary ergodic process in which $E\{X^2(t)\}$ is finite, both definitions give the same result[26]. In statistical terms this means that C_ℓ is consistently estimated (on account of the property of asymptotic convergence) by equation 2.15.

The autocorrelation function is then defined, on the above assumption, as

$$\rho_\ell = C_\ell / E\{X^2(t)\} \tag{2.16}$$

where $-1 < \rho_\ell < +1$, $\rho_{-\ell} = \rho_\ell$ for all ℓ and $\rho_0 = 1$; the continuous set of values $\rho_\ell, \ell \geqslant 0, \ldots$, constitute a theoretical correlogram. Estimates of ρ_ℓ from observed sequences are denoted here by r_ℓ and are called serial correlations[27]. From an observed discrete sequence $x_t, t = 1, 2, 3, \ldots, N$, the serial correlation coefficients r_ℓ can be obtained by correlating the sequences $(x_1, x_2, x_3, \ldots, x_{N-\ell})$ and $(x_{1+\ell}, x_{2+\ell}, x_{3+\ell}, \ldots, x_N)$, with means $\bar{x}' = (N-\ell)^{-1} \sum_{i=1}^{N-\ell} x_i$ and $\bar{x}'' = (N-\ell)^{-1} \sum_{i=i}^{N-\ell} x_{i+\ell}$, as follows.

$$r_\ell = N(N-\ell)^{-1} \left[\sum_{t=1}^{N-\ell} \left\{ (x_t - \bar{x}')(x_{t+\ell} - \bar{x}'') \right\} \right] \Big/ \left[\left\{ \sum_{t=1}^{N-\ell} (x_t - \bar{x}')^2 \right\} \left\{ \sum_{t=1}^{N-\ell} (x_{t+\ell} - \bar{x}'')^2 \right\} \right]^{1/2} \tag{2.17}$$

This is based on the well-known definition of the correlation coefficient (which dates back to the work of Francis Galton and Karl Pearson). However, generally in the case of large samples, the statistics $\bar{x}'$ and $\bar{x}''$ could be replaced by the sample mean $\bar{x} = N^{-1} \sum_{t=1}^{N} x_t$. Also, the term $N(N-\ell)^{-1}$ can be closely

---

[26] The ergodic theorem is explained by Yaglom (1962, pp. 16–22).
[27] Here, the inspiration has come from the dictionary of Kendall and Buckland (1971). In some texts, for example, in that of Davis (1941), serial correlations denote, in general, correlations between observations from two different series; included in the same class are autocorrelations which pertain to a single series. By these definitions, however, the autocorrelations can mean either the sample or population values.

approximated by unity for small or moderate values of ℓ as N increases. Hence,

$$r_\ell = \left[\sum_{t=1}^{N-\ell} \left\{ (x_t - \bar{x})(x_{t+\ell} - \bar{x}) \right\} \right] \bigg/ \sum_{t=1}^{N} (x_t - \bar{x})^2 \qquad (2.18)$$

A graph of r_ℓ against ℓ is termed a serial correlogram.

Note that, in small samples, the difference between equations 2.17 and 2.18 becomes more pronounced when ℓ increases if the end observations differ significantly from the overall mean $\bar{x}$. The formula given by equation 2.17 is used, therefore, for practical purposes when sample sizes are small; here smallness is of the order of 50 or less[28].

The serial correlogram is a very useful tool for investigating the structure of a time series with regard to how observations separated by fixed periods of time are interrelated; it is assumed for simplification that the trend component is removed. In a stationary series (that is, in a series without strict periodicities or large-scale fluctuations) the r_ℓ values die away as ℓ increases. A few different types of correlograms are now considered, each corresponding to a particular type of time series.

2.5.1 Periodic time series

The autocorrelogram for any time series with a cyclic component will itself be periodic. For example, consider the following sinusoidal series which has a period p, an amplitude λ and a phase ϕ which is uniformly distributed over the range $(0, 2\pi)$.

$$X(t) = \lambda \sin \left(\frac{2\pi t}{p} + \phi \right)$$

Clearly, $E\{X(t)\} = 0$. It follows from the orthogonal properties explained above that $E\{X(t)^2\} = \lambda^2/2$; hence, $\text{var}\{X(t)\} = \lambda^2/2$. Also, it can be shown that

$$E\{X(t)X(t+\ell)\} = \lambda^2 E \left[\sin\left\{ \frac{2\pi t}{p} + \phi \right\} \sin\left\{ \frac{2\pi(t+\ell)}{p} + \phi \right\} \right]$$

$$= \lambda^2 \{\cos(2\pi\ell/p)\}/2$$

Hence,

$$\rho_\ell = E\{X(t)X(t+\ell)\}/\text{var}\{X(t)\}$$

$$= \cos(2\pi\ell/p) \qquad (2.19)$$

Figure 2.7 shows the serial correlogram of monthly inflows to Caban Coch

[28] The merits of different formulae for r_ℓ are discussed in hydrological literature; see, for example, Fiering and Jackson (1971). Jenkins and Watts (1968, pp. 182–3) recommend the use of equation 2.18 from the spectral viewpoint and from other theoretical considerations. By and large, for the samples usually encountered, the differences are irrelevant; also, they are generally swamped by errors from the assumption of stationarity.

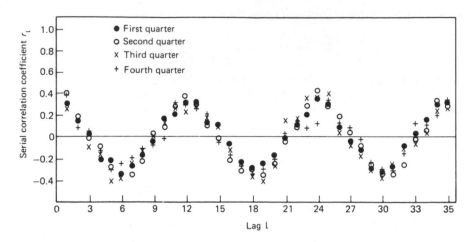

Figure 2.7 Serial correlograms of monthly inflows to Caban Coch Reservoir, Wales for the period 1917 to 1966, where the data are divided into four equal non-overlapping sections and serial correlations are estimated from each section

Reservoir in Wales; the annual period is clearly seen here. Because the sequence x_t does not, of course, behave like a perfect sinusoidal function, the correlogram has an amplitude of less than unity unlike that given by equation 2.19. Another point is that the phase ϕ in the original series is completely lost. This is also shown by the correlogram of monthly precipitation at Colombo in Sri Lanka (figure 2.8); the period here is 6 months as expected from monsoon effects.

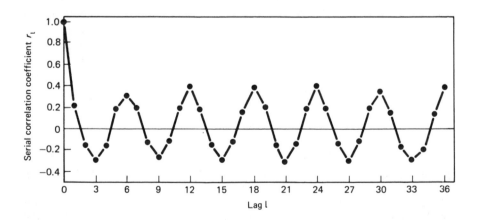

Figure 2.8 Serial correlogram of monthly precipitation at Colombo, Sri Lanka

2.5.2 Non-periodic dependent time series

The lag-one serial correlation in observed (non-periodic) sequences, such as in annual data sets, increases with the strength of carry-over effects within the catchment or in the atmosphere. Higher-lag serial correlations are similarly affected. Values of r_1 from 140 world-wide observed sequences of annual river flows are given by Yevjevich (1963). For example, in the St Lawrence River at Ogdensburgh, New York, $r_1 = 0.721$, whereas in the John Day River at McDonald Ferry, Oregon, $r_1 = 0.065$. For monthly, daily and other types of data, serial correlation tends to increase, as already noted, with the closeness of the spacing Δt of the observations; it is also enhanced over short lags by the seasonal effect.

The variance of the serial correlations r_ℓ in a dependent sequence is somewhat complicated even for large samples from a normal population. However, on the hypothesis that the autocorrelations ρ_k are non-zero for $k \leq q$, say, and are zero for $k > q$, then the variance of the r_ℓ can be approximated by

$$\text{var}(r_\ell) \approx \left(1 + 2 \sum_{k=1}^{q} r_k^2 \right) \Big/ N, \quad \ell > q \tag{2.20}$$

Also, in the same range of lags the r_ℓ values have an approximate normal distribution with a mean of zero[29]. This result is made use of in the formulation of linear stochastic models in chapter 4.

2.5.3 Independent time series

For a serially independent series the autocovariance coefficients as defined by equation 2.15 are (theoretically) equal to zero except when $i = 0$, in which case it is equal to the variance. Hence, $E(r_\ell) \approx 0, \ell \neq 0$, and $r_0 = 1$. The $r_\ell, \ell \neq 0$, values are distributed approximately as a normal variate with zero mean and variance given by

$$\text{var}(r_\ell) \approx 1/N \tag{2.21}$$

which follows from equation 2.20. This provides an approximate test of significance[30].

Example 2.6   From a sequence of 100 random numbers the following serial correlation coefficients $r_\ell, \ell = 1, 2, \ldots, 10$, are calculated using equation 2.17: $-0.08, +0.02, -0.15, -0.14, +0.10, -0.13, -0.15, +0.01, +0.15, +0.09$. Are the 100 numbers serially independent at the 5% level of significance?

The null hypothesis is that the numbers are not serially correlated, in which

---

[29] See Bartlett (1978).
[30] Anderson (1942) has done original research in this field. His work on serial correlations in hypothetical circular time series leads to a more complicated expression for var (r_ℓ). Significance tests used, for example, by Roesner and Yevjevich (1966) are based on this. However, because an objective test procedure, such as the portmanteau test explained in chapter 4, is required for model verification, equation 2.21 is retained for preliminary puposes.

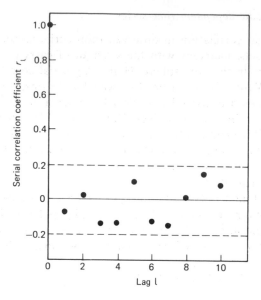

Figure 2.9   Serial correlogram of a sequence of random numbers

case the r_ℓ values have an approximate normal distribution as defined above. Accordingly, the test criterion is that if $|r_\ell| > 1.96/N^{1/2}$, that is, $|r_\ell| > 0.196$, the hypothesis is rejected. The serial correlogram is shown in figure 2.9. Hence the null hypothesis is not rejected.

2.6 Spectral methods

The correlogram described above is, of course, a function of time and is therefore said to belong to the time domain. A complementary method of analysing the dependence structure of a time series is found in the frequency domain by means of the spectrum, the term frequency being used here in the harmonic sense and not in the sense of the histogram.

As known historically in the study of optics, from the time of Newton, when a beam of white sunlight passes through a prism, it is decomposed into a set of fundamental coloured lights, according to the length of the energy waves; each of these has a frequency bandwidth in the spectrum of pure coloured lights in which violet and red have the highest and lowest frequencies respectively. Any particular mixed colour can be thought of as a combination of fundamental colours, and here the relative strength of the individual components is important. By analogy, a time series can be regarded as a combination of basic frequencies of occurrence of random variables. The role of the spectrum is to decompose a time series on a frequency basis, and the objective in this part of the analysis is to estimate the frequencies and their relative amplitudes.

Basically, the spectrum can be defined by using the method of harmonic analysis explained in section 2.4. As before, consider N items of data spaced at equal intervals Δt, where the fundamental (which means total) period $p = N\Delta t$; the harmonic constituents have frequencies of $i = 1, 2, 3, \ldots, p/2$ cycles over period p. Note that p can span over any period such as the length of an observed sequence, although in the case pertaining to equations 2.9 to 2.13 it is restricted to the annual cycle. A graph of half the squares of amplitudes $(\hat{\alpha}_i^2 + \hat{\beta}_i^2)/2$ against frequency i, where $\hat{\alpha}_i$ and $\hat{\beta}_i$ are the estimated values of the constants of each harmonic by using equations 2.12 and 2.13, is called the estimated sample spectrum; also, a mathematical function fitted through the points is called the estimated spectral density function. This approach is, of course, empirical; the theoretical spectrum is explained in the next section.

A plot of this kind is referred to as a line spectrum because it shows vertical lines representing the values of $(\hat{\alpha}_i^2 + \hat{\beta}_i^2)/2$ or a discrete spectrum. The alternative name periodogram is due to Schuster (1898) who originally suggested the form of equation 2.8, and this type of variance decomposition in which $(\hat{\alpha}_i^2 + \hat{\beta}_i^2)/2$ is the variance associated with each frequency. During the early part of this century many investigations were made through periodogram analysis on the possible effects on meteorological data of the sunspot cycle which has a mean period of 11 years, as discussed in chapter 1. In addition, the Bruckner cycle which is somewhat irregular with a mean period of 35 years and other astronomical rhythms have been examined[31].

However, the emphasis is no longer on the detection of hidden periodicities which cannot be supported on a physical basis unlike, say, that of the annual cycle. Besides, the periodogram is disadvantageous for, although it provides unbiased estimators of the spectrum at the respective frequencies, the variance does not decrease to zero when the sample size tends to infinity. In other (statistical) words, the ordinates of the periodogram are not consistent estimators of spectral densities. Interpretation from a periodogram is, therefore, difficult with excessive scatter of neighbouring values and the occurrence of unexpected peaks. Furthermore, sample spectra from different sections of a data set resemble each other only in their overall aspects[32].

On the other hand, the continuous spectrum, as defined in the following subsection, provides when applied to stochastic processes a fair representation of the manner in which the different oscillatory movements of a variable are

---

[31] For example, Moore (1914, chapter 2) applied Fourier and harmonic analysis to rainfall in the Ohio Valley which was found to have a significant period of 8 years. Usually in this approach values of $(\alpha_i^2 + \beta_i^2)/2$ are plotted against the period $N\Delta t/i$ of harmonics in units of time, whereas in modern spectral analysis the ordinates are frequencies. Kendall and Stuart (1976, pp. 477, 480) compare the two diagrams for the Beveridge wheat price index referred to in section 2.4.1. Elsewhere, the periodogram was applied to 14 annual river-flow sequences from four continents by Andel and Balek (1971) who found apparent periodicities of 5 to 34 years; a test of significance due to Fisher (1929) was used here.

[32] This is shown, for example, by Adamowski (1971).

distributed in terms of frequencies. This could be compared with a histogram which depicts the relative strength of values within different class intervals of magnitude. Although smoothing is also required here, techniques are well advanced and, in addition, the more stable large sample behaviour is helpful.

2.6.1   Estimation of smoothed spectrum through autocorrelation function

The conventional method of estimation is to make a harmonic analysis of the autocorrelogram. This is based on the conclusions drawn from section 2.5.1 that periodic movements in time series can be preserved through the autocorrelation function; although, as noted then, information on phase differences is lost in the process of estimation, this is not important in the case of stationary processes.

The variance spectrum $s^*(f)$ and the autocovariance function C_ℓ of a continuous process, as given by equation 2.15, where f denotes frequency in cycles per unit time and ℓ refers to lag, were shown by Wiener (1930) and Khintchine (1934) to be Fourier transforms of each other[33]. This means that, over an infinite range,

$$s^*(f) = \int_{-\infty}^{+\infty} C_\ell \exp(-2\pi j f \ell)\,d\ell$$

$$= \int_{-\infty}^{+\infty} C_\ell \cos(2\pi f \ell)\,d\ell \tag{2.22}$$

in which $j = (-1)^{1/2}$ and

$$C_\ell = \int_{-\infty}^{+\infty} s^*(f) \exp(2\pi j f \ell)\,df$$

$$= \int_{-\infty}^{+\infty} s^*(f) \cos(2\pi f \ell)\,df \tag{2.23}$$

provided the integrals as defined above are finite. The theory is partly based on the fact that the autocorrelation function is symmetrical, that is, $\rho_\ell = \rho_{-\ell}$ for $\ell = 1, 2, 3, \ldots$, or in other words the function is an even one.

The part of the total variance in a time series that is attributed to a particular bandwidth $f = f_1$ to $f = f_2$ is given by

$$\int_{f_1}^{f_2} s^*(f)\,df$$

This function of the variance is termed the power within the frequency band by electrical engineers with reference to the dissipation of power in a resistor by an electrical signal, and for this reason the term power spectrum is used. For a covariance stationary series it is convenient to divide $s^*(f)$ by the variance σ^2. In

---

[33] Proof of Wiener's theorem is given also by Lee (1960, pp. 93–6).

this way, $s(f) = s^*(f)/\sigma^2$, which is called the (normalised) spectral density function, is defined by replacing C_ℓ in equation 2.22 by the autocorrelation function ρ_ℓ.

For a discrete stationary series for which the autocorrelations are considered at fixed intervals of time, Δt units apart, the integral on the right-hand side of equation 2.22 becomes a summation. Note that $d\ell$ should then be deleted and $\ell\Delta t$ should be written for ℓ. Hence

$$s^*(f) = \sum_{\ell = -\infty}^{\infty} C_{\ell\Delta t}\cos(2\pi f\ell\,\Delta t), \qquad -1/2\Delta t \leqslant f < 1/2\Delta t$$

Now let $s^*(f)$ and the summation be multiplied by $\cos(2\pi fk\Delta t)df$ and integrated from $-1/2\Delta t$ to $1/2\Delta t$, these limits being applicable because of the nature of the cosine function. Then

$$\int_{-1/2\Delta t}^{1/2\Delta t} s^*(f)\cos(2\pi fk\Delta t)df$$

$$= \sum_{k = -\infty}^{\infty} C_{\ell\Delta t}\int_{-1/2\Delta t}^{1/2\Delta t} \cos(2\pi f\ell\Delta t)\cos(2\pi fk\Delta t)\,df$$

$$= C_{k\Delta t}, \qquad k = 0, \pm 1, \pm 2, \ldots$$

by using the fact that

$$\int_{-1/2\Delta t}^{1/2\Delta t} \cos(2\pi f\ell\Delta t)\cos(2\pi fk\Delta t)\,df \begin{cases} = \frac{1}{2}, & k = \ell, -\ell \text{ but } k \neq 0 \\ = 1, & k = \ell = 0 \\ = 0 \text{ otherwise} \end{cases}$$

Accordingly, $1/2\Delta t$ is the highest frequency in cycles per unit time (or 0.5 cycle per sampling interval) for which information is sought. It is termed the Nyquist frequency after the Swedish telecommunications engineer Harry Nyquist. Incidentally, if f is replaced by ω radians per unit time, the factor 2π is omitted from the cosine terms and the Nyquist frequency becomes, $\pi/\Delta t$ radians per unit time.

The serial correlation coefficients r_ℓ are calculated using equation 2.18 for lags $\ell = 1, 2, 3, \ldots, M$, where M, which is called the truncation point, corresponds to the limiting frequency in the above discussion. Here, the choice of M is subjective; for N items of data, M could be in the range $N/5$ to $N/10$, but more about this follows. It is seen from the foregoing that the spectrum is expressed by means of cosine terms only and that the coefficients of the sine terms are zero. Also, the wavelengths, which are the periods in units of time, of the harmonics are $2M, 2M/2, 2M/3, \ldots, 2$. Equation 2.22 can then be written by using an index k, which is equal to $2fM$, where f is the frequency in cycles per unit time, in the normalised operational form

$$\hat{s}_k' = \left\{ r_0 + 2\sum_{\ell = 1}^{M-1} r_\ell \cos(\pi k\ell/M) + r_M\cos(\pi k) \right\} \bigg/ M \qquad (2.24)$$

in which usually $k = 1, 2, 3, \ldots, M$. This gives the raw estimated spectral density function[34].

It should be noted that low values of M result in bias and the loss of important information in the serial correlogram; this would lead to excessive smoothing in the spectral densities. At the other extreme, high values of M will lead to high variance and a spectrum which is not clear. A practical approach to the choice of M is to make two or three sets of calculations initially by using different values of M and then to study the sensitivity. Also, examination of the (empirical) serial correlation function is beneficial here.

It is obvious that values of r_ℓ become less reliable when ℓ increases because these are calculated from fewer observations. Therefore, it is reasonable to give less weight to values of r_ℓ at the higher lags. This is achieved by multiplying the cosine terms in equations 2.22 and 2.24 by a set of unequal weights γ_ℓ. The function that defines these is referred to as a lag window, an example of which is the following.

$$\gamma_\ell = \{1 + \cos(\pi\ell/M)\}/2 \tag{2.25}$$

This particular weighting method, known as the Tukey lag window, is equivalent to the hanning procedure which Tukey named after J. von Hann, an Austrian meteorologist[35]. In the hanning method, the raw estimates obtained from equation 2.24 are simply smoothed by means of a weighted moving average of three terms as follows.

$$\hat{s}_k = 0.25\hat{s}'_{k-1} + 0.5\hat{s}'_k + 0.25\hat{s}'_{k+1} \tag{2.26}$$

Alternatively, the hamming method due to R. W. Hamming which takes the form

$$\hat{s}_k = 0.23\hat{s}'_{k-1} + 0.54\hat{s}'_k + 0.23\hat{s}'_{k+1} \tag{2.27}$$

could be used. This is given here merely for completeness.

Equations 2.26 and 2.27 are applicable for $k = 2, 3, 4, \ldots, M-1$. The terminal spectral estimates $\hat{s}_1$ and $\hat{s}_M$ are obtained by giving double weights of $(0.5, 0.5)$ and $(0.54, 0.46)$ to the end and penultimate values ($\hat{s}'_1, \hat{s}'_2, \hat{s}'_{M-1}$ and $\hat{s}'_M$) respectively through the two methods.

Figure 2.10 shows the spectral density function obtained by using equations 2.24 and 2.26, with $M = k = 50$, from 50 years of monthly flow observations in

---

[34] The divisor M in equation 2.24 makes the area under the (normalised) spectral density function equal to unity. Actually, the divisor should be $2M$, but then there should also be a 2 after the sign of equality to replace the double infinite range in equation 2.22. If frequency is measured in radians per unit time, M should be replaced by π. Some authors, for example, Blackman and Tukey (1958, p. 35) and Craddock (1965), have omitted the divisor.

[35] Note also that there are other windows; see, for example, Jenkins and Watts (1968, chapter 7). The one employed by Parzen (1961) is the preferred alternative because it does not produce negative values. However, it appears that the advantage in its use for practical purposes, over the one described here, is not significant.

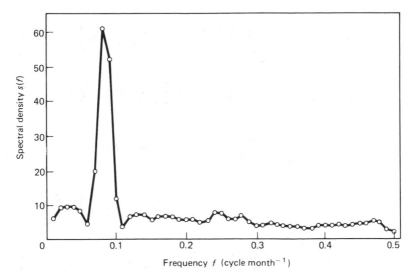

Figure 2.10   Smoothed spectral density function for monthly flows in Derwent at Yorkshire Bridge, England, where spectral densities are calculated at points shown and interpolated and the annual cycle is shown by the sharp peak at 0.08 cycle month^{-1}

the Derwent at Yorkshire Bridge in England. Note the sharp peak representing the annual cycle around $f = 0.08$ cycle month^{-1}.

An important point is that a trend-like movement in a time series appears as a low-frequency noise at, and adjacent to, $k = 0$. Although values in the spectrum near the left terminal are subject to higher sampling errors, it would be advantageous if the trend could be estimated and removed. There can, of course, be peaks elsewhere in the spectrum. Such sharply rising high values indicate rhythmic movements; higher irregularities in cyclical movements lead to peaks with broad bases, whereas at the other extreme a sine curve, which represents a perfect periodicity but is not a practical possibility, will give rise to a vertical line on the spectrum at the appropriate frequency.

It should be noted that individual points are not of great importance by themselves. Indeed, the spectrum ought to be viewed as a whole. The problems of inference and interpretation notwithstanding, the spectral shape gives an indication of the type of mathematical model that generates the series, and it is to obtain this type of information that the spectrum is perhaps best suited.

Example 2.7   The first 16 serial correlation coefficients from the total annual flows in the Gota near Sjotop-Vanersborg, Sweden, for the period 1807 to 1957 are given below. The data are taken from Yevjevich (1963), and the r_l values are computed from equation 2.18. Use equation 2.24 to evaluate the spectral density function with $M = 16$, and hence find the smoothed spectral density function through the hanning procedure given by equation 2.26.

Because the spectrum has no sharp peaks the conclusion is that there are no regular cycles of wavelengths 3 to 32 years. However, the higher spectral

Serial correlation coefficients

0.458	-0.004	-0.091	-0.055	-0.046	0.009	0.018	-0.016	-0.052	-0.002
0.024	0.007	-0.062	0.046	0.107	0.034				

$R_l = r_l \cos(\pi k/16)$

Index k		1	2	3	4	5	6	7	8	9	10	11
Wave-length 32/k years		32	16	10.7	8	6.4	5.3	4.6	4	3.6	3.2	2.9
$\pi k/16$		0.1963	0.3927	0.5890	0.7854	0.9817	1.1781	1.3744	1.5708	1.7671	1.9635	2.1598
lag l	r_l											
0	1.000	1.000	1.000	1.000	1.000	1.000	1.000	1.000	1.000	1.000	1.000	1.000
1	0.458	0.449	0.423	0.381	0.324	0.254	0.175	0.089	0	-0.089	-0.175	-0.254
2	-0.004	-0.004	-0.003	-0.002	0	0.002	0.003	0.004	0.004	0.004	0.003	0.002
3	-0.091	-0.076	-0.035	0.018	0.064	0.089	0.084	0.051	0	-0.051	-0.084	-0.089
4	-0.055	-0.039	0	0.039	0.055	0.039	0	-0.039	-0.055	-0.039	0	0.038
5	-0.046	-0.026	0.018	0.045	0.033	-0.009	-0.042	-0.038	0	0.038	0.042	0.009
6	0.009	0.003	-0.006	-0.008	0	0.008	0.006	-0.003	-0.009	-0.003	0.006	0.008
7	0.018	0.004	-0.017	-0.010	0.013	0.015	-0.005	-0.018	0	0.018	0.007	-0.015
8	-0.016	0	0.016	0	-0.016	0	0.016	0	-0.016	0	0.016	0
9	-0.052	0.010	0.048	-0.029	-0.037	0.043	0.020	-0.051	0	0.051	-0.020	-0.043
10	-0.002	0.001	0.001	-0.002	0	0.002	-0.001	-0.001	0.002	-0.001	-0.001	0.002
11	0.024	-0.013	-0.009	0.024	-0.017	-0.005	0.022	-0.020	0	0.020	-0.022	0.005
12	0.007	-0.005	0.0	0.005	-0.007	0.005	0	-0.005	0.007	-0.005	0	0.005
13	-0.062	0.052	-0.024	-0.012	0.044	-0.061	0.057	-0.034	0	0.034	-0.057	0.061
14	0.046	-0.042	0.033	-0.018	0	0.018	-0.033	0.042	-0.046	0.042	-0.033	0.018
15	0.107	-0.015	0.099	-0.089	0.076	-0.059	0.041	-0.021	0	0.021	-0.041	0.059
16	0.034	-0.034	0.034	-0.034	0.034	-0.034	0.034	-0.034	0.034	-0.034	0.034	-0.034
$2\sum_{l=1}^{15} R_l$		0.418	1.088	0.684	1.062	0.682	0.683	-0.088	-0.226	0.081	-0.718	-0.390
$\tilde{s}_k$		1.384	2.122	1.650	2.096	1.648	1.717	0.878	0.808	1.047	0.316	0.576
$\hat{s}_k$		1.753	1.819	1.879	1.777	1.738	1.490	1.070	0.885	0.804	0.564	0.446

densities in respect of the lower frequencies (or higher wavelengths) and the lower densities at the other end of the spectrum indicate an autoregressive type of dependence in the data. This type of behaviour is explained in section 2.6.2 and the next example.

The complementary term spectral window (or kernel function) λ_f is given for the Fourier transform, in the frequency domain, of the lag window. For example, the Tukey spectral window

$$\lambda_f = M[2\pi f M\{1 - (2fM)^2\}]^{-1} \sin(2\pi fM) \tag{2.28}$$

corresponds to the lag window given by equation 2.25. The effective width of a spectral window is called the bandwidth, and it is equal to $8\pi/3M$ for the Tukey spectral window. If the truncation point M is decreased, the variance and the resolution, by which we can distinguish between sharp peaks, decrease with the widening of the bandwidth, but the bias increases; an increase in M has the opposite effect.

Another point regarding equispaced sampling is that, if the interval at which observations are made is too large, a high-frequency sinusoid, of the continuous time series which is discretised, could be mistakenly identified as one with a lower frequency. This can be understood more clearly by firstly superimposing two sine curves with equal amplitudes but where the frequency of one is, say, seven times that of the other and secondly by considering the points of intersection as the sampling times. What Tukey calls aliasing is then said to occur.

2.6.2 *Some theoretical spectra*

A theoretical random process in which the variables that constitute it are mutually independent (that is, if we refer to equation 2.15, $C_\ell = 0$ for $\ell \neq 0$) and are identically distributed is termed white noise by analogy with white light in optics which in effect is a mixture of equal proportions, in terms of spectral power, of coloured lights. It follows that the white noise process, in which the frequency constituents are uniformly distributed, could be represented on the spectrum by a horizontal line which encloses unit area in the case of the spectral density function. However, this ideal condition of equal proportions of various frequencies is only approximated in practice[36]. On the other hand, if the variables are serially correlated, the process is named red noise after the low-frequency end of the spectrum. A first-order autoregressive process AR(1) or Markov process is one in which, as explained in chapter 4, the variables ξ_t can be represented by $\xi_t = \rho_1 \xi_{t-1} + \eta_t$, where η_t is a white noise process and both ξ_t and η_t have zero mean and finite variance. It is easy to show that this process has the spectral density function

---

[36] A theoretical continuous series in which there is no autocorrelation (that is, $\rho_\ell = 0$ for $\ell \neq 0$) is purely hypothetical with the implication of infinite variance, but we can visualise a natural or generated sequence to which this condition is applicable; nevertheless, the crude spectrum of the sample would still be oscillatory.

$$s_k = \bar{s}(1 - \rho_1^2)/\{1 + \rho_1^2 - 2\rho_1\cos(\pi k/M)\} \tag{2.29}$$

where $\bar{s}$ is the spectral density of the white noise process. Similarly, for the second-order autoregressive process $\xi_t = \alpha_1\xi_{t-1} + \alpha_2\xi_{t-2} + \eta_t$, given in chapter 4, the spectral density function takes the form

$$s_k = \bar{s}(1 - \rho_1\alpha_1 - \rho_2\alpha_2)/\{1 + \alpha_1^2 + \alpha_2^2 - 2\alpha_1(1 - \alpha_2)\cos(\pi k/M)$$

$$- 2\alpha_2\cos(2\pi k/M)\} \tag{2.30}$$

in which $\alpha_1 + \alpha_2 < 1$, $\alpha_1 - \alpha_2 > -1$ and $-1 < \alpha_2 < 1$ for stationary conditions[37].

2.6.3 Prewhitening

Regardless of the value of M that is adopted, some 'leakage' occurs through the process of averaging. This means that, if high frequencies are found in parts of the spectrum, they will influence neighbouring values. To circumvent this problem, Blackman and Tukey (1958) suggested the method of prewhitening. As implied, the procedure is to flatten the spectrum by filtering the sequence of data so that the spectrum appears more like a white noise spectrum than that of figure 2.10. A common method of prewhitening in hydrology is to standardise and remove periodicity from, say, an observed monthly sequence x_t, $t = 1, 2, 3, \ldots$, where $\tau = 1, 2, \ldots, 12$ are the calendar months, by using the formula

$$\xi_{t,\tau} = (x_{t,\tau} - m_\tau)/\sigma_\tau \tag{2.31}$$

However, results are affected by the periodic m_τ and s_τ values obtained from a sample (section 2.4)[38]. Another type of prewhitening is the removal of trend or low-frequency oscillation, as discussed in section 2.3.

2.6.4 Confidence limits

It has been shown that $v\,\hat{s}_k/s_k$ is distributed approximately as a chi-squared χ^2 variable in which the degrees of freedom v depend on the lag window used and s_k denotes the population spectral density[39]. For the Tukey window,

$$v = 2.67N/M \tag{2.32}$$

when N items of data are used for the spectral estimates. Hence, it follows that at a level of significance α, the $(1 - \alpha)\,100\%$ confidence limits of the (smoothed) spectral density estimates are

$$v\hat{s}_k/\chi^2_{v,\,1-\alpha/2} \quad \text{and} \quad v\hat{s}_k/\bar{\chi}^2_{v,\,\alpha/2} \tag{2.33}$$

---

[37] See, for example, Kendall (1976, p. 83) and applications made by Julian (1967) and by Gilman et al. (1963). The autocorrelation functions of the AR(1) and AR(2) processes will be found in chapter 4.

[38] The correlograms and spectra of sequences standardised in this way are shown by Roesner and Yevjevich (1966).

[39] See section 3.5 for the chi-squared distribution and degrees of freedom.

Expressed as a statement of probability this means that

$$\Pr(\chi^2_{v,\,1-\alpha/2} < v\hat{s}_k/s_k \leqslant \chi^2_{v,\,\alpha/2}) = 1 - \alpha \qquad (2.34)$$

where Pr denotes probability. It should be noted that asymptotic (that is, large sample) properties are used here to give confidence limits for different points on the spectrum, but, strictly speaking, the lines joining these limits are not confidence bands for the spectrum as a whole[40].

Example 2.8 Evaluate the spectral density function of the Markov process $\xi_t = \rho_1 \xi_{t-1} + \eta_t$ for which r_1, the estimate of ρ_1, is 0.25. If this represents the prewhitened spectral density function estimated from 600 monthly flows in the Derwent at Yorkshire Bridge, England, determine its 95 % confidence limits for values k, in equation 2.29, equal to 1, 5, 10, 20, 30, 40 and 50 and $M = 50$.

Initially, note from figure 2.10 that, apart from the single peak, the general pattern suggests a gradual decay unlike that for white noise. Now, for the Markov process,

$$\hat{s}_k = 2(1 - 0.25^2)/\{1 + 0.25^2 - 0.50\cos(\pi k/50)\}$$

$$= 1.875/\{1.0625 - 0.50\cos(\pi k/50)\} \qquad (2.35)$$

For estimating the confidence limits, $v = 2.67 \times 600/50 = 32$ degrees of freedom and, for $\alpha = 0.05$, $\chi^2_{v,\,\alpha/2} = 49.50$, $\chi^2_{v,\,1-\alpha/2} = 18.27$. Figure 2.11 shows the smoothed spectral density function of the Derwent data, prewhitened by means of equation 2.31 and estimated through a computer routine. The confidence limits given by equation 2.33 are applied in this example to the spectral densities $\hat{s}_k$ obtained from equation 2.35. Before applying the Markov process it would be useful to ascertain whether the condition $r_k \approx r_1^{|k|}$ (explained in chapter 4) is applicable to the serial correlation coefficients r_k, $k = 1, 2, 3, 4, \ldots$, of the prewhitened sequence.

Prior to concluding from figure 2.11 that the given Markov process is a reasonable approximation to that represented by the prewhitened Derwent flows or whether a more complicated model is required, additional data ought to be analysed. Alternatively, split sample tests may be taken, or the truncation point M (in equation 2.24) may be changed. An important question is whether the low-frequency oscillations in the estimated spectral densities are due to sampling fluctuations. Other diagnostic methods for this type of model are given in chapter 4.

2.6.5 Fast Fourier transform

An alternative and much faster method of estimating the spectral densities, called the fast Fourier transform (FFT), is based on the original periodogram approach in which Fourier coefficients are estimated by using equations 2.12 and 2.13. For a discrete sequence x_t, $t = 1, 2, 3, \ldots, N$, the Fourier transform is

[40] A method of measuring the reliability of spectral estimates is given by Lomnicki and Zaremba (1957) and is described by Yevjevich (1972b, pp. 95–100).

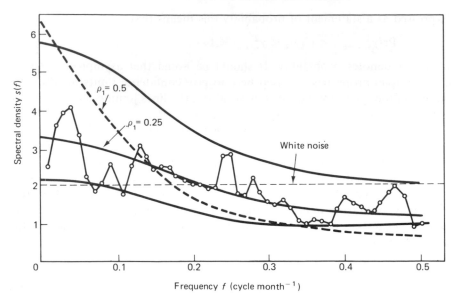

Figure 2.11 Estimated smoothed spectral density functions of prewhitened monthly flows in Derwent at Yorkshire Bridge, England: the estimated spectral density function is given by the oscillatory line; full smooth curves denote the Markov process $\xi_t = 0.25\xi_{t-1} + \eta_t$ and its 95 % confidence limits; the Markov process $\xi_t = 0.5\xi_{t-1} + \eta_t$ and the white noise process are represented by the broken curve and the broken horizontal line respectively

given by

$$X_k = N^{-1} \sum_{t=1}^{N} x_t \exp(-j2\pi tk/N) \tag{2.36}$$

where $j = (-1)^{1/2}$ and k is an index. In the FFT method, the sequence length N is decomposed into factors and the sequence is decomposed into subsequences. For a simple form of decomposition such as $N = 2^r$, where r is an integer, the number of real operations is of the order $2N \log_2(N)$ by this procedure in contrast with the N^2 operations required through the direct approach. This could result in vast savings in computer time.

The disadvantages are that sample lengths N cannot usually be factorised effectively, if at all, for time-saving purposes. This necessitates the addition of zeros, and to circumvent the distortions from these additions a technique called tapering is required. Moreover, problems may arise on account of aliasing, explained in subsection 2.6.1, and 'leaking' of significant harmonics to other frequencies. Also, there could be confusion because results differ significantly from those obtained by the continuous spectrum method[41]. These difficulties

[41] Edge and Liu (1970) investigate these differences.

notwithstanding, the use of the FFT method is obviously economical for extensive or repetitive work, in research, for instance[42]. However, sample sizes in hydrology and associated fields are limited (which means that the FFT is not expected to cause a substantial saving in time). Also, the serial correlations need to be computed in most cases. Therefore, the methods given in subsection 2.6.1 are still being used in practical applications.

2.7 Further remarks on spectrum and serial correlogram

Those advocating the use of the spectrum often extol its properties to the detriment of correlogram analysis. Indeed, raw spectral estimates at neighbouring frequencies are independent, whereas successive points on the correlogram are correlated. However, both functions are distorted in the presence of non-stationary behaviour; it is for this reason that attempts should be made initially to eliminate non-stationarities, as described earlier. What is perhaps more difficult is the interpretation of a spectrum from highly non-normal data.

Furthermore, extraordinary behaviour of a different type is seen in observed spectra of hydrological data from some parts of the world, in which oscillations, though almost regular, differ significantly from the sinusoidal pattern. In such cases sharp peaks arise in the spectra at frequencies which are subharmonics of the fundamental frequency; echoing is then said to occur—an undesirable byproduct of the method of analysis[43]. We should not conclude that these peaks represent periodicities in a deterministic sense. (Note that confirmation is possible through cross spectral analysis explained in section 2.9.) On the other hand, there could be corroboration on physical grounds as in the case of the 6-monthly cycle shown in figure 2.11. Like that in figure 2.11, the structure of the serial correlogram provides proof of the particular type of underlying periodicity.

This type of occurrence highlights the need to study both the serial correlogram and the spectrum in a complementary way[44]. Even in more straightforward situations it might be advantageous to do so. As already noted, the serial correlogram illustrates the strength of dependence between values separated in time, whereas the spectrum shows the relative significance of different frequencies of oscillation, through a decomposition of variance. Although information found in one is reflected in the other (for example, there is a relationship between the smoothness of the spectrum and the rate at which the correlogram converges to zero) a conjunctive study, in the face of uncertainty,

[42] For a worked example and references, see Jenkins and Watts (1968, pp. 314–7). Detailed explanations are also given by Cooley et al. (1977), by Bendat and Piersol (1971, chapter 9) and by Otnes and Enochson (1972, chapters 4, 7).
[43] See, for example, Quimpo (1967), Roesner and Yevjevich (1966) and Koopmans (1974, p. 199). Kendall and Stuart (1976, p. 481) give the theory for a repetitive triangular type of oscillation.
[44] See also Quimpo (1968) and the discussion by C. C. Kisiel.

enhances their potential use[45].

For the diagnosis and estimation of linear stochastic models, the correlogram has direct appeal, as shown in chapter 4. However, for input–output processes and in spatially correlated systems, such as the one explained in the following sections, spectral methods are more conducive to physical interpretation.

2.8   Cross correlogram

The covariance function C_ℓ which measures the linear dependence between items ℓ time units apart in the time series $X(t), t > 0$, with zero mean is defined for a covariance stationary process by equation 2.15. Quite often it is useful for modelling and other purposes to determine the dependence structure between two series $\{X(t), t\varepsilon T\}$ and $\{Y(t), t\varepsilon T\}$ not only at concurrent times but with one series leading or lagging the other by ℓ time units[46]. An example of this is the linear dependence between river flows at a downstream station and antecedent rainfall in the river catchment. Such a cross covariance function is defined by the following equations.

$$C_{XY}(\ell) = E\{X(t)\,Y(t+\ell)\} \tag{2.37}$$

$$C_{YX}(\ell) = C_{XY}(-\ell) = E\{X(t+\ell)\,Y(t)\} \tag{2.38}$$

in which the two series have zero means and E is the expectation operator[47]. Note that $C_{XY}(\ell) \neq C_{XY}(-\ell)$ because this is not an even function, in contrast with the equality $C_\ell = C_{-\ell}$ which follows directly from equation 2.15.

The cross correlation function of the two series $X(t)$ and $Y(t)$, with means $E(X)$ and $E(Y)$ and variances var (X) and var (Y), is given by

$$\rho_{XY}(\ell) = E[\,\{X(t) - E(X)\}\,\{Y(t+\ell) - E(Y)\}/\{\text{var}(X)\text{var}(Y)\}^{1/2}] \tag{2.39}$$

(and, similarly, $\rho_{YX}(\ell)$ corresponds to equation 2.38). These are estimated from two sets of observations $(x_t, y_t; t = 1, 2, 3, \ldots, N)$ with estimated means $\bar{x}$ and $\bar{y}$, by the sample cross correlation coefficients

$$r_{xy}(\ell) = \left\{\sum_{t=1}^{N-\ell} (x_t - \bar{x})(y_{t+\ell} - \bar{y})\right\} \bigg/ \left[\left\{\sum_{t=1}^{N} (x_t - \bar{x})^2\right\}\right.$$

$$\left. \times \left\{\sum_{t=1}^{N} (y_t - \bar{y})^2\right\}\right]^{1/2} \tag{2.40}$$

---

[45] Some applications of correlograms and spectra are also given by Panofsky and Brier (1958), by Chow and Kareliotis (1970) and by Kottegoda (1970).
[46] The relevance and effectiveness of two-site models are discussed by Kottegoda and Yevjevich (1977); see chapter 4.
[47] These definitions for C_{XY} and C_{YX} (as given by equations 2.37 and 2.38 and equation 2.40) for $r_{xy}(\ell)$, which have also been adopted by Box and Jenkins (1976, chapter 11), are not followed universally. The opposite interpretation is given, for instance, by Granger and Hatanaka (1964).

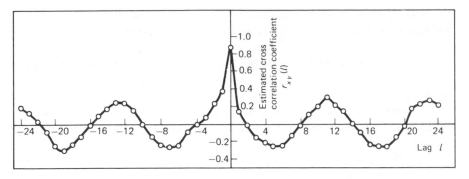

Figure 2.12 Empirical cross correlation function of monthly inflows (X series) to Alwen Reservoir, Wales, and the mean rainfall (Y series) over the catchment area of 25.6 km^2, in which the preservation of the annual cycle, the peak at zero lag and the differences between $r_{xy}(\ell)$ and $r_{xy}(-\ell)$ for each ℓ, $\ell = 1, 2, 3, \ldots$, should be noted

for lag $\ell = 0, 1, 2, \ldots$. Similarly, the sample cross correlation coefficients for negative lags, which are equal to the coefficients $r_{yx}(\ell)$ for positive lags, are obtained by changing the numerator of equation 2.40 to correspond to equation 2.38. This gives a cross correlogram for $l = 0, \pm 1, \pm 2, \ldots$. An example is shown in figure 2.12; note the preservation of the joint periodic effects.

2.9 Cross spectral analysis

In order to determine how the low- and high-frequency fluctuations in two series are related, an analysis in the frequency domain is required. The normalised cross spectrum so obtained is complementary to the cross correlogram which is in the time domain. Information on the relationships between the frequencies in the time series obtained from cross spectral analysis includes their phase differences (note that phase is not taken into account in the autocorrelation and spectral functions) and coherence which is comparable with cross correlation in its classical sense. There is also a form of spectral regression coefficient called gain.

Theoretically, the cross spectral density function of a pair of time series is a Fourier transformation of their cross correlation function; the theory is analogous to that pertaining to equation 2.22. For a frequency ω in radians per unit time, a lag window γ_ℓ (which is necessary, as before, for estimation) and truncation point M of the cross correlations, the estimated cross spectral density function is given by

$$\hat{s}_{xy}(\omega) = \left\{ \sum_{\ell=-M}^{M} \gamma_\ell r_{xy}(\ell)\cos(\omega\ell) \right\} \Big/ \pi \qquad (2.41)$$

Here, $\omega = 2\pi f$, in which f is the frequency in cycles per unit time. $\hat{s}_{xy}(\omega)$ is, in fact, a complex quantity and is therefore subdivided for operational purposes into a real part called the (in phase) normalised sample cospectrum given by

$$\hat{c}_{xy}(\omega) = \left[\gamma_0 r_{xy}(0) + \sum_{\ell=1}^{M} \gamma_\ell \left\{ r_{xy}(\ell) + r_{xy}(-\ell) \right\} \cos(\omega\ell) \right] \bigg/ \pi \quad (2.42)$$

Note that the cospectrum represents the distribution of the lag-zero cross correlation over different frequencies. Then there is an imaginary part called the normalised (out-of-phase) sample quadrature spectrum which takes the form

$$\hat{q}_{xy}(\omega) = \left[\sum_{\ell=1}^{M} \gamma_\ell \{ r_{xy}(\ell) - r_{xy}(-\ell) \} \sin(\omega\ell) \right] \bigg/ \pi \quad (2.43)$$

where $\hat{s}_{xy} = \hat{c}_{xy}(\omega) - j\hat{q}_{xy}(\omega)$ in which $j = (-1)^{1/2}$. Also, a real function called the normalised cross amplitude spectrum

$$\hat{\beta}_{xy}(\omega) = \{ \hat{c}_{xy}^2(\omega) + \hat{q}_{xy}^2(\omega) \}^{1/2} \quad (2.44)$$

can be obtained from the cospectrum and quadrature spectrum. This measures the association between the amplitudes in the two series at the same frequency ω.

A very useful relationship is the phase spectrum defined by

$$\hat{\phi}_{xy}(\omega) = \tan^{-1} \{ -\hat{q}_{xy}(\omega)/\hat{c}_{xy}(\omega) \} \quad (2.45)$$

which shows whether the components of frequency in one series lead or lag those in the other at the same frequency ω. Of equal importance is the estimated coherence (or squared coherency) spectrum

$$\hat{C}_{xy}(\omega) = \hat{\beta}_{xy}^2(\omega)/\hat{s}_x(\omega)\hat{s}_y(\omega) \quad (2.46)$$

in which the denominator is the product of the normalised sample spectral density functions of the two series. The coherence function which takes values between 0 and 1 measures the interdependence between the frequency components in the two series at frequency ω; coherence is analogous to the square of the correlation coefficient. Whereas the cross correlogram of figure 2.12 shows that the cross correlation between two series is high at lags 12, 24 and so on, the coherence function contrasts the frequencies in the two series that are mutually related with those that might be spurious or unsystematic. Note that, in order to reduce the bias in $\hat{C}_{xy}(\omega)$, the two series ought to be initially realigned in time if necessary, so that the estimated cross-correlated function peaks at zero lag; for instance, when correlating rainfall and river flow this function may not peak at zero lag if short time units are used. Again, useful information can be obtained from the gain function of the $Y(t)$ series on the $X(t)$ series (by referring to section 2.8) at frequency ω. This is comparable with the regression coefficient of the $Y(t)$ series on the $X(t)$ series and is estimated from

$$\hat{g}_y(\omega) = \hat{\beta}_{xy}(\omega)/\hat{s}_x(\omega) \quad (2.47)$$

A study of the aforementioned relationships enables us to assess the non-

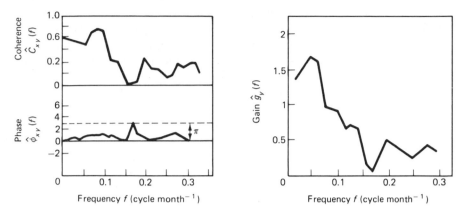

Figure 2.13   Coherence, phase and gain functions for monthly precipitation at Auburn, California, and monthly run-off of the Middle Fork American River near Auburn. (From Yevjevich (1972b), by courtesy of the author)

linearities and interactions involved in time series and should lead to the formulation of more realistic models[48]. For practical purposes it is sufficient to plot two or three of the functions, including coherency, against frequency. An example is shown in figure 2.13 in which frequencies f are given in cycles per unit time. Note, from the coherency spectrum, the strong coherence between the two sequences in the annual cycle ($f = 0.08$) and in the lower frequencies. However, the higher-frequency fluctuations are incoherent (or unrelated). The main implication here is that any additional peaks which might be observed in the spectrum of the output sequence, as discussed in section 2.8, are spurious. Again, the information in the gain function provides further confirmation. On the other hand, the interpretation of the phase function is less certain. In general, if $X(t+r)$ is in phase with $Y(t)$, which means that corresponding peaks occur at times $t+r$ and t respectively, $\phi_{xy}(\omega) = \omega r$, provided that the processes are linear, serially and bilaterally[49].

2.10   Concluding remarks

The lack of complete understanding of the physical processes involved and the

[48] Practical inferences from the coherence spectrum and its physical interpretation are discussed by Kisiel (1969, pp. 48, 62–8), and Tukey (1965) stresses the importance of the approach. Examples of cross spectral analysis are given by Buorodimos and Oguntuase (1974), by Chatfield and Pepper (1971), by Kisiel and Duckstein (1974) and by Gunnerson (1966). One of the basic applications in this area is that on marketing research by Barksdale and Guffey (1972). Applications to mean monthly temperatures in Berlin and Vienna and to other temperature sequences are given by Brillinger (1975, pp. 209–219). See also a comprehensive study by Rodríguez-Iturbe (1967). Brillinger (1975), Rodríguez-Iturbe (1967) and Jenkins and Watts (1968, chapters 8–11) explain the cross spectral analysis of multiple series, in addition.
[49] See Jenkins and Watts (1968, p. 349).

consequent uncertainties in the magnitudes and frequencies of future events have highlighted the importance of time series analysis. The methods explained here are for the purpose of examining historical sequences of time series. In addition, crossing properties, runs, range and the Hurst phenomenon are explained in chapter 5. These studies and procedures would enable, amongst other things, realistic forecasts or simulations to be made through the type of models explained in chapter 4.

The subject matter herein pertains almost exclusively to deterministic or systematic aspects. In addition, a complete specification of the random component, which as noted is an important requirement in stochastic models, is necessary. For this purpose, therefore, the estimation and practical use of probability functions that are appropriate to the underlying stochastic processes are examined in the next chapter.

References

Adamowski, K. (1971). Spectral density of a river flow time series. *J. Hydrol.*, **14**, 43–52

Andel, J., and Balek, J. (1971). Analysis of periodicity in hydrological sequences. *J. Hydrol.*, **14**, 66–82

Anderson, R. L. (1942). Distribution of the serial correlation coefficient. *Ann. Math. Statist.*, **13**, 1–13

Anderson, T. W. (1971). *Analysis of Time Series*, Wiley, New York

Avara, E. P. (1975). Some effects of autocorrelated and crosscorrelated noise on the analysis of variance. *Proceedings of the 4th Conference on Probability and Statistics in Atmospheric Sciences, Tallahassee, Florida, 18–21 November 1975*, American Meteorological Society, Lancaster, Pennsylvania, preprints, pp. 139–42

Bailey, N. T. J. (1964). *The Elements of Stochastic Processes*, Wiley, New York

Barksdale, H. C., and Guffey, H. J., Jr. (1972). An illustration of cross-spectral analysis in marketing. *J. Marketing Res.*, **9**, 271–8

Bartholomew, D. J. (1973). *Stochastic Models for Social Processes*, 2nd edn, Wiley, New York

Bartlett, M. S. (1978). *An Introduction to Stochastic Processes with Special Reference to Methods and Applications*, 3rd edn, Cambridge University Press, Cambridge

Bendat, J. S., and Piersol, A. G. (1971). *Random Data: Analysis and Measurement Procedures*, Wiley, New York

Beveridge, W. H. (1921). Weather and harvest cycles. *Econ. J.*, **31**, 429–52

Blackman, R. B., and Tukey, J. W. (1958). *The Measurement of Power Spectrum from the Point of View of Communication Engineering*, Dover Publications, New York

Bourodimos, E. L., and Oguntuase, A. M. (1974). Cross-spectral analysis of rainfall and runoff for Raritan and Mullica River basins in New Jersey. *J. Hydrol.*, **21**, 61–79

Box, G. E. P., and Jenkins, G. M. (1976). *Time Series Analysis: Forecasting and Control*, revised edn, Holden Day, San Francisco, California

Brier, G. W. (1961). Some statistical aspects of long-term fluctuations in solar and atmospheric phenomena. *Ann. N. Y. Acad. Sci.*, **95**, 173–87

Brillinger, D. R. (1975). *Time Series, Data Analysis and Theory*, Holt, Rinehart and Winston, New York

Brown, R. G. (1963). *Smoothing, Forecasting and Prediction of Discrete Time Series*, Prentice-Hall, Englewood Cliffs, New Jersey

Buishand, T. A. (1977). Stochastic modelling of daily rainfall sequences. *Mededelingen Landbouwhogeschool Wageningen, Netherlands*, **77**, No. 3.

Bullard, K. L., Yevjevich, V., and Kottegoda, N. T. (1977). Effect of misestimating harmonics in periodic hydrologic parameters. *Colo. St. Univ., Fort Collins, Hydrol. Papers*, No. 88

Buys-Ballot, C. H. D. (1847). *Les Changements Périodiques de Température*, Utrecht

Chatfield, C. (1975). *The Analysis of Time Series: Theory and Practice*, Chapman and Hall, London

Chatfield, C., and Pepper, M. P. G. (1971). Time series analysis: an example from geophysical data. *Appl. Statist.*, **20**, 217–38

Chow, Ven Te, and Kareliotis, S. J. (1970). Analysis of stochastic hydrologic systems. *Water Resour. Res.*, **6**, 1569–82. (1972). Letters. *Water Resour. Res.*, **8**, 154–65

Christiansen, J. E. (1967). Indications of changing relationships between precipitation and streamflow with time. *Proceedings of the International Conference on Water for Peace*, vol. 4, *Water Supply Technology*, United States Government Printing Office, Washington, D.C., pp. 731–9

Cliff, A. D., and Ord, J. K. (1973). *Spatial Autocorrelation*, Pion, London

Cooley, J. W., Lewis, P. A. W., Welch, P. D. (1977). The fast Fourier transform and its application to time series. *Statistical Methods for Digital Computers* (eds K. Enslein, A. Ralston and H. S. Wilf), Wiley, New York

Craddock, J. M. (1957). An analysis of the slower temperature variations at Kew Observatory by means of mutually exclusive band pass filters. *J. R. Statist. Soc. A*, **120**, 387–97

——(1965). The analysis of meteorological time series in forecasting. *Statistician*, **15**, 167–90

Davis, H. T. (1941). *The Analysis of Economic Time Series*, Principia Press, Bloomington, Indiana

Dawdy, D. R. (1972). Discussion on 'Analysis of stochastic hydrologic systems' by Ven Te Chow and S. J. Kareliotis. *Water Resour. Res.*, **8**, 154–6

Doob, J. L. (1953). *Stochastic Processes*, Wiley, New York

Draper, N. R., and Smith, H. (1966). *Applied Regression Analysis*, Wiley, New York

Durbin, J. (1962). Trend elimination by moving-average and variate-difference filters. *Bull. Int. Statist. Inst.*, **39**, 131–41

Edge, B. L., and Liu, P. C. (1970). Comparing power spectra computed by

Blackman–Tukey and fast Fourier transform. *Water Resour. Res.*, **6**, 1601–10

Fiering, M. B., and Jackson, B. (1971). *Synthetic Streamflows*, Water Resources Monograph 1, American Geophysical Union, Washington, D.C.

Fisher, R. A. (1929). Tests of significance in harmonic analysis. *Proc. R. Soc. London A*, **125**, 54–9

Gilman, D. L., Fuglister, F. J., and Mitchell, J. M., Jr. (1963). On the power spectrums of 'red noise'. *J. Atmos. Sci.*, **20**, 182–4

Granger, C. W. J., and Hatanaka, M. (1964). *Spectral Analysis of Economic Time Series*, Princeton University Press, Princeton, New Jersey

Grenander, U., and Rosenblatt, M. (1966). *Statistical Analysis of Stationary Time Series*, 2nd edn, Wiley, New York

Gunnerson, C. G. (1966). Optimizing sampling intervals in tidal estuaries. *J. Sanit. Eng. Div., Am. Soc. Civ. Eng.*, **92** (SA2), 103–25

Hannan, E. J. (1970). *Multiple Time Series*, Wiley, New York

Holloway, J. L., Jr. (1958). Smoothing and filtering of time series and space fields. *Adv. Geophys.*, **4**, 351–89

Jenkins, R. H., and Watts, D. G. (1968). *Spectral Analysis and its Applications*, Holden Day, San Francisco, California

Julian, P. R. (1967). Variance spectrum analysis. *Water Resour. Res.*, **3**, 831–45

Karlin, S., and Taylor, H. M. (1975). *A First Course in Stochastic Processes*, 2nd edn, Academic Press, New York

Keeping, E. S. (1967). Distribution-free methods in hydrology. *Statistical Methods in Hydrology, Proceedings of the 5th Hydrology Symposium, McGill University*, 1966, Queen's Printer, Ottawa, pp. 211–47

Kendall, M. G. (1976). *Time Series*, 2nd edn, Griffin, London

Kendall, M. G., and Buckland, W. R. (1971). *A Dictionary of Statistical Terms*, 3rd edn, Haffner, New York

Kendall, M. G., and Stuart, A. (1973). *The Advanced Theory by Statistics*, vol. 2, 3rd edn, Griffin, London

——(1976). *The Advanced Theory of Statistics*, vol. 3, 3rd edn, Griffin, London

Khintchine, A. (1934). Korrelationstheorie der Stationären Stochastichen Prozesse. *Mathematische Annalen*, **109**, 604–15

Kisiel, C. C. (1969). Time series analysis of hydrologic data. *Adv. Hydrosci.*, **5**, 1–119

Kisiel, C. C., and Duckstein, L. (1974). Time and frequency domain identification of a casual bivariate stochastic process. *Proceedings of the 1971 Warsaw Symposium on Mathematical Models in Hydrology, Warsaw*, vol. 1, International Association of Scientific Hydrology, Paris, pp. 364–71

Koopmans, L. H. (1974). *The Spectral Analysis of Time Series*, Academic Press, New York

Kottegoda, N. T. (1970). Statistical methods of river flow synthesis for water resources Assessment. *Proc. Inst. Civ. Eng.*, paper 7339S, suppl. XVIII

Kottegoda, N. T., and Yevejevich, V. (1977). Preservation of correlation in generated hydrologic samples through two-station models. *J. Hydrol.*, **33**, 99–121

Lee, Y. W. (1960). *Statistical Theory of Communications*, Wiley, New York

Lomnicki, Z. A., and Zaremba, S. R. (1957). On estimating the spectral density function of a stochastic process. *J. R. Statist. Soc. B*, **19**, 13–37

Moore, H. L. (1914). *Economic Cycles: Their Law and Cause*, Macmillan, New York

Natural Environmental Research Council (1975). *Flood Studies Report*, Natural Environmental Research Council, London

Otnes, R. K., and Enochson, L. (1972). *Digital Time Series Analysis*, Wiley, New York

Panofsky, H. A., and Brier, G. W. (1958). *Some Applications of Statistics to Meteorology*, Mineral Industries Extension Services, Pennsylvania State University, University Park, Pennsylvania

Papoulis, A. (1965). *Probability, Random Variables and Stochastic Processes*, McGraw-Hill, New York

Parzen, E. (1961). Mathematical considerations in the estimation of spectra. *Technometrics*, **3**, 167–90

——(1962). *Stochastic Processes*, Holden Day, San Francisco, California

Quimpo, R. G. (1967). Stochastic model of daily river flow sequences. *Colo. St. Univ., Fort Collins, Hydrol. Papers*, No. 18

——(1968). Autocorrelations and spectral analysis in hydrology. *J. Hydraul. Div., Am. Soc. Civ. Eng.*, **94** (HY2), 363–73. (1969). Discussion closure. *J. Hydraul. Div., Am. Soc. Civ. Eng.*, **95** (HY6), 2148–50

Rodríguez-Iturbe, I. (1967). The application of cross-spectral analysis to hydrologic time series. *Colo. St. Univ., Fort Collins, Hydrol. Papers*, No. 24

Roesner, L. A., and Yevjevich, V. M. (1966). Mathematical models for time series of monthly precipitation and monthly runoff. *Colo. St. Univ., Fort Collins, Hydrol. Papers*, No. 15

Schuster, A. (1898). On the investigation of hidden periodicities. *Terr. Magn.*, **3**, 13–41

Slutzky, E. (1937). The summation of random causes as the source of cyclic processes. *Econometrica*, **5**, 105–46

Sudler, C. E. (1927). Storage required for the regulation of streamflow. *Trans. Am. Soc. Civ. Eng.*, **91**, 622–60

Tukey, J. W. (1965). Data analysis and the frontiers of geophysics. *Science*, **148**, 1283–9

Wallis, J. R., and Matalas, N. C. (1971). Correlogram analysis revisited. *Water Resour. Res.*, **7**, 1448–59

Wold, H. (1954). *A Study in the Analysis of Stationary Time Series*, 2nd edn, Almqvist and Wiksell, Stockholm

Wiener, N. (1930). Generalized harmonic analysis. *Acta Mathematica*, **55**, 117–258

Yaglom, A. M. (1962). *An Introduction to the Theory of Stationary Functions*, Prentice-Hall, Englewood Cliffs, New Jersey

Yevjevich, V. (1963). Fluctuations of wet and dry years, part I. *Colo. St. Univ., Fort Collins, Hydrol. Papers*, No. 1

——(1972a). Structural analysis of hydrologic time series. *Colo. St. Univ., Fort Collins, Hydrol. Papers*, No. 56

——(1972b). *Stochastic Processes in Hydrology*, Water Resources Publications, Fort Collins, Colorado

——(1974). Determinism and stochasticity in hydrology. *J. Hydrol.*, **22**, 225–38

Yule, G. U. (1921). On the time-correlation problem, with especial reference to the incorrect variate-difference correlation method (with discussion), *J. R. Statist. Soc.*, **84**, 497–537

3 Probability functions and their use

Specification of the distributions of random variables is important for the formulation of mathematical models explained in the next two chapters and in the application of probabilistic methods treated in chapters 7, 8 and 9. For instance, the preservation of extreme values and other properties, explained in chapters 5 and 6, in a realistic manner is dependent on the appropriate choice of probability functions.

Univariate continuous distribution functions applicable to hydrological time series are discussed here. In particular, relevant members of the Pearson family are examined, and the type III function is treated in detail. The chapter includes several other types such as Johnson's S_B and S_U curves. Methods of estimating parameters through moments and maximum likelihood are given. This is followed by detailed explanations of the chi-squared and Kolmogorov–Smirnov goodness-of-fit tests with examples. In addition, procedures for generating random numbers with normal, gamma and other distributions are presented, and computer programmes are given. Complementary material is found in chapter 6 which pertains to the estimation and use of various distribution functions applicable to high flows; this includes the lognormal distribution and discrete types such as the binomial and Poisson distributions. The interpretations and general philosophy of probabilities are discussed in chapter 9.

3.1 Probability distributions of hydrological data

A sample of data is comprised of items of various magnitudes. Relevant information on their relative magnitudes can be given diagrammatically by a histogram through class frequencies within chosen intervals. To form such a diagram the ordinates are divided, for scaling purposes, by the total number of observations. If the class intervals are decreased and the sample size is increased, the histogram becomes, in the limit, a probability density curve; unit area is enclosed between it and the horizontal axis. For most natural processes, this type of curve tends to zero at its left and right extremities. In general, it could be represented mathematically by a probability density function.

The flow in a river at a particular instant of time, the annual rainfall over a catchment area and the maximum 24-hour temperature in a city are examples of random variables, so named because of uncertainty in the outcome of events. A random variable has an associated probability density function and is often referred to as a variate[1]. If a continuous variable X takes a value x, then its probability density for this value is usually denoted by $f(x)$. The probability that X takes any value in an interval x_1 to x_2 is given by

$$\Pr(x_1 < X \leqslant x_2) = \int_{x_1}^{x_2} f(x)\,dx \tag{3.1}$$

If x_1 is the lowest possible value (equal to $-\infty$ in the limit) which X can take, the probability in equation 3.1 is denoted by $F(x_2)$ and, in general, by $F(x)$, where $0 \leqslant F(x) \leqslant 1$; $F(x)$ is termed the (cumulative probability) distribution function.

Similarly, the joint probability that the random variables X and Y take values in the intervals (x_1, x_2) and (y_1, y_2) respectively can be described by the bivariate distribution function

$$\Pr(x_1 < X \leqslant x_2, y_1 < Y \leqslant y_2) = \int_{x_1}^{x_2} \int_{y_1}^{y_2} f(x, y)\,dx\,dy \tag{3.2}$$

in which the bivariate probability density function $f(x, y)$ represents a three-dimensional surface enclosing unit volume. Now $f(x)$ and $f(y)$ are called the marginal or univariate probability density functions of the X and Y populations respectively. Also, if the values of X and Y are statistically independent, $f(x, y) = f(x)f(y)$, but this may not be true in applications. The concept can be extended in a straightforward manner to a multivariate probability distribution of three or more random variables.

Often there is the need to incorporate empirical probability density functions in a mathematical model. The accepted practice is to infer from the particular sample the general form of a hypothetical infinite population of which the data are a random sample and to estimate the parameters of this population. Tests on goodness of fit between the hypothetical and observed probability densities or distributions are then made. This approach is based on the assumption that the hydrologic regime is time invariant, which means that long-term non-stationarities are not considered to be significant.

The uncertainties of the inferences made should not be forgotten because, in several cases, a historical sample of data may not fully represent the population. This is of importance if large-scale extrapolations are planned. For example, it

---

[1] Standard normal variates and gamma variates, for instance, will be referred to in the text.

could be a record of a dry 50-year period within a 500-year climatic oscillation, or, on the other hand, unusually high flood flows may be included. Verification of this might be carried out by correlation with longer sequences of flow data, if available, or associated phenomena such as rainfall, from the same region or climatic zone.

From early times a great deal of the theory of mathematical statistics and probability has been based on the assumption of normality in distribution. If a random variable X is normally distributed, its probability density function is given by

$$f(x) = \{\sigma(2\pi)^{1/2}\}^{-1}\exp\{-(x-\mu)^2/2\sigma^2\}, \qquad -\infty \leqslant x \leqslant \infty \qquad (3.3)$$

where the mean μ and the standard deviation σ of the population are the two parameters which completely specify the function. This function can also be written in the standard form

$$f(z) = (2\pi)^{-1/2}\exp(-z^2/2) \qquad (3.4)$$

where $z = (x-\mu)/\sigma$ and $-\infty \leqslant z \leqslant \infty$; this represents a bell-shaped function with a maximum ordinate of $1/(2\pi)^{1/2}$ and points of inflection at $z = 1, -1$. It should be noted that the first σ term in equation 3.3 is required to make the area between the curve $y = f(x)$ and the x axis equal to unity[2].

Similarly, by referring to equation 3.2, if z_1 and z_2 denote the values of the random variables from the X and Y populations which, say, take the place of z in equation 3.4, then the standardised bivariate normal frequency function is given by

$$f(z_1, z_2) = \{2\pi(1-\rho^2)^{1/2}\}^{-1}\exp\{-(z_1^2 - 2\rho z_1 z_2 + z_2^2)/(2-2\rho^2)\} \qquad (3.5)$$

where ρ is the coefficient of correlation between the X and Y populations; application of this function is discussed in chapter 7. A more general form of equation 3.5 can be written to represent the multivariate normal density function involving more than one variable.

By normal we used to imply that any data set which does not conform with the properties of the normal distribution is exceptional. The normal curve is known to have originated in the eighteenth century by De Moivre, and it was

---

[2] Tables of $f(z)$ and the distribution function $F(z)$ are commonly found. Note that, for large z, $F(z) \approx 1 - f(z)/z$, for $z > 0$; for $z = 1, 5, 2, 2.5$ and 3, errors are $2.14, 0.44, 0.08$ and 0.01% respectively, with $F(z)$ being underestimated. The following approximation holds for all $z > 0$ (Abramowitz and Stegun, 1964, p. 932) with an error of less than 1×10^{-5}.

$$F(z) \approx 1 - f(z)(0.436\,183\,6b - 0.120\,167\,6b^2 + 0.937\,298\,0b^3)$$

where $b = 1/(1 + 0.332\,67z)$. For a given $F(z)$, the inverse function for z, $z > 0$, can be approximated by solving the cubic

$$0.044\,715z^3 + z - (\pi/8)^{1/2}\ln[F(z)/\{1 - F(z)\}] = 0$$

errors are less than 1% for $z < 3.0$; see Page (1977). For a more accurate inverse function, see Beasley and Springer (1977).

developed as a mathematical tool notably by Gauss and Laplace. Because its initiation should perhaps be attributed to more than one person, the adjective normal is preferred here to alternatives such as gaussian.

The reasoning for normality or asymptotic (that is, when applied to large samples) normality in distribution is largely based on the central limit theorem. The theorem is due to Lindeberg, Liapounoff and Laplace, and it states basically that the sum of N identically distributed mutually independent random variables with finite variances tends to be normally distributed as N tends to infinity[3].

A great deal has also been written on the normal law of error, subsequent to the research of Gauss in astronomy. Use of the normal function is advantageous because its statistical properties are well established. Such virtues notwithstanding, the only justification that can be found is in the observations that are recorded. As for its asymptotic properties, it could be argued that these are mainly of academic interest if we consider the finite time spans, such as the period of usefulness of a reservoir for the design of which the data are to be used. An important question is the sensitivity of the form of distribution function on the main hydrological characteristics; this will be discussed in chapters 5 and 6.

Except for certain annual series, empirical distributions of hydrological data are not commonly normal, which is a specific symmetric type. This is because the density functions are physically bounded by left terminals which are positive or zero in the limit. On the side of high flows the tails are long, and there is greater uncertainty regarding their shapes and lengths. In many cases empirical data which describe various other phenomena in nature are also non-normal in distribution. In fact, as early as 1879, Galton, the founder of biometrics, warned about some of the absurdities which the use of the normal function leads to[4].

For these reasons and because of the preponderance of relatively low values, the probability density functions are asymmetrical. With the mean greater than the mode (which is at the position of maximum density) the coefficient of asymmetry or skewness is positive in a hydrological density function. Another point is that, in discrete (averaged) time series, the coefficient of skewness tends to increase with the closeness in the spacing of the data. This means that the skewness in distributions of daily data is greater than that in monthly data, and annual data are comparatively normal in distribution, by the central limit theorem.

Hydrologists, as well as other applied scientists, have sought theoretical justification for the choice of particular probability functions. For instance, it is known that the normal, lognormal and gamma functions are applicable if a series of events can be attributed to an infinitely large number of additive,

[3] The central limit theorem and the normal law of error are discussed in most statistical texts, for example those by Feller (1968) and by Gnedenko (1968). Lucid explanations are also found in the *Encyclopaedia Brittanica* (1932, 1969). Support for normality has been given, for instance, by Daw (1966).
[4] Galton's work is referred to, for instance, by Kottler (1950). Heath (1967) notes the non-normality in natural distributions.

multiplicative or squares of independent causal factors respectively. These arguments are, however, difficult to validate for river flows and other natural phenomena which change in time and space with the complexities of underlying processes and their interactions. Indeed, it would be more realistic to think that observed events are caused by interdependent factors of various types, which can be additive, multiplicative, exponential and so on.

These analytical difficulties have led to applications of heuristic curve-fitting methods. To meet the practical requirements, systems of distribution or probability density functions have been suggested. Such a system, if it is an adequate one, should be capable of representing a whole range of observed distributions. Because of uncertainty and lack of information regarding natural processes, more weight is usually given to goodness of fit in the choice of system and a particular member than to the mathematical soundness of its origin or justification on some hypothetical physical grounds. However, there are other considerations.

In making the final choice, feasibility of computation, estimation and application could be the decisive factors. Then there is also the question of sensitivity with regard to design variables such as reservoir capacities and lengths of spillways; however, these aspects are not examined here. For practical purposes, a particular function should not have too many parameters for its specification. This may be four in the limit to be reduced to three or two if sample limitations and uncertainties in estimation warrant.

3.2 Pearson density functions

A system which has been used extensively in many fields is that originated by Pearson. In one of his better-known papers, Fisher (1922) stated that 'we may instance the development by Pearson of a very extensive system of skew curves . . . a body of work which has enormously extended the power of modern statistical practice'. After several decades of experimentation over a wide sphere and in spite of the apparently diminishing interest in curve fitting, many will agree with these remarks. Pearson's system of frequency curves is logical and practical and covers a wide range of empirical distributions found in various fields[5].

The system is based on the following differential equation in which y is the ordinate of a probability density function $f(x)$ at a distance x from the origin, and d, c_0, c_1 and c_2 are constants.

$$dy/dx = y(x - d)/(c_0 + c_1 x + c_2 x^2) \qquad (3.6)$$

The different types of functions depend on the nature of the roots of the

---

[5] The first published work on the applications of these curves in hydrology is by Foster (1924). Reference to the Pearson system is also found in the work of Goodrich (1927) and the ensuing discussion, which deal with empirical methods for plotting asymmetrically distributed data; see also Slade (1936).

equation

$$c_0 + c_1 x + c_2 x^2 = 0 \qquad (3.7)$$

Density functions obtained through equation 3.6 have a single mode (which is equidistant from the points of inflection) at $x = d$ if d is not a root of equation 3.7. The left and right termini of a function may be finite or infinite (with $dy/dx = 0$) or one of each kind. It will, of course, be possible to obtain a better fit to the data by the inclusion of additional constants such as c_3 and c_4, that is, by expanding the polynomial part (in parentheses) of equation 3.6; however, there is no advantage in doing so on account of likely sampling errors in available data sets. Because the objective is to estimate the distribution function and the parameters that define the population and not those which closely fit a sample, the incorporation of additional terms may be misleading.

The numbers originally assigned to the various Pearson densities seem to be arbitrary; they comprise a total of twelve functions. Of the different types, the type III (gamma) function has been used in a variety of applications such as in hydrology and meteorology. The other forms suited to data which have probability densities with finite left terminals and positive skewness are the type I (beta), type VI (inverted beta or beta of the second kind) and type V (inverted gamma) functions. These are listed in table 3.1 and the different derivations are based on the roots of equation 3.7; of these the gamma and beta forms have, in their general Pearson types, three and four parameters respectively which are positive in all cases. As a whole, these types are widely representative, and in common they have a finite left terminal ξ known as the location parameter and unbounded right tails except for the type I curve which terminates at $\xi + \lambda$. The parameters γ and δ of these functions modify the shape; λ is a scale parameter and $e(= 2.718\,28 \ldots)$ is the exponential constant. Also, it is important to note that the functions $\Gamma(\gamma) = \int_0^\infty x^{\gamma-1} e^{-x} \, dx$ and $B(\gamma, \delta) = \int_0^1 x^{\gamma-1} (1-x)^{\delta-1} \, dx = \Gamma(\gamma)\Gamma(\delta)/\Gamma(\gamma+\delta)$ are the (complete) gamma and beta functions respectively; the adjective incomplete is used in this context if the upper limit of integration is less than the maximum for the function. Now, if $\xi = 0$ and $\lambda = 1$, the number of parameters are reduced by two so that types III and I have the same basic form as in the definitions for $\Gamma(\gamma)$ and $B(\gamma, \delta)$ respectively. Again, restoration of the

Table 3.1   Four Pearson densities with finite left terminals and positive skewness

Type	Density function; $\gamma, \delta, \lambda, \xi > 0$; $x \geqslant \xi$; for type I only; $\xi \leqslant x \leqslant \xi + \lambda$	Roots of equation 3.7
I	$f(x) = (x-\xi)^{\gamma-1}\{1 - (x-\xi)/\lambda\}^{\delta-1}/\lambda^\gamma B(\gamma, \delta)$	Real and opposite in sign
III	$f(x) = (x-\xi)^{\gamma-1} e^{-(x-\xi)/\lambda}/\lambda^\gamma \Gamma(\gamma)$	c_2 is zero and there is only one root, $-c_0/c_1$
V	$f(x) = (x-\xi)^{\gamma-1} e^{-\gamma/(x-\xi)} \lambda^\gamma/\Gamma(\gamma)$	Real and equal
VI	$f(x) = (x-\xi)^{\gamma-1} \lambda^\delta/(x+\lambda-\xi)^{\gamma+\delta} B(\gamma, \delta)$	Real and of the same sign

scale parameter gives in the case of the type III function, the commonly used (two-parameter) gamma density function (the distribution function of which is the incomplete gamma function, subject to scaling effects).

3.2.1   Type I function

Because the roots of equation 3.7 are real and opposite in sign, equation 3.6 may be written as

$$\frac{d\{\log(y)\}}{dx} = \frac{x-d}{a_1(x-a_2)(a_3-x)}$$

$$= \frac{1}{a_1(a_3-a_2)}\left(\frac{a_2-d}{x-a_2}+\frac{a_3-d}{a_3-x}\right) \tag{3.8}$$

Hence,

$$f(x) = k_0(x-a_2)^{(a_2-d)/a_1(a_3-a_2)}(a_3-x)^{-(a_3-d)/a_1(a_3-a_2)}$$
$$a_2 \leqslant x \leqslant a_3 \tag{3.9}$$

where k_0 is the constant of integration. If we write $\xi, \xi+\lambda, \gamma-1$ and $\delta-1$ for a_2, a_3 and the two power constants respectively and if we use a new constant $k_1 = k_0 \lambda^{\delta-1}$, equation 3.9 becomes

$$f(x) = k_1(x-\xi)^{\gamma-1}\{1-(x-\xi)/\lambda\}^{\delta-1}, \qquad \xi \leqslant x \leqslant \xi+\lambda \tag{3.10}$$

Substituting z for $(x-\xi)/\lambda$, $0 \leqslant z \leqslant 1$, and equating the area enclosed by the probability density curve to 1, which, as already noted, is the basic requirement for all probability density functions, we obtain

$$k_1 \int_0^1 z^{\gamma-1}\lambda^{\gamma-1}(1-z)^{\delta-1}\lambda\,\delta z = 1 \tag{3.11}$$

From the definition of the complete beta function, $k_1 = 1/\lambda^\gamma B(\gamma, \delta)$. Hence the type I function can be written in the form

$$f(x) = (x-\xi)^{\gamma-1}\{1-(x-\xi)/\lambda\}^{\delta-1}/\lambda^\gamma B(\gamma, \delta), \qquad \xi \leqslant x \leqslant \xi+\lambda \tag{3.12}$$

The function is J shaped if $\gamma < 1$, and this can represent probability densities of daily rainfall totals. If in addition $\delta < 1$, a U-shaped function is obtained which has been used to represent probability densities of cloud intensities[6].

---

[6] Several applications of the type I function have been made in hydrology, for example, by Johnson and Tattersall (1971).

3.2.2 Type III function

For this type, $c_2 = 0$. Accordingly, equation 3.6 can be expressed as

$$\frac{d\{\log(y)\}}{dx} = \frac{x-d}{c_0 + c_1 x}$$

$$= \frac{1}{c_1} - \frac{d + c_0/c_1}{c_0 + c_1 x} \qquad (3.13)$$

Hence

$$f(x) = e^{k_0 + x/c_1}(c_0 + c_1 x)^{-(d + c_0/c_1)/c_1}, \qquad x \geqslant -c_0/c_1 \qquad (3.14)$$

where e^{k_0} is the constant of integration. If we change $-(d + c_0/c_1)/c_1$ to $\gamma - 1$, divide by $c_1^{\gamma-1}$ and substitute $-\xi$ for c_0/c_1 and $-\lambda$ for c_1, equation 3.14 can be written, by using a new constant $k_1 = e^{k_0 - c_0/c_1^2} c_1^{\gamma-1}$, in the form

$$f(x) = k_1 e^{-(x-\xi)/\lambda}(x-\xi)^{\gamma-1}, \qquad \xi \leqslant x \leqslant \infty \qquad (3.15)$$

Substituting z for $(x-\xi)/\lambda$, $0 \leqslant z \leqslant \infty$, and because unit area should be enclosed by a probability density curve, we obtain

$$k_1 \int_0^\infty e^{-z} z^{\gamma-1} \lambda^{\gamma-1} \lambda \, dz = 1 \qquad (3.16)$$

Using the definition of the (complete) gamma function gives $k_1 = \lambda^{-\gamma}/\Gamma(\gamma)$. This leads to the type III function

$$f(x) = (x-\xi)^{\gamma-1} e^{-(x-\xi)/\lambda} / \lambda^\gamma \Gamma(\gamma), \qquad \xi \leqslant x \leqslant \infty \qquad (3.17)$$

If $\gamma = 1$, this becomes an exponential function (see section 6.9); if $\gamma < 1$, it is J shaped, that is, $f(x) = \infty$ at the origin.

3.2.3 Type V function

From the characteristics in Table 3.1

$$\frac{d\{\log(y)\}}{dx} = \frac{x-d}{a_1(x-a_2)^2}$$

$$= \frac{1}{a_1(x-a_2)} + \frac{a_2-d}{a_1(x-a_2)^2} \qquad (3.18)$$

Hence,

$$f(x) = k_0(x-a_2)^{1/a_1} e^{-(a_2-d)/a_1(x-a_2)}, \qquad x \geqslant a_2 \qquad (3.19)$$

where k_0 is the constant of integration. Changing a_2, $1/a_1$ and $(a_2-d)/a_1$ to ξ, $(-\gamma-1)$ and λ respectively gives

$$f(x) = k_0(x-\xi)^{-\gamma-1} e^{-\lambda/(x-\xi)}, \qquad \xi \leqslant x \leqslant \infty \qquad (3.20)$$

The constant k_0 is found by substituting $1/z$ for $(x - \xi)/\lambda$, $0 \leqslant z \leqslant \infty$, and by analysing as in the case of the type III function. Hence, the function can be written

$$f(x) = (x - \xi)^{-\gamma - 1} e^{-\lambda/(x - \xi)} \lambda^{\gamma}/\Gamma(\gamma), \qquad \xi \leqslant x \leqslant \infty \qquad (3.21)$$

3.2.4 Type VI function

From the tabulated characteristics,

$$\frac{d\{\log(y)\}}{dx} = \frac{x - d}{a_1(x - a_2)(x - a_3)} \qquad (3.22)$$

By following the procedure used for the type I function,

$$f(x) = k_0(x - a_2)^{(a_2 - d)/a_1(a_2 - a_3)}(x - a_3)^{-(a_3 - d)/a_1(a_2 - a_3)} \qquad (3.23)$$

By changing constants

$$f(x) = k_1(x - \xi)^{\gamma - 1}(x + \lambda - \xi)^{-\delta - \gamma}, \qquad \xi \leqslant x \leqslant \infty \qquad (3.24)$$

The constant k_1 is found by substituting $z/(1 - z)$ for $(x - \xi)/\lambda$, $0 \leqslant z \leqslant 1$, and by integrating as for the type I function. Therefore,

$$f(x) = (x - \xi)^{\gamma - 1}(x + \lambda - \xi)^{-\delta - \gamma} \lambda^{\delta}/B(\gamma, \delta) \qquad (3.25)$$

represents the type VI function. This function is J shaped if $\gamma < 1$.

3.3 Estimation by method of moments

Pearson applied the method of moments[7] in order to fit probability density functions to samples of data. Commenting on the procedure, Fisher (1922) stated, 'Perhaps the most extended use of the criterion of consistency has been developed by Pearson in the method of moments. In this method, which is without question of great practical utility, different forms of frequency curves are fitted by calculating as many moments of the sample as there are parameters to be evaluated. The parameters chosen are those of an infinite population of the specified type having the same moments as those calculated from the sample.' Here, the word consistency means that, if $\tilde{\theta}$, say, is a consistent estimator of θ, it converges (in probability) to the required parameter.

In a random sample of data $x_i, i = 1, 2, \ldots, N$, with estimated mean $\bar{x}$, the nth central moment μ_n is estimated by the statistic m_n as follows.

$$m_n = N^{-1} \sum_{i=1}^{N} (x_i - \bar{x})^n \qquad (3.26)$$

The first central moment is zero and the second gives an estimate of the

---

[7] According to Fisher, this dates back to Bessel, Gauss and Thiele. The moment-generating function, explained in chapter 6, is complementary to this section.

variance; the multiplication of this by $N/(N-1)$ makes it unbiased. If $\bar{x}$ in equation 3.26 is replaced by zero, then this gives the estimated nth moment m'_n about the origin; the first moment is the sample mean.

In order to predetermine which type of probability density curve suits the data best, it is useful to know the moment coefficients $\beta_1 = \mu_3^2/\mu_2^3$ and $\beta_2 = \mu_4/\mu_2^2$ of the series. These coefficients, estimated by the statistics b_1 and b_2 by using the sample moments given by equation 3.26, are also called the moment ratios or beta coefficients. The square root of the first is in fact the coefficient of asymmetry or skewness, and the second is the coefficient of kurtosis.

3.3.1　Graphical procedure

A practical means of making an initial choice of a probability distribution is through a diagram of kurtosis against skewness on which curves or zones between curves which mathematically represent the three- or four-parameter functions respectively, as listed in table 3.1, are drawn. These curves are shown in figure 3.1; also given here are points representing the estimated values of kurtosis and skewness from some samples of river-flow data which have been

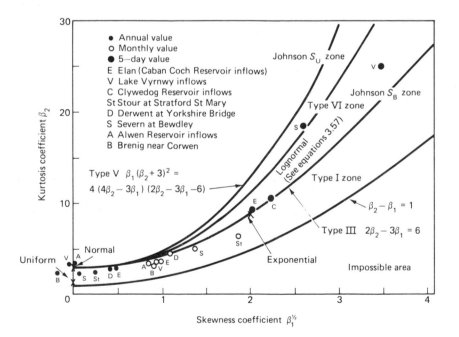

Figure 3.1　Locations or boundaries of Pearson- and Johnson-type functions with estimated values from historical samples and in which points representing exponential, normal and uniform functions are also shown, with coefficients of kurtosis and skewness (9, 2), (3, 0) and (1.8, 0) respectively

discretised to form annual, monthly and 5-day (pentad) series[8]. The point ($\beta_2 = 3$, $\beta_1^{1/2} = 0$), at which the curves of the type III and V functions originate, represents the normal function; the estimated values of β_2 and $\beta_1^{1/2}$ for a particular series increase from this point when the time unit on which it is based is decreased, as mentioned in section 3.1. For the assessment of sampling errors and the choice of distribution functions, knowledge of the distributions of $b_1^{1/2}$ and b_2, the estimated coefficients of skewness and kurtosis, is required.

3.3.2 Sampling errors in estimates of skewness and kurtosis

The distribution of the *estimated skewness* $b_1^{1/2}$ is asymptotically normal. However, for small samples of less than, say, $N = 200$ items from a non-normal population, the probability density of $b_1^{1/2}$ is asymmetrical, with the skewness increasing for higher values of skewness in the parent population. From the work of Fisher it is known that, as normality is approached, the standard error of $b_1^{1/2}$ is $\{6N(N-1)/(N-2)(N+1)(N+3)\}^{1/2}$ which tends to $(6/N)^{1/2}$ for large samples. On the other hand, if the sample is drawn from a *normal* universe, the probability density function of b is symmetrical, and Fisher's formula for the standard error is applicable. Note that the standard errors given here are, in a strict sense, applicable only to serially independent data.

As for the distribution of the *estimated kurtosis* b_2, much larger samples are required than for $b_1^{1/2}$ if an approximation to normality is to be justified[9]. Results of computer experiments are useful in attempting to resolve the uncertainty here. For instance, D'Agostino and Pearson (1973) obtained the probability distribution of b_2 through computer simulation of small samples from a *normal* population. Generation of random numbers will be explained in section 3.7. For example, it was found that for samples of 50, 100, 150 and 200 items, the 95 % confidence limits of b_2 are 4.35, 2.07; 4.02, 2.27; 3.85, 2.37; 3.74, 2.44 respectively[10]. The results show that the positive skewness in the distribution of b_2 decreases as N increases. For large samples from a normal population, the coefficient $b_2 - 3$ of excess may be compared with $(24/N)^{1/2}$, which is the asymptotic standard error[11]. However, if the parent population is highly *non-*

---

[8] It would be more appropriate for some purposes, such as the application of Box–Jenkins models, which will be explained in chapter 5, if the moments of estimated independent residuals are used as shown by Kottegoda (1970, 1972). Svanidze (1974) in a study on skewness and kurtosis has given values of b_1 and b_2 for 200 annual flow series from many parts of the world; see also the earlier work of Matalas (1963) on low flows and the work of Gupta (1970) and of Snyder (1972). Furthermore, Markovic (1965) studied the distributions of annual rainfall and run-off data from 2506 stations in the United States. Note that there is also a criterion used by Pearson for this purpose, as given for instance, by Elderton and Johnson (1969, p. 41).

[9] In recent years there has been a fresh impetus of papers on tests for normality especially in *Biometrika* in which Geary's test was published in 1935.

[10] In each pair, the higher and lower values have probabilities of non-exceedance equal to 0.975 and 0.025 respectively.

[11] See also Pearson and Hartley (1972, pp. 36–40).

normal, there is great uncertainty regarding the sampling distribution of b_2 when sample sizes are small.

3.3.3   *Reasons for frequent use of type III function*

The central position of the curve representing the type III function in figure 3.1, around which the points appear to be scattered, seems to justify the popularity of this function. Also, it needs only three parameters for definition, which is one less than for the beta types. Here, we must bear in mind the likely errors of sampling, the magnitudes of which might be gauged by evaluating the coefficients in split samples. Therefore, initial acceptance of the function could be based on close proximity to the curve. There is, of course, no certainity in such inferences, and, even if a point lies exactly on the curve, it does not necessarily follow that the probability density is identical with the type III function but that it is a good approximation to it[12].

3.3.4   *Method of moments applied to type III function*

As shown in 3.2.2, the general form for this probability density function is

$$f(x) = (x - \xi)^{\gamma - 1} e^{-(x - \xi)/\lambda} / \lambda^{\gamma} \Gamma(\gamma)$$

Because this function is defined through three parameters, it is necessary to evaluate the first three moments. The nth moment of the area enclosed by the function and the x axis about a vertical axis, say, y', through the left terminal if the function is

$$\mu'_n = \int_{\xi}^{\infty} f(x)(x - \xi)^n \, dx \tag{3.27}$$

Substituting for $f(x)$ and changing $(x - \xi)/\lambda$ to z, $0 \leqslant z \leqslant \infty$, with $dx = \lambda \, dz$, we obtain

$$\mu'_n = \lambda^n \int_{0}^{\infty} z^{\gamma + n - 1} e^{-z} \, dz / \Gamma(\gamma) \tag{3.28}$$

From the definition $\Gamma(\gamma) = \int_{0}^{\infty} z^{\gamma - 1} e^{-z} \, dz$ it follows that

$$\mu'_n = \lambda^n \Gamma(\gamma + n) / \Gamma(\gamma) \tag{3.29}$$

Integration by parts gives

$$\Gamma(\gamma + n) = \int_{0}^{\infty} z^{\gamma + n - 1} e^{-z} \, dz$$

$$= [-z^{\gamma + n - 1} e^{-z}]_{0}^{\infty} + \int_{0}^{\infty} e^{-z} (\gamma + n - 1) z^{\gamma + n - 2} \, dz \tag{3.30}$$

---

[12] Note also that the location of the lognormal function, which will be introduced in section 3.6, is almost central; this gives justification for its frequent use.

The lower limit in the first term on the right-hand side is zero. By successive differentiation (with respect to z) of the numerator and denominator of $z^{\gamma+n-1}/e^z$ until the power of z in the numerator is negative the upper limit is also found to be zero. (This is through l'Hospital's rule; alternatively, we may apply a Taylor series expansion to the denominator and then divide by the numerator.) The second term on the right-hand side is equivalent to $(\gamma+n-1)\Gamma(\gamma+n-1)$. Hence

$$\Gamma(\gamma+n) = (\gamma+n-1)\Gamma(\gamma+n-1)$$

and from equation 3.29 by successive substitutions

$$\mu'_n = \lambda^n(\gamma+n-1)(\gamma+n-2)\ldots(\gamma+1)\gamma \qquad (3.31)$$

from which the first three moments about the left terminal are

$$\mu'_1 = \lambda\gamma$$
$$\mu'_2 = \lambda^2(\gamma+1)\gamma$$
$$\mu'_3 = \lambda^3(\gamma+2)(\gamma+1)\gamma \qquad (3.32)$$

Consider a sample of data $x_i, i = 1, 2, \ldots, N$, the histogram of which seems to fit the type III function, given by equation 3.17, on the basis of the estimated moment coefficients and the corresponding curve in figure 3.1. Let $x' = x - \xi$. Also, let $\bar{x}$ and $\bar{x}'$ denote respectively the estimated means or first moments about the axes of y and y', through the left terminal from which the x' values are measured. It follows that .

$$\bar{x} = \bar{x}' + \tilde{\xi}, \qquad x - \bar{x} = x' - \bar{x}' \qquad (3.33)$$

where $\tilde{\xi}$ is the estimator of ξ. The estimated second central moment, that is, variance with $\sum$ denoting $\sum\limits_{i=1}^{N}$, is given by

$$m_2 = \sum (x - \bar{x})^2/N$$
$$= \sum (x' - \bar{x}')^2/N - m'_2 - (m'_1)^2 \qquad (3.34)$$

where m'_i is the estimated ith moment about the y' axis and $m'_1 = \bar{x}'$. Equating these two sample moments to the moments of function 3.17 given by the first two equations 3.32 respectively and simplifying, we find that $m_2, \tilde{\gamma}$ and $\tilde{\lambda}$ are related as follows.

$$m_2 = \tilde{\lambda}^2\tilde{\gamma} \qquad (3.35)$$

where $\tilde{\gamma}$ and $\tilde{\lambda}$ denote moment estimators of these parameters. In the same way, the estimated third central moment is

$$m_3 = \sum (x - \bar{x})^3/N$$
$$= \sum (x' - \bar{x}')^3/N \qquad (3.36)$$

After expanding the right-hand side and regrouping, we obtain

$$m_3 = m'_3 - 3m'_1 m'_2 + 2(m'_1)^3 \tag{3.37}$$

By substituting m'_3 for μ'_3 and so on from equations 3.32 and by simplifying, the relationship between m_3, $\tilde{\lambda}$ and $\tilde{\gamma}$ becomes

$$m_3 = 2\tilde{\lambda}^3 \tilde{\gamma} \tag{3.38}$$

The estimator g_1 of γ_1, the skewness coefficient, equals $m_3/m_2^{3/2}$. Therefore, using equations 3.35 and 3.38, we get

$$\tilde{\gamma} = 4/g_1^2 \tag{3.39}$$

This result is applicable also to the gamma density function. From equations 3.35 and 3.39, changing $m_2^{1/2}$ to the estimated standard deviation s gives

$$\tilde{\lambda} = sg_1/2 \tag{3.40}$$

From the first of equations 3.32 and from equation 3.33

$$\begin{aligned} \tilde{\xi} &= \bar{x} - \bar{x}' \\ &= \bar{x} - \tilde{\lambda}\tilde{\gamma} \\ &= \bar{x} - 2s/g_1 \end{aligned} \tag{3.41}$$

3.4 Maximum likelihood method of estimation

The concept of maximum likelihood (ML) was originated by Daniel Bernoulli about 200 years ago. The ML method of estimating parameters is due to Fisher. This optimisation procedure has been accepted as a more efficient method when compared with the method of moments for most distributions. Again we quote Fisher (1922), 'The criterion of efficiency is satisfied by those statistics which when derived from large samples tend to a normal distribution with the least possible standard deviation.' Efficiencies of estimators can be compared by their variances. However, one drawback in ML estimation is that the exact form of the distribution must be known.

Let the random sample x_1, x_2, ..., x_N be part of a population, the distribution of which depends on, say, the three parameters γ, λ and ξ. Then, $L(x_1, x_2, \ldots, x_N | \gamma, \lambda, \xi)$ is called the likelihood of the sample. For a given density function $f(x)$ and a set of parameters there could be an infinite number of different samples from the same population. The likelihood function is defined as

$$L = \prod_{i=1}^{N} f(x_i | \gamma, \lambda, \xi) \tag{3.42}$$

in which $L(.)$ is replaced by L and $f(x_i | \gamma, \lambda, \xi)$ denotes the probability density for a particular value x_i and a set of parameters γ, λ and ξ.

The likelihood L changes with variations in the values of the three parameters; by the ML method a set of parameters that maximises L is found from an infinite number of sets, each of which could define the population of the given form. The parameters estimated in this way give the highest prior probability to the known sample or, in other words, makes the sample most likely. When applying the ML method, a set of partial differential equations and constraints should be satisfied in the case of unimodal likelihood functions with zero slope at maximum value[13]. These are as follows.

$$\frac{\partial L}{\partial \gamma} = 0, \quad \frac{\partial L}{\partial \lambda} = 0, \quad \frac{\partial L}{\partial \xi} = 0, \quad \frac{\partial^2 L}{\partial \gamma^2} < 0, \quad \frac{\partial^2 L}{\partial \lambda^2} < 0, \quad \frac{\partial^2 L}{\partial \xi^2} < 0 \quad (3.43)$$

3.4.1 *Maximum likelihood method applied to type III function*

For the three-parameter type III function, estimates of γ, λ and ξ are obtained so that L is maximised. It is more convenient here, as in several other applications, to maximise the natural logarithm ln of L; the same results are obtained in this way. From equations 3.42 and 3.17

$$L^* = -N\gamma \ln(\lambda) - N \ln\{\Gamma(\gamma)\} + (\gamma - 1)\sum \ln(x_i - \xi) - \sum (x_i - \xi)/\lambda \quad (3.44)$$

where L^* and $\sum$ denote $\ln(L)$ and $\sum\limits_{i=1}^{N}$ respectively.

From the partial derivatives of equation 3.44, the following three equations are obtained for the ML estimators $\hat{\gamma}$, $\hat{\lambda}$ and $\hat{\xi}$.

$$\partial L^*/\partial \gamma = -N \ln(\hat{\lambda}) - N\psi(\hat{\gamma}) + \sum \ln(x_i - \hat{\xi}) = 0 \qquad (3.45)$$

$$\partial L^*/\partial \lambda = -N\hat{\gamma}/\hat{\lambda} + \sum (x_i - \hat{\xi})/\hat{\lambda}^2 = 0 \qquad (3.46)$$

$$\partial L^*/\partial \xi = -(\hat{\gamma} - 1)\sum (x_i - \hat{\xi})^{-1} + N/\hat{\lambda} = 0 \qquad (3.47)$$

in which

$$\psi(\gamma) = d[\ln\{\Gamma(\gamma)\}]/d\gamma$$

is the psi or digamma function[14]. From equation 3.46

$$\hat{\gamma}\hat{\lambda} = N^{-1}\sum (x_i - \hat{\xi}) \qquad (3.48)$$

The elimination of $\hat{\lambda}$ from equations 3.47 and 3.48 gives

$$\hat{\gamma} = \sum (x_i - \hat{\xi})^{-1}/\{\sum (x_i - \hat{\xi})^{-1} - N^2/\sum (x_i - \hat{\xi})\} \qquad (3.49)$$

and, rearranging equation 3.45, we obtain

$$\psi(\hat{\gamma}) = N^{-1}\sum \ln(x_i - \hat{\xi}) - \ln(\hat{\lambda}) \qquad (3.50)$$

An asymptotic relationship exists between $\psi(\gamma)$ and the so-called Bernoulli

---

[13] These criteria are not applicable in every case; one of the exceptions is the rectangular or uniform density function $f(x) = 1/\lambda$, $\xi \leqslant x \leqslant \xi + \lambda$ (Mood et al., 1974, pp. 282, 283). The ML method is also explained in other books; see, for example, Fisz (1963).
[14] This function and its derivatives are tabulated by Davis (1935); shorter tables are given by Abramowitz and Stegun (1964, pp. 267–73).

numbers B_n which can be obtained by equating terms in the series expansion

$$z/(e^z - 1) = \sum_{n=0}^{\infty} B_n z^n/n!$$

that is, after dividing z by $(z + z^2/2 + z^3/6 + z^4/24 \ldots)^{15}$. This relationship is given by

$$\psi(\gamma) = \ln(\gamma) - (2\gamma)^{-1} - \sum_{n=1}^{\infty} B_{2n}/2n\gamma^{2n}$$

$$= \ln(\gamma) - (2\gamma)^{-1} - (12\gamma^2)^{-1} + (120\gamma^4)^{-1} - (252\gamma^6)^{-1}$$

$$+ (240\gamma^8)^{-1} - (132\gamma^{10})^{-1} + \ldots \tag{3.51}$$

The parameters γ, λ and ξ may be estimated iteratively as follows[15].

Initially, ξ is equated to the lowest item of data or the value obtained by the method of moments; after this, γ and λ are estimated from equations 3.49 and 3.48 respectively. Then, $\psi(\gamma)$ is calculated from equation 3.51 by using only the given seven terms of the right-hand side. Almost in every case, the first iterative value of $\psi(\gamma)$ is quite different from the right-hand side of equation 3.50. Therefore, the value of ξ should be incremented (or decremented) by using progressively smaller increments, and the procedure should be repeated until this equation is closely satisfied. In this way the ML estimates of γ, λ and ξ are obtained. Because λ is positive for positive skewness, it is seen from equation 3.47 that $\gamma > 1$. This entails that the ML method cannot be applied to J-shaped functions which by the method of moments have coefficients of skewness greater than 2. For $\gamma > 2$, tabulated values and those computed through equation 3.51 are the same for five significant figures. If $1 < \gamma \leqslant 2$, $\psi(\gamma)$ is easily obtained by using the recurrence formula[16] $\psi(\gamma) = \psi(\gamma + 1) - 1/\gamma$.

One of the first applications of the ML method was by Thom (1958) in meteorology. He suggested the use of only one term of the expansion containing Bernoulli numbers in equation 3.51. This leads to an explicit equation without recourse to iteration. A table giving correction factors to estimated values of γ, necessitated by the reduction in terms of equation 3.51, is given by Thom. However, if values of γ are low, corrections to the other parameters may also be necessary[17].

---

[15] Bernoulli numbers are referred to by Kendall and Buckland (1971, p. 13), by Johnke *et al.* (1960) and by Abramowitz and Stegun (1964, pp. 259, 804, 810).
[16] This follows directly from the relationship $\Gamma(\gamma + 1) = \gamma\Gamma(\gamma)$ derived above.
[17] This method is also described by Markovic (1965) and by Yevjevich (1972). Moran (1957) who applied the ML method and the two-parameter gamma function to flood data from Australia argues in its favour. Support is also found from the results of computer experiments of Matalas and Wallis (1973) which indicate that ML estimates have less bias and variance than those through moments. On the other hand, Greenwood and Durand (1960) doubt whether the additional labour is worthwhile. The work of Pearson and Hartley (1972, tables 37, 38) and the work of Shenton and Bowmah (1972) are also relevant in this context.

3.4.2 *Comparison of maximum likelihood method and method of moments*

Using likelihood tests, Fisher found that the method of moments is inefficient unless the likelihood function is nearly symmetrical. The efficiency decreases sharply when the parameter γ is decreased[18]. However, the efficiency of estimators is difficult to evaluate as it usually requires knowledge of the true distribution. Furthermore, most studies of efficiency yield results which are only applicable to large samples.

The simpler method of moments is advantageous because there are no restrictive assumptions regarding the parent population. Its shortcoming is that estimates of moments are subject to sampling errors which could be large for the higher moments.

Results from the application of the two methods to the type III function are given in table 3.2. Annual river-flow data from Yevjevich (1963), in which catchment retention effects have been removed and the data are reduced to unit mean, are used for this purpose. Tests show that the data are serially independent at the 5 % level of significance, and type III functions are indicated by figure 3.1 and the method of moments. For each station the first set of parameters is obtained by the method of moments and the second by the ML method. (In some of the other data series examined, $\xi < 0$ and ML solutions could not be obtained in a few cases.) It is found that, with not more than 10 iterations, computed values of $\psi(\gamma)$ are equal to those from equations 3.48 with five significant figures. As the form of the underlying distribution is unknown, there need not be great concern that different estimates of parameters are obtained by the two methods. In application, the main interest usually lies on the magnitudes of the extreme values at probabilities such as 0.99 and 0.01; a few calculations will bring out the differences[19].

Standard gamma variates u for particular values of the shape parameter γ and the probability $F(u)$ of non-exceedance are given in table 3.3; for extensive tables, the work of Wilk *et al.* (1962) or that of Pearson and Hartley (1972, pp. 6, 7) should be consulted. This pertains to the gamma function $f(z) = e^{-z}z^{\gamma-1}/\Gamma(\gamma)$. For example, if $\gamma = 2$ and $F(u) = 0.99$, $u = 6.6384$. This means that

$$0.99 = \int_0^{6.6384} e^{-z}z^{\gamma-1}\,dz/\Gamma(\gamma)$$

Because of the linear relationship between the gamma function and the Pearson type III function, if λ and ξ are the scale and location parameters, the corresponding Pearson type III variate x is equal to $6.6384\lambda + \xi$.

By using table 3.3, the Pearson type III variates calculated by the moments and ML methods can be compared at a probability of non-exceedance equal to

---

[18] This is explained by Kendall and Stuart (1973, p. 69).
[19] Elderton and Johnson (1969, p. 195) and Hawkins (1972) give more reasons to support the method of moments.

Table 3.2 Pearson type III function applied to six annual series of river-flow data

Station, Period	Standard deviation	Skewness	Kurtosis	First series correlation coefficient	Lowest value	Moments and ML estimates of parameters		
						ξ	γ	λ
Pecos River near Anton Chico, New Mexico, U.S.A., 1911 to 1957	0.712	1.45	5.2	0.133	0.083	0.017 0.034	1.90 1.89	0.516 0.511
Kaweah River near Three Rivers, California, U.S.A., 1903 to 1956	0.520	1.04	3.8	0.108	0.226	0.000 0.131	3.71 2.85	0.270 0.305
Magnetawan River near Burks Falls, Canada, 1913 to 1953	0.235	0.84	3.9	0.209	0.523	0.441 0.258	5.65 10.54	0.099 0.070
Bungyip River at Bungyip, Victoria, Australia, 1907 to 1948	0.372	1.41	5.5	0.075	0.479	0.472 0.405	2.01 2.75	0.262 0.216
Goulburn River, near Murchison, Victoria, Australia, 1881 to 1954	0.453	0.94	4.1	0.179	0.223	0.039 0.073	4.51 4.26	0.213 0.218
Tama River, near Atsumi, Japan, 1918 to 1955	0.409	1.47	5.6	−0.020	0.447	0.444 0.403	1.85 2.38	0.300 0.251

Table 3.3 Standard gamma variates ard probabilities

Probability of non-exceedance	Standard gamma variate for shape parameter γ =														
	0.1	0.5	1	2	3	4	5	6	8	10	12	14	16	18	22
0.001	0.0000	0.0000	0.0010	0.0454	0.1905	0.4286	0.7394	1.1071	1.9708	2.9605	4.0424	5.1954	6.4053	7.6621	10.2881
0.010	0.0000	0.0001	0.0101	0.1486	0.4360	0.8232	1.2791	1.7853	2.9061	4.1302	5.4282	6.7824	8.1811	9.6163	12.5740
0.020	0.0000	0.0003	0.0202	0.2147	0.5672	1.0162	1.5295	2.0891	3.3071	4.6183	5.9959	7.4237	8.8914	10.3915	13.3493
0.050	0.0000	0.0020	0.0513	0.3554	0.8177	1.3663	1.9701	2.6130	3.9808	5.4254	6.9242	8.4639	10.0360	11.6343	14.8937
0.100	0.0000	0.0079	0.1054	0.5318	1.1021	1.7448	2.4326	3.1519	4.6561	6.2213	7.8293	9.4696	11.1353	12.8216	16.2436
0.200	0.0000	0.0321	0.2231	0.8244	1.5350	2.2968	3.0895	3.9037	5.5761	7.2892	9.0309	10.7940	12.5739	14.3675	17.9872
0.300	0.0000	0.0742	0.3567	1.0973	1.9138	2.7637	3.6336	4.5171	6.3122	8.1329	9.9716	11.8237	13.6864	15.5576	19.3204
0.400	0.0001	0.1375	0.5108	1.3764	2.2851	3.2113	4.1477	5.0910	6.9914	8.9044	10.8262	12.7546	14.6881	16.6258	20.5111
0.500	0.0006	0.2275	0.6931	1.6783	2.6741	3.6721	4.6709	5.6702	7.6692	9.6687	11.6684	13.6681	15.6679	17.6678	21.6676
0.600	0.0037	0.3542	0.9163	2.0223	3.1054	4.1753	5.2366	6.2919	8.3898	10.4757	12.5532	14.6243	16.6904	18.7525	22.8668
0.700	0.0174	0.5371	1.2040	2.4392	3.6156	4.7622	5.8904	7.0056	9.2089	11.3873	13.5480	15.6954	17.8325	19.9610	24.1978
0.800	0.0694	0.8212	1.6094	2.9943	4.2790	5.5150	6.7210	7.9060	10.2325	12.5188	14.7767	17.0133	19.2338	21.4394	25.8195
0.900	0.2662	1.3528	2.3026	3.8897	5.3223	6.6808	7.9936	9.2747	11.7709	14.2060	16.5981	18.9580	21.2924	23.6061	28.1843
0.950	0.5804	1.9207	2.9957	4.7439	6.2958	7.7537	9.1535	10.5130	13.1481	15.7052	18.2075	20.6686	23.0971	25.4992	30.2404
0.980	1.1190	2.7059	3.9120	5.8339	7.5166	9.0841	10.5804	12.0270	14.8166	17.5098	20.1352	22.7094	25.2434	27.7444	32.6683
0.990	1.5885	3.3174	4.6052	6.6384	8.4059	10.0451	11.6046	13.1085	16.0000	18.7831	21.4899	24.1391	26.7429	29.3096	34.3548
0.999	3.3637	5.4138	6.9078	9.2334	11.2289	13.0622	14.7941	16.4547	19.6262	22.6574	25.5893	28.4461	31.2436	33.9926	39.3748

0.99 (because the records are short, hardly any confidence could be put in values extrapolated further)[20]. For instance, for the Kaweah River (table 3.2), $x = 2.58$ and 2.61 and, for the Magnetawn River, $x = 1.69$ and 1.62 from the two methods respectively. However, greater differences are found over the low-flow sections of the distributions, and these could be gauged from the values of ξ given in table 3.2. For example, flows with a 0.01 probability of non-exceedance calculated by the two methods for six stations compare as follows: 0.087, 0.102; 0.192, 0.251; 0.600, 0.572; 0.512, 0.484; 0.264, 0.278; 0.482, 0.468. On the other hand, there is uncertainty regarding the choice of distribution; for instance, the lognormal function (see section 3.6.2) can also be fitted to the data by using the tests given in the next section, and in this way another set of extreme values is obtained.

Firm conclusions cannot, of course, be drawn by examining one set of data. However, when we consider the uncertainties regarding the choice of distribution and the level of accuracy required, the differences in the results from the two methods are not of special significance. Tukey (1962) has stated that 'Data analysis must progress by approximate answers, at best . . .', and this is quite relevant in the general context. It means here that the simpler method of moments can usually provide answers for practical situations. In the rare cases when sufficient information is available to apply the ML method, this would provide better estimates[21].

3.5 Goodness-of-fit tests

A goodness-of-fit test is required in order to ascertain whether a theoretical distribution can be fitted to a distribution observed through a set of measurements. The fit is usually determined by means of a criterion which depends on the differences between the observed and theoretical density functions or distributions. The chi-squared and Kolmogorov–Smirnov goodness-of-fit tests are described in this section.

3.5.1 Chi-squared test

The well-known chi-squared test has been widely used since its inception by Karl Pearson around 1900. The test is based on the density function which is divided into cells through class intervals. Originally, equal class intervals were suggested for this purpose; however, a better method is to follow Mann and

[20] Simple linear interpolations of values in table 3.3 are taken. Numerical methods of interpolation are described by Hamming (1973) and in other books, for example, Pearson and Hartley (1972, pp. 134–41 and tables 6.6–6.9).
[21] The method of moments and the ML method can be applied to the two-parameter gamma function by using only the first two moments and two partial differential equations (Moran, 1957) respectively following a simpler procedure than for the type III function. Elsewhere, Hoadley (1968) has shown estimation procedures for four-parameter functions which use the first three moments and the left terminal if known. The ML method becomes extremely tedious when applied to four-parameter functions; Greenwood and Durand (1960) discuss its use for the type V function.

Wald (1942) and to divide the total area under the density function into equal *areas*. In this way the unequal class intervals are obtained. An inverse function, applied through a computer subroutine, may be used for this purpose[22].

To explain the criterion, let the ordinates of the density function be multiplied by N and let a histogram be formed on the basis of these class intervals with the total area enclosed also equal to N. Then the statistic

$$X^2 = \sum_{i=1}^{\ell} (O_i - E_i)^2 / E_i \qquad (3.52)$$

is calculated where E_i and O_i are the expected and observed numbers of items as given by the areas under the enlarged density function and histogram respectively for each class interval i, $i = 1, 2, \ldots, \ell$. If the fit is perfect, $X^2 = 0$, but, even if the choice of function and estimates of parameters are absolutely correct, inevitable sampling fluctuations result in a small positive value of X^2. In order to test whether the appropriate probability density function is being fitted, a level of significance is used, as explained below, to ascertain whether the value of X^2 obtained is not significantly high. It should be noted that X^2 is positive and that no consideration is given to the signs and locations of the differences in equation 3.52; this could diminish the overall usefulness of tests such as this. However, the test is thought to be satisfactory when applied to serially independent data with $N > 50$ and with not less than 5 items in each interval.

Asymptotically, that is, when N tends to infinity, the probability density of the discrete X^2 variable can be approximated by the continuous χ^2 density[23]. This density was originally discovered in the second half of the nineteenth century and was developed subsequently by Pearson. As shown by Fisher, it is equivalent to the sum of squares of independent standard normal variates and is therefore of the gamma type. The density function of χ^2 is given by

$$f(\chi^2) = (\chi^2)^{\gamma - 1} e^{-\chi^2/\lambda} \lambda^{-\gamma} / \Gamma(\gamma) \qquad (3.53)$$

in which the gamma scale parameter $\lambda = 2$ and shape parameter $\gamma = v/2$. Here v denotes the degrees of freedom, which Good (1973) defines as the number of observations less the number of necessary relations among these observations. In this context, if k is the number of parameters to be estimated (for example, $k = 3$ for a Pearson type III function), then $v = \ell - 1 - k$ are the degrees of freedom[24]. The purpose of incorporating v is to make the test less dependent on the function tested.

---

[22] See, for example, Beasley and Springer (1977), Best and Roberts (1975) and Cran *et al.* (1977) for the normal, gamma and beta integrals respectively. Reference may also be made to Wilk *et al.* (1962), to Pearson and Hartley (1972) or to Pearson (1957).

[23] Note that this is not an exact test. In fact equation 3.52 is an approximation obtained by taking only the first term in a logarithmic series expansion consequent to maximising the likelihood of the joint occurrences of events in each interval (Johnson and Leone, 1977, pp. 274-7).

[24] In fact, the term the degrees of freedom (which is due to R. A. Fisher and is analogous to that of a dynamical system) cannot be clearly defined in simple terms. Another point is

The probability $\Pr(\chi^2)$ of chi squared is obtained by integrating equation 3.53 between limits 0 and X^2. If $1 - \Pr(\chi^2) \geqslant \alpha$, then the hypothesis that the probability density of the population is the same as that of the function fitted is accepted at the level α of significance. This is the probability of making a type I error; that is, α is the probability of rejecting a hypothesis when it should be accepted[25]. On the other hand, we may accept a hypothesis when it should be rejected with probability β; a type II error is then made. We shall discuss these further at the end of subsection 3.5.2.

Therefore, for the condition that $\Pr(X^2 \leqslant \chi^2_{v,\alpha}) = 1 - \alpha$, a simple test procedure is to determine whether $X^2 \leqslant \chi^2_{v,\alpha}$. Values of $\chi^2_{v,\alpha}$ are given in standard tables for various levels of significance and degrees of freedom; these can also be obtained from table 3.3 by using equation 3.53. (This will be shown in example 3.1.) For large values of v, χ^2 tends to be normally distributed; if z_α is the value which a standard normal deviate exceeds with probability α, then, for $v > 30$, $\chi^2 \approx v\{1 - 2/9v + z_\alpha(2/9v)^{1/2}\}^3$ by the Wilson–Hilferty transformation[26].

There is, however, uncertainty regarding ℓ, the number of class intervals to be chosen[27]. By following the work of Mann and Wald (1942) and Williams (1950), if the level of significance $\alpha = 0.05$, values of $\ell = 39, 35, 30, 23, 15, 12$ and 9 may suffice for sample sizes $N = 2000, 1500, 1000, 500, 200, 100$ and 50 respectively. For other values of N and α the formula $\ell = 2\{2(N-1)^2/z_\alpha^2\}^{1/5}$, where z_α is the value which a standard normal deviate exceeds with probability α, with reference to equations 3.4 and 3.1 (for example, if $\alpha = 0.05$, $z_\alpha = 1.645$) can be used with the proviso that $N/\ell \geqslant 5$.

Example 3.1   Annual flows of the Bungyip River at Bungyip, Victoria, Australia for the period 1907 to 1948, taken from Yevjevich (1963), are given below.

Annual flows (modular (zero-mean) units)

0.626	0.855	0.743	1.294	0.897	1.067	0.479	0.681	1.124	1.317
1.035	0.631	1.126	0.681	0.909	1.949	1.539	0.866	0.816	0.836
0.943	1.000	1.203	1.315	1.309	0.794	2.312	1.179	1.051	0.979
0.488	1.0591	0.739	0.982	0.827	0.606	0.674	0.686	0.813	1.156
0.879									

---

that, strictly speaking, equation 3.53 is applicable with $\gamma = (\ell - 1 - k)/2$ only if the parameters are estimated by the ML method and this should be applied to the grouped data and not to the individual items (Kendall and Stuart, 1973, p. 447).

[25] Basically, it means that, if we know the parameters and the true form of the density function and its parameters and if 100 random samples from the same population are tested at some future date, it is expected that $\Pr(\chi^2)$ will exceed 0.95, say, in five samples. For the broader implications of the significance level, see, for example, Barnard (1947).

[26] Some values of z_α may be taken from the second and third columns of table 6.9.

[27] Kendall and Stuart (1973, chapter 30) discuss this problem.

Fit a Pearson type III function and test for goodness of fit by the chi-squared method using the 5 % level of significance.

The parameters of the Pearson type III function are estimated by the method of moments, and values given in table 3.2 (which are $\tilde{\xi} = 0.472$, $\tilde{\gamma} = 2.01$ and $\tilde{\lambda} = 0.262$) are used as estimates. The standard gamma variates under $\gamma = 2$ in table 3.3 are taken; these are then multiplied by 0.262 and are incremented by 0.472 to give the Pearson type III variates. From the suggestions given above, ℓ ought to be 8. However, ℓ is taken as 10 so that table 3.3 can be used for the sake of this example. The expected number in each class is 4.1, if we assume equal probabilities. Class intervals and calculations are as tabulated below.

Probability of non-exceedance	Lower limit of class interval	Observed number O_i in class	Expected number E_i in class	$(O_i - E_i)^2 / E_i$
0.90	1.491	4	4.1	0.002
0.80	1.257	4	4.1	0.002
0.70	1.111	5	4.1	0.198
0.60	1.002	3	4.1	0.295
0.50	0.912	4	4.1	0.002
0.40	0.833	6	4.1	0.880
0.30	0.759	4	4.1	0.002
0.20	0.688	2	4.1	1.076
0.10	0.611	6	4.1	0.880
0.00	0.472	3	4.1	0.295

The value of X^2 which is the sum of the items in the last row is 3.632. If we apply equation 3.53 with $\gamma = 3$ (obtained from $(10 - 1 - 3)/2$) and $\lambda = 2$ (which is invariable), the value of $\chi^2_{6, \alpha}$ from table 3.3 for $\alpha = 0.05$ (that is, the probability of non-exceedance equals 0.95) is $2 \times 6.2958 = 12.59$. Therefore, the data fit the Pearson type III function at the 5 % level of significance because $X^2 < \chi^2_{6, \alpha}$.

3.5.2 Kolmogorov–Smirnov goodness-of-fit test

This goodness-of-fit test is of more recent origin and is based on the (cumulative) distribution function. Kolmogorov (1933) originally derived the statistic, and the test procedure was developed by Smirnov (1948) and by others.

For a sample of size N, the criterion is the maximum (vertical) difference between a theoretical distribution function $F(x)$ and the empirical or sample distribution function $F_N(x)$, which is a step function. Let x_i, $i = 1, 2, \ldots, N$, be a random sample of serially independent observations of a random variable X with continuous probability distribution function $F(x) = \Pr(X_i \leqslant x)$; the x_i values are ordered so that x_N is the highest. $F_N(x) = k/N$, where k is the number of x_i values which are less than or equal to a particular value x; note that $F_N(x)$

$= 0$ for $x < x_1$ and $F_N(x) = 1$ for $x \geqslant x_N$. If the null hypothesis that the sample has the assumed distribution is to be accepted, $F(x)$ should be close to $F_N(x)$ for the whole range of the function. In order to quantify the closeness, define $D_N = \max |F_N(x) - F(x)|$. Then the Kolmogorov–Smirnov statistic D_N is a random variable and $L(z)$, the limiting (cumulative) distribution function of $N^{1/2}D_N$, is given by

$$L(z) = \lim_{N \to \infty} \{\Pr(N^{1/2}D_N \leqslant z)\} \qquad (3.54)$$

where the left-hand side denotes the asymptotic probability Pr that $N^{1/2}D_N$ is less than or equal to a particular value z. Smirnov (1948) gives the following probability distribution of $N^{1/2}D_N$.

$$L(z) = (2\pi)^{1/2}z^{-1} \sum_{k=1}^{\infty} \exp\{-(2k-1)^2\pi^2 z^{-2}/8\} \qquad (3.55)$$

It is important to note that $L(z)$ is independent of the form which $F(x)$ takes.

The test proceeds as follows. Given a sample of size N and a level α of significance, if $\Pr(D_N \leqslant D_{N,\alpha}) = 1 - \alpha$, it is necessary to know the value $D_{N,\alpha}$ (which D_N exceeds 100 $\alpha\%$ of the time). The limiting distribution $L(z)$ given by equations 3.54 and 3.55 holds approximately for N not less than 35; in fact, there is very good agreement if N exceeds 85. Accordingly, for $\alpha = 0.01, 0.05$ and 0.10, large sample values of $N^{1/2}D_{N,\infty}$ are 1.63, 1.36 and 1.225 respectively[28].

For smaller samples, values of $D_{N,\alpha}$ are given in the following table[29].

Table 3.4   Values of $D_{N,\alpha}$

N	$D_{N,0.05}$	$D_{N,0.01}$
15	0.338	0.404
16	0.328	0.392
17	0.318	0.381
18	0.309	0.371
19	0.301	0.363
20	0.294	0.356
25	0.27	0.36
30	0.24	0.29
35	0.23	0.27
> 35	$1.36/N^{1/2}$	$1.63/N^{1/2}$

Example 3.2   The total annual flows of the Severn at Bewdley for the period 1921 to 1968 are tabulated below in millimetres of equivalent rainfall over the

[28] Values of $L(z)$ for z ranging from 0.28 to 3.0 in increments of 0.1 are listed by Smirnov (1948); see also Gnedenko (1968, pp. 497, 498).
[29] This is based on a (non-mathematical) paper by Massey (1951) after Feller (who simplified Kolmogorov's original proof) and Doob. Tables are also given by Birnbaum (1952), Miller (1956) and Beyer (1968, p. 426).

catchment. If the mean and standard deviation are 473.8 mm and 98.4 mm respectively, ascertain whether the normal distribution fits the data at a significance level $\alpha = 0.05$. The data are taken to be serially independent[30].

Annual flow (mm)									
305	427	570	562	443	440	566	583	437	603
600	494	287	300	461	535	428	414	542	500
429	354	409	420	404	579	466	462	380	515
597	424	365	652	416	378	536	589	455	716
416	421	371	282	572	581	518	533		

The 48 items of data tabulated above are ranked in ascending order: 282, 287, . . ., 603, 652, 716. Then the step function $F_N(x)$ is computed from these values and is drawn as shown in figure 3.2. Note that $F_N(x) = 1.0$ for $x \geqslant 716$; $F(x) = 47/48$ for $716 \geqslant x \geqslant 652$; $F_N(x) = 46/48$ for $652 \geqslant x \geqslant 603$ and so on; also at the left extremity, $F_N(x) = 1/48$ for $287 \geqslant x \geqslant 282$; $F_N(x) = 0$ for $x < 282$. Then $F(x)$ is drawn by using the mean and standard deviation and a table giving the area $\Phi(z)$ under the standard normal function between limits 0.5 and z. Points on the $F(x)$ curve may be verified using the second and third columns of table 6.9. For example, $F(x) = 0.9$ for $x = 1.282 \times 98.4 + 473.8 = 600$ and $F(x) = 0.2$ for $x = -0.842 \times 98.4 + 473.8 = 391$.

The observed maximum absolute difference D_N between the two functions is 0.10 and $N^{1/2}D_N = (48)^{1/2} \times 0.10 = 0.69$. Because $N^{1/2}D_N < 1.36$, the null hypothesis is accepted at the $\alpha = 0.05$ level of significance. It should be noted that when measuring vertical distances the measurements are taken from the left extremities of the steps if $F_N(x) > F(x)$ and at points where $F_N(x) < F(x)$ measurements are taken from the right extremities of the step[31]. The conclusion tallies with the information given in figure 3.1 with regard to the point corresponding to the annual data of the River Severn.

Alternatively, confidence limits can be drawn for $\alpha = 0.05$, as shown in figure 3.2 through two broken lines that are vertically $D_{N,\alpha}$ above and $D_{N,\alpha}$ below $F(x)$.

[30] As in the chi-squared test, the data should be serially independent, a condition which seems to be relaxed to some extent in practice; Weiss (1978) gives an empirical correction to the Kolmogorov–Smirnov statistic for a second-order autoregressive process. Furthermore, table 3.4 is not applicable, strictly speaking, when the parameters are estimated from the data, but then the test is thought to be a conservative one; a table is given by Lilliefors (1967) and Kendall and Stuart (1973, p. 477) make further comments. Alternatively, parameters estimated from one-half of a sequence may be used to test the distribution of the other half as shown by Kottegoda (1970); however, this results in a loss of information.

[31] In this connection, D'Agostino and Noether (1973) warn that some computer programmes for the test have been incorrectly formulated.

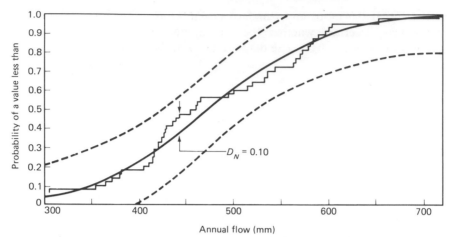

Figure 3.2 Annual flow data of Severn at Bewdley for the period 1921 to 1968 tested for normality by the Kolmogorov–Smirnov method: full curve represents normal distribution; broken curves represent 95 % confidence limits

Because $F_N(x)$ is confined within these limits the null hypothesis is accepted at the chosen level of significance.

A practical procedure, which is useful if two or more theoretical functions are tested and compared, is to set the confidence limits by means of two-step functions which are $D_{N,\alpha}$ above and $D_{N,\alpha}$ below $F_N(x)$. The theoretical curves are then drawn. Of course, the step functions and curves are bounded vertically by 0 and 1.

Example 3.3   Fit the step function representing the data in example 3.1 with a Pearson type III (cumulative) distribution function, and test for goodness of fit at the 5 % level of significance using the Kolmogorov–Smirnov method.

The data are ranked in ascending order as in example 3.2, and the step function is drawn by following the same procedure; this is shown in figure 3.3. The percentage points of the theoretical Pearson type III function are calculated from table 3.3 by the method explained in example 3.1, and a smooth curve is drawn through these points in figure 3.3.

The maximum vertical difference between the step and fitted functions is 0.07. The product of this and $(41)^{1/2}$ is 0.45 which is less than the critical value of 1.36. Hence, the hypothesis that the Pearson type III function fits the Bungyip River data is accepted at the 5 % level of significance. Again, confidence limits can be drawn as explained in example 3.2. Also, it is found that the same conclusion is reached, if the ML method of estimation is used.

It is known that, at the 50 % power level, the Kolmogorov–Smirnov test detects smaller deviations in probability distributions than the chi-squared test[32]. By power is meant the chance of detecting that the chosen distribution

[32] See, for example, Massey (1951).

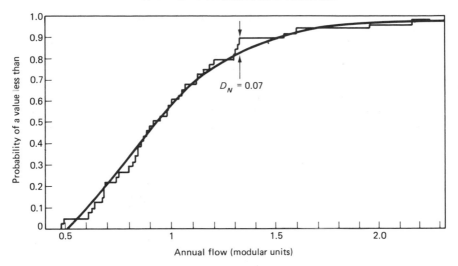

Figure 3.3 Annual flow data of Bungyip at Bungyip, Victoria, for the period 1907 to 1948 fitted with Pearson type III function (to obtain modular units, annual flows are divided by the mean)

function fits the empirical distribution of observed data as opposed to that of an alternative hypothesis. The power is also equal to $1 - \beta$, where β is the probability of making a type II error, as explained in subsection 3.5.1. To achieve the same sensitivity as in the Kolmogorov–Smirnov test with N values, a larger sample of $N^{5/4}$ items is required if the chi-squared test is applied[33]. Furthermore, in contrast with the X^2 statistic which has an asymptotic χ^2 distribution, the test based on D_N is distribution free (that is, it does not depend on the marginal distribution of the data) for finite values of N and continuous distribution functions[34].

3.5.3 Kolmogorov–Smirnov two-sample test

The goodness-of-fit test in a particular form devised by Smirnov could also be used to determine whether two samples of data are from the same population or whether they are identically distributed, for a specific α. If $D_{M,N}$ is the maximum (vertical) difference between the empirical step functions representing two independent samples of size M and N, that is, $D_{M,N} = \max |F_M(x) - F_N(x)|$, where $F_M(x)$ is defined in the same way as $F_N(x)$, then $L(z)$ given by equation 3.55 is also the limiting cumulative distribution of $\{MN/(M+N)\}^{1/2} D_{M,N}$.

---

[33] See Kendall and Stuart (1973, p. 476).
[34] By the minimum χ^2 test, however, estimates of distribution parameters may be chosen so as to minimise the X^2 differences (Kendall and Stuart, 1973, pp. 96–8). The procedure will make the test statistic distribution free, but it is difficult to apply.

Expressed as a statement of probability corresponding to equation 3.54, this becomes

$$L(z) = \lim_{M,N \to \infty} (\Pr[\{MN/(M+N)\}^{1/2}D_{M,N} \leqslant z]) \qquad (3.56)$$

Example 3.4　Divide the data given in example 3.2 into two samples, so that the first contains items 1 to 30 of the data and the second is formed with the remaining 18 values. Ascertain whether the two samples are from the same population.

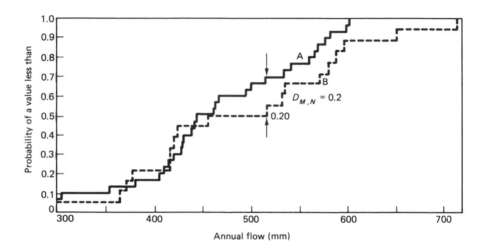

Figure 3.4　Kolmogorov–Smirnov two-sample test applied to annual flow data of Severn for the period 1921 to 1950 (sample A) and for the period 1951 to 1968 (sample B)

The items of data in each sample are ranked separately, and the step functions are computed. These are drawn as shown in figure 3.4. It is found that the observed maximum difference $D_{M,N} = 0.2$. The result could be obtained directly from the computed values of $F_N(x)$ and $F_M(x)$, but the figure illustrates fully the differences in distributions. By substituting, $\{MN/(M+N)\}^{1/2} = \{30 \times 18/48\}^{1/2} = 3.35$. Therefore, $\{MN/(M+N)\}^{1/2}D_{M,N} = 0.67$. Because this is less than 1.36, the null hypothesis that the samples are from the same population is not rejected with $\alpha = 0.05$. Note that the asymptotic distribution of the Kolmogorov–Smirnov statistic is used although M and N are not large. However, the resulting errors from samples of this size are not of practical significance[35].

[35] Critical values of $D_{M,N}$ for $M, N < 15$ are tabulated by Beyer (1968, p. 428) and are found for $M, N < 25$ in the work of Pearson and Hartley (1972, table 55). The exact distribution of $D_{M,N}$ is rather complicated; see Kim and Jennrich (1973) and the extensive tables given. Kendall and Stuart (1973, pp. 505–21) give other two-sample tests.

3.5.4   *Remarks on curve fitting*

In some practical situations, curve fitting becomes more of an art than an exact science. For instance, when sample sizes are small, two or more curves may fit an observed distribution equally well. Then we might choose the function which from general experience is the best suited for the purpose and is also easy to implement, say, for data generation. At the other extreme, if a distribution of, say, daily data is to be fitted, no single function may pass the statistical tests. In such a case, we might need to improvise by fitting, for example, exponentials separately to the high flows and low flows and an appropriate function to the rest of the data. However, consideration should also be given to the more advanced types given in the following section.

3.6   Other families of probability functions

Amongst other probability functions and methods, transformations to normality constitute one main area of interest. Johnson's system described in subsection 3.6.2 is in this category. Another method is to use a polynomial to modify a standard function. Also, there are other types such as mixed and stable distributions and the Weibull function.

3.6.1   *General transformations*

Towards the end of the last century, whilst non-normal distributions were gaining acceptance from knowledge of observed data in diverse fields, many writers suggested simple transformations to normality. For example, if x represents an observed sequence, it could be ascertained whether the transformation $y = (x - \xi)^\delta$ makes the y sequence close to normality in distribution if an optimum set of parameters δ and ξ is chosen[36].

A simpler type is the transformation to normality given by $y = \log(x - \xi)$ and originated by Galton, who like Karl Pearson was a biologist. This is now known as the lognormal distribution with a maximum of three parameters, and unlike many *ad hoc* transformations has a physical backing in certain applications[37].

3.6.2   *Johnson's system*

Johnson (1949) developed the bounded S_B and the unbounded S_U functions in his system of frequency curves generated by methods of translation (a word originally used by Edgeworth in this context). The three-parameter lognormal

[36] More recently, when transforming precipitation data, Stidd (1953) used the cube root and subsequently the nth root (Stidd, 1970). Also, Young and Pisano (1968) employed minimum skewness transformations in generating data at several sites. The modern approach, due to Box and Cox (1964), and methods of estimation will be given in subsection 4.6.2.

[37] Examples are found in the breaking of rocks and particles and in sediment transport as shown by Aitchison and Brown (1957) and by Kottler (1950).

function S_L has a central place in Johnson's system. The regions of applicability with respect to kurtosis and skewness in the data are shown in figure 3.1. The zone of the S_B curves with bounded values of kurtosis is below the curve for the lognormal function, which is represented by the parametric equations

$$\beta_1 = (\omega - 1)(\omega + 2)^2 \qquad\qquad (3.57)$$

$$\beta_2 = \omega^4 + 2\omega^3 + 3\omega^2 - 3, \qquad \omega \geqslant 1$$

(where ω is a dummy variable) and is above the line $\beta_2 - \beta_1 = 1$. It includes the whole of the Pearson type I zone and part of the type VI zone. The S_U zone is unrestricted above the lognormal curve.

The underlying theme in Johnson's system of frequency functions is that there is a function $f(.)$ such that the related z values given by

$$z = \gamma + \delta f\{(x - \xi)/\lambda\} \qquad\qquad (3.58)$$

have a standard normal distribution. The distribution of the original X population is defined through four parameters. Two of these parameters, ξ and λ, only govern the left extremity and the scale of the X population respectively. The shape of the distribution is affected by the other parameters, γ and δ.

If we write y for $(x - \xi)/\lambda$, Johnson's system may be classified as follows.

(1) *Lognormal*   In this case $f(y) = \ln(y)$. Because the constant λ of $\ln(y)$ can be combined with γ, the constant λ of equation 3.58 becomes redundant. Therefore, the distribution of the X population has three parameters[38]. Also, $\xi \leqslant x \leqslant \infty$.

(2) S_B *family* This is of the form $f(y) = \ln\{y/(1 - y)\}$ and $\xi \leqslant x \leqslant \xi + \lambda$. (Fisher's z transformation $\frac{1}{2}\ln\{(1 + r)/(1 - r)\}$ of the correlation coefficient r is comparable in form.) After estimating the mean, standard deviation, skewness and kurtosis of the X population, the shape parameters γ and δ and the mean and standard deviation of the Y population can be found from tables[39]. Because $x = y\lambda + \xi$, ξ and λ can be estimated from the means and standard deviations of the X and Y population. Johnson and Tattersall (1971), for instance, give an application of the S_B curve.

(3) S_U *family* In this case, $f(y) = \sinh^{-1}(y) = \ln\{y + (y^2 + 1)^{1/2}\}$. The first moment and the second, third and fourth central moments are obtained after substituting for y and transforming to the exponential form. As for the S_B family, tables can be used to estimate the parameters[40].

3.6.3   Use of polynomial functions

In general, a particular frequency function $f(x)$ can be modified by using a

[38] The lognormal distribution will be analysed in section 6.5.
[39] See Pearson and Hartley (1972, table 36). Equations for the moments are given by Johnson and Kotz (1970, chapter 12).
[40] Pearson and Hartley (1972, tables 34, 35) and Elderton and Johnson (1969, pp. 126–8). A computer algorithm of fitting Johnson curves is given by Hill *et al.* (1976).

polynomial series $b_i(x)$ to obtain a new function $g(x)$ as follows.

$$g(x) = f(x) \sum_{i=0}^{\ell} b_i(x) \tag{3.59}$$

Two specific cases are the normal density function modified by Hermite polynomials and the gamma function modified by Laguerre polynomials. Series expansion methods involving the normal function originated with the Gram–Charlier series type A introduced at the start of this century; perhaps more credit is due to the economist Edgeworth who produced a similar series about 70 years ago which had considerable applications in astronomy and physics[41].

3.6.4 Additional types and methods

Besides the functions described here the Weibull probability density function given by

$$f(x) = (c/\lambda)\{(x - \xi)/\lambda\}^{c-1} \exp[-\{(x - \xi)/\lambda\}^c] \tag{3.60}$$

where $x \geq \xi > 0$, $c > 0$, $\lambda > 0$, has been fitted to flow data from the United States; ξ and λ are location and scale parameters respectively and the shape parameter c varies with skewness. However, its use in modelling stream flows is limited, and this is because in many cases it does not fit observed distributions. On the other hand, the Weibull function can represent probabilities such as run lengths of dry weather.

Because of the intuitive reasoning that variables from which natural processes derive are not identically distributed, mixtures of two or more probability functions have been suggested. In general, these involve the normal, gamma and the Pearson family of distributions.

In addition, a complex family called stable distributions has been suggested, on theoretical grounds, for application to economic time series, such as incomes, stocks and shares; Pareto and Levy were the pioneers. Characteristically, the tails of the density functions are thicker than those of the normal and exponential functions. However, their use in natural time series is yet to be justified[42].

In contrast with the transformations to normality and the polynomial series which are based on the density function $f(x)$, a (cumulative) distribution function of the type $F(x) = 1 - 1/(1 + x^a)^b$ was suggested by Burr in 1942. Tukey's lambda distribution $x = F(x)^\lambda - \{1 - F(x)\}^\lambda$ is of a similar type. A more generalised form of this is the Wakeby distribution $x = m + a[1 - \{1 - F(x)\}^b] - c[1 - \{1 - F(x)\}^{-d}]$, $x > m$, which is due to H. A. Thomas, Jr[43].

---

[41] See Kendall and Stuart (1977, chapter 6) and Tao et al. (1976).
[42] See Kottegoda (1978). A simple treatment of the Weibull function is given by Siddall (1972, pp. 309–17).
[43] Landwehr et al. (1978) have applied the Wakeby distribution. The Burr and Tukey distributions are given by Kendall and Stuart (1977, chapter 6) and by Ramberg (1975) respectively.

3.7   Random numbers: generation and transformations

Random numbers are required for two main purposes. In the first place they are essential for the generation of data sets through the models explained in the next two chapters. For data generation, the numbers should have a specific distribution. This is determined by the distributions of historical data on the basis of the the goodness-of-fit tests described in section 3.5. Secondly, random numbers are needed for studying the sampling properties of statistics when analytical solutions cannot be found. An example of this is the experimental procedure mentioned in subsection 3.3.2 to determine the sampling distribution of the estimated kurtosis b_2.

Roulette wheels such as those at Monte Carlo were originally used in obtaining random numbers, hence the term Monte Carlo methods. Since then, investigators have tried coin tossing, numbers in a telephone directory and subsequently tables of random numbers. The modern method is, of course, to use a computer routine. In this section methods of generating uniformly distributed random numbers are shown. Procedures for transformation to the distributions described in this chapter are then given[44].

3.7.1   Generation of uniform random numbers

Nearly all large computers have library subroutines to generate random numbers that have a uniform density, $f(x) = 1$, $0 \leqslant x \leqslant 1$. The output from these subroutines should be checked to ascertain whether the numbers are satisfactory for the purposes to be served. Some of the tests performed are on distribution, serial correlation, the first three or more moments, runs up and down, runs above and below certain levels and extreme values.

In the mixed congruent or modular method a random number x_i is obtained by using an equation of the type

$$x_i = (ax_{i-1} + b) \text{ (modulo } d) \tag{3.61}$$

where the integer constants a, b and d and the initial value x_0 (called the seed) are preassigned; the notation modulo d signifies that x_i is the remainder obtained after dividing $ax_{i-1} + b$ by d. Finally, all the x_i values are divided by d.

The quality of the results depends on the magnitudes of the constants a, b and d and their relationships, but the type of computer used will impose constraints. The main criterion is that the period, after which the original numbers are unavoidably repeated, should be as long as possible; this period increases as d increases. In practice, d is set equal to the word length, that is, to the number of bits retained as a unit in the computer. Also, the constants b and d should not have any common factors. As regards the constant a, its value needs to be sufficiently high; low values of this constant may not give good quality standard

---

[44] For explanations and proofs, see, for example, Hull and Dobell (1962), Tocher (1963) and Abramowitz and Stegun (1964, section 26.8).

normal random deviates after the transformation explained in the next subsection[45].

In order to reduce the serial dependence in the series, a second set of numbers, with the equation

$$y_i = (a'y_{i-1} + b')(\text{modulo } d') \tag{3.62}$$

and the initial value y_0, may be generated and combined alternately with the first. Different sequences of random numbers will be obtained by changing the initial values x_0 and y_0. The numbers generated by these methods are called pseudorandom because by fixing the constants we can predict the entire sequence[46].

Quite often the constants b and b' are omitted as in the original multiplicative congruential method of D. H. Lehmer in 1948. Incidentally, he put a equal to 23.

Figure 3.5 shows a FORTRAN subroutine which can be used to generate random numbers with uniform density. Here, KA, KB, NA and NB are the constants a, a', d and d' respectively of equations 3.61 and 3.62. It will be seen that the constants b' and d' have been omitted; the addition of constants XA and XB merely ensures (with a 3% increase in time) that zero values are not generated. Note that it would be expedient to change the subroutine to a function if the tests are excluded.

A chi-squared test on distribution is performed, and the first NAM serial correlation coefficients are printed. A test to ascertain whether the mean, variance and skewness are close to 1/2, 1/12 and 0 respectively is included. (These values may be verified by applying the method of moments to the case, $f(x) = 1, 0 \leqslant x \leqslant 1$.) Additional tests, for example, on runs and extremes might be added[47].

This subroutine should not be used to replace one provided by a computer, if that is found after testing to produce excellent results. It is given primarily so that readers may follow a useful procedure. If a satisfactory standard routine is not available, this may be adapted.

Another techniques which can be carried out on a pocket calculator is the mid-square method[48]. The procedure is to select a four-digit integer as the initial

---

[45] Lewis et al. (1969) suggest that a should be approximately but not exactly equal to $d^{1/3}$; see also Hammersley and Handscomb (1964) and Knuth (1969) on the choice of constants.

[46] According to von Neumann (1951), the outstanding Hungarian mathematician whose work we shall cite in many instances, 'Anyone who considers arithmetical methods of producing random digits is, of course, in a state of sin', for 'there is no such thing as a random number—there are only methods to produce random numbers'.

[47] For recent algorithms and tests for random numbers, see Lewis et al. (1969) and Chen (1971). Some non-congruent generators are discussed by Marsaglia and Bray (1968), and the references given in these papers deal with the bias and more stringent tests. An extensive discussion and examination of the methods and tests are also given by Maisel and Gnugnoli (1972).

[48] This technique is due to J. von Neumann and is described by Taussky and Todd (1956).

```
      SUBROUTINE RAND(SQ)
      COMMON/A/NX,NUM,NAM,NOT
      COMMON/B/LA,LB
C
C  SUBROUTINE GENERATES NX RANDOM NUMBERS WITH UNIFORM DENSITY IN
C  INTERVAL(0,1).INITIALIZE LA,LB WITH VALUES(E.G.1000567,2257333) ABOVE
C  10**6. IF NOT=1 CHI-SQUARED TOTAL FROM NUM CLASS INTERVALS,NAM SERIAL
C  CORRELATION COEFFICIENTS AND MOMENT STATISTICS ARE PRINTED AND RANDOM
C  NUMBERS LISTED. IF NOT=0 ONLY THE LIST IS PRINTED. IF NOT=2 TESTS ARE
C  MADE WITHOUT A LIST. IF NOT EXCEEDS 2 THE TESTS AND LIST ARE OMITTED.
C
      DIMENSION SQ(10000),P(100),NO(100),CO(20)
C
C  LIST CONSTANTS.
      ARC=1./FLOAT(NUM)
      AQ=FLOAT(NX)/FLOAT(NUM)
      MI=NUM-1
      KA=5**5
      KB=7**5
      NA=2**35-31
      NB=2**31-1
      ZA=FLOAT(NA)
      ZB=FLOAT(NB)
      XA=1.0/(2.0*ZA)
      XB=1.0/(2.0*ZB)
C
C  GENERATE RANDOM NUMBERS FROM TWO SERIES ALTERNATELY.
      DO 1 I=1,NX,2
      LA=MOD(KA*LA,NA)
      SQ(I)=FLOAT(LA)/ZA+XA
      LB=MOD(KB*LB,NB)
    1 SQ(I+1)=FLOAT(LB)/ZB+XB
      IF(NOT.GT.2) RETURN
      IF(NOT.LT.2) WRITE(6,2)  (SQ(J),J=1,NX)
    2 FORMAT(2X,10F11.8)
      IF(NOT.EQ.0) RETURN
C
C     COMPUTE MEAN, VARIANCE AND SKEWNESS.
      AL=FLOAT(NX)
      SA=0.
      SB=0.
      SC=0.
      DO 3 J=1,NX
      SQJ=SQ(J)
      SA=SA+SQJ
      SB=SB+SQJ*SQJ
    3 SC=SC+SQJ*SQJ*SQJ
      AV=SA/AL
      VAR=SB/AL-AV*AV
      ST=SQRT(VAR)
      SKEW=(SC/AL-3.*AV*SB/AL+2.*AV**3)/ST**3
      WRITE (6,4) AV,VAR,SKEW
    4 FORMAT(//,2X,6HMEAN =,F7.5,5X,10HVARIANCE =,F7.5,5X,
     125HCOEFFICIENT OF SKEWNESS =,F7.5)
```

Figure 3.5 FORTRAN subroutine to generate random uniform variates. The first generator used (see values for KA and NA) has also been tested by Lewis *et al.* (1969). For a calculator or small computer, KA = 997, KB = 809, NA = 7607 and NB = 9601, can be recommended, but the period is only about twice NA

```
C
C   COMPUTE CHI-SQUARED STATISTIC.
      P(1)=ARC
      DO 5 N=2,MI
5     P(N)=P(N-1)+ARC
      DO 6 N=1,NUM
      NO(N)=0
6     CONTINUE
      DO 7 N=1,NX
      IF(SQ(N).GT.P(1)) GO TO 7
      NO(1)=NO(1)+1
7     CONTINUE
      DO 8 K=2,MI
      DO 8 N=1,NX
      IF(SQ(N).GT.P(K)) GO TO 8
      IF(SQ(N).LE.P(K-1)) GO TO 8
      NO(K)=NO(K)+1
8     CONTINUE
      DO 9 N=1,NX
      IF(SQ(N).LE.P(MI)) GO TO 9
      NO(NUM)=NO(NUM)+1
9     CONTINUE
      CHIN=0.
      DO 10 N=1,NUM
      CHIN=CHIN+(FLOAT(NO(N))-AQ)**2/AQ
10    CONTINUE
      WRITE(6,11) NUM,AQ
11    FORMAT(//,2X,1CHNUMBERS IN,I4,2X,21HEQUAL CLASS INTERVALS,
     131HCOMMENCING WITH LOWEST INTERVAL,8X,
     131HEXPECTED NUMBER IN EACH CLASS =,F6.0)
      WRITE(6,12) (NO(N),N=1,NUM)
12    FORMAT(2X,3CI4)
      WRITE(6,13) CHIN
13    FORMAT(2X,2CHCHI-SQUARED TOTAL = ,F8.2)
C
C   COMPUTE SERIAL CORRELATION COEFFICIENTS.
      WRITE(6,14)
14    FORMAT(//,51H SERIAL CORRELATION COEFFICIENTS FOR LAGS 1 2 3 ETC)
      S=0.0
      T=0.0
      DO 15 N=1,NX
      SQN=SQ(N)
      S=S+SQN
15    T=T+SQN*SQN
      AV=S/AL
      T=T-AL*AV*AV
      DO 17 K=1,NAM
      S=0.0
      I=NX-K
      DO 16 L=1,I
16    S=S+(SQ(L)-AV)*(SQ(L+K)-AV)
17    CO(K)=S/T
      WRITE(6,18) (CO(K),K=1,NAM)
18    FORMAT(10F10.5)
      RETURN
      END
```

Figure 3.5   (contd.)

number. Then this number is squared to obtain a seven- or eight-digit number; if there are only seven digits in the squared number, a zero is added in front. Thereafter the middle four digits form the next random integer, and the procedure is followed repeatedly to obtain as many random numbers as required. Finally, all the random integers are divided by 10 000. The main shortcoming in this method is that periods are comparatively short. This means that the same set of numbers is repeated after a shorter period than in the congruent method; the cycle depends on the initial number. Note also that the technique can be applied in general to numbers with $2n$ digits.

3.7.2 *Transformation to normal distribution*

The random numbers of uniform density could be transformed to suit a specific density function. Box and Muller (1958) originated a procedure for generating normal deviates. In this method, two random standard normal deviates (n_i, n_{i+1}) are produced from two random uniform variates $(u_i, u_{i+1}, 0 \leqslant u_i < 1.0)$ by the transformation

$$n_i = \{-2\ln(u_i)\}^{1/2} \cos(2\pi u_{i+1})$$

$$n_{i+1} = \{-2\ln(u_i)\}^{1/2} \sin(2\pi u_{i+1}) \tag{3.63}$$

In figure 3.6, a listing of a subroutine is given[49].

3.7.3 *Generation of gamma variates*

An efficient method of producing gamma variates was originated by Von Jöhnk (1964)[50]. The operational steps are as follows.

(1) Estimate parameter γ which affects the shape of the fitted gamma function. This is denoted by B in SUBROUTINE GAMMA of figure 3.6.

(2) Let $\gamma = k + p$, where k is zero or a positive integer and $0 \leqslant p \leqslant 1.0$.

(3) Generate a series of uniform random variates u_i, $0 < u_i < 1.0$, $i = 1$, 2, . . ., t, . . ., n.

(4) Let $A_t = u_t^{1/p}$ and $B_t = u_{t+1}^{1/(1-p)}$. Starting with the initial pair of variates, with $t = 1$, check whether the constraint $A_t + B_t < 1$ is satisfied. (Then, $A_t/(A_t + B_t)$ is taken as a standard beta variate with parameters p and $1 - p$.) Otherwise reject u_t and u_{t+1}, and repeat this step by using the next pair of variates and so on if necessary. In practice, the constraint holds in about four cases out of five.

(5) A series of standard gamma variates $g_{i,\gamma}$, $i = 1, 2, 3, . . ., s$, with shape parameter γ is obtained from

$$g_{i,\gamma} = -A_t(A_t + B_t)^{-1} \ln(u_{t+2}) - \sum_{\ell=1}^{k} \ln(u_{t+2+\ell}) \tag{3.64}$$

[49] A proof of this transformation is given by Tocher (1963, pp. 33, 34). Senne (1974) gives tests on normal deviates and, for recent research which points to improved results from the use of only a sine function in equation 3.63, see Golder and Settle (1976).

[50] This has been proved independently by Whittaker (1972); for other techniques, see Cheng (1977).

```
      SUBROUTINE ANORM (SQ,NX)
C
C  SUBROUTINE TO TRANSFORM NX UNIFORM RANDOM NUMBERS IN INTERVAL (0,1)
C  AND ARRAY SQ TO NX INDEPENDENT STANDARD NORMAL VARIATES.
C
      DIMENSION SQ(2000)
      NYY=NX-1
      AN=8.*ATAN(1.)
      DO 1 N=1,NYY,2
      AA=SQRT(-2.*ALOG(SQ(N)))
      SQN=SQ(N+1)
      SQ(N)=AA*COS(AN*SQN)
    1 SQ(N+1)=AA*SIN(AN*SQN)
      RETURN
      END
      SUBROUTINE GAMMA(SQ,SH)
      COMMON/C/NY
      COMMON/D/B
C
C  SUBROUTINE TO GENERATE NY RANDOM GAMMA VARIATES USING A MAXIMUM OF NX
C  RANDOM NUMBERS WITH UNIFORM DENSITY IN THE INTERVAL (0,1). PARAMETER
C  B MUST COME FROM MAIN PROGRAM. WORKS SATISFACTORILY FOR B IN INTERVAL
C  (0.08,32). B=P+K WITH P IN INTERVAL (0,1) AND K IS ZERO OR A POSITIVE
C  INTEGER. P IS EQUATED TO ZERO IF WITHIN 5 PERCENT OF ITS LIMITS. NX
C  MAY BE LIMITED TO NY*(B+3.5) APPROXIMATELY. IF P=0 , NX=K*NY. PROGRAM
C  WORKS FASTER WITH TWO IF STATEMENTS REMOVED FROM DO LOOP 7 AND TWO
C  EXTERNAL LOOPS OR SUBROUTINES ADDED FOR (1) P=0.0 AND (2) K=0.
C
      DIMENSION SH(200),SQ(10000)
      K=B
      P=B-FLOAT(K)
      DO 1 J=1,NY
    1 SH(J)=0.0
C
C  ADJUST P IF WITHIN FIVE PERCENT OF ITS LIMITS
      IF(P.GT.0.95) K=K+1
      IF(P.LT.0.05.OR.P.GT.0.95) P=0.0
      LY=1
      DO 7 MY=1,NY
    2 IF(P-.01) 5,5,3
    3 AA=SQ(LY)**(1./P)
      PB=SQ(LY+1)**(1./(1.-P))
      CC=AA+BB
      LY=LY+2
C
C  REJECT UNIFORM DEVIATES IF CONSTRAINT IS NOT SATISFIED
      IF(CC-1.) 4,3,3
    4 SH(MY)=-(AA/CC)*ALOG(SQ(LY))
      LY=LY+1
C
C  TRANSFORMATION RELATED TO INTEGRAL PART OF SHAPE PARAMETER
      IF(K) 7,7,5
    5 DO 6 J=1,K
      SH(MY)=SH(MY)-ALOG(SQ(LY))
    6 LY=LY+1
    7 CONTINUE
      RETURN
      END
```

Figure 3.6   FORTRAN subroutines to generate standard normal variates and gamma
variates. These are based on the Box–Muller and Von Jöhnk methods

(in which $t = 1 + 2r_1$, $4 + k + 2(r_1 + r_2)$, $7 + k + 2(r_1 + r_2 + r_3)$, . . ., $3s - 2 + (s$

$- 1)k + 2 \sum\limits_{t=1}^{s=1} r_i$, where the r_i, $i = 2, \ldots, s$, are pairs of rejected numbers (step 4);

although, for all i, the integers r_i are generally zero or unity they could, with sharply decreasing probability, be higher). The second term on the right-hand side of equation 3.64 is omitted if k is zero, that is, for skewness greater than 2, when γ is estimated by the method of moments. If p is nearly zero (or unity), only this term is used in the equation with appropriate adjustment in the suffix of u.

3.7.4 *Random variates with other densities*

Transformation of gamma variates to other types of Pearson densities given in table 3.1 is possible by using the different relationships which each of these have with the chi-squared density. Let $g_{i,\gamma}$ and $g_{i,\delta}$, $i = 1, 2, \ldots, s$, represent two independent series of random gamma variates with shape parameters γ and δ respectively. Then the series $g_{i,\gamma}/(g_{i,\gamma} + g_{i,\delta})$ has the beta density (type I) with shape parameters γ and δ. Likewise, the series $g_{i,\gamma}/g_{i,\delta}$ has the inverse beta density (type VI) with shape parameters γ and δ and the series $1/g_{i,\gamma}$ has the inverse gamma density (type V) with the shape parameter γ for $i = 1, 2, \ldots, s$ in every case. By multiplying each of the variates in a series by the scale parameter λ and by adding the location parameter ξ the numbers can be transformed to the appropriate Pearson type[51].

Transformation to other functions is also possible from uniform random variates, and currently many computers have such facilities[52]. For example, the series $-\ln(u_i)/\lambda$, $i = 1, 2, 3, \ldots$, has the exponential (cumulative) distribution function $F(x) = 1 - \exp(-\lambda x)$.

3.8   Other comments and further reading

A practical use of distribution functions is shown in figure 3.7. Here, distributions of data generated by using the Pearson type III and normal distributions in autoregressive models, which are explained in chapter 4, are compared with the distribution of historical 5-day flow data for two stations in Wales. The distributions in the original data are evaluated from 11-year subsamples to show the variations within the periods of records. This shows that the normal distribution is inappropriate when sampling intervals are small; this

---

[51] The Von Jöhnk procedure is suitable only when γ and δ are small; alternatives are given by Atkinson and Whittaker (1976).
[52] In order to transform uniformly distributed numbers u_t to any type x_t with common distribution $F(x)$, we calculate the inverse $F^{-1}(u_t)$ or find a suitable approximation to it. The fundamentals of this approach and the rejection method are explained by Maisel and Gnugnoli (1972, chapter 8); see also Tocher (1903, chapter 1, 2). Butler (1970) gives an inverse algorithm to suit any purpose. Snow (1968) deals with transformation to the Poisson distribution. For a comprehensive bibliography on random number generation and testing, see Sowey (1978) and his earlier work.

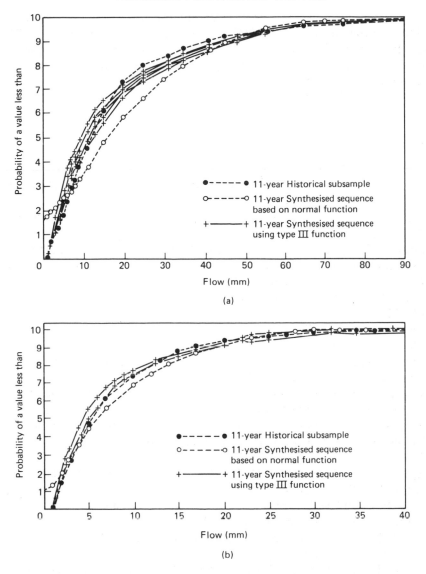

Figure 3.7 Probability distributions of subsamples of historical data and typical sequences of synthesised data based on an autoregressive model and a 5-day time unit for two river-flow stations (a) Elan Valley at Caban Coch Reservoir and (b) River Wye at Cadora in Wales

was confirmed by goodness-of-fit tests. Of course, the sensitivity of distributions to design choice remains to be examined.

The material in this chapter does not constitute a comprehensive treatment of continuous probability functions. For further reading, the following references are recommended in increasing order of sophistication: Johnson and Leone (1977); Elderton and Johnson (1969); Ord (1972); Johnson and Kotz (1970). Also, Hastings and Peacock (1975) have produced a useful handbook on 25 univariate distributions with moments, graphs and methods of random number generation. However, for multivariate distributions the work of Johnson and Kotz (1972) should be consulted.

References

Abramowitz, M., and Stegun, I. A. (eds) (1964). Handbook of mathematical functions. *Natl Bur. Stand. (U.S.), Appl. Math. Sec., Publ.*, No. 55; *Handbook of Mathematical Functions*, Dover Publications, New York

Aitchison, J., and Brown, J. A. C. (1957). *The Lognormal Distribution*, Cambridge University Press, London

Atkinson, A. C., and Whittaker, J. (1976). A switching algorithm for the generation of beta random variables with at least one parameter less than 1. *J. R. Statist. Soc. A*, **139**, 462–7

Barnard, G. A. (1947). The meaning of a significance level, *Biometrika*, **34**, 179–82

Beyer W. H. (ed.) (1968). *Handbook of Tables in Probability and Statistics*, Chemical Rubber Co., Ohio

Beasley, J. D., and Springer, S. G. (1977). The percentage points of the normal distribution. *Appl. Statist.*, **26**, 118–21

Best, D. J., and Roberts, D. E. (1975). The percentage points of the χ^2 distribution. *Appl. Statist.*, **24**, 385–8

Birnbaum, Z. W. (1952). Numerical tabulation of the distribution of Kolmogorov's statistic for finite sample size. *J. Am. Statist. Assoc.*, **47**, 425–41

Box, G. E. P., and Cox, D. R. (1964). An analysis of transformations. *J. R. Statist. Soc. B.*, **26**, 211–52

Box, G. E. P., and Muller, M. E. (1958). A note on the generation of random normal deviates. *Ann. Math. Statist.*, **29**, 610–11

Butler, E. L. (1970). General random number generator (G5). *Commun. Assoc. Comput. Mach.*, **13**, 49–52

Chen, E. H. (1971). A random normal number generator for 32-bit-word computers. *J. Am. Statist. Assoc.*, **66**, 400–3

Cheng, R. C. H. (1977). The generation of gamma variables with non-integral shape parameter. *Appl. Statist.*, **26**, 71–5

Cran, G. W., Martin, K. J., and Thomas, G. E. (1977). A remark on algorithms, AS63: the incomplete beta integral, AS64: inverse of the incomplete beta function ratio. *Appl. Statist.*, **26**, 111–14

D'Agostino, R., and Noether, G. E. (1973). On the evaluation of the Kolmogorov statistic. *Am. Statist.*, **27**, 81–2

D'Agostino, R., and Pearson, E. S. (1973). Tests for departure from normality.

Empirical results for the distributions of b_2 and $\sqrt{b_1}$. *Biometrika*, **60**, 613–22

Davis, H. T. (1935). *Tables of the Higher Mathematical Functions*, vol. 2, Principia Press, Bloomington, Indiana

Daw, R. H. (1966). Why the normal distribution? *J. Inst. Actuaries Students Soc.*, **18**, 2–15

Elderton, W. P., and Johnson, N. L. (1969). *Systems of Frequency Curves*, University Press, Cambridge, Massachusetts

Encyclopaedia Brittanica (1932), vol. 18, The Encyclopaedia Brittanica Co. Ltd, London, pp. 529–39

Encyclopaedia Brittanica (1969), vol. 18, William Benton, Chicago, Illinios, pp. 570–9

Feller, W. (1968). *Introduction to Probability Theory and its Applications*, vol. 1, 3rd edn, Wiley, New York

Fisher, R. A. (1922). On the mathematical foundations of theoretical statistics. *Philos. Trans. A*, **222**, 309–68

Fisz, M. (1963). *Probability Theory and Mathematical Statistics*, 3rd edn, Wiley, New York

Foster, H. A. (1924). Theoretical frequency curves and their application to engineering problems. *Trans. Am. Soc. Civ. Eng.*, **87**, 142–203

Gnedenko, B. V. (1968). *The Theory of Probability*, 4th edn (translated from the Russian by S. D. Seckler), Chelsea, New York

Golder, E. R., and Settle, J. G. (1976). The Box–Muller method of generating pseudo-random normal deviates. *Appl. Statist.*, **25**, 12–20

Good, I. J. (1973). What are degrees of freedom? *Am. Statist.*, **27**, 227–8

Goodrich, R. D. (1927). Straight line plotting for skew frequency distributions. *Trans. Am. Soc. Civ. Eng.*, **91**, 1–118

Greenwood, J. A., and Durand, D. (1960). Aids for fitting the gamma distribution by maximum likelihood. *Technometrics*, **2**, 55–65

Gupta, V. L. (1970). Selection of frequency distribution models. *Water Resour. Res.*, **6**, 1193–8

Hammersley, J. M., and Handscomb, D. C. (1964). *Monte Carlo Methods*, Methuen, London

Hamming, R. W. (1973). *Numerical Methods for Scientists and Engineers*, 2nd edn, McGraw-Hill, New York

Hastings, N. A. J., and Peacock, J. B. (1975). *Statistical Distributions*, Butterworths, London

Hawkins, R. H. (1972). Discussion on two-distribution method for flood-frequency analysis. *J. Hydraul. Div., Proc. Am. Soc. Civ. Eng.*, **98** (HY10), 1885–7

Heath, D. F. (1967). Normal or lognormal: approximate distributions. *Nature (London)*, **213**, 1159–60

Hill, I. D., Hill, R., and Holder, R. L. (1976). Fitting Johnson curves by moments, algorithms AS 99. *Appl. Statist.*, **25**, 180–9

Hoadley, A. B. (1968). Use of the Pearson densities for approximating a skew density whose left terminal and first three moments are known. *Biometrika*, **55,** 559–63

Hull, T. E., and Dobell, A. R. (1962). Random number generators. *Soc. Ind. Appl. Math. Rev.*, **4,** 230–54

Johnke, Emde and Lösh (1960). *Tables of Higher Functions*, 6th edn, McGraw-Hill, New York

Johnson, D., and Tattersall, K. H. (1971). Hydrological data analysis for water resources problems. *J. Water Eng.*, **25,** 181–200

Johnson, N. L. (1949). Systems of frequency curves generated by methods of translation. *Biometrika*, **36,** 149–76

Johnson, N. L., and Kotz, S. (1970). *Continuous Univariate Distributions*, vols 1, 2, Houghton Mifflin, Boston, Massachusetts

—— (1972). *Continuous Multivariate Distributions*, vol. 4, Wiley, New York

Johnson, N. L., and Leone, F. C. (1977). *Statistics and Experimental Design in Engineering and the Physical Sciences*, vol. 1, 2nd edn, Wiley, New York

Kendall, M. G., and Buckland, W. R. (1971). *A Dictionary of Statistical Terms*, 3rd edn, Haffner, New York

Kendall, M. G., and Stuart, A. (1973). *The Advanced Theory of Statistics*, vol. 2, 3rd edn, Griffin, London

—— (1977). *The Advanced Theory of Statistics*, vol. 1, 4th edn, Griffin, London

Kim, P. J., and Jennrich, R. I. (1973). Tables of the exact sampling distribution of the two-sample Kolmogorov–Smirnov criterion, $D_{mn} > m \leqslant n$. *Selected Tables in Mathematical Statistics*, vol. 1 (eds. H. L. Harter and D. B. Owen), American Mathematical Society, Providence, Rhode Island, pp. 79–170

Knuth, D. E. (1969). *The Art of Computer Programming*, vol. 2, *Seminumerical Algorithms*, Addison-Wesley, Reading, Massachusetts

Kolmogorvo, A. (1933). Sulla determinazione empirica di una legge di distribuzione. *Giornale dell Instituto Italiano degli Attuari*, **4,** 83–91

Kottegoda, N. T. (1970). Statistical methods of river flow synthesis for water resources assessment. *Proc. Inst. Civ. Eng.*, paper 7339S, suppl. XVIII

—— (1972). Stochastic five daily stream flow model. *J. Hydraul. Div., Proc. Am. Soc. Civ. Eng.*, **98** (HY9), 1469–85

—— (1978). Tail behaviour of riverflow probability densities. *Proceedings of the International Symposium on Risk and Reliability in Water Resources, Waterloo, Canada*, preprints

Kottler, F. (1950). The distribution of particle sizes. *J. Franklin Inst.*, **250,** 339–56

Landwehr, J. M., Matalas, N. L., and Wallis, J. R. (1978). Some comparisons of flood statistics in real and log space. *Water Resour. Res.*, **14,** 902–20

Lewis, P. A. W., Goodman, A. S., and Miller, J. M. (1969). A pseudo-random number generator for the system/360. *IBM Syst. J.*, **8,** 136–46

Lilliefors, H. W. (1967). On the Kolmogorov–Smirnov test for normality with mean and variance unknown. *J. Am. Statist. Assoc.*, **62,** 399–402

Maisel, H., and Gnugnoli, G. (1972). *Simulation of Discrete Stochastic Systems*,

Science Research Associates, Chicago, Illinois

Mann, H. B., and Wald, A. (1942). On the choice of the number of class intervals in the application of the chi square test. *Ann. Math. Statist.*, **13**, 306–17

Markovic, R. D. (1965). Probability functions of best fit to distributions of annual precipitation and runoff. *Colo. St. Univ., Fort Collins, Hydrol. Papers*, No. 8

Marsaglia, G., and Bray, T. A. (1968). One-line random number generators and their use in combinations. *Commun. Assoc. Comput. Mach.*, **11**, 757–9

Massey, F. J., Jr. (1951). The Kolmogorov–Smirnov test for goodness of fit. *J Am. Statist. Assoc.*, **46**, 68–78.

Matalas, N. C. (1963). Probability distributions of low flows. *U.S. Geol. Survey, Prof. Paper*, No. 434-A

Matalas, N. C., and Wallis, J. R. (1973). Eureka! it fits a Pearson type 3 distribution. *Water Resour. Res.*, **9**, 281–9

Miller, L. H. (1956). Table of percentage points of Kolmogorov Statistics. *J. Am. Statist. Assoc.*, **51**, 111–21

Mood, A. M., Graybill, F. A., and Boes, D. C. (1974). *Introduction to the Theory of Statistics*, McGraw-Hill, New York

Moran, P. A. P. (1957). The statistical treatment of flood flows. *Trans. Am. Geophys. Un.*, **38**, 519–23

von Neumann, J. (1951). Various techniques used in connection with random digits. *Natl Bur. Stand. (U.S.), Appl. Math. Ser.*, **12**, 36–8

Ord, J. K. (1972). *Families of Frequency Distributions*, Griffin, London

Page, E. (1977). Approximations to the cumulative normal function and its inverse for use on a pocket calculator. *Appl. Statist.*, **26**, 75–6

Pearson, K. (1957). *Tables of the Incomplete Γ-Function*, Cambridge University Press, Cambridge

Pearson, E. S., and Hartley, H. O. (eds) (1972). *Biometrika Tables for Statisticians*, vol. 2, Cambridge University Press, Cambridge

Ramberg, J. S. (1975). A probability distribution with application to Monte Carlo simulation studies. *Statistical Distributions in Scientific Work*, vol. 2 (eds C. P. Patil, S. Kotz and J. K. Ord), D. Reidal Publishing Company, Dordrecht, pp. 51–64

Senne, K. D. (1974). Machine independent Monte Carlo evaluation of the performance of dynamic stochastic systems. *J. Stochastics*, **1**, 215–38

Shenton, L. R., and Bowman, K. O. (1972). Further remarks on maximum likelihood estimates for the gamma distribution. *Technometrics*, **14**, 725–33

Siddall, J. N. (1972). *Analytical Decision Making in Engineering Design*, Prentice-Hall, Englewood Cliffs, New Jersey

Slade, J. J., Jr. (1936). An asymptotic probability function. *Trans. Am. Soc. Civ. Eng.*, **101**, 35–104

Smirnov, N. (1948). Table for estimating the goodness of fit of empirical distributions. *Ann. Math. Statist.*, **19**, 279–81

Snow, R. H. (1968). Algorithm 342: generator of random numbers satisfying the Poisson distribution. *Commun. Assoc. Comput. Mach.*, **11**, 819–20

Snyder, W. M. (1972). Fitting of distribution functions by nonlinear least squares, *Water Resour. Res.*, **8**, 1423–32

Sowey, E. R. (1978). A second classified bibliography on random number generating and testing. *Int. Statist. Rev.*, **46**, 89–102

Stidd, C. K. (1953). Cube-root-normal distributions. *Trans. Am. Geophys. Un.*, **34**, 31–5

—— (1970), The *n*th root normal distribution of precipitation. *Water Resour. Res.*, **6**, 1095–103

Svanidze, G. G. (1974). Mathematical models of run-off for the computation of storage reservoirs. *Proceedings of the Warsaw 1971 Symposium on Mathematical Models in Hydrology*, vol. 1 International Association of Scientific Hydrology, Paris, pp. 408–13

Tao, P. C., Yevjevich, V., and Kottegoda, N. T. (1976). Distributions of hydrologic independent stochastic components. *Colo. St. Univ., Fort Collins, Hydrol. Papers*, No. 82

Taussky, O., and Todd, J. (1956). Generation and testing of pseudo-random numbers. *Symposium on Monte Carlo Methods* (ed. H. A. Meyer), Wiley, New York, p. 16

Thom, H. C. S. (1958). A note on the gamma distribution. *Mon. Weath. Rev.*, **86**, 117–22

Tocher, K. D. (1963). *The Art of Simulation*, Hodder and Stoughton, London

Tukey, J. W. (1962). The future of data analysis. *Ann. Math. Statist.*, **33**, 1–67

Von Jöhnk, M. D. (1964). Evzeugung von betaverteilten und gammaverteilten Zufallszahlem. *Metrika*, **8**, 5–15

Weiss, M. S. (1978). Modification of the Kolmogorov–Smirnov statistic for use with correlated data. *J. Am. Statist. Assoc.*, **73**, 872–5

Whittaker, J. (1972). A note on the generation of gamma random variables with non-integral shape parameter. *Floods and Droughts, Proceedings of the 2nd International Hydrology Symposium*, Colorado State University Press, Fort Collins, Colorado

Wilk, M. B., Gnanadesikan, R., and Huyett, M. J. (1962). Probability plots of the gamma distribution. *Technometrics*, **4**, 1–20

Williams, C. A. Jr. (1950). On the choice of the number and width of classes for the chi-square test of goodness of fit. *J. Am. Statist. Assoc.*, **45**, 77–86

Yevjevich, V. (1963). Fluctuations of wet and dry years, part I. *Colo. St. Univ., Fort Collins, Hydrol. Papers*, No. 1

Yevjevich, V. (1972). *Probability and Statistics in Hydrology*, Water Resources Publications, Fort Collins, Colorado

Young, G. K., and Pisano, W. C. (1968), Operational hydrology using residuals. *J. Hydraul. Div., Proc. Am. Soc. Civ. Eng.*, **94** (HY 4), 909–23

4 Linear stochastic models

This chapter concerns types of linear models that are used to represent stochastic processes. The purpose is to generate likely future sequences of data for design and planning. In general, the models are formulated so that the current value of a variable is the weighted sum of past values and random numbers which represent unknown effects.

Autoregressive, moving-average and Box–Jenkins autoregressive moving-average (ARMA) and autoregressive integrated moving-average (ARIMA) models are explained here. Initially, it is assumed that trend and periodicity are removed prior to application, through the methods described in chapter 2. Then, section 4.7 deals specifically with seasonal models. A separate section pertains to transformations to normality and other methods of dealing with non-normal data. This is followed by an extension of univariate models for multisite data generation. Short-term forecasting procedures based on ARMA models and Kalman filtering are also included. Other practical uses of stochastic models are indicated.

4.1 Introduction to data generation and assumptions

The data used in the design, planning and operational studies of water resource schemes could be restricted to historical records. However, a serious drawback may then result, because a particular sequence of observations does not occur in an identical form over a future period. Consider, for example, the record of annual flows in the Göta River, Sweden, for the period 1907 to 1957, shown in figure 4.1c. This may be taken as the basis for water resource assessments over, say, the next 50 years. The true form of the projected flows represented by the broken lines is, of course, unknown, but we can suggest from experience that the properties of the time series as explained in chapter 2 will be propagated. This is evident from the traces of the two previous 50-year historical records, shown in figure 4.1, which could be viewed as realisations of the process studied. However, some important characteristics such as runs of low flows and extreme events may vary.

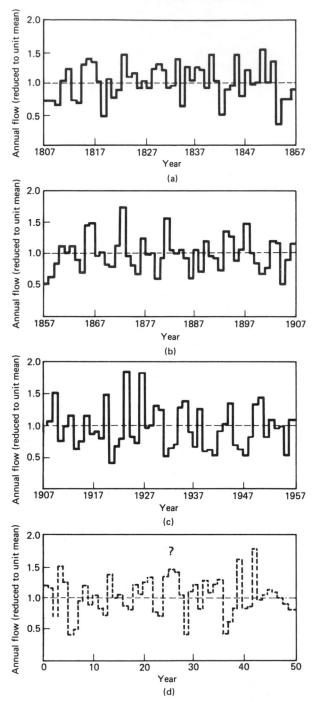

Figure 4.1   (a), (b), (c) Historical record and (d) future design period in Göta near
Sjötop-Vänersborg (Lake Vänern outflows), Sweden

The role of stochastic models taken up in this and the next chapter is to produce computer-generated likely sequences of future flows. Generated data sets are particularly useful in determining the reliabilities of maintaining specific supplies from complex systems.

It is important to note the assumptions on which the concept and the application of stochastic models are based. These are listed as follows.

(i) In the first instance, if recorded sequences do not adequately represent a process, a practically useful analysis cannot be made. It is assumed, therefore, that the sample represents the population to a sufficient degree. It is also implied here that the conditions of stationarity (and ergodicity) are invoked; on the other hand, non-stationary models can be formulated such as the seasonal and ARIMA models described in this chapter.

(ii) Secondly, it should be possible to identify and rectify errors of measurement and recording, if these exist, from a preliminary analysis of the data. Also, any enforced effects on the time series caused, for instance, by river diversions or by the construction of dams must be accounted for so that the series represents natural events as they occur.

(iii) Lastly, the model, on the one hand, should be manageable in form; on the other hand, it ought to maintain the pertinent statistical and hydrological characteristics of the process, so that the various types of events and sequences that are likely to occur are generated in a realistic manner.

In practice, these conditions cannot be fully met, and there are often many violations; indeed, accurate analyses and ideal models are not physically attainable entities. Nevertheless, the best possible use must be made of the available data, and, with such considerations in mind, a model which is sufficiently flexible and is at the same time parsimonious with respect to its parameters should satisfy general purposes. However, there should be a proviso here that the parameters can be estimated with some degree of confidence and that the effect on the design of likely errors in them and in model choice can be assessed.

4.2 Linear autoregressive models

In a linear autoregressive model, the current value of a variable is equated to the weighted sum of a preassigned number of past values and a variate that is completely random; here, the word linear merely signifies that the current value is dependent additively upon the past values and not, for example, on their squares or square roots. This type of model is a first approximation to many natural processes. It is particularly applicable to flow in a river which is supplemented by time-dependent components of ground water, surface run-off, catchment retention and the like. In addition, the precipitation process itself provides justification; as explained in chapter 1, this is strongly associated with atmospheric circulatory systems and oceanic temperatures that may persist over long time intervals.

The method dates back to the classical work of Markov (1907). The basic theory is due to Yule (1921, 1927) and Walker (1931); Yule who was evidently disenchanted with periodogram analysis especially with the 'disturbed periodic movement' of sunspot numbers suggested a procedure based on serial correlation (so named originally by him). Subsequently, Wold (1954) made a theoretical analysis of models of this type, and, more recently, Box and Jenkins (1976) presented a systematic methodology[1].

The model is applied to the stochastic component ξ_t (with reference to equation 2.1) which is treated as a random variable. This means that trend and seasonality are assumed to be removed and that the residual is covariance stationary. It is postulated that the value ξ_t at time t is constituted from the weighted sum of p values at times $t-1, t-2, \ldots, t-p$ and a random number η_t; the η_t, $t = 0, \pm 1, \pm 2, \ldots$, values are mutually independent and identically distributed. Autoregressive models of different orders p are analysed below; the procedure for estimating p is given in section 4.5.

4.2.1   pth-order model

The pth-order linear autoregressive model $AR(p)$ takes the form

$$\xi_t = \phi_{p,1}\xi_{t-1} + \phi_{p,2}\xi_{t-2} + \phi_{p,3}\xi_{t-3} + \ldots + \phi_{p,p}\xi_{t-p} + \eta_t$$

$$= \sum_{i=1}^{p} \phi_{p,i}\xi_{t-i} + \eta_t \tag{4.1}$$

where $\phi_{p,i}$, $i = 1, 2, 3, \ldots, p$ are the autoregressive parameters or weights. The properties of ξ_t and η_t are $E(\xi_t) = E(\eta_t) = 0$, $\text{var}(\xi_t) = E(\xi_t^2) = \sigma_\xi^2$, $\text{var}(\eta_t) = E(\eta_t^2) = \sigma_\eta^2$, $\rho_k = E(\xi_t\xi_{t-k})/\sigma_\xi^2$ and, for $k = 1, 2, 3, \ldots, E(\eta_t\eta_{t-k}) = E(\eta_t\xi_{t-k}) = 0$; the last equality merely signifies that the current random number is independent of past values of the process. As in previous notation, E denotes the expected or mean value of the term within the parentheses and the variance is abbreviated to var.

Henceforth it is assumed without loss of generality that the variance σ_ξ^2 of the stochastic component is equal to one. This means that, in application, the numbers generated through such equations as equation 4.1 should be multiplied by the standard deviation of the variable modelled and the mean should then be added to each number. These and other model parameters are estimated from observed sequences.

4.2.2   Estimation of autoregressive parameters

If equation 4.1 is multiplied by ξ_{t-1} and expectations are taken,

---

[1] Box–Jenkins models are explained more briefly by Anderson (1976), for instance.

$$E(\xi_t \xi_{t-1}) = \phi_{p,\,1} E(\xi_{t-1} \xi_{t-1}) + \phi_{p,\,2} E(\xi_{t-2} \xi_{t-1}) + \phi_{p,\,3} E(\xi_{t-3} \xi_{t-1})$$

$$+ \ldots + \phi_{p,\,p} E(\xi_{t-p} \xi_{t-1}) + E(\eta_t \xi_{t-1}) \tag{4.2}$$

Because $E(\eta_t \xi_{t-1}) = 0$ and on account of the other properties given above, it follows that

$$\rho_1 = \phi_{p,\,1} + \phi_{p,\,2}\rho_1 + \phi_{p,\,3}\rho_2 + \ldots + \phi_{p,\,p}\rho_{p-1} \tag{4.3}$$

Furthermore, if equation 4.1 is multiplied by $\xi_{t-2}, \xi_{t-3}, \ldots, \xi_{t-p}$ in turn and if expectations are taken after each multiplication, p relationships called the Yule–Walker equations are obtained. These can be represented in matrix form by

$$
\begin{bmatrix}
\rho_1 \\
\rho_2 \\
\rho_3 \\
\cdot \\
\cdot \\
\cdot \\
\rho_p
\end{bmatrix}
=
\begin{bmatrix}
1 & \rho_1 & \rho_2 & \cdots & \rho_{p-1} \\
\rho_1 & 1 & \rho_1 & \cdots & \rho_{p-2} \\
\rho_2 & \rho_1 & 1 & \cdots & \rho_{p-3} \\
\cdot & \cdot & \cdot & & \cdot \\
\cdot & \cdot & \cdot & & \cdot \\
\cdot & \cdot & \cdot & & \cdot \\
\rho_{p-1} & \rho_{p-2} & \rho_{p-3} & \cdots & 1
\end{bmatrix}
\begin{bmatrix}
\phi_{p,\,1} \\
\phi_{p,\,2} \\
\phi_{p,\,3} \\
\cdot \\
\cdot \\
\cdot \\
\phi_{p,\,p}
\end{bmatrix}
\tag{4.4}
$$

or briefly

$$\rho_p = P_p \phi_p$$

A necessary condition for stationarity is that the autocorrelation matrix P_p is positive definite, that is, the determinant and all its principal minors are zero or positive. Therefore,

$$\phi_p = P_p^{-1} \rho_p \tag{4.5}$$

In order to solve equation 4.5, serial correlation coefficients $r_1, r_2, \ldots, r_p$ are substituted in P_p and ρ_p, and hence the Yule–Walker estimates of the autoregressive parameters $\phi_{p,\,1}, \phi_{p,\,2}, \ldots, \phi_{p,\,p}$ are obtained. For a normal linear process, this gives the approximate ML or least-squares estimates[2]. Detailed procedures are described in subsections 4.2.4 to 4.2.6. However, the order of the model is unknown, and this problem is taken up in section 4.5.

The above-mentioned conditions for stationarity can also be specified through the so-called characteristic equation

$$b^p - \phi_{p,\,1} b^{p-1} - \phi_{p,\,2} b^{p-2} - \ldots - \phi_{p,\,p} = 0 \tag{4.6}$$

where b is a dummy variable, by stating that the roots of the equation (which means the values of b which satisfy it) should lie inside the unit circle given by $b^2 = 1$. Accordingly, if equation 4.6 is written as

---

[2] See Jenkins and Watts (1968, pp. 192–3).

$$\prod_{i=1}^{p} (b - \pi_i) = 0 \tag{4.7}$$

then $|\pi_i| < 1$ for $i = 1, 2, \ldots, p$.

4.2.3　Variance of independent variables

By squaring both sides of equation 4.1 and taking expectations it follows that, because each of the expected values $E(\eta_t \xi_{t-1})$, $E(\eta_t \xi_{t-2})$, $\ldots$, $E(\eta_t \xi_{t-p})$ are equal to zero,

$$1 = \phi_{p,1}\rho_1 + \phi_{p,2}\rho_2 + \phi_{p,3}\rho_3 + \ldots + \phi_{p,p}\rho_k + \sigma_\eta^2 \tag{4.8}$$

Hence, σ_η^2, which is the variance of the independent variables η_t, is given by

$$\sigma_\eta^2 = 1 - \phi_{p,1}\rho_1 - \phi_{p,2}\rho_2 - \phi_{p,3}\rho_3 - \ldots - \phi_{p,p}\rho_p$$
$$= 1 - R^2 \tag{4.9}$$

where

$$R^2 = \phi_{p,1}\rho_1 + \phi_{p,2}\rho_2 + \phi_{p,3}\rho_3 + \ldots + \phi_{p,p}\rho_p$$

is called the coefficient of determination or the square of the multiple correlation coefficient[3].

4.2.4　First-order model

The first-order autoregressive model AR(1) is known familiarly as a Markov model[4]. It is given by

$$\xi_t = \phi_{1,1}\xi_{t-1} + \eta_t \tag{4.10}$$

If this equation is multiplied throughout by ξ_{t-1} and if expectations are taken, because $E(\eta_t \xi_{t-1}) = 0$ in addition to the assumptions $E(\xi_t)^2 = 1$ and $E(\xi_t) = 0$, it follows that

$$\phi_{1,1} = \rho_1 \tag{4.11}$$

where ρ_1 is the lag-one autocorrelation coefficient and $-1 < \rho_1 < 1$. Also, from equation 4.9, the variance of the independent variables η_t is given by

$$\sigma_\eta^2 = 1 - \rho_1^2 \tag{4.12}$$

Again, if equation 4.10 is multiplied in turn by ξ_{t-1}, ξ_{t-2}, ξ_{t-3}, $\ldots$ and ξ_{t+1}, ξ_{t+2}, ξ_{t+3}, $\ldots$,

$$\rho_k = \rho_1^{|k|}, \qquad k = 0, \pm 1, \pm 2, \pm 3 \tag{4.13}$$

---

[3] R^2 varies with the chosen model and is a measure of the predictability of a time series; Nelson (1976) gives a rigorous interpretation.
[4] This can also be stipulated in terms of probabilities by a (first-order) Markov chain which is applied to reservoir problems in chapter 7.

In a physical sense, this is suggestive of base flow recession behaviour (from the ground-water component of river flows).

Example 4.1   The mean and standard deviation of the annual flows in the Severn at Bewdley in England are 4.7 and 0.958 respectively in units of 100 mm of equivalent rainfall over the catchment; also, the first serial correlation coefficient $r_1 = 0.324$. Generate three items of data (for times t, $t+1$ and $t+2$) using a Markov model and the following independent standard normal variates η_t: 0.87, -0.65, 1.15. In order to use equation 4.10, multiply the η_t values by the standard deviation $s_\eta = (1 - r_1^2)^{1/2} = 0.946$ (from equation 4.12). Assume that $\tilde{\xi}_{t-1} = 0$, that is, $x_{t-1} = 4.7$.

$$\begin{aligned}
\tilde{\xi}_t &= 0.324 \times 0 + 0.946 \times 0.87 &&= 0.823, && x_t = 0.958\tilde{\xi}_t + 4.7 &&= 5.49 \\
\tilde{\xi}_{t+1} &= 0.324 \times 0.823 - 0.946 \times 0.65 &&= -0.348, && x_{t+1} = 0.958\tilde{\xi}_{t+1} + 4.7 &&= 3.94 \\
\tilde{\xi}_{t+2} &= -0.324 \times 0.348 + 0.946 \times 1.15 &&= 0.975, && x_{t+2} = 0.958\tilde{\xi}_{t+2} + 4.7 &&= 5.63
\end{aligned}$$

4.2.5 *Second-order model*

The second-order autoregressive model AR(2) takes the form

$$\xi_t = \phi_{2,1}\xi_{t-1} + \phi_{2,2}\xi_{t-2} + \eta_t \tag{4.14}$$

From the Yule–Walker equation of section 4.2.2,

$$\rho_1 = \phi_{2,1} + \phi_{2,2}\rho_1$$

and

$$\rho_2 = \phi_{2,1}\rho_1 + \phi_{2,2} \tag{4.15}$$

As explained before, estimates $\hat{\phi}_{2,1}$ and $\hat{\phi}_{2,2}$ of the parameters are obtained by substituting the estimated serial correlation coefficients r_1 and r_2 for ρ_1 and ρ_2. Hence,

$$\hat{\phi}_{2,2} = (r_2 - r_1^2)/(1 - r_1^2) \tag{4.16}$$

and

$$\hat{\phi}_{2,1} = r_1 \quad \hat{\phi}_{2,2}r_1 = r_1(1 - r_2)/(1 - r_1^2) \tag{4.17}$$

The stationarity constraints on $\phi_{2,1}$ and $\phi_{2,2}$ are determined as follows. From equations 4.6 and 4.7, because $\pi_1 = \{\phi_{2,1} - (\phi_{2,1}^2 + 4\phi_{2,2})^{1/2}\}/2$, $\pi_2 = \{\phi_{2,1} + (\phi_{2,1}^2 + 4\phi_{2,2})^{1/2}\}/2$, $|\pi_1| < 1$ and $|\pi_2| < 1$, it follows that $-1 < \phi_{2,2} < 1$, $\phi_{2,1} + \phi_{2,2} < 1$ and $\phi_{2,2} - \phi_{2,1} < 1$. It can also be shown that, for stationary conditions, $\rho_1^2 < (\rho_2 + 1)/2$ and $-1 < \rho_1, \rho_2 < +1$.

Example 4.2   Annual flows in the Göta River near Sjötop-Vänersborg (Lake Vänern outflows), Sweden, for the period 1807 to 1957 are reduced to unit mean and are tabulated by Yevjevich (1963). The estimated standard deviation is 0.182, and the first and second serial correlation coefficients are 0.458 and -0.004. It is found that a second-order process provides a satisfactory fit to the data. Generate three additional values using the following independent standard normal variates: 1.352, -0.532, 0.789.

$$\hat{\phi}_{2,1} = r_1(1 - r_2)/(1 - r_1^2) = 0.458 \times 1.004/(1 - 0.458^2) = 0.582$$

$$\hat{\phi}_{2,2} = (r_2 - r_1^2)/(1 - r_1^2) = (-0.004 - 0.458^2)/(1 - 0.458^2) = -0.271$$

From equation 4.9,

$$\hat{R}^2 = \hat{\phi}_{2,1}r_1 + \hat{\phi}_{2,2}r_2 = 0.582 \times 0.458 + 0.271 \times 0.004$$

$$\hat{\sigma}_\eta^2 = 1 - \hat{R}^2 = 0.856^2$$

Assuming that

$\check{\xi}_t = 0.582 \times 0 - 0.271 \times 0 + 0.856 \times 1.352$	$= 1.157,$	$x_t = 0.182\check{\xi}_t + 1$	$= 1.211$
$\check{\xi}_{t+1} = 0.582 \times 1.157 - 0.271 \times 0 - 0.856 \times 0.532$	$= 0.218,$	$x_{t+1} = 0.182\check{\xi}_{t+1} + 1$	$= 1.040$
$\check{\xi}_{t+2} = 0.582 \times 0.218 - 0.271 \times 1.157 + 0.856 \times 0.789$	$= 0.489,$	$x_{t+2} = 0.182\check{\xi}_{t+2} + 1$	$= 1.089$

4.2.6   General recursive formulae

Equations 4.16 and 4.17 can be written in the form

$$\hat{\phi}_{2,2} = (r_2 - \hat{\phi}_{1,1}r_1)/(1 - \hat{\phi}_{1,1}r_1)$$

and

$$\hat{\phi}_{2,1} = \hat{\phi}_{1,1} - \hat{\phi}_{2,2}\hat{\phi}_{1,1}$$

Proceeding in a similar manner from the second- to the third- and so on to higher-order models, we can obtain the estimates of a general pth- order model recursively through a pivotal reduction[5] of equation 4.4. The formulae are

$$\hat{\phi}_{p,p} = \left(r_p - \sum_{j=1}^{p-1} \hat{\phi}_{p-1,j}r_{p-j} \right) \bigg/ \left(1 - \sum_{j=1}^{p-1} \hat{\phi}_{p-1,j}r_j \right) \tag{4.18}$$

$$\hat{\phi}_{p,j} = \hat{\phi}_{p-1,j} - \hat{\phi}_{p,p}\hat{\phi}_{p-1,p-j}, \qquad j = 1, 2, 3, \ldots, p-1 \tag{4.19}$$

A computer programme for estimating $\phi_{p,i}, i = 1, 2, \ldots, p$ by this method is given in figure 4.2. Note that these may not be the best estimates. Alternatively, least-squares estimates that minimise

$$\sum_{t=1}^{N} \left(\check{\xi}_t - \sum_{i=1}^{p} \phi_{p,i}\check{\xi}_{t-i} \right)^2$$

where $\check{\xi}_t, t = 1, 2, \ldots, N$, is an observed sequence and $\check{\xi}_{t-i} = 0$ if $t - i < 1$ can be found. There are other sophisticated methods[6]. However, the type of variations between properties of subsamples of historical data, as shown in figures 4.3 to 4.5, is indicative of a general uncertainty of the process. For this reason, refined methods of estimation may not be practically worthwhile.

---

[5] See Durbin (1960).
[6] See, for example, Box and Jenkins (1976, chapter 7) and Hipel et al. (1977) for the ML and modified least-squares methods.

```
      SUBROUTINE AUTO(D,NN,LL)
      DIMENSION D(3000),R(50),Y(50),Z(50)
C
C  NN & LL DENOTE NUMBER OF DATA ITEMS AND MAXIMUM AUTOREGRESSIVE MODEL
C  ORDER RESPECTIVELY. FIRST COMPUTE LL SERIAL CORRELATION COEFFICIENTS.
C
      WRITE(6,1)
1     FORMAT(1HU,51H SERIAL CORRELATION COEFFICIENTS FOR LAGS 1 2 3 ETC)
      S=0.0
      T=0.0
      DO 2 N=1,NN
      DN=D(N)
      S=S+DN
2     T=T+DN*DN
      AV=S/FLOAT(NN)
      T=T-FLOAT(NN)*AV*AV
      DO 4 K=1,LL
      S=0.0
      I=NN-K
      DO 3 L=1,I
3     S=S+(D(L)-AV)*(D(L+K)-AV)
4     R(K)=S/T
      WRITE(6,5) (R(K),K=1,LL)
5     FORMAT(10F10.5)
C
C  OBTAIN RECURSIVE ESTIMATES OF AUTOREGRESSIVE PARAMETERS AND RESIDUAL
C  VARIANCE FOR MODELS OF ORDER 1 TO LL.
C
6     FORMAT(1HO,44H PARAMETERS OF AUTOREGRESSIVE MODEL OF ORDER,I5)
      N=1
      WRITE(6,6) N
      WRITE(6,7) R(1)
7     FORMAT(10F10.5)
      SS=(1.0+R(1))*(1.0-R(1))
      SZ=SS*(FLOAT(NN)-1.0)/(FLOAT(NN)-3.0)
      WRITE(6,8) SZ
8     FORMAT(21H RESIDUAL VARIANCE = ,F10.5)
      Y(1)=R(1)
      DO 12 N=2,LL
      WRITE(6,6) N
      NM=N-1
      AA=R(N)
      BB=1.0
      DO 9 I=1,NM
      AA=AA-Y(I)*R(N-I)
9     BB=BB-Y(I)*R(I)
      Z(N)=AA/BB
      DO 10 I=1,NM
10    Z(I)=Y(I)-Z(N)*Y(N-I)
      DO 11 I=1,N
11    Y(I)=Z(I)
      WRITE (6,7) (Z(I),I=1,N)
      SS=SS*(1.0-Z(N))*(1.0+Z(N))
      SZ=SS*(FLOAT(NN)-FLOAT(N))/(FLOAT(NN)-1.0-2.0*FLOAT(N))
12    WRITE(6,8) SZ
      RETURN
      END
```

Figure 4.2 FORTRAN subroutine to compute serial correlation coefficients and estimate parameters of autoregressive models using the Yule–Walker equations

4.3   Partial autocorrelations

The set of parameters $\phi_{1,1}$, $\phi_{2,2}$, $\phi_{3,3}$, ... which are the last coefficients of autoregressive models of order 1, 2, 3, ... respectively constitute the so-called partial autocorrelation function (PAF). In general, the partial autocorrelation $\phi_{p,p}$ is the autocorrelation remaining in the series after fitting a model of order p -1 and removing the linear dependence. Indeed, both the order and type of model are indicated by the PAF.

If we return to the particular case of autoregressive models, it is important to note that, whereas the autocorrelation function decreases to zero only at an infinite lag, in an autoregressive process of order p the partial autocorrelations $\phi_{k,k}$ are theoretically zero for $k > p$. Therefore, the sample PAF is an important tool in determining the order of the model if the serial correlation function suggests that the process could be approximated by a linear autoregressive model. The PAF is also useful for identifying other types of processes, as explained in the following sections, and its role as a diagnostic tool is summarised in subsection 4.5.4.

For an autoregressive process of order p, the variance of the estimated partial autocorrelations is given by

$$\text{var}(\hat{\phi}_{k,k}) \approx 1/N, \qquad k > p \tag{4.20}$$

where N is the sample length. A test procedure could be devised by demarcating, say, 95 % confidence limits which are $1.96/N^{1/2}$ above and below the horizontal axis of the sample PAF. This is on the assumption that the distribution of a partial serial correlation coefficient with zero expectation is approximately normal[7]. If the parent time series is autoregressive in form, then the order p of the model would be indicated on the plot when the $\hat{\phi}_{k,k}$ values for $k > p$ are not significantly different from zero. Examples of serial correlograms and sample PAFs from three sets of annual data are given in figures 4.3 to 4.5. The serial correlation and the estimated PAF are shown here for the annual flows in three rivers from Africa, North America and Europe. Interpretations will be taken up in subsequent sections.

---

[7] See Anderson (1942). However, the distribution may be significantly different from normal if $N < 30$.

Figure 4.3   Serial correlograms and estimated partial autocorrelograms of annual flows in Göta near Sjötop–Vänersborg (Lake Vänern outflows), Sweden, for the period 1807 to 1957: broken lines denote 95 % confidence limits: (a) serial correlograms of 50-year subsequences; (b) estimated partial autocorrelograms of 50-year subsequences; (c) serial correlogram of 150-year sequence; (d) estimated partial autocorrelogram of 150-year sequence; (e) serial correlograms of estimated independent residuals $\hat{\eta}_t$ of 150-year sequence in which the AR(1) and AR(2) models used are given by $\xi_t = 0.0458\xi_{t-1} + \eta_t$ and $\xi_t = 0.582\xi_{t-1} - 0.271\xi_{t-2} + \eta_t$ respectively.

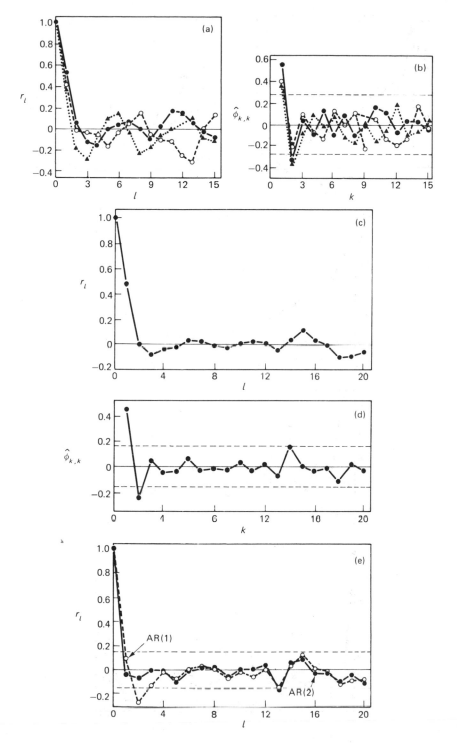

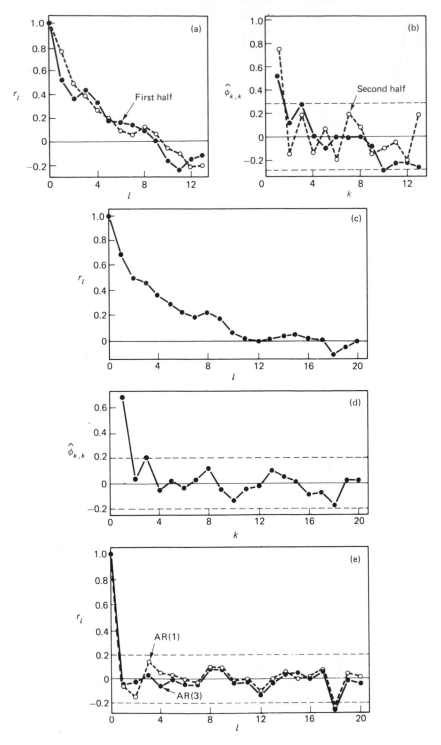

An ancillary method for choosing k is to draw a plot of estimated residual variance

$$s_\eta^2(k) \approx \{(N-k)/(N-2k-1)\} \prod_{i=1}^{k} (1 - \hat{\phi}_{i,i}^2) s_\xi^2 \tag{4.21}$$

(where s_ξ^2 is the variance of the stochastic component) for model lengths $k = 1, 2, 3, \ldots$. Accordingly, a suitable order $k = p$ of a model is the order for which the residual variance is a minimum, or more appropriately (in practical situations) if the residual variance for models of order greater than p does not decrease significantly[8].

4.4   Moving-average models

In contradistinction to autoregressive processes, a moving-average process MA(q) of order q is one in which the current value of a random variable is the weighted sum of $q+1$ random numbers. Here, the weight assigned to the currently added random number is unity, and random numbers generated at antecedent times are multiplied by $-\theta_{q,1}, -\theta_{q,2}, \ldots, -\theta_{q,q}$ respectively. Accordingly, the model takes the form

$$\xi = \eta_t - \theta_{q,1}\eta_{t-1} - \theta_{q,2}\eta_{t-2} - \cdots - \theta_{q,q}\eta_{t-q}$$

$$= \eta_t - \sum_{j=1}^{q} \theta_{q,j}\eta_{t-j} \tag{4.22}$$

The stochastic component ξ_t is equivalent in this case to the output from a linear filter with a white noise η_t input[9]. As before, $E(\xi_t) = 0$ and $E(\xi_t^2) = 1$; also, $E(\eta_t\eta_{t-k}) = 0$ for $k \neq 0$. Hence, by squaring equation 4.22 and taking expectations, the variance of the random component is given by

$$\sigma_\eta^2 = 1/(1 + \theta_{q,1}^2 + \theta_{q,2}^2 + \ldots + \theta_{q,q}^2) \tag{4.23}$$

Then multiplying the left-hand side of equation 4.22 by ξ_{t-k} and the right-hand side by $\eta_{t-k} - \theta_{q,1}\eta_{t-1-k} - \theta_{q,2}\eta_{t-2-k} \quad \cdots \quad \theta_{q,q}\eta_{t-q-k}$, taking expectations

[8] See Jenkins and Watts (1968, pp. 197–8). An example will be given in section 4.6.
[9] In an infinite-order moving average process, a necessary constraint for stationarity is that the sum of the squared weights should be less than infinity (Mandelbrot, 1976).

Figure 4.4   Serial correlograms and estimated partial autocorrelograms of annual flows in St Lawrence, at Ogdensburgh, New York, for the period 1860 to 1957: broken lines denote 95% confidence limits: (a) serial correlograms of half-sequences; (b) estimated partial autocorrelograms of half-sequences; (c) serial correlogram of 97-year sequence; (d) estimated partial autocorrelogram of 97-year sequence; (e) serial correlograms of estimated independent residuals $\hat{\eta}_t$ of 97-year sequence in which the AR(1) and AR(3) models used are given by $\xi_t = 0.695\xi_{t-1} + \eta_t$ and $\xi_t = 0.670\xi_{t-1} - 0.107\xi_{t-2} + 0.200\xi_{t-3} + \eta_t$ respectively

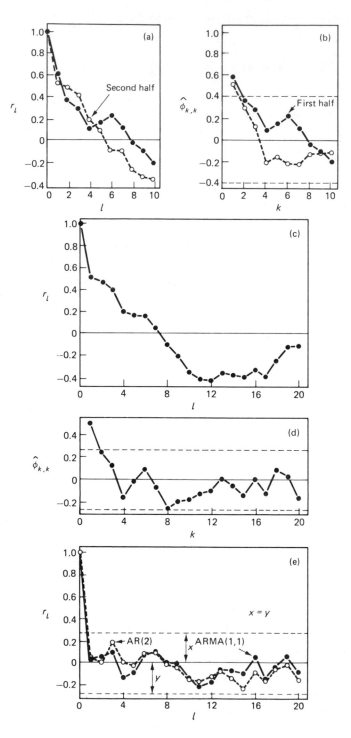

and substituting for σ_η^2 from equation 4.23, we obtain

$$\rho_k = (-\theta_{q, k} + \theta_{q, 1}\theta_{q, k+1} + \theta_{q, 2}\theta_{q, k+2} + \ldots + \theta_{q, q-k}\theta_{q, q})/$$
$$(1 + \theta_{q, 1}^2 + \theta_{q, 2}^2 + \ldots + \theta_{q, q}^2), \quad k = 1, 2, 3, \ldots, q \quad (4.24)$$

and

$$\rho_k = 0, \quad k > q$$

where ρ_k is the lag-k autocorrelation coefficient.

For the first-order moving-average model MA(1), therefore,

$$\rho_1 = -\theta_{1, 1}/(1 + \theta_{1, 1}^2) \quad (4.25)$$

Hence, $\theta_{1, 1}$ can be estimated from the roots of the equation

$$\hat{\theta}_{1, 1}^2 + \hat{\theta}_{1, 1}/r_1 + 1 = 0 \quad (4.26)$$

It is seen that one root is the reciprocal of the other and the root which satisfies the invertibility constraint $|\hat{\theta}_{1, 1}| > 1$ is the initial estimate of the moving-average parameter[10]. However, such an estimate is found to be inefficient. (This means that, for some other value of $\theta_{1, 1}$, generated data could look more like the historical data.) The suggested procedure is to estimate $\theta_{1, 1}$ by minimising the sum of squares of the residuals which is $\sum_{t=1}^{N} \tilde{\varepsilon}_t^2$, where $\tilde{\varepsilon}_1 = \tilde{\xi}_1, \tilde{\varepsilon}_2 = \tilde{\xi}_2 + \theta_{1, 1}\tilde{\varepsilon}_1, \tilde{\varepsilon}_3 = \tilde{\xi}_3 + \theta_{1, 1}\tilde{\varepsilon}_2$ and $\tilde{\xi}_t, t = 1, 2, 3, \ldots, N$, is an observed sequence. The alternative ML procedure is much more difficult for estimation.

4.5 Box–Jenkins models: formulation and identification

The models described in sections 4.2 to 4.4 are special types of the so-called Box–Jenkins class of models. Of these, the ARMA model, which includes the

[10] An MA(q) process is stationary. In addition if the roots of its characteristic equation $b^q + \theta_{q, 1}b^{q-1} + \theta_{q, 2}b^{q-2} + \ldots + \theta_{q, q} = 0$ are less than one in absolute value, it is invertible. This means that it could then be converted into a stationary autoregressive process, that is, a process with a convergent set of parameters. Finite-order moving-average models are generally inappropriate for direct application in hydrology. They are included here as a prelude to the ARMA and ARIMA models of section 4.5.

Figure 4.5 Serial correlograms and estimated partial autocorrelograms of annual flows in Niger at Koulikoro, Mali, Africa, for the period 1906 to 1957: broken lines denotes 95% confidence limits: (a) serial correlograms of half-sequences; (b) estimated partial autocorrelograms of half-sequences; (c) serial correlogram of 51-year sequence; (d) estimated partial autocorrelogram of 51-year sequence; (e) serial correlograms of estimated independent residuals $\tilde{\eta}_t$ of 51-year sequence in which the AR(2) and ARMA(2, 2) models used are given by $\xi_t = 0.402\xi_{t-1} + 0.248\xi_{t-2} + \eta_t$ and $\xi_t = 0.84\xi_{t-1} + \eta_t - 0.40\eta_t$ respectively

autoregressive, the moving-average and the mixed types, is commonly applied to stationary time series. Then there is the non-stationary ARIMA type, and it encompasses all the other models in its group.

A backshift operator B is used in defining the models, so that by using the notation of the previous sections $B\xi_t = \xi_{t-1}$, $B^2\xi_{t-2}$ and in general $B^p\xi_t = \xi_{t-p}$; likewise, $B^q\eta_t = \eta_{t-q}$. There is also a difference operator ∇ such that $\nabla\xi_t = (1-B)\xi_t = \xi_t - \xi_{t-1}$, $\nabla^2\xi_t = (1-B)^2\xi_t = (\xi_t - \xi_{t-1}) - (\xi_{t-1} - \xi_{t-2}) = \xi_t - 2\xi_{t-1} + \xi_{t-2}$ and in general $\nabla^d\xi_t = (1-B)^d\xi_t$. This type of differencing is referred to in subsection 2.3.1 with other filtering methods. It is useful in transforming a non-stationary series to one that is stationary. Here, the difference operator is only applied in the ARIMA type of models described in subsection 4.5.3.

With this notation, the AR(1) and MA(1) models are $(1 - \phi_{1,1}B)\xi_t = \eta_t$ and $\xi_t = (1 - \theta_{1,1}B)\eta_t$ respectively. Because these are equivalent to $\xi_t = (1 - \phi_{1,1}B)^{-1}\eta_t = (1 - \theta_{\infty,1} - \theta_{\infty,2} - \dots)\eta_t$ and $(1 - \theta_{1,1}B)^{-1}\xi_t = (1 - \phi_{\infty,1} - \phi_{\infty,2} - \dots)\xi_t = \eta_t$ respectively, it follows that AR(1) $\equiv$ MA(∞) and MA(1) $\equiv$ AR(∞). It can also be shown that the same results hold for all finite AR(p) and MA(q) processes.

The next important requirement is a methodology for identifying the type of model which adequately represents an observed sequence. This means that we should be able to make the best possible choice from the autoregressive, moving-average and mixed models.

4.5.1 *Autoregressive moving-average ARMA(p, q) model*

The mixed autoregressive moving-average model ARMA(p, q) is specified by combining equations 4.1 and 4.22.

$$\xi_t = \phi_{p,1}\xi_{t-1} + \phi_{p,2}\xi_{t-2} + \dots + \phi_{p,p}\xi_{t-p} + \eta_t - \theta_{q,1}\eta_{t-1}$$
$$- \theta_{q,2}\eta_{t-2} - \dots - \theta_{q,q}\eta_{t-q} \tag{4.27}$$

The effect of linear aquifers and independent rainfall amounts justifies the approximate representation of river-flow processes through ARMA models. They are also analogous to those conceptual models in parametric hydrology that are based on linear reservoirs[11].

Equation 4.27 may be written as

$$\phi_p(B)\xi_t = \theta_q(B)\eta_t \tag{4.28}$$

where

$$\phi_p(B) = 1 - \phi_{p,1}B - \phi_{p,2}B^2 - \dots - \phi_{p,p}B^p \tag{4.29}$$

and

$$\theta_q(B) = 1 - \theta_{q,1}B - \theta_{q,2}B^2 - \dots - \theta_{q,q}B^q \tag{4.30}$$

[11] For further discussions on physical interpretations of ARMA and other stochastic models, see Moss (1972) and Dooge (1972).

Equations 4.29 and 4.30 represent two polynomials of order p and q respectively. The prerequisites for stationarity and invertibility respectively are that the roots of the equations $\phi_p(B) = 0$ and $\theta_q(B) = 0$ or that these roots, which are also termed the zeros of B, should lie outside the unit circle. (These conditions are applicable to $AR(p)$ and $MA(q)$ processes respectively.)

The estimation of the parameters of the $ARMA(p, q)$ model is not a straightforward procedure. An algorithm can be formulated for the purpose by following the method used for the basic $ARMA(1, 1)$ model in the next subsection[12]. With regard to the number of parameters, parsimony has been suggested. This means that $p + q$ ought to be a minimum. For example, an $ARMA(1, 1)$ model is preferable to an $AR(3)$ model if it is found that both types fit an observed sequence.

4.5.2 Autoregressive moving-average ARMA(1, 1) model

In the class of mixed models, the simplest is the $ARMA(1, 1)$ model

$$\xi_t = \phi_{1, 1}\xi_{t-1} + \eta_t - \theta_{1, 1}\eta_{t-1} \tag{4.31}$$

Let $E(\eta_t) = E(\xi_t) = 0$, $E(\xi_t^2) = 1$, $\rho_k = E(\xi_t\xi_{t-k})$ and $E(\xi_t\eta_{t-1}) = \rho_{\xi, \eta}(-1)$. As noted before, $E(\eta_t\eta_{t-k}) = 0$ for $k \neq 0$ and $E(\eta_t\xi_{t-k}) = 0$ for any integer $k > 0$. Initially, if equation 4.31 is multiplied by ξ_t and expectations are taken, it follows that

$$1 = \phi_{1, 1}\rho_1 + E\{\eta_t(\phi_{1, 1}\xi_{t-1} + \eta_t - \theta_{1, 1}\eta_{t-1})\} - \theta_{1, 1}\rho_{\xi, \eta}(-1)$$
$$= \phi_{1, 1}\rho_1 + \sigma_\eta^2 - \theta_{1, 1}\rho_{\xi, \eta}(-1) \tag{4.32}$$

Then, by multiplying equation 4.31 by η_{t-1} and ξ_{t-1} in turn and taking expectations,

$$\rho_{\xi, \eta}(-1) = (\phi_{1, 1} - \theta_{1, 1})\sigma_\eta^2 \tag{4.33}$$

and

$$\rho_1 = \phi_{1, 1} - \theta_{1, 1}\sigma_\eta^2 \tag{4.34}$$

Hence,

$$\sigma_\eta^2 = (1 - \phi_{1, 1}^2)/(1 + \theta_{1, 1}^2 - 2\phi_{1, 1}\theta_{1, 1}) \tag{4.35}$$

and

$$\rho_1 = (1 - \phi_{1, 1}\theta_{1, 1})(\phi_{1, 1} - \theta_{1, 1})/(1 + \theta_{1, 1}^2 - 2\phi_{1, 1}\theta_{1, 1}) \tag{4.36}$$

Also, by multiplying equation 4.31 by ξ_{t-k}, where $k \geqslant 2$, and by taking expectations,

$$\rho_k = \phi_{1, 1}\rho_{k-1} \tag{4.37}$$

---

[12] See Box and Jenkins (1976, pp. 201–3) for the $ARMA(p, q)$ model.

An initial estimate $\hat{\phi}_{1,1}$ of $\phi_{1,1}$ is obtained from r_2/r_1 (where r_1 and r_2 are the lag-one and lag-two serial correlation coefficients) by using equation 4.37. The substitution of $\hat{\phi}_{1,1}$ and r_1 in equation 4.36 gives an initial estimate $\hat{\theta}_{1,1}$ of $\theta_{1,1}$. Then, given the stationarity and invertibility constraints

$$-1 < \phi_{1,1} < +1 \text{ and } -1 < \theta_{1,1} < +1 \tag{4.38}$$

a grid search is made, and the two parameters are estimated by minimising the sum of squares of the residuals which is $\sum_{t=1}^{N} \tilde{\varepsilon}_t^2$, where $\tilde{\varepsilon}_1 = \tilde{\xi}_1, \tilde{\varepsilon}_2 = \tilde{\xi}_2 - \phi_{1,1}\tilde{\xi}_1$ $+ \theta_{1,1}\tilde{\varepsilon}_1, \tilde{\varepsilon}_3 = \tilde{\xi}_3 - \phi_{1,1}\tilde{\xi}_2 + \theta_{1,1}\tilde{\varepsilon}_2, \ldots$, and $\tilde{\xi}_t$, $t = 1, 2, 3, \ldots, N$, is an observed sequence[13]. Note that, if $\phi_{1,1}$ is at or too close to its limits, as given by 4.38, non-stationary behaviour is indicated, in which case an ARIMA model seems to be appropriate.

Example 4.3   Annual flows in the Niger at Koulikoro (some 60 miles downstream of Bamako in Mali), Africa, for the period 1906 to 1957 are reduced to unit mean and are tabulated by Yevjevich (1963). The estimated standard deviation is 0.242, and the first and second serial correlation coefficients are 0.535 and 0.463 respectively. Estimate an initial set of parameters of an ARMA(1, 1) model (which can be fitted to the data). From a least-squares fitting procedure it is found that the set of estimated parameters $\hat{\phi} = 0.84$ and $\hat{\theta} = 0.40$ provides a near-optimal fit. Generate three additional values using the following independent standard normal deviates: $+1.123$, -0.821, -0.342. From equation 4.37, $\hat{\phi}_{1,1} = 0.865$; from equation 4.36, $\hat{\theta}_{1,1} = 0.502$. From equation 4.35, $\hat{\sigma}_\eta = 0.777$ for $\hat{\phi}_{1,1} = 0.84$ and $\hat{\theta}_{1,1} = 0.40$. With $\tilde{\xi}_{t-1} = \tilde{\eta}_{t-1} = 0$,

$$\tilde{\xi}_t = 0.84 \times 0 + 0.777(1.123 - 0.40 \times 0) = 0.873, x_t = 0.242\tilde{\xi}_t + 1 = 1.211$$
$$\tilde{\xi}_{t+1} = 0.84 \times 0.873 + 0.777(-0.821 - 0.40 \times 1.123) = -0.254, x_{t+1} = 0.242\tilde{\xi}_{t+1} + 1 = 0.939$$
$$\tilde{\xi}_{t+2} = -0.84 \times 0.254 + 0.777(-0.342 + 0.40 \times 0.821) = -0.224, x_{t+2} = 0.242\tilde{\xi}_{t+2} + 1 = 0.946$$

4.5.3   *Autoregressive integrated moving-average ARIMA(p, d, q) model*

The ARIMA model is a generalised version of the ARMA model which can account for non-stationary behaviour by means of a dth-order difference operator ∇^d. By using the notation explained above it can be represented by

$$\phi_p(B)\nabla^d \xi_t = \theta_q(B)\eta_t \tag{4.39}$$

---

[13] A graphical procedure is useful for estimation. Its main purpose is for smoothing the effects of sampling fluctuations. Points with values of $\phi_{1,1}$ and $\theta_{1,1}$ (constrained by equation 4.38) as coordinates are marked on a square, and the corresponding sums S of squares are noted by these grid intersections. Then contours which join equal values of S are drawn and parameter estimates are found from the minimum S point, for example, as discussed by Chatfield and Prothero (1973, p. 302). Non-linear estimation procedures are described by Box and Jenkins (1976, chapter 7). One of the first applications of ARMA models in hydrology was by Carlson *et al.* (1970).

By changing the variable ξ_t, this can be transformed to an ARMA(p, q) type. For example, if $\psi_t = \nabla^d \xi_t$,

$$\phi_p(B)\psi_t = \theta_q(B)\eta_t \tag{4.40}$$

This means that, if $\phi(B)$ and $\theta(B)$ are defined by equations 4.29 and 4.30 respectively, the series ψ_t is generated by an ARMA(p, q) process; correspondingly, ξ_t is of the ARIMA(p, d, q) type. In practice, a minimum value of d is found so that the process given by equation 4.40 satisfies the necessary constraints. As Box and Jenkins (1976) postulate, the parameters p, d and q need not be greater than 2 for practical purposes.

Consider the case when ξ_t is generated by an ARIMA(1, 1, 1) process. Initially, the non-stationary series ξ_t is transformed into a stationary series ψ_t by differencing as follows.

$$\psi_t = \xi_t - \xi_{t-1} \tag{4.41}$$

Then the parameters of the ARMA(1, 1) model are estimated. For example, if $\hat{\phi}_{1,1} = 0.8$ and $\hat{\theta}_{1,1} = 0.6$, the process is generated by $(1 - 0.8B)(1 - B)\xi_t = (1 - 0.6B)\eta_t$; that is, $(1 - 1.8B + 0.8B^2)\xi_t = (1 - 0.6B)\eta_t$, or more specifically $\xi_t = 1.8\xi_{t-1} - 0.8\xi_{t-2} + \eta_t - 0.6\eta_{t-1}$. An ARIMA(2, 2, 2) process can be similarly investigated by replacing the right-hand side of equation 4.41 by $\xi_t - 2\xi_{t-1} + \xi_{t-2}$ and using equation 4.40 appropriately.

There is, however, a basic philosophical point which deters us from using an ARIMA model for generating future sequences. This concerns the high probability, if this type of model is indicated, that the climatological and physiographical factors which caused non-stationary behaviour in the first place will change. Then the model maker is faced with the same type of situation that arises if a trend is detected. These problems could only be resolved intuitively. Procedures for identification and estimation are now taken up.

4.5.4 Model identification and estimation

An iterative procedure for fitting the Box–Jenkins types of models is given in figure 4.6. This is performed recursively, the essential steps being identification, estimation and verification of the model type, order and parameters. As already mentioned, the serial correlogram is the initial requirement. Methods of estimating the autocorrelations ρ_i are given in chapter 2. The estimation of the partial autocorrelations $\phi_{i,i}$ is equally important. The procedures adopted are almost inevitably subjective on account of sampling fluctuations, complications arising from unremoved non-stationary effects and the interdependence in the serial correlations. However, the general shapes of the serial correlation and the sample partial autocorrelation functions are useful as a basis for identification. The expected behaviour of the autocorrelation function is in direct contrast with that of the partial autocorrelation function of a stationary process. For instance, in a Markov (that is, first-order autoregressive) process, the autocorrelations decrease exponentially, whereas the partial autocorrelations are

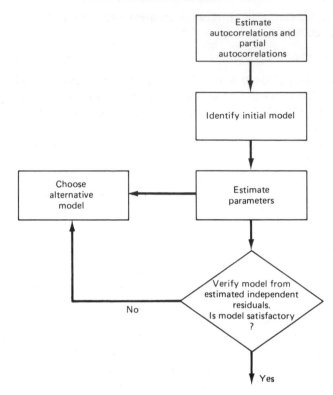

Figure 4.6   Iterative recursive procedure for Box–Jenkins models

theoretically zero except for $\phi_{1,1}$, which is non-zero. The situation is reversed in the case of a first-order moving-average process. On the other hand, in an ARMA(1, 1) process, both functions decay exponentially after the first lag. For identifying these and other types, table 4.1 is given as a guide for identification.

Initially, the shapes of the sample functions are examined, for practical identification purposes. Then, if the indications are that the process is an autoregressive type, a significance test is made to determine its order. This is based on the assumption that the estimated partial autocorrelations $\hat{\phi}_{i,i}$, $i > p$, of an AR(p) process are normally distributed with zero mean and variance $1/N$, where N is the number of observations[14]. Similarly for an MA(q) process, the serial correlations r_ℓ, $\ell > q$, are taken to be normally distributed with zero mean and variance given by equation 2.20.

Methods of estimating the parameters of the different types of models are as given in sections 4.2, 4.3 and 4.4.

After identification and estimation, diagnostic checking (that is, verification)

[14]   See Anderson (1942) and Quenouille (1949).

Table 4.1 Identification of Box–Jenkins models using autocorrelation and partial autocorrelation functions

Model type	Autocorrelation function	Partial autocorrelation function
AR(1), first-order autoregressive (Markov)	Exponential decrease	$\phi_{1,1} \neq 0$ $\phi_{i,i} = 0$ for $i = 2, 3, 4, \ldots$
AR(p), pth-order autoregressive	Mixed type of damping from lag 1	$\phi_{i,i} \neq 0$ for $i \leqslant p$ $\phi_{i,i} = 0$ for $i > p$
MA(1), first-order moving-average	$\rho_1 \neq 0$ $\rho_i = 0$ for $i = 2, 3, 4, \ldots$	Exponential decrease
MA(q), qth-order moving-average	$\rho_i = 0$ for $i > q$ $\rho_i \neq 0$ for $i \leqslant q$	Mixed type of damping from lag 1
ARMA(1, 1), autoregressive moving-average	Exponential decrease after lag 1	Exponential decrease after lag 1
ARMA(p, q), autoregressive moving-average	Mixed type of damping after lag $q + 1$	Mixed type of damping after lag $p - q$

is made by testing the residuals thus obtained for independence. For the general ARMA(p, q) model described in subsection 4.5.1 which takes the form

$$\phi(B)\xi_t = \theta(B)\eta_t$$

the estimated residuals are, therefore, $\hat{\eta}_t = \hat{\theta}^{-1}(B)\hat{\phi}(B)\hat{\xi}_t$; here, $\hat{\theta}$ and $\hat{\phi}$ are polynomials (in B) in which the coefficients are the estimated parameters, and $\hat{\xi}_t$, $t = 1, 2, 3, \ldots, N$, is an observed sequence. To clarify this, consider a pth-order autoregressive model $\phi(B)\xi_t = \eta_t$ given explicitly by equation 4.1. In this case, the residuals are estimated as follows.

$$\tilde{\eta}_t = \tilde{\xi}_t - \sum_{k=1}^{p} \hat{\phi}_{p,k} \tilde{\xi}_{t-k} \qquad (4.42)$$

where $\tilde{\xi}_{t-k} = 0$, if $t - k < 1$. Likewise for the moving-average model given by equation 4.22, estimated residuals are found from

$$\tilde{\eta}_t = \tilde{\xi}_t + \sum_{k=1}^{q} \hat{\theta}_{q,k} \tilde{\eta}_{t-k} \qquad (4.43)$$

where $\tilde{\eta}_{t-k} = 0$, if $t - k < 1$. Similarly, the estimated residuals obtained by applying the ARMA(p, q) model are given by

$$\tilde{\eta}_t = \tilde{\xi}_t - \sum_{k=1}^{p} \hat{\phi}_{p,k} \tilde{\xi}_{t-k} + \sum_{k=1}^{q} \hat{\theta}_{q,k} \tilde{\eta}_{t-k} \qquad (4.44)$$

where $\tilde{\xi}_{t-k} = \tilde{\eta}_{t-k} = 0$, if $t - k < 1$.

If the ARMA(p, q) family of models do not fit the observed sequence, the (non-stationary) ARIMA(p, d, q) types may be tried. Accordingly, dth-order differencing is carried out on the observed $\tilde{\xi}_t$ sequence, as explained in subsection 4.5.3 to form the sequence $\tilde{\psi}_t = \nabla^d \tilde{\xi}_t$, $t = 1, 2, 3, \ldots$. Here, a minimum value of d is chosen by trial and error so that a model from the ARMA(p, q) family can be fitted to the $\tilde{\psi}_t$ sequence, as previously discussed.

For purposes of graphical verification, serial correlations r_ℓ of the estimated residuals $\tilde{\eta}_t$ are obtained after fitting the appropriate model, from those represented by equations 4.42, 4.43 and 4.44. Then confidence limits are drawn on the serial correlogram so obtained to test the hypothesis that the $\tilde{\eta}_t$ values have an independent normal distribution, in which case the r_ℓ values are approximately normally distributed with zero mean and variance approximately equal to $1/N$, where N is the number of items of data. Examples are given in figures 4.3e, 4.4e and 4.5e. However, this graphical procedure is considered to be inadequate except for preliminary purposes, mainly because it is applied to the estimated residuals and not to the true residuals which are unknown. This could mean that a sample in which serial correlation is not significant according to the test may be part of an autocorrelated population. On the other hand, rejection of the null hypothesis when only one value is significant may sometimes be incorrect.

The Box–Pierce portmanteau lack-of-fit test attempts to provide answers to these points. This is applied collectively to a set of serial correlations r_ℓ of an estimated sequence of residuals $\tilde{\eta}_t$. The first k values of r_ℓ are used for the purpose where k is sufficiently large (say, of the order of 10 to 25). For an ARIMA(p, d, q) process, the statistic

$$Q = n \sum_{\ell=1}^{k} r_\ell^2 \qquad (4.45)$$

has a χ^2 distribution with $v = k - p - q$ degrees of freedom; also, $n = N - d$. The drawback is that the test has low power particularly for small values of N, the sample size[15].

Example 4.4　From the annual flows of the Fox River near Berlin, Wisconsin, U.S.A., for the period 1898 to 1957, as given by Yevjevich (1963), the r_ℓ, $\ell = 1$, 2, . . ., 15, values of the estimated residuals $\tilde{\eta}_t$ after fitting a Markov model with estimated parameter $\hat{\phi}_{1,1} = 0.393$ are as follows: 0.0497, −0.1650, −0.1159, 0.0174, −0.0129, −0.0311, −0.0265, −0.0970, 0.0201, 0.0407, 0.0443, 0.0478,

---

[15] Davies *et al.* (1977) give a modified test. Another approximate way of checking for white noise is through the cumulative periodogram; this makes use of the fact that the theoretical periodogram of white noise has equal ordinates (see subsection 2.6.2). Examples of the periodogram and portmanteau tests are given by Box and Jenkins (1976, pp. 290–8).

1:1051, -0.0972, -0.1489: $n = 59$, and we find (a) $k = 10$, $Q = 3.35$, $v = 10 - 1 = 9$. Using the notation of section 3.5, $\chi^2_{9, \, 0 \cdot 95} = 3.35$, which means that, on average, in 19 samples out of 20, values of Q will be greater than 3.35. Also (b) $k = 15$, $Q = 6.12$, $v = 15 - 1 = 14$, $\chi^2_{14, \, 0 \cdot 9625} \approx 6.12$. This suggests that the Markov model is a quite reasonable approximation.

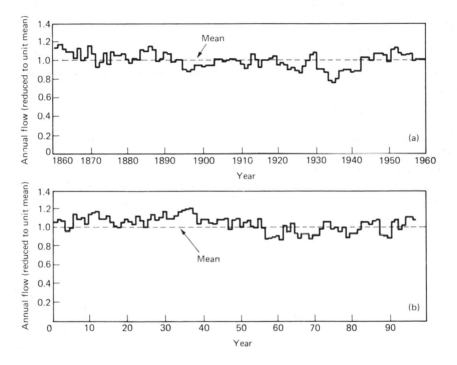

Figure 4.7 (a) 97-year historical and (b) 97-year generated flow data of St Lawrence at Ogdensburgh, New York, in which the AR(3) model $\xi_t = 0.670\xi_{t-1} - 0.107\xi_{t-2} + 0.200\xi_{t-3} + \eta_t$ was used

In figure 4.7, the 97-year historical sequence of annual flows in the St Lawrence at Ogdensburgh, New York, is compared with a generated sequence by using the AR(3) model $\xi_t = 0.670\xi_{t-1} - 0.107\xi_{t-2} + 0.200\xi_{t-3} + \eta_t$. In contrast, the flows in the Danube at Orsova, Romania, are independently distributed; 120-year historical and generated sequences are compared in figure 4.8. On the other hand, one of two or more models seem to be suitable for the Niger flows as indicated in figure 4.5. In such cases the most simple model that does not contradict the data should be chosen (a rule that is termed Occam's razor). This means that the model with the least number of parameters should be chosen and that the autoregressive and other less complicated models are

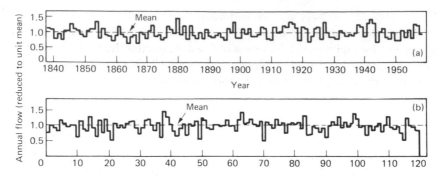

Figure 4.8 (a) 120-year historical and (b) 120-year generated flow data of Danube at Orsova, Romania, in which the independent model $\xi_t = \eta_t$ was used

preferred[16]. The serial correlograms of the historical and generated river flows in the St Lawrence are compared in figure 4.9a. Note the high sampling fluctuations, which is in contrast with the correlograms of the Danube flows shown in figure 4.9b.

4.6 Application to non-normal series

The models discussed in the previous sections are assumed to be applied to discrete series that are transformed to second-order stationarity. It is implied, therefore, that the distribution of the random component, for instance in equation 4.1, is normal. This approximation would generally suffice in the case of annual series as discussed in chapter 3. However, modifications may be necessary for coping with monthly and other more closely spaced data.

If the stochastic component ξ_t is non-normally distributed with skewness γ_ξ, then the skewness γ_η to be incorporated in the random component η_t depends on the model and its parameters. An alternative procedure is to transform observed values so that the distributions are normal. This section deals with these methods. The associated problem of seasonality is the subject of the next section.

[16] From theoretical considerations, Akaike (1974) suggests that we should choose the model with the minimum AIC $= -2\ln(\mathrm{ML}) + 2(p+q)$, where p, q pertain to the ARMA$(p+q)$ models, AIC denotes the Akaike information criterion and ML the maximum likelihood. Elsewhere, comparative studies are made by Granger and Morris (1976); See also McClave (1978).

Figure 4.9 Serial correlograms of historical and generated flow data of (a) St Lawrence at Ogdensburgh, New York, and (b) Danube at Orsova, Romania, in which the models used to generate data sequences are given in figures 4.7 and 4.8 captions and the first generated sequences correspond to those shown in figures 4.7 and 4.8: broken lines denote 95% confidence limits for the serially independent flows in the Danube

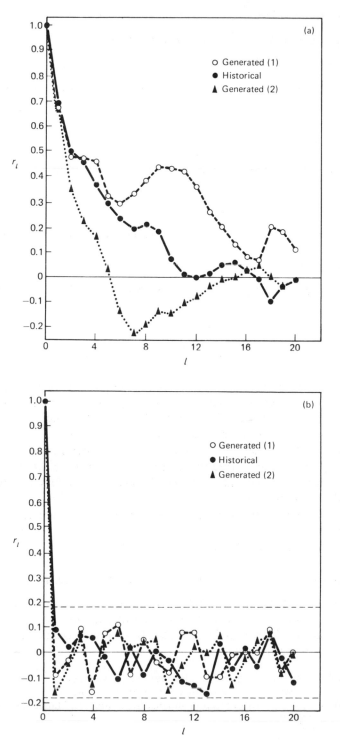

4.6.1 Preservation of skewness in Markov model

As given by equation 4.10, the model is of the form

$$\xi_t = \phi_{1,1}\,\xi_{t-1} + \eta_t$$

where $\phi_{1,1} = \rho_1$ is the lag-one autocorrelation coefficient. By cubing both sides and taking expectations,

$$E(\xi_t^3) = E(\rho_1^3\,\xi_{t-1}^3 + 3\rho_1^2\,\xi_{t-1}^2\,\eta_t + 3\rho_1\,\xi_{t-1}\,\eta_t^2 + \eta_t^3)$$

Because ξ_{t-1} and η_t are independent, the expectations of the second and third terms on the right are zero. Also, $\sigma_\eta^2 = 1 - \rho_1^2$ from equation 4.12, and $E(\xi_t) = E(\eta_t) = 0$. Therefore,

$$\gamma_\eta = \gamma_\xi (1 - \rho_1^3)/(1 - \rho_1^2)^{3/2} \qquad (4.46)$$

in which, for estimation purposes, ρ_1 is replaced by r_1, its sample estimate[17].

4.6.2 Box–Cox transformations

Box and Cox (1964) suggest the following method of transforming an observed value x.

$$
\begin{aligned}
y &= (x^\lambda - 1)/\lambda, & \lambda \neq 0 \\
&= \ln(x), & \lambda = 0
\end{aligned}
\qquad (4.47)
$$

The parameter λ could be chosen so that the skewness of the transformed series is a minimum. However, the efficiency of this approach is very low compared with the more sophisticated ML method. Hinkley (1977) suggests a simpler procedure. For each of the different values of $\lambda = 0, \pm 0.5, \pm 1.0, \ldots$, the sample mean $\bar{y}$, the standard deviation $\hat{\sigma}_y$ (or the more robust interquartile range) and the median $\hat{\zeta}_y$ are calculated from the transformed data. Then the statistics $d_\lambda = (\bar{y} - \hat{\zeta}_y)/\hat{\sigma}_y$ are compared and interpolated if necessary, to find the value of λ for which d_λ is a minimum.

A further refinement is to introduce a second parameter by replacing x with $x - \xi$, say. Of special interest is the situation when $\lambda = 0$ in equation 4.47. This is the case in which the variable has a lognormal distribution[18].

4.6.3 Data generation using Markov model and lognormal distribution

Consider the transformation $Y = \ln(X - \xi)$, where X has mean μ and variance σ_X^2; Y is normally distributed with mean μ_Y and variance σ_Y^2 and ξ is a location parameter, which could be negative; also, the lag-ℓ autocorrelation coefficients are ρ_ℓ and $\rho_{\ell,Y}$ respectively.

---

[17] Equation 4.45 has been used by Matalas (1967) and by others.
[18] The lognormal distribution is introduced in section 3.6 and will be examined in section 6.3. With regard to data generation and bias in parameters, Matalas (1967) made an important contribution.

It can be shown that

$$\mu = \exp(\mu_Y + \sigma_Y^2/2) + \xi \tag{4.48}$$

and

$$\sigma^2 = \{\exp(2\mu_Y + \sigma_Y^2)\}\{\exp(\sigma_Y^2) - 1\} \tag{4.49}$$

Also,

$$\gamma_1 = \{\exp(3\sigma_Y^2) - 3\exp(\sigma_Y^2) + 2\}\{\exp(\sigma_Y^2) - 1\}^{-3/2} \tag{4.50}$$

where γ_1 is the coefficient of skewness of the population[19]. By substituting sample estimators g_1, s^2 and $\bar{x}$ in the left-hand side of equations 4.50, 4.49 and 4.48 respectively, estimators s_y^2, $\bar{y}$ and $\hat{\xi}$ of the parameters σ_Y^2, μ_Y and ξ are obtained, in that order. The relationship between ρ_ℓ and $\rho_{\ell,Y}$ is determined by using equations 4.48 and 4.49 as follows.

$$E(X_t X_{t+\ell}) = E[\{\exp(Y_t) + \xi\}\{\exp(Y_{t+\ell}) + \xi\}]$$
$$= E\{\exp(Y_t + Y_{t+\ell}) + \xi\exp(Y_t) + \xi\exp(Y_{t+\ell}) + \xi^2\}$$

From equation 4.48, $E\{\exp(Y_t)\} = \exp(\mu_Y + \sigma_Y^2/2)$. It follows that

$$E\{\exp(Y_t + Y_{t+\ell})\} = \exp\{2\mu_Y + \tfrac{1}{2}\mathrm{var}(Y_t + Y_{t+\ell})\}$$
$$= \exp\{2\mu_Y + \sigma_Y^2(1 + \rho_{\ell,Y})\}$$

Therefore, again using equation 4.48,

$$\mathrm{cov}(X_t, X_{t+\ell}) = E\{(X_t - \mu)(X_{t+\ell} - \mu)\}$$
$$= E(X_t X_{t+\ell}) - \mu^2$$
$$= [\exp\{2\mu_Y + \sigma_Y^2(1 + \rho_{\ell,Y})\} + 2\xi\exp(\mu_Y + \sigma_Y^2/2) + \xi^2]$$
$$- \{\exp(\mu_Y + \sigma_Y^2/2) + \xi\}^2$$
$$= \exp\{2\mu_Y + \sigma_Y^2(1 + \rho_{\ell,Y})\} - \exp(2\mu_Y + \sigma_Y^2)$$

Hence, by using equation 4.49,

$$\rho_\ell = \mathrm{cov}(X_t, X_{t+\ell})/\sigma^2$$
$$= \{\exp(\sigma_Y^2 \rho_{\ell,Y}) - 1\}\{\exp(\sigma_Y^2) - 1\}^{-1} \tag{4.51}$$

By substituting the (estimated) lag-one serial correlation coefficient r_1 for ρ_1 in equation 4.51, an estimator $r_{1,Y}$ of $\rho_{1,Y}$ is obtained. The generating equation for

[19] These three formulae are obtained through the method of moments (see section 3.3 and specifically section 6.3). The basic quadratic nature of variances and covariances is made use of in the derivation that follows; equation 4.51 can also be proved by using the moment-generating function (see section 6.3). This relationship was given originally by Yevjevich (1966) and was extended by Mejía and Rodríguez-Iturbe (1974). The lognormal distribution has been used, for instance, by Beard (1965) and by Codner and McMahon (1973).

the Markov lognormal model is

$$X_t = \xi + \left[\exp\{ \mu_Y (1 - \rho_{1,Y}) \} \right] (X_{t-1} - \xi)^{\rho_{1,Y}} \exp(\sigma_Y \eta_t) \tag{4.52}$$

in which η_t is an independent standard normal variate with a zero mean and a variance $1 - \rho_{1,Y}^2$.

An alternative and more direct method is to use the second of the Box–Cox transformations, $y = \log(x)$. Then the parameters of, say, the Markov model are estimated from the sequence y, and, finally, antilogarithms are taken on the generated data. However, this method has two disadvantages: firstly, zero values cannot be transformed, and for this reason an arbitrary small value is sometimes added to all observed values; secondly, statistical and other properties of generated data may differ significantly from the properties of historical data. On the other hand, all values produced will be positive, unlike in the application of equation 4.52. Negativity in generated data will be discussed in chapter 5 in relation to crossings.

4.6.4 *Dealing with non-normal distributions in general*

Generating random variables with gamma and other distributions is explained in chapter 3. For application purposes the differences in skewness of the stochastic component ξ_t and the random component η_t, as given by equation 4.46 for the Markov model, should be noted.

A practical method is to calculate the skewness and other distribution properties from the estimated independent residuals which for a Markov model is given by $\tilde{\eta}_t = \tilde{\xi}_t - r_1 \tilde{\xi}_{t-1}$, where $\tilde{\xi}_t$ is an observed standardised variable[20]. This can be extended to the more complicated models by using appropriate forms of $\tilde{\eta}_t$, as given by equations 4.42 to 4.44. However, it should be borne in mind that all these procedures are subject to sampling errors. Here, distributions are deduced from estimated independent residuals which may be distorted from model errors and bias in estimated parameters. The uncertainties may be resolved to some extent by tests on generated data; this will be discussed in section 4.10.

4.7 Seasonal models

In hydrology, seasonal models applicable to monthly series were originally used by Thomas and Fiering (1962) and by Roesner and Yevjevich (1966) using Yevjevich's (1966) method. Let $x_{t,\tau}$ represent the flow in month t, where $t, t = 1, 2, \ldots, 12N$ (and N is the number of years), corresponds to the calendar month τ, $\tau = 1, 2, \ldots, 12$. Then, seasonality is preserved by equating the standardised variables ξ_t used, for example, in equation 4.1 to the residuals $(x_{t,\tau} - \mu_\tau)/\sigma_\tau$, in which μ_τ and σ_τ represent the mean and the standard deviation respectively for

[20] See Kottegoda (1970). Other procedures are described by Phatarfod (1976) and Moran (1970).

the calendar month τ. This method is known as prewhitening and is explained in subsection 2.6.3. Model formulations are discussed here. The alternative Box–Jenkins seasonal model is also given. Finally, shot noise and other daily models are explained.

4.7.1 Autoregressive seasonal models

The pth-order autoregressive seasonal model which corresponds to equation 4.1 takes the form

$$X_{t,\tau} = \mu_\tau + \sigma_\tau \sum_{i-1}^{p} \phi_{p,i}(X_{t-i,\tau-i} - \mu_{\tau-i})/\sigma_{\tau-i} + \sigma_\tau \eta_t \tag{4.53}$$

in which $E(\eta_t) = E(\eta_t \eta_{t-k}) = 0$ for $k \neq 0$ and $\operatorname{var}(\eta_t) = E(\eta_t^2) = 1 - R^2$; note that, if $\tau - i \leqslant 0$, $\tau - i$ should be replaced by $\tau - i + 12$. The order p and the autoregressive parameters $\phi_{p,i}$ are estimated from the standardised ξ_t series.

Because μ_τ and σ_τ have to be estimated from short historical samples, harmonic fitted statistics $\hat{\mu}_\tau$ and $\hat{\sigma}_\tau$, as explained in section 2.4, have been substituted in equation 4.53 for estimating the autoregressive parameters[21]. However, the resulting $\tilde{\xi}_t$ series and hence the autoregressive parameters may be significantly affected by sampling errors. This could happen when the sample statistics m_τ and s_τ are used or when their harmonic fitted estimates $\hat{\mu}_\tau$ and $\hat{\sigma}_\tau$ are substituted for the unknown parameters μ_τ and σ_τ. The advantage in the harmonic model is that it needs fewer parameters; also these are less affected by sample sizes.

A further generalisation of this model is possible by making $\phi_{p,i}$ seasonal[22], but usually the differences between the seasonal parameters are not significant.

Example 4.5 It is thought that the periodicities in the monthly flow of the Brenig River in Wales could be approximated by a simple sinusoidal function (without recourse to a least-squares fit) for the monthly means and a similar function with a different amplitude for the monthly standard deviations. The highest and lowest values in each of the two sets of 12-month statistics correspond to January and July respectively; the magnitudes in millimetres of equivalent rainfall over the catchment are tabulated.

Month	Mean m_τ	Standard deviation s_τ
January ($\tau = 1$)	124	51
July ($\tau = 7$)	28	20

---

[21] See, for example, Roesner and Yevjevich (1966) who applied a first-order model to monthly flow data; a second-order model for daily river flows was suggested by Quimpo (1968), and Kottegoda (1972) used a fourth-order model for generating 5-day data.

[22] See Yevjevich (1972).

Using the random numbers $-0.3213, 1.3144, 0.1023$ which are taken from an independent standard normal population and assuming a first-order autoregressive model, obtain values for the flows in January, February and March of a hypothetical year. The first serial correlation coefficient r_1 of the standardised series is 0.3, and it may be assumed that in December of the previous year the flow was equal to the mean flow for December.

The mean of the monthly means is given by $\hat{\mu} = (m_1 + m_7)/2 = (124 + 28)/2 = 76;$ $(m_1 - m_7)/2 = (124 - 28)/2 = 48$. The mean of the monthly standard deviations equals $(s_1 + s_7)/2 = (51 + 20)/2 = 35.5;$ $(s_1 - s_7)/2 = 15.5$.

Month	Mean m_τ	Standard deviation s_τ
January $(\tau = 1)$	$76 + 48 \sin(3 \times 2\pi/12) = 124.0$	$35.5 + 15.5 \sin(3 \times 2\pi/12)$ $= 51.0$
February $(\tau = 2)$	$76 + 48 \sin(4 \times 2\pi/12) = 117.6$	$35.5 + 15.5 \sin(4 \times 2\pi/12)$ $= 48.9$
March $(\tau = 3)$	$76 + 48 \sin(5 \times 2\pi/12) = 100.0$	$35.5 + 15.5 \sin(5 \times 2\pi/12)$ $= 43.3$
July $(\tau = 7)$	$76 + 48 \sin(9 \times 2\pi/12) = 28.0$	$35.5 + 15.5 \sin(9 \times 2\pi/12)$ $= 20.0$

The first-order model, in which ε_t values have zero mean and unit variance, is given by

$$
\begin{aligned}
\xi_t &= r_1 \xi_{t-1} + (1 - r_1^2)^{1/2} \varepsilon_t & &= 0.3 + 0.955\varepsilon_t \\
\xi_1 &= 0 + 0.954 \times (-0.3213) & &= -0.307, & \hat{x}_{1,1} &= \hat{\xi}_1 s_1 + m_1 = 108 \\
\xi_2 &= 0.3 \times (-0.307) + 0.954 \times 1.3144 & &= 1.162, & \hat{x}_{2,2} &= \hat{\xi}_2 s_2 + m_2 = 174 \\
\xi_3 &= 0.3 \times (1.162) + 0.954 \times 0.1023 & &= 0.446, & x_{3,3} &= \hat{\xi}_3 s_3 + m_3 = 119
\end{aligned}
$$

Serial correlograms, estimated partial autocorrelograms and residual variance of 5-day flows in the Severn at Bewdley are shown in figure 4.10. Again, figure 4.11 shows serial correlograms of 11-year subsamples of unadjusted x_t and adjusted ξ_t 5-day inflow data to Caban Coch Reservoir in Wales; enveloping curves representing generated data are also drawn. In both cases AR(4) models are chosen. Another point is that the serial correlations may not be stationary throughout the year. Recognising this, Thomas and Fiering (1962) formulated a model through which correlations between flows in consecutive months can be maintained.

4.7.2 Thomas–Fiering seasonal model

This takes the form

$$
X_{t,\tau} = \mu_\tau + \sigma_\tau \rho_\tau (X_{t-1, \tau-1} - \mu_{\tau-1})/\sigma_{\tau-1} + \sigma_\tau \eta_t \tag{4.54}
$$

in which

$$
\rho_\tau = E\{(X_{t,\tau} - \mu_\tau)(X_{t-1, \tau-1} - \mu_{\tau-1})\}/\sigma_\tau \sigma_{\tau-1}
$$

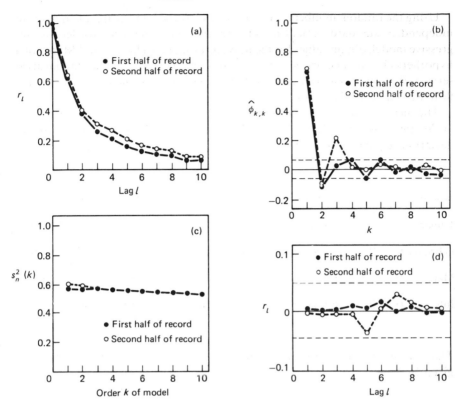

Figure 4.10 (a) Serial correlograms of estimated residuals, (b) estimated partial autocorrelograms, (c) residual variance and (d) serial correlograms of estimated residuals by the AR(4) model of 5-day flows in Severn at Bewdley, England (48-year record): broken lines denote 95% confidence limits

is the coefficient of correlation between the flows in months τ and $\tau - 1$. For the random component $E(\eta_t) = E(\eta_t \eta_{t-k}) = 0$ for $k \neq 0$. Also, from subsection 4.2.3 and 4.2.4, var $(\eta_t) = 1 - \rho_\tau^2$.

If skewness is to be maintained, then by using a similar derivation as in subsection 4.6.1 the coefficient of skewness to be applied to the random component in month τ is given by

$$\gamma_{\eta, \tau} = (\gamma_\tau - \rho_\tau^3 \gamma_{\tau-1})/(1 - \rho_\tau^2)^{3/2} \tag{4.55}$$

where γ_τ is the coefficient of skewness in $X_{t, \tau}$, $t = 1, 2, 3, \ldots$.

The drawback here is that with short records significant differences in the ρ_τ values may not be found. Besides, ρ_τ could be zero for particular months of the year, partly on account of random climatic movements within the year.

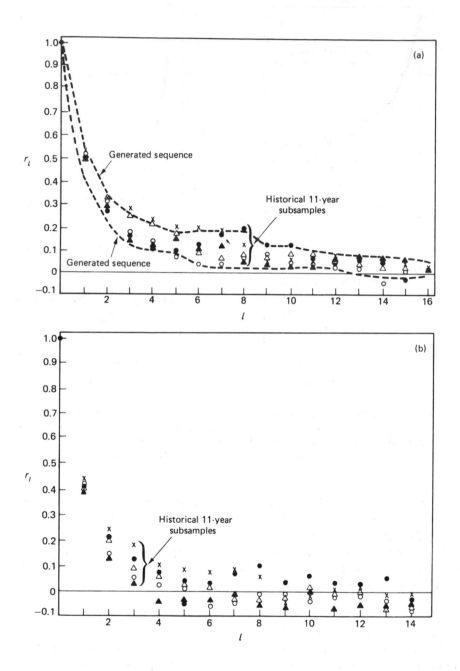

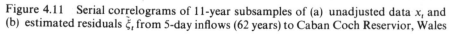

Figure 4.11   Serial correlograms of 11-year subsamples of (a) unadjusted data x_t and (b) estimated residuals $\tilde{\xi}_t$ from 5-day inflows (62 years) to Caban Coch Reservoir, Wales

4.7.3 Box–Jenkins seasonal model

An ARIMA type model can also be used for generating data in which seasonal effects are accounted for. Backshift operators such as $B^s \xi_t = \xi_{t-s}$ are used for this purpose when events s time units apart are identically distributed; for example, if the annual cycle is to be represented through a monthly series, $s = 12$. Consider initially a model of the type ARIMA(1, 0, 1) which is, of course, equivalent to ARMA(1, 1). It is given by $(1 - \Phi B^{12}) \xi_t = (1 - \Theta B^{12}) \psi_t$, that is, $\xi_t - \Phi \xi_{t-12} = \psi_t - \Theta \psi_{t-12}$ where Φ and Θ are parameters and ψ_t is a standardised residual. The next step is to apply a difference operator which is given by

$$\nabla_s \xi_t = (1 - B^s) \xi_t$$

$$= \xi_t - \xi_{t-s}$$

$$\nabla_s^2 \xi_t = (1 - B^s)^2 \xi_t$$

$$= \xi_t - 2\xi_{t-s} + \xi_{t-2s}$$

and, in general, $\nabla_s^D \xi_t = (1 - B^s)^D \xi_t$. Accordingly, the seasonal ARIMA$(P, D, Q)_s$ model is represented by

$$\Phi_P(B^s) \nabla_s^D \xi_t = \Theta_Q(B^s) \psi_t \tag{4.56}$$

However, the residual $\psi(t) = \Theta_Q^{-1}(B^s) \Phi_P(B^s) \nabla_s^D \xi_t$ is usually not independent, mainly because the short-lag autocorrelation structure is not incorporated in the model. For this reason, it is necessary to formulate a multiplicative seasonal model which, in the general case, is the combination of two ARIMA types and is denoted by $(p, d, q) \times (P, D, Q)_s$. The complete seasonal model then takes the form

$$\Phi_P(B^s) \phi_p(B) \nabla_s^D \nabla^d \xi_t = \Theta_Q(B^s) \theta_q(B) \eta_t \tag{4.57}$$

where η_t is a standardised independent variable.

For example, a multiplicative ARIMA(2, 0, 0) × (1, 1, 1)$_{12}$ model (applied to monthly data) is given by $(1 - \phi_1 B - \phi_2 B^2)(1 - \Phi_1 B^{12})(1 - B^{12}) \xi_t = (1 - \Theta_1 B^{12}) \eta_t$. In application, the procedure is first to obtain a differenced sequence $\nabla_{12} \tilde{\xi}_t = \xi_t - \tilde{\xi}_{t-12}$ from a sample of observed data ξ_t, $t = 1, 2, 3, \ldots, N$. (For simplicity, the double-suffix notation for parameters in section 4.5 is not adopted here.) Then the estimates $\hat{\Phi}_1$ and $\hat{\Theta}_1$ are found by applying a seasonal ARMA(1, 1)$_{12}$ model to the differenced sequence. Finally, an AR(2) model is applied to the residuals from the seasonal model. The generating equation, found by expanding the product $(1 - \phi_1 B - \phi_2 B^2)(1 - \Phi_1 B^{12})(1 - B^{12})$ and substituting for the B terms, is as follows.

$$\xi_t = \phi_1 \xi_{t-1} + \phi_2 \xi_{t-2} + (1 + \Phi_1) \xi_{t-12} - (\phi_1 + \phi_1 \Phi_1) \xi_{t-13}$$

$$- (\phi_2 + \phi_2 \Phi_1) \xi_{t-14} - \Phi_1 \xi_{t-24} + \phi_1 \Phi_1 \xi_{t-25} + \phi_2 \Phi_1 \xi_{t-26}$$

$$+ \eta_t - \Theta_1 \eta_{t-12}$$

This type of model is applicable, strictly speaking, only when the monthly standard deviations are not seasonal[23].

4.7.4   Models for daily flows: problems and references

When applied to daily flows the autoregressive and general Box–Jenkins models described in this chapter have limitations, which could be serious. One reason is that, because daily data have highly non-normal distributions, extreme values and properties such as runs and crossings are not maintained through models that were devised originally for normal processes[24]. Of equal significance is the fact that the rapid ascensions and slow recessions that are associated with individual rainfall events are not specifically modelled[25].

A particular method of preserving such time-irreversible characteristics is through filtered Poisson processes explained by Parzen (1962) and applied in hydrology by Weiss (1977); Bernier (1970) was perhaps the first to suggest the approach[26]. In application, a continuous series $X(t)$ of river flows is considered to be generated by a number $N(t)$ of 'rainfall shots' Y_m in the interval $(-\infty, t)$; $N(t)$ is a Poisson process with mean v. In effect, the flow at time t is contributed by pulses $Y_m \exp\{-b(t - \tau_m)\}$, $m = 0 \pm 1 \pm 2, \ldots$, which are zero for $t < \tau_m$. Here, the magnitude of a shot Y_m is an independent exponentially distributed random variable with mean θ; b is the decay (or hydrograph recession) rate and τ_m denotes random arrival times of shots which are analogous to the times that rain storms start. The variable m is considered to extend backwards to $-\infty$, so that

$$X(t) = \sum_{m=-\infty}^{N(t)} Y_m \exp\{-b(t - \tau_m)\} \qquad (4.58)$$

The model parameters v, θ and b in the Weiss (1977) model are estimated from the means, the standard deviations and the lag-one serial correlations in the data for each month. The integration of equation 4.58 between limits t and $t - 1$ gives the following discrete process.

$$X_t = e^{-bs} X_{t-s} + \eta_t \qquad (4.59)$$

which has a gamma density function. The advantage here is that the positively skewed innovation term η_t has a positive probability of being exactly zero in contrast with the random component in an AR(1) process. Exponentially

---

[23] Applications are given by McKerchar and Delleur (1974).

[24] With reference to a given magnitude or level, a run is a sequence of events, all of which are above the level or alternatively all are below the level, and a crossing (of the level) occurs at the commencement as well as the end of the run. Further details will be given in chapter 5.

[25] The autoregressive daily flow process was originally investigated by Quimpo (1968) and was extended empirically to model hydrograph properties by Payne et al. (1969).

[26] Shot noise was originally used to analyse the quantum effect of fluctuations of electric current in vacuum tubes; see Doi (1978) for similar applications.

distributed random numbers (subsection 3.7.4) with means $1/v$ and θ are used for generating the times between the random arrivals and the magnitudes of the shots respectively. This so-called single-shot noise model is replaced by a double-shot noise model if we attempt to maintain base flow and surface run-off processes separately. Seasonality is accounted for by using a different set of parameters for each calendar month.

The main shortcomings are on account of undesirable fluctuations on the recessions with faster decay rates and excessive carry-over effects between months, and biased parameters. Also, coefficients of skewness in generated data tend to be higher than in historic data. Another inadequacy is the basic assumption of independence in storm events.

Realistic daily flow models ought to deal with these basic requirements. They should also cope with the dependency in rainfall inputs, which could be approximated by Markov chains. In this area Yakowitz (1973) suggested a non-linear autoregressive type of operational model to generate daily flows in an arid region of the United States where flows may be zero at times, and the ascension and recession behaviour is generally sharp. For the Rillito river flows to which the method was applied, a fifth-order Markov chain is required. There will, of course, be problems associated with non-arid areas especially with regard to large catchments in which several tributaries, each with its own pattern of rainfall, contribute to the flow at a particular point in a river. This means that some deterministic aspects of river flow need to be incorporated in a model for daily flows.

In the Treiber and Plate (1975) model, daily flows are assumed to be the output of a non-linear system. The days in which input pulses (or rainfall shots) occur, pulse magnitudes and the system function are estimated from the flows. A Markov chain is used to produce sequences of dry and wet days, and the pulses for the wet days are generated by an autoregressive process with an exponential random component. Seasonal effects are preserved in the same way as in the Weiss (1977) model. Shortcomings are partly on account of negative pulses which need to be arbitrarily adjusted and the assumptions made in the generating equations.

Disaggregration models in which monthly flows, for example, are split up to form daily flows constitute another area (Beard, 1967; Valencia and Schaake, 1973). There are problems here partly on account of discontinuities at the ends of months which Mejia and Rouselle (1976) attempt to solve. These have, in fact, been treated as multisite models which are taken up in the next section. A different approach to the generation of daily flows is to interpolate pentad data to form daily units (Kottegoda, 1972; Green, 1973).

4.8 Multisite data generation

For the planning, design and operational studies of water resource systems, concurrent sequences of flow data are required at more than one site. This section deals with models which can be used to generate data sets for this purpose. These models should be formulated so that important relationships between the time series are preserved, together with the properties of the individual series. For instance, rivers in a particular region tend to rise and recess at about the same times because of the proximity of catchment areas and possible similarities in catchment characteristics. Such correlations within the multiple time series are strengthened if the high flows are caused by frontal systems, the effects of which are widespread; this becomes more obvious when short-interval data are used.

An analysis of multiple time series is presented by Quenouille (1957). He considers three types of models which are, in effect, extensions of the univariate autoregressive, moving-average and mixed models explained in sections 4.2, 4.3 and 4.4. The treatment here is limited to the autoregressive type which was initiated in hydrology by Matalas (1967). An essential requirement is to incorporate the matrices of lag-zero and lag-one correlation coefficients; higher-lag models are also included. Initially, a basic two-station model is explained.

4.8.1 Two-site models

Models for generalising concurrent data at two sites are formulated so that the covariance and cross covariance properties are maintained. In general, they are concerned only with the lag-one serial correlation coefficients ρ_1 and ρ_2 in the flows in the two sites and the lag-zero cross correlation coefficients ρ, apart from preserving the means and standard deviations[27]. A particular model which serves the purposes is given by

$$\xi_{1,t} = \rho_1 \xi_{1,t-1} + (1 - \rho_1^2)^{1/2} \lambda_{1,t} \tag{4.60}$$

$$\xi_{2,t} = \rho_2 \xi_{2,t-1} + \alpha \lambda_{1,t} + \beta \lambda_{2,t} \tag{4.61}$$

where $\xi_{1,t}$ and $\xi_{2,t}$ represent the standardised flows at the two sites, respectively, and $\lambda_{1,t}$ and $\lambda_{2,t}$ are two independent identically distributed standardised variates generated at time t. The parameters α and β are chosen so that $E(\xi_{1,t}\xi_{2,t}) = \rho$ and $E(\xi_{2,t}^2) = 1$.

Because $E(\xi_{2,t-1}\lambda_{1,t}) = E(\xi_{2,t-1}\lambda_{2,t}) = E(\lambda_{1,t}\lambda_{2,t}) = 0$, by squaring equation 4.61, it follows that $1 = \rho_2^2 + \alpha^2 + \beta^2$.

Again, if the left-hand side and the right-hand side of equation 4.60 are multiplied by the left-hand side and the right-hand side of equation 4.61 respectively,

$$\rho = \rho_1 \rho_2 \rho + \alpha (1 - \rho_1^2)^{1/2}$$

---

[27] The Box–Jenkins notation $\rho_{1,1}(1)$, $\rho_{2,2}(1)$ and $\rho_{1,2}(0)$ will be adopted in the next subsection in place of ρ_1, ρ_2 and ρ respectively, which are used only in this subsection in order to simplify the ensuing formula given by equations 4.62 and 4.63. Other models are given by Fiering (1964), by Lawrance (1976) and by Kahan (1974).

Hence,

$$\alpha = \rho(1 - \rho_1\rho_2)/(1 - \rho_1^2)^{1/2} \tag{4.62}$$

$$\beta^2 = \frac{(1 - \rho_1^2)(1 - \rho_2^2) - \rho^2(1 - \rho_1\rho_2)^2}{1 - \rho_1^2} \tag{4.63}$$

4.8.2 First-order multisite autoregressive model

It is assumed that series of flows of each site are standardised to zero mean and unit variance after initially removing trend and seasonality. When applied to m stations the $m \times 1$ vector $\xi_t = (\xi_{1,t}, \xi_{2,t}, \ldots, \xi_{m,t})^T$, in which T denotes transpose, represents the flows at time t. The model takes the form

$$\xi_t = A\xi_{t-1} + B\eta_t \tag{4.64}$$

where A and B are two $m \times m$ matrices of parameters and $\eta_t = (\eta_{1,t}, \eta_{2,t}, \ldots, \eta_{m,t})^T$ is an $m \times 1$ vector of independent standard normal deviates, generated at time t, which are also independent of the elements of vector ξ_{t-1}. The matrices A and B ensure that the lag-zero, lag-one and lag-minus-one cross correlations between the m time series are maintained in addition to the lag-one serial correlations for each series. In order to determine the elements of these two matrices, the first operation required is to post-multiply equation 4.64 throughout by ξ_{t-1}^T and to take expectations. Accordingly,

$$E(\xi_t\xi_{t-1}^T) = AE(\xi_{t-1}\xi_{t-1}^T) + BE(\eta_t\xi_{t-1}^T)$$

From the prior assumptions, $E(\eta_t\xi_{t-1}^T) = 0$. Hence, this equation may be written

$$M_1 = AM_0 \tag{4.65}$$

where M_1 in an $m \times m$ matrix in which the element of the ith row and jth column is $E(\xi_{i,t}\xi_{j,t-1}) = \rho_{i,j}(-1)$ which is the lag-one cross correlation between the ith and jth series. Here, the (-1) in $\rho_{i,j}(-1)$ signifies that, in the cross correlation, the jth series is lagged behind the ith series by one time unit when computing the sum of the cross product terms, the notation used in equations 2.37, 2.38 and 2.39 being adopted; likewise, $E(\xi_{i,t-1}\xi_{j,t})$ is denoted by $\rho_{i,j}(+1)$. As noted in chapter 2, $\rho_{i,j}(-1) \neq \rho_{i,j}(+1)$ for $i \neq j$; for the diagonal elements of M_1, however, which represent the lag-one serial correlations of each of the series $\rho_{i,i}(-1) = \rho_{i,i}(+1)$. The matrix M_0 represents the lag-zero cross correlations between the series. (Also, it follows that M_1 is asymmetric, whereas M_0 is symmetric.) Hence, from equation 4.65,

$$A = M_1M_0^{-1} \tag{4.66}$$

from which A can be estimated by substituting the estimated correlation coefficients in the matrices M_1 and M_0.

In order to estimate B, equation 4.64 is post-multiplied throughout by ξ_t^T, and expectations are taken. Hence,

$$E(\xi_t \xi_t^T) = AE(\xi_{t-1} \xi_t^T) + BE(\eta_t \xi_t^T)$$

$$= AE(\xi_t \xi_{t-1}^T)^T + BE\{\eta_t (A\xi_{t-1} + B\eta_t)^T\}$$

$$= AE(\xi_t \xi_{t-1}^T)^T + BE(\eta_t \xi_{t-1}^T)A^T + BE(\eta_t \eta_t^T)B^T$$

Because $E(\eta_t \xi_{t-1}^T) = 0$ and $E(\eta_t \eta_t^T)$ is an identity matrix,

$$M_0 = AM_1^T + BB^T \tag{4.67}$$

If

$$C = BB^T \tag{4.68}$$

which accordingly is a symmetrical matrix, it follows from equations 4.68, 4.67 and 4.66 that

$$C = M_0 - M_1 M_0^{-1} M_1^T \tag{4.69}$$

from which C can be estimated by substituting the estimated matrices M_0 and M_1.

In contrast with matrix A, B does not have a unique set of solutions. One method which is comparatively straightforward is to assume that B is lower triangular[28]. Accordingly, B, B^T and C are written as follows.

$$BB^T = \begin{bmatrix} b_{1,1} & 0 & 0 & . & . & 0 \\ b_{2,1} & b_{2,2} & . & . & . & . \\ . & . & . & . & . & 0 \\ . & . & . & . & . & 0 \\ . & . & . & . & . & . \\ b_{m,1} & b_{m,2} & . & . & . & b_{m,m} \end{bmatrix} \begin{bmatrix} b_{1,1} & b_{2,1} & . & . & . & b_{m,1} \\ 0 & b_{2,2} & . & . & . & b_{m,2} \\ 0 & . & . & . & . & . \\ . & . & . & . & . & . \\ . & . & . & . & . & . \\ 0 & . & . & . & 0 & b_{m,m} \end{bmatrix}$$

$$C = \begin{bmatrix} c_{1,1} & c_{2,1} & . & . & . & c_{m,1} \\ c_{2,1} & c_{2,2} & . & . & . & c_{m,2} \\ . & . & . & . & . & . \\ . & . & . & . & . & . \\ . & . & . & . & . & . \\ c_{m,1} & c_{m,2} & . & . & . & c_{m,m} \end{bmatrix}$$

The diagonal elements are found from

$$b_{1,1} = (c_{1,1})^{1/2}$$

$$b_{2,2} = (c_{2,2} - b_{2,1}^2)^{1/2}$$

---

[28] The idea originated from Young (1968). Matalas (1967) suggested the use of principal components following Fiering (1964); see also Lawrance and Kottegoda (1977).

In general,

$$b_{k,k} = (c_{k,k} - b_{k,k-1}^2 - b_{k,k-2}^2 - \ldots - b_{k,1}^2)^{1/2} \tag{4.70}$$

For these relationships to hold, C should be positive definite; thus the parameters are constrained as follows.

$$c_{1,1} \geqslant 0$$

$$c_{2,2} \geqslant b_{2,1}^2$$

$$c_{3,3} \geqslant b_{3,2}^2 + b_{3,1}^2$$

.

.

.

$$c_{k,k} \geqslant b_{k,k-1}^2 + b_{k,k-2}^2 + \ldots + b_{k,1}^2 \tag{4.71}$$

Also, it follows from equation 4.68 that the elements in the kth row are given by

$$b_{k,1} = c_{k,1}/b_{1,1}$$

$$b_{k,2} = (c_{k,2} - b_{2,1}b_{k,1})/b_{2,2}$$

$$b_{k,3} = (c_{k,3} - b_{3,1}b_{k,1} - b_{3,2}b_{k,2})/b_{3,3}$$

In general,

$$b_{k,j} = (c_{k,j} - b_{j,1}b_{k,1} - b_{j,2}b_{k,2} - \ldots - b_{j,j-1}b_{k,j-1})/b_{j,j} \tag{4.72}$$

Example 4.6 Equation 4.64 is used to generate simultaneous sequences for monthly data for the Teme at Tenbury Wells (w) and for the Severn at Bewdley (b). The following cross correlations are estimated from the historical data after standardising to zero mean and unit variance.

$$\hat{\rho}_{(w,b)}(-1) = 0.397$$

$$\hat{\rho}_{(b,w)}(-1) = 0.272$$

$$\hat{\rho}_{(b,w)} = 0.845$$

and the serial correlations are estimated as follows.

$$\hat{\rho}_w(1) = 0.403$$

$$\hat{\rho}_b(1) = 0.338$$

The estimated means and standard deviations of the January and February flows at Tenbury Wells are as follows.

$$\bar{x}_{w,\text{Jan}} = 60.8, \qquad \bar{x}_{w,\text{Feb}} = 47.5$$

$$s_{w,\text{Jan}} = 31.4, \qquad s_{w,\text{Feb}} = 29.8.$$

Generate the first two values of data for the Teme, which are for January and February, using the following random numbers for the elements in vector $\boldsymbol{\eta}_t$: -0.134, -0.268, 1.639 and 0.134.

Assume that the synthetic data for December at the two sites are equal to the mean values for this month at the respective sites.

$$M_0 = \begin{bmatrix} 1.000 & 0.845 \\ 0.845 & 1.000 \end{bmatrix}$$

$$M_1 = \begin{matrix} \text{(w)} \\ \text{(b)} \end{matrix} \begin{matrix} \text{(w)} & \text{(b)} \\ \begin{bmatrix} 0.403 & 0.397 \\ 0.272 & 0.338 \end{bmatrix} \end{matrix}$$

If d denotes the determinant of M_0, $d = 1.0 - 0.845^2 = 0.286$. Hence

$$M_0^{-1} = \begin{bmatrix} 1.000/d & -0.845/d \\ -0.845/d & 1.000/d \end{bmatrix} = \begin{bmatrix} 3.497 & -2.955 \\ -2.955 & 3.497 \end{bmatrix}$$

Therefore,

$$A = M_1 M_0^{-1} = \begin{bmatrix} 0.236 & 0.197 \\ -0.048 & 0.378 \end{bmatrix}$$

Also,

$$C = BB^T$$

$$= M_0 - AM_1^T$$

$$= \begin{bmatrix} 1.000 & 0.845 \\ 0.845 & 1.000 \end{bmatrix} - \begin{bmatrix} 0.236 & 0.197 \\ -0.048 & 0.378 \end{bmatrix} \begin{bmatrix} 0.403 & 0.272 \\ 0.397 & 0.338 \end{bmatrix}$$

$$= \begin{bmatrix} 0.827 & 0.714 \\ 0.714 & 0.885 \end{bmatrix}$$

Assuming that B is lower triangular, using equations 4.70 and 4.72, we obtain

$$b_{1,1} = (c_{1,1})^{1/2} = (0.827)^{1/2} = 0.909$$

$$b_{2,1} = c_{2,1}/b_{1,1} = 0.714/0.909 = 0.785$$

$$b_{2,2} = (c_{2,2} - b_{2,1}^2)^{1/2} = (0.885 - 0.785^2)^{1/2} = 0.518$$

Hence,

$$B = \begin{bmatrix} 0.909 & 0 \\ 0.785 & 0.518 \end{bmatrix}$$

If $\tilde{\xi}_{\text{Jan}} = (\tilde{\xi}_{w,\text{Jan}} \; \tilde{\xi}_{b,\text{Jan}})^T$ is a column vector which denotes the generated standardised flows at Tenbury Wells and Bewdley respectively in January,

$$
\begin{bmatrix} \tilde{\xi}_{w,\text{Jan}} \\ \tilde{\xi}_{b,\text{Jan}} \end{bmatrix} = \begin{bmatrix} 0.236 & 0.197 \\ -0.048 & 0.378 \end{bmatrix} \begin{bmatrix} 0.000 \\ 0.000 \end{bmatrix}
$$
$$
+ \begin{bmatrix} 0.909 & 0 \\ 0.785 & 0.518 \end{bmatrix} \begin{bmatrix} -0.134 \\ -0.268 \end{bmatrix}
$$

in which the column vector with zero elements signify that the antecedent standardised values are zero. Hence,

$$
\tilde{\xi}_{w,\text{Jan}} = -0.909 \times 0.134 = -0.122
$$

and

$$
\tilde{\xi}_{b,\text{Jan}} = -0.785 \times 0.134 - 0.518 \times 0.268 = -0.244
$$

Proceeding to the next time increment, we obtain

$$
\begin{bmatrix} \tilde{\xi}_{w,\text{Feb}} \\ \tilde{\xi}_{b,\text{Feb}} \end{bmatrix} = \begin{bmatrix} 0.236 & 0.197 \\ -0.048 & 0.378 \end{bmatrix} \begin{bmatrix} -0.122 \\ -0.244 \end{bmatrix}
$$
$$
+ \begin{bmatrix} 0.909 & 0 \\ 0.785 & 0.518 \end{bmatrix} \begin{bmatrix} 1.639 \\ 0.134 \end{bmatrix}
$$

Hence,

$$
\tilde{\xi}_{w,\text{Feb}} = -0.236 \times 0.122 - 0.197 \times 0.244 + 0.909 \times 1.639 = 1.413
$$

Lastly, from the above standardised values, the generated flows at Tenbury Wells in January and February are as follows.

$$
\tilde{\xi}_{w,\text{Jan}} \times s_{w,\text{Jan}} + \bar{x}_{w,\text{Jan}} = -0.122 \times 31.4 + 60.8 = 57.0
$$

and

$$
\tilde{\xi}_{w,\text{Feb}} \times s_{w,\text{Feb}} + \bar{x}_{w,\text{Feb}} = 1.413 \times 29.8 + 47.5 = 89.6
$$

In order to assess the bias and variance in the correlation coefficients, pertaining to models of these types, statistics were computed from 200 sequences of generated annual data by using a two-site model (equations 4.60 and 4.61) and a multisite model (equation 4.64) for two stations on the French Broad River, U.S.A. Results are shown in figure 4.12 through frequency polygons and are compared with historical statistics. The least bias and variance are for the lag-zero cross correlation. As regards the lag-one cross correlations, the multisite model which is devised to maintain these is, contrary to expectations, not vastly superior for that purpose. Bias in correlation is discussed by Marriott and Pope (1954), by Quenouille (1956), by McGregor

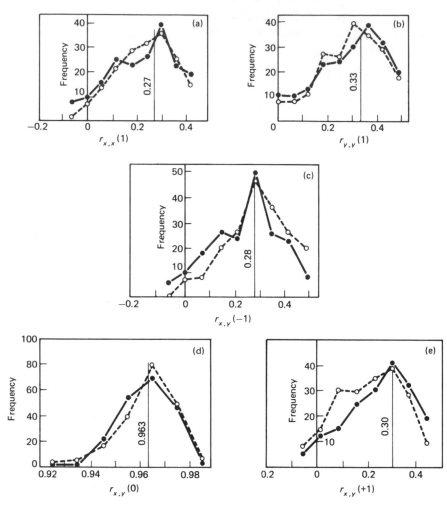

Figure 4.12 Frequency polygons of serial correlations and estimated cross correlations from 2×200 generated 54-year annual samples of the French Board River at Ashville, North Carolina (X series), and near Newport, Tennessee (Y series), using two-site (broken lines) and multisite model (full lines): vertical lines represent estimates from historical data: (a) lag-one serial correlations, site X; (b) lag-one serial correlations, site Y; (c) lag-minus-one estimated cross correlations; (d) lag-zero estimated cross correlations; (e) lag-plus-one estimated cross correlations

(1962) and by Kendall (1976, pp. 91–3); a detailed experimental study is made by Kottegoda and Yevjevich (1977).

4.8.3 Higher-order multisite autoregressive models

The first-order multisite model can be extended to form a general autoregressive type of model

$$\boldsymbol{\xi}_t = \sum_{\ell=1}^{p} \boldsymbol{A}_\ell \boldsymbol{\xi}_{t-\ell} + \boldsymbol{B}\boldsymbol{\eta}_t \qquad (4.73)$$

Let $\boldsymbol{M}_0$ and $\boldsymbol{M}_\ell, \ell = 1, 2, \ldots, p$, denote the $m \times m$ lag-zero and lag-ℓ correlation matrices in respect of the correlated $\boldsymbol{\xi}$ component. Here, the matrix $\boldsymbol{M}_0$ is as defined after equation 4.65. However, $\boldsymbol{M}_\ell$ is such that its diagonal elements are the lag-ℓ serial correlations at each of the m stations, in order, and the general (i,j)th element is $E(\xi_{i,t}\xi_{j,t-\ell}) = \rho_{i,j}(-\ell)$ which is the lag-ℓ cross correlation coefficient between the ith and jth series with the jth series lagged behind the ith series by ℓ time units. Then, by post-multiplying equation 4.73 by $\boldsymbol{\xi}_{t-i}^{\mathrm{T}}$ and taking expectations,

$$\boldsymbol{M}_i = \sum_{\ell=1}^{p} \boldsymbol{A}_\ell \boldsymbol{M}_{i-\ell}, \qquad i = 1, 2, \ldots, p \qquad (4.74)$$

The simultaneous equations given by equation 4.74 can be written

$$[\boldsymbol{M}_1 \boldsymbol{M}_2 \ldots \boldsymbol{M}_p] - [\boldsymbol{A}_1 \boldsymbol{A}_2 \ldots \boldsymbol{A}_p] \begin{bmatrix} \boldsymbol{M}_0 & \boldsymbol{M}_1 & \cdot & \cdot & \cdot & \boldsymbol{M}_{p-1} \\ \boldsymbol{M}_1^{\mathrm{T}} & \boldsymbol{M}_0 & \cdot & \cdot & \cdot & \boldsymbol{M}_{p-2} \\ \cdot & & \cdot & \cdot & \cdot & \cdot \\ \cdot & & & \cdot & \cdot & \cdot \\ \cdot & & & & \cdot & \cdot \\ \boldsymbol{M}_{p-1}^{\mathrm{T}} & \boldsymbol{M}_{p-2}^{\mathrm{T}} & \cdot & \cdot & \cdot & \boldsymbol{M}_0 \end{bmatrix}$$

that is,

$$[\boldsymbol{A}_1 \boldsymbol{A}_2 \ldots \boldsymbol{A}_p] = [\boldsymbol{M}_1 \boldsymbol{M}_2 \ldots \boldsymbol{M}_p] \begin{bmatrix} \boldsymbol{M}_0 & \boldsymbol{M}_1 & \cdot & \cdot & \boldsymbol{M}_{p-1} \\ \boldsymbol{M}_1^{\mathrm{T}} & \boldsymbol{M}_0 & \cdot & \cdot & \boldsymbol{M}_{p-2} \\ \cdot & & \cdot & \cdot & \cdot \\ \cdot & & \cdot & \cdot & \cdot \\ \cdot & & & \cdot & \cdot \\ \boldsymbol{M}_{p-1}^{\mathrm{T}} & \boldsymbol{M}_{p-2}^{\mathrm{T}} & \cdot & \cdot & \boldsymbol{M}_0 \end{bmatrix}^{-1} \qquad (4.75)$$

Similarly, by post-multiplying equation 4.73 by $\boldsymbol{\xi}_t^{\mathrm{T}}$ and taking expectations,

$$\boldsymbol{M}_0 = \sum_{\ell=1}^{p} \boldsymbol{A}_\ell \boldsymbol{M}_\ell^{\mathrm{T}} + \boldsymbol{B}\boldsymbol{B}^{\mathrm{T}}$$

and

$$\boldsymbol{B}\boldsymbol{B}^{\mathrm{T}} = \boldsymbol{M}_0 - \sum_{\ell=1}^{p} \boldsymbol{A}_\ell \boldsymbol{M}_\ell^{\mathrm{T}} \qquad (4.76)$$

The matrices A_i, $i = 1, 2, \ldots$, can be obtained by solving equation 4.75 after the matrix multiplications on the right[29].

If $BB^T = C$, say, then, by assuming a triangulation matrix for B as in the first-order model, the elements of B can be found.

4.8.4 *Further comments on multisite models*

The order of a multisite autoregressive model could be estimated from the serial correlations and estimated partial autocorrelations of the individual series; here similarities amongst the different series are expected. There are problems, however, if the distribution is not multivariate normal. In such cases, transformations which result in approximate normality as described in section 4.6 could be used. Alternatively, the marginal distributions of the estimated residuals, given for instance for the first-order model by

$$\eta_t = \hat{B}^{-1}(\tilde{\xi}_t - \hat{A}\tilde{\xi}_{t-1}) \tag{4.77}$$

which follows from equation 4.42 can be examined, and skewness and other properties can be calculated. This means in practice that the distribution of the m elements of the column vector η_t are investigated by using the estimated matrices A and B and the historical data ξ_t, $t = 1, 2, \ldots, N$. By using the methods in chapter 3, the distributions of the random numbers are then transformed to suitable distributions[30].

Another difficulty might arise when historical sequences of different lengths are used for estimating the correlation matrices. In such a case, constraints may be violated, which is equivalent to stating that C given by equation 4.68 is not positive definite. Methods have been suggested for circumventing this problem (about which there will be more in subsection 4.10.1); we can, for instance, infill the missing sections through iterative regressions applied to data at the different sites[31].

The method can be extended to monthly data by using the seasonal means and standard deviations in the same way as in section 4.7; this has been used by Young and Pisano (1968). A more direct solution was indicated by Bernier (1970) and is shown by Salas and Pegram (1977).

4.9 Short-term forecasting

One of the practical applications of time series analysis and stochastic models is in short-term forecasting. Methods have been developed in recent years which

---

[29] Pegram and James (1972) suggest a simplification to reduce computations, by assuming that the A_i matrices are diagonal matrices. See also Ledolter (1978).

[30] Moran (1970) indicates how a mulivariate gamma process may be applied.

[31] Earlier, Fiering (1968) suggested a method through which a correlation matrix is made positive definite by adjusting the eigenvalues and hence the variances of the principal components of the correlation matrix. Also, Crosby and Maddock (1970) found a positive definite matrix C using the ML method of Anderson (1957).

could be used to control water resource systems over immediate time horizons. An effective forecasting procedure necessitates the efficient use of current and past information, the best-fitting mathematical models which should be changed or modified if necessary and the updating of parameters.

Primitive methods of forecasting were based on the last observed value or a mean value from a historical record. Then moving averages, as explained in section 2.3.1, were introduced. Exponential smoothing is one of the other procedures that can be used[32]. Here, the forecast $\hat{x}_t(1)$ at time $t + 1$ is dependent on the current and past observations x_t, x_{t-1}, . . ., as follows.

$$\hat{x}_t(1) = \alpha x_t + \alpha(1-\alpha)x_{t-1} + \alpha(1-\alpha)^2 x_{t-2} + \alpha(1-\alpha)^3 x_{t-3} + \ldots \tag{4.78}$$

in which the constant α, $0 < \alpha < 1$ is heuristically fitted. A more flexible and systematic method of smoothing errors and of making short-term forecasts is by means of the Box–Jenkins models described in section 4.5. These models which are useful operationally for generating likely future sequences can also be adopted to produce a set of expected values; however, this is only practicable over the immediate future because the variance of the forecast function increases with time. The forecasting approach is explained here. Also included is the Kalman filter method of recursive estimation.

4.9.1 Forecasting with $ARMA(p, q)$ model

The model given by equation 4.27 can be used to produce a value x_t representing, say, annual flow with mean μ at time t; it is assumed that the series is free of trend and periodicity. That is,

$$\phi_p(B)(X_t - \mu) = \theta_q(B)\eta_t \tag{4.79}$$

in which, as before, η_t is the random component with zero mean.

For the purpose of forecasting a value $X_{t+\ell}$ at time t, where ℓ is the lead time of the forecast, equation 4.79 is written

$$X_{t+\ell} = \mu + \phi_{p,1}(X_{t+\ell-1} - \mu) + \phi_{p,2}(X_{t+\ell-2} - \mu) + \ldots$$
$$+ \phi_{p,p}(X_{t+\ell-p} - \mu) + \eta_{t+\ell} - \theta_{q,1}\eta_{t+\ell-1}\,\theta_{q,2}\eta_{t+\ell-2}$$
$$- \ldots - \theta_{q,q}\eta_{t+\ell-q} \tag{4.80}$$

Alternatively, $X_{t+\ell}$ can be equated to an infinite sum of current and previous shocks (a term commonly used for random effects) follows.

$$X_{t+\ell} = \mu + (1 + \psi_1 B + \psi_2 B^2 + \ldots)\eta_{t+\ell} \tag{4.81}$$

where $\psi_1, \psi_2, \ldots$ are a set of constants. The weights $\psi_1, \psi_2, \psi_3, \ldots$ are found by

[32] See Wheelwright and Makridakis (1977) and Toyoda et al. (1969).

combining equations 4.80 and 4.81 as follows.

$$(1 - \phi_{p,1}B - \phi_{p,2}B^2 - \ldots - \phi_{p,p}B^p)(1 + \psi_1 B + \psi_2 B^2 + \ldots)$$
$$= (1 - \theta_{q,1}B - \theta_{q,2}B^2 - \ldots - \theta_{q,q}B^q) \qquad (4.82)$$

Then, by equating the coefficients of B, B^2, B^3, $\ldots$,

$$\psi_1 = \phi_{p,1} - \theta_{q,1}$$
$$\psi_2 = \phi_{p,1}\psi_1 + \phi_{p,2} - \theta_{q,2}$$
$$\psi_3 = \phi_{p,1}\psi_2 + \phi_{p,2}\psi_1 + \phi_{p,3} - \theta_{q,3} \qquad (4.83)$$

and so on.

Equations 4.80 or 4.81 may be used as a forecast function. The optimal or minimum mean square error forecast of lead ℓ and at time t is $\hat{x}_t(\ell) = [X_{t+\ell}]$ which is the expectation of $X_{t+\ell}$, conditional on X_t, X_{t-1}, X_{t-2}, $\ldots$. This is obtained by using all the currently available information. Therefore, from equation 4.80,

$$\hat{x}_t(\ell) = \mu + \phi_{p,1}[X_{t+\ell-1} - \mu] + \phi_{p,2}[X_{t+\ell-2} - \mu] + \ldots$$
$$+ \phi_{p,p}[X_{t+\ell-p} - \mu] + [\eta_{t+\ell}] - \theta_{q,1}[\eta_{t+\ell-1}]$$
$$- \theta_{q,2}[\eta_{t+\ell-2}] - \ldots - \theta_{q,q}[\eta_{t+\ell-q}] \qquad (4.84)$$

Again, from equation 4.81, the forecast can also be given as follows.

$$\hat{x}_t(\ell) = \mu + [\eta_{t+\ell}] + \psi_1[\eta_{t+\ell-1}] + \psi_2[\eta_{t+\ell-2}]$$
$$+ \ldots + \psi_\ell[\eta_t] + \psi_{\ell+1}[\eta_{t-1}] + \ldots \qquad (4.85)$$

When forecasting, an X variable within square brackets such as $[X_{t-i}]$ is replaced by the observed value x_{t-i} if $i = 0, 1, 2, 3, \ldots$. With this notation, $[X_{t+i}]$ denotes a forecast $\hat{x}_t(i)$ of lead time i made at time origin t, if $i = 1, 2, 3, \ldots$.

As regards the shocks, the conditional expectation $[\eta_{t+i}] = 0$, in equations 4.84 and 4.85, for $i = 1, 2, 3, \ldots$, because it represents an unknown future error. This means that in the right-hand side of equation 4.85 all the terms between μ and $\psi_\ell[\eta_t]$ will be zero. However, $[\eta_{t-i}]$ denotes the one-step-ahead forecast error at time origin $t - i - 1$, for $i = 0, 1, 2, \ldots$, that is,

$$[\eta_{t-i}] = x_{t-i} - \hat{x}_{t-i-1}(1) \qquad (4.86)$$

in which x_{t-i} is the observed value at time $t - i$ and $\hat{x}_{t-i-1}(1)$ is the forecast of this value, made at time $t - i - 1$.

From equations 4.81 and 4.85 (in which the conditional expectations of future shocks are equated to zero) the minimum mean square forecast error for lead time ℓ at time t is

$$e_t(\ell) = x_{t+\ell} - \hat{x}_t(\ell)$$
$$= \eta_{t+\ell} + \psi_1 \eta_{t+\ell-1} + \ldots + \psi_{\ell-1}\eta_{t+1} \qquad (4.87)$$

Because $E(\eta_{t+\ell}\eta_{t+\ell-i}) = 0$ for $i \neq 0$ and $E(\eta_{t+\ell}^2) = 1$,

$$\text{var}\{e_t(\ell)\} = (1 + \psi_1^2 + \psi_2^2 + \ldots + \psi_{\ell-1}^2)\sigma_\eta^2 \tag{4.88}$$

If we assume that the $e_t(\ell)$ values are normally distributed with variance given by equation 4.88, confidence limits can be calculated for each forecast as shown in the following example.

Example 4.7 The annual flows (reduced to unit mean) in the St Lawrence at Ogdensburgh can be represented by the model

$$X_{t+\ell} = 1 + 0.670(X_{t+\ell-1} - 1) - 0.107(X_{t+\ell-2} - 1)$$
$$+ 0.200(X_{t+\ell-3} - 1) + \eta_{t+\ell}$$

The observed flows for the period 1938 to 1941 are as follows: 0.905, 0.897, 0.872, 0.884. These are in reduced form with a mean of unity and are taken from Yevjevich (1963). Using the year 1940 as the base, forecast the next five values and calculate the 95% confidence limits given that $\hat{\sigma}_\eta = 0.060$. (From equation 4.9, $\sigma_\eta = \sigma_X(1 - R^2)^{1/2}$, where $\sigma_X^2 = \text{var}(X)$.) Then, with 1941 as the time base, update the forecasts.

Using equation 4.84 and substituting for the conditional expectations, we find that the forecasts, with $t = 1940$, are as follows.

For 1941

$$\hat{x}_t(1) = 1 + 0.670(x_t - 1) - 0.107(x_{t-1} - 1) + 0.200(x_{t-2} - 1)$$
$$= 1 + 0.670(0.872 - 1) - 0.107(0.897 - 1) + 0.200(0.905 - 1)$$
$$= 0.906$$

For 1942

$$\hat{x}_t(2) = 1 + 0.670\{\hat{x}_t(1) - 1\} - 0.107(x_t - 1) + 0.200(x_{t-1} - 1)$$
$$= 0.930$$

For 1943

$$\hat{x}_t(3) = 1 + 0.670\{\hat{x}_t(2) - 1\} - 0.107(\hat{x}_t(1) - 1) + 0.200(x_t - 1)$$
$$= 0.938$$

For 1944

$$\hat{x}_t(4) = 1 + 0.670\{\hat{x}_t(3) - 1\} - 0.107(\hat{x}_t(2) - 1) + 0.200(\hat{x}_t(1) - 1)$$
$$= 0.947$$

For 1945

$$\hat{x}_t(5) = 1 + 0.670(\hat{x}_t(4) - 1) - 0.107(\hat{x}_t(3) - 1) + 0.200(\hat{x}_t(2) - 1)$$
$$= 0.957$$

Then, from equation 4.83, in which the moving-average parameters are zero,

$$\psi_1 = 0.670$$

$$\psi_2 = 0.670 \times 0.670 - 0.107$$

$$= 0.342$$

$$\psi_3 = 0.670 \times 0.342 - 0.107 \times 0.670 + 0.200$$

$$= 0.357$$

$$\psi_4 = 0.670 \times 0.357 - 0.107 \times 0.342 + 0.200 \times 0.670$$

$$= 0.337$$

By using equation 4.88, the 95 % confidence limits of the forecasts are as follows.

For 1941

$$0.906 \pm 1.96 \times 1.0 \times 0.060$$

$$= 1.024, 0.788$$

For 1942

$$0.930 \pm 1.96 \times (1.449)^{1/2} \times 0.060$$

$$= 1.072, 0.788$$

For 1943

$$0.938 \pm 1.96 \times (1.566)^{1/2} \times 0.060$$

$$= 1.085, 0.791$$

For 1944

$$0.947 \pm 1.96 \times (1.693)^{1/2} \times 0.060$$

$$= 1.100, 0.794$$

For 1945

$$0.957 \pm 1.96 \times (1.807)^{1/2} \times 0.060$$

$$= 1.115, 0.799$$

A forecast of lead $\ell + 1$ made at time t can be updated from the next time base $t + 1$, by using equation 4.85 and its conditional expectations, as discussed. It follows from equations 4.85 and 4.86 that

$$\hat{x}_{t+1}(\ell) = \hat{x}_t(\ell + 1) + \psi_\ell[\eta_{t+1}]$$
$$= \hat{x}_t(\ell + 1) + \psi_\ell\{x_{t+1} - \hat{x}_t(1)\}$$

Therefore, if $t + 1$ stands for 1941, $\hat{x}_{t+1}(\ell) = \hat{x}_t(\ell + 1) + \psi_\ell(0.884 - 0.906)$ $= \hat{x}_t(\ell + 1) - 0.022\psi_\ell$. By substituting $\ell = 1, 2, 3$ and 4, the updated forecasts for the 4 years commencing 1942 are given below with the previous forecasts in parentheses.

$$0.930 - 0.022 \times 0.670 = 0.915(0.930)$$

$$0.938 - 0.022 \times 0.342 = 0.930(0.938)$$

$$0.947 - 0.022 \times 0.357 = 0.939(0.947)$$

$$0.957 - 0.022 \times 0.337 = 0.950(0.957)$$

(The same results are obtained through equation 4.85 with $t = 1941$.)

When the lead times are varied by using the same time origin, as in example 4.7, the forecast errors are correlated[33]. This means that a sequence of forecasts, considered as a whole, tends to be either above or below the sequence of future flows when they are actually recorded. Likewise, forecast errors at the same lead time but at different time origins are generally correlated. On the other hand, a sequence of optimal one-step-ahead forecast errors are uncorrelated.

In the next example, forecasts are made using a ARMA(1, 1) model. The forecasting process is initiated by equating unknown η_t values to zero.

Example 4.8   The following are the annual flows (reduced to unit mean) in the Niger at Kouliko, Mali, for the period 1951 to 1955, as given by Yevjevich (1963): 1.385, 1.060, 1.280, 1.352, 1.333. Using the model, we obtain

$$X_{t+\ell} = 1 + 0.82(X_{t+\ell-1} - 1) + \eta_{t+\ell} - 0.40\eta_{t+\ell-1}$$

with $E(\eta_{t+\ell}) = E(\eta_{t+\ell-1}) = 0$, forecast values up to 1955, with the years 1951 and 1952 as time bases, given that $\hat{\sigma}_\eta = 0.195$ (by multiplying $\hat{\sigma}_\eta$ from equation 4.35 by $s = 0.242$). Also find the 95% confidence limits.

The one-step-ahead forecast function is

$$\hat{x}_t(1) = 0.18 + 0.82x_t - 0.40[\eta_t]$$

Here, $[\eta_t] = x_t - \hat{x}_{t-1}(1)$, but this is equated to zero for the initial time base (the resulting errors will, of course, tend to decrease as subsequent time bases are taken up and forecasts are updated). For $\ell = 2, 3, 4, \ldots$,

$$\hat{x}_t(\ell) = 1 + 0.82\{\hat{x}_t(\ell - 1) - 1\}$$

With 1951 as the time base t the forecasts are as follows.

For 1952

$$\hat{x}_t(1) = 0.18 + 0.82 \times 1.385$$

$$= 1.316$$

For 1953

$$\hat{x}_t(2) = 0.18 + 0.82 \times 1.316$$

$$= 1.259$$

[33] This is shown by Box and Jenkins (1976, pp. 158–60).

For 1954

$$\hat{x}_t(3) = 0.18 + 0.82 \times 1.259$$

$$= 1.212$$

For 1955

$$\hat{x}_t(4) = 0.18 + 0.82 \times 1.212$$

$$= 1.174$$

The forecasts are updated, in the year $t = 1952$, as given below.
For 1953

$$\hat{x}_t(1) = 0.18 + 0.82 \times 1.060 - 0.40(1.060 - 1.316)$$

$$= 1.152$$

For 1954

$$\hat{x}_t(2) = 0.18 + 0.82 \times 1.152$$

$$= 1.125$$

For 1955

$$\hat{x}_t(3) = 0.18 + 0.82 \times 1.125$$

$$= 1.103$$

From equations 4.83,

$$\psi_1 = 0.82 - 0.40$$

$$= 0.420$$

$$\psi_2 = 0.82 \times 0.42$$

$$= 0.344$$

$$\psi_3 = 0.82 \times 0.344$$

$$= 0.282$$

If we use equation 4.87, the 95 % confidence limits of the forecasts with 1951 as the time base are as follows.
For 1952

$$1.316 \pm 1.96 \times 0.195$$

$$= 1.698,\ 0.934$$

For 1953

$$1.259 \pm 1.96 \times 1.08 \times 0.195$$

$$= 1.672,\ 0.846$$

For 1954

$$1.212 \pm 1.96 \times 1.14 \times 0.195$$

$$= 1.648, 0.776$$

For 1955

$$1.174 \pm 1.96 \times 1.17 \times 0.195$$

$$= 1.621, 0.727$$

Again, with 1952 as the time base, the confidence limits are as given below.

For 1953

$$1.152 \pm 1.96 \times 0.195$$

$$= 1.534, 0.770$$

For 1954

$$1.125 \pm 1.96 \times 1.08 \times 0.195$$

$$= 1.538, 0.712$$

For 1955

$$1.103 \pm 1.96 \times 1.14 \times 0.195$$

$$= 1.539, 0.667$$

The forecasts from 1951 are compared with the historical values in figure 4.13. Also shown are the 95% confidence limits of the forecast.

If an ARMA(2, 2) model is used, note that, when forecasts are made with the second and third subsequent time bases, $[\eta_{t-1}] = x_{t-1} - \hat{x}_{t-2}(1)$.

These methods can be extended to forecast monthly or daily flows by incorporating a seasonal component. For this purpose the autoregressive seasonal model of subsection 4.7.1 may be used[34].

An alternative to the Box–Jenkins models are the so-called adaptive types, which have the potential of overcoming some of the limitations shown in the above examples[35]. This is attempted by updating the model parameters prior to forecasting by using the previous estimates of the model parameters and a function of the prediction error process; accordingly, the models can cope with short-term non-stationary behaviour.

[34] McMichael and Hunter (1972) forecast daily temperatures and river flows. McKercher and Delleur (1974), Delleur et al. (1976), Chatfield and Prothero (1973) and Thompson and Tiao (1971) apply Box–Jenkins models. Stochastic difference equations are used by Rao and Kashyap (1974) and by Clarke (1974) to forecast daily and 3-hourly flows respectively; see also Tillotson and Cluckie (1977).

[35] Examples are given by Jazwinski (1969) and by Wheelwright and Makridakis (1973, 1977), but they need not necessarily be advantageous over simpler types such as exponential smoothing, as shown by Ekern (1976).

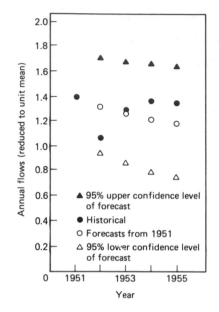

Figure 4.13   Short-term forecasting of annual flows in Niger at Koulikoro, Mali, Africa, by use of an ARMA(1, 1) model

4.9.2   *Filtering methods of real-time forecasting*

In recent years recursive least-squares estimation and signal enhancement procedures developed by control engineers have been applied to water resource systems. These date back to the work of Wiener and Kolmogorov and, in a fundamental sense, to the least-squares methods used originally by Gauss, in estimating planetary orbits and by Legendre in other work[36].

The need for filters is because all natural systems are subject to random or unknown influences, termed noise. Filters are devised so that the underlying signals or deterministic movements can be estimated and modelled. The basis for the original Wiener filter is that a measurement process $y(t)$ in continuous time t is represented by

$$y(t) = s(t) + \eta(t) \tag{4.89}$$

where $s(t)$ is a multivariate normal signal process with known autocorrelations and cross correlations and where $\eta(t)$ is a normal white noise process[37]. The

---

[36] More recently, Plackett originated methods of updating estimates of parameters in a linear regression model. A perspective of recursive approaches to time series analysis with the Kalman filter method is given by Young (1974); see also the review of linear prediction methods by Makhoul (1975). Other interesting introductions are given by Sorenson (1970) and by Anderson (1971).

[37] See Wiener (1949).

spectrum of $s(t)$ generally decreases with increasing frequency as shown by figure 2.11; as regards $\eta(t)$, the robustness of the filter allows for slight departures from the flat spectrum that is theoretically required. An optimum Wiener filter finds a minimum least-squares error estimate $\hat{s}(t)$ of $s(t)$, given a set of measurements $y(t)$. One possible deterrent is that it involves work in the frequency domain. Also, it is assumed that the process is stationary or that a suitable transformation is available.

The Kalman or Kalman–Bucy filter and other extended forms constitute the currently popular recursive technique of estimating the state of a system in the presence of noise[38]. Its advantages are that stationarity is not a prerequisite and that application is in the time domain. This can undoubtedly play an important role in real-time forecasting of hydrological time series. Elsewhere, it has been used effectively, for example, to control the flight of a space rocket which is subject to unknown disturbances but is well defined dynamically.

The Kalman filtering system is described by the following two equations which represent a dynamic linear model. Firstly, $x_k = (x_1, x_2, \ldots, x_n)_k^T$, which denotes the true state of the system (for example, flows, levels, water quality indices) at time $t_k \varepsilon T$, is represented through an $n \times 1$ vector by the system equation

$$x_{k+1} = \phi_{k+1,k} x_k + \eta_k \tag{4.90}$$

Here, $\phi_{k+1,k}$ is an $n \times n$ matrix of parameters which represents the state transition from time t_k to t_{k+1}, and η_k is a $n \times 1$ vector of normal white noise which effects the state at time t_k. The parameters of the ϕ matrix are estimated from the model, for example, an autoregressive or an ARMA model, which represents the state; in the time-invariant case, which is generally assumed, $\phi_{k+1,k} = \phi$. Secondly, the observation or measurement equation

$$y_k = H_k x_k + \varepsilon_k \tag{4.91}$$

relates the measured data, given by the $p \times 1$ vector $y_k = (y_1, y_2, \ldots, y_p)_k^T$ to the state. Here, H_k is a $p \times n$ observation matrix at time t_k, and ε_k is a $p \times 1$ vector of normal white noise which denotes the random differences between the observations and the state at time t_k.

The vectors η_k and ε_k have zero means and variances $E(\eta_k \eta_j^T) = Q_k \delta_{k,j}$ and $E(\varepsilon_k \varepsilon_j^T) = R_{k,j}$ respectively, where $\delta_{k,j} = 0$ except that (when $k = j$) $\delta_{k,k} = 1$; also $E(\eta_k \varepsilon_j^T) = 0$. For simplification, the non-zero variances are made time invariant and are denoted by Q and R respectively (without the suffixes k).

An estimate $\hat{x}_{k|k}$ of x_k is made from the measured data y_k by minimising the mean square estimate $E\{(\hat{x}_{k|k} - x_k)^T (\hat{x}_{k|k} - x_k)\}$. Note that neither the observations nor the model estimates represent the true state. The state estimation procedure outlined here is an attempt to obtain optimum values. For this purpose the previous best estimates $\hat{x}_{k-1|k-1}, \hat{x}_{k-2|k-2}, \ldots$ are used as follows.

---

[38] See Kalman (1960), Kalman and Bucy (1961) and earlier work by Swerling (1959). Details of an application to velocity measurements is given by Sorenson (1968).

$$\hat{x}_{k|k} = \phi_{k,k-1}\hat{x}_{k-1|k-1} + K_k(y_k - H_k\phi_{k,k-1}\hat{x}_{k-1|k-1}) \qquad (4.92)$$

in which K_k is called the Kalman gain matrix and is given by

$$K_k = P_{k|k-1}H_k^T(H_kP_{k|k-1}H_k^T + R)^{-1} \qquad (4.93)$$

Here,

$$P_{k|k-1} = E\{(\hat{x}_{k|k-1} - x_k)(\hat{x}_{k|k-1} - x_k)^T\} \qquad (4.94)$$

is the covariance of the error in the predicted estimate based on observations up to time t_{k-1}, and it is extrapolated as follows.

$$P_{k|k-1} = \phi_{k,k-1}P_{k-1|k-1}\phi_{k,k-1}^T + Q \qquad (4.95)$$

Also, $\hat{x}_{k|k-1} = \phi_{k,k-1}\hat{x}_{k-1|k-1}$ is the best estimate of x_k based on observations up to t_{k-1}, and

$$P_{k|k} = E\{(\hat{x}_{k|k} - x_k)(\hat{x}_{k|k} - x_k)^T\} \qquad (4.96)$$

is the updated covariance matrix of the estimation errors; this is found from

$$P_{k|k} = P_{k|k-1} - K_kH_kP_{k|k-1} \qquad (4.97)$$

Note that, in equation 4.93, K_k depends on $P_{k|k-1}$ and the covariance matrix R of the observation errors. The elements of H_k which relate the measurements to the state usually have the values one or zero in water resource applications; another simplification is to make ϕ time invariant. Thus equations 4.92, 4.93, 4.95 and 4.97 represent the Kalman filter, but, prior to implementing the recursive procedure, the matrices $x_{k|k}$ and $P_{k|k}$ need to be initialised. This is done somewhat arbitrarily in practice; however, any distortion caused does, in general, decrease with time[39].

Amongst the practical difficulties that may be encountered are those in estimating the noise covariances Q and R. Several computer algorithms are suggested for the purpose, but these may require modifications in practice[40]. In this context, the problem of divergence, which usually arises from the modelling of errors, is of concern. This means basically that the error variances may increase with time. Attempts to remedy the situation are sometimes made by discarding information from distant observations or by magnifying the influence of the noise processes[41]. These problems notwithstanding, Kalman filtering provides a practical method of obtaining estimates recursively.

[39] Linear regression model applications of the Kalman filter and the extended Kalman filter for forecasting daily flows and water quality are given by Young (1974). Lettenmaier and Burges (1976) have applied the technique to water quality parameters. See also the numerical example on radar measurements by Hovanessian (1976, pp. 143–9) and the comprehensive work of Gelb (1974, chapter 4). Duong et al. (1975) elaborate on state space concepts and Harrison and Stevens (1976) present the statistical theory. For other hydrological applications, see Todini and Bouillot (1976), Szöllöse-Nagy (1976) and Maissis (1977) .
[40] See Szöllösi-Nagy (1975).
[41] See Jazwinski (1969, 1970), and the more recent work by Brewer (1976).

4.10   Practical applications and general comments

Section 4.9 deals with an important practical application of stochastic models for the purpose of short-term forecasting. Another operational procedure, where these models may be used, is the infilling of missing values in hydrological data.

4.10.1   *Infilling missing flow data*

Consider a situation where a section of a record is incomplete, whereas long records covering the missing section are available for neighbouring gauging stations. Such cases often arise in the application of multisite models. Usually, the main reason for the lack of concurrent data sets is because flow records at some stations have commenced many years after.

Prior to data generation, simulation of a complex water resource system is possible by using historical data if complete data sets are available at all stations. If long sections of data are missing rather than a few items, a stochastic approach by using time series models is required in order to maintain the covariance matrices; this is not possible through a simple regression model. However, an infinite number of sequences that preserve the covariance matrices estimated from the known sequences are realisable. For data generation purposes, Kottegoda and Elgy (1977) use the first-order multisite model

$$Y_{t+1} = A(\, Y_t^{\mathrm{T}} \, X_{t+1}^{\mathrm{T}} \, X_t^{\mathrm{T}})^{\mathrm{T}} + B\eta_{t+1}$$

in which flows at stations Y are infilled by using current and antecedent flows at stations X. This entails many estimation problems such as those discussed by Anderson (1957) and already noted in subsection 4.8.4. Iterative methods of determining the parameters of A and B by using previously infilled data are set out.

4.10.2   *Comments on testing generated data*

If we return to data generation methods in general, their greatest potential seems to be in the simulation of large systems. Here, we should bear in mind the assumptions and limitations of stochastic models, as outlined in section 4.1. As regards the validity and choice of models, the question is often asked about the best methods of testing generated data. From the practising engineer's viewpoint, the preservation of statistics, such as the mean, the standard deviation and the short-lag serial correlation, is not particularly important, because it is known that, on average, these will be maintained. Of greater concern in comparative assessments are aspects such as the yield and reliability of a system, the duration curves and other hydrological properties; runs, run sums, crossings and extreme values are also important. In other words, it is more purposeful to examine the properties that are not specifically incorporated in the models[42]. The necessity to ascertain how realistic generated data are on the

[42] Some tests of this type are used by Kottegoda (1970).

basis of such criteria cannot be overstressed. These will be taken up in chapter 5.

4.10.3   *Applications of data generation methods*

In the United States, Beard (1965) pioneered the practical use of several data generation methods. Particular examples of operational techniques are those of Young and Pisano (1968) who used a first-order multisite model to produce monthly data for eight stations and the daily flow generation by Payne *et al.* (1969) which was cited earlier. Another case study in which the lognormal distribution is used is presented by Gupta and Fordham (1972). Regulation of river basins of the Severn and the Wye in the United Kingdom has necessitated infilling and data generation (Hamlin and Kottegoda, 1971, 1974; Hamlin *et al.*, 1976). Elsewhere, O'Donnell *et al.* (1972) discuss the practicalities of using an autoregressive lognormal daily flow model for the Dart in southern England and Vardar in Yugoslavia. Data generation has also been used in various reservoir studies with the use of economic concepts as, for example, in the work by Jettmar and Young (1975). Numerous other applications have been made to supplement systems engineering techniques, as will be explained in chapter 8.

4.10.4   *Other properties and models*

The models examined in this chapter are based almost exclusively on short-lag serial correlations. The frequent use of such models is partly because available samples are usually of limited size and because any latent long-term movements are difficult to assess. For the same reasons, care and judgement are called for in application[43]. A scrutiny of some long sequences of historical data reveals properties of particular significance in hydrology which need to be investigated.

Of particular relevance in long-term assessments of reservoir storage is the work of H. E. Hurst. In the next chapter the so-called Hurst phenomenon is explained, in addition to runs, crossing properties, reservoir depletions and range. Also, operational models, such as the fractional gaussian noise types, devised specifically for hydrological situations are included.

References

Akaike, H. (1974). A new look at the statistical model identification. *IEEE Trans. Autom. Control*, **19**, 716–23

Anderson, B. D. O. (1971). A qualitative introduction to Wiener and Kalman–Bucy Filters. *Proc. Inst. Radio Electron. Eng. Aust.*, March, 93–103

Anderson, O. D. (1976). *Time Series Analysis and Forecasting—The Box–Jenkins Approach*, Butterworths, London

---

[43] Some of the many problems in hydrology are examined by Borgman and Amorocho (1970); for preserving long-term effects, Fiering (1967, chapter 7) suggested a twenty-lag model.

Anderson, R. L. (1942). Distribution of the serial correlation coefficient. *Ann. Math. Statist.*, **13**, 1–13

Anderson, T. W. (1957). Maximum likelihood estimates for a multivariate normal distribution when some observations are missing. *J. Am. Statist. Assoc.*, **52**, 200–3

Beard, L. R. (1965). Use of interrelated records to simulate streamflow. *J. Hydraul. Div., Am. Soc. Civ. Eng.*, **91** (HY5), 13–22.

—— (1967). Simulation of daily streamflow. *Proceedings of the International Hydrology Symposium*, vol. 1, *Fort Collins, Colorado*, pp. 624–32

Bernier, J. (1970). Inventaire des modèles des processus stochastiques applicables à la description des débits journaliers des rivières. *Rev. Int. Statist. Inst.*, **38**, 49–61

Borgman, L. E., and Amorocho, J. (1970). Some statistical problems in hydrology. *Rev. Int. Statist. Inst.*, **38**, 82–96

Box, G. E. P., and Cox, D. R. (1964). An analysis of transformations. *J. R. Statist. Soc. B*, **26**, 211–52

Box, G. E. P., and Jenkins, G. M. (1976). *Time Series Analysis: Forecasting and Control*, revised edn, Holden Day, San Francisco, California

Brewer, H. W. (1976). Identification of the noise in a Kalman filter. *Control and Dynamic Systems, Advances in Theory and Applications*, vol. 12 (ed. C. T. Leondes), Academic Press, New York, pp. 491–579

Carlson, R. E., MacCormick, A. J. A., and Watts, D. G. (1970). Application of linear random models to four annual streamflow series. *Water Resour. Res.*, **6**, 1070–8

Chatfield, C., and Prothero, D. L. (1973). Box–Jenkins seasonal forecasting: problems in a case-study, with discussion. *J. R. Statist. Soc. A*, **136**, 295–352

Clarke, R. T. (1974). The representation of a short period of experimental catchment data by a linear stochastic difference equation. *Proceedings of the 1971 Warsaw Symposium on Mathematical Models in Hydrology*, vol. 1, International Association of Scientific Hydrology, Paris, pp. 3–16

Codner, G. P., and McMahon, T. A. (1973). Lognormal streamflow generation models re-examined. *J. Hydraul. Div., Am. Soc. Civ. Eng.*, **99** (HY9), 1421–31

Crosby, D. S., and Maddock, T., III (1970). Estimating coefficients of a flow generator from monotone samples of data. *Water Resour. Res.*, **6**, 1079–86

Davies, N., Triggs, C. M., and Newbold, P. (1977). Significance levels of the Box–Pierce portmanteau statistic in finite samples. *Biometrika*, **64**, 517–22

Delleur, J. W., Tao, P. C., and Kavvas, M. L. (1976). An evaluation of the practicality and complexity of some rainfall and runoff time series models. *Water Resour. Res.*, **12**, 953–70

Doi, K. (1978). Physical reality of shot noise model for the short-term variability of cyg X-1. *Nature (London)*, **275**, 197–8

Dooge, J. C. I. (1972). Mathematical models of hydrologic systems. *Modelling of Water Resource Systems*, vol 1 (ed. A. K. Biswas), Harvest House, Montreal, pp. 170–88

Duong, N., Winn, C. B., and Johnson, G. R. (1975). Modern control concepts in hydrology. *IEEE Trans. Syst. Manage. Cybern.*, **5**, 46–53

Durbin, J. (1960). The fitting of time-series models. *Rev. Int. Statist. Inst.*, **28**, 233–44

Ekern, S. (1976). Forecasting with adaptive filtering: a critical re-examination. *Oper. Res. Q.*, **27**, 705–15

Fiering, M. B. (1964). Multivariate technique for synthetic hydrology. *J. Hydraul. Div., Am. Soc. Civ. Eng.*, **90** (HY5), 43–60

—— (1967). *Streamflow Synthesis*, Macmillan, London

—— (1968). Schemes for handling inconsistent matrices. *Water Resour. Res.*, **4**, 291–7

Gelb, A. (ed.) (1974). *Applied Optimal Estimation*, Massachusetts Institute of Technology Press, Cambridge, Massachusetts

Granger, C. W. J., and Morris, M. J. (1976). Time series modelling and interpretation. *J. R. Statist. Soc. A*, **139**, 246–57

Green, N. M. D. (1973). A synthetic model for daily streamflow. *J. Hydrol.*, **20**, 351–64

Gupta, V. L., and Fordham, J. W. (1972). Streamflow synthesis—a case study. *J. Hydraul. Div., Am. Soc. Civ. Eng.*, **98** (HY6), 1049–55

Hamlin, M. J., and Kottegoda, N. T. (1971). Extending the record of the Teme. *J. Hydrol.*, **12**, 100–16

—— (1974). The preparation of a data set for hydrological system analysis. *Design of Water Resources Projects with Inadequate Data*, vol. 1, *Symposium, Madrid*, 1973, *Int. Assoc. Sci. Hydrol. Publ.*, No. 108, pp. 163–77

Hamlin, M. J., Kottegoda, N. T., and Kitson, T. (1976). Control of a river system with two reservoirs. 1974 *Symposium on the Control of Water Resource Systems, Haiffa, Israel, J. Hydrol.*, **28**, 155–73

Harrison, P. J., and Stevens, C. F. (1976). Bayesian forecasting. *J. R. Statist. Soc. B*, **38**, 205–47

Hinkley, D. (1977). On quick choice of power transformation. *Appl. Statist.*, **26**, 67–9

Hipel, K. W., McLeod, A. I., and Lennox, W. C. (1977). Advances in Box–Jenkins modelling, 1, model construction. *Water Resour. Res.*, **13**, 567–75

Hovanessian, S. A. (1976). *Computational Mathematics in Engineering*, Lexington Books, Lexington, Massachusetts

Jazwinski, A. H. (1969). Adaptive filtering. *Automatica*, **5**, 475–85

—— (1970). *Stochastic Processes and Filtering Theory*, Academic Press, New York

Jenkins, R. H., and Watts, D. G. (1968). *Spectral Analysis and its Applications*, Holden Day, San Francisco, California

Jettmar, R. U., and Young, G. K. (1975). Hydrologic estimation and economic regret. *Water. Resour. Res.*, **11**, 648–56

Kahan, J. P. (1974). A method for maintaining cross and serial correlations and the coefficient of skewness under generation in the linear bivariate regression model. *Water Resour. Res.*, **10**, 1245–8

Kalman, R. E. (1960). A new approach to linear filtering and prediction problems. *J. Basic Eng., Trans. Am. Soc. Mech. Eng. D*, **82**, 35–45

Kalman, R. E., and Bucy, R. S. (1961). New results in linear filtering and prediction theory. *J. Basic Eng., Trans. Am. Soc. Mech. Eng. D*, **83**, 95–108

Kendall, M. G. (1976). *Time Series*, 2nd edn, Griffin, London

Kottegoda, N. T. (1970). Statistical methods of river flow synthesis for water resources assessment, with discussion. *Proc. Inst. Civ.·Eng.*, paper 7339S, suppl. XVIII, 415–42

—— (1972). Stochastic five daily stream flow model. *J. Hydraul. Div., Am. Soc. Civ. Eng.*, **98** (HY9), 1469–85

Kottegoda, N. T., and Elgy, J. (1977). Infilling missing flow data. *Proceedings of the 3rd International Hydrology Symposium, Fort Collins, Colorado*, preprints

Kottegoda, N. T., and Yevjevich, V. (1977). Preservation of correlation in generated hydrologic samples through two-station models. *J. Hydrol.*, **33**, 99–121

Lawrance, A. J. (1976). A reconsideration of the Fiering two-station model. *J. Hydrol.*, **29**, 77–85

Lawrance, A. J., and Kottegoda, N. T. (1977). Stochastic modelling of riverflow time series, with discussion. *J. R. Statist. Soc. A*, **140**, 1–47

Ledolter, J. (1978). The analysis of multivariate time series applied to problems in hydrology. *J. Hydrol.*, **36**, 327–52

Lettenmaier, D. P., and Burges, S. J. (1976). Use of state estimation techniques in water resource system modelling. *Water Resour. Bull.*, **12**, 83–99. (1977). Discussion. *Water Resour. Bull.*, **13**, 161–7, 1289–91

McClave, J. T. (1978). Estimating the order of autoregressive models: the max χ^2 method. *J. Am. Statist. Assoc.* **73**, 122–8

McGregor, J. R. (1962). The approximate distribution of the correlation between two stationary linear Markov series. *Biometrika*, **49**, 379–88

McKerchar, A. I., and Delleur, J. W. (1974). Application of seasonal parametric linear stochastic models to monthly flow data. *Water Resour. Res.*, **10**, 246–55

McMichael, F. C., and Hunter, J. S. (1972). Stochastic modelling of temperature and flow in rivers. *Water Resour. Res.*, **8**, 87–98

Maissis, A. H. (1977). Optimal filtering techniques for hydrological forecasting. *J. Hydrol.*, **33**, 319–30

Makhoul, J. (1975). Linear prediction: a tutorial review. *Proc. IEEE*, **63**, 561–80

Mandelbrot, B. B. (1976). Note on the definition and the stationarity of fractional gaussian noise. *J. Hydrol.*, **30**, 407–9

Markov, A. A. (1907). Investigation of a noteworthy case of dependent trials. *Izvestiya Rossiiskoi Akademii Nauk*, **1**

Marriott, F. H. C., and Pope, J. A. (1954). Bias in the estimation of autocorrelations. *Biometrika*, **41**, 390–402

Matalas, N. C. (1967). Mathematical assessment of synthetic hydrology. *Water Resour. Res.*, **3**, 937–45

Mejía, J. M., and Rodríguez-Iturbe, I. R. (1974). Correlation links between normal and log normal processes. *Water Resour. Res.*, **10**, 689–90

Mejía, J. M., and Rousselle, J. (1976). Disaggregration models in hydrology revisited. *Water Resour. Res.*, **12**, 185–6

Moran, P. A. P. (1970). Simulation and evaluation of complex water systems operations. *Water Resour. Res.*, **6**, 1737–42

Moss, M. E. (1972). Reduction of uncertainties in autocorrelation by the use of physical models. *Proceedings of the International Symposium on Uncertainties in Hydrologic and Water Resource Systems*, vol. 1, 11–14 December 1972, *University of Arizona, Tucson*, pp. 203–29

Nelson, C. R. (1976). The interpretation of R^2 in autoregressive moving average time series models. *Am. Statist.*, **30**, 175–80

O'Donnell, T., Hall, M. J., and O'Connell, P. E. (1972). Some applications of stochastic hydrological models. *Modelling of Water Resource Systems*, vol. 1 (ed. A. K. Biswas), Harvest House, Montreal, pp. 250–62

Parzen, E. (1962). *Stochastic Processes*, Holden Day, San Francisco, California

Payne, K., Neuman, W. R., and Kerri, K. D. (1969). Daily streamflow simulation. *J. Hydraul. Div., Am. Soc. Civ. Eng.*, **95** (HY4), 1163–79

Pegram, G. G. S., and James, W. (1972). Multilag multivariate autoregressive model for the generation of operational hydrology. *Water Resour. Res.*, **8**, 1074–6

Phatarfod, R. M. (1976). Some aspects of stochastic reservoir theory. *J. Hydrol.*, **30**, 199–217

Quenouille, M. H. (1949). Approximate tests of correlation in time series. *J. R. Statist. Soc. B*, **11**, 68–84

—— (1956). Notes on bias in estimation. *Biometrika*, **43**, 353–60

—— (1957). *The Analysis of Multiple Time Series*, Statistical Monographs No. 1, Griffin, London

Quimpo, R. G. (1968). Stochastic analysis of daily riverflows. *J. Hydraul. Div., Am. Soc. Civ. Eng.*, **94** (HY1), 43–57

Rao, R. A., and Kashyap, R. L. (1974). Stochastic difference equation modelling of hydrologic processes. *Proceedings of the 1971 Warsaw Symposium on Mathematical Models in Hydrology*, vol. 1, International Association of Scientific Hydrology, Paris, pp. 140–50

Roesner, L. A., and Yevjevich, V. M. (1966). Mathematical models for time series of monthly precipitation and monthly runoff. *Colo. St. Univ., Fort Collins, Hydrol. Papers*, No. 15

Salas, J. D., and Pegram, G. G. S. (1977). A seasonal multivariate multilag autoregressive model in hydrology. *Proceedings of the 3rd International Hydrology Symposium, Fort Collins, Colorado*, preprints

Sorenson, H. W. (1968). Controllability and observability of linear, stochastic, time-discrete control systems. *Adv. Control Syst.*, **6**, 95–158

—— (1970). Least squares estimation: from Gauss to Kalman. *IEEE Spectrum*, **7**, 63–8

Swerling, P. (1959). A proposed stagewise differential correction procedure for satellite tracking and prediction, *J. Astronaut. Sci.*, **6**; *Rand Corp., Santa Monica, Calif., Rep.*, No. P-1292

Szöllösi-Nagy, A. (1975). An adaptive identification and prediction algorithm for the real-time forecasting of hydrologic time series. *Proceedings of the International Symposium and Workshop on the Application of Mathematical Models in Hydrology and Water Resource Systems*, International Association of Scientific Hydrology, Bratislava, preprints

—— (1976). An adaptive identification and prediction algorithm for the real-time forecasting of hydrological time series. *Hydrol. Sci. Bull.*, **21**, 163–76

Thomas, H. A., and Fiering, M. B. (1962). Mathematical synthesis of streamflow sequences for the analysis of river basins by simulation. *Design of Water Resource Systems* (eds A. Maass *et al.*), Harvard University Press, Cambridge, Massachusetts, chapter 12, pp. 459–93

Thompson, H. E., and Tiao, G. C. (1971). Analysis of telephone data: a case study of forecasting seasonal time series. *Bell J. Econ. Manage. Sci.*, **2**, 515–41

Tillotson, A., and Cluckie, I. D. (1977). Linear models for flow estimation and prediction. *Proceedings of the 3rd International Hydrology Symposium, Fort Collins, Colorado*, preprints

Todini, E., and Bouillot, D. (1976). A rainfall run-off Kalman filter model. *System Simulation in Water Resources* (ed. G. C. Vansteenkiste), North-Holland, Amsterdam

Toyoda, J., Toriumi, N., and Inoue, Y. (1969). An adaptive predictor of river flow for on line control of water resource systems. *Automatica*, **4**, 175–81

Treiber, B., and Plate, E. J. (1975). A stochastic model for the simulation of daily flows. *Proceedings of the International Symposium and Workshop on the Application of Mathematical Models in Hydrology and Water Resource Systems*, International Association of Scientific Hydrology, Bratislava, preprints

Valencia, R. D., and Schaake, J. C., Jr. (1973). Disaggregation processes in stochastic hydrology. *Water Resour. Res.*, **9**, 580–5

Walker, Sir Gilbert (1931). On periodicity in series of related terms. *Proc. R. Soc. London A*, **131**, 518–32

Weiss, G. (1977). Shot noise models for synthetic generation of multisite daily streamflow data. *Water Resour. Res.*, **13**, 101–8

Wheelwright, S. C., and Makridakis, S. (1973). An examination of the use of adaptive filtering in forecasting. *Oper. Res. Q.*, **24**, 55–64

—— (1977). *Forecasting Methods for Management*, 2nd edn, Wiley, New York

Wiener, N. (1949). *The Extrapolation, Interpolation and Smoothing of Stationary Time Series*, Wiley, New York

Wold, H. (1954). *A Study in the Analysis of Stationary Time Series*, 2nd edn,

Almqvist and Wiksell, Stockholm

Yakowitz, S. J. (1973). A stochastic model for daily river flows in an arid region. *Water Resour. Res.*, **9**, 1271–85

Yevjevich, V. M. (1963). Fluctuations of wet and dry years, part I, research data assembly and mathematical models. *Colo. St. Univ., Fort Collins, Hydrol. Papers*, No. 1

—— (1966). Stochastic problems in the design of reservoirs. *Water Research* (eds A. V. Kneese and S. C. Smith), John Hopkins Press, Baltimore, pp. 375–411.

—— (1972). Structural analysis of hydrologic time series, *Colo. St. Univ., Fort Collins, Hydrol. Papers*, No. 56

Young, G. K. (1968). Discussion of 'Mathematical assessment of synthetic hydrology' by N. C. Matalas. *Water Resour. Res.*, **4**, 681–3

Young, G. K., and Pisano, W. C. (1968). Operational hydrology using residuals. *J. Hydraul. Div., Am. Soc. Civ. Eng.*, **94** (HY4), 909–23

Young, P. (1974). Recursive approaches to time series analysis. *J. Inst. Math. Its Appl.*, **10**, 209–29

Yule, G. U. (1921). On the time correlation problem with special preference to the variate-difference correlation method. *J. R. Statist. Soc.*, **84**, 497–537

—— (1927). On a method of investigating periodicities in disturbed series, with special reference to Wolfer's sunspot numbers. *Philos. Trans. A*, **226**, 267–98

5 Special properties and models

This chapter concerns properties of special significance in hydrology. In the general class of crossing properties, theoretical aspects of runs, run lengths and sums are explained, and their practical relevance is discussed. Reservoir storage analysis which follows includes the Rippl diagram and the concepts of deficit and range. In this context the Hurst phenomenon, which has been an important subject of research and some controversy within the hydrological world and outside, is described, and the associated theoretical treatment of the rescaled range is taken up. Fractional gaussian processes which maintain the Hurst effect over very long time spans are explained. The final sections pertain to models that generate fractional noise and the broken-line model which is outlined. To aid the practitioner, some computer subroutines are provided.

5.1 Runs and crossing properties

There does not appear to be a universally accepted method of defining droughts in hydrometeorology. However, one criterion which has practical significance pertains to the deficits with respect to (or excursions below) a specified level or rate of flow in a river. The duration of a deficit is known as a run length. In general, a run is defined as a sequence of observations of the same kind preceded and succeeded by one or more observations of a different kind[1]. Corresponding to the run length, the magnitude of the deficit is known as a run sum. Such characteristics of a time series belong to a general class called crossing properties.

To explain these specifically, consider the crossing level u in figure 5.1 which shows a section $(0, T)$ of a stationary discrete time series ξ_t with zero mean and variance σ_ξ^2. Downcrossings of this level occur at times B and I because the flows at these times are less than u, whereas flows at the antecedent times A and H respectively are greater than u. The corresponding deficit run lengths are ℓ_1 and

---

[1] See Mood (1940).

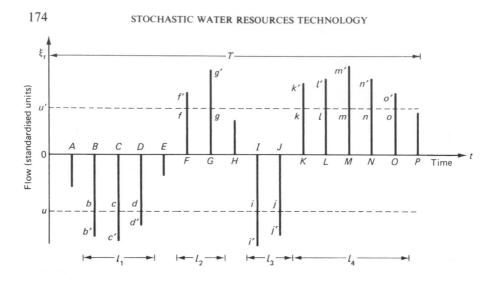

Figure 5.1   Crossing properties of a discrete time series; deficit run lengths ℓ_1, ℓ_3 at level u; surplus run lengths ℓ_2, ℓ_4 at level u'; downcrossings of level u at B and I with deficit run sums $bb' + cc' + dd'$ and $ii' + jj'$ respectively; upcrossings of level u' at F and K with surplus run sums $f'f + g'g$ and $k'k + \ell'\ell + m'm + n'n + o'o$ respectively

ℓ_3. Also, the quantities $bb' + cc' + dd'$ and $ii' + jj'$ are known as the deficit run sums.

Here, u can represent the level in a river which should be maintained in order to meet water supply demands. Alternatively, u may be relevant to the minimum rate of flow required for pollution control. Again it could be the lowest acceptable level for navigation purposes. Then the deficit run sums represent the quantities that need to be released, for example, from a regulating reservoir. Furthermore, the design and operation of hydroelectric schemes and the sizing of pumps are related to crossings and run sums.

Likewise, the durations and magnitudes of flows above a fixed high level such as u' in figure 5.1, known as the surplus run lengths and the sums with respect to this level, are of importance for flood control purposes. In the case shown, upcrossings of level u' occur at times F and K, and the surplus run lengths are ℓ_2 and ℓ_4. The run sums, given by $f'f + g'g$, $k'k + \ell'\ell + m'm + n'n + o'o$ and so on, can be regarded as the storage reservation that needs to be made in a reservoir for the abatement of floods downstream.

Numbers of level crossings too have an important physical relevance. The analysis of rare floods and, in general, the theory of extreme values, dealt with in the next chapter, are relevant to the crossings of levels remote from the mean. In addition, the mean number of crossings which characterise a time series are of interest to river engineers. They also provide a check on the credibility of a stochastic model when generated data are examined. In general, the number of crossings at various levels, as well as the mean run lengths and sums, are useful criteria in the analysis of time series.

5.1.1 *Theoretical aspects*

The theory of crossings probably began with the work of Rice (1945). He showed that the expectation of the number of downcrossings of a level u (which is equal to the expectation of the number of upcrossings of the same level) of a stationary normal stochastic process ξ_t with zero mean and variance σ_ξ^2 in an interval $0 \leqslant t \leqslant T$ is given by

$$E\{N_T^-(u)\} = T(2\pi)^{-1}(\lambda_2/\sigma_\xi^2)^{1/2} \exp(-u^2/2\sigma_\xi^2) \tag{5.1}$$

in which λ_2 is the second moment of the spectral density function $f(\omega)$, where ω is the frequency in cycles per unit time; in general,

$$\lambda_r = \int_0^\infty \omega^r f(\omega)d\omega$$

Also, if $C''(0)$ is the second derivative of the covariance function at the origin,

$$\lambda_2 = -C''(0) \tag{5.2}$$

It follows that, for the mean level $(u = 0)$, $E\{N_T^-(0)\} = T(2\pi)^{-1}$ $\{-C''(0)/\sigma_\xi^2\}^{1/2}$ in this way, the mean number of crossings of the zero level characterises a particular time series.

The applicability of equations such as equation 5.1 is unfortunately limited because of the fundamental non-normal nature of hydrologic time series, as explained in chapter 3. Another apparent disadvantage is that practical investigations are made in discrete time[2].

If we consider again the discrete case shown in figure 5.1, let $L^-(u)$ and $S^-(u)$ denote a deficit run length and deficit run sum, respectively, in the interval $(0, T)$, where T is large. As before, $N_T^-(u)$ denotes the number of downcrossings in $(0, T)$; this is also the number of deficit runs in the same interval. If $\Pr(\xi_{t-1} > u, \xi_t < u)$ is the probability of a downcrossing at time t, the expected number of downcrossings (or upcrossings) in $(0, T)$ is

$$E\{N_T^-(u)\} = \Pr(\xi_{t-1} > u, \xi_t < u)T \tag{5.3}$$

For a discrete time series we can give the expected values of the deficit run length and the deficit run sum as follows.

$$E\{L^-(u)\} = \Pr(\xi_t < u)/\Pr(\xi_{t-1} > u, \xi_t < u) \tag{5.4}$$

and

$$E\{S^-(u)\} = E\{L^-(u)\} \, E(u - \xi_t | \xi_t < u) \tag{5.5}$$

[2] Cramér and Leadbetter (1967) have extended the theory to run lengths and sums, whereas Tick and Shaman (1966) consider aspects which are not necessarily normal. See also the review of the literature given by Leadbetter (1972). In application, Rodríguez-Iturbe (1969) adopted the continuous gaussian theory to the 150-year sequence of annual flows in the Rhine at Basle and found close agreement between the observed and theoretically expected values of crossings, run lengths and sums. Later, Nordin and Rosbjerg (1970) studied 12 annual river-flow sequences from North America, Asia and Europe.

where the vertical line means conditional to the inequality on the right.

A programme for computing the numbers of crossings, run lengths and sums is given in figure 5.2. One purpose this can serve is for comparing crossing properties in generated and historical data as a means of testing the validity of postulated models; the usefulness of such a procedure derives from the versatility of crossing properties. The results from the application of an AR(1) model, given by $\xi_t = \rho_1 \xi_{t-1} + \eta_t$, to 5-day data are shown in figure 5.3. The

```
      SUBROUTINE CROSS (R,NM,BM,STD)
      DIMENSION R(2000),Q(7),NX(7),JX(7),SX(7)
C
C   AT LOW CROSSING LEVELS Q(K),K=1,2,....,6, EQUAL TO BM-STD(K-1)/2 WHERE
C   BM AND STD ARE MEAN AND STANDARD DEVIATION, SUBROUTINE FINDS NUMBER
C   L=NX(K) OF DOWNCROSSINGS, TOTAL DEFICIT RUN LENGTHS JJ=JX(K) AND
C   TOTAL DEFICIT RUN SUMS SS=SX(K) IN SEQUENCE R(N), N=1,2,....,NM. TO
C   FIND UPCROSSINGS,SURPLUS RUN LENGTHS AND SUMS AT HIGH CROSSING LEVELS
C   CHANGE FOLLOWING:- Q(K)=BM+STD*FLOAT(K-1)/2.0; 2 IF(R(N)-Q(K)) 1,1,3;
C   3 IF(R(N-1)-Q(K)) 4,1,1;
C   9 FORMAT(1H0,51H  UP CROSSINGS   TOTAL SURPLUS RUN LENGTHS AND SUMS).
C
      DO 8 K=1,6
      Q(K)=BM+STD*FLOAT(1-K)/2.0
      L=0
      N=1
      SS=0.0
      JJ=0
1     S=0.0
      J=0
      N=N+1
      IF(N-NM) 2,2,7
2     IF(R(N)-Q(K)) 3,1,1
3     IF(R(N-1)-Q(K)) 1,1,4
4     J=J+1
      S=S+Q(K)-R(N)
      N=N+1
      IF(N-NM) 5,5,7
5     IF(Q(K)-R(N)) 6,6,4
6     L=L+1
      JJ=JJ+J
      SS=SS+S
      GO TO 1
7     NX(K)=L
      JX(K)=JJ
8     SX(K)=SS
      WRITE(6,9)
9     FORMAT(1H0,51H DOWN CROSSINGS   TOTAL DEFICIT RUN LENGTHS AND SUMS)
      WRITE(6,10) (Q(K),K=1,6)
      WRITE(6,11) (NX(K),K=1,6)
      WRITE(6,12) (JX(K),K=1,6)
      WRITE(6,13) (SX(K),K=1,6)
10    FORMAT(6H  FLOW,20X,6F15.2)
11    FORMAT(11H  CROSSINGS,15X,6I15)
12    FORMAT(18H  TOTAL RUN LENGTH,8X,6I15)
13    FORMAT(15H  TOTAL RUN SUM,11X,6F15.2)
      RETURN
      END
```

Figure 5.2   FORTRAN subroutine to evaluate empirical crossing properties in a discrete sequence

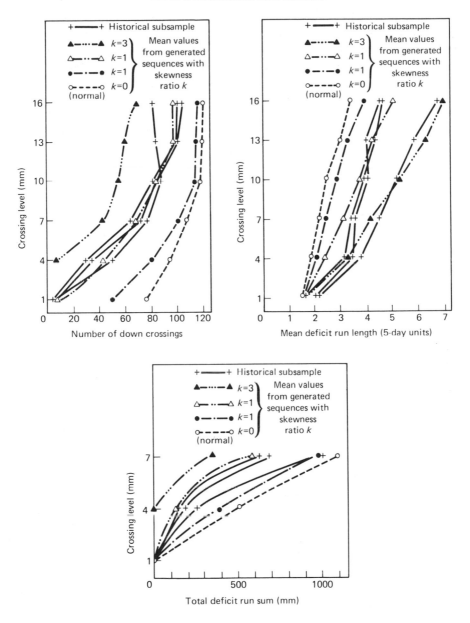

Figure 5.3 Crossing properties of 5-day flows in Irfon at Abernant, Wales, and data generated with AR(1) (Markov) model: catchment area, 33 km; historical mean, 18.6 mm; variance, 349 mm; skewness, 1.87; 11-year subsamples from 33-year record. Data generated using $X_{t,\tau} = \mu_\tau + \sigma_\tau \rho_1 (X_{t-1,\tau-1} - \mu_{\tau-1})/\sigma_{\tau-1} + \sigma_\tau (1 - \rho_1^2)^{1/2} \varepsilon_t$, where μ_t, σ_τ^2, are seasonal means and variances respectively for $\tau = 1, 2, \ldots, 73$, ρ_1 is the lag-one autocorrelation coefficient of standardised flows $E(\varepsilon_\tau) = E(\varepsilon_t \varepsilon_{t-1}) = 0$; var $(\varepsilon_t) = 1$ and $E\{(\varepsilon_t - \mu)^3\} = k\gamma_1$, $k = 0, 1, 2, 3$, where $\gamma_1 = E\{(X_{t,\tau} - \mu_X)^3\} \{\text{var}(X_{t,\tau})\}^{3/2}$

method of preserving skewness which is given in subsection 4.6.1 is relevant in this context. However, in this particular study the skewness applied to the random component η_t is in turn made equal to 0, γ_ξ, $2\gamma_\xi$ and $3\gamma_\xi$, where γ_ξ is the coefficient of skewness in the stochastic component, the sample estimate of which is 1.87 in this case. The investigation shows that crossing properties are oversensitive to the coefficient of skewness maintained in the model. It is seen that increasing the skewness results in an increase in the run lengths but in a decrease in the run sums and crossings. Of special interest is the minimum skewness that needs to be applied in a model to eliminate the generation of negative values (with subzero crossing levels)[3].

5.1.2 Some properties of independent discrete series

Consider an independent and identically distributed discrete series $X_t, t = 1, 2, 3, \ldots$, which represents, say, the total precipitation at a particular site during the tth year. Let $F(x)$ denote the common distribution function of the X_t series. Also, let $q = F(u) = \Pr(X \leqslant u)$, where u is a crossing level and $p = 1 - q$. Then, if $+1$ and -1 signify that X_t is greater than (or equal to) u and less than u respectively, the probability distribution of surplus run lengths is given by

$$\Pr(L^+ = \ell) = \Pr(X_{i+2} = X_{i+3} = \ldots = X_{i+\ell} = 1, X_{i+\ell+1} = -1 \mid X_i$$
$$= -1, X_{i+1} = 1)$$
$$= p^\ell q^2 / pq = p^{\ell-1} q \tag{5.6}$$

for $\ell = 1, 2, 3, \ldots$, which is a geometric distribution. Also it can be shown that the expected value and variance of surplus run lengths is

$$E(L^+) = 1/q, \qquad \text{var}(L^+) = p/q^2 \tag{5.7}$$

Note that for deficit run lengths L^- the probabilities p and q should be interchanged in equations 5.6 and 5.7. A useful outcome is that the mean run length is equal to 2 if the median value, for which $p = q = 0.5$, is taken as the crossing level.

An alternative way to estimate runs is to condition them on the number of X values which are represented by $+1$ or -1. The expected total number and variance of runs $N = N_i^+ + N_i^-$ are then given by

$$E(N) = 1 + 2nm/(n+m)$$
$$\text{var}(N) = 2nm(2nm - n - m)/\{(n+m)^2(n+m-1)\} \tag{5.8}$$

where n and m represent the numbers of values above and below the chosen crossing level, respectively[4].

If long runs are observed in a given sequence, which is the same as having only

---

[3] These results are from Kottegoda (1974).
[4] See Fraser (1976, pp. 569, 570). Simplified proofs are given by Brunk (1965, pp. 359, 360).

a few runs, it indicates some type of grouping due to a serial correlation, to a periodic movement or perhaps to a trend. In fact, a runs test can be formulated to test for independence on the basis of equation 5.8. The significance test is made on the assumption that N is normally distributed, the null hypothesis being that the sequence is independent. This is supplementary to the tests on time series given in chapter 2 and is included here in the general context of crossing properties.

Example 5.1   Annual flows in the Danube at Orsova, Romania, for the period 1837 to 1886 and in the St Lawrence for the period 1860 to 1909 are tabulated below. They are taken from longer sequences that are reduced to unit mean as tabulated by Yevjevich (1963). The estimated median values are 0.976 and 1.017 respectively, and values above the median are underlined.

Annual flows in Danube

1.178	1.222	0.844	1.000	0.796	1.092	1.094	1.315	1.122	1.109
0.954	0.892	1.092	1.135	1.142	1.396	0.813	1.152	0.846	0.809
0.732	0.913	1.161	0.984	0.773	0.604	0.876	0.948	0.641	1.030
0.969	0.833	1.079	1.295	0.891	0.932	0.768	0.807	1.241	1.124
0.986	1.461	0.939	1.246	0.799	1.220	0.904	0.831	1.000	0.796

Annual flows in St Lawrence

1.142	1.179	1.134	1.104	1.104	1.021	1.129	1.005	1.034	1.158
1.075	0.930	0.984	1.084	0.959	1.092	1.046	1.046	1.075	1.013
0.963	1.063	1.042	1.121	1.050	1.154	1.117	1.001	1.021	1.088
1.075	0.951	1.005	1.005	0.897	0.884	0.905	0.947	0.947	0.938
0.942	0.947	1.005	1.013	0.988	1.001	1.013	1.088	1.000	0.959

If j represents the observed number of runs with respect to the median, determine whether the sequences are independent.

Substituting $n = m = 25$ in equation 5.8, we find that $E(N) = 26$ and $\mathrm{var}(N) = 12.24$. Therefore, j can be given in standard units as $z = (u - 26)/(12.24)^{1/2}$. For the Danube data, $j = 24$ and hence $z = -2/(12.24)^{1/2} = -0.57$. Because $-1.96 < z < 1.96$ the hypothesis of independence is not rejected. However, for the St Lawrence data, $j = 14$ and $z = -12/(12.24)^{1/2} = -3.43$. Therefore, the hypothesis of independence is rejected, which confirms the information given in figure 4.4.

This is a faster method of testing for independence than the serial correlogram tests given in chapters 2 and 4, but all run tests have low power, in a relative sense[5]. Nevertheless, it can be used for preliminary work and for comparative purposes as shown here.

5.1.3 Runs in hydrology: references to other works

Run sums of independent normal variates were determined analytically by Downer et al. (1967). Subsequently, Llamas and Siddiqui (1969) extended the theory of run lengths and run sums to independent gamma variates. For a Markov process, the approximate distributions of run lengths were found by Saldarriaga and Yevjevich (1970); later, Sen (1976) presented an exact method. Again, Millan (1972) obtained the conditional distribution of the longest run lengths in a finite sample of a Markov process. More recently, Guerrero–Salazar and Yevjevich (1975) investigated the largest run sums in a finite sequence and the longest run lengths and run sums in the bivariate case of two concurrent sequences. In the more complicated cases (such as in mutually dependent and serially correlated series) data generation methods were used, seasonal components being initially removed for monthly time series. Of particular relevance in this context is the combinational analysis of David and Barton (1962) and the work of Cramér (1946), of Cox and Miller (1965) and of Feller (1968); Fisz (1963, chapter 11) outlines the theory of runs.

5.2 Rippl diagram and reservoir storage

The systematic approach to reservoir design dates back to the work of Rippl (1883) an Austrian engineer. The commonly used method for studying reservoir behaviour known as the Rippl or mass diagram. Basically, this is a time plot of cumulative inflows to a reservoir formed from an observed sequence. For example, if $x_1, x_2, \ldots, x_N$ denote a historical record at unit intervals of time, the ordinates of the mass diagram are given by

$$S_t = \sum_{i=1}^{t} x_i, \qquad t = 1, 2, \ldots, N \tag{5.9}$$

Let $\bar{x}_N = S_N/N$. Also, let the withdrawal rate from the reservoir be constant and equal to $\alpha \bar{x}_N$ per unit time. The factor α where $0 < \alpha < 1$ is introduced on account of evaporation and seepage losses from the reservoir and is known as the degree of development or draft rate. Only constant withdrawal rates are considered here, but the theory can be easily modified to cope with seasonal variations in α when using monthly data, say.

In order to determine, by means of a mass diagram, the capacity of a reservoir required to supply $\alpha \bar{x}_N$ per unit time, the first step is to determine the minimum j

---

[5] Wallis and Matalas (1971) give some empirical results. As explained in chapter 3, if β is the type II error, that is, the probability of accepting a hypothesis when it should be rejected, the power is $1 - \beta$.

which satisfies the constraint.

$$x_j \geqslant \alpha \bar{x}_N > x_{j+1}, \qquad j = 1, 2, \ldots, N-1 \tag{5.10}$$

Suppose this corresponds to time $j = k_1$, the following two computations are made.

(i) The length ℓ_1 of depletion period during which the reservoir level is throughout below the level at time k_1; ℓ_1 is the maximum ℓ for which the following constraint is satisfied.

$$\alpha \bar{x}_N \ell - \sum_{i=1}^{\ell} x_{k_1+i} \geqslant 0 \tag{5.11}$$

This means that at time $k_1 + \ell_1 + 1$, the reservoir is at or above the level at time k_1.

(ii) The deficit

$$d_1 = \max_{1 \leqslant m \leqslant \ell_1} \left(\alpha \bar{x} m - \sum_{i=1}^{m} x_{k_1+i} \right) \tag{5.12}$$

Let the value of m which maximises equation 5.12 be m_1. In order to find the next local maximum $j = k_2$, after time $\ell_1 + k_1$, the constraint 5.10 is now applied for times $j = k_1 + \ell_1 + 1, k_1 + \ell_1 + 2, k_1 + \ell_1 + 3, \ldots, N-1$, until satisfied. Then by using equation 5.11, ℓ_2 is found, and equation 5.12 gives d_2 and m_2. After this procedure is repeated for the entire sequence, the following statistics are evaluated. The maximum deficit is given by

$$d_{max}^{(\alpha)} = \max(d_i), \qquad i = 1, 2, 3, \ldots$$

for a withdrawal rate $\alpha \bar{x}$. Let

$$d_{max}^{(\alpha)} = d_j, \text{ say}$$

with a duration $m_{max} = m_j$. The length of longest depletion is given by

$$\ell_{max}^{(\alpha)} = \max(\ell_i), \qquad i = 1, 2, 3, \ldots$$

for a withdrawal rate $\alpha \bar{x}$.

The main design requirement here is the maximum deficit $d_{max}^{(\alpha)}$ which is the minimum reservoir capacity required to supply $\alpha \bar{x}$ per unit time. Of additional interest is the length $\ell_{max}^{(\alpha)}$ of the longest depletion.

To illustrate the use of the Rippl diagram, annual flows in the Niger, reduced to unit mean, are examined in figure 5.4; the gauging station is at Koulikoro, some 60 miles downstream of Bamako in Mali, Africa. Computations show that, for example, $d_{max}^{(0.85)} = 0.67$ and $\ell_{max}^{(0.85)} = 12$. A listing of a subroutine which can be used for the purpose is given in figure 5.5; this also takes into account any depletions at the commencement or end of a sequence. Note that the initial reservoir storage does not enter the computations.

A sequence of low values before the commencement of a record or successive high values after the end of it could effect the results, but we cannot verify this

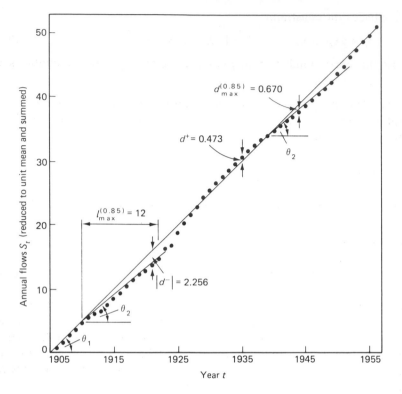

Figure 5.4 Rippl diagram for annual flows in Niger at Koulikoro, Mali, Africa, for the period 1906 to 1956: $S_t = \sum\limits_{i=1}^{t} x_i, x_i = 1, 2, \ldots, x_N$; sample mean $\bar{x} = S_N/N = \tan\theta_1$. For withdrawal rate $\alpha\bar{x} = \tan\theta_2, \alpha = 0.85$, $d_{max}^{(\alpha)}$ is the maximum deficit and $\ell_{max}^{(\alpha)}$ is the length of longest depletion d_N^+ and d_N^- are maximum and minimum accumulated departures from mean; adjusted range $r_N^* = d_N^* + |d_N^-|$

Annual flow (reduced to unit mean and summed)

0.732	1.521	2.791	3.594	4.637	5.483	6.012	6.617	7.517	8.409
9.366	10.401	11.303	12.106	12.783	13.744	14.752	16.179	17.708	18.799
20.075	21.476	22.817	24.128	25.260	26.411	27.468	28.417	29.353	30.473
31.305	32.261	33.144	33.905	34.709	35.354	36.126	36.772	37.574	38.570
39.387	40.472	41.371	42.351	43.736	44.796	46.076	47.428	48.761	49.644
50·999									

because the sample is limited. That is to say, if additional data were available, the answers might be different. In the mass curve analysis known as the sequent peak algorithm an attempt is made to resolve the problem by supposing that the historical data repeats itself; only two such periods are required for the

```
      SUBROUTINE DEFCIT(R,NM,BM,IY,KK)
      DIMENSION R(2000),Q(7),RS(7),IS(7),IL(7),JL(7),JS(7)
C
C     FOR WITHDRAWAL RATES Q(K)=BM(21-K)/20,K=1,2,....,7, WHERE BM=MEAN SUB-
C     ROUTINE FINDS MAXIMUM DEEICITS RS(K)=S IN SEQUENCE R(N),N=1,2,...,NM,
C     WHERE R(1) OCCURS AT TIME IY. IT ALSO FINDS COMMENCING YEARS IS(K)
C     AND DURATIONS IL(K)=M OF DEFICITS, AND LENGTHS OF LONGEST DEPLETIONS
C     JL(K)=M WITH COMMENCING YEARS JS(K).
C
      DO 8 K=1,7
      Q(K)=BM*FLOAT(21-K)/20.0
      S=0.0
      N=1
      M=0
      RS(K)=0.0
      IL(K)=0
      IS(K)=0
      JL(K)=0
      JS(K)=0
1     S=S+Q(K)-R(N)
      IF(S)6,6,2
2     M=M+1
      IF(S-RS(K)) 4,4,3
3     RS(K)=S
      IS(K)=N-M+IY
      IL(K)=M
4     IF(M-JL(K)) 7,7,5
5     JS(K)=N-M+IY
      JL(K)=M
      GO TO 7
6     S=0.0
      M=0
7     N=N+1
      IF(N-NM) 1,1,8
8     CONTINUE
      WRITE(6,9) (Q(K),K=1,7)
      WRITE(6,10) (RS(K),K=1,7)
      WRITE(6,11) (IS(K),K=1,7)
      WRITE(6,12) (IL(K),K=1,7)
      WRITE(6,13) (JL(K),K=1,7)
      WRITE(6,11) (JS(K),K=1,7)
9     FORMAT(1H0,19X,8H RELEASE,7F9.2)
10    FORMAT(1H0,11X,16H MAXIMUM DEFICIT,7F9.2)
11    FORMAT(12X,16H COMMENCING YEAR,7I9)
12    FORMAT(19X,9H DURATION,7I9)
13    FORMAT(1H0,27HLENGTH OF LONGEST DEPLETION,7I9)
      RETURN
      END
```

Figure 5.5   FORTRAN subroutine to compute maximum deficits and longest reservoir depletions with times of commencement and durations

calculations[6]. For the Niger data, however, results are unaltered.

The basic difference between deficits and the (deficit) run sums shown in figure 5.1 is that short-term excursions above a crossing level ($u = \alpha \bar{x}$) are allowed for in the Rippl diagram method. Note also that for a realistic

[6] This is due to H. A. Thomas, Jr., and is also explained by Fiering (1967, pp. 38–43). Similar procedures have been suggested by S. N. Kritskiy and M. F. Menkel (Klemeš,

assessment of reservoir capacity, storage volumes should be added to $d_{max}^{(\alpha)}$ to cater for minimum storage, estimated siltation, losses through evaporation and other requirements.

The main shortcoming in the methods based on the Rippl diagram is that the historical sequence of length N is assumed to recur over a future design period of length N. It is, of course, impossible to make such a N-year forecast, but one approach which attempts to tackle future uncertainties for design purposes is through range analysis.

5.3 Range analysis

Range analysis in hydrology commenced with the work of Hurst (1951, 1956) who found heuristically an approximate relationship between the rescaled range (defined below) and the sample size. His studies were based on about 800 sequences of hydrological and geophysical data from various parts of the world. These included river flows, precipitation amounts, temperatures, lake levels, atmospheric pressures, growth of tree rings, sunspot numbers and thickness of deposits in lakes. Apart from natural observed sequences, Hurst *et al.* (1964) investigated numerous other variables such as the cost-of-living indices and wheat prices together with some trivial data sets. The sample sizes of the data ranged from 40 to 2000 years.

5.3.1 *Hurst phenomenon*

For an observed sequence $x_1, x_2, \ldots, x_N$, with $E(x) = \mu$, the range is defined by

$$r_N = \max\{0, \ \max_{1 \leqslant i \leqslant N} (x_1 + x_2 + \ldots + x_i - i\mu)\}$$

$$- \min\{0, \ \min_{1 \leqslant i \leqslant N} (x_1 + x_2 + \ldots + x_i - i\mu)\} \tag{5.13}$$

This is sometimes referred to as the crude range.

It is advantageous for practical purposes to calculate the difference between the maximum d_N^+ and the minimum d_N^- of the accumulated departures from the sample mean $\bar{x} = \sum_{i=1}^{N} x_i/N$. This gives the adjusted range r_N^*. Thus

$$r_N^* = \max_{1 \leqslant i \leqslant N} (x_1 + x_2 + \ldots + x_i - i\bar{x}) -$$

$$\min_{1 \leqslant i \leqslant N} (x_1 + x_2 + \ldots + x_i - i\bar{x}) \tag{5.14}$$

$$= d_N^+ + |d_N^-|$$

1978) and by Hazen (1914). On critical period analysis, see Hall *et al.* (1969). Tschannerl (1971) discusses the resulting loss in net benefits arising from inadequate sample information prior to reservoir construction. Wallis and Matalas (1972) give some experimental results from using generated data.

Note that, for $i = N$, the terms within each set of parentheses in equation 5.14 sum to 0, but this does not necessarily apply to the corresponding terms in equation 5.13; hence, we have the addition of two zeros in the equation for r_N.

The adjusted range is also shown in Figure 5.4. There are two basic differences between r_N^* and $d_{max}^{(\alpha)}$, the deficit estimated from the mass curve analysis described in section 5.2. Firstly, the degree of development α is equal to 1.0, for the range. Secondly, the minimum d_N^- can occur before d_N^+ in range analysis, whereas $d_{max}^{(\alpha)}$ is the maximum of the differences between each peak and its subsequent trough on the plot of accumulated departures from $\alpha\bar{x}$; however, this disparity does not arise if we use the sequent peak algorithm. To understand the range more clearly, consider a hypothetical situation in which the observed flow sequence is routed through a reservoir of capacity r_N^* with initial storage $|d_N^-|$ and a constant withdrawal rate $\bar{x}$ (including losses) per unit time. Under these conditions, the reservoir will be full on one or more occasions without overflowing, it will empty at least once and the withdrawal rate will be maintained throughout.

In order to compare the results from different observed sequences, the range is divided by the standard deviation s_N estimated by

$$s_N = N^{-1/2} \left\{ \sum_{i=1}^{N} (x_i - \bar{x})^2 \right\}^{1/2}$$

to give the adjusted rescaled range

$$r_N^{**} = r_N^*/s_N \tag{5.15}$$

This division by the standard deviation is a unique feature in Hurst's work. Of greater significance is the relation

$$r_N^{**} = (N/2)^K \tag{5.16}$$

where K is deemed to be constant for an observed sequence, which he established empirically. It was found that the exponent K varies from 0.46 to 0.96 with a mean of 0.73 and a standard deviation of 0.09 in the sequences which Hurst examined. For the individual groups of data analysed such as river flows we expect less variation.

Example 5.2   Flows in the Tano River in Japan have been recorded since 1918. The first ten items of annual data, from a complete data set which is reduced to unit mean, are approximated as follows: 1.1, 1.5, 1.4, 0.9, 1.7, 0.7, 1.1, 0.4, 0.8, 2.4. If the estimated standard deviation of flows is 0.58, calculate the adjusted range and hence the exponent K in Hurst's equation.

The sample mean is $\bar{x} = 1.2$ and $N = 10$.

$x_i - \bar{x}$	-0.1	0.3	0.2	-0.3	0.5	-0.5	-0.1	-0.8	-0.4	1.2
$\sum(x_i - \bar{x})$	-0.1	0.2	0.4	0.1	0.6	0.1	0	-0.8	-1.2	0

$$d_N^+ = 0.6, \qquad d_N^- = -1.2, \qquad r_N^* = 0.06 + 1.2 = 1.8$$
$$r_N^{**} = 1.8/0.58 = 3.1$$
$$K = \log(r_N^{**})/\log(N/2) = 0.70$$

(By using equation 5.13 with $\mu = 1.0$, the range (or crude range) equals 2.0.)

Hurst (1956) also derived the theoretically expected value of the adjusted range. He used some coin-tossing experiments to show that, for independent standard normal variates, the asymptotic result

$$E(R_N^*) = (\pi/2)^{1/2}N^{1/2} \approx 1.253 \times N^{1/2} \tag{5.17}$$

holds[7]. Feller (1951) gave an independent and rigorous derivation of the same result, which is applicable to stationary independent random variables with finite variance regardless of distribution. Note that the result is valid only if N is large, say, greater than 1000. He also showed that the variance of R_N^{**} is

$$\text{var}(R_N^{**}) = (\pi^2/6 - \pi/2)N$$
$$= 0.074N \tag{5.18}$$

This holds approximately for $N \geqslant 50$.

Analogous to equation 5.16, the more general form

$$E(R_N^{**}) = cN^h \tag{5.19}$$

has been adopted by Mandelbrot and Wallis (1968) and by others in which the exponent h is the *Hurst coefficient* and c is another constant[8]. It was postulated that a natural process is characterised by a population value of h; the small sample estimate of h is denoted by H. The fact that values of $H \neq 0.5$ are found in observed natural sequences whereas, for a normal independent or ARMA type process, the asymptotic value of h is 0.5 has become known as the *Hurst phenomenon*.

[7] A summary of Hurst's theoretical approach is given by Anis and Lloyd (1975).
[8] Hurst used equation 5.16 so that $E(R_N^*) = 1$ for $N = 2$ in his attempts to find the best possible fits to the data used, but this restriction may cause bias.

Figure 5.6   FORTRAN subroutine to compute values of adjusted rescaled range. (On C cards change SQ to R and interchange at STARTING TIMES and SUBSAMPLE SIZES.)

```
      SUBROUTINE ADRSN(R,NM)
      DIMENSION R(2000),RSR(15)
C
C     SUBROUTINE COMPUTES ADJUSTED RESCALED RANGE RSR(KK) IN SEQUENCE
C     SQ(N), N=1,2,...,NM, AT STARTING TIMES JS=3,4,5,7,10,20,40,70,100,
C     200,400,700,1000,2000 AND SUBSAMPLE SIZES JT=1,100,200,300,...,1400.
C
      WRITE(6,1)
1     FORMAT(//,60X,'RESCALED RANGE')
      WRITE(6,2)(JT,JT=100,1400,100)
2     FORMAT(1H0,6X,'T',6X,'1',14I7,3X,'MEAN')
      WRITE(6,3)
3     FORMAT(7X,'S')
      K=1
      JS=2
4     CONTINUE
      IF(JS.EQ.5) K=2
      IF(JS.EQ.7) K=3
      IF(JS.EQ.10) K=10
      IF(JS.EQ.20) K=20
      IF(JS.EQ.40) K=30
      IF(JS.EQ.100) K=100
      IF(JS.EQ.200) K=200
      IF(JS.EQ.400) K=300
      IF(JS.EQ.1000) K=1000
      IF(JS.EQ.2000) K=2000
      IF(JS.EQ.4000) K=3000
      JS=JS+K
      AN=FLOAT(JS)
      SM=0.0
      IF(JS.GT.NM) GO TO 12
      IF(JS.GT.9000) GO TO 12
      KK=0
      DO 5 JP=1,15
5     RSR(JP)=0.0
      JT=1
      KA=99
6     JAM=JT+JS-1
      IF(JAM.GT.NM) GO TO 9
      IF(JT.GT.1400) GO TO 9
      KK=KK+1
      AG=0.0
      BG=0.0
      DO 7 JZ=JT,JAM
      RJZ=R(JZ)
      AG=AG+RJZ
7     BG=BG+RJZ*RJZ
      AG=AG/AN
      ST=SQRT(BG/AN-AG*AG)
      SUM=0.0
      RPOS=0.0
      RNEG=0.0
      DO 8 JZ=JT,JAM
      SUM=SUM+R(JZ)-AG
      IF(SUM.LT.RNEG) RNEG=SUM
8     IF(SUM.GT.RPOS) RPOS=SUM
      RSR(KK)=(RPOS-RNEG)/ST
      JT=JT+KA
      KA=100
      GO TO 6
9     SS=0.0
      DO 10 JD=1,KK
10    SS=SS+RSR(JD)/FLOAT(KK)
      WRITE(6,11) JS,(RSR(JP),JP=1,15),SS
11    FORMAT(//,3X,I5,16F7.2)
      GO TO 4
12    RETURN
      END
```

5.3.2   Estimation of Hurst coefficient h

Mandelbrot and Wallis (1969a, b) proposed a graphical procedure for estimating h, through a so-called pox diagram. This involves computations which use equation 5.15 of the rescaled range $r_{t,n}^{**}$ based on different subsequence sizes $n \leqslant N$, from the same record, in contrast with the use of the complete sample size N as in the estimation of K from equation 5.16; t denotes the starting points of the subsequences which are also varied. Computed values are plotted on a double logarithmic graph of $r_{t,n}^{**}$ against n. If R_n^{**} denotes the estimated mean of the $r_{t,n}^{**}$ with n fixed and t a variable, the estimate H of h is the slope of straight line fitted by eye to the plot of $\overline{R}_n^{**}$ against n for $n > n_0$; here, $n_0 \approx 20$ is taken as the arbitrary upper limit of the so-called initial transient stage. For these computations, values of t and n are chosen so that the information abstracted is maximised as far as possible whilst minimising the amount of overlapping between subsequences. Suggested values can be found from the subroutine listed in figure 5.6 for evaluating the mean rescaled range; lower values of t than those given may be required for small sample sizes.

   In general, estimates of h are biased because the slope h depends on n. That is, $E(\overline{R}_n^{**}) \approx n^{h(n)}$, whereas we are attempting to estimate $\lim_{n \to \infty} \{h(n)\} = h$, in which $h(n)$ is the local exponent[9]. This should be considered in section 5.4.

5.3.3   Range and rescaled range in small samples

The interpretation of the Hurst phenomenon given above, which is the commonly accepted one, is undoubtedly important from theoretical considerations. However, for practical purposes knowledge of the small sample behaviour of the range statistics is required. This subsection summarises the theoretical contributions that have practical significance[10]. Firstly, independent identically distributed standard normal variates are considered. For this adjusted range, Solari and Anis (1957) proved that

$$E(R_N^*) = (N/2\pi)^{1/2} \sum_{i=1}^{N-1} \{i(N-i)\}^{-1/2} \tag{5.20}$$

Subsequently, Anis and Lloyd (1976) established that, for the rescaled adjusted range,

---

[9] Alternative 'F Hurst' procedures are suggested by Wallis and Matalas (1970). Other references will be given in section 5.4. Several authors, for example, Bloomer and Sexton (1974), have commented on the sampling variability.

[10] The original work on the crude range by Anis and Lloyd (1953) is also relevant here. Some investigators have supplemented their analytical works by data generation methods to determine the effects (on the expectation of the range) of withdrawal rates linearly dependent on storage, and also of serial correlation, periodicity and skewness in the inflow data; see, for example, Melentijevich (1965), Yevjevich (1967) and Salas (1972).

$$E(R_N^{**}) = (1/\pi)^{1/2} \left[\Gamma\{ (N-1)/2 \}/\Gamma(N/2) \right] \sum_{i=1}^{N-1} \{ (N-i)/i \}^{1/2} \quad (5.21)$$

Again, for a sequence of inputs from a gamma population with a two-parameter density function $f(x) = x^{\gamma-1}e^{-x/\lambda}/\lambda^\gamma \Gamma(\gamma)$ (where γ and λ are the shape and scale parameters respectively, as defined in chapter 3), Anis and Lloyd (1975) give

$$E(R_N^*) = 2\gamma^{-1/2}N^{-\gamma N}\,\Gamma(\gamma N) \sum_{i=1}^{N-1} i^{i\gamma-1}(N-i)^{(N-i)\gamma} \Big/ $$
$$\Gamma(i\gamma)\Gamma(N\gamma - i\gamma), \qquad N = 1, 2, 3, \ldots \qquad (5.22)$$

One important outcome of the theoretical work on the rescaled range as given by equation 5.21 is that for finite sequences of independent normal variates the exponent h in equation 5.19 is significantly greater than 0.5. The asymptotic value, $h = 0.5$, is reached only when N is much larger than the sample sizes found in practice. Likewise, Hurst's exponent K defined by equation 5.16 undergoes transitory behaviour but at a slower rate. Values of $E(R_N^{**})$, $K(N)$ and $h(N)$ are given in table 5.1 for some values of N. Evaluation of $E(R_N^{**})$ is made from equation 5.21 and the local exponent $h(N)$ is defined by $\left[\log\{ E(R_{N+1}^{**}) \} - \log\{ E(R_{N-1}^{**}) \} \right]/\log\{ (N+1)/(N-1) \}$. Also $K(N) = \log\{ E(R_N^{**}) \}/\log(N/2)$.

Table 5.1   Variation of $E(R_N^{**})$, $K(N)$ and $h(N)$ independent with N in normal deviates

Sample size N	Adjusted rescaled range $E(R_N^{**})$	Hurst exponent $K(N)$	Local exponent $h(N)$
10	3.023	0.687	0.627
15	4.611	0.664	0.593
30	5.844	0.652	0.577
40	6.890	0.644	0.567
50	7.813	0.639	0.561
100	11.453	0.623	0.544
200	16.621	0.610	0.531
500	26.900	0.596	0.522
1000	38.497	0.587	0.514

5.3.4   Explanations of Hurst phenomenon and experiments

Results in table 5.1 show that Hurst's formula (equation 5.16) gives an exponent $K(N)$ that is biased upwards relative to the local exponent $h(N)$ estimated from equation 5.19. More importantly, transience, that is, the decrease of the exponent to 0.5 as N increases, can account for the Hurst phenomenon in independent normal variates.

As seen in chapter 3, observed sequences are not, in essence, normally distributed. However, computer experiments show that the adjusted rescaled range r_N^{**} is seemingly insensitive to changes in the marginal distribution[11]. This is in contrast with the adjusted range r_N^* which becomes independent of the distribution only when N is large, perhaps greater than 1000 in highly skewed data[12].

The important characteristic of natural time series is persistence. This is the property by which high flows tend to follow high flows and low flows tend to follow low flows. A particular method of measuring persistence is through the serial correlogram. The effect of (positive) serial correlation on the adjusted rescaled range can be demonstrated by generating data sets using the AR(p) and ARMA (p, q) models described in chapter 4. In this way $K(N)$ and $h(N)$ are found to take on values greater than those for independent variates given in table 5.1. These differences increase with increases in the serial correlations. However, they decrease for very large sample sizes; furthermore, it has been shown analytically that when N becomes very large the Hurst coefficient tends to the asymptotic value of 0.5 for ARMA processes[13]. It follows from all of this that the preasymptotic periods, over which the Hurst coefficient is greater than 0.5, are much larger than those from independent variates. From the practical viewpoint, because sample sizes investigated by Hurst were less than 2000, it seems reasonable to assume that serial correlation can, at least, partly account for the observed Hurst phenomenon.

Another explanation put forward of the Hurst phenomenon is non-stationarity of the mean time series. Examples of this, such as the changes in the mean flow in the Volga at Volgograd shown in figure 1.5, are found in chapter 1. Hurst (1957) also suggested a novel card experiment to simulate these conditions. This is explained here for its historical interest. The procedure is to label each card in a pack of 52 with a number from the set ($\pm 1, \pm 3, \pm 5, \pm 7$). These numbers are approximately normally distributed if they are distributed as follows: one of the sevens, four of the fives, eight of the threes and thirteen of the ones. To begin with, the pack is shuffled, a card is drawn at random and replaced

---

[11] See, for example, Salas *et al.* (1977). The robustness of the r_N^** statistic is discussed by Mandelbrot and Wallis (1969c).

[12] Moran (1964) originally investigated the range of gamma independent variates.

[13] See Siddiqui (1976) who also showed that, if the stable distribution described in subsection 3.6.4 is applicable, which is of course hypothetical, the asymptotic value of the coefficient is $1/v$, where v is the characteristic exponent of this distribution. The comparable study of Boes and Salas (1973) is also of academic interest. In addition, results of several empirical works have been published. For instance, Matalas and Huzzen (1967) used an AR(1) model, given by $\xi_t = \rho_1 \xi_{t-1} + (1 - \rho_1)^{1/2} \varepsilon_t$, where ρ_1 is the lag-one autocorrelation coefficient and the ε_t values are independent standard normal variates. They found that, if $\rho_1 = 0.3$, $\bar{K}(50) = 0.71$ and $\bar{K}(1000) \approx 0.63$; however, if $\rho_1 = 0.7$, $\bar{K}(50) \approx 0.80$ and $\bar{K}(1000) = 0.7$ in which the mean values of K are estimated from 10 000 sequences. O'Connell (1974) found that the short-term Hurst effect can be maintained through ARMA models. Similar computer experiments were carried out by Hipel and McLeod (1978) and by Salas *et al.* (1977). Salas *et al.* and Gomide (1978) claim that the types of dates used by Hurst (1951, 1956) can be generated by ARMA models on the r_N^{**} criterion. Also, empirical distributions of r_N^{**} are given by Wallis and O'Connell (1973).

after noting its number, say, -5. Then 26 cards are dealt and the five highest cards are removed from this hand of 26 and replaced by the five lowest from the other hand. Next, a joker is added to the first hand which is again shuffled. From this reduced set of 27, cards are drawn at random one at a time and are replaced after noting the numbers sequentially, the pack being shuffled after each draw. When the joker is drawn, the entire procedure is repeated. Note that, if a positive number, say, $+3$, is drawn after shuffling the pack of 52 cards, the three lowest cards from this hand are replaced by the three highest from the other. In this way a sequence can be extended to give a required number of variates with exponent $K = 0.73$ which is the mean of the coefficient in Hurst's original study.

Other more sophisticated computer experiments have recently been made to produce sequences with time-varying means[14]. In fact, these may be adapted to give a range of Hurst coefficients. However, the correlation structure in the sequences so generated are found to be of the ARMA(1, 1) type. Therefore, it appears that such procedures are not warranted in practice.

To conclude, it can be said that both serial correlation and non-stationarity can account for the Hurst effect over finite time horizons. Indeed, many natural processes seem to have both these properties in varying degrees so that it is difficult to identify the effect of each.

In contrast with the aforementioned techniques, fractional gaussian models are specifically devised to preserve the Hurst phenomenon over almost infinite time spans, on the premise that it is caused by intransient effects. Accordingly, they are termed infinite memory models. Strictly speaking, the simple AR(1) model and the more complicated ARMA models also possess infinite memories, but the correlograms are of the exponential type (as given, for example, by equation 4.13) so that the influence, on the present, of events in the distant past is negligible.

The models described in the following sections are operational ones. It appears that there are no physical reasons to support them, but we could say the same regarding some of the models used in flood estimation such as the log Pearson type III function described in the next chapter[15]. They are, in effect, sophisticated and versatile generators of data (complementary to the classical models described in chapter 4) which take the place of Hurst's card experiment described above.

---

[14] A more general procedure is described by Boes and Salas (1978) for use on a computer. Likewise, Klemeš (1974) carried out computer experiments with a normally varying mean and exponentially distributed time epochs t to obtain a range of values of the Hurst coefficient. Potter (1976), who also suggests that non-stationarity is an explanation of the Hurst phenomenon, found that segments of some precipitation records from the United States have widely different K values. This is shown on a much wider scale in the numerous data sets listed by Hurst (1956); for example, the maximum and minimum K values from 100-year segments of the Nile flow data are 0.86 and 0.38.

[15] On the contrary, Scheidegger (1970) has commented on the physical inplausibility of fractional gaussian models. Indeed, earlier versions had to be modified on account of some unrealistic features, as explained in section 5.4.

5.4   Fractional gaussian noise

Soon after the results of Hurst's studies became known some leading statisticians, for example, Moran (1959, p. 66), expressed the view that the Hurst phenomenon is due to an extraordinary type of serial correlation structure. Inspired by the work of Hurst, Mandelbrot (1965) constructed a class of random processes called fractional gaussian noises (FGNs) which are shown to exhibit the N^h behaviour with $h > 0.5$ for infinite values of N. A distinguishing feature of these processes is that unlike the ARMA types, all of which follow the asymptotic $N^{0.5}$ law, they do not belong to the brownian domain of attraction. Here, the term brownian describes, broadly speaking, a physical phenomenon in which some variable is in a continuous state of random fluctuation. It is named after the Scottish botanist Robert Brown who, in 1827, observed 'rapid oscillatory motion' in pollen grains suspended in water: such motions are evidently caused by continual molecular impacts. The displacements of the particles in time were shown by Einstein, in his quantitative theory, to be normally distributed[16]. Elsewhere, the study of brownian motion was pursued heuristically by Bachelier, as evidenced, for example, by his 'Theorie de la speculation', and rigorously as a (continuous) stochastic process by Wiener, hence the term Bachelier–Wiener process. The mathematics is, of course, sophisticated; simplified definitions relevant to the text are given below.

As implied, FGN processes differ in their autocorrelation structure from ARMA processes. The basic difference can be given by their relative measures of persistence which, if we follow the definition of Taylor (1938) in his studies of turbulence, may be regarded as the integral of the autocorrelation function from lag zero to lag infinity. Accordingly, persistence is finite for all types of ARMA processes as in equation 4.13. On the contrary, the integral of the autocorrelogram of an FGN process is infinite[17].

The term fractional arises from the type of spectral density function $s(f)$ of FGN. This is of the form f^{1-2h}, where f denotes frequency and h, which is conditional to $0 < h < 1$ and $h \neq 0.5$, is the (fractional) Hurst coefficient. For white noise, h takes on the (asymptotic) value of 0.5 which means that, as noted in chapter 2, its spectrum is horizontal. On the other hand, the corresponding spectral slope of a realisation of FGN, with $0.5 < h < 1.0$, has limits 0 and 1.0, that is, on a double-logarithmic plot.

5.4.1   Joseph and Noah effects

For hydrological generation, FGNs specifically attempt to preserve in a time series the natural characteristic of having, on occasion, long periods of low flows

[16]   See Einstein (1906).
[17]   Details of FGNs which follow are partly based on the work of Mandelbrot and Van Ness (1968) and of Mandelbrot and Wallis (1968, 1969a); an original appraisal of Hurst's work was made by Mandelbrot (1965). Mandelbrot (1977) has used these concepts in his general study of forms appearing in nature, such as the length of the coast line of Britain which of course depends on the step taken to measure it.

or long periods of high flows. This is called the Joseph effect. It follows directly from the property of infinite persistence which the noises possess. The other main point is that extremely high flows or, alternatively, extremely low flows occur sometimes in nature. This characteristic of a river-flow series is termed the Noah effect[18]. However, this property may not be maintained through gaussian processes without a skewed innovation as discussed earlier in regard to crossing properties.

5.4.2 *Fractional brownian motion*

If the brownian motion random process is denoted by $B(t)$, it is important to note that the increments $B(t + u) - B(t)$ are normally distributed with mean zero and variance u. Furthermore, brownian motion satisfies the asymptotic $N^{0.5}$ law of Hurst and Feller. It is also said to be a self-similar process (a term which had been used by previous writers). This self-similarity means, roughly speaking, that distribution properties are unaltered when the time scale is changed. Here, it means that the random variates $B(t + u) - B(t)$ and $\{B(t + ur) - B(t)\}/r^{0.5}$ have the same distribution. The same scaling effect is reflected in the distribution of the rescaled range which is accordingly proportional to $N^{0.5}$.

Now the main interest is in the structure of fractional brownian motion (FBM). This is, in effect, a form of moving average of the increments $dB(t) = B(t + dt) - B(t)$ of (continuous) brownian motion. To obtain FBM the past increments, $dB(u)$ are weighted by $(t - u)^{h - 0.5}$, where h is a parameter to give

$$B_h(t) = \int_{-\infty}^{t} (t - u)^{h - 0.5} \, dB(u), \qquad -\infty < t < \infty \tag{5.23}$$

The parameter h is, in fact, the Hurst coefficient, and the increments are normal (gaussian) white noise. The FBM process too is self-similar, but it follows the N^h law, where $h \neq 0.5$ and where the random variates $B_h(t + u) - B_h(t)$ and $\{B_h(t + ur) - B_h(t)\}/r^h$ have identical distributions. Thus brownian motion may be thought of as a special case of FBM.

Discrete-time fractional Brownian motion (DTFBM), which will be denoted by $b_t(h)$, is formed by taking the unit increment of $B_h(t)$ up to time t as follows.

$$b_t(h) = B_h(t) - B_h(t - 1)$$
$$= \int_{t-1}^{t} k_h(t - u) \, dB(u) \tag{5.24}$$

where $k_h(t - u)$ is a continuously varying kernel function, as defined by equation 5.23 and given explicitly below.

---

[18] The biblical connotations of these two colourful terms are, firstly, the seven fat and seven lean years of Joseph, son of Jacob, or more appropriately in the Nile flows, not far from the land of Joseph, and, secondly, the devastating floods in the Euphrates basin, consequent to forty days and nights of incessant rain, from which Noah, his family and the animals escaped in an ark of gopherwood.

5.4.3   Approximations to fractional gaussian noise

For practical purposes a sample realisation of discrete-time fractional gaussian noise (DTFGN) is needed from the $b_t(h)$ value given by equation 5.24. However, it is difficult to evaluate this integral on a computer. Therefore, certain approximations to FGN have been suggested. These are formed as follows.

(i) A grid of n, say, equispaced points is set up over each time interval, and at each point an independent normal variate with zero mean and variance $1/n$ is generated. By this approximation, a high-frequency error term is introduced; this means that short-run properties may not be maintained realistically.

(ii) The integral limits of $-\infty$ and t for the variable u are replaced by the finite span $-M + t < u < t$, where M is the memory of the process. This introduces a low-frequency error term which may impair the Joseph effect; specifically, at $N > 3M$, the rescaled range becomes proportional to $N^{0.5}$.

(iii) After selecting the grid n, the kernel function $k_h(t - u)$ is given in a simplified form as shown below.

For the so-called type I approximation to DTFGN with the grid $n = 10$, the exact kernel function is equivalent to $u^{h-0.5}$ for $0 \leqslant u \leqslant 1$ and to $u^{h-0.5} - (u - 1)^{h-0.5}$ for $1 \leqslant u \leqslant \infty$. The type II approximation is based on a grid $n = 1$ and is therefore a much cruder version. Its practical advantage is that the computer output is ten times faster. In this case, the kernel function takes the approximate form $(h - 0.5)u^{h-1.5}$. In order to clarify the FGN-generating mechanism, the simpler type II approximation is explained below.

5.4.4   Type II approximation to fractional gaussian noise

FGNs based on the type II approximation, conditional to a Hurst coefficient h and a memory M, are generated by

$$X_t^{(\text{II})} = (h - 0.5) \sum_{u=t-M}^{t-1} (t - u)^{h-1.5} \eta_u, \qquad 1/2 < h < 1 \qquad (5.25)$$

where η_u, $u = 0, \pm 1, \pm 2, \pm 3, \ldots$, are independent standard normal variates. Hence, for $t = 1$,

$$X_1^{(\text{II})} = (h - 0.5)(1^{1.5-h}\eta_0 + 2^{1.5-h}\eta_{-1} + 3^{1.5-h}\eta_{-2} + \cdots$$
$$+ M^{1.5-h}\eta_{-M+1})$$

and, for $t = 2$,

$$X_2^{(\text{II})} = (h - 0.5)(1^{1.5-h}\eta_{+1} + 2^{1.5-h}\eta_0 + 3^{1.5-h}\eta_{-1} + \cdots$$
$$+ M^{1.5-h}\eta_{-M+2})$$

In this way a series of mutually dependent variates $X_t^{(\text{II})}$, $t = 1, 2, 3, \ldots, N$, in which the rescaled range is proportional to N^h, is obtained. Note that, in order to generate a single FGN variate, M random variates η_u are required. The recommended value for M is 20000. In order to generate the next variate, the last random variate is discarded, and a new random variate is produced, but the same set of M weights is used.

As mentioned, the introduction of a rough grid $n = 1$ results in a high-frequency error. Because such effects are undesirable, Matalas and Wallis (1971) introduced a filtering parameter p, which is an arbitrarily chosen integer greater than 1. For this purpose, equation 5.25 is modified as follows.

$$X_t^{(\text{II}')} = (h - 1/2) \sum_{u = pt - M}^{pt - 1} (pt - u)^{h - 1 \cdot 5} \eta_u$$

In application, the same set of weights is used as for equation 5.25. The difference is that to generate $X_{t+1}^{(\text{II}')}$ the last p random variates used for $X_t^{(\text{II}')}$ are discarded and p new random variates are added to the start of the sequence of η_u.

The main drawback in all the type I and type II approximations to FGN is the excessive computer time required. To remedy the situation, Mandelbrot (1971) postulated a fast fractional gaussian noise generator (FFGN). This is summarised in the next subsection[19].

5.4.5 Fast fractional gaussian noise

In order to derive the FFGN the low-frequency properties of the covariance function of the DTFBM which is given by

$$C_\ell(h) = \{(\ell + 1)^{2h} - 2\ell^{2h} + (\ell - 1)^{2h}\}/2 \qquad (5.26)$$

is reproduced. In this way, the autocorrelations are positive for all ℓ, for $0.5 < h \leqslant 1$, and the integration of the covariance function between limits 0 and ∞ in infinite, but $C_\ell(0.5) = 0$, for all ℓ.

The construction of FFGN requires two additive components. The first component $X_t^{(\text{L})}$ concerns low-frequency effects and is found by weighting N standardised AR(1) (that is, Markov) normal processes. The main point in its formulation is that the covariance structure of DTFBM given by equation 5.26 holds for large lags in the approximate form

$$C_\ell'(h) = h(2h - 1)\ell^{2h - 2} \qquad (5.27)$$

For all practical purposes the differences between $C_\ell(h)$ and $C_\ell'(h)$ is insignificant. Hence,

$$X_t^{(\text{L})} = \sum_{n = 1}^{N} W_n X_t(GM \mid n, B) \qquad (5.28)$$

where $X_t(GM \mid n, B)$ is a standardised AR(1) normal process with a suggested lag-one autocorrelation equal to $\exp(-B^{-n})$ and normal independent variates. The parameter B takes a value in the suggested range 2 to 4, but computer experiments show that variations within this range are not over-sensitive to a

[19] Further details are also given by Lawrance and Kottegoda (1977) and by Chi et al. (1973).

design parameter such as reservoir capacity. The weights W_n are given by

$$W_n^2 = h(2h - 1)(B^{1-h} - B^{h-1})B^{-2(1-h)n}/\Gamma(3 - 2h) \tag{5.29}$$

which is obtained from equations 5.27 and 5.28 as shown in the literature[20]. It was originally suggested that $N = N(T)$ should be functional to the desired sample size T, but $N = 15$ to 20 is found to suffice in practice. The generation of $X_t^{(L)}$ can be followed by the subroutine given in figure 5.7.

```
      SUBROUTINE FFGN(SQ)
      READ (5,1) NY,NZ,H,B,GAM
    1 FORMAT(2I6,3F6.3)
      DIMENSION SQ(2000),RD(20,200),C(25),CC(25),W(25)

C
C   SUBROUTINE GENERATES NY FAST FRACTIONAL GAUSSIAN NOISE NUMBERS WITH
C   PARAMETERS B,H AND NZ=N(T). REQUIRES NY*NZ INDEPENDENT STANDARD
C   NORMAL VARIATES. GAM = COMPLETE GAMMA FUNCTION OF (3-2H).
C   HIGH FREQUENCY COMPONENT NEEDS TO BE ADDED.
C
      AWN=H*(2.0*H-1.0)*(B**(1.0-H)-B**(H-1.0))/GAM
      BWN=-2.0*(1.0-H)
      DO 2 N=1,NZ
      C(N)=1.0/EXP((1.0/B)**FLOAT(N))
      CC(N)=SQRT(1.0-C(N)*C(N))
    2 W(N)=SQRT(AWN*B**(BWN*FLOAT(N)))
      JJ=0
      DO 4 NA=1,NZ
      DO 4 NB=1,NY
      JJ=JJ+1
      RD(NA,NB)=SQ(JJ)
      IF(NB-1) 3,4,3
    3 NC=NB-1
      RD(NA,NB)=RD(NA,NC)*C(NA)+RD(NA,NB)*CC(NA)
    4 CONTINUE
      DO 6 NB=1,NY
      SUM=0.0
      DO 5 NA=1,NZ
    5 SUM=SUM+RD(NA,NB)*W(NA)
    6 SQ(NB)=SUM
      RETURN
      END
```

Figure 5.7   FORTRAN subroutine to generate FFGN

The second component $X_t^{(H)}$, which is added to correct the high-frequency errors resulting from $X_t^{(L)}$, is a separate single AR(1) normal process with zero mean. Its variance is $1 - B^{h-1}(2h^2 - h)/\Gamma(3 - 2h)$ and its lag-one autocorrelation $2^{2h-1} - 1 + \sum_{n=1}^{N(t)} W_n(1 - r_n) - B^{-(1-h)}h(2h - 1)/\Gamma(3 - 2h)$. Finally, FFGN is obtained by the addition

$$X_t^{(f)} = X_t^{(L)} + X_t^{(H)} \tag{5.30}$$

The reduction in computer time is such that about 2000 $X_t^{(f)}$ variates can be generated in the time taken to generate one $X_t^{(II)}$ variate with $M = 20\,000$. For

[20] See, for example, Lawrance and Kottegoda (1977).

Table 5.2 Adjusted range, adjusted rescaled range, maximum deficit and length of longest deficit for annual flows (reduced to unit mean) in Göta near Sjötop-Vänersborg (Lake Vänern outflows), Sweden, for the period 1807 to 1957 using historical data, AR(2) model and FFGN model

Model		Adjusted range	Adjusted rescaled range	$\alpha = 1.0$		$\alpha = 0.95$		$\alpha = 0.90$		$\alpha = 0.85$		$\alpha = 0.80$	
				$d_{max}^{(1.0)}$	$\ell_{max}^{(1.0)}$	$d_{max}^{(0.95)}$	$\ell_{max}^{(0.95)}$	$d_{max}^{(0.90)}$	$\ell_{max}^{(0.90)}$	$d_{max}^{(0.85)}$	$\ell_{max}^{(0.85)}$	$d_{max}^{(0.80)}$	$\ell_{max}^{(0.80)}$
Historical non-overlapping, 50-year subsamples	First	2.30	13.18	1.41	32	0.86	16	0.63	9	0.43	8	0.23	5
	Second	1.64	9.32	0.89	32	0.57	9	0.43	5	0.33	3	0.23	3
	Third	1.74	9.21	1.74	25	1.41	18	0.91	15	0.47	10	0.28	4
AR(2) model 50-year subsamples	Max.	2.57	13.00	2.57	32	1.42	32	0.63	12	0.47	6	0.37	3
	Mean	1.61	8.83	1.49	32	0.92	16	0.58	9	0.47	5	0.34	4
	Min.	1.24	7.99	0.75	12	0.41	6	0.38	4	0.21	3	0.13	2
FFGN model, 50-year subsamples $h = 0.6$	Max.	2.18	12.01	2.19	33	1.19	23	0.62	9	0.40	8	0.35	3
	Mean	1.75	9.61	1.58	27	0.90	17	0.55	9	0.39	5	0.28	3
	Min.	1.05	5.73	0.82	25	0.50	13	0.30	6	0.25	4	0.20	2
$h = 0.7$	Max.	2.56	14.05	2.56	33	1.56	27	0.68	11	0.45	8	0.43	6
	Mean.	2.04	12.22	1.83	27	1.10	20	0.64	10	0.45	6	0.36	4
	Min.	1.36	7.50	1.03	17	0.82	9	0.62	5	0.43	4	0.30	3
$h = 0.8$	Max.	2.85	15.64	2.85	32	1.85	27	0.86	20	0.48	8	0.38	8
	Mean	2.27	12.45	2.05	27	1.30	22	0.78	13	0.48	8	0.33	5
	Min.	1.05	5.77	1.05	26	0.77	16	0.51	6	0.37	6	0.24	4

operational purposes, the output from the models can be transformed so that the means and variances of observed sequences are maintained.

Example 5.3   Table 5.2 shows the adjusted range r_N^*, the adjusted rescaled range r_N^{**}, the maximum deficit $d_{max}^{(\alpha)}$ and the length of longest depletion $\ell_{max}^{(\alpha)}$ for degrees of development given by $\alpha = 1.0, 0.95, 0.90, 0.85$ and 0.80 in the annual flows of the Göta River near Sjötop-Vänersborg, Sweden, for the period 1807 to 1957. The data, which is reduced to unit mean, is taken from Yevjevich (1963) and is divided into non-overlapping 50-year subsamples. The results are compared with those from the AR(2) model given by $\xi_t = 0.583\xi_{t-1} - 0.271\xi_{t-2} + n_t$. Then the computations are repeated by using the output from a FFGN model with $h = 0.6, h = 0.7$ and $h = 0.8$, after generating 50-year sequences with a total of 25 in each case.

It might be concluded on the basis of the given criteria and the results given that the AR(2) model is sufficient for generating likely future sequences of annual data in this particular application. However, conditions over a future design period may be different from those of the recent past, as evidenced, for instance, by the range analysis of the Nile record by Hurst (1956). Therefore, an attempt should be made to establish a probability distribution of deficits or reservoir yield, say. For this purpose, short historical records may be biased and ought to be extended, wherever feasible, by regression. Another point is that shorter time intervals such as months or days are required for operational studies of reservoirs, particularly the smaller ones which supply non-irrigation needs. In such cases ARMA models may not adequately reproduce the critical reservoir statistics from the historical data[21].

To give a second application of the technique, the FFGN model is applied to 5-day inflows to Caban Coch Reservoir in Wales where the historical record commenced in 1908. The estimated mean $\bar{x}$ and the variance s^2 are 18 mm and 372 mm^2 respectively of equivalent rainfall over the catchment area of 184 km^2, and the estimated coefficient of skewness is given by $g_1 = 2.05$. The Hurst coefficient is estimated as 0.60, as shown by figure 5.8 by using the subroutine in figure 5.6; the data are prewhitened for this purpose. On account of the unknown but expectedly high sampling error in the estimate of h, values of $h = 0.8, 0.7$ and 0.6 were experimented with; the range $0.6 < h < 0.5$ was ignored because the resulting noise is approximately white. Plots of maximum deficits and probabilities of exceedance are given in figure 5.9 for withdrawal rates $\alpha\bar{x}$, $\alpha = 0.7, 0.8$ and 0.9.

A useful outcome of this experiment is that it gives a possible range of values for the future. It is seen here that, in order to approximate closely the properties in the past record which are of interest here, a value of h in the range of 0.6 to 0.7 needs to be maintained[22]. One method of tackling future uncertainties on

---

[21] This has been found, for instance, by Askew *et al.* (1971). Probability distributions in storage calculations began with the work of Hazen (1914). See, for example, Hufschmidt and Fiering (1966) and Burges and Linsley (1971).

[22] In order to find a better estimate of h from recorded data, Kottegoda (1970) suggests, for approximately normally distributed data, an average value based on the slopes of

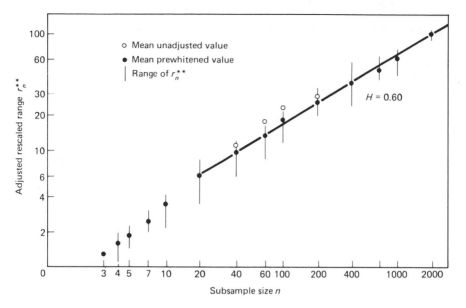

Figure 5.8   Plot of adjusted rescaled range r_n^{**} against subsample size n of 5-day inflows to Caban Coch Reservoir, Wales

account of environmental and climatic effects is through bayesian decision theory which will be explained in chapter 9. This involves loss and benefit functions, the concept of expected opportunity loss and the subjective assessment of probabilities, say, of different values of h, based on all available information.

An interesting alternative model of a similar type is based on the simple broken-line process of Ditlevson (1969).

5.5   Broken-line models

A simple broken-line process is derived from the linear interpolation between uniformly spaced independent normal variates with zero means. When two or more of such processes each with a preassigned variance and starting point are added, we obtain a broken-line process. This may be regarded as an approximation to FGN, and just as in the derivation of FFGN the asymptotic behaviour of the covariance function can be closely approximated through

double logarithmic plots of $E(R_n^{**})$ against n, $E(R_n^*)$ against n and $s(f)$ against f is taken. Young and Jettmar (1976) used equation 4.27, the serial correlogram and a least-squares estimate of h, whereas Hipel and McLeod (1978) obtained an ML estimator. In the face of future uncertainties and an account of likely modelling errors, however, these refinements could be merely academic.

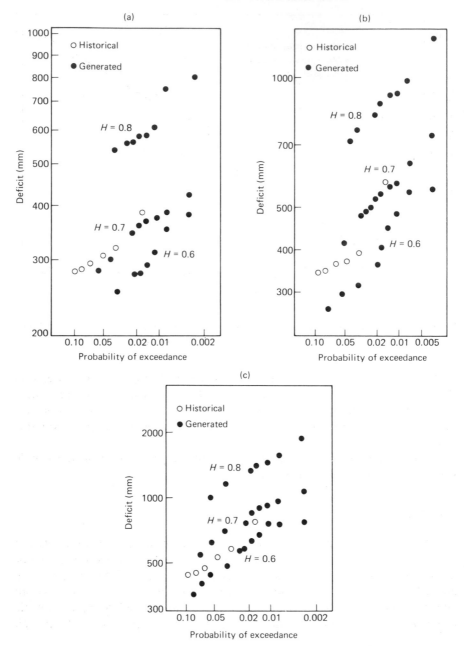

Figure 5.9   Plots of deficit against probability of exceedance for 5-day inflows to Caban Coach Reservoir, Wales, and data generated using FFGN model with $H = 0.8, 0.7$ and 0.6, and for outflow $\alpha\bar{x}$, where $\bar{x}$ is the estimated mean and (a) $\alpha = 0.7$, (b) $\alpha = 0.8$ and (c) $\alpha = 0.9$

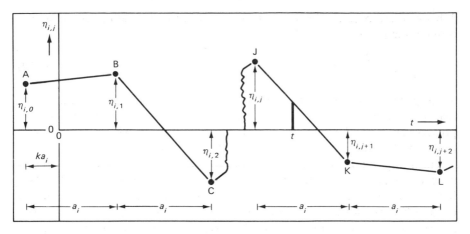

Figure 5.10 Simple broken-line (continuous) process i, formed by interpolating at times t between points A, B, C, . . ., J, K. L, . . ., which have ordinates normally distributed with zero mean and variance σ_i and abscissae $-ka_i, a_i - ka_i, 2a_i - ka_i, \ldots$. Broken-line process ξ_t is formed by summing simple broken-line processes $\beta_i(t)$, $i = 1, 2, \ldots, n$, at times t. (See, for example, the thick vertical line at t)

equation 5.27, which is the way in which the Hurst behaviour is modelled. Basically, it is a continuous process that is somewhat non-normal.

A simple broken-line process $\beta_i(t)$ is shown in figure 5.10. The points A, B, C, . . ., J, K, L, . . ., have equal projections of length a_i on the time axis and their ordinates are normally distributed each with mean zero and variance σ_i^2. Point A is set back with respect to the time origin by ka_i, where the k are uniformly distributed in the interval $(0, 1)$.

It follows that, in general,

$$\beta_i(t) = \eta_{i, j} + \frac{t + ka_i - ja_i}{a_i}(\eta_{i, j+1} - \eta_{i, j})$$

$$ja_i - ka_i \leqslant t \leqslant (j + 1)a_i - k_i a_i \qquad (5.31)$$

Also, it can be shown that

$$\mathrm{var}\{\beta_i(t)\} = 2\sigma_i^2 / 3 \qquad (5.32)$$

and the lag-ℓ covariance is given by

$$C_i(\ell) = \begin{cases} 1 - \frac{3}{4}(\ell/a_i)^2\,(2 - (\ell/a_i)), & 0 \leqslant \ell \leqslant a_i \\ \frac{1}{4}(2 - \ell/a_i)^3, & a_i < \ell \leqslant 2a_i \\ 0, & 2a_i < \ell < \infty \end{cases} \qquad (5.33)$$

A broken-line process ξ_t is formed in discrete time by adding, say, n simple broken-line processes $\beta_i(t)$. Thus

$$\xi_t = \sum_{i=1}^{n} \beta_i(t) \tag{5.34}$$

To implement this model we need to determine n, a_i and σ_i, $i = 1, 2, \ldots, n$, making a total of $2n + 1$ parameters. The high-frequency properties are preserved by a suitable choice of parameter values through which the covariance function of ξ_t and an observed sequence are matched.

The fitting technique for preserving low frequencies partly follows the FFGN model, as regards parameters B and H. However, there is a limited advantage here in that crossing properties can be maintained when flows are approximately normal. The application is based on equation 5.1 in which the second derivative λ_2 of the covariance function at the origin is estimated from the serial correlogram by a finite-difference method. In summation, the method is seen to be useful, at least in some respects, and has flexibility. The main drawback, however, is that it has numerous parameters to estimate unless certain assumptions are made[23].

5.6   Final comments

The purpose of this chapter has been to explain certain hydrological properties that are complementary to those treated in chapter 2 and for the maintenance of which the classical methods described in chapter 4 may not suffice. Techniques are provided here for dealing with the various problems. It should not be forgotten that these models can only cope with nature's complexities in approximate ways. For operational purposes, therefore, too much stress should not be placed on their physical relevance. As regards model choice, any given recipe for selection would be subjective to some extent, because statistical tests are generally insensitive for the purpose. Each case may merit a different approach depending on which criteria are important. Of greater concern are the possible effects on estimated parameters which may arise from future climatological and environmental variations. Until climatologists and others can produce definite answers, we may need to resort to decision theory with economic functions for design purposes, as outlined in chapter 9.

Data generation methods can play a useful role in the simulation of complex water resource systems[24]. In this way the performance of a system may be analysed under different conditions. However, the behaviour and reliability of a

---

[23] Mejia *et al.* (1972) take $a_i = a_1 q^{i-1}$ and $\sigma_i = \sigma_1 (a_1/a_i)^{1/2}$. This reduces the parameters to three: a_1, q and n. For further details, see Garcia *et al.* (1972), Mejia *et al.* (1974) and Lawrance and Kottegoda (1977). Limitations pointed out by Mandelbrot (1972) are mainly on account of its coarse approximation to an infinite memory process.

[24] A detailed example of simulation is given by Steinberg (1968).

single reservoir with variable withdrawal rates can be investigated, and its optimum capacity can be found by more direct methods, if the inflow data are independent or have a Markov type of dependent structure. The relevant probabilistic analysis and methods are explained in chapter 7, and the operational aspects are dealt with in chapter 8, but prior to that the important Noah property in hydrology is taken up in the next chapter.

References

Anis, A. A., and Lloyd, E. H. (1953). On the range of partial sums of a finite number of independent normal variates. *Biometrika*, **40**, 35–42

—— (1975). Skewed inputs and the Hurst effect. *J. Hydrol.*, **26**, 39–53

—— (1976). The expected value of the adjusted rescaled Hurst range of independent normal summands. *Biometrika*, **63**, 111–16

Askew, A. J., Yeh, W. G. H., and Hall, W. A. (1971). A comparative study of critical drought simulation. *Water Resour. Res.*, **7**, 52–62

Bloomer, R. J. G., and Sexton, J. R. (1974). Problems encountered in synthetic river flow generation procedures. *Proceedings of the* 1971 *Warsaw Symposium on Mathematical Models in Hydrology*, vol. 1, International Association of Scientific Hydrology, Paris, pp. 91–103

Boes, D. C., and Salas, J. D. (1973). On the expected range and expected adjusted range of partial sums of exchangeable random variables. *J. Appl. Prob.*, **10**, 671–7

—— (1978). Nonstationarity of the mean and the Hurst phenomenon. *Water Resour. Res.*, **14**, 135–43

Brunk, H. D. (1965). *An Introduction to Mathematical Statistics*, 2nd edn, Blaisdell, Waltham, Massachussetts

Burges, S. J., and Linsley, R. K. (1971). Some factors influencing required reservoir storage. *J. Hydraul. Div., Proc. Am. Soc. Civ. Eng.*, **97** (HY7), 977–91. (1972). Discussion. *Proc. Am. Soc. Civ. Eng.*, **98** (HY4), 717–18; (HY11), 2038–9

Chi, M., Neal, E., and Young, G. K. (1973). Practical application of fractional brownian motion and noise to synthetic hydrology. *Water Resour. Res.*, **9**, 1523–33

Cox, D. R., and Miller, H. D. (1965). *The Theory of Stochastic Processes*, Methuen, London

Cramér, H. (1946). *Mathematical Methods of Statistics*, Princeton University Press, Princeton, New Jersey

Cramér, H., and Leadbetter, M. R. (1967). *Stationary and Related Stochastic Processes*, Wiley, New York

David, F. N., and Barton, D. E. (1962). *Combinatorial Chance*, Griffin, London

Ditlevson, O. (1969). *Extremes and First Passage Times with Applications in Civil Engineering*, Danmarks Ingeniorakademi, Copenhagen

Downer, R. N., Siddiqui, M. M., and Yevjevich, V. (1967). Application of runs to hydrologic droughts. *Proceedings of the International Hydrology Symposium*, vol. 1, *Fort Collins, Colorado*, pp. 496–505

Einstein, A. (1906). Zur Theorie der Brownschen Bewegung. *Annalen der Physik*, *IV*, **19**, 371–81

Feller, W. (1951). The asymptotic distribution of the range of sums of independent random variables. *Ann. Math. Statist.*, **22**, 427–32

—— (1968). *Introduction to Probability Theory and its Applications*, vol. 1, 3rd edn, Wiley, New York

Fiering, M. B. (1967). *Streamflow Synthesis*, Macmillan, London

Fisz, M. (1963). *Probability Theory and Mathematical Statistics*, 3rd edn, Wiley, New York

Fraser, D. A. S. (1976). *Probability and Statistics: Theory and Applications*, Duxbury Press, North Scituate, Massachusetts

Garcia, L. E., Dawdy, D. R., and Mejía, J. M. (1972). Long memory monthly streamflow simulation by broken line model. *Water Resour. Res.*, **8**, 1100–5

Gomide, F. L. S. (1978). Markovian inputs and the Hurst phenomenon. *J. Hydrol.*, **37**, 23–45

Guerrero-Salazar, P., and Yevjevich, V. (1975). Analysis of drought characteristics by the theory of runs. *Colo. St. Univ., Fort Collins, Hydrol. Papers*, No. 80

Hall, W. A., Askew, A. J., and Yeh, W. W. G. (1969). Use of the critical period in reservoir analysis. *Water Resour. Res.*, **5**, 1205–15

Hazen, A. (1914). Storage to be provided in impounding reservoirs for municipal water supply. *Trans. Am. Soc. Civ. Eng.*, **77**, 1539–640

Hipel, K. W., and McLeod, A. I. (1978). Preservation of the rescaled adjusted range, part one—a reassessment of the Hurst phenomenon. *Water Resour. Res.*, **14**, 491–508

Hufschmidt, M. M., and Fiering, M. B. (1966). *Simulation Techniques for Design of Water Resource Systems*, Harvard University Press, Cambridge, Massachusetts

Hurst, H. E. (1951). Long term storage capacity of reservoirs (with discussion). *Trans. Am. Soc. Civ. Eng.*, **116**, paper 2447, 770–808

—— (1956). Methods of using long term storage in reservoirs (with discussion). *Proc. Inst. Civ. Eng.*, part I, **5**, paper 6049, 519–90

—— (1957). A suggested statistical model of some time series which occur in nature. *Nature (London)*, **180**, 494

Hurst, H. E., Black, R. P., and Simaika, Y. M. (1964). *Long-Term Storage, An Experimental Study*, Constable, London

Klemeš, V. (1974). The Hurst phenomenon—a puzzle? *Water Resour. Res.*, **10**, 675–88

—— (1978). Discussion on 'Sequent peak procedure: minimum reservoir capacity subject to constraint on final storage' by K. W. Potter. *Water Resour. Bull.*, **14**, 991–3

Kottegoda, N. T. (1970). Applicability of short-memory models to English riverflow data. *J. Inst. Water Eng.*, **24**, 481–9. (1971). Communication. *J. inst. Water Eng.*, **25**, 128–31

Kottegoda, N. T. (1974). Effect of skewness in three stochastic riverflow models on crossing properites of synthesized data. *Water Resour. Res.*, **10**, 446–56

Lawrance, A. J., and Kottegoda, N. T. (1977). Stochastic modelling of riverflow time series (with discussion). *J. R. Statist. Soc. A*, **140**, 1–47

Leadbetter, M. R. (1972). Point processes generated by level crossings. *Stochastic Point Processes* (ed. N. R. Lewis), Wiley, New York, pp. 436–67

Llamas, J., and Siddiqui, M. M. (1969). Runs of precipitation series. *Colo. St. Univ., Fort Collins, Hydrol. Papers*, No. 33

Mandelbrot, B. B. (1965). Une classe de processus stochastiques homothétiques à soi; application à la loi climatologique de H. E. Hurst. *Comptes Rendus de L'Académie des Sciences de Paris*, **260**, 3274–7

—— (1971). A fast fractional gaussian noise generator. *Water Resour. Res.*, **7**, 543–53

—— (1972). Broken line process derived as an approximation to fractional noise. *Water Resour. Res.*, **8**, 1354–6

—— (1977). *Fractals, Form, Chance, and Dimension*, Freeman, San Francisco, California

Mandelbrot, B. B., and Van Ness, J. W. (1968). Fractional brownian motions, fractional noises and applications. *Soc. Ind. Appl. Math. Rev.*, **10**, 422–37

Mandelbrot, B. B., and Wallis, J. R. (1968). Noah, Joseph and operational hydrology. *Water Resour. Res.*, **4**, 909–20. (1969). Letters and correction. *Water Resour. Res.*, **5**, 915–20, 1164

——(1969a). Computer experiments with fractional gaussian noises, parts 1, 2 and 3. *Water Resour. Res.*, **5**, 228–67. (1969). Correction. *Water Resour. Res.*, **5**, 1164

—— (1969b). Some long-run properties of geophysical records. *Water Resour. Res.*, **5**, 321–40

—— (1969c). Robustness of the rescaled range R/S in measurement of noncyclic long run statistical dependence. *Water Resour. Res.*, **5**, 967–88

Matalas, N. C., and Huzzen, C. S. (1967). A property of the range of partial sums. *Proceedings of the International Hydrology Symposium*, vol. 1, *Fort Collins, Colorado*, pp. 252–7

Matalas, N. C., and Wallis, J. R. (1971). Statistical properties of multivariate fractional noise processes. *Water Resour. Res.*, **7**, 1460–8

Mejía, J. M., Dawdy, D. R., and Nordin, C. F. (1974). Streamflow simulation, 3, the broken line process and operational hydrology. *Water Resour. Res.*, **10**, 242–5

Mejía, J. M., Rodríguez–Iturbe, I., and Dawdy D. R. (1972). Streamflow simulation, 2, the broken line process as a potential model for hydrologic simulation. *Water Resour. Res.*, **8**, 931–41

Melentijevich, M. J. (1965). The analysis of range with output linearly dependent upon storage. *Colo. St. Univ., Fort Collins, Hydrol. Papers*, No. 15

Millan, J. (1972). Drought impact on regional economy. *Colo. St. Univ., Fort Collins, Hydrol. Papers*, No. 55

Mood, A. M. (1940). The distribution theory of runs. *Ann. Math. Statist.*, **11**, 367–92

Moran, P. A. P. (1959). *The Theory of Storage*, Wiley, New York

—— (1964). On the range of cumulative sums. *Ann. Inst. Statist. Math., Tokyo*, **16**, 109–12

Nordin, C. F., and Rosbjerg, D. M. (1970). Applications of crossing theory in hydrology. *Bull. Int. Assoc. Sci. Hydrol.*, **15**, 27–43

O'Connell, P. E. (1974). A simple stochastic modelling of Hurst's law. *Proceedings of the 1971 Warsaw Symposium on Mathematical Models in Hydrology*, vol. 1, International Association of Scientific Hydrology, Paris, pp. 169–87

Potter, K. W. (1976). Evidence for non-stationarity as a physical explanation of the Hurst phenomenon. *Water Resour. Res.* **12**, 1047–52

Rice, S. O. (1945). Mathematical analysis of random noise. *Bell Syst. Tech. J.*, **24**, 46–156

Rippl, W. (1883). The capacity of storage reservoirs for water supply. *Proc. Inst. Civ. Eng.*, **71**, 270–8

Rodríguez-Iturbe, I. (1969). Applications of the theory of runs to hydrology. *Water Resour. Res.*, **5**, 1422–6

Salas, J. D. (1972). Range analysis for storage problems of periodic-stochastic processes. *Colo. St. Univ., Fort Collins, Hydrol. Papers*, No. 57

Salas, J. D., Boes, D. C., Yevjevich, V., and Pegram, G. G. S. (1977). On the Hurst phenomenon. *Proceedings of the 3rd International Hydrological Symposium, Fort Collins, Colorado*, preprints

Saldarriaga, J., and Yevjevich, V. (1970). Application of run-lengths to hydrologic series. *Colo. St. Univ., Fort Collins, Hydrol. Papers*, No. 40

Scheidegger, A. E. (1970). Stochastic models in hydrology. *Water Resour. Res.*, **6**, 750–5

Sen, Z. (1976). Wet and dry periods of annual flow series. *J. Hydraul. Div., Proc. Am. Soc. Civ. Eng.*, **102** (HY10), 1503–14

Siddiqui, M. M. (1976). The asymptotic distribution of the range and other functions of partial sums of stationary processes. *Water Resour. Res.*, **12**, 1271–6

Solari, M. E., and Anis, A. A. (1957). The mean and variance of the maximum of the adjusted partial sums of a finite number of independent normal variates. *Ann. Math. Statist.*, **28**, 706–16

Steinberg, R. M. (1968) Reservoir system simulation. *Range of Choice in Water Management* (ed. R. K. Davis), Johns Hopkins, Baltimore, Maryland

Taylor, G. I. (1938). The spectrum of turbulence. *Proc. R. Soc. London A*, **164**, 476–90

Tick, L. J., and Shaman, P. (1966). Sampling, rate and appearance of stationary gaussian processes. *Technometrics*, **8**, 91–106

Tschannerl, G. (1971). Designing reservoirs with short streamflow records. *Water Resour. Res.*, **7**, 827–33

Wallis, J. R., and Matalas, N. C. (1970). Small sample properties of H and K-estimators of the Hurst coefficient h. *Water Resour. Res.*, **6**, 1583–94

—— (1971). Correlogram analysis revisited. *Water Resour. Res.*, **7**, 1448–59

—— (1972). Sensitivity of reservoir design to the generating mechanisms of inflows. *Water Resour. Res.*, **8**, 634–41

Wallis, J. R., and O'Connell, P. E. (1973). Firm reservoir yield—how reliable are historic hydrological records? *Hydrol. Sci. Bull.*, **18**, 347–65

Yevjevich, V. M. (1963). Fluctuations of wet and dry years, part I, research data assembly and mathematical models. *Colo. St. Univ., Fort Collins, Hydrol. Papers*, No. 1

—— (1967). Mean range of linearly dependent normal variables with application to storage problems. *Water Resour. Res.*, **3**, 663–71

Young, G. K., and Jettmar, R. V. (1976). Modelling monthly hydrologic persistence. *Water Resour. Res.*, **12**, 829–35

6 Statistical treatment of floods

A flood is an unusually high stage in a river that can cause damage to adjacent areas. Floods vary spatially and temporally in magnitude and are often measured through their peak discharges. The structural and hydraulic designs of dams and bridges are based on such extreme flows in water courses. Furthermore, the frequency of occurrence, the maximum stage reached, the volume of flood water, the area inundated and the duration of floods are of importance to the civil engineer when planning and designing roads, buildings and structures. In addition, there are dependent economic problems such as flood-plain zoning and flood insurance.

The peak flow and hydrograph of a flood are controlled by many complex and interrelated factors. In the first place, the amount, intensity and areal extent of the causative storm, antecedent precipitation, accumulated snow, temperature and vegetation are significant climatic (or climatically affected) factors. Secondly, physiographical properties such as the size, shape, slopes and orientation of the catchment, especially in relation to storm movements and isohyetal lines, channel and flood-plain storage and soil composition exert a large influence. In addition, man-made or natural changes in catchment characteristics and hydraulic parameters of flow cause further complications.

On account of these complexities, hydrologists have had to resort to statistical methods. The main objective in this approach is to estimate the magnitudes that are exceeded with specific probabilities. This chapter is for the purpose of describing and critically examining the methods of flood estimation. These include the use of type I (Gumbel), II and III extreme value, lognormal, Pearson type III, log Pearson type III, binomial, Poisson and multinomial distributions. In addition, the peaks-over-threshold method is explained. Empirical methods of regional flood frequency analysis and fundamentals of the probable maximum flood technique are also described[1].

[1] Auxiliary treatment through unit hydrograph theory for calculating flood volumes, durations and the like are outside the scope of this text and reference may be made, for example, to Wilson (1974) and to the Natural Environmental Research Council (1975, vol. 1, chapters 5, 6).

6.1 Annual maximum series and return periods

Although floods are high flows which occur at varying intervals of time, it facilitates the analysis to study flood events within constant intervals of time. Also, it is preferable to choose an interval of 1 year rather than, say, a period of 3 months which brings in additional complications because of the seasonal effect.

Let the random variable X_i denote the maximum instantaneous flow in year i, $i = 1, 2, 3, \ldots$, at a gauging station. These X_i values are said to constitute an annual maximum series. In practice, an observed sequence $x_i, i = 1, 2, 3, \ldots N$, is used to make probabilistic estimates of flood flows. Quite often the annual maxima are taken from discrete daily mean flows, and except for flashy rivers (which rise and fall rapidly at times of flood) these have an approximate linear relationship with the instantaneous peaks[2].

Initially, the treatment will be confined to annual maximum series. The alternative approach is to analyse a so-called partial duration series. This pertains to peak flows that exceed a given threshold value and is the subject of section 6.9.

In all statistical flood studies, a particularly important concept is that of the return period T. This is associated with a fixed magnitude of flood discharge called the T-year flood and is, in fact, the average time interval between exceedances of that magnitude[3]. As will be defined in subsection 6.3.3, T is the reciprocal of probability with which a variate exceeds the given magnitude. This can also be explained in terms of percentiles, the method of describing distributions by identifying particular points on the distribution function; for example, the 10-year flood is the ninetieth percentile of the distribution of annual floods. Note that there will be some T-year periods in which the T-year flood will be exceeded more than once and other such periods in which the highest flood is less than the T-year flood[4].

6.2 Distribution of extreme values

Extreme value theory, which is used in flood estimation, dates back to Fréchet (1927) and to Fisher and Tippett (1928). To explain the fundamentals, consider a set of independent random variables $W_j, j = 1, 2, 3, \ldots, n$, with a common cumulative distribution function $G(x)$, where x is an observed value and n is the

---

[2] See, for example, Gumbel (1958a).

[3] The term return period was originally used by Fuller (1914) who was also the first to apply frequency methods in flood estimation.

[4] Specifically, if 10 000 years of data are available, there will be, on average, no flood in excess of the 100-year flood in about 37 of the 100 centuries. Also, the expectation is that in each of about 37 other centuries there will be one such flood, and in the remaining period two or more such floods would occur in each century. It is assumed here that the flood peaks are mutually independent; the calculations are based on the Poisson distribution explained in section 6.9.

number of equispaced data points within a fixed period of, say, 1 year. Also, let $\{W_{(1)}, W_{(2)}, W_{(3)}, \ldots, W_{(n)}\}$ represent the ordered set of the same variables in which $W_{(1)}$ is the smallest and $W_{(n)}$ is the largest. The distribution of $W_{(n)}$ is given by

$$\Pr\{W_{(n)} \leqslant x\} = Q_n(x)$$
$$= \Pr(W_1 \leqslant x)\Pr(W_2 \leqslant x)\Pr(W_3 \leqslant x)\ldots\Pr(W_n \leqslant x)$$
$$= \{G(x)\}^n \tag{6.1}$$

in which Pr denotes probability.

As n increases indefinitely, $Q_n(x)$ approaches one of three asymptotic types known as the types I, II and III extreme value distributions. In the first type, X is an unbounded variable; the second and third types deal with variables with lower and upper limits respectively. Because the type I distribution was extensively developed and applied to flood events by Gumbel (1958a), it is often referred to as the Gumbel distribution[5]. A simplified derivation of this now follows.

6.3 Gumbel distribution

The Gumbel distribution of extreme values results from any initial distribution of the exponential type. Examples of these are the normal and gamma distributions; the right tails of their density functions converge to the exponential form for large values of the variable. Accordingly, $g(x)$, which is the derivative of $G(x)$ in equation 6.1, can be approximated to the form $\lambda e^{-\lambda x}$. This leads to a probability of non-exceedance given by $G(x) = 1 - e^{-\lambda x}$. Therefore, from equation 6.1

$$Q_n(x) = \Pr\{W_{(n)} \leqslant x\}$$
$$= (1 - e^{-\lambda x})^n \tag{6.2}$$

By changing the location and scale, equation 6.2 can be written as $Q_n(x) = [1 - \exp\{-\alpha(x - u)\}/n]^n$, where u and α are the location and dispersion parameters respectively. Hence,

$$\lim_{n \to \infty} \{Q_n(x)\} = F(x)$$
$$= \exp\{-e^{-\alpha(x-u)}\} \tag{6.3}$$

which is the Gumbel (double-exponential) distribution function[6]. Originally, Fisher and Tippett (1928) using a functional relation derived the general form of

---

[5] 'It seems that the rivers know the theory,' said Gumbel (1967) in what was to be his last address to engineering hydrologists, 'It remains to convince the engineers—not only in underdeveloped countries—of the validity of this analysis.' Court (1952) gives a simple explanation of the Gumbel procedure as originally formulated.

[6] For a rigorous mathematical proof, see Gumbel (1958a, pp. 156–9), Kendall and Stuart (1977, pp. 352–6) or Bury (1975, pp. 369–71). The particular limit theorem is proved in subsection 6.8.2.

equation 6.3 and the other two types of extreme value distributions included in section 6.4.

If we follow the notation of Gumbel (1958a) and substitute the value y of a reduced (that is, dimensionless) random variate Y where

$$y = \alpha(x - u) \tag{6.4}$$

the basic form of the Gumbel distribution becomes

$$F(y) = \exp(-e^{-y}) \tag{6.5}$$

the density function of which is

$$f(y) = dF(y)/dy$$
$$= e^{-y}\exp(-e^{-y}) \tag{6.6}$$

6.3.1 Moment-generating function

The moments of a function such as the Gumbel distribution can be obtained through its moment-generating function (MGF). For a random variate Y with moments of all orders (as explained in section 3.3) and a probability density function $f(y)$, the MGF is defined as

$$M_Y(t) = E(e^{tY})$$

$$= \int_{-\infty}^{+\infty} e^{ty}f(y)\,dy \tag{6.7}$$

where E denotes expectation (that is, expected value) and t is a dummy variable[7]. From the series expansion of e^{tY},

$$M_Y(t) = E\{1 + tY + (tY)^2/2! + (tY)^3/3! + \ldots\} \tag{6.8}$$

6.3.2 Statistical properties

By substituting $z = e^{-y}$, which makes $dz/dy = -e^{-y}$, it follows from equations 6.6 and 6.7 that for the Gumbel distribution

$$M_Y(t) = \int_0^\infty z^{-t}e^{-z}\,dz$$

Replacing $-t$ in the right-hand side by $(1-t)-1$ it is seen, from the standard form of the gamma function given in section 3.2, that

$$M_Y(t) = \Gamma(1-t) \tag{6.9}$$

[7] Note that in the more advanced books the characteristic function $E(e^{iYt})$, which is the expectation of a complex function, is used in place of the MGF.

From equations 6.8 and 6.9, therefore, the rth moment of the Y population is given by

$$\mu_r'(Y) = \frac{d^r}{dt^r} \Gamma(1-t) \Big|_{t=0} \tag{6.10}$$

for the Gumbel distribution. It follows, by taking the derivative of $M_Y(t)$ and by putting $t = 0$, that

$$\mu_1'(Y) = \frac{d}{dt} \Gamma(1-t) \Big|_{t=0}$$

$$= -\Gamma(1-t)\psi(1-t) \Big|_{t=0}$$

$$= -\psi(1) \tag{6.11}$$

where $\psi(t) = d[\ln\{\Gamma(t)\}]/dt$ is the psi function in subsection 3.4.1; this is also called the digamma function. From tables, $\psi(1) = -0.5772$, which is known as Euler's constant[8]. Hence,

$$E(y) = \mu_1'(Y) = 0.5772$$

where, as noted, y is a reduced variate. Also,

$$\mu_2'(Y) = \Gamma(1-t) \left[\frac{d\psi(1-t)}{dt} + \{\psi(1-t)\}^2 \right] \Big|_{t=0} \tag{6.12}$$

where $d\psi(t)/dt = \psi'(t)$ is the trigamma function and is tabulated in some books[9]. Now $\psi'(1) = \pi^2/6$. Hence, $\mu_2'(Y) = \pi^2/6 + (0.5772)^2$ and var $(Y) = \mu_2(Y) = \mu_2'(Y) - \{\mu_1'(Y)\}^2 = \pi^2/6$, which approximates to 1.6449. Similarly, by using the multigamma functions, $\psi''(1)$ and $\psi^{(3)}(1)$, it can be shown that the coefficient of skewness is 1.1396 and the coefficient of kurtosis is 5.4000.

Because the skewness and higher coefficients are the same for both Y and X populations, the only changes that arise in fitting are those of location and dispersion as given by equation 6.4. The maxima and minima of the density function $f(y)$ are found from the derivative of $f(y)$ in equation 6.6 and these are at $y = \infty$, $-\infty$ and 0, the first two of which are the minimum points and the third is a maximum point (showing that the mode is above the origin for the variate Y). The median value, obtained by setting $F(y)$ in equation 6.5 to 0.5, is 0.3665. Also, the maximum ordinate which occurs at $y = 0$ is $1/e = 0.3679$, which is a constant for both the X and Y populations. These properties and the shape of the Gumbel density function are shown in figure 6.1, in which comparison is made with the normal density function.

[8] See, for example, Abramowitz and Stegun (1964, pp. 267–71).
[9] See, for example, Tribus (1969, p. 112).

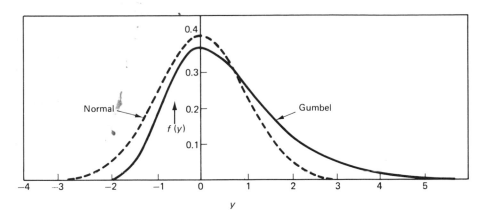

Figure 6.1   Gumbel and normal density functions compared

6.3.3   Definition of return period

Let the reduced random variates Y_i denote the maximum floods in years $i, i = 1,$ 2, 3, ..., respectively. Then, if the Y_i values are serially independent, the probability that the time interval $\tilde{T}$ between exceedances of a flood magnitude y (in reduced units) equals n is given by

$$\Pr(\tilde{T} = n) = \Pr(Y_1 < y)\Pr(Y_2 < y) \dots \Pr(Y_{n-1} < y)\Pr(Y_n > y)$$

$$= \{\Pr(Y < y)\}^{n-1}\Pr(Y > y)$$

For the second equality we assume that the Y_i values are identically distributed. This geometric distribution corresponds to equation 5.6. Here, the variable n can take any value from 1 to ∞, and the expected value $E(\tilde{T})$ is found from the properties of the geometric distribution as follows.

$$E(\tilde{T}) = \sum_{n=1}^{\infty} n\Pr(\tilde{T} = n)$$

$$= \sum_{n=1}^{\infty} n\{1 - \Pr(Y > y)\}^{n-1}\Pr(Y > y)$$

$$= 1/\Pr(Y > y)$$

The return period T is commonly written instead of $E(\tilde{T})$ above[10].

---

[10]   Lloyd (1970) has shown that the variance of T is $\{1 - \Pr(Y > y)\}/\{\Pr(Y > y)\}^2$. If the flood events are serially correlated, the variance is greater; the return period is then given by $T = 1/\Pr(Y_n > y \mid Y_{n-1} < y)$.

6.3.4 *Relationship between Gumbel variate and return period*

From equation 6.5 and subsection 6.3.3

$$1 - \exp(-e^{-y}) = 1/T \tag{6.13}$$

Hence,

$$y = -\ln\{\ln(T) - \ln(T-1)\} \tag{6.14}$$

Now

$$y = -\ln\{-\ln(1 - 1/T)\}$$
$$= -\ln\{-(-1/T) + \tfrac{1}{2}(-1/T)^2 - \tfrac{1}{3}(-1/T)^3 + \ldots\}$$

from Maclaurin's theorem. If only three terms are used in the series expansion,

$$y \approx -\ln(1/T + 1/2T^2 + 1/3T^3) = \ln\{6T^3/(6T^2 + 3T + 2)\}$$

Hence, the approximations

$$y \approx \ln(T - 1/2) \quad \text{or} \quad y \approx \ln(T) \tag{6.15}$$

may be used in place of equation 6.14 for $T > 10$ years if errors up to 0.5 % and 2.5 % respectively can be tolerated; the second approximation is sufficient for all practical purposes when $T > 25$ years.

   Equation 6.14 gives a non-linear relationship between the value y of the reduced variate and the return period T. A few pairs of values (y, T) are as follows: 0, 1.58 (most probable flood); 0.3665, 2 (median flood); 0.5772, 2.33 (mean flood); 1.2459, 4.00; 3.9019, 50.00; 4.6002, 100.00; 6.2136, 500.00. Engineers and hydrologists have been plotting experimental data on special types of paper since Hazen (1914), a civil engineer, originated the graphical linearisation of the normal distribution. The method is used as a verification of the suitability of one or more assumed distributions for a given sample of data.

6.3.5 *Probability paper*

Gumbel probability paper (suggested originally by Powell (1943)) may be drawn as follows. Initially, values of the return period T, such as 1.01, 1.1, 1.2, 1.3, 1.5, 2, 3, 4, 5, 10, 15, 20, 30, 40, 50, 60, 100, 200 and 250, are selected. After computing the corresponding values of the reduced variate y by using equation 6.14, vertical lines spaced at distances directly proportional to the differences between the y values are drawn, and the return periods T are shown correspondingly against these lines (figure 6.2). In this way the y values are on a linear scale, but the return periods T are on a double-exponential scale, as given by equation 6.13. On the other hand, if a graph of x against y is drawn on arithmetic paper, a straight-line plot

$$x = y/\alpha + u \tag{6.16}$$

which follows from equation 6.4, will give the flood magnitudes x for various y

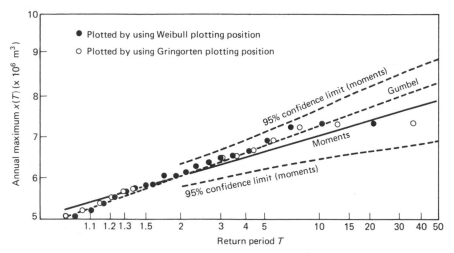

Figure 6.2   Gumbel distribution fitted to annual maxima from daily inflows to Caban Coch Reservoir for the period 1909 to 1928

values. However, it is more meaningful to relate x to the return periods T rather than to the y values. Therefore, the scales are chosen accordingly, and from equations 6.14 and 6.16 the relationship of x against T is given by

$$x(T) = u - \ln\{\ln(T) - \ln(T - 1)\}/\alpha \qquad (6.17)$$

This shows that a straight line could be fitted if the observed values are plotted on Gumbel paper. It provides a quick verification of fit without using the goodness-of-fit tests described in chapter 3; a good fit would justify the acceptance of the Gumbel distribution. When plotting the data, however, the true return periods associated with each of the items of data are not known. Therefore, the accepted practice is to use what is termed a plotting position[11].

6.3.6   Plotting positions

Let m denote the rank of N items of annual maxima which are ordered so that the first value ($m = 1$) is the largest and the smallest ($m = N$) is placed last[12]. One possible method, first applied to flood flows in California, is to take m/N as the probability of exceedance. Accordingly, $1/T(= 1 - F(x)) = m/N$, but the smallest has a probability of exceedance equal to 1, which is not found on probability paper. An alternative plotting position is to make $T = N/(m - 1)$, but the drawback is that the largest flood cannot be plotted because it has a

[11] Gumbel (1958a, pp. 32–6) gives conditions for the choice of a plotting position; for example, it should be possible to plot all the observations. Also, the plotting position ought to depend on the assumed distribution.
[12] For plotting purposes, it is convenient to reverse the conventional method of ordering as defined in section 6.2.

return period of infinity, or in other words a probability of zero. Hazen (1930), a pioneer in flood studies, suggested the alternative $T = N/(m - 1/2)$ in order to plot all the data. This was objected to by Gumbel (1958b) on the grounds that the highest flood has a return period of $2N$. Instead, he recommended the use of the Weibull plotting position $T = (N + 1)/m$ for the Gumbel distribution. Subsequently, Gringorten (1963) showed that $T = (N + 0.012)/(m - 0.44)$ is a better approximation as an unbiased plotting position for this distribution. To explain the meaning of bias in this context, consider a sample of N annual maxima, from which ℓ subsamples each of length N/ℓ (with $N/\ell > 30$, say) are formed and in which the values in each subsample are ranked in order. Then, an unbiased plotting position is such that, if average values of the same rank from different samples are plotted and if ℓ is indefinitely large, these values will lie on a line which represents the distribution of the population[13]. Further comments on plotting positions from the viewpoint of the practising engineer will be given in section 6.7.

Four of the commonly used plotting positions are given in table 6.1. Also shown are the return intervals for the largest, second largest and smallest flood from a sample of 100 items.

Table 6.1   Plotting positions

Plotting position	Usage	For $N = 100$		
		T for $m = 1$ (100-year flood)	T for $m = 2$ (50-year flood)	T for $m = 100$ (1.01-year flood)
Weibull, $T = (N + 1)/m$	Used by Gumbel	101	50.5	1.01
Gringorten, $T = (N + 0.12)/(m - 0.44)$	Extreme value distributions	179	64	1.01
Hazen, $T = N/(m - \frac{1}{2})$	Gamma distribution	200	66.7	1.01
Blom, $T = (N + \frac{1}{4})/(m - \frac{3}{8})$	Normal (and lognormal) distributions	160.4	61.7	1.01

6.3.7   Method-of-moments fitting procedure

From the relationship $Y = \alpha(X - u)$ in equation 6.4,

$$E(y) = \alpha\{E(X) - u\} \tag{6.18}$$

[13] For discussions on plotting positions, see Benson (1962b), Stipp and Young (1971) and the Natural Environmental Research Council (1975, vol. 1, chapter 2); also, Langbein (1960) gives simple derivations for some plotting positions; the treatment by Kimball (1960) and Barnett (1975) is more sophisticated.

and

$$\text{var}(Y) = \alpha^2 \text{var}(X) \tag{6.19}$$

where var denotes variance. Therefore if we substitute 0.5772 for $E(y)$ and $\pi^2/6$ for var(y) (from the results previously obtained in subsection 6.3.2) and sample estimators $\bar{x}$ and s^2, for $E(X)$ and var(X) respectively, the moment estimators of the parameters α and u are

$$\tilde{\alpha} = 1.282/s \tag{6.20}$$

and

$$\tilde{u} = \bar{x} - 0.45s \tag{6.21}$$

Hence, from equations 6.17, 6.20 and 6.21,

$$\tilde{x}(T) = \bar{x} - s[0.4500 + 0.7797 \ln\{\ln(T) - \ln(T-1)\}] \tag{6.22}$$

Using this formula a theoretical straight line could be drawn on the Gumbel graph paper of $x(T)$ against T to represent a sample of annual maxima x_1, x_2, x_3, . . ., x_N with estimated mean $\bar{x}$ and standard deviation s respectively. Two points would obviously suffice to define this line, and the Gringorten plotting position can be used to represent the data. This is, of course, on the assumption, which is not necessarily true, that the data are distributed in this way.

Example 6.1   Ranked annual maxima from mean daily inflows to Caban Coch Reservoir during the period 1909 to 1928 are as follows.

Annual maxima ($\times 10^6$ m^3)									
7.31	7.30	7.22	6.90	6.64	6.53	6.48	6.38	6.30	6.12
6.07	6.06	5.82	5.81	5.75	5.65	5.51	5.37	5.20	5.08

Plot the data on Gumbel paper, and estimate the mean and standard deviation from the sample. Using these statistics, fit a straight line to the data. Estimate the 50-year flood.

Let x_i, $i = 1, 2, \ldots, N$, denote the maxima where $N = 20$ and let $\sum$ denote $\sum_{i=1}^{N}$. The estimated mean $\bar{x} = \sum x_i/N = 6.175 \times 10^6$ m^3 and $s = \{(\sum x_i^2/N - \bar{x}^2)N/(N-1)\}^{1/2} = 0.6746 \times 10^6$ m^3 is the estimated standard deviation[14].

Equations 6.20 and 6.21 provide estimates $\tilde{\alpha} = 1.9011$ and $\tilde{u} = 5.8714$ of the parameters, and the Gringorten plotting position $T = (N + 0.12)/(m - 0.44)$

[14] This formula is used by Gumbel (1941) to compute what he terms 'the observed standard deviation'. As a matter of interest, if the x_i values are normally distributed, then in order to obtain a strictly unbiased estimate of s, the quantity $K = 2\{\Gamma(N/2)\}^2/[\Gamma\{(N-1)/2\}]^2$, in which Γ denotes the complete gamma function, should replace the divisor $N-1$ in the formula; see, for example, Holtzman (1950).

gives the return periods as follows: 35.9, 12.9, 7.86, 5.65, 4.41, 3.62, 3.07, 2.66, 2.35, 2.10, 1.91, 1.74, 1.60, 1.48, 1.38, 1.29, 1.21, 1.15, 1.08 and 1.03. The ranked values are plotted, and a straight line is then fitted by using the method of moments. This is done by calculating two values from equation 6.22, such as $\tilde{x}(2) = 6.06$ and $\tilde{x}(50) = 7.92$. These two points define the (full) straight line of $x(T)$ against T.

Figure 6.2 shows that, if the two largest values are disregarded, the Gumbel distribution as fitted by the method of moments provides a good fit to the data. It is quite possible that this sample is biased downwards and the two highest values represent return periods less than 20 years. Unfortunately, there is no satisfactory method of verifying this, but we could, in the first instance, fit the Gumbel distribution by different methods and see whether there is a significant change in the results.

6.3.8 Gumbel's fitting method

In Gumbel's fitting method, the estimation of the parameters u and α are based on the Weibull plotting position $T = (N + 1)/m$, where N is the sample size and m is the rank commencing with the largest value. If we use Gumbel's notation, the procedure is to evaluate the mean $\bar{y}_N$ and the standard deviation $\sigma_N = \{\Sigma(y - \bar{y}_N)^2/N\}^{1/2}$ of the N values of the reduced variate Y, after substituting each of the values $m = 1, 2, 3, \ldots, N$ in $T = (N + 1)/m$ and then calculating the corresponding y values from equation 6.14. It will, of course, be more convenient here to refer to tables of $\bar{y}_N$ and σ_N such as those provided by Gumbel (1954, 1958a). Alternatively, refer to table 6.2, which is more accurate.

Table 6.2 Expected means $\bar{y}_N$ and standard deviations σ_N of Gumbel reduced variates

N	$\bar{y}$	σ_N	N	$\bar{y}_N$	σ_N	N	$\bar{y}_N$	σ_N
16	0.5154	1.0306	33	0.5388	1.1225	50	0.5485	1.1607
17	0.5177	1.0397	34	0.5396	1.1256	51	0.5489	1.1623
18	0.5198	1.0481	35	0.5403	1.1285	52	0.5493	1.1638
19	0.5217	1.0557	36	0.5411	1.1313	53	0.5497	1.1653
20	0.5236	1.0628	37	0.5417	1.1339	54	0.5501	1.1668
21	0.5252	1.0694	38	0.5424	1.1365	55	0.5504	1.1682
22	0.5268	1.0755	39	0.5430	1.1390	56	0.5508	1.1695
23	0.5282	1.0812	40	0.5436	1.1413	57	0.5511	1.1709
24	0.5296	1.0865	41	0.5442	1.1436	58	0.5515	1.1722
25	0.5309	1.0914	42	0.5448	1.1458	59	0.5518	1.1734
26	0.5321	1.0961	43	0.5453	1.1479	60	0.5521	1.1747
27	0.5332	1.1005	44	0.5458	1.1499	70	0.5548	1.1854
28	0.5343	1.1047	45	0.5463	1.1518	80	0.5569	1.1938
29	0.5353	1.1086	46	0.5468	1.1537	90	0.0586	1.2007
30	0.5362	1.1124	47	0.5472	1.5555	100	0.5600	1.2065
31	0.5371	1.1159	48	0.5477	1.1573	∞	0.5772	1.2825
32	0.5380	1.1193	49	0.5481	1.1590			

Therefore, substituting $\bar{y}_N$ for $E(Y)$ and σ_N^2 for var(Y) and the sample estimators $\bar{x}$ and s^2 for $E(x)$ and var(x) respectively in equation 6.18 and 6.19, we obtain the following.

$$\tilde{\alpha}' = \sigma_N/s \tag{6.23}$$

and

$$\tilde{u}' = \bar{x} - \bar{y}_N s/\sigma_N \tag{6.24}$$

Hence, from equations 6.17, 6.23 and 6.24,

$$\tilde{x}'(T) = \bar{x} - (s/\sigma_N)[\bar{y}_N + \ln\{\ln(T) - \ln(T-1)\}] \tag{6.25}$$

Example 6.2   Plot the extreme value data from example 6.1 using the Weibull plotting position. Hence, fit a straight line using Gumbel's fitting procedure, and estimate the 50-year flood.

The ordered return periods $T = (N+1)/m$ are as follows: 21, 10.5, 7, 5.25, 4.2, 3.5, 3, 2.625, 2.333, 2.1, 1.909, 1.75, 1.615, 1.5, 1.4, 1.313, 1.235, 1.167, 1.105, 1.05. As a matter of interest, the corresponding y values are calculated as follows: 3.02, 2.302, 1.87, 1.554, 1.302, 1.089, 0.903, 0.735, 0.581, 0.436, 0.298, 0.166, 0.0355, -0.0940, -0.2254, -0.361, -0.506, -0.666, -0.855, -1.113, from which $\bar{y}_N = 0.5236$ and $\sigma_N = 1.0628$; these tally with the values given in table 6.2. (Substituting the computed values from example 6.1 of $\bar{x}$ and s in equations 6.23 and 6.24, we find $\tilde{\alpha}' = 1.5754$ and $\tilde{u}' = 5.8426$.) From equation 6.25, $\tilde{x}'(2) = 6.08$ and $\tilde{x}'(50) = 8.32$. These two points define the broken line in figure 6.2. Notice that the differences between the plotted points are mainly in the high and low values.

6.3.9   *Frequency factors for Gumbel distribution*

Following Chow (1951, 1964), we can write equations 6.22 and 6.25 in the form

$$x(T) = \mu + K(T)\sigma \tag{6.26}$$

to represent the population of annual maxima. That is to say, an annual maximum with return period T is the sum of the mean and a constant $K(T)$ times the standard deviation of the maxima. The function $K(T)$, for a particular T, depends on the form of the density function of the maxima. It is clear from equation 6.22 that, for the Gumbel distribution and the method-of-moments procedure,

$$K(T) = -[0.4500 + 0.7797\ln\{\ln(T) - \ln(T-1)\}] \tag{6.27}$$

Some values of $K(T)$ are given in table 6.3.

Table 6.3   Values of $K(T)$ using the method of moments

T	10000	1000	500	200	100	50	20	10	2.33	1.5
$K(T)$	6.73	4.94	4.39	3.68	3.14	2.59	1.87	1.30	0	-0.38

For Gumbel's method of fitting, it follows from equation 6.25 that

$$K(T) = -[\bar{y}_N + \ln\{\ln(T) - \ln(T-1)\}]/\sigma_N \tag{6.28}$$

For a given sample of size N, $\bar{y}_N$ and σ_N are known, and this formula can be used to calculate $K(T)$ through Gumbel's method for any value of T.

6.3.10   Confidence limits

It can be shown that the variance of the T-year flood estimated, from a sample of size N with an estimated variance s^2, by Gumbel's fitting method is

$$\text{var}\{\tilde{x}'(T)\} = (s^2/N)[1 + 1.14W(T)\{(N-1)/N\}^{1/2}$$
$$+ W(T)^2(1.1 - 0.6/N)] \tag{6.29}$$

where $W(T) = \{\bar{y}_N - y(T)\}/\sigma_N$ in which $y(T)$ is the value of y obtained from equation 6.14 and $\bar{y}_N$ and σ_N are the mean and standard deviation respectively of the N y values[15].

Then, if we assume that the sampling distribution of the T-year flood is normal, the $100(1-\alpha)\%$ confidence limits of $\tilde{x}(T)$ are

$$\tilde{x}'(T) \pm z_{\alpha/2}[\text{var}\{x'(T)\}]^{1/2}$$

where $z_{\alpha/2}$ is the value which a standard normal deviate exceeds with probability $\alpha/2$. Strictly speaking, the normal distribution is applicable only when N is large, say, of the order of 200 or greater and if $\tilde{x}'(T)$ behaves as an arithmetic mean.

For the method-of-moments fitting procedure, the variance of the estimated T-year flood is given by

$$\text{var}\{\tilde{x}(T)\} = (s^2/N)[1 + 1.14K(T) + K(T)^2\{0.6 + 0.5N/(N-1)\}] \tag{6.30}$$

for which equation 6.27 gives the $K(T)$ function

Example 6.3   Using the data in example 6.1 and equation 6.30, calculate the 95% confidence limits of the population value of $\tilde{x}(T)$, for $T = 2, 5, 10, 20, 30, 50$.

$$s^2/N = 0.6746^2/20$$
$$= 0.02276$$
$$\{0.6 + 0.5N/(N-1)\} = 0.6 + 10/19$$
$$= 1.1263$$

The calculations are given in table 6.4.

---

[15] Lowery and Nash (1970) and Kaczmarek (1957) give derivations; see also the World Meteorological Organisation (1974, p. 5.26).

Table 6.4 95% confidence limits by moments method

T	$K(T)$	$\mathrm{var}\{\hat{x}(T)\}$	$\hat{x}(T)\} = \bar{x} + K(T)s$	$1.96[\mathrm{var}\{\hat{x}(T)\}]^{1/2}$	Upper confidence limit	Lower confidence limit
50	2.592	0.2622	7.92	1.00	8.92	6.92
30	2.189	0.2024	7.65	0.88	8.53	6.77
20	1.866	0.1604	7.44	0.79	8.23	6.65
10	1.305	0.1002	7.06	0.62	7.68	6.44
5	0.7195	0.0547	6.66	0.46	7.12	6.20
2	−0.1642	0.0192	6.06	0.27	6.33	5.79

6.3.11   *Maximum likelihood method of estimation*

The ML method of estimation is described in section 3.4. From equations 6.4, 6.5 and 6.6 the probability distribution and density functions of the Gumbel distribution are given by

$$F(x) = \exp\{-e^{-(x-u)\alpha}\}$$

and

$$f(x) = \alpha e^{-(x-u)\alpha}\exp\{-e^{-(x-u)\alpha}\}$$

respectively. For a sample x_i, $i = 1, 2, \ldots, N$, the log likelihood function, $L^*(x_1, x_2, \ldots, x_N \mid u, \alpha)$, which is conditional to the values u and α of the parameters, is given by

$$L^* = -\sum(x_i - u)\alpha - \sum e^{-(x_i - u)\alpha} + N\ln(\alpha) \tag{6.31}$$

where $\sum$ denotes $\sum\limits_{i=1}^{N}$. The partial derivatives of equation 6.31 are

$$\partial L^*/\partial\alpha = -\sum(x_i - u) + \sum(x_i - u)e^{-(x_i - u)\alpha} + N/\alpha \tag{6.32}$$

and

$$\partial L^*/\partial u = N\alpha - \sum \alpha e^{-(x_i - u)\alpha} \tag{6.33}$$

The ML estimators $\hat{u}$ and $\hat{\alpha}$ of the parameters are obtained by setting $\partial L^*/\partial\alpha = 0$, $\partial L^*/\partial u = 0$. For the ML conditions therefore, from equation 6.33

$$\exp(\hat{u}\hat{\alpha}) = N \Big/ \sum\exp(-\hat{\alpha}x_i) \tag{6.34}$$

and, from equation 6.32 after substituting from equations 6.33 and 6.34 and simplifying,

$$1/\hat{\alpha} = \bar{x} - \sum\{x_i\exp(-\hat{\alpha}x_i)\}\Big/\sum\exp(-\hat{\alpha}x_i) \tag{6.35}$$

where $\bar{x} = \sum x_i/N$. Also, from equation 6.34,

$$\hat{u} = -(1/\hat{\alpha})\ln\{1/N)\sum\exp(-\hat{\alpha}x_i)\} \tag{6.36}$$

A simple method for solving equations 6.35 and 6.36 is to estimate an initial value of α by the method of moments and then to substitute it in the right-hand side of equation 6.35; the reciprocal of equation 6.35 will give the next trial value. Therefore, the third value of α is made equal to the weighted average of the first and second, and equation 6.35 is used again to obtain a fourth value; here, the most recent value deserves a greater weight. The routine is repeated till equation 6.35 holds, and then, if $\hat{\alpha}$ is substituted in equation 6.36, $\hat{u}$ is found[16]. All these

---

[16] Gumbel (1958b, pp. 231–4) explains the methods of B. F. Kimball. Elsewhere, a procedure to find numerical solutions for $\hat{\alpha}$ and $\hat{u}$ is given by Jenkinson (1969, pp. 205–9), and this is followed by the Natural Environmental Research Council (1975, vol. 1, pp. 85–9). Also, Panchang (1969) shows how to obtain a solution iteratively.

trial-and-error methods could be easily implemented through a digital computer. However, a pocket calculator was used for the short sequence in the next example.

Example 6.4   Fit the Gumbel distribution by the ML method to the data given in example 6.1. Estimate the parameters and the 50-year flood.

The first trial value of parameter α is made equal to 1.9011, which is obtained from example 6.1. After substituting this in the right-hand side of equation 6.35, the second estimate of 1.6201 is obtained from the reciprocal. Another trial value of α, say, $(2 \times 1.6201 + 1.9011)/3 = 1.7138$ used in the right-hand side of equation 6.35 gives the next estimate of 1. 7351. Finally, $\hat{\alpha} = 1.726$ is thought to be sufficiently accurate (considering the data) and, from equation 6.36, $\hat{u} = 5.861$. Also, $\hat{x}(50) = 8.12$ from equation 6.17. This estimate of the 50-year flood is higher than the value obtained by the method of moments but is less than that from Gumbel's method.

In order to place confidence limits on the $\hat{x}(T)$ values found by the ML method, it can be assumed that these are asymptotically normally distributed. The standard error function which is required is somewhat complicated; the procedure is comparable with that used by Moran (1957).

Comments on the use of the ML method such as its dependence on an assumed distribution are given in section 3.4. Of course, any other method which assumes a particular probability model will give unsatisfactory results if the probability model is itself incorrect. This point is taken up again in section 6.7. There has been criticism by Gumbel (1967) that the ML method gives undue weight to the smaller values; although this may not be a fair criticism, it should not be forgotten that engineers looking for practical means of extrapolation tend to give more attention to the larger values in the data[17].

6.3.12   *Limitations in Gumbel method*

It should be noted that the limiting form of the extreme value distribution is reached extremely slowly. On theoretical considerations, the value of n in equation 6.1 should be extremely large, perhaps greater than 10^9, for the asymptotic form (equation 6.3) to hold. On the contrary, n is taken as 365 when applied to discrete daily series[18].

In applications it is found that there is a serial dependence and periodicity in the data, from which the extremes are drawn. This is generally true of daily and shorter-interval hydrological or meteorological data. However, Watson (1954) has shown that the limiting distribution will also hold when the process is of a certain moving-average type. On the other hand, Gumbel (1967) has warned about errors of estimation arising from cycles, pseudocycles and trend-like movements. Furthermore, the theory is not strictly valid if the extreme values are not identically distributed. This happens when there are different causative

---

[17] There are also other fitting procedures such as Downton's method, as used, for example, by Huxham and McGilchrist (1969).

[18] See, for example, Gumbel (1958a, p. 4).

factors for floods such as frontal rains, thunderstorms and melting of snow.

There is also another operational point. Because the left extremities of density functions of the X and Y populations are at $-\infty$, some negative values can be generated by the Gumbel probability model. For the reduced random variate Y, it follows from equation 6.4 (as could be visualised from figure 6.1) that the probability of a negative value is $1/e = 0.3679$. If we consider a practical case, it is found that, by substituting in equation 6.27, $K(1.01) = -1.6424$, which is applicable for a very low value that is exceeded by the annual maxima in 99 years out of 100. Hence, if $\sigma > 0.6089\mu$ in equation 6.26, a negative flood will occur on average once in 100 years. However, for the estimated value of the standard deviation σ in example 6.1, this period is much longer than 100 years.

Finally, as for other probability distribution functions, sampling errors in the estimates of parameters may be quite large, the implication being that extrapolations may be subject to large errors. Benson (1960) showed that for a hypothetical sample of 1000 items of flood data from a known Gumbel population, parameters estimated from independently chosen subsamples (such as those from a set of 40 subsamples of 25-year periods) are vastly different. It was seen that straight-line plots representing these subsamples have widely varying intercepts and gradients, the variabilities increasing, as expected, in inverse proportion to the subsample lengths. It is found, for instance, that to estimate values of 50- and 100-year floods which are within 25 % of the correct value, 95 % of the time, minimum sample lengths of 39 and 48 years respectively are required. Again, for the estimation of a 50-year flood with a maximum error of 10 %, record lengths of 90 or 110 are required for chances of success equal to 80 % or 95 % of the time respectively.

6.4   General extreme value distribution

As already noted, the Gumbel or type I extreme value distribution is a particular type of the asymptotic or limiting distribution applicable to extreme values. The two-parameter Gumbel distribution is advantageous in the theoretical treatment of flood events, but because of the limitations in application it would be appropriate to consider also the practicability of the other two extreme value asymptotic distributions. The types II and III extreme value distributions are three parametric and their (asymptotic) forms can be obtained if we initially write $G(a_n x)$ in equation 6.1 in place of $G(x)$ and equate a_n to $n^{-\ell}$ and n', where ℓ is a positive constant[19]. Readers may bypass this section on a first reading; however, the distributions are used for regional analysis in section 6.10.

6.4.1   *Type II extreme value distribution*

If we follow the notation in equations 6.2 and 6.3, the asymptotic type II extreme

[19] See Jenkinson (1955) for applications in hydrometeorology and Gumbel (1958a, b) for the theory.

value distribution is given by

$$\lim_{N \to \infty} [\Pr\{W_{(n)} \leqslant x\}] = \exp[-\{(u-\varepsilon)/(x-\varepsilon)\}^{\alpha}] \qquad (6.37)$$

where Pr denotes probability of non-exceedance and $W_{(n)}$ is a random variable representing the maximum flood in any year, of which x is a particular value; $x \geqslant \varepsilon$ and $u \geqslant \varepsilon$. This is also known as the Fréchet distribution.

From equations 6.3 and 6.37

$$x = \varepsilon + (u - \varepsilon)\exp(y/\alpha) \qquad (6.38)$$

where y is the type I extreme value (Gumbel) reduced variate. Because of the positive exponential form (for $\alpha > 0$), x increases faster than for the Gumbel distribution, when y is increased. Therefore the distribution can be represented by a curve which is *concave upwards* on Gumbel probability paper. Now, if x is displaced by ε, its natural logarithm will bear a linear relationship with y. If the assumption $\varepsilon = 0$ holds, a straight line of x against y can be drawn on a special type of Gumbel probability paper that has a vertical logarithmic scale to represent this distribution in its two-parameter form; alternatively we may plot $\log(x)$ against y on ordinary Gumbel probability paper.

6.4.2   *Type III extreme value distribution*

If we use similar notation as in the type II distribution, the probability of non-exceedance in this case is given by

$$\lim_{N \to \infty} [\Pr\{W_{(n)} \leqslant x\}] = \exp[-\{(\omega-x)/(\omega-u)\}^{\alpha}] \qquad (6.39)$$

where $x \leqslant \omega$; $u \leqslant \omega$. The relationship between x and y is of the form

$$x = \omega - (\omega - u)\exp(-y/\alpha) \qquad (6.40)$$

This is a negative exponential type, and, therefore, it can be represented by a curve which is *concave downwards* on Gumbel probability paper. Note that this is of the same type as the Weibull function given by equation 3.60.

6.4.3   *General formula for extreme value distribution*

Corresponding to equations 6.39 and 6.40, Jenkinson (1969) suggested a single equation of the type

$$x = u + (1/\alpha)\{1 - \exp(-ky)\}/k \qquad (6.41)$$

to represent the relationships between x and y of the three types of asymptotic extreme value distributions in which u, α and k are parameters of location, scale and shape respectively. This is called the general extreme value (GEV) distribution. By substituting the series expansion of $\exp(-ky)$ in equation 6.41 and by then dividing by k, it is seen that the special case $k = 0$ leads to the linear relationship for x against y which characterises the type I extreme value distribution as given by equation 6.4. The type II extreme value distribution is applicable when $k < 0$, and, if $k > 0$, the type III distribution is signified; these two are represented by equations 6.38 and 6.40 respectively.

In order to evaluate the T-year flood by this method, equation 6.41 is written

$$x(T) = u + z(T)/\alpha \tag{6.42}$$

where the value $z(T)$ of the standardised variate Z is given by

$$z(T) = \{1 - \exp(-ky)\}/k \tag{6.43}$$

in which y and T are related as shown by equation 6.14.

The method of sextiles applied by Jenkinson (1969) gives approximate estimates of k, u and α as follows. The infinite population of Z values, the probability distribution of which can be given as a function of k and y through equation 6.43, is considered to be arranged in increasing order and to be divided into six groups of equal size. Denote the mean of the variates in the ith sextile group by $\mu_{Z,i}$, where $i = 1$ represents the large sextile, and the mean and standard deviation of these six mean values by μ_Z and σ_Z respectively. Then, let the corresponding X values also be divided into six groups in the same way. This is done in a sample of data by ordering the items and by dividing them into six equal or nearly equal groups. Let $\mu_{X,i}$ denote the population mean of the variates in the ith sextile group; also, let the mean and standard deviation of these six values be

$$\mu = \sum_{i=1}^{6} \mu_{X,i}/6$$

and

$$\sigma = \left\{ \sum_{i=1}^{6} (\mu_{X,i} - \mu)^2/6 \right\}^{1/2}$$

respectively. From equation 6.42, by taking expectations and by equating variances

$$\mu = u + \mu_Z/\alpha \tag{6.44}$$

and

$$\sigma = \sigma_Z/\alpha \tag{6.45}$$

The relationships between the shape parameters k (which is common to both X and Z populations), μ_Z, σ_Z and a shape ratio $r - (\mu_{Z,5} - \mu_{Z,6})/(\mu_{Z,1} - \mu_{Z,2})$ are given in table 6.5. (From the above definition, using equations 6.43, 6.7 and 6.9, $\mu_Z = \{1 - \Gamma(1 + k)\}/k$. However, to calculate σ_Z and r, we need to use the inverse gamma function, explained in subsection 3.5.1.)

The shape ratio r, which is the same for the Z and X populations from equation 6.42, is estimated from the sample-based statistics $\hat{\mu}_{x,i}$ by $\hat{r}$ $= (\hat{\mu}_{x,5} - \hat{\mu}_{x,6})/(\hat{\mu}_{x,1} - \hat{\mu}_{x,2})$. By interpolation, the corresponding estimates $\hat{k}$,

Table 6.5   Shape parameter k, mean μ_Z standard deviation σ_Z, and shape ratio r of dimensionless Z population of GEV variates

k	μ_Z	σ_Z	r
−0.5	1.54	2.85	0.08
−0.4	1.22	2.24	0.11
−0.3	0.99	1.83	0.16
−0.2	0.82	1.55	0.23
−0.1	0.69	1.35	0.32
0	0.58	1.20	0.44
0.1	0.49	1.09	0.59
0.2	0.41	1.01	0.79
0.3	0.34	0.95	1.05
0.4	0.28	0.92	1.39
0.5	0.23	0.89	1.83
0.6	0.18	0.88	2.39
0.7	0.13	0.87	3.13

$\hat{\mu}_z$ and $\hat{\sigma}_z$ are found from table 6.5, after which equations 6.44 and 6.45 are used to calculate $\hat{u}$ and $\hat{\alpha}$.

Example 6.5   Annual maxima from daily naturalised flows of the Derwent at Yorkshire Bridge for the period 1936 to 1971 are ranked in descending order in table 6.6. The sextile means $\hat{\mu}_{x,\,1}, \hat{\mu}_{x,\,2}, \hat{\mu}_{x,\,3}, \hat{\mu}_{x,\,4}, \hat{\mu}_{x,\,5}$ and $\hat{\mu}_{x,\,6}$ are also given in table 6.6. Estimate the parameters of a GEV distribution to be fitted to the data, and hence calculate $\hat{x}(60)$, $\hat{x}(40)$, $\hat{x}(20)$, $\hat{x}(10)$, $\hat{x}(5)$, $\hat{x}(3)$, $\hat{x}(2)$, $\hat{x}(1.5)$ and $\hat{x}(1.1)$. Plot these values and the given annual maxima on Gumbel probability paper.

Table 6.6

Ranked annual maxima ($\times 10^6$ m^3)

8.68	4.27	3.49	3.09	2.58	2.30
6.28	4.17	3.47	3.05	2.47	2.28
5.59	3.89	3.44	2.86	2.46	2.15
5.42	3.76	3.40	2.83	2.44	2.13
4.54	3.59	3.20	2.63	2.40	2.12
4.50	3.58	3.12	2.59	2.38	2.02
$\hat{\mu}_{x,\,1}$	$\hat{\mu}_{x,\,2}$	$\hat{\mu}_{x,\,3}$	$\hat{\mu}_{x,\,4}$	$\hat{\mu}_{x,\,5}$	$\hat{\mu}_{x,\,6}$
5.84	3.88	3.35	2.84	2.46	2.17

$$\hat{r} = (\hat{\mu}_{x,\,5} - \hat{\mu}_{x,\,6})/(\hat{\mu}_{x,\,1} - \hat{\mu}_{x,\,2})$$
$$= 0.29/1.96$$
$$= 0.15$$

From table 6.5 for $\hat{r} = 0.15$, $\hat{k} = -0.32$. The negative sign of $\hat{k}$ shows that the type II extreme value distribution is applicable; also, $\hat{\mu}_z = 1.04$ and $\hat{\sigma}_z = 1.91$. The estimated mean and standard deviation of the sextile means are respectively $\hat{\mu} = 3.42$ and $\hat{\sigma} = 1.22$. From equation 6.45, $\hat{\alpha} = \hat{\sigma}_z/\hat{\sigma} = 1.91/1.22 = 1/0.64$, and, from equation 6.44, $\hat{u} = 3.42 - 0.64 \times 1.04 = 2.75$. The $\hat{x}(T)$ values are obtained as shown in table 6.7 from equations 6.14 and 6.41.

Table 6.7   Computations of $\hat{x}(T)$ for type II extreme value distribution

T	y	$\exp(-\hat{k}y)$	$\hat{z}(T)$	$x(T)$
60	4.09	3.70	8.43	8.14
40	3.68	3.24	7.01	7.24
30	3.38	2.95	6.10	6.66
20	2.97	2.59	4.96	5.92
10	2.25	2.05	3.30	4.86
5	1.50	1.62	1.93	3.98
3	0.90	1.33	1.05	3.42
2	0.37	1.12	0.39	3.00
1.5	−0.09	0.97	−0.09	2.69
1.1	−0.87	0.76	−0.76	2.26

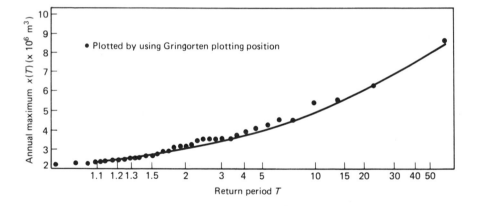

Figure 6.3   GEV distribution fitted by Jenkinson's sextile method to annual maxima from daily flows in Derwent at Yorkshire Bridge for the period 1936 to 1971

The annual maxima from table 6.6 are plotted in figure 6.3 by using the Gringorten plotting position, and the values in table 6.7 give the smooth curve.

The ML equations for the GEV distribution are, of course, more complicated than those for the Gumbel distribution[20].

[20] See Jenkinson (1969, pp. 199–205) and the Natural Environmental Research Council (1975, vol. 1, pp. 96–7).

6.5   Lognormal distribution

The general theory of the lognormal distribution, which is introduced in chapter 3, and its method of application to extreme values are given herein[21].

6.5.1   *Theoretical considerations*

Chow (1954) considered that the occurrence of a flood flow denoted, say, by the random variable X is the result of the joint multiplicative action of a vast number of meteorological and geographical effects, $X_1, X_2, X_3, \ldots, X_r$. That is, $X = X_1 X_2 X_3 \ldots X_r$. If r is infinitely large, log X is the sum of an infinite number of independent variates, and, accordingly, it is normally distributed by the central limit theorem (see section 3.1). The less satisfactory aspects of this approach are that some of the effects are interdependent (such as mean rainfall and elevation or storm intensity and catchment size, shape and orientation), and there could be great difficulty in identifying them. Because of dependency, the process should strictly be modelled by a multivariate distribution. Furthermore, in practice it is likely that the interactions of the contributory effects are of various types, such as additive, multiplicative, exponential and so on. So, the lognormal distribution can only provide an approximation to real world situations just as when other theoretical distributions are applied to flood flows.

In general, let $Y = \ln(X - \xi)$ be normally distributed with the parameters μ_Y as mean and σ_Y as standard deviation. This means that the random variable X of which an observed value given by

$$x = \exp(y) + \xi \tag{6.46}$$

is assumed to have a three-parameter lognormal distribution. It should be noted that the lognormal distribution is equally applicable when 10 (or any other number) is the base of the logarithms, which will only cause a change in scale[22]. The probability density function for the Y population is

$$f(y) = \sigma_Y^{-1}(2\pi)^{-1/2}\exp\{-(y-\mu_Y)^2/2\sigma_Y^2\} \tag{6.47}$$

The parameters μ_Y and σ_Y are obtained by the method of moments (section 3.3) as follows.

$$E\{\exp(Y)\} = \int_{-\infty}^{\infty} \exp(y)f(y)\mathrm{d}y$$
$$= \sigma_Y^{-1}(2\pi)^{-1/2}\exp(\mu_Y + \sigma_Y^2/2)$$

[21] Hazen (1914) and Horton (1914) originally applied the distribution to flood flows, and, subsequently, Chow (1954) derived the underlying theory; Kalinske (1946), Matalas (1967) and Sangal and Biswas (1970) have also made notable contributions. For an extensive treatment, see Aitchison and Brown (1957).
[22] The value y corresponds to z in equation 3.58; μ_Y and σ_Y correspond to γ and δ respectively and parameter λ is redundant as noted in section 3.6.2.

$$\times \int_{-\infty}^{\infty} \exp[-\{y - \mu_Y - \sigma_Y^2\}^2 / 2\sigma_Y^2] dy$$

the integral part of which is equal to the unit area enclosed by a normal probability density curve, defined functionally by the parameters $\mu_Y + \sigma_Y^2$ and σ_Y.

$$E\{\exp(Y)\} = \exp(\mu_Y + \sigma_Y^2/2) \tag{6.48}$$

From equations 6.46 (by taking expectations) and 6.48

$$\mu = \exp(\mu_Y + \sigma_Y^2/2) + \xi \tag{6.49}$$

where $E(X) = \mu$ is the mean of the X population. Because $E(2Y) = 2\mu_Y$ and $\text{var}(2Y) = 4\sigma_Y^2$, from equations 6.46 and 6.48

$$E\{(X - \xi)^2\} = \exp\{2\mu_Y + 2\sigma_Y^2\} \tag{6.50}$$

The variance σ^2 of the X population is equal to $E(X^2) - \mu^2$. Hence, it follows from equations 6.49 and 6.50 that

$$\sigma^2 = \{\exp(2\mu_Y + \sigma_Y^2)\} \{\exp(\sigma_Y^2) - 1\} \tag{6.51}$$

Also, from $E(X - \mu)^3$ and by using equations 6.46, 6.49 and 6.51, it can be shown that the skewness coefficient $\gamma_1 = \sigma^{-3} E\{(X - \mu)^3\}$ of the X population and σ_Y are related as follows.

$$\gamma_1 = \{\exp(3\sigma_Y^2) - 3\exp(\sigma_Y^2) + 2\} / \{\exp(\sigma_Y^2) - 1\}^{3/2} \tag{6.52}$$

This formula is used to estimate σ_Y when fitting a three-parameter lognormal distribution[23].

Equation 6.49 can be easily adapted for the two-parameter lognormal distribution in which $\xi = 0$. Also, in this case if $V = \sigma/\mu$, the coefficient of variation of the X population, it can be shown that (Aitchinson and Brown, 1957)

$$\gamma_1 = V^3 + 3V \tag{6.53}$$

One advantage that the lognormal distribution has over the Gumbel distribution is that it is more flexible for curve fitting because the skewness is not fixed.

For the three-parameter case in which $y = \ln(x - \xi)$,

$$x(T) = \exp(\mu_Y + z_T' \sigma_Y) + \xi \tag{6.54}$$

[23] The formula is used in chapter 4; see also Matalas (1967). Sangal and Biswas (1970) suggested an alternative fitting procedure using the median ζ of the X population; if $\alpha = \xi/\mu$, $\beta = \zeta/\mu$ and $V = \sigma/\mu$,

$$2\alpha^3(1 - \beta) + \alpha^2(V^2 + \beta^2 - 5 + 4\beta) + 2\alpha(2 - \beta V^2 - \beta - \beta^2) + \beta^2 V^2 - 1 + \beta^2 = 0$$

This is solved iteratively to find α and hence ξ; then we proceed as in the two-parameter case. However, Burges et al. (1975) have found from Monte Carlo experiments that the estimator using the median has a larger variance and bias than that based on skewness γ_1 as given by equation 6.52 except perhaps when $\gamma_1 < 0.51$.

The ML method of estimation is far more complicated; Giesbrecht and Kempthorne (1976) discuss the approach and cite earlier work.

6.5.2 Probability paper

Normal probability paper was devised by Hazen (1914) for determining probabilities of reservoir yield. Subsequently, Whipple (1916) used logarithmic probability paper to test, for example, the distributions of microscopic organisms in water. The normal density function for a variate X is given by equation 3.3, and equation 3.4 represents the standard normal density function $f(z)$, where $z = (x - \mu)/\sigma$.

If x is normally distributed, a graph of x against z will give on arithmetic graph paper a straight line with intercept μ and gradient σ. Each x value is associated with a z value which has a fixed probability of non-exceedance. It is more useful, on the other hand, to plot values of the integral

$$\Phi(z) = (2\pi)^{-1/2} \int_{-\infty}^{z} \{\exp(-t^2/2)\} \, dt \qquad (6.55)$$

on the horizontal scale to represent corresponding z values[24]. This is given as a percentage on some types of normal probability paper in which the top and bottom scales are in units of $\{1 - \Phi(z)\} 100$ and $\Phi(z) 100$ respectively. As noted in section 6.1, the return period $T = 1/\{1 - \Phi(z)\}$.

Lognormal probability paper is produced in the same way except that the vertical scale is logarithmic so that the data need not be transformed to logarithms. If the lognormal law holds, it is expected that a long sequence of annual maxima will give a straight-line plot with a gradient of σ_Y, and an intercept of μ_Y on the vertical representing $\Phi(z) = 0.5$, if the vertical scale is transformed to logarithms and the horizontal scale is converted from $\Phi(z)$ to z.

Example 6.6 Ranked annual maximum daily flows in the Severn at Bewdley for the period 1940 to 1968 are given below. In order to see the fit of a two-parameter lognormal distribution, plot the values on lognormal probability paper. Fit a straight line by the method of moments, and estimate $x(10)$.

Ranked annual maximum daily flows ($m^3 \, s^{-1}$)

793	768	747	747	711	683	660	648	624	585
585	546	529	528	500	469	465	465	465	455
451	445	422	419	381	347	316	311	300	

The annual maxima are plotted in figure 6.4 by using the Weibull plotting position $T = (N + 1)/m$; the Blom plotting position has been recommended by

---

[24] See the commonly available tables of the normal distribution or the second and third columns of table 6.9.

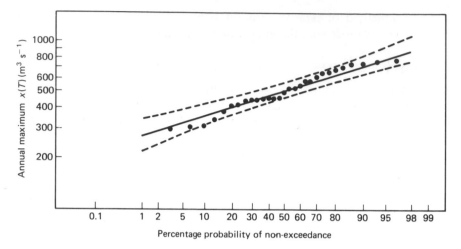

Figure 6.4 Two-parameter lognormal distribution fitted to annual maxima from daily mean flows in Severn at Bewdley for the period 1940 to 1968: broken lines denote 95% confidence limits

Gringorten (1963) for the normal (or lognormal) distribution.

The estimated mean and the standard deviation of the sample are $\bar{x} = 529.8$ and $s = 144.5$ respectively. From equations 6.49 (in which $\xi = 0$) and 6.51, the estimated mean $\bar{y}$ and the standard deviation s_y of the Y population are $\bar{y} = \ln(\bar{x}) - s_y^2/2 = 6.237$ and $s_y = [\ln\{(s/\bar{x})^2 + 1\}]^{1/2} = 0.2679$ respectively. From tables of the normal distribution, $\Phi(2.054) = 0.98$ and $\Phi(2.326) = 0.99$. Therefore, $\tilde{x}(50)$, which corresponds to $\Phi(z) = 0.98$, is equal to $\exp(6.237 + 2.054 \times 0.2679) = 886$, and $x(1.01)$, for which $\Phi(z) = 0.01$, equals $\exp(6.237 - 2.326 \times 0.2679) = 274$. These two values correspond to probabilities of non-exceedance equal to 98% and 1% respectively and define the straight line in figure 6.4. The 10-year flood $\tilde{x}(10)$ corresponds, of course, to a probability $(1 - 1/10) \times 100 = 90\%$ of non-exceedance. Its magnitude is 720 m s^{-1} from the straight-line plot, or it is theoretically equal to $\exp(6.237 + 1.282 \times 0.2679) = 720.6$.

6.5.3 Frequency factors

From equation 6.26

$$K(T) = \{x(T)/\mu - 1\}/V$$

where $V = \sigma/\mu$. For the two-parameter case in which $y = \ln(x)$, $x(T) = \exp(\mu_y + z'_T \sigma_y)$, where z'_T is the value which a standard normal deviate exceeds with probability $1/T$, as given by

$$1/T = (2\pi)^{-1/2} \int_{z'_T}^{\infty} \exp(-t^2/2)dt$$

and the variable Y is normal with a mean μ_Y and a standard deviation σ_Y. Substituting from equations 6.49 (in which $\xi = 0$) and 6.51, we obtain

$$K(T) = V^{-1}(\{1/(V^2 + 1)^{1/2}\}\exp[z'_T\{\ln(V^2 + 1)\}^{1/2}] - 1) \qquad (6.57)$$

This gives the frequency factor for the two-parameter lognormal distribution which is related as shown to the corresponding standard normal deviate z'_T and the coefficient of variation V of the X population. A similar, but more complicated, expression for the frequency factor of the three-parameter lognormal distribution could be given by using z'_T and the three parameters μ_Y, σ_Y and ξ.

Example 6.7   For the data given in example 6.6, estimate the $K(T)$ factor for $T = 20$ and hence $\hat{x}(20)$. Also, estimate the return period of the mean annual flood and the magnitude of the median annual flood.

From equation 6.56 and tables of the standard normal distribution, $\phi(1.6449)$ $= 1 - 1/20$, that is, $z'_{20} = 1.6449$. The sample estimate of the coefficient of variation $V = s/\bar{x} = 144.5/529.8 = 0.273$. Hence, from equation 6.57, $K(20)$ $= 1.829$ and, from equation 6.26, $\hat{x}(20) = 530 + 1.829 \times 144.5 = 794$. This tallies closely with the value from figure 6.4 which has a 95 % probability of non-exceedance. For the mean annual flood, $K(T) = 0$ in equation 6.57. Therefore,

$$\exp[z'_T\{\ln(V^2 + 1)\}^{1/2}] = (V^2 + 1)^{1/2}$$

Hence, $\hat{z}'_T = \{\ln(\hat{V}^2 + 1)\}^{1/2}/2 = 0.1339$. Because $1 - \Phi(0.1339) = 1/2.24$ from tables, the return period of the mean annual flood is given by $T = 2.24$, corresponding to which $\hat{x}(2.24) = \bar{x} = 529.8$. This value has a probability of non-exceedance equal to $(1 - 1/2.24) \times 100 = 55.3\%$ on the horizontal scale of figure 6.4. For the median annual flood, $T = 2$ and $z'_2 = 0.0$ if the distribution is normal. Therefore, from equation 6.57, $\hat{K}(T) = \{1/(\hat{V}^2 + 1)^{1/2} - 1\}/V = -0.1292$, and, from equation 6.26, $\hat{x}(2) = 529.8 - 0.1292 \times 144.5 = 511$, which tallies with the intercept on the 50 % probability line in figure 6.4.

6.5.4   *Confidence limits*

For the two-parameter case the logarithm of the estimate of the T-year flood $x(T)$ is related to $\bar{y}$ and s_y, the estimated values of the parameters μ_Y and σ_Y, as follows from equation 6.54.

$$\ln\{\hat{x}(T)\} = \bar{y} + z'_T s_y$$

where z'_T which is defined by equation 6.56 has a probability of exceedance $1/T$. Now $\text{cov}(\bar{y}, s_y) = 0$, because $\bar{y}$ and s_y are independent[25]. Also, $\text{var}(\bar{y}) = \sigma_Y^2/N$ and $\text{var}(\sigma_Y) = \sigma_Y^2/2N$. These quantities are estimated by s_y^2/N and $s_y^2/2N$ respectively. Hence,

$$\text{var}[\ln\{\hat{x}(T)\}] = s_y^2/N + z'^2_T s_y^2/2N$$

---

[25] Shuster (1973) shows that the statistics y and s_y^2 are independent.

where N is the sample size. The $100(1-\alpha)\%$ confidence limits of $x(T)$, the population value of the T-year flood, is given by

$$\exp\{\ln\{\tilde{x}(T)\} \pm z_{\alpha/2}(\text{var}[\ln\{\tilde{x}(T)\}])^{1/2}\} \qquad (6.58)$$

where $z_{\alpha/2}$ is the value which is exceeded with probability $\alpha/2$ by a standard normal deviate[26].

Example 6.8   Using the data given in example 6.6, compute and plot the 95% confidence limits for $T = 1.01, 1.05, 1.25, 2, 5, 20$ and 100.

Now $s_y = 0.2679$ and $N = 29$; therefore, $s_y^2/N = 0.002\,475$ and $s_y^2/2N = 0.001\,237$. The confidence limits are shown in table 6.8 and figure 6.4.

Table 6.8   95% confidence limits with lognormal distribution fitted to annual maximum flows of Severn at Bewdley

T	z'_T	$(\text{var}[\ln\{\tilde{x}(T)\}])^{1/2}$	$\ln\{\tilde{x}(T)\}$	Upper confidence limit	Lower confidence limit
100	2.3263	0.0958	6.8599	1150	790
20	1.6449	0.0763	6.6773	922	684
5	0.8416	0.0579	6.4621	717	572
2	0	0.0497	6.2367	563	464
1.25	−0.8416	0.0579	6.0112	457	364
1.05	−1.6449	0.0763	5.7960	382	283
1.01	−2.3263	0.0958	5.6135	331	227

Example 6.9   Fit a three-parameter lognormal distribution to the data given in example 6.6. Here, estimate $x(50)$ and $x(1.01)$.

For the $N(=29)$ items of data from the X population, the coefficient of skewness γ_1 is estimated as follows,

$$g_1 = \{N^2\sum x^3 - 3N\sum x\sum x^2 + 2(\sum x)^3\}/N(N-1)(N-2)s^3 \qquad (6.59)$$

where $s = [\{\sum x^2 - (\sum x)^2/N\}/(N-1)]^{1/2}$ and $\sum$ denotes summation of N values. Hence $g_1 = 0.2515$, and, as obtained in example 6.5, $\bar{x} = 529.8$ and $s = 144.5$ which are the sample estimates of μ and σ. From equation 6.52, s_y, the estimate of σ_y, equals 0.0835 and from equations 6.51 and 6.49, $\bar{y} = 7.451$ and $\tilde{\xi} = -1212$, which are the estimates of μ_y and ξ respectively. Hence, $\tilde{x}(50) = \exp(7.451 + 2.054 \times 0.0835) - 1212 = 845$, and $\tilde{x}(1.01) = \exp(7.451 - 2.326 \times 0.0835) - 1198 = 220$.

Because g_1 is small and $\tilde{\xi}$ is negative, it does not seem worthwhile to fit this distribution here. Under more favourable conditions the theoretical straight line passing through the two points such as $\tilde{x}(5)$ and $\tilde{x}(1.01)$ may be compared with the line representing the two-parameter distribution for visual goodness of fit with the plotted points.

[26] Bias in small samples may be corrected by using the tables of Student's t distribution instead.

6.5.5 Bias in skewness and Hazen's correction

It should be noted that the estimator given by equation 6.59 is unbiased only if the population is normal which is not true in practice. Because g_1 is known to have a definite downward bias when calculated from a lognormal population, Hazen (1930) suggested the use of an empirical correction factor of $1 + 8.5/N$ for the coefficient of skewness[27]. Thus the revised estimator becomes

$$g'_1 = \{N\sum x^3 - 3N(\sum x)(\sum x^2) + 2(\sum x)^3\}(1 + 8.5/N)/N(N-1)(N-2)s^3$$

$$(6.60)$$

Example 6.10 For the data given in example 6.6, fit a three-parameter lognormal distribution using Hazen's correction for skewness. Hence, estimate $x(50)$ and $x(1.01)$.

From example 6.9, $\bar{x} = 529.8$, $s = 144.5$ and $g'_1 = (1 + 8.5/29) \times 0.2511 = 0.3252$. From equations 6.52, 6.51 and 6.49 the following estimates of σ_Y, μ_Y and ξ are obtained: $s_y = 0.1077$, $\bar{y} = 7.193$ and $\tilde{\xi} = -808$. Hence, from equation 6.54, $\tilde{x}(50) = \exp(7.193 + 2.054 \times 0.1077) - 808 = 851$ and $\tilde{x}(1.01) = \exp(7.193 + 2.326 \times 0.1067) - 808 = 227$

6.5.6 Regional skewness

On account of sampling errors in estimates of skewness, it has been suggested that an average value should be taken over a hydrologically homogeneous region. The drawback is that such a region could be difficult to define, and in practice boundaries are marked somewhat arbitrarily. Results show that estimates of skewness for stations within a region have high variability and poor correlation with physiographic and meteorologic factors. Furthermore, such estimates are biased when outliers ('surprisingly high values') are present. More about these aspects will be found in sections 6.10 and 6.11.

State-averaged values of skewness for logarithmically transformed flood data from the United States range from 0.6 in the eastern states to -0.5 in Illinois[28]. The country has also been partitioned into 14 regions for this purpose. From flood records at 1351 selected stations, means of the skewness of untransformed data range from 3.0 in the south to 0.9 in the southwest and northeast[29]. In the

---

[27] Wallis *et al.* (1974) have found from Monte Carlo studies that Hazen's correction gives an unbiased estimate over a small range such as $0.5 < \gamma_1 < 2$ for the lognormal distribution. They also noted that the average bias factor in the estimated skewness is a function of the skewness and the distribution, and, subsequently, Bobée and Robitaille (1975) proposed formulae for adjustment. Regardless of bias corrections a single estimate of the coefficient of skewness is subject to high sample fluctuations, but the absolute magnitude of the statistic does not exceed $(N-2)/(N-1)^{1/2}$, as shown by Kirby (1974).

[28] See Hardison (1974).

[29] See Matalas *et al.* (1975).

United Kingdom, corresponding regional averages of skewness of flood data vary from 4.36 in the southeast to 1.04 in the northeast[30].

6.6   Pearson type III function applied to extreme values

The Pearson type III function is explained and methods of estimating the parameters are given in sections 3.2 to 3.4. The function which was applied originally to flood flows by Foster (1924) has no rigorous analytical basis, but its usefulness for curve-fitting purposes has been demonstrated[31].

6.6.1   Frequency factors

As shown in subsection 3.2.2, the Pearson type III function is given by

$$f(x) = (x - \xi)^{\gamma - 1} \exp\{-(x - \xi)/\lambda\}/\lambda^{\gamma}\Gamma(\gamma), \qquad \xi \leqslant x \leqslant \infty \qquad (6.61)$$

where γ, λ and ξ are the three parameters. By using the transformation

$$z = (x - \xi)/\lambda \qquad (6.62)$$

the standard gamma function

$$f(z) = z^{\gamma - 1}\exp(-z)\Gamma(\gamma) \qquad (6.63)$$

is obtained. The integral of this, with finite upper limit $u(T)$ and $0 \leqslant F(u) \leqslant 1$,

$$F(u) = \int_0^{u(T)} z^{\gamma - 1}\exp(-z)\mathrm{d}z\Gamma(\gamma) \qquad (6.64)$$

is extensively tabulated by Wilk et al. (1962). The T-year flood

$$x(T) = \xi + u(T)\lambda \qquad (6.65)$$

is obtained after replacing z in equation 6.62 by $u(T)$, the standard gamma variate, which is also given in table 3.3 for some values of γ and $F(u) = 1 - 1/T$. Then, substituting from equations 3.40 and 3.41 in equation 6.65, we obtain the following estimator by the method of moments.

$$\check{x}(T) = \bar{x} + s\{u(T)g_1/2 - 2/g\} \qquad (6.66)$$

where $\bar{x}$, s and g_1 are the estimators of the mean, the standard deviation and the coefficient of skewness respectively of the X population. Equation 6.66 corresponds to the general form of equation 6.26 and the frequency factors $K(T) = u(T)\gamma_1/2 - 2/\gamma_1$ are given in table 6.9 for some values of the probability $F(u)$ of non-exceedance and the coefficient of skewness γ_1. As noted from equation 3.39, $\gamma = 4/\gamma_1^2$, and this links table 6.9 to table 3.3. For more comprehensive tables, reference should be made to Harter (1969).

---

[30] See the Natural Environmental Research Council (1975).
[31] As shown by the Natural Environmental Research Council (1975) and by others such as Majumdar and Sawhney (1965).

Table 6.9 Frequency factors for Pearson type III function

Return period T	Probability of non-exceedance F(u)	Frequency factors for coefficient of skewness γ_F =																
		0	0.2	0.4	0.6	0.8	1.0	1.2	1.4	1.6	1.8	2.0	2.5	3.0	3.5	4.0	4.5	5.0
1.0001	0.0001	-3.719	-3.299	-2.899	-2.525	-2.184	-1.884	-1.628	-1.418	-1.247	-1.111	-1.000	-0.800	-0.667	-0.571	-0.500	-0.444	-0.400
1.0010	0.0010	-3.090	-2.808	-2.533	-2.268	-2.017	-1.786	-1.577	-1.394	-1.238	-1.107	-0.999	-0.800	-0.667	-0.571	-0.500	-0.444	-0.400
1.0101	0.0100	-2.326	-2.178	-2.029	-1.880	-1.733	-1.588	-1.449	-1.318	-1.197	-1.087	-0.990	-0.799	-0.667	-0.571	-0.500	-0.444	-0.400
1.0204	0.0200	-2.054	-1.945	-1.834	-1.720	-1.606	-1.492	-1.379	-1.270	-1.166	-1.069	-0.980	-0.798	-0.666	-0.571	-0.500	-0.444	-0.400
1.0256	0.0250	-1.960	-1.864	-1.764	-1.663	-1.559	-1.455	-1.352	-1.250	-1.152	-1.060	-0.975	-0.797	-0.666	-0.571	-0.500	-0.444	-0.400
1.0526	0.0500	-1.645	-1.586	-1.524	-1.458	-1.389	-1.317	-1.243	-1.168	-1.093	-1.020	-0.949	-0.790	-0.665	-0.571	-0.500	-0.444	-0.400
1.1111	0.1000	-1.282	-1.258	-1.231	-1.200	-1.166	-1.128	-1.086	-1.041	-0.994	-0.945	-0.894	-0.771	-0.660	-0.570	-0.500	-0.444	-0.400
1.2500	0.2000	-0.842	-0.850	-0.855	-0.857	-0.856	-0.852	-0.844	-0.832	-0.817	-0.799	-0.777	-0.711	-0.636	-0.562	-0.498	-0.444	-0.400
2	0.5000	0.000	-0.033	-0.067	-0.099	-0.132	-0.164	-0.195	-0.225	-0.254	-0.281	-0.307	-0.360	-0.396	-0.413	-0.413	-0.400	-0.379
5	0.8000	0.842	0.830	0.816	0.800	0.780	0.758	0.733	0.705	0.675	0.643	0.609	0.518	0.420	0.322	0.226	0.137	0.058
10	0.9000	1.282	1.301	1.317	1.329	1.336	1.340	1.340	1.337	1.329	1.318	1.303	1.250	1.180	1.096	1.001	0.900	0.795
20	0.9500	1.645	1.700	1.750	1.797	1.839	1.877	1.910	1.938	1.962	1.981	1.996	2.012	2.003	1.971	1.920	1.853	1.773
	0.9750	1.960	2.053	2.142	2.227	2.308	2.384	2.455	2.521	2.582	2.638	2.689	2.793	2.867	2.913	2.933	2.931	2.909
50	0.9800	2.054	2.159	2.261	2.359	2.453	2.542	2.626	2.706	2.780	2.848	2.912	3.048	3.152	3.226	3.274	3.298	3.300
100	0.9900	2.326	2.472	2.615	2.755	2.891	3.023	3.149	3.271	3.388	3.499	3.605	3.845	4.051	4.225	4.368	4.483	4.573
1000	0.9990	3.090	3.377	3.666	3.956	4.244	4.531	4.815	5.095	5.371	5.642	5.908	6.548	7.152	7.720	8.253	8.752	9.220
10000	0.9999	3.719	4.153	4.597	5.047	5.501	5.957	6.412	6.867	7.318	7.766	8.210	9.299	10.354	11.373	12.357	13.305	14.220

Example 6.11   Ranked annual maximum flows of the Derwent at Longbridge Weir for the period 1936 to 1962 are given below. Plot the data using the Hazen plotting position, given in table 6.1, on normal probability paper, and fit a curve to represent the Pearson type III function. Estimate $x(10)$.

Ranked annual maximum flows ($m^3 s^{-1}$)

269	258	228	180	167	144	143	143	142	126
124	117	115	110	109	108	106	102	102	99
98	95	87	85	81	77	68			

The estimated mean and standard deviation are $\bar{x} = 129.00$ and $s = 51.84$, and the skewness coefficient g_1, estimated by equation 6.60, is equal to 2.056. The coefficient of skewness is aproximated to 2.0, and the frequency factors are found from table 6.9; calculations are given in table 6.10.

Table 6.10   Pearson type III function fitted to flood flows in Derwent at Longbridge

Return period T	Probability of non-exceedance $F(u)$	Frequency factor $K(T)$	$\hat{x}(T)$
1.001	0.001	−0.999	77.2
1.01	0.01	−0.990	77.7
1.02	0.02	−0.980	78.2
1.05	0.05	−0.949	79.8
1.11	0.10	−0.894	82.7
1.25	0.20	−0.777	88.7
2.00	0.50	−0.307	113
5	0.80	0.609	161
10	0.90	1.303	197
20	0.95	1.996	232
50	0.98	2.912	280
100	0.99	3.605	316

The plotted points and the theoretical curve are shown in figure 6.5. $\hat{x}(10)$ = 196 $m^3 s^{-3}$.

6.6.2   Two-parameter gamma function

The gamma probability density function

$$f(x) = x^{\gamma - 1} \exp(-x/\lambda)/\lambda^{\gamma} \, \Gamma(\gamma), \qquad 0 \leqslant x < \infty \tag{6.67}$$

which has been applied to flood flows, for instance, by Moran (1957) is a simpler version of the Pearson type III function given above with the location parameter

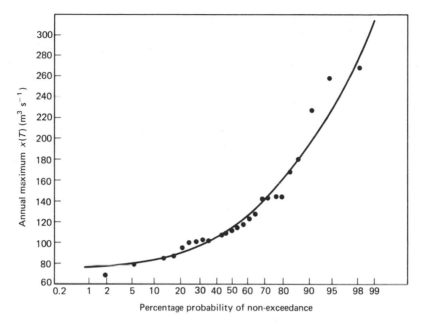

Figures 6.5　Pearson type III distribution fitted to annual maxima for daily flows in Derwent at Longbridge Weir for the period 1936 to 1962

$\xi = 0$. The parameters γ and λ may be estimated by the method of moments from the mean $\bar{x}$ and the standard deviation s if we use equation 3.35 and the first equation of equation 3.32. Hence, $\hat{\lambda} = s^2/\bar{x}$ and $\hat{\gamma} = \bar{x}^2/s^2$.

Obviously, this will not fit a given sequence of data better than the type III function will. However, if goodness-of-fit tests show that neither is rejected, the two-parameter function may be used.

Example 6.12　For the data given in example 6.11, estimate $x(20)$ by using the gamma function given by equation 6.67.

As shown above, $\hat{\lambda} = 51.84^2/129.00 = 20.83$ and $\hat{\gamma} = (129/51.84)^2 = 6.192$. For $T = 20$, the probability of non-exceedance is given by $F(u) = 1 - 1/20 = 0.95$ with reference to equation 6.64. From table 3.3, the standard gamma variate $u(T)$ is 10.77 which is obtained by interpolation for $\gamma = 6.19$. Hence, $\hat{x}(20) = u(T)\lambda = 10.77 \times 20.83 = 224$.

6.6.3　*Log Pearson type III function*

When the Pearson type III function is applied to the logarithms (to any base) of the flood flows, the distribution function is termed the log Pearson type III function. If $x = e^y$, then from equation 6.66

$$x(T) = \exp[y + s_y\{u(T)g_y/2 - 2/g_y\}] \tag{6.68}$$

where $\bar{y}$, s_y and g_y denote the estimators of the mean, the standard deviation and the skewness of the Y population for which, by comparing equations 6.26 and 6.68, $\tilde{K}(T) = u(T)g_y/2 - 2/g_y$. When referring to table 6.9 for this frequency factor, if skewness is negative which is quite possible for logarithmically transformed flood flows, the following procedure should be adopted. Replace each pair of co-ordinates $\{\gamma_Y, F(u)\}$ by $\{|\gamma_Y|, 1 - F(u)\}$, and then change the sign; for example, if $\gamma_Y = -1.0$, $K(10)$ which corresponds to $F(u) = 0.9$ is obtained from the row for $F(u) = 0.1$ and is equal to 1.128 after changing the sign. The log Pearson type III distribution was recommended for general use by the American Water Resources Council[32].

Example 6.13   Plot the data given in example 6.11 on lognormal probability paper, using the Blom plotting position from table 6.1, and fit the log Pearson type III function. Estimate $x(10)$ by this method.

$\bar{y} = 4.796$, $s_y = 0.3495$ and $g'_y = 1.0696$, which is approximated to 1.0 and table 6.9 is referred to. The calculations are given in table 6.11.

Table 6.11   Log Pearson type III function fitting to flood flows in Derwent at Longbridge

Return period T	Probability of non-exceedance $F(u)$	Frequency function $K(T)$	$\tilde{x}(T)$
1.001	0.001	−1.786	65
1.01	0.01	−1.588	69
1.02	0.02	−1.492	72
1.05	0.05	−1.317	76
1.11	0.10	−1.128	82
1.25	0.20	−0.852	90
2.00	0.50	−0.164	114
5	0.80	0.758	158
10	0.90	1.340	193
20	0.95	1.877	233
50	0.98	2.542	294

The plotted points and the theoretical curve are shown in figure 6.6 from which $\tilde{x}(10) = 193 \text{ m}^3 \text{ s}^{-1}$.

Note that the log Pearson type III function has a lower limit $\exp(\xi_Y)$ when skewness is positive[33]. This is estimated by $\exp(\bar{y} - 2s_y/g'_y)$ through the method of moments. If $y = 10^x$, the limit becomes $\exp\{(\bar{y} - 2s_y/g'_y)\ln(10)\}$. For the given data, the lower limit is 57. On the contrary, if skewness is negative, the log Pearson type III variates are bound by an equal upper limit. This necessitates careful consideration in application.

[32] See Benson (1968). This was originally suggested by L. R. Beard. Confidence limits for $x(T)$ when the Pearson type III or log Pearson type III distributions are applicable involves a procedure suggested by Moran (1957) which is partly numerical. This is also given by Santos (1970) and by Condie (1977).
[33] See Gilroy (1972).

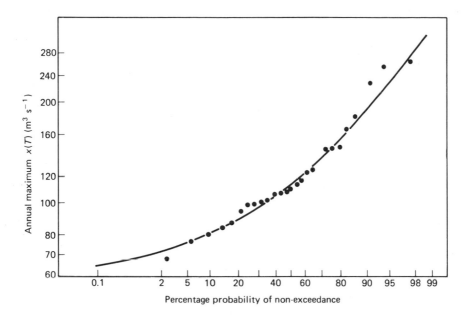

Figure 6.6   Log Pearson type III distribution fitted to annual maxima for daily flows in
              Derwent at Longbridge Weir for the period 1936 to 1962

6.7   Discussion on frequency methods of flood estimation

The distributions given in the preceding sections have been used extensively in
the estimation of flood-flow probabilities. Although each of them has had
support on theoretical or empirical grounds, it seems reasonable to think that no
ordinary probability function can fully represent the complicated flood-
producing factors which change in time and space owing to natural causes or
man's actions. Therefore, some degree of subjectivity is unavoidable, if we
consider the present state of the art. Graphical techniques do indeed provide a
convenient method of choosing between different distributions; however, long
extrapolations may be unreliable even if good fits are obtained.

Studies involving comparisons between probability distributions have been
made recently. Firstly, six distributions were applied to records of length 40 to
97 years from 10 selected stations by the work group on flow frequency methods
appointed by the Hydrological Committee of the United States Water
Resources Council[34]. These are the Gumbel, log Gumbel (that is, a two-
parameter type II extreme value distribution), two-parameter gamma, log
Pearson type III, lognormal and lognormal modified by the Hazen method.
Their recommendation was that the log Pearson type III distribution, of which

[34] See Benson (1968).

the lognormal distribution is a special case, should be used with the proviso that, if the data show evidence of a significant difference, the best-fitting distribution should be adopted.

In order to assess the relative suitabilities of the distributions, an empirical goodness-of-fit test was used by the United States work group. They thought that more information could be obtained from such a procedure than through one of the statistical goodness-of-fit tests described in chapter 3 in which a single abnormal value could cause rejection It is interesting to recall that Gumbel (1943) too had expressed some dissatisfaction over the chi-squared test when applied to flood flows. In the particular method adopted by the United States team, a sequence of data was ranked, and the items were plotted at points, say, $\{x_D(T), T\}$, where D signifies the data, on log Gumbel probability paper by using the Weibull plotting position. Then, for each station and each of the return periods $T = 2, 5, 10, 25$ and 50, the absolute differences between interpolated values on the broken straight lines joining the plotted points and the theoretical values $\tilde{x}(T)$ for each function were calculated. These differences were then reduced to dimensionless units by dividing by the interpolated values $x_D(T)$. The criterion on which the log Pearson type III function was chosen is the average of these differences.

One of the criticisms levelled against the American report is that it does not show how to deal with samples containing outliers (surprisingly high values)[35]. The question of whether to include such discordant values with the rest of the sample data has been recurring over the part 100 years or more in studies on astronomy and other natural phenomena; many publications on the subject are found in the journal *Technometrics*. However, an engineer who has to face up to such a situation could benefit perhaps more from personal judgement than by using a complicated statistical fuction as formulated, for example, by Grubbs (1950). In this, associated rainfall data and the physical reasons for any extraordinary event ought to be examined. The subjective nature of decision making, implied by the word surprising, is stressed by Collett and Lewis (1976) who also point out the relevance of presentation, scale and pattern of the data in perceiving outliers; however, if an objective statistical criterion is used, the word discordant should be used in place of the word surprising. Anscombe (1960) compares a rejection rule to a domestic fire insurance policy, the choice of which depends on the answers to such questions as the following.

(1) What is the premium?
(2) How much protection does the policy give in the event of fire?
(3) How much danger really is there of a fire?

The answer to the last question will be as obvious to the prudent hydrologist as to the householder who is aware that many homes are destroyed by fire.

In the extensive report by the Natural Environmental Research Council

---

[35] If low flows are being examined, an outlier is, on the other hand, a surprisingly low value.

(1975), the empirical distributions of 35 annual maximum flow sequences from the United Kingdom and Ireland, selected on a reliability basis were fitted with each of 7 theoretical functions. These are the Gumbel, GEV, gamma, log gamma, Pearson type III, log Pearson type III and lognormal distributions. The record lengths ranged from 31 years to 88 years in the United Kingdom catchments; the maximum and minimum lengths of the Irish records are 44 years and 23 years respectively. Chi-squared and Kolmogorov–Smirnov goodness-of-fit tests and three indices based on probability plots, in which the standardised measure is similar to that adopted by the American group except that the divisor is the mean of the annual maxima from the record instead of the $x_D(T)$ values which are dependent on the plotting position. Not surprisingly, the three-parameter distributions such as the log Pearson type III and the GEV functions were found to fit the data better than the two-parameter functions. The Natural Environmental Research Council (1975) chose the type II extreme value function for extrapolation on a regional and national basis. It was also found, from several preliminary statistical tests carried out, that there is persistence in 2 and trend in 6 of the chosen 28 United Kingdom records, although these are not allowed for in the formulation of the theoretical functions. Such departures from ideal conditions have been encountered in applications elsewhere, and the imposed limitations should be borne in mind.

The main shortcomings in the annual maximum series method of flood estimation can be summarised as follows. Firstly, the true probability distribution, if it exists, is obscured owing to sampling errors, and, therefore, extrapolation should be treated with caution. When using graphical techniques a suitable choice of plotting position is desirable if it results in minimum bias. However, this criterion is based on repeated sampling from a hypothetical population, whereas in practical situations only a single sample is available. The point is that distortions at high return periods arising from an incorrect plotting position may be totally swamped by errors caused by an inappropriate probability model. It seems, therefore, that unwarranted emphasis can be given to the choice of a plotting position. Secondly, estimates of parameters are also subject to errors. The method of moments is generally affected by sampling errors in the estimates of moments. Moran (1957), amongst others, advocated the ML method of estimation. However, the importance associated with the ML method may not be justifiable when the assumptions on which the probability model are based are themselves incorrect.

One possible alternative is to use bayesian decision theory as explained in chapter 9. An example is given by Davis et al. (1972) for flood control on the Rillito Creek in Arizona; here, the decision variable is the height of dikes to be constructed. Results are, however, highly dependent on the cost or benefit function used and are also based on this assumed distribution[36]. Other possible solutions to the problem are described in section 6.12.

---

[36] The economic effect of floods, flood protection works and insurance are discussed by Brown (1972).

6.8 Binomial, Poisson and multinomial distributions

Another type of question which a practising engineer would ask concerns the probabilities of occurrence of floods of very high return periods within an economic life span of, say, a spillway dam. This is required in evaluating the risks involved. The answer could be given without specifying the probability distribution of the flood events and the values of the parameters, but, of course, the flood magnitude associated with the given return period is dependent on this distribution; it means that errors in estimating the true return period of a high flood magnitude will affect the value of risk.

The binomial distribution has been used for this purpose[37]. The Poisson and multinomial distributions are also applicable; the first is used as an approximation to the binomial and a joint probability, when two or more exceedance levels are considered, is calculated from the second.

6.8.1 *Binomial distribution*

The values in a serially independent annual maximum series could be thought of as either an exceedance (success) or a non-exceedance (failure) of a fixed value with probabilities of occurrence equal to p and $1 - p$ respectively. This two-sided Bernoulli random variable, which was formally described by James Bernoulli in the days when probability theory was mainly applied to games of chance, leads to the binomial probability distribution

$$B(M = m \,|\, N, \; p) = \binom{N}{m} p^m (1 - p)^{N - m} \qquad (6.69)$$

of M successes in N independent identically distributed Bernoulli trials. The theory is derived in the following example.

Example 6.14 Calculate the probability of having two 10-year annual maximum flood events, in a 5-year period, assuming that the events are serially independent.

Let $x(10)$ denote the flood magnitude which has a return period of 10 years. The joint probability of having two 10-year flood events, each of which is equal to or greater than $x(10)$, with a probability of occurrence $p(= 0.1)$, and three flood events each of which is less than $x(10)$ in magnitude, with probability of occurrence $1 - p$ is given by $p^2 (1 - p)^3$ for an independent sequence. The five flood events can be arranged in 5! different ways, but the two 10-year flood events are classed together because there is no need to identify them individually; the other three are similarly included together in a separate class. Therefore, the total number of different arrangements of the two types of flood events is $5!/2! \; 3! = 10$. (If P_1 denotes p and P_2 denotes $1 - p$, the 10 different sequences could be denoted by $P_1 P_1 P_2 P_2 P_2$, $P_1 P_2 P_1 P_2 P_2$, $P_1 P_2 P_2 P_1 P_2$, $P_1 P_2 P_2 P_2 P_1$, $P_2 P_1 P_1 P_2 P_2$, $P_2 P_1 P_2 P_1 P_2$, $P_2 P_1 P_2 P_2 P_1$, $P_2 P_2 P_1 P_1 P_2$,

[37] See, for example, Markowitz (1971).

$P_2 P_2 P_1 P_2 P_1$ and $P_2 P_2 P_2 P_1 P_1$.) Hence, the required probability equals

$$\binom{5}{2} p^2 (1-p)^3 = 10 \times 0.1^2 \times 0.9^3 = 0.0729.$$

6.8.2 Poisson distribution

Under certain conditions the binomial can be approximated by the Poisson distribution. If $p = a/N$ (for example, if $p = 0.01$ which signifies a 100-year flood and $N = 40$, then $a = 0.4$), equation 6.66 can be written in the following form.

$$B(M = m \,|\, N, p) = \binom{N}{m} (a/N)^m (1 - a/N)^{N-m}$$

$$= N(N-1)(N-2) \ldots (N-m+1)(N^m m!)^{-1} a^m$$

$$\times (1 - a/N)^N (1 - a/N)^{-m}$$

If m and a are fixed,

$$\lim_{N \to \infty} \{N(N-1)(N-2) \ldots (N-m+1) N^{-m}\} = 1$$

and

$$\lim_{N \to \infty} \{(1 - a/N)^{-m}\} = 1$$

From a series expansion,

$$\ln\{1/(1-t)\} = -\ln(1-t)$$

$$= t + t^2/2 + t^3/3 + t^4/4 + \ldots$$

Now, if $b = (1 - a/N)^N$,

$$\ln(b) = N \ln(1 - a/N)$$

$$= -a - a^2/2N - a^3/3N^2 \ldots$$

Therefore,

$$\lim_{N \to \infty} (1 - a/N)^N = e^{-a}$$

Hence, for large N, the binomial is approximated by the Poisson probability distribution

$$P(M = m \,|\, a) = a^m e^{-a}/m! \tag{6.70}$$

and this is justifiable if p is small, say, not more than 0.10, and N is large.

Example 6.15 The probability of at least one 100-year flood in a 40-year period is $1 - P(M = 0 \,|\, a) = 1 - (40 \times 0.01)^0 e^{-40 \times 0.01}/0! = 0.33$. Note that the probability of no 100-year floods is subtracted from unity.

6.8.3   *Multinomial distribution*

The probability of having, in a sequence of N annual maxima, $M_1, M_2, M_3, \ldots,$ M_r events with probabilities of occurrence equal to $p_1, p_2, p_3, \ldots, p_r$ respectively is given by the multinomial distribution,

$$M(M_1 = m_1, M_2 = m_2, \ldots, M_r = m_r \,|\, N, p_1, p_2, \ldots, p_r)$$

$$= p_1^{m_1} p_2^{m_2} \ldots p_r^{m_r} (1 - p_1 - p_2 \ldots - p_r)^{N - m_1 - m_2 \ldots - m_r}$$

$$\times N!/m_1!m_2! \ldots m_r!(N - m_1 - m_2 - \ldots - m_r)! \qquad (6.71)$$

where

$$\sum_{i=1}^{r} M_i \leqslant N$$

The set of probabilities p_i, $i = 1, 2, 3, \ldots, r$, can be expressed in terms of the return intervals T_i, $i = 1, 2, 3, \ldots, r$, as follows.

$$p_1 = 1/T_1$$

$$p_2 = 1/T_2 - 1/T_1$$

$$p_3 = 1/T_3 - 1/T_2$$

$$p_r = 1/T_r - 1/T_{r-1}$$

The theory can be easily derived using the same type of arguments as in example 6.14, and it is obvious that the binomial is a special case of the multinomial distribution.

Example 6.16   Calculate the probability of having, in a 5-year sequence of annual maxima, four 5-year floods of which two are 10-year floods. $N = 5$; $m_1 = 2$; $m_2 = 2$; $p_1 = 0.1$; $p_2 = 0.2 - 0.1 = 0.1$. Hence, the required probability is $0.1^2 \times 0.1^2 \times 0.8^1 \times 5!/2!2!1! = 0.0024$.

6.8.4   *Limitations*

It is important to note that these calculations are based on the assumption that the flood events are serially independent and identically distributed. Moreover, as in the choice of the basic extreme value models, the method ignores alterations in natural and environmental factors. On account of man's actions such as urbanisation, channel improvements, construction of dams and irrigation works there will be further changes in the underlying distributions[38].

Hitherto, only annual maximum series were considered. As already mentioned in section 6.7, these have limitations which casts doubts on extrapolated values. In order to increase the information found in high flows from a short sample of data, the peaks-over-threshold method, in which estimates are based on more than one value per year, is used.

---

[38] See, for example, Kazmann (1972, pp. 615, 616).

6.9   Peaks-over-threshold method

The peaks-over-threshold (POT) method concerns the distribution of the number and magnitude of peak flows that exceed a threshold such as x_b in figure 6.7 which shows part of a continuous record of flow in a river. Such peak flows are said to constitute a partial duration series. The threshold level x_b may be raised or lowered so as to involve a desirable number of peaks per year; this chosen number may be in the range from 3 to 5.

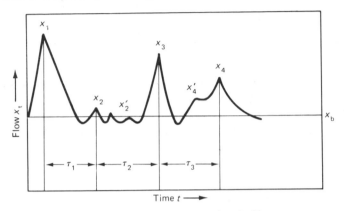

Figure 6.7   Peaks over a threshold

In order to make the analysis tractable, it is assumed that the individual peaks $x_1, x_2, x_3, x_4, \ldots$ represent independent hydrometeorological events or, in other words, that these are not serially correlated. This means that peaks such as x_2' and x_4' which do not have definite ascensions and recessions and which seem to be associated with x_2 and x_4 respectively are not considered. In practice, the selection has to be done empirically[39].

Also of interest is the distribution of the interevent (also called waiting or recurrence) times τ_i, $i = 1, 2, 3, \ldots$, between successive exceedances. The joint distribution of the τ_i values specify a stochastic process which is found by the times of peak flows exceeding x_b. The term renewal process is applicable if the τ_i values are independent and identically distributed. This cannot, of course, be strictly true because of seasonal variations. For example, the times between summer thunderstorms are different from those between cyclonic rains in winter. Moreover, if snow is contributory, the times of melting may be distributed differently.

If on average there are a peaks per year which exceed the threshold, then the number M of POT events per year is a random variable which has the Poisson probability distribution

[39] For example, the Natural Environmental Research Council (1975, vol. 1, p. 46) suggests that 'peaks should be separated in time by 3 times the time to peak and that the flow should decrease between peaks to two-thirds of the first peak'.

$$P(M = m \mid a) = a^m e^{-a}/m! \tag{6.72}$$

where m is a particular value which M takes.

Also, the probability of exceedance of the τ_i values has the exponential distribution

$$\Pr(\tau_i > \tau) = e^{-m\tau} \tag{6.73}$$

in which the parameter $1/m$ is the mean of the τ_i values, as shown below.

The magnitudes X of the peaks which exceed x_b are also assumed to be exponentially distributed so that the probability of exceedance of a particular value $x(T)$ which has a recurrence interval of T years is given by

$$\Pr\{X > x(T) \mid X > x_b\} = e^{-\lambda\{x(T)-x_b\}}$$

where λ is a constant and the vertical line inside the brackets denotes conditional to. Because the probability of exceedance is the reciprocal of the return interval, in the POT analysis the T-year flood is that which on average is exceeded once in aT events compared with once in T events in the annual maximum series. It follows that

$$e^{-\lambda\{x(T)-x_b\}} = 1/aT \tag{6.74}$$

and

$$x(T) = x_b + \{\ln(a) + \ln(T)\}/\lambda \tag{6.75}$$

For a given set of exceedances $X_{(1)}, X_{(2)}, X_{(3)}, \ldots, X_{(N)}$, which are serially independent and ranked in ascending order so that $X_{(1)}$ is the lowest,

$$\Pr(x_{(1)} < x) = 1 - e^{-(x-x_b)/(1/N\lambda)} \tag{6.76}$$

The expectation of a variate with an exponential distribution $F(x) = 1 - e^{-\lambda x}$ is given by

$$E(X) = \int_0^\infty x\lambda e^{-\lambda x}\,dx$$

$$= [-xe^{-\lambda x}]_0^\infty + \int_0^\infty e^{-\lambda x}\,dx,$$

integrating by parts.

Because $\lim_{x \to \infty}(xe^{-\lambda x}) = 0$, for the same reasons given after equation 3.30, $E(X) = 1/\lambda$. Correspondingly, it follows from equation 6.74 that

$$\mu = x_b + 1/\lambda \tag{6.77}$$

where μ is the mean of the $X_{(i)}$ population with the sample estimator

$$\bar{x} = \sum_{i=1}^N x_{(i)}/N$$

Also, from equation 6.76, the expected value of the lowest item is given by

$$E(X_{(1)}) = x_b + 1/N\lambda \tag{6.78}$$

Now $\bar{x}$ and $x_{(1)}$ are sufficient estimators of μ and x_b respectively, where according to the definition by Fisher (1922) an estimator t, say, is sufficient for a parameter θ, say, if the distribution of a sample, given t, does not depend on θ. Therefore, the following estimator for λ is obtained from equation 6.77.

$$\hat{\lambda}' = 1/(\bar{x} - x_{(1)}) \tag{6.79}$$

By taking expectations and by substituting from equations 6.77 and 6.78

$$E(\hat{\lambda}') = \lambda N/(N-1)$$

Then the following unbiased estimator for λ is obtained by substituting the last result in equation 6.79 for $E(\hat{\lambda}')$.

$$\hat{\lambda}' = \{(N-1)/N\}/(\bar{x} - x_{(1)}) \tag{6.80}$$

Again, for x_b, the following unbiased estimator is obtained from equation 6.78.

$$\hat{x}_b = x_{(1)} - 1/N\hat{\lambda} \tag{6.81}$$

The POT method is useful for estimating the magnitudes and frequency of events which have low return periods T. Its main importance is in the design of cofferdams or culverts. However, for $T > 10$, Langbein (1949) has shown that $x(T)$ calculated from the POT method differs very little from that calculated from an annual maximum series.

Example 6.17 Peak daily flows in the River Derwent at Yorkshire Bridge which exceed 19 m³ s⁻¹ are tabulated below for the period 1933 to 1937.

Daily flows (m³ s⁻¹)

1933		1936	
Feb. 1	21.16	Mar. 8	20.46
Mar. 3	30.71	Mar. 9	20.51
Mar. 4	28.39	Sep. 7	28.21
Nov. 15	19.06	Nov. 9	20.12
		Nov. 12	20.23
1934		Nov. 15	22.17
		Nov. 17	19.92
None		Dec. 14	26.73
1935			
Feb. 15	36.62	1937	
Feb. 16	41.04	Jan. 6	29.55
Oct. 9	28.54	Feb. 14	20.65
Oct. 27	35.09	Mar. 17	22.88
Oct. 28	30.65	Mar. 18	33.15
Oct. 29	23.11	Mar. 19	24.87
Oct. 30	23.39	Dec. 2	32.35
Oct. 31	24.21	Dec. 22	29.17
Nov. 4	22.96		
Nov. 17	27.87		
Nov. 20	21.37		
Nov. 21	21.99		

Using a suitable threshold value, estimate the following.

(1) The probability of at least two exceedances of the threshold in 1 year.
(2) The probability of having a 3-year period without any exceedances.
(3) The magnitude of a 5-year flood.

(This sample is too short for practical purposes and is only used here merely to explain the procedure.) The following POT values are taken as serially independent values with an average of three per year; 21.16, 30.71, 41.04, 28.54, 35.09, 22.96, 27.87, 21.99, 28.21, 22.17, 26.73, 29.55, 33.15, 32.35, 29.17. The lowest value $x_{(1)} = 21.16$ and the mean $\bar{x} = 28.71$.

(1) Using equation 6.72, $a = 3$, $P(M = 0|3) = 3^0 e^{-3}/0! = 0.0498$ and $P(M = 1|3) = 3^1 e^{-3}/1! = 0.1494$. The probability of at least two exceedances per year is $1 - P(M = 0|3) - P(M = 1|3) = 0.8008$ which tallies with the visual evidence of four cases out of five.

(2) By using equation 6.73, $P(\tau_i > 3) = \exp(-3 \times 3) = 0.0001$, which is an exceedingly low probability of having a 3-year period without an exceedance.

(3) From equations 6.80, 6.81 and 6.75, $\hat{\lambda} = (14/15)/(28.71 - 21.16) = 0.1236$, $\hat{x}_b = x_{(1)} - 1/N\hat{\lambda} = 20.62$ and $\hat{x}(5) = 20.62 + 8.09 \ln(3 \times 5) = 42.53$.

6.10   Regional flood frequency analysis

The limitations in single-site data are, in summary, that a sequence may be too short to represent the population of flood events adequately, even without considering possible non-stationarities. In addition, the critical values in the records may be subject to serious errors of measurement. On account of such deficiencies, hydrologists have resorted to regionalisation, that is, to combining the information in several records from a homogeneous zone or region. This would hopefully lead to a more realistic estimation of floods of given return periods.

Initially, there is the problem of defining the boundary of such a region. One way to demarcate a region is so that the hydrologic or response characteristics of the catchment areas within it are comparable. These may be assessed through unit hydrographs, lag times and flow duration curves. Alternatively, physical and climatological characteristics may be the overriding criteria in the choice. Finally, and this is probably the easiest method, regions could be defined through existing geographical boundaries; also, areas of similar soils or geology and land use maps have been employed particularly in the United States[40].

There are two main objectives in regional analysis. The first is to extrapolate flood estimates to sites with scanty or no data. In regional studies a multiple regression formula of the type

$$x(T) = aB^b C^c D^d \dots K^k$$

[40] See, for example, the numerous references in Schulz et al. (1973).

is generally assumed for $x(T)$ in which $B, C, \ldots, K$ are the parameters or factors and $b, c, d, \ldots, k$ are regression constants[41]. Then a linear regression equation is obtained through a logarithmic transformation. Initially, a distribution such as the log Pearson type III is fitted to the observed flood data, separately for each station. From the station curves, estimated values $\hat{x}(T)$ are obtained for a particular value of T and are regressed by using a step-forward method, with catchment and other characteristics. These variables are tested in turn for significance before they are included in the equation. The procedure, at any step, is to select the independent variable which maximises the squared partial correlation coefficients, given the $\hat{x}(T)$ and the variables selected before[42].

In the report by the Natural Environmental Research Council (1975), the mean flood, which has a return period of 2.33 years for the Gumbel distribution, is correlated to significant catchment characteristics. The parameters used are as follows: catchment area (km²); STMFRQ, the number of stream junctions, shown on a $1:25000$ map divided by A; S1085, stream gradient which is calculated from 10% to 85% of the stream length from the gauge; RSMD, net 1-day rainfall (which is rainfall less a weighted mean soil moisture deficit) with a 5-year return period; LAKE, proportion of catchment draining through a lake; SOIL, an index of catchment soils in the range of 0.15 to 0.50 calculated from $0.15S_1 + 0.3S_2 + 0.4S_3 + 0.45S_4 + 0.5S_5$, where S_1, S_2, S_3, S_4 and S_5 are the fractions of the catchment area covered by five soil types in increasing order of perviousness; URBAN, the urban fraction of the catchment[43].

For example, the regression equation for the central region of the United Kingdom is

$$\hat{x}(2.33) = 0.0213(\text{AREA})^{0.94}(\text{STMFRQ})^{0.27}(\text{S}1085)^{0.16}$$

$$\times (\text{SOIL})^{1.23}(\text{RSMD})^{1.03}(1+\text{LAKE})^{-0.85} \qquad (6.82)$$

At the same time a dimensionless flood sequence is obtained for a region after dividing the observed values from the various catchments by the estimated mean for the particular catchment. In this way floods from different catchments can be compared directly; originally, engineers used catchment area as a divisor. A region curve is then drawn from the ordered set of data on normal and Gumbel probability paper by using appropriate plotting positions. These curves are similar to figures 6.2 or 6.5 except that the vertical axes are marked in units of $x(T)/x(2.33)$, in which $x(2.33)$ is the (Gumbel) mean annual maximum flood. It is noted from the report by the Natural Environmental Research Council

---

[41] For example, Benson (1962a) used the following parameters for the northeastern United States: N-year annual peak discharge; drainage area; main-channel slope; percentage of surface storage area plus 0.5%; N-year rainfall intensity; average January degrees below freezing; orographic factor.

[42] Standard methods of regression are explained for example by Fryer (1966). Most computers have routines for this type of work.

[43] Regional studies have also been made for the United Kingdom by Nash and Shaw (1966) and by Cole (1966).

(1975) that the type II extreme value distribution seems to provide the best fit for distributions of flood events on a regional basis. Accordingly, parameters of this distribution are calculated for ten regions in the United Kingdom and one for the whole of Ireland. The limits of the regional values of parameters in equation 6.41 are $0 \leqslant k \leqslant -0.325$, $0.77 \leqslant u \leqslant 0.87$ and $0.18 \leqslant \alpha \leqslant 0.28$ with mean values of $-0.2, 0.8$ and 0.24 respectively. By using the second approximation of equation 6.15, the national (United Kingdom) equation suggested by the Natural Environmental Research Council (1975) is

$$\hat{x}(T)/\hat{x}(2.33) = -0.4 + 1.20T^{0.2} \tag{6.83}$$

It should be noted that the presence of an outlier, say, x_{max}, which is an extremely high flow such as a 1000-year flood within a short sample, will give an upward bias to the mean flow as given by equation 6.82 or by a similar regression equation. Now, the median flood flow x_{med} is known to be a more stable statistic than the mean $x(2.33)$; the Natural Environmental Research Council (1975) found that $x(2.33)/x_{med} \approx 1.07$ for United Kingdom data and recommended that, if in a particular case $x_{max} > 3x_{med}$, $\hat{x}(2.33)$ should be equated to $1.07x_{med}$.

Regionalisation is sometimes used to extend floods temporarily in order to estimate the frequency of floods of high return periods. According to Kritsky and Menkel (1969), hydraulic structures in the Soviet Union are designed to pass maximum floods which occur on average once in 1000 or 10 000 years. This has been achieved by combining flood records from the Volga, Dneiper and other river basins. However, because of spatial correlation between flood events, the return period of a critical flood event could be much less than, say, the hypothetical 1000-year period obtained by combining 20 records of length 50 years. The influence of correlation, in this so-called station–year method, is examined by Carrigan (1971).

Finally, if we return to the general regional approach, its main shortcoming is that the highest floods within a region are often caused by a single meteorological event. The same could also apply to the second, third and other critical floods. When this happens there seems to be little virtue in using regionalisation because we cannot obtain more information than in a single-station analysis. At the other extreme, if the crucial floods are caused by local convective precipitation, orographic effects or the melting of snow rather than through cyclonic systems which are often widespread, the standard error in the regression may be too high, and the method is of doubtful value for spatial extrapolation, on account of significant differences between the flood-producing characteristics of the individual catchments.

6.11   Probable maximum precipitation

The inadequacies in the frequency approach are discussed in previous sections. Even if long records are available, there is uncertainty regarding estimated values. For instance, regardless of the largest observed flow, it is inevitable that a

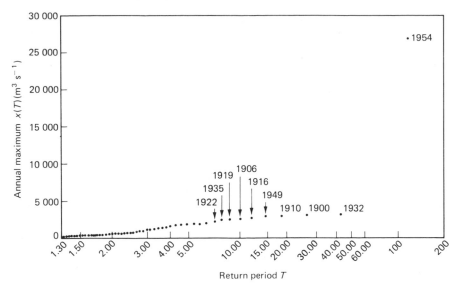

Figure 6.8 Annual maximum peak flows in Pecos near Shumla, Texas, for the period 1900 to 1968: Gringorton plotting position is used; return periods of less than 1.3 years are not shown. Years in which the ten highest flows occurred are given. Note the flood which occurred on 28 June 1954 as shown at the top. Prior to October 1954, the gauging station was 13 miles downstream at Pecos, Texas

much larger flood will occur in the future, and it is in the application to abnormally high flows that frequency methods are the least satisfactory. An example is shown in figure 6.8 which is a Gumbel plot from 67 years of annual maxima in the Pecos River near Shumla, Texas. The maximum flow in 1954 is an outlier which, if ignored and calculated on the basis of the other 66 items of data, has a return period of more than 10^{11} years. This is clearly a flood event which cannot be accounted for by conventional methods! Other examples from the United States are the floods in Virginia during August 1969 due to hurricane Camille, which were about ten times those recorded earlier, and this was followed by the catastrophic events in Rapid City, South Dakota. However, the largest flood damage, estimated at three billion dollars, was caused in June 1972 by hurricane Agnes in the eastern United States during June 1972, and the greatest flooding elsewhere during recent decades occurred in Bangladesh during November 1970 as a result of a tropical cyclone[44].

Although such freak events are possible almost everywhere, it is rational to assume from a knowledge of physics that there is an upper limit to maximum floods, however impractical its definition might seem, in the same way that other natural phenomena have their own ends or bounds. To quote Horton (1936), 'A

[44] Information on other outliers in flood data from the United States is given by Hardison (1973).

small stream cannot produce a major Mississippi flood just as an ordinary barnyard fowl cannot lay an egg a yard in diameter: it would transcend nature's capabilities under the circumstances.' We could also add other impossible cases such as a man of age 200 years, a woman 10 feet tall and a snake 1 mile long.

In this sense, the unbounded right tails of commonly postulated frequency functions for flood flows are not realistic. The question then arises what the upper limit should be, and this will be of particular interest in the design of large dams, the failure of which can have a serious effect on lives and property. In order to find a practical solution to the problem, hydrometeorologists have developed the technique of probable maximum precipitation (PMP).

It is easy to imagine that, when observed storms are transposed from neighbouring catchments to an area above a particular observation site, extreme flood flows which exceed the magnitudes of observed events could occur at this site. Storm maximisation obtained by considering dew points, wind velocities, condensation of cloud particles and other criteria related to storm efficiency increases this effect. However, all the meteorological factors associated with maximum floods cannot be accounted for, because of the limitations in the knowledge of atmospheric processes and also because of the lack of data. Because of these shortcomings, the approach is subjective and it has aroused a great deal of controversy[45]. Nevertheless, in the United States, design floods are based on the PMP method if the dam heights are greater than 60 feet, and a United States committee has considered the safety of large dams on this basis[46]. Then, the unit hydrograph method is used to obtain the probable maximum flood from the PMP. The method is also followed in Australia. The following is an outline of the basic principles.

Because the upper limit of high floods cannot be satisfactorily defined, no structure which is designed to cope with these extraordinary events could be absolutely safe. On the other hand, the design of, say, a spillway dam that can pass the flood caused by the highest possible precipitation is conceivable, if the flood is obtained by maximising all the factors simultaneously, but the cost of such a structure would be prohibitive. Besides, there is uncertainty regarding these 'maximum' factors. For engineering expediency, therefore, PMP has been defined as the magnitude of rainfall over a catchment area that would result in a flood flow of which there is 'virtually no risk of being exceeded'[47]. There have also been other definitions, and a discussion on these is given by Alexander (1965). In this context it is important to note here that in some areas the melting of snow is an important contributory factor.

As for the term storm transposition used in hydrometeorology, with its area of extent and physical boundaries, a region of meteorological homogeneity is best regarded as one in which every catchment within it can have precipitation events with similar inflow wind movement and storm mechanisms but with

[45] See, for example, Gumbel (1958b), Yevjevich (1968) and Benson (1973).
[46] This is reported, for instance, by Gray (1974).
[47] See Myers (1969).

variations in the total moisture charge and frequency of occurrence. There is also another important point to bear in mind. This concerns the types of storms which we are justified in transposing. Whereas thunderstorms lend themselves easily to transposition with hardly any reservation regarding distance, hurricanes are effective only in certain coastal areas[48]. Also, there are limits to transposition in mountainous zones, and storms observed in one catchment cannot be considered to occur in another if the difference in elevation is excessive (say, more that about 1500 feet). By the same token, the shape and orientation of rainfall patterns associated with frontal rains should not be altered. Therefore, it follows that a hydrometeorological analysis of this type requires careful judgement.

When faced with inadequate data, PMP analysts estimate the moisture of a storm from surface dew points. This approximation is reasonable for heavy storms when the column of air is saturated and the vertical temperature gradient is equivalent to the saturated pseudoadiabatic lapse rate which is a decrease of about $0.5\,^{\circ}$C per 100 m above the surface. The importance of the dew point stems from the fact that there is an increase of about 9 % in precipitation for every $1\,^{\circ}$C increase in the dew point; dew points over oceanic surfaces are of special significance. Maps giving the variation in precipitation water with dew points and elevations (of orographic barriers to inflowing air) are given with examples by Weisner (1970) and by the Tennessee Valley Authority (1961). In elementary applications of the method recorded precipitation–depth–duration curves are increased directly in proportion to the amounts of water that can be precipitated in the two catchment areas[49].

It has also been suggested that an empirical factor $K(T)$ times the standard deviation should be used in addition to the mean of a maximum precipitation sequence as an initial approximation to the PMP in the form given by equation 6.26. For instance, Hershfield (1961) found that, in a key group of 24-hour United States stations, $K(T)$ has an upper limit of 15. Meanwhile, Alexander (1963), in order to provide a measurably probabilistic basis to the problem, related the return period T_c of PMP in a catchment area A_c to the rank r, in descending order where $r = 1, 2, 3, \ldots, N_e$, of observed maximum precipitation events in the homogeneous zone, of area A_h, as follows.

$$T_c = N_e A_h / r A_c$$

[48] See, for example, Lane (1948, chapter 1).
[49] For practical application in the Tennessee valley area, see the Tennessee Valley Authority (1961). A manual for the estimation of PMP is given by the World Meteorological Organisation (1973). Calculations involving other criteria are also given by Weisner (1970) and elsewhere by Miller (1973). As regards national maps of maximum precipitation and other aspects of analysis and design, reference may be made, for example, to Chow (1964, sections 9, 21, 25), Linsley et al. (1949), Berry et al. (1945) and the Natural Environmental Research Council (1975).

6.12   Other methods and comments

A different approach to flood estimation is possible through the generation of large samples of data by means of the daily flow time series models explained in chapter 4. Kottegoda (1972, 1973) has examined the possibilities through a linear autoregression model; the work of Green (1973) and Quimpo (1967) are relevant. Of more recent origin is the shot noise model of Weiss (1977) and the model of Treiber and Plate (1975) based on a deterministic system function (see chapter 4). One of the main purposes in this approach is to estimate parameters of a probability model from very large samples of data. However, there are problems regarding the correct formulation of daily models and the estimates of their parameters, and on average the uncertainties in this method may balance those in conventional frequency methods of flood estimation. Nevertheless, the output should be useful for simulation of complex systems.

Monte Carlo methods could also indicate improved decision-oriented methods to counteract uncertainty in flood estimation, although practicalities are yet not clear. For instance, extensive computer studies were made by Slack *et al.* (1975) on the choice of distribution between normal, Gumbel, lognormal or Weibull distributions for high-flow data generated on the basis of these distributions. Their criterion is the minimum expected design loss with square root, linear and quadratic loss functions and variable scaling factors; the sample space was defined through skewness (in the third and fourth distributions), sample size and return period. If $\hat{x}(T)$ and $x(T)$ denote the estimated and true values respectively of the design flood (in the authors' notation) an underdesign loss occurs if $\hat{x}(T) < x(T)$ and vice versa. On the basis of expected opportunity losses, the normal does not seem to be disadvantageous, regardless of whether we identify the underlying distribution of floods or not. However, with limited information on skewness and detailed information on the relative scale of overdesign to underdesign losses, a substantial reduction in opportunity losses occurs. In a subsequent work, it was found that the assumed distribution which minimises the expected design loss is quite stable with respect to N, the sample size[50].

Because longer records of rainfall are usually available, attempts have been made to obtain improved estimates of frequencies of high flows from rainfall events. However, antecedent conditions, for instance, are highly variable, and because gauged rainfall data may not be representative of catchment rainfall there is high scatter in plots of rainfall against river flow. On the other hand, there is a central tendency for the return intervals in the two sides to be theoretically equal in the long run, but in a practical situation this property is not of much use[51].

If we return now to the POT approach examined in section 6.9, perhaps its main drawback is that the data are not identically distributed. As an improvement, Todorovic and Rouselle (1971) formulated a seasonal model (see

[50]   See Wallis *et al.* (1976).
[51]   See Larson and Reich (1973) and the discussion of their paper by Whittaker (1973).

also Todorovic (1978)). For this type of analysis, harmonic fitted cumulative sums of the mean number of exceedances of the threshold value in 17 periods of 20 days and 1 of 25 days within an annual cycle are initially computed. The probability distribution of the largest POT value in, say, the summer season is given by

$$\Pr(X_{su} < x) = \exp(-M_{sp}^{-x/\mu_{sp}} - M_{su}^{-x/\mu_{su}})$$

in which M_{sp} is the difference between the mean number of exceedances at the end and start of the spring season and μ_{sp} is the expectation of the POT value during the spring season; M_{su} and μ_{su} have similar connotations with respect to the summer season. The original work of Todorovic and his coworkers is commendable; nevertheless, the main problem of estimating the magnitudes of flood peaks for specified high return periods still remain, on account of the fact that the distributions of the annual maximum and partial duration series merge rather quickly.

On the subject of annual maxima flows, Singh and Sinclair (1972) proposed an empirical five-parameter distribution comprising two normal distributions in order to model the reverse curvatures frequently seen in probability plots. In spite of better fits to sample data which is anticipated, there could be serious doubts about the true form of the population distribution as estimated by this method. The idea of mixed distributions is intuitively correct, but empirical curve-fitting methods cannot provide permanent solutions. Indeed, the future of objective treatment of high flows must lie on a rigorous mathematical and physical approach without restrictive assumptions.

6.13 Final remarks and summary

As mentioned before, great uncertainty is associated with the estimation of the probabilities of rare floods. This seems to be inevitable because, firstly, there is insufficient information at present to define empirically the right tails of density functions of high flows. Secondly, because of the underlying complexities that are unaccounted for, theoretical models are inadequate for dealing with the important problems. Therefore, a definite set of rules cannot be given in the foreseeable future for flood estimation, and any decisions taken will be subject to personal bias. More confidence could, of course, be placed in the estimation of average or more likely events.

In the hydraulic design of a structure, such as a culvert for which the criterion is a high flow with a return period of about 5 to 10 years, the POT method should normally provide satisfactory answers when the available sequence of data is sufficiently long, perhaps more than 30 years. Large floods which affect the design of structures such as dams could be estimated through a probability function chosen from a selected few that fit the data. This may suffice for practical purposes when samples are sufficiently long and return intervals are commensurate with sample lengths. An indication of the likely errors which arise even in such cases is given in subsection 6.2.1; these errors would escalate when incorrect probability models are chosen or on account of non-stationarities. If the estimation involves an extrapolation far beyond the data sample, then the regional method is suggested which is also the best way by which floods at ungauged sites could be estimated. It is important here to bear in mind the limitations which this entails, such as bias and standard errors due to lack of representative data and incorrectly defined regional boundaries respectively.

This means that estimates of floods of high return intervals are generally subject to serious errors. As regards very high floods that are a threat to life and property, the most feasible method of tackling this problem at present is by the PMP technique. Although the concept is subjective and the method tends to become arbitrary in practice, it helps to provide an engineering solution which takes into account the relevant information and uncertainties.

References

Abramowtiz, M., and Stegun, L. (eds) (1964). Handbook of mathematical functions. *Natl Bur. Stand., Appl. Math. Ser. Publ.*, No. 55; *Handbook of Mathematical Functions*, Dover Publications, New York

Aitchison, J., and Brown, J. A. C. (1957). *The Lognormal Distribution*, Cambridge University Press, London

Alexander, G. N. (1963). Using the probability of storm transposition for estimating the frequency of rare floods. *J. Hydrol.*, **1**, 46–57

——(1965). Discussion of 'hydrology of spillway design: large structures—adequate data'. *J. Hydraul Div., Proc. Am. Soc. Civ. Eng.*, **91** (HY1), 211–19

Anscombe, F. J. (1960). Rejection of outliers. *Technometrics*, **2**, 123–47

Barnett, V. (1975). Probability plotting methods and order statistics. *Appl. Statist.*, **24**, 95–108

Benson, M. A. (1960). Characteristics of frequency curves based on a theoretical 1000-year record. *U.S., Geol. Surv., Water-Supply Paper*, No. 1543-A, 51–94

——(1962a). Factors influencing the occurrence of floods in a humid region of diverse terrain. *U.S., Geol. Surv., Water-Supply Paper*, No. 1580-B

——(1962b). Plotting positions and economics of engineering planning. *J. Hydraul. Div., Proc. Am. Soc. Civ. Eng.*, **88** (HY6), 57–71. (1963). Discussion closure. *J. Hydraul. Div., Proc. Am. Soc. Civ. Eng.*, **89** (HY6), 251–2

—— (1968). Uniform flood-frequency estimating methods for federal agencies. *Water Resour. Res.*, **4**, 891–908. (1969). Comments. *Water Resour. Res.*, **5**, 910–11. (1970). Comments. *Water Resour. Res.*, **6**, 998–9

—— (1973). Thoughts on the design of design floods. *Floods and Droughts, Proceedings of the 2nd International Hydrology Symposium*, 11–13 September 1972, Water Resource Publications, Fort Collins, Colorado, pp. 27–33

Berry, F. A., Bollay, E., and Beers, N. R. (eds) (1945). *Handbook of*

Meteorology, McGraw-Hill, New York

Bobée, B., and Robitaille, R. (1975). Correction of bias in the estimation of the coefficient of skewness. *Water Resour. Res.*, **11**, 851–4

Brown, J. P. (1972). *The Economic Effect of Floods*, Springer, Berlin

Burges, S. J., Lettenmaier, D. P., and Bates C. L. (1975). Properties of the three-parameter log normal probability distribution. *Water Resour. Res.*, **11**, 229–35

Bury, K. V. (1975). *Statistical Models in Applied Science*, Wiley, New York

Carrigan, P. H., Jr. (1971). A flood frequency relation based on regional record maxima. *U.S., Geol. Surv., Prof. Paper*, No. 434-F

Chow, V. T. (1951). A general formula for hydrologic frequency analysis. *Trans. Am. Geophys. Un.*, **32**, 231–7. (1952). Discussion. *Trans. Am. Geophys. Un.*, **33**, 277–82

——(1954). The log-probability law and its engineering applications. *Proc. Am. Soc. Civ. Eng.*, **80**, paper 536, 1–25

——(1964). *Handbook of Applied Hydrology*, McGraw-Hill, New York

Cole, G. (1966). An application of the regional analysis of flood flows. *Proceedings of the Symposium on River Flood Hydrology, March* 1965, Institution of Civil Engineers, London, session B, paper 3

Collett, D., and Lewis, T. (1976). The subjective nature of outlier rejection procedures. *Appl. Statist.*, **25**, 228–37

Condie, R. (1977). The log Pearson type 3 distribution: the T-year event and its asymptotic standard error by maximum likelihood theory. *Water Resour. Res.*, **13**, 987–91

Court, A. (1952). Some new statistical techniques in geophysics. *Adv. Geophys.*, **1**, 45–85

Davis, D. R., Kisiel, C. C., and Duckstein, L. (1972). Bayesian decision theory applied to design in hydrology. *Water Resour. Res.*, **8**, 33–41

Fisher, R. A. (1922). On the mathematical foundations of theoretical statistics. *Philos. Trans. A*, **222**, 309–68

Fisher, R. A., and Tippett, L. H. C. (1928). Limiting forms of the frequency distribution of the largest or smallest member of a sample. *Proc. Camb. Philos. Soc.*, **24**, 180–90

Foster, H. A. (1924). Theoretical frequency curves and their applications to engineering problems. *Trans. Am. Soc. Civ. Eng.*, **87**, 142–203

Fréchet, M. (1927). Sur la loi de probabilité de l'écart maximum. *Annales de la Société Polonaise de Mathematique*, **6**, 92–117

Fryer, H. C. (1966). *Concepts and Methods of Experimental Statistics*, Allyn and Bacon, London

Fuller, W. E. (1914). Flood flows. *Trans. Am. Soc. Civ. Eng.*, **77**, 564–617

Giesbrecht, F., and Kempthorne, O. (1976). Maximum likelihood estimation in the three-parametric lognormal distribution. *J. R. Statist. Soc. B*, **38**, 257–63

Gilroy, E. J. (1972). The upper bound of a log-Pearson type 3 random variable with negatively skewed logarithms. *U.S., Geol. Surv., Prof. Paper*, **800**, B273–5

Gray, D. A. (1974). Safety of dams—bureau of reclamation. *J. Hydraul. Div., Am. Soc. Civ. Eng.*, **100** (HY2), 267–77

Green, N. M. D. (1973). A synthetic model for daily streamflow. *J. Hydrol.*, **20**, 351–64

Gringorten, I. I. (1963). A plotting rule for extreme probability paper. *J. Geophys. Res.*, **68**, 813–4

Grubbs, F. E. (1950). Sample criteria for testing outlying observations. *Ann. Math. Statist.*, **21**, 27–58

Gumbel, E. J. (1941). The return period of flood flows. *Ann. Math. Statist.*, **12**, 163–90

——(1943). On the reliability of the classical chi-square test. *Ann. Math. Statist.*, **14**, 253–63

——(1954). Statistical theory of extreme valves and some practical applications. *Natl Bur. Stand., Appl. Math. Ser., Publ.*, No. 33

——(1958a). *Statistics of Extremes*, Columbia University Press, New York

——(1958b). Theory of floods and droughts. *J. Inst. Water Eng.*, **12**, 157–84 (1959). Communications. *J. Inst. Water Eng.*, **13**, 71–102

——(1967). Extreme value analysis of hydrologic data. *Statistical Methods in Hydrology, Proceedings of the 5th Hydrology Symposium, McGill University*, 1966, Queen's Printer, Ottawa, pp. 147–81

Hardison, C. H. (1973). Probability distribution of extreme floods, highways and the catastrophic floods of 1972. *Proceedings of the 52nd Annual General Meeting of the Highway Research Board*, National Academy of Sciences, Washington, D.C., No. 479, pp. 42–5

——(1974). Generalized skew coefficients of annual floods in the United States and their application. *Water Resour. Res.*, **10**, 745–52

Harter, H. L. (1969). A new table of percentage points of the Pearson type III distribution. *Technometrics*, **11**, 177–87

Hazen, A. (1914). Storage to be provided in impounding reservoirs for municipal water supply. *Trans. Am. Soc. Civ. Eng.*, **77**, 1539–640

——(1930). *Flood Flows*, Wiley, New York

Hershfield, D. M. (1961). Estimating the probable maximum precipitation. *J. Hydraul. Div., Am. Soc. Civ. Eng.*, **87** (HY5), 99–116

Holtzman, W. H. (1950). The unbiased estimate of the population variance and standard deviation. *Am. J. Psychol.*, **63**, 615–17

Horton, R. E. (1914). Discussion on 'Flood flows' by W. E. Fuller. *Trans. Am. Soc. Civ. Eng.*, **77**, 663–70

——(1936). Hydrologic conditions as affecting the results of the application of method of frequency analysis to flood records. *U.S., Geol. Surv., Water-Supply Paper*, No. 771, 433–50

Huxham, S. H., and McGilchrist, C. A. (1969). On the extreme value distribution for describing annual flood series. *Water Resour. Res.*, **5**, 1404–5

Jenkinson, A. F. (1955). The frequency distribution of the annual maximum (or minimum) values of meteorological elements. *Q. J. R. Meteorol. Soc.*, **81,** 158–71

——(1969). Estimation of maximum floods. *World Meteorol. Organ., Tech. Note*, No. 98, chapter 5, 183–257

Kaczmarek, Z. (1957). Efficiency of the estimation of floods with a given return period, vol. 3, International Association of Scientific Hydrology, Toronto, pp. 145–59

Kalinske, A. A. (1946). On the logarithmic-probability law. *Trans. Am. Geophys. Un.*, **27,** 709–11

Kazmann, R. G. (1972). *Modern Hydrology*, 2nd edn, Harper and Row, New York

Kendall, M. G., and Stuart, A. (1977). *The Advanced Theory of Statistics*, vol. 2, 4th edn, Griffin, London

Kimball, B. F. (1960). On the choice of plotting positions on probability paper. *J. Am. Statist. Assoc.*, **55,** 546–60

Kirby, W. (1974). Algebraic boundedness of sample statistics. *Water Resour. Res.*, **10,** 220–2

Kottegoda, N. T. (1972). Flood evaluation—can stochastic models provide an answer? *Proceedings of the International Symposium on Uncertainties in Hydrology and Water Resources Systems*, vol. 1, 11–14 *December 1972, University of Arizona, Tucson*, pp. 105–14

——(1973). Flood estimation by some data generation techniques. *Floods and Droughts, Proceedings of the 2nd International Hydrology Symposium*, 11–13 *September* 1972, Water Resource Publications, Fort Collins, Colorado, pp. 189–99

Kritsky, S. N. and Menkel, M. F. (1969). On principles of estimation methods of maximum discharge. *Floods and their Computation*, vol. 1, International Association of Scientific Hydrology, Belgium, No. 84, pp. 29–41

Lane, F. W. (1948). *The Elements Rage*, Country Life, London

Langbein, W. B. (1949). Annual floods and the partial-duration flood series. *Trans. Am. Geophys. Un.*, **30,** 879–81

——(1960). Plotting positions in frequency analysis. *U.S., Geol. Surv., Water-Supply Paper*, No. 1543-A, 48–51

Larson, C. L., and Reich, B. M. (1973). Relationships of observed rainfall and runoff intervals. *Floods and Droughts, Proceedings of the 2nd International Hydrology Symposium*, 11–13 *September* 1972, Water Resource Publications, Fort Collins, Colorado, pp. 34–43

Linsley, R. K., Kohler, M. A., and Paulhus, J. L. H. (1949). *Applied Hydrology*, McGraw-Hill, New York

Lloyd, E. H. (1970). Return periods in the presence of persistence. *J. Hydrol.*, **10,** 291–8

Lowery, M. D., and Nash, J. E. (1970). A comparison of methods of fitting the double exponential distribution. *J. Hydrol.*, **10,** 259–75

Majumdar, K. C., and Sawhney, R. P. (1965). Estimates of extreme values by different distribution functions. *Water Resour. Res.*, **1,** 429–34

Markowitz, E. M. (1971). The chance a flood will be exceeded in a period of years. *Water Resour. Bull.*, **7**, 40–53

Matalas, N. C. (1967). Mathematical assessment of synthetic hydrology. *Water Resour. Res.*, **3**, 937–45

Matalas, N. C., Slack, J. R., and Wallis, J. R. (1975). Regional skew in search of a parent. *Water Resour. Res.*, **11**, 815–26

Miller, J. F. (1973). Probable maximum precipitation—the concept, current, procedures and the outlook. *Floods and Droughts, Proceedings of the 2nd International Hydrological Symposium, 11–13 September* 1972, Water Resource Publications, Fort Collins, Colorado, pp. 50–61

Moran, P. A. P. (1957). The statistical treatment of flood flows. *Trans. Am. Geophys. Un.*, **38**, 519–23

Myers, V. A. (1969). The estimation of extreme precipitation as the basis for design flood—resume of practice in the United States. *Floods and their Computation*, vol. 1, International Association of Scientific Hydrology, Belgium, No. 84, pp. 84–104

Nash, J. E., and Shaw, B. L. (1966). Flood frequency as a function of catchment characteristics. *Proceedings of the Symposium on River Flood Hydrology, March* 1965, Institution of Civil Engineers, London, session C, paper 6

Natural Environmental Research Council (1975). *Flood Studies Report*, Natural Environment Research Council, London

Panchang, C. M. (1969). Improved precision of future high floods. *Floods and their Computation*, vol. 1, International Association of Scientific Hydrology, Belgium, No. 84, pp. 51–9

Powell, R. W. (1943). A simple method of estimating flood frequencies. *Civ. Eng.*, **13**, 105–6

Quimpo, R. G. (1967). Stochastic model of daily river flow sequences. *Colo. St. Univ., Fort Collins, Hydrol. Papers*, No. 18

Sangal, B. P., and Biswas, A. K. (1970). The 3-parameter lognormal distribution and its application in hydrology. *Water Resour. Res.*, **6**, 505–15

Santos, A., Jr. (1970). The statistical treatment of flood flows. *Water Power*, **22**, 63–7

Schulz, E. F., Koelzer, V. A., and Mahmood, K. (eds) (1973). *Floods and Droughts, Proceedings of the 2nd International Hydrology Symposium, 11–13 September* 1972, Water Resource Publications, Fort Collins, Colorado

Schuster, J. (1973). A simple method of teaching the independence of $\overline{X}$ and s^2. *Am. Statist.*, **27**, 29–30

Singh, K. P., and Sinclair, R. A. (1972). Two-distribution method for flood-frequency analysis. *J. Hydraul Div., Proc. Am. Soc. Civ. Eng.*, **98** (HY1), 29–44

Slack, J. R., Wallis, J. R., and Matalas, N. C. (1975). On the value of information to flood frequency analysis. *Water Resour. Res.*, **11**, 629–47

Stripp., J. R., and Young, G. K., Jr. (1971). Plotting positions for hydrologic frequencies. *J. Hydraul. Div., Proc. Am. Soc. Civ. Eng.*, **97** (HY1), 219–22

Tennessee Valley Authority (1961). *Floods and Flood Control*, Tennessee Valley

Authority, Knoxville, Tennessee

Todorovic, P. (1978). Stochastic models of floods. *Water Resour. Res.*, **14**, 345–56

Todorovic, P., and Rouselle, J. (1971). Some problems of flood analysis. *Water Resour. Res.*, **7**, 1144–50

Treiber, B., and Plate, E. J. (1975). A stochastic model for the simulation of daily flows. *Proceedings of the International Symposium and Workshop on the Application of Mathematical Models in Hydrology and Water Resources System*, International Association of Scientific Hydrology, Bratislava, preprints

Tribus, M. (1969). *Rational Descriptions, Decisions and Designs*, Pergamon, New York

Wallis, J. R., Matalas, N. C., and Slack, J. R. (1974). Just a moment! *Water Resour. Res.*, **10**, 211–19

——(1976). Effect of sequence length *n* on the choice of assumed distribution of floods. *Water Resour. Res.*, **12**, 457–71

Watson, G. S. (1954). Extreme values in samples from *M*-dependent stationary stochastic processes. *Ann. Math. Statist.*, **25**, 798–800

Weisner, C. J. (1970). *Hydrometeorology*, Chapman and Hall, London

Weiss, G. (1977). Shot noise models for synthetic generation of multisite daily streamflow data. *Water Resour. Res.*, **13**, 101–8

Whipple, G. C. (1916). The element of chance in sanitation. *J. Franklin Inst.*, **182**, 205–27

Whittaker, J. (1973). Discussion on 'Relationship of observed rainfall and runoff recurrence intervals' by C. L. Larson and B. M. Reich. *Floods and Droughts, Proceedings of the 2nd International Hydrology Symposium, 11–13 September 1972*, Water Resource Publications, Fort Collins, Colorado, pp. 108–9

Wilk, M. B., Gnanadesikan, R., and Hugett, M. J. (1962). Probability plots for the gamma distribution. *Technometrics*, **4**, 1–20

Wilson, E. M. (1974). *Engineering Hydrology*, 2nd edn, Macmillan, London

World Meteorological Organisation (1973). Manual for estimation of probable maximum precipitation. *Oper. Hydrol. Rep.*, No. 1, *World Meteorol. Organ.*, Geneva, *Publ.*, No. 332.

——(1974). Guide to hydrometeorological practices. *World Meteorol. Organ.*, Geneva, *Publ.*, No. 168

Yevjevich, V. (1968). Misconceptions in hydrology and their consequences. *Water Resour. Res.*, **4**, 225–32. (1969). Comments and reply. *Water Resour. Res.*, **5**, 535–41

7 Probability theory applied to reservoir storage

Stochastic models applicable to hydrologic time series and extreme events are investigated in earlier chapters. Such models are important for the simulation of complex water resource systems and for flood estimation purposes. However, in the design of individual reservoirs where one of the main criteria is the probability of failure, a more direct approach can be adopted if the inflow data are independent or have a Markov type of dependence. The choice between alternatives is usually made so that this probability does not exceed a stipulated value, which depends on the purposes served. Also important is the average number of times a reservoir will spill or empty during a given period. Another interesting outcome is the probability of first time emptiness.

Probability theory applied to reservoir storage problems is explained at a basic level in this chapter. The credit goes to Moran (1954) who initiated a theory based on serially independent reservoir inflows with a fixed distribution. Moran's theory has been extended in the past 20 years with notable practical contributions, amongst others, by Gould (1961) who incorporated failures within a year. Subsequently, Lloyd (1963) developed a probability theory for serially correlated inflows. In addition, probabilities of reservoir levels are dependent on probability distributions of seasonal inflows and their interrelations.

Details and examples of these methods are given here. As an introduction, some aspects of the associated theory of queues are considered.

7.1 Queueing theory and water storage

Queueing or waiting theory began around 1909 with the work of the Danish scientist A. K. Erlang after attempts to find a solution to random demands on the Copenhagen automatic telephone system and consequent congestion in telephone traffic. The general class of problems of this type involves the arrival of 'customers' at a service station where a queue is formed prior to service; here, the rates of arrival and completion of service are variable. The theory is now an important branch of the post-war science named operations research[1].

In the field of water resources, storage in a reservoir is analogous to queues. If the reservoir is treated as a service station, the probability distribution of inflows may be regarded as one of arrival rates, and, accordingly, the discharges from storage become the service function[2].

Of particular interest are the probabilities of high and low levels of storage. These are determined through 'probability-routing' methods which date back to the work of Saverenskiy (1940). However, Moran (1954, 1955, 1959) is credited with the initiation of storage theory, which required, as he found it, a mathematical treatment different from queueing theory.

Moran's theory of reservoirs is based on the special type of stochastic process called a Markov process (named after the Russian mathematician A. A. Markov) which we studied in chapter 4; the discrete case is termed a Markov chain. These are important tools in the application of probability theory to real world situations in which uncertainty is a major problem.

7.2 Definition of Markov chain

A continuous stochastic process $\{Z(t), t \geqslant 0\}$, where $Z(t)$ is a random variable which measures for instance the water level in a reservoir, is said to be a *first-order Markov process*, if for a set of time points $t_1 < t_2 < \ldots < t_n$ (which are in a parameter set T, called the index set of the process as explained in chapter 2) the conditional distribution of the random variable $Z(t_n)$ can be defined in terms of only $Z(t_{n-1})$. This means that the history of the process prior to time t_{n-1} is assumed to be irrelevant to the value taken currently in time. Expressed as a statement of probability,

$$\Pr\{Z(t_n) \leqslant z_n \,|\, Z(t_{n-1}) = z_{n-1}, Z(t_{n-2}) = z_{n-2}, \ldots, Z(t_1) = z_1\}$$
$$= \Pr\{Z(t_n) \leqslant z_n \,|\, Z(t_{n-1}) = z_{n-1}\} \tag{7.1}$$

where Pr denotes probability, $z_1, z_2, \ldots, z_n$ is a set of real numbers and the vertical bars mean conditional to the equalities on the right[3].

Note that a second-order Markov process can be represented by adding the term $Z(t_{n-2}) = z_{n-2}$, preceded by a comma, before the closing brackets on the

---

[1] Operations research will be introduced in the next chapter. Details of queueing theory are given by Cox and Smith (1961), by Gross and Harris (1974), by Hillier and Lieberman (1974, chapters 9, 10), by Gillett (1976) and by Shamblin and Stevens (1974, chapter 8); the treatment by Moran (1959) and in the *Journal of Applied Probability* is more sophisticated.

[2] The application of queueing theory to a reservoir was originally made by Langbein (1958); in the case studied, inflows are serially correlated and output is a linear function of storage. Also, Fiering (1962) applied the theory to a multipurpose reservoir.

[3] This definition corresponds to that of Parzen (1962, p. 188). For further information, see, for example, Lloyd (1974), *Encyclopaedia Brittanica* (1977) and Cox and Miller (1965, chapters 1, 3).

right-hand side of equation 7.1. This represents a process in which the 'memory' lasts over two intervals of time[4]. Higher-order processes may be similarly defined.

In general, a discrete time first-order Markov process described by a sequence of random variables $Z_t, t = 0, 1, 2, \ldots$, with discrete state space is referred to as a first-order Markov chain or simply as a Markov chain. The state space, as mentioned in chapter 2, is the set of possible values which the random variable takes; it is said to be discrete if it contains a finite or, statistically speaking, an enumerable infinity of points[5].

7.3   Moran's theory of reservoirs

The pioneering work of Moran and others led to the use of Markov chains in the application of probability theory to storage problems. This section deals with the general theory and the underlying assumptions; a worked example is also included.

7.3.1   *Application of Markov chains and assumptions made*

Storage in a reservoir changes continuously with time and is dependent on previous inflows, which could have significant serial correlation, a large variance and non-normal distributions which change seasonally. In addition, storage is, of course, influenced by rates of withdrawal. Other factors such as losses through evaporation and seepage and a reduction in capacity through siltation also affect reservoir levels. Because such complexities are theoretically unassailable, Moran made the following simplifying assumptions.

(1) Discrete time units are considered, continuous time processes being complicated because they require the solutions to a system of integral equations.

(2) The reservoir is replenished during the wet season, and withdrawal is made instantaneously at the end of an annual period. These assumptions may be appropriate for conditions in the reservoirs of the Snowy Mountains in southeast Australia which supposedly stimulated Moran's interest in reservoir theory. However, in general, it may be assumed that inflows and withdrawals

---

[4] The word memory in this sense merely signifies the number of antecedent values required to describe the current value in time. On the other hand, as shown by equation 4.13, the dependency in a Markov process extends over an infinite time span, though with a fast exponential decrease rate.

[5] A. A. Markov assumed at the turn of the century, as in the above definition of a Markov chain and in what is followed in the book by Isaacson and Madsen (1976) for instance, that the time parameter is discrete and that the number of states is finite. Revuz (1975, p. 316) uses the word process when time is continuous and the word chain in the discrete case regardless of state conditions, whereas Chung (1967) and Billingsley (1961) refer to a denumerable and a finite state space respectively, when defining a Markov chain. Note that the book by Revuz is less sophisticated than the others and contains several numerical examples, though they are not directly relevant to the practitioner.

occur continuously throughout the year: however, when the reservoir level is low, the demand is restricted to the available water.

(3) The discrete series of inflows are not serially correlated and have a fixed probability distribution. The effects of serial correlation and seasonality are considered later in this chapter.

(4) Losses are neglected. This is not a serious departure from reality for, although losses are largely influenced by reservoir levels and temperatures, they may be approximately accounted for in the amounts withdrawn.

The probability distribution of storage in a reservoir could then be represented by a simple Markov chain. In order to apply the theory, let a sequence of discrete serially independent flows X_t, obtained by summing continuous flows between successive time intervals $t - 1$ to t, for $t = 1, 2, 3, \ldots$, be routed through a reservoir of effective capacity C. Annual river-flow data are generally appropriate for this purpose. On the same time scale, and at the end of the corresponding time intervals, the reservoir contents are given by the series of states $Z_t, t = 1, 2, 3, \ldots$; also, let the initial state, at time $t = 0$, be Z_0. To define the state space, the reservoir capacity is divided into $c + 1$ mutually exclusive and exhaustive states through a set of $c + 2$ class boundaries as shown in figure 7.1 (in which $c = 9$). If the annual demand is Y, then $Z_t = Z_{t-1} + X_t - Y$; this is subject to $0 \leqslant Z_t \leqslant C$ in which the left constraint is applicable when the demand can only be partly met, if at all, and the right one is imposed if spilling occurs. Then

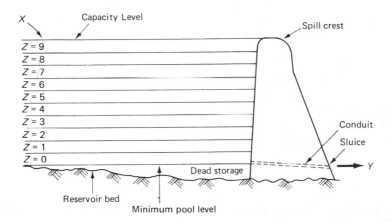

Figure 7.1   Finite reservoir states (Z), inflow (X) and outflow (Y). A Z value denotes a particular reservoir state or storage between two limits; the boundaries of a state are given by the two horizontal lines at the top and bottom of it. In the classical method, volumetric increments or differences between state boundaries with respect to $Z = 1$, $2, \ldots, c - 1$ are equal, and each increment is twice that for $Z = c$ (full) or 0(empty); here, $c = 9$. By the alternative definition, all the increments are equal, but full and empty reservoir states signify that the storage is at capacity and minimum pool levels respectively

the conditional probability that the reservoir is in state i at time t, given that it was in state j, at time $t - 1$, is denoted by

$$q_t(i, j) = \Pr(Z_t = i \mid Z_{t-1} = j) \tag{7.2}$$

If the storage distribution has a simple (that is, a first-order) Markov chain structure and at antecedent times the contents were equal to $j, k, \ell, \ldots$, this conditional probability is equal to

$$\Pr(Z_t = i \mid Z_{t-1} = j, Z_{t-2} = k, Z_{t-3} = \ell, \ldots) \tag{7.3}$$

Note that the addition here of the conditions $Z_{t-2} = k, Z_{t-3} = \ell, \ldots$ does not affect the probability because, as already mentioned, the Markov property implies that the probability that a reservoir is in a particular state at a time t can be fully determined by the state at a time $t - 1$.

The set of $q_t(i, j)$ values is termed the matrix of *one-step probabilities*. The problem is further simplified if these probabilities are independent of time t, in which case the process is said to be homogeneous in time. This means that

$$\Pr(Z_t = i \mid Z_{t-1} = j) = \Pr(Z_{t-k} = i \mid Z_{t-k-1} = j) \tag{7.4}$$

for $k = 1, 2, 3, \ldots$. The analysis which follows will be restricted to (discrete) homogeneous processes.

The collection of homogeneous one-step transition probabilities $q(i, j)$ are denoted in matrix notation by Q, which is a square matrix of order $c + 1$ in which the element of the ith row and the jth column is $q(i, j)$, as follows.

$$
\begin{array}{c}
\text{previous state } j \\[4pt]
\begin{array}{cccccc}
 & (0) & (1) & (2) & \cdots & (c)
\end{array} \\
Q = \begin{array}{c} \text{current} \\ \text{state } i \end{array}
\begin{array}{c}
(0) \\ (1) \\ (2) \\ \vdots \\ (c)
\end{array}
\left[
\begin{array}{ccccc}
q(0,0) & q(0,1) & q(0,2) & \cdots & q(0,c) \\
q(1,0) & q(1,1) & q(1,2) & \cdots & q(1,c) \\
q(2,0) & q(2,1) & q(2,2) & \cdots & q(2,c) \\
\vdots & \vdots & \vdots & & \vdots \\
q(c,0) & q(c,1) & q(c,2) & \cdots & q(c,c)
\end{array}
\right]
\end{array}
\tag{7.5}
$$

Note that $0 \leqslant q(i, j) \leqslant 1$, for $i, j = 0, 1, \ldots, c$; and also $\sum_i q(i, j) = 1$, which means that each of the columns sums to unity. The matrix Q of one-step transition probabilities is called a stochastic matrix because it has these two properties and is, in addition, square[6]. Another point is that the columns are not

[6] This method of representing Q is adopted by Moran (1954), by Gould (1961), by Harris (1965) and by Lloyd (1974). In other works, for instance, those by Isaacson and Madsen (1976), by Ross (1972), by Feller (1968), by Cox and Miller (1965), by Klemeš (1971) and by Venetis (1969a) the previous and current states are reversed so that the *rows* sum to unity.

identical; this follows from the Markov-dependent properties which are not equal for all the pairs of states.

It is conventional in practice to take 0 as the lowest state with the reservoir empty or nearly empty and state c as the highest state when the reservoir is at, or around, capacity level. The volumetric increments or differences between adjacent state boundaries with respect to states $1, 2, \ldots, c-1$ are equal according to Moran (1954); each increment is twice that for states 0 (empty) and c (full) respectively. By the Saverenskiy (1940) definition, all the increments are equal, but full and empty reservoir states signify that the storage is at capacity and minimum pool levels respectively. In application the number of reservoir states range from 5 to 30. The larger number is sometimes taken in order to minimise the errors in the computed probabilities of the end states, an outcome of the first assumption in subsection 7.3.1; also, the differences resulting from the two definitions will then be reduced. More about this follows.

7.3.2 Unconditional probabilities and n-step transition probabilities

Let the column vector $P_t = [p_t(0) \; p_t(1) \ldots p_t(c)]^T$, where T denotes transpose, represent the unconditional or marginal probabilities of the reservoir contents at time t in which the element $p_t(j)$ is the probability $\Pr(Z_t = j)$.

The relationship between P_t and P_{t+1}, the vector of unconditional probabilities of reservoir states at time $t+1$, is given by

$$P_{t+1} = QP_t \tag{7.6}$$

This follows from the well-known relationship between conditional and unconditional probabilities.

$$\Pr(Z_{t+1} = i) = \Pr(Z_{t+1} = i | Z_t = 0)\Pr(Z_t = 0)$$
$$+ \Pr(Z_{t+1} = i | Z_t = 1)\Pr(Z_t = 1) + \ldots$$
$$+ \Pr(Z_{t+1} = i | Z_t = c)\Pr(Z_t = c) \tag{7.7}$$

A total of $c+1$ equations similar to equation 7.7 can then be written corresponding to the $c+1$ elements of the vector P_{t+1}. The right-hand side terms of these equations are identifiable with the corresponding elements obtained from the product QP_t in equation 7.6.

Furthermore, applying equation 7.6 to the points $t+1$ and $t+2$ on the time scale, we find that

$$P_{t+2} = QP_{t+1}$$
$$= Q(QP_t)$$
$$= Q^2 P_t$$
$$= Q^{(2)} P_t \tag{7.8}$$

where $Q^{(2)}$ denotes the two-step transition matrix of conditional probabilities (with time homogeneity). This is equal, as shown, to the square of Q, the one-step transition matrix. In general, if the process commenced at time 0,

$$P_n = Q^n \times P_0$$

$$= Q^{(n)} P_0 \tag{7.9}$$

in which $Q^{(n)} = QQ \ldots Q$ is the n-step transition matrix of conditional probabilities. The relationship $Q^{(\ell + m)} = Q^{(\ell)} Q^{(m)}$, which follows from equations 7.8. and 7.9 is known as the Chapman–Kolmogorov identity.

7.3.3 Steady state probabilities

When n increases, the elements of matrix $Q^{(n)}$ approach under ergodic conditions (as defined in chapter 2) the so-called steady state values with identical columns. Each column is equivalent to a vector Π, known as the long-run or invariant distribution. This is the limiting vector of unconditional probabilities, that is,

$$\lim_{n \to \infty} (P_n) = \Pi$$

$$= [\pi(0)\pi(1) \ldots \pi(c)]^T \tag{7.10}$$

and, of course, the elements of Π sum to unity. The limiting matrix from $Q^{(n)}$ is therefore

$$\lim_{n \to \infty} \{Q^{(n)}\} = \begin{bmatrix} \pi(0) & \pi(0) & \ldots & \pi(0) \\ \pi(1) & \pi(1) & \ldots & \pi(1) \\ \cdot & \cdot & & \cdot \\ \cdot & \cdot & & \cdot \\ \cdot & \cdot & & \cdot \\ \pi(c) & \pi(c) & & \pi(c) \end{bmatrix} \tag{7.11}$$

If a reservoir is commissioned at time 0, the steady state (also referred to as an equilibrium state) unconditional probabilities (the vector Π) are the probabilities of the various reservoir states after time t when t is very large or theoretically after an infinite length of time. It is easily seen from equation 7.9 by applying the conditions of equations 7.10 and 7.11 that the elements of the vector Π are independent of those in the vector P_0. This means that regardless of the initial state of the reservoir or its probability vector we could predict, subject to underlying assumptions, the probabilities which the reservoir states will eventually take. Now consider the case when equation 7.6 is applied to times n and $n + 1$, when n is very large. Because P_n and P_{n+1} each tend to be equal to Π, it follows that

$$\Pi = Q\Pi \tag{7.12}$$

This enables the steady state vector Π to be solved as shown below[7].

[7] A more rigorous proof is given by Kemeny and Snell (1960, pp. 99, 100).

In practice, the limiting matrix given by equation 7.11 is closely approximated after, say, n multiplications QQQ .... The value n, which could be about 10 in practice, depends on the capacity and number of reservoir states, the variance and other distribution properties of the inflows and the rate of withdrawal.

In order to calculate the $\pi(i)$, $i = 0, 1, \ldots, c$, a set of $c + 1$ simultaneous equations is obtained from equation 7.12, but this dependent set of $c + 1$ equations has an infinite number of solutions. We shall have $c + 1$ *independent* equations if one of these is replaced by

$$\pi(0) + \pi(1) + \ldots + \pi(c) = 1 \tag{7.13}$$

To explain the method of application, two examples are given; in the four cases of example 7.1, the state space $S = \{0, 1\}$.

Example 7.1(a)   Initially, a simplified form of a a common type is considered.

$$Q = \begin{bmatrix} 1/3 & 1/2 \\ 2/3 & 1/2 \end{bmatrix}$$

$$Q^{(2)} = \begin{bmatrix} 16/36 & 15/36 \\ 20/36 & 21/36 \end{bmatrix}$$

$$Q^{(3)} = \begin{bmatrix} 92/216 - 0.4259 & 93/216 = 0.4306 \\ 124/216 = 0.5741 & 123/216 = 0.5694 \end{bmatrix}$$

$$Q^{(4)} = \begin{bmatrix} 556/1296 = 0.4290 & 555/1296 = 0.4282 \\ 740/1296 = 0.5710 & 741/1296 = 0.5718 \end{bmatrix}$$

This shows a fast approach to the steady state distribution,

$$\Pi = [3/7 = 0.4286 \quad 4/7 = 0.5714]^{\mathrm{T}}$$

Here, the solutions $\pi = 3/7$ and $\pi_1 = 4/7$ are obtained from the simultaneous equations $\pi_0 + \pi_1 = 1$ and $\pi_0 = (1/3)\pi_0 + (1/2)\pi_1$, which follow from equation 7.13 and by substituting Q in equation 7.12, respectively.

Example 7.1(b)   A totally different example is now taken up.

$$Q = \begin{bmatrix} 1 & 0 \\ 0 & 1 \end{bmatrix}$$

$$Q^{(n)} = \begin{bmatrix} 1 & 0 \\ 0 & 1 \end{bmatrix}$$

Because the states do not communicate and consequently $Q^{(n)} = Q$, steady state conditions cannot be reached[8]. It is implied that inflows are equal to the outflow

---

[8] If all pairs of states communicate, the Markov chain is said to be irreducible.

(plus losses), a situation which negates the purpose of a reservoir. The chain described by the matrix is not ergodic, for, in this case, transitions are not possible from one state to any other state.

Example 7.1(c)   The next case deals with a special case of the type in example 7.1(a).

$$Q = \begin{bmatrix} 1/2 & 1/2 \\ 1/2 & 1/2 \end{bmatrix}$$

$$Q^{(n)} = \begin{bmatrix} 1/2 & 1/2 \\ 1/2 & 1/2 \end{bmatrix}$$

Here, steady state conditions hold for all n. However, a stochastic matrix with equal elements is rarely encountered in application to reservoir storage.

Example 7.1(d)   Finally, an extreme case of the type in example (a) is examined.

$$Q = \begin{bmatrix} 9/10 & 1/10 \\ 1/10 & 9/10 \end{bmatrix}$$

Note that, in this case, the columns converge at a slower rate than in example 7.1(a); here,

$$\Pi = [1/2 \quad 1/2]^{\mathrm{T}}$$

Example 7.2   The annual inflows $X_t, t = 1, 2, 3, \ldots$, to a reservoir are serially independent; X_t may be considered to be one of the following volumetric units: 1, 2, 3, 4 and 5, where each unit is 5×10^6 m^3. The inflow data when converted to the above units are approximately normally distributed with a mean of 3 and a standard deviation of 1. The reservoir capacity is 3 units, and the annual demand including losses is 3 units. Also, the storage is, at any time, in one of the following states.

State 0, empty, with storage not exceeding $\frac{1}{2}$ unit.
State 1, one-thirds full, with storage exceeding $\frac{1}{2}$ unit but not exceeding $1\frac{1}{2}$ units.
State 2, two-thirds full, with storage exceeding $1\frac{1}{2}$ units but not exceeding $2\frac{1}{2}$ units.
State 3, full, with storage exceeding $2\frac{1}{2}$ units.

Thus, the reservoir state space $S = \{0, 1, 2, 3\}$.
The reservoir is commissioned on 1 January 1980.

(a) Determine the elements of the one-step annual transition matrix on the assumption that the process is homogeneous in time.
(b) If the reservoir is initially full, what are the probabilities of the various states on (i) 1 January 2080 and on (ii) 1 January 1982?

(c) If the reservoir is initially full, what is the probability that the reservoir (i) will not be empty during the first 3 years of operation and (ii) will be empty for the first time around 1 January 1983?

(d) What is the return period for a full reservoir?

Note initially that the conversion of continuously distributed inflows and reservoir storages into discrete units may introduce errors at the boundaries between reservoir states. Design alternatives tend to be unaffected by these as the number of units and states increase.

(a) From the tables of the normal distribution, the probabilities of the five types of inflows are approximated as follows for $t = 0, 1, 2, \ldots$.

$$\Pr(X_t = 1) = 0.061$$

$$\Pr(X_t = 2) = 0.245$$

$$\Pr(X_t = 3) = 0.388$$

$$\Pr(X_t = 4) = 0.245$$

$$\Pr(X_t = 5) = 0.061$$

The one-step transition probabilities $q(i, j)$, $i, j, = 0, 1, 2, 3, 4$, are as follows.

$$
\begin{aligned}
q(0, 0) &= \Pr(X_t \leqslant 3) = 0.694 \\
q(1, 0) &= \Pr(X_t = 4) = 0.245 \\
q(2, 0) &= \Pr(X_t = 5) = 0.061 \\
q(3, 0) &= \Pr(X_t \geqslant 6) = 0.000 \\
\hline
&\qquad\qquad\qquad\quad 1.000
\end{aligned}
$$

$$
\begin{aligned}
q(0, 1) &= \Pr(X_t \leqslant 2) = 0.306 \\
q(1, 1) &= \Pr(X_t = 3) = 0.388 \\
q(2, 1) &= \Pr(X_t = 4) = 0.245 \\
q(3, 1) &= \Pr(X_t \geqslant 5) = 0.061 \\
\hline
&\qquad\qquad\qquad\quad 1.000
\end{aligned}
$$

$$
\begin{aligned}
q(0, 2) &= \Pr(X_t \leqslant 1) = 0.061 \\
q(1, 2) &= \Pr(X_t = 2) = 0.245 \\
q(2, 2) &= \Pr(X_t = 3) = 0.388 \\
q(3, 2) &= \Pr(X_t \geqslant 4) = 0.306 \\
\hline
&\qquad\qquad\qquad\quad 1.000
\end{aligned}
$$

$$q(0, 3) = \Pr(X_t < 1) = 0.000$$
$$q(1, 3) = \Pr(X_t = 1) = 0.061$$
$$q(2, 3) = \Pr(X_t = 2) = 0.245$$
$$q(3, 3) = \Pr(X_t \geqslant 3) = 0.694$$

$$\overline{1.000}$$

Hence, the one-step transition matrix is given by

previous state j

$$Q = \begin{matrix} & & & (0) & (1) & (2) & (3) \\ & & (0) & \begin{bmatrix} 0.694 & 0.306 & 0.061 & 0.000 \\ \text{current} & (1) & 0.245 & 0.388 & 0.245 & 0.061 \\ \text{state} & (2) & 0.061 & 0.245 & 0.388 & 0.245 \\ i & (3) & 0.000 & 0.061 & 0.306 & 0.694 \end{bmatrix} \end{matrix}$$

(b) (i) The following simultaneous equations are obtained by using equation 7.12.

$$-0.306\pi(0) + 0.306\pi(1) + 0.061\pi(2) \qquad\qquad = 0$$
$$0.245\pi(0) - 0.612\pi(1) + 0.245\pi(2) + 0.061\pi(3) \quad = 0$$
$$0.061\pi(0) + 0.245\pi(1) - 0.612\pi(2) + 0.245\pi(3) \quad = 0$$
$$0.061\pi(1) + 0.306\pi(2) - 0.306\pi(3) \quad = 0$$

One of these equations, preferably a long one, is then replaced by

$$\pi(0) + \pi(1) + \pi(2) + \pi(3) = 1.0$$

and the solutions obtained are given below[9].

$$\pi(0) = 0.273$$
$$\pi(1) = 0.227$$
$$\pi(2) = 0.227$$
$$\pi(3) = 0.273$$

That is,

$$\Pi = [0.273 \quad 0.227 \quad 0.227 \quad 0.273]^{\mathrm{T}}$$

[9] For hand calculations a useful modus operandi is gaussian (or Gauss–Jordan) elimination as used, for example, by Strang (1976, pp. 2–6). If the set of simultaneous equations in example 7.2(b)(i) is represented by $A\Pi = 0$, basically this involves a reduction of the square matrix A by elementary row operations to a triangular one, from which stepwise solutions to Π are found.

which gives the probabilities of the various states after a long period, such as 100 years.

(b) (ii) The initial vector of unconditional probabilities $P_0 = [0 \; 0 \; 0 \; .1]^T$, and, from equation 7.8, $P_2 = Q^2 P_0$.

Because the elements of the column vector P_0 are zero except the last which is unity the column vector P_2 is equal to the vector formed by the elements of the last column of the product QQ, that is,

$$[q^{(2)}(0, 3) \quad q^{(2)}(1, 3) \quad q^{(2)}(2, 3) \quad q^{(2)}(3, 3)]^T$$

where

$q^{(2)}(0, 3) = 0.694 \times 0.000 + 0.306 \times 0.061 + 0.061 \times 0.245 + 0.000 \times 0.694$
$\quad = 0.034$
$q^{(2)}(1, 3) = 0.245 \times 0.000 + 0.388 \times 0.061 + 0.245 \times 0.245 + 0.061 \times 0.694$
$\quad = 0.126$
$q^{(2)}(2, 3) = 0.061 \times 0.000 + 0.245 \times 0.061 + 0.388 \times 0.245 + 0.245 \times 0.694$
$\quad = 0.280$
$q^{(2)}(3, 3) = 0.000 \times 0.000 + 0.061 \times 0.061 + 0.306 \times 0.245 + 0.694 \times 0.694$
$\quad = 0.560$

Hence,

$$P_2 = [0.034 \quad 0.216 \quad 0.280 \quad 0.560]^T$$

(c) (i) Given the initial vector of unconditional probabilities, in order to determine the unconditional probabilities of first time emptiness after a period of t years of operation of the reservoir ($t = 1, 2, 3, \ldots$) the elements of the first column of the one-step transition matrix Q are adjusted so that when the reservoir reaches an empty state it remains empty thereafter. In this particular case an absorption state is set up by changing the first element to unity and the other elements in the first column to zero. Note that, column is changed to unity in this particular case; on the other hand, if a full reservoir is of interest, the last element of the last column should be changed to unity and similarly other theoretical absorption states may be utilised[10].

The adjusted matrix of transition probabilities is given by

$$Q' = \begin{bmatrix} 1.000 & 0.306 & 0.061 & 0.000 \\ 0.000 & 0.388 & 0.245 & 0.061 \\ 0.000 & 0.245 & 0.388 & 0.245 \\ 0.000 & 0.061 & 0.306 & 0.694 \end{bmatrix}$$

[10] Probabilities of absorption have been used in the cases of random walks and gambler's ruin; see, for example, Mosteller (1965, problems 36, 37). The general theory is discussed by Feller (1968, chapters 14, 15) in his classical work, by Gnedenko (1960, pp. 128–32) and by Parzen (1962, chapter 6). For a simpler explanation, see Shamblin and Stevens (1974, pp. 66–72) Reardon (1970) and Benjamin and Cornell (1970) give applications to reservoir problems. Incidentally, if a transition probability $q(i, j) = 1$ for $i \neq j$, a 'reflection' barrier is made.

The cumulative probabilities of a first-time-empty reservoir can be obtained by using Q'. By premultiplying the vector P_t of unconditional probabilities at time t by the one-step transition matrix Q' to obtain the vector of unconditional probabilities at time $t + 1$, which is P_{t+1}, it is ensured that the probability of emptiness at the end of year t is included in the probability of emptiness after $t + 1$ years. For further clarification the various probability routes during the first 3 years of operation of a reservoir which is initially full are shown in figure 7.2. Note that, at the nodes, transition probabilities denoted by lines leading out to the right sum to 1. These are, with respect to nodes from top to bottom, the elements in the columns, from left to right, of Q'. The nodes of the figure in the column marked 1 year represent the unconditional probabilities $p_1(i)$, $i = 0, 1, 2, 3$. The next column denotes the unconditional probabilities $p_2(i)$ obtained by multiplying the antecedent values in turn by the elements in the corresponding row of transition probabilities, as shown by the probability routes, and by then summing. In this problem the main interest is with regard to the $p_t(0)$, $t = 1, 2, \ldots$; however, the probabilities $p_t(i)$ for $i \neq 0$ are required at each stage for the next transition from t to $t + 1$. As in the previous case

$$P_0 = [0 \quad 0 \quad 0 \quad 1]^T$$

$$P_1 = Q'P_0$$

$$= [0.000 \quad 0.061 \quad 0.245 \quad 0.694]^T$$

$$P_2 = Q'P_1$$

$$= \begin{bmatrix} 1.000 & 0.306 & 0.061 & 0.000 \\ 0.000 & 0.388 & 0.245 & 0.061 \\ 0.000 & 0.245 & 0.388 & 0.245 \\ 0.000 & 0.061 & 0.306 & 0.694 \end{bmatrix} [0.000 \quad 0.061 \quad 0.245 \quad 0.694]^T$$

$$= [0.034 \quad 0.126 \quad 0.280 \quad 0.560]^T$$

That is, $p_2(0) = 0.034$.

It will be noted that, because $p_1(0) = 0.0$, changing $q(i, 0)$ for $i = 0, 1, 2, 3$ has no effect on P_2, the same result being obtained as for question (b) (ii); however, this is not true for $P_3, P_4, \ldots$. Again,

$$P_3 = Q'P_2$$

$$= \begin{bmatrix} 1.000 & 0.306 & 0.061 & 0.000 \\ 0.000 & 0.388 & 0.245 & 0.061 \\ 0.000 & 0.245 & 0.388 & 0.245 \\ 0.000 & 0.061 & 0.306 & 0.694 \end{bmatrix} [0.034 \quad 0.126 \quad 0.280 \quad 0.560]^T$$

The first element of vector P_3, that is, $p_3(0) = 0.034 + 0.126 \times 0.306 + 0.280$

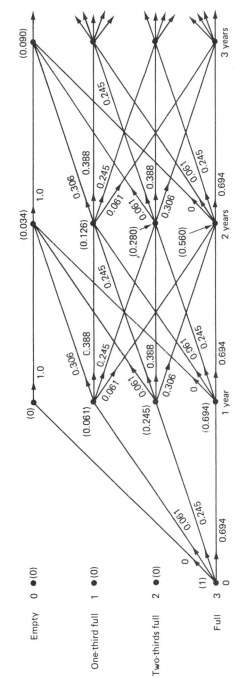

Fig. 7.2 Transition of probability routes for absorption in empty state. Unconditional probabilities are shown within parentheses at each nodal point. The sets of conditional probabilities from the top to the bottom nodal points represent the columns (from left to right) of the transition probability matrix Q. To obtain Q', the first column has been modified so that there are no transitions from an empty state

$\times 0.061 = 0.090$. Therefore the probability of having storages greater than $\frac{1}{2}$ unit during the first 3 years of operation is $1 - 0.090 = 0.910$.

(c) (ii) Because of the absorption state, $p_2(0)$ includes the probabilities of first time emptiness after 1 year and 2 years. Likewise, $p_3(0)$ includes the probabilities of first time emptiness after 1 year, 2 years and 3 years as seen from the arrows leading to the top row of nodes in figure 7.2. Therefore, the probability of an empty reservoir for the first time at the end of the third year is $p_3(0) - p_2(0) = 0.056$.

(d) From the answer to (b)(i) the steady state probability of a full reservoir is 0.273. This is the long-run probability (after the memory of the initial state is lost in the process of continuous transitions) of having a full reservoir in any year. Hence, the return period of a full reservoir is $1/0.273 = 3.66$ years. This means that, on average, the reservoir will be full once in 3.66 years or 3 times in 11 years.

7.4   Gould method for failures within a year

The theory developed by Moran was modified, to some extent, by Gould (1961) in his application to monthly data. Probabilities of various reservoir states at the end of a year are evaluated for the cases when both inflows and outflows are continuous, but, as in many other applications, discrete reservoir states are taken. The main point is that the empirical routing procedure which is followed allows probabilities of failure within a year to be computed. In this way serial correlation in monthly data is accounted for; however, annual flows are assumed to be independent as in the Moran model.

An empty state is reached when the reservoir contents are equal to the dead storage, with reference to figure 7.1, and the term full signifies that the reservoir is at capacity level; both end conditions conform to the Saverenskiy definition. However, it should be noted that, in the Gould method, failure means that the stipulated monthly demand cannot be met during a particular year from the sum of the reservoir contents at the end of the previous year and the inflows during the current year.

The elements of the matrix of one-step transition probabilities are obtained by counting the proportion of time from, say, N years of monthly data, when the reservoir is initially in a state $i, i = 0, 1, \ldots, c$, and ends in each of the $c + 1$ states. Relative frequencies are also used to obtain the probabilities of failure for each initial state. These are separately listed and are represented by an additional row at the top of the transition matrix.

A further modification which may be adopted is that, when the reservoir is less than half full, the withdrawal rate is reduced. In the same way any other release rule may be adopted; furthermore, evaporation losses can be incorporated. Also, if the final state is near the boundary between two states a probability due to 1/2 year is added on the tally sheet to each state instead of allocating the year to one particular row. Although this is subjective, it may be useful for short records.

The method is based on the premise that an observed sequence reflects the stream-flow distribution better than a fitted theoretical function. However, records may be biased, particularly short ones, and may not often include extreme flow sequences that are crucial in reservoir design. From experience it is known that a minimum period of 30 to 50 years is required for practically meaningful results. The record examined in the following example is limited to 10 years for illustrative purposes.

Example 7.3   The monthly total flows in the Derwent at Yorkshire Bridge, England, are listed in table 7.1, in millimetres of equivalent rainfall over the catchment area, for the period 1930 to 1939. A reservoir is planned with an effective capacity of 300 mm to meet monthly demands (or maximum thereof) of 60 mm from October to March and of 80 mm from April to September. The reservoir contents are divided into five states: an empty state (0), states 1 to 3 with limits 1 to 100, 101 to 200 and 201 to 299 respectively, and a full state (4). Assuming that on 1 January of any year the reservoir storage is equal to one of the following: 0 mm, 50 mm, 150 mm, 250 mm and 300 mm, corresponding to the respective initial states, determine the steady state probabilities and the overall probability of failure.

Table 7.1   Monthly flows in Derwent at Yorkshire Bridge, England

Year	Monthly flows (mm)												
	Jan.	Feb.	Mar.	Apr.	May	Jun.	Jul.	Aug.	Sep.	Oct.	Nov.	Dec.	Total
1930	132	52	77	83	44	37	110	89	110	124	131	94	1083
1931	162	152	45	99	41	104	70	115	100	29	114	57	1088
1932	150	24	49	125	104	24	45	27	66	158	102	67	941
1933	74	107	155	26	32	30	26	12	11	71	85	21	650
1934	90	25	92	47	52	19	32	46	27	120	99	144	793
1935	94	168	81	79	21	30	18	12	65	216	207	140	1131
1936	110	80	141	53	24	43	83	47	113	104	161	123	1082
1937	152	177	143	91	51	23	46	18	14	34	44	113	906
1938	128	64	46	28	36	64	97	28	32	171	128	121	943
1939	199	101	80	65	52	25	94	66	30	64	164	134	1074

Given an initial reservoir state j, the years, if any, in which the final state i is reached for $i, j = 0, 1, 2, 3, 4$, are listed in table 7.2. In addition, the years in which failure occurs during 1 or more months are given in table 7.2 in the row F at the top, for each of the different initial states.

The values given in table 7.2 can be verified as follows. For instance, if the initial storage on 1 January 1933 is 0 mm (stage 0) the storages at the commencements of the following 12 months are 14 mm, 61 mm, 156 mm, 102 mm, 54 mm, 4 mm, 0 mm, 0 mm, 0 mm, 11 mm, 36 mm and 0 mm. This means that the reservoir fails to meet the demand in July, August and September and is empty on 31 December 1933. Next consider the other extreme case of an

Table 7.2   Transition years

Current state	Previous state				
	0	1	2	3	4
F	1932	1933	1933	1933	1933
	1933	1934	1934		
	1934	1935			
	1935	1938			
	1938				
0	1933	1933	1933	1933	1933
1	1937	1937	1937	1937	1937
2	1932	1932	1934		
	1934	1934			
3	1930	1930	1931	1931	1931
	1931	1931	1932	1932	1932
	1936	1936	1938	1934	1934
	1938	1938			
	1939	1939			
4	1935	1935	1930	1930	1930
			1935	1935	1935
			1936	1936	1936
			1939	1938	1938
				1939	1939

initially full reservoir. Then the corresponding storages for 1933 are 300 mm, 300 mm, 300 mm, 246 mm, 198 mm, 148 mm, 94 mm, 26 mm, 0 mm, 11 mm, 36 mm and 0 mm. The reservoir is again empty at the end of the year, and for this condition a failure occurs in September. It follows, therefore, that the year 1933 should be included throughout the two top rows[11].

The matrix of one-step transition probabilities is estimated after dividing the number of entries in each cell of table 7.2, except those of the top row by 10 (the number of years of data). This is given by

[11] A graphical procedure is described by Gould (1961). The first requirement is an underlay in which the boundaries and midpoints of all reservoir states, except the terminal ones, are marked on two verticals that are 12 1-month units apart and are situated at the left and right extremities of the underlay. In addition, two horizontal lines denoting the capacity and empty levels of the reservoir are drawn. Then each year of record is represented separately on a transparent paper called an overlay; here, a sequence of 1 year is represented by a broken line that consecutively joins a zero point and the 12 cumulative 1-month inflows less withdrawals during the year. These overlays are (in turn) horizontally aligned and are moved vertically on the overlay, with readjustments if the upper and lower boundaries are crossed, to determine the reservoir states at the end of each year, corresponding to a particular initial state.

$$Q = \begin{bmatrix} 0.1 & 0.1 & 0.1 & 0.1 & 0.1 \\ 0.1 & 0.1 & 0.1 & 0.1 & 0.1 \\ 0.2 & 0.2 & 0.1 & 0.0 & 0.0 \\ 0.5 & 0.5 & 0.3 & 0.3 & 0.3 \\ 0.1 & 0.1 & 0.4 & 0.5 & 0.5 \end{bmatrix}$$

Using equations 7.12 and 7.13, we obtain

$$-0.9\pi(0) + 0.1\pi(1) + 0.1\pi(2) + 0.1\pi(3) + 0.1\pi(4) = 0$$

$$0.1\pi(0) - 0.9\pi(1) + 0.1\pi(2) + 0.1\pi(3) + 0.1\pi(4) = 0$$

$$0.2\pi(0) + 0.2\pi(1) - 0.9\pi(2) \qquad\qquad = 0$$

$$0.5\pi(0) + 0.5\pi(1) + 0.3\pi(2) - 0.7\pi(3) + 0.3\pi(4) = 0$$

$$\pi(0) + \quad \pi(1) + \quad \pi(2) + \quad \pi(3) + \quad \pi(4) = 1$$

This gives the following steady state probabilities to two significant figures (further accuracy is not warranted because of the short sample).

$$\pi(0) = 0.10$$

$$\pi(1) = 0.10$$

$$\pi(2) = 0.05$$

$$\pi(3) = 0.11$$

$$\pi(4) = 0.64$$

By comparing the results from examples 7.2 and 7.3 it appears that the consequence of using a fitted symmetrical distribution is that a more systematic set of steady state probabilities is obtained.

The column vector

$$\Pi = [0.10 \quad 0.10 \quad 0.05 \quad 0.11 \quad 0.64]^{\mathrm{T}}$$

gives the steady state probabilities of the various states at the start of any year. Correspondingly, the row vector

$$F = [0.5 \quad 0.4 \quad 0.2 \quad 0.1 \quad 0.1]$$

obtained from the top row of table 7.2 denotes the probabilities of failure during a year based on the relative frequency and corresponding to each of the five initial conditions. Hence, it follows that the overall probability of failure is $F\Pi = 0.17$.

It should be mentioned that the given 10-year sample is biased because it contains a very severe drought period. Another point, which is a practical one, is that it may be more meaningful if the water year is taken to end on 30 September, that is, just before the wet season commences. However, this brings out the undesirable feature of this method, from a mathematical viewpoint, that the transition matrix depends on the commencing month.

As noted, the probabilities evaluated are subject to sampling errors in the estimated elements of Q. In order to assess the range of such errors, each element could be considered to be approximately binomially distributed with mean p, say, and variance $p(1 - p)/n$, where n is the number of years of data; however, this is valid only if the serial correlation is not significant. On this basis, the element 0.6 in Q has approximate confidence limits of 0.3 to 0.9. Of course, if long records are available, the width of the confidence band is vastly reduced.

7.5 Serial correlation and seasonal changes in inflows

Moran's exposition was followed by works of a more advanced theoretical nature by Kendal (1957) who considered an infinite reservoir, unlike Moran's finite reservoir with a bottom and a top level, and a gamma type of inflow distribution. Kendall's paper was presented to the Royal Statistical Society who convened a dam theory symposium[12]. The degree of sophistication in these papers is expectedly high. However, a reservoir theory specifically oriented to practical situations was required; the main problems to be tackled concerned seasonality and serial correlation.

7.5.1 *Serially correlated inflows*

Recognising the need to minimise the gap between theory and practice, Lloyd (1963) extended Moran's theory taking into account the serial correlation of inflows. A bivariate Markov chain was formulated to describe the simultaneous behaviour of correlated inflows and reservoir states on the assumption that the inflows too follow a Markov chain. That is, instead of writing the probability of transition from state Z_{t-1} to state Z_t in equation 7.5, probabilities of transititions from (Z_{t-1}, X_{t-1}) to (Z_t, X_t) are entered. For a theoretical solution we need to know the transition probabilities of the inflow distribution; for this purpose, the inflow probabilities are entered against each reservoir state. Consequently, the solution of steady state probabilities requires a large number of simultaneous equations, although this does not call for a radical change in the approach.

If the transitition probability matrix is symmetrical and outflows are equal to the mean inflows, it is found that, for a reservoir with $c + 1$ states and a three-

---

[12] The works of Prabhu (1958) and of Weesakul (1961) were based on a finite demand. Gani (1957), like Prabhu, theorised on geometric and Poisson input distributions. These authors also considered probabilities of first emptiness. For pre-1967 bibliographies on advanced statistical treatment of reservoirs including continuous inflows, see Lloyd (1967), Prabhu (1964) and Moran (1959).

valued symmetrical inflow distribution, the probability of a full or empty reservoir is $1/\{c+1-\rho(c-1)\}$, where ρ is the lag-one autocorrelation coefficient. These probabilities reduce to $1/(c+1)$ for serially independent inflows. *This shows that the probabilities of emptiness and of spilling increases when the correlation in the inflows increases.* The particular method is applicable to steady state conditions with normally distributed inflows[13]. A numerical example of a bivariate Markov chain will be given in the next example.

7.5.2 *Effect of seasonality on probability of emptiness*

In seeking a solution to seasonal changes in the probability distribution of inflows within an annual cycle, Lloyd and Odoom (1964) suggested the division of a year into k seasons and the use of a different one-step transition matrix for each season. Solutions to simultaneous equations relating the steady state probabilities of reservoir states at the end of a year are made after multiplying the transition matrices in the appropriate order, but this had been envisaged earlier by Moran (1954). The practicalities of a variable-season model were originally investigated by White (1965).

Harris (1965) followed the work of Moran and Gould in his practically useful case study of the Alwen Reservoir in Wales. The year is divided into a winter season (October to March) and a summer season (April to September). Also, the inflows in the summer are taken to be independent of the inflows in winter, a reasonable assumption in this particular application. The demands from the reservoir during winter and summer, which include statutory compensation releases for downstream users, were assumed constant for the season (although, of course, it varies from month to month). Furthermore, it is found that the distribution of the historical seasonal inflows to Alwen Reservoir is approximately normal. On this basis, a matrix of one-step transition probabilities is formulated for each season. If we denote these as S (summer) and W (winter), it follows from the assumption of intraseasonal independence that the annual matrix $Q = SW$. Hence, the steady state probabilities are evaluated as in example 7.2. Incidentally, it is found in the Alwen case study that Q^8 gives the steady matrix with identical columns to four significant figures.

7.5.3 *Application of bivariate Markov chain*

As seen from the above subsections, the problem becomes complicated when the reservoir inflows have significant correlation between seasons. If the probability distributions of the summer and winter inflows approach normality, the model can be based on the bivariate normal distribution[14].

---

[13] Simplifying the work of Lloyd (1963) in order to investigate the effect of variable release rules, Klemeš (1970) suggested a one-step transition matrix of the form RG, where R consists of ones and zeros and G contains the inflow distribution. However, this does not reduce the computational load.

[14] See, for example, the National Bureau of Standards (1959). The bivariate model distribution has been used by Harris *et al.* (1965).

For a univariate normal inflow distribution, as explained in chapter 3, the probabilities are equivalent to segmental areas under the normal function. If the inflow distributions are to be treated as bivariate because of significant cross correlation, the joint probabilities are found from differences in volumes enclosed by the three-dimensional surface. Note that, when referring to tables of the bivariate normal distribution, the appropriate table is the one which corresponds, as closely as possible, to the observed coefficient of correlation between the sets of seasonal inflows.

For non-normal inflow distributions, however, with interseasonal correlation, an analytical solution does not seem to be feasible. In the following simplified example, the conditional probabilities are evaluated empirically (by counting) from an observed sample of data.

Example 7.4 A reservoir of two (volumetric) units capacity is to be constructed to supply a constant demand of 1 unit per season of 6 months (that is, winter or summer). Inflows to the reservoir are 0 and 1 units in summer and 1 or 2 units in winter. For given winter inflows, the conditional probabilities of inflows in the following summer are as follows.

Inflow in following summer	*Conditional probability for winter inflow =*	
	1	2
0	0.3	0.6
1	0.7	0.4

Likewise, for given summer inflows, the conditional probabilities of inflows in the following winter are given below.

Inflow in following winter	*Conditional probability of summer inflow =*	
	0	1
1	0.5	0.3
2	0.5	0.7

The reservoir state space $S = (0, 1)$, where state 0 signifies that the reservoir contents are not more than 1 unit, and state 1 represents contents of more than 1 unit. However, the initial contents are assumed to be either 0.5 units (state 0) or 1.5 units (state 1) by following the procedure in example 7.3. The seasonal inflows are incorporated in tables 7.3 and 7.4 of the bivariate transition probabilities.

Table 7.3   Matrix **W** of transition probabilities for winter

| | | | | *Transition probability of reservoir state (at start of winter season) =* | | | |
| | | | | 0 *Winter inflow =* | | 1 *Winter inflow =* | |
				1	2	1	2
Reservoir state at end of winter season =	0	Inflow in following = summer	0	0.3	0	0	0
			1	0.7	0	0	0
	1	Inflow in following = summer	0	0	0.6	0.3	0.6
			1	0	0.4	0.7	0.4

Zero probabilities denote impossible transitions. For example, with initial contents and winter inflows totalling 2.5 units, the reservoir cannot be in state 0 after meeting the demand of 1 unit (see first and second entries in second column). The non-zero probabilities are taken from the first table.

Table 7.4   Matrix **S** of transition probabilities for summer

| | | | | *Transition probability of reservoir state (at start of summer season) =* | | | |
| | | | | 0 *Summer inflow =* | | 1 *Summer inflow =* | |
				0	1	0	1
Reservoir state at end of summer season =	0	Inflow in following = winter	1	0.5	0.3	0.5	0
			2	0.5	0.7	0.5	0
	1	Inflow in following = winter	1	0	0	0	0.3
			2	0	0	0	0.7

The annual matrix of transition probabilities $Q = SW$ is as follows.

$$Q = \begin{bmatrix} 0.36 & 0.30 & 0.15 & 0.30 \\ 0.64 & 0.30 & 0.15 & 0.30 \\ 0 & 0.12 & 0.21 & 0.12 \\ 0 & 0.28 & 0.49 & 0.28 \end{bmatrix}$$

In the first column of Q, for example, the first and second entries are obtained from $0.5 \times 0.3 + 0.3 \times 0.7 = 0.36$ and $0.5 \times 0.3 + 0.7 \times 0.7 = 0.64$. The vector of steady state probabilities is given by

$$\Pi = [\pi(0|1) \quad \pi(0|2) \quad \pi(1|1) \quad \pi(1|2)]^{\mathrm{T}}$$

The elements of Π denote the long-run probabilities of states 0 and 1 in the reservoir at the end of a year (that is, at the end of summer) conditional to inflows of 1 or 2 units in the following winter. Proceeding as in examples 7.2 and 7.3, we obtain

$$-0.64\pi(0|1) + 0.30\pi(0|2) + 0.15\pi(1|1) + 0.30\pi(1|2) = 0$$

$$\pi(0|1) + \pi(0|2) + \pi(1|1) + \pi(1|2) = 1$$

$$0.12\pi(0|2) - 0.79\pi(1|1) + 0.12\pi(1|2) = 0$$

$$0.28\pi(0|2) + 0.49\pi(1|1) - 0.72\pi(1|2) = 0$$

Hence, $\pi(0|1) = 0.31$, $\pi(0|2) = 0.39$, $\pi(1|1) = 0.09$ and $\pi(1|2) = 0.21$. This means that the total probability of a reservoir state of 0 at the end of a year is $\pi(0|1) + \pi(0|2) = 0.70$. Also, the total probability of a reservoir state of 1 at the end of a year is $\pi(1|1) + \pi(1|2) = 0.30$.

   In practice, a much larger number of inflow units and reservoir states are required, and this, of course, causes a great increase in the work load. It is also necessary, in the design of reservoirs, to repeat the computations with different reservoir volumes and withdrawal rates[15].

7.5.4   Other practical considerations

It is found that, for a given reservoir, inflow distribution and release rule, the estimated probability of emptiness changes as the number of stipulated

[15] An empirical method devised by Harris et al. (1965) is to evaluate initially the probability of failure assuming that seasonal inflows are independent and then to multiply this by a correlation factor which takes values of 1.25, 1.5, 1.95 and 2.65 for correlation coefficients of 0.3, 0.4, 0.5 and 0.6 respectively, between the summer and winter inflows; see also Cole (1966). Furthermore, for serially correlated inflows, Gould (1966) suggested that the percentage of failure, $p = 100F$ obtained on the assumption of serial independence should be increased by $1.7r(p+7)$ where r is the lag-one serial correlation coefficient.

reservoir states increases. However, if the Saverenskiy (1940) definition of state boundaries (equispaced with two end states) is followed, a fewer number of reservoir states than for the Moran (1954) version (used in example 7.2) will give a close approximation to the solution that will be obtained with a large number, say, 30, states[16]. On the other hand, the Moran definition is practically more purposeful because reservoirs are rarely at the limiting (full or empty) states and also on account of the inconsistencies in the transitions at the boundary states. In summary, it is thought that 10 reservoir states may suffice for design purposes, if we bear in mind the likely sampling fluctuations in the historical data; this may be reduced to five states for rough calculations.

There are other considerations, for example, the coefficient of variation for lognormal or gamma distributed inflows. For design purposes a useful practical exercise is to draw graphs of probabilities of emptiness against reservoir capacity for each demand rate or release rule[17].

7.6   Associated topics, other works and comments

In recent years several developments of Moran's theory have been made. Some of the more relevant works are reviewed here. Apart from reservoir studies, it is important to note the use made of Markov chains in meteorology, during the past few decades.

7.6.1   *Applications in meteorology*

The theory explained in the preceding sections can be easily adopted to calculate the probabilities of wet and dry days as shown in the following example.

Example 7.5   Let the state space for weather on any day in a particular area be $S = (0, 1)$ where 0 and 1 signify dry weather (D) and rain (R) respectively. If it rains on day n, the probability of having rain on day $n + 1$ is 3/5; also the probability of having rain on day $n + 1$ given that it is dry on day n is 1/3. Determine the probability of having rain on day $n + 3$, given that day n is dry.

The one-step transition matrix is

$$Q = \begin{array}{c} \text{day} \\ n+1 \end{array} \begin{array}{c} \text{(D)} \\ \text{(R)} \end{array} \left[\begin{array}{cc} 2/3 & 2/5 \\ 1/3 & 3/5 \end{array} \right]$$

Assuming a first-order Markov chain and time homogeneity, we obtain

[16] See Doran (1975) and Klemeš (1977).
[17] For the engineering viewpoint, see, for example, Reardon (1970) and Joy and McMahon (1972).

$$Q^{(3)} = \begin{bmatrix} 2/3 & 2/5 \\ 1/3 & 3/5 \end{bmatrix} \begin{bmatrix} 2/3 & 2/5 \\ 1/3 & 3/5 \end{bmatrix} \begin{bmatrix} 2/3 & 2/5 \\ 1/3 & 3/5 \end{bmatrix}$$

$$= \begin{array}{c} \text{day} \\ n+3 \end{array} \begin{array}{c} \\ \text{(D)} \\ \text{(R)} \end{array} \begin{bmatrix} \overset{\text{day } n}{\overset{\text{(D) \quad (R)}}{374/675}} & 602/1125 \\ 301/675 & 523/1125 \end{bmatrix}$$

The probability of a dry day 3 days later, conditional to an initial dry day, is 374/675. Note that this is 4114/4050 of the long-run probability of 6/11 which is obtained from equations 7.12 and 7.13.

Similar to the transition matrix in this example, a modified 4×4 matrix can be set out to represent the weather on days $n+1$ and $n+2$, conditional to the weather on days n and $n+1$. In the same way, an 8×8 matrix may be formulated to account for the conditional probabilities involving an additional day's weather.

A notable work in this field is that by Gabriel and Neumann (1962) who applied a Markov chain model to occurrences or non-occurrences of daily rainfall at Tel Aviv in terms of conditional probabilities p_1 and p_0, where

$$p_1 = \text{Pr(wet day | previous day wet)}$$

$$p_0 = \text{Pr(wet day | previous day dry)}$$

The probabilities of lengths of wet or dry runs are geometrically distributed. This means that the probability of a wet run of length k is

$$(1 - p_1)p_1^{k-1} \tag{7.14}$$

which conforms with equation 5.6. Similarly, the probability of a dry spell of length m is

$$p_0(1 - p_0)^{m-1} \tag{7.15}$$

In this way, the probabilities of wet or dry runs in a given population can be calculated[18]. However, the geometric distribution may be inadequate if the persistence increases for the first few days of a wet run, although it fits the Tel Aviv data (as no doubt other distributions do as well)[19].

[18] Further use of the work of Gabriel and Neumann (1962) is made by Cox and Miller (1965, examples 3.2–3.6). In addition, Gabriel and Neumann found expressions for the parameters of a normal distribution fitted to the number of wet days in large samples. However, the probabilities of specific wet spells as a function of a finite sample size are more difficult to evaluate. See the related urn problem on run lengths of black and white balls by David and Barton (1962, p. 90) and the less rigorous work by Weiss (1964).

[19] See Green (1964). Note also the applications in meteorology by Brooks and Carruthers (1953, chapter 16), Green (1970), Hershfield (1971) and Crovelli (1973). Lowry and Guthrie (1968) estimate the order of a Markov chain using a goodness-of-fit test in application to daily precipitation from the United States. However, Farmer and

7.6.2   Summary of other works and scope for future

An interesting application of Moran's theory of reservoirs was made by Jarvis (1964) to the Ord River project in western Australia. One important modification was the variable release rule which he adopted, taking into account the reservoir state at the time of application. Jarvis also followed the theory of Weesakul (1961) to determine the probabilities of first emptiness. In another study, Dyck and Schramm (1965) modified Langbein's technique to account for the seasonal changes and serial correlation in monthly inflows to a multipurpose reservoir using the Pearson type III function.

Several noteworthy papers on probability methods were read at the Reservoir symposium in Medmenham, England. For example, the joint action of several reservoirs in a river basin for flood control purposes was considered by Gani (1965). Practical applications with operational advice were presented by White (1965) amongst others.

Elsewhere, Venetis (1969a, b), studied the distribution of failures during a period of reservoir operation. He followed the works of Moran and Gould but incorporated probability-generating functions. In addition, Venetis (1969c) considered a stochastic model of monthly reservoir storage in which the inflows constitute a first-order autoregressive process approximated by a Markov chain. Numerical examples are included in Venetis (1969a, b, c).

In a similar vein, Klemeš (1971) made a comparative study of the Moran and Gould methods with respect to safe and failure transitions. A modification of the Gould method was suggested and illustrated through numerical four-valued transition matrices. Subsequently, Klemeš (1974) presented a theory for the probability distribution of outflows which have a linear relationship with storage for both serially independent and Markovian inflows. Also on the same topic, Pegram (1974) found that the probability of a zero outflow is not influenced to an appreciable degree by the form of the transition probability matrix representing a series of Markovian inflows. In a somewhat different context Phatarfod (1976) compares analytical methods and gamma Markov data generation techniques for determining the reservoir size, reliability and draft relationship.

Specific areas in which further mathematical work would be beneficial are reservoir theories with variable outflows, multiple systems and non-normal non-Markovian correlated inflows with associated time-dependent probabilities of reservoir states. Judging from recent publications in the *Journal of Applied Probability*, we can say that some progress is being made on these topics. However, as Phatarfod (1976) puts it, 'mathematicians have ventured into more and more esoteric areas using only the imagery of the reservoir problem'. The urgent need, therefore, as in general queueing theories, is to bridge the gap between theory and the level of practical application.

Homeyer (1974) find that Markov models are inadequate for estimating the probabilities of consecutive dry days, in a particular climatic region. Chin (1977) gives methods of testing the order of a Markov chain.

References

Benjamin, J. R., and Cornell, C. A. (1970). *Probability, Statistics and Decision for Civil Engineers*, McGraw-Hill, New York

Billingsley, P. (1961). *Statistical Inference for Markov Processes*, University of Chicago Press, Chicago, Illinois

Brooks, C. E. P., and Carruthers, N. C. (1953). *Handbook of Statistical Methods in Meteorology*, H. M. Stationary Office, London, pp. 281–339

Chin, E. H. (1977). Modelling daily precipitation occurrence process with Markov chain. *Water Resour. Res.*, **13**, 949–56

Chung, K. L. (1967). *Markov Chains with Stationary Transition Probabilities*, 2nd edn, Springer, Berlin

Cole, J. A. (1966). Application of two season statistics to reservoir yield calculations. *Proceedings of the International Association of Scientific Hydrology Symposium, Garda, Italy*, pp. 590–1

Cox, D. R., and Miller, H. D. (1965). *The Theory of Stochastic Processes*, Methuen, London

Cox, D. R., and Smith, W. L. (1961). *Queues*, Monographs on Applied Probability and Statistics, Methuen, London

Crovelli, R. A. (1973). Stochastic models for precipitation. *Proceedings of the International Symposium on Uncertainties in Hydrologic and Water Resource Systems*, vol. 1, *11–14 December 1972, University of Arizona, Tucson*, pp. 284–98

David, F. N., and Barton, D. E. (1962). *Combinatorial Chance*, Griffin, London

Doran, D. G. (1975). An efficient transition definition for discrete state reservoir analysis: the divided interval technique. *Water Resour. Res.*, **11**, 867–73

Dyck, S., and Schramm, M. (1966). Queuing theory and multipurpose reservoir design. *Proceedings of the International Association of Scientific Hydrology Symposium, Garda, Italy*, paper 2(71), pp. 707–10

Encyclopaedia Britannica (1977), vol. 14, 15th edn, William Benton, Chicago, Illinois, pp. 1113–15

Farmer, E. E., and Homeyer, J. W. (1974). The probability of consecutive rainless days. *Water Resour. Bull.*, **10**, 914–24

Feller, W. (1968). *Introduction to Probability Theory and its Applications*, vol. 1, 3rd edn, Wiley, New York

Fiering, M. B. (1962). Queuing theory and simulation in reservoir design. *Trans. Am. Soc. Civ. Eng.*, **127**, part I, paper 3367, 1114–44

Gabriel, K. R., and Neumann, J. (1962). A Markov chain model for daily rainfall occurrence at Tel Aviv. *Q. J. R. Meteorol. Soc.*, **88**, 90–5

Gani, J. (1957). Problems in the probability theory of storage systems. *J. R. Statist. Soc. B*, **19**, 181–206

——(1965). Flooding models. *Proceedings of the Reservoir Yield Symposium, 21–23 September 1965*, Water Research Association, Medmenham, paper 4, pp. 4-1–4-16

Gillett, B. E. (1976). *Introduction to Operations Research, A Computer Oriented Algorithmic Approach*, McGraw-Hill, New York

Gnedenko, B. V. (1968). *The Theory of Probability*, 4th edn (translated from Russian by B. D. Seckler), Chelsea, New York

Gould, B. W. (1961). Statistical methods for estimating the design capacity of dams. *J. Inst. Eng. Aust.*, **33**, 405–16

——(1966). Communication on 'Probability of reservoir yield failure using Moran's steady state method and Gould's probability writing method' by R. A. Harris. *J. Inst. Water Eng.*, **20**, 141–6

Green, J. R. (1964). A model for rainfall occurrence. *J. R. Statist. Soc. B.*, **26**, 345–53

——(1970). A generalized probability model for sequences of wet and dry days. *Mon. Weath. Rev.*, **98**, 238–41

Gross, D., and Harris, C. M. (1974) *Fundamentals of Queuing Theory*, Wiley, New York

Harris, R. A. (1965). A probability of reservoir yield failure using Moran's steady state probability method and Gould's probability routing method. *J. Inst. Water Eng.*, **19**, 302–28

Harris, R. A., Dearlove, R. E., and Morgan, M. (1965). Reservoir yield, 2, serially correlated inflows and subsequent attainment of steady state probabilities, *Water Res. Assoc., Medmenham, Tech. Paper*, No. 45

Hershfield. D. M. (1971). Parameter estimation for wet-dry sequences. *Water Resour. Bull.*, **7**, 441–6

Hillier, F. S., and Lieberman, G. J. (1974). *Operations Research*, 2nd edn, Holden Day, San Francisco, California

Isaacson, D. L., and Madsen, R. W. (1976). *Markov Chains—Theory and Applications*, Wiley, New York

Jarvis, C. L. (1964). An Application of Moran's theory of dams to the Ord River project, western Australia. *J. Hydrol.*, **2**, 232–47

Joy, C. S., and McMahon, T. A. (1972). Reservoir-yield estimation procedures. *Civ. Eng. Trans., Inst. Eng. Aust.*, **14**, 28–36

Kemeny, J. G., and Snell, J. L. (1960). *Finite Markov Chains*, Van Nostrand, Princeton, New Jersey

Kendall, D. G. (1957). Some problems in the theory of dams. *J. R. Statist. Soc. B.*, **19**, 207–33

Klemeš, V. (1970). A two-step probabilistic model of storage reservoir with correlated inputs. *Water Resour. Res.*, **6**, 756–67

——(1971). On one difference between the Gould and Moran storage models. *Water Resour. Res.*, **7**, 410–4

——(1974). Probability distribution of outflow from a linear reservoir. *J. Hydrol.*, **21**, 305–14

——(1977). Discrete representation of storage for stochastic reservoir optimization. *Water Resour. Res.*, **13**, 149–58

Langbein, W. B. (1958). Queuing Theory and Water Storage. *J. Hydraul. Div., Am. Soc. Civ. Eng.*, **84** (HY5), 1811-1–1811-24

Lloyd, E. H. (1963). A probability theory of reservoirs with serially correlated inputs, *J. Hydrol.*, **1**, 99–128

——(1967). Stochastic reservoir theory. *Adv. Hydrosci.*, **4**, 281–339

——(1974). What is, and what is not, a Markov chain. *J. Hydrol.*, **22**, 1–28

Lloyd, E. H., and Odoom, S. (1964). Probability theory of reservoirs with seasonal input. *J. Hydrol.*, **2**, 1–10

Lowry, W. P., and Guthrie, D. (1968). Markov chains of order greater than one. *Mon. Weath. Rev.*, **96**, 798–801

Moran, P. A. P. (1954). A probability theory of dams and storage systems. *Aust. J. Appl. Sci.*, **5**, 116–24

——(1955). A probability theory of dams and storage systems, modifications of the release rule. *Aust. J. Appl. Sci.*, **6**, 117–30

——(1959). *The Theory of Storage*, Methuen, London

Mosteller, F. (1965). *Fifty Challenging Problems in Probability*, Addison-Wesley, Reading, Massachusetts

National Bureau of Standards (1959). Tables of the bivariate normal distribution function and related functions. *U.S. Dep. Comm., Washington, D.C., Appl. Math. Ser.*, No. 50

Parzen, E. (1962). *Stochastic Processes*, Holden Day, San Francisco, California

Pegram, G. G. S. (1974). Factors affecting draft from a Lloyd reservoir. *Water Resour. Res.*, **10**, 63–6

Phatarfod, R. M. (1976). Some aspects of stochastic reservoir theory. *J. Hydrol.*, **30**, 199–217

Prabhu, N. U. (1958). Some exact results for the finite dam. *Ann. Math. Statist.*, **29**, 1234–43

——(1964). Time dependent results in storage theory. *J. Appl. Prob.*, **1**, 1–64

Reardon, T. J. (1970). Storage yield and probability from an engineer's viewpoint (with discussion). *Civ. Eng. Trans., Inst. Eng. Aust.*, **12**, 119–24, 168, 169

Revuz, D. (1975). *Markov Chains*, North-Holland, Amsterdam

Ross, S. M. (1972). *Introduction to Probability Models*, Academic Press, New York

Saverenskiy, A. D. (1940). Metod rascheta regulirovaniya stoka. *Gidrotekhnicheskoe Stroitel'stvo*, No. 2, 24–8

Shamblin, J. E., and Stevens, G. T., Jr. (1974). *Operations Research, a Fundamental Approach*, McGraw-Hill, New York

Strang, G. (1976). *Linear Algebra and its Applications*, Academic Press, New York

Venetis, C. (1969a). Conditional probabilities of failures in reservoir operation for the Moran–Gould model. *Water Resour. Res.*, **5**, 514–18. (1970). Comments. *Water Resour. Res.*, **6**, 1427–32

——(1969b). On the distribution of the frequency of reservoir deficit, *J. Hydrol.*, **8**, 341–6. (1970). Correction. *J. Hydrol.*, **10**, 103–4. Discussion. *J. Hydrol.*, **10**, 199–201

——(1969c). A stochastic model of monthly reservoir storage. *Water Resour. Res.*, **5**, 729–34. (1970). Correction. *Water Resour. Res.* **6**, 351

Weesakul, B. (1961). First emptiness of a finite dam. *J. R. Statist. Soc. B*, **23**, 343–51

Weiss, L. L. (1964). Sequences of wet or dry days described by a Markov chain probability model. *Mon. Weath. Rev.*, **92**, 169–76

White, J. B. (1965). Probability of emptiness, II, a variable-season model. *Proceedings of the Reservoir Yield Symposium*, *21–23 September* 1965, Water Research Association, Medmenham, paper 6, pp. 6-1–6-11

8 Stochastic programming methods in systems engineering

The application of optimisation and decision theory in water resource engineering is evidenced by a proliferation of research activities during the past two decades. Originally, such methods were based on a deterministic approach, on the assumption that system inputs are known or could be replaced by their mean values. In recent times, however, the scope and diversity of planning and design has increased. Therefore, the need has arisen for a more flexible methodology, one that can cope, in some practical way, with incomplete information and uncertainty beyond the mean and variance. Nowhere is this more appropriate than in hydrological situations where nature appears to behave in an unpredictable manner.

The subject of this chapter is, broadly speaking, a continuation of the probabilistic concepts introduced in chapter 7, but procedures herein are directed more towards operational policies. Systems engineering techniques such as linear and dynamic programming are explained; the emphasis is on chance constraints and other stochastic aspects. Game theory is also discussed together with non-linear and other programming methods. The next chapter deals with terminal decisions under risk and uncertainty.

8.1 Historical background

Primitive methods of optimisation, that is, seeking the 'best' solution have been used from prehistoric times. For example, we learn from Virgil how a legendary queen founded Carthage by choosing a semicircular plot of land, with the sea as its linear boundary, thereby maximising the area for a given perimeter. Also, it appears that at the ancient Temple of Apollo (the god of prophesy) a council of priests sang verses giving optimal solutions to problems presented by the audience. Elsewhere, it is known that the ancient Egyptians were concerned with the optimisation of taxes on farmlands along the Nile which benefit from deposits after annual flooding.

Nature seems to adopt optimum methods everywhere, and man needs to optimise for his advancement whether in simple curve fitting, in investment strategies or in the design and operation of water resource systems. Although it is a goal which is always sought, an objective meaning to an optimum solution could be given only through mathematical expressions relating variables.

The first important application in optimisation theory came with the classical methods of calculus introduced in the seventeenth century. Then followed refinements for solving constrained problems, such as Lagrange multipliers. This involves the multiplication of the constraint functions by a set of dummy variables and the addition of these to the function to be optimised; the Lagrange function so formed is differentiated with respect to each of the basic variables. There were also the methods of variational calculus, used originally by Newton to design a ship's hull by minimising the drag of water. The procedure here is, basically, to determine the optimum of an integral involving a finite number of unknown functions[1].

With the phenomenal progress of civilisation during the twentieth century and the economic boom of the 1950s, technological and managerial problems needing optimisation were becoming increasingly difficult to solve by analytical methods. This was partly because of the large number and nature of constraints involved. Consequently, numerical solutions were sought by those concerned. Such efforts led to the science known as operations research. It was originated in England around 1940 under the leadership of Professor Blackett of the University of Manchester, in order to meet military objectives during World War II; Professor Blackett's highly successful multidisciplinary team comprised scientists and mathematicians. In the next two decades, applications were made over a wide range of activities such as in industry and business, with vast developments taking place during the latter stages in the United States. During this period, the advent of the electronic computer and mathematical developments were of particular significance. The occupation became known as the systems approach, and the area of activity is commonly referred to as systems engineering[2].

8.2 Introduction to systems engineering

A system is a collection of various components; for instance, a water resource system may have reservoirs, treatment plants, pipelines and other constituents. These components may be real or abstract. The systems approach concerns the

---

[1] The subject was developed by Euler and Lagrange after initiation by the Bernouillis. These classical methods have serious limitations when applied to large systems. Detailed explanations of them are beyond the scope of this book; see, for example, Siddall (1972). Objective and constraint functions will be explained in subsection 8.3.2.
[2] In this context the word engineering means basically to put together a system, and system engineers are, quite often, not engineers (Checkland, 1970).

interactions between different components of a system and not its internal behaviour.

Mathematically, a system is described by a model, the purpose of which is to find a rational solution to a problem. The analyst must take account of the factors that affect a system and must make use of all the available information and ideally the best expertise and experience. Again, it is important to note that the systems approach concerns the interactions between different components of a system and not its internal mechanism.

Thus systems engineering is a methodology for finding the 'best' course of action or an optimal set of solutions, where there is a choice between alternatives. For its implementation, the objectives and system constraints should be clearly stated. These may be controlled by economic, technological, sociological, environmental, legal and other possible effects[3].

The general aspects and objectives of the methods are as outlined. Prior to further elaboration, a fundamental point ought to be made. This pertains to the difference between static and dynamic optimisation, as shown in figure 8.1. The static case leads to an optimal point where there is a choice between two or more variables, after utility curves (which join points of equal value) are initially drawn. Examples of these are linear and non-linear programming techniques explained in the following sections as well as direct search and gradient methods. On the other hand, the solution in a dynamic case is an optimal path as sought, for instance, through the sequential policy-making techniques of dynamic programming, treated in section 8.4, and the calculus of variations.

Note that each problem requires a different approach with varying degrees of adoption and innovation as necessary. Another consideration is the level of simplicity or accuracy that is warranted and the manageability which this entails[4]. Accordingly, the problem must be defined with sufficient precision. An equally important philosophy is the methodology for setting out the problem.

In formulating an optimising technique we should declare the overall objectives (for instance, in conjunctive water resource schemes) or goals to be attained. When maximising benefits or minimising costs, the questions to whom or for what purpose should be borne in mind. Furthermore, we must specify criteria, we must list priorities and we must demarcate constraints prior to setting out alternative courses or policies. In summary, the main steps in the application of the systems approach can be specified as follows[5].

(1) State the problem and set out the objectives.
(2) Specify the criteria to serve the objectives.

[3] McMillan and Gonzalez (1973), O'Laoghaire and Himmelblau (1974), Siddall (1972), Hall and Dracup (1970) and the Meta Systems Incorporated (1975) give further details of the systems approach. Basic ideas and historical background on systems thinking are given by Kramer and de Smit (1977).
[4] Bellman (1957), for instance, refers to a 'straight and narrow path between the pitfalls of oversimplification and the morass of overcomplication'.
[5] This classification is more objective oriented than that of Churchman et al. (1957) which, as given also by Shamblin and Stevens (1974), is problem oriented.

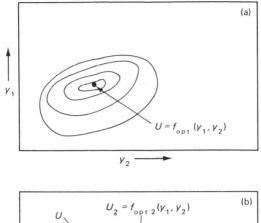

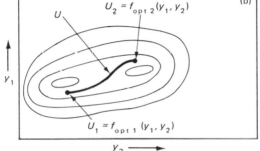

Figure 8.1   Static and dynamic cases of optimisation in two dimensions: (a) static case, U denotes optimal point; (b) dynamic case, U denotes optimal path

(3) Assign priorities in the case of multiple objectives.
(4) Demarcate the constraints and quantify the uncertainties.
(5) Classify the alternative courses or policies.
(6) Outline the final course in general terms.
(7) Set the final course in detail.

Quite often in large-scale systems there is a need for multilevel and multigoal planning on account of natural, political, legal and other constraints. When there is a diversity of objectives, a screening stage, involving an hierarchy or ranking of alternative choices, may be necessary. The ultimate aim is that scarce water resources are transformed into specific uses in time and space, thereby maximising social benefit.

In cases where there are conflicting objectives on the same level, the theory of games may be utilised. As outlined in section 8.5, this involves two or more 'players' (who could be, for example, countries or organisations) with opposing objectives. The action space and pay-off functions of the individual players determine the final outcome.

The aforementioned procedures, when applied directly, imply that solutions are sought through deterministic models. There is, however, a widespread need for a more flexible stochastic approach, because of uncertainty and incomplete information. Also a cut-off level is applied in studying phenomena, on account of negligible or unknown factors. Again, measurement errors are usually inevitable and are often lumped in time and space. All of this highlights the importance of stochasticity in model formulation. A direct method of implementation is by describing random variables through their probability distributions.

Randomness is also used in the lottery of rewards on which game theory and decision theory are based. It is important to note that there can be a personal bias in estimates of probabilities; in this connection, subjectivity is implied in many areas of decision making, particularly in the bayesian methods explained in chapter 9.

It should be remembered that uncertainties are present not only in inputs but also in outputs. Furthermore, in real world situations, objectives too may not be deterministic. As an example, consider the differential feedback game of a torpedo which is aimed at a ship; on account of conflicting pursuits, strategies in such a situation are stochastic, changing continuously on receipt of new evidence.

A schematic approach to optimal decisions in a stochastic water resource system is given in figure 8.2. This illustrates the explicit stochastic or optimum benefits approach in which decisions or policies are such that expected benefits are maximised or expected costs are minimised. The inputs to this system are treated as stochastic variables, which are described by marginal probability density functions and parameters α; also, deterministic variables T such as trend and seasonality will effect the input. The decision variables are given by D and Y_j which denote a set of outputs, conditional to decision j, which have marginal probability densities.

An alternative to the method given above for choosing between two or more decisions is the implicit stochastic or statistical trials approach. In this case an optimum sequence of decisions is determined from relative proportions of successful trials on the basis of maximum present values. Here, generated sequences are used as random realisations, and the output probability functions shown in figure 8.2 are replaced by a set of vectors. This is used in complex situations where explicit procedures are not feasible[6]. Apart from these two methods, simulation is adopted, for instance, in reservoir studies where operation rules are tested by routing sequences of data; more about this important aspect follows.

If we follow the outline of the principles of operations research given above, specific methods of implementation, which are suitable for water resource

[6] The terms explicit and implicit stochastic have been used, for instance, by Roefs and Bodin (1970) and Croley (1974). Examples of the first kind are given by Gablinger and Loucks (1970) and of the second kind by Young (1967) and by Hall and Howell (1963); Roefs (1968) reviews early applications in reservoir management.

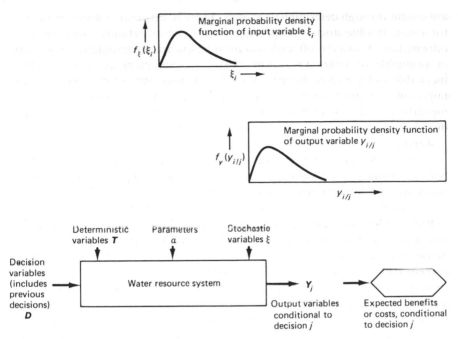

Figure 8.2 Optimal decision making in a stochastic water resource system. This illustrates the explicit stochastic approach in which the expected benefits or costs are optimised. Alternatively, the implicit stochastic approach may be adopted in which generated sequences of input data are used

systems, are now explained. The emphasis will be on those procedures through which randomness can be accounted for. The first technique taken up is that of linear programming which has considerable appeal because of its simplicity. This will be followed by the more flexible approach of dynamic programming.

8.3 Linear programming

Linear programming (LP) is a relatively unsophisticated technique of systems engineering. Here, the word programming means the selection of an optimum allocation of resources after initial description and specification[7].

8.3.1 General considerations for water resource applications

A water resource system may consist of direct abstraction, underground or

[7] The basic idea of LP dates back to the Russian mathematician L. V. Kantorovich (Dantzig, 1963, pp. 22, 23; Tintner and Sengupta, 1972). However, the American G. B. Dantzig (1963) is commonly regarded as the father of this modern science; he has acknowledged that the word programming was suggested to him by T. C. Koopmans.

other sources combined with one or more reservoirs. Such a system may supply water for consumptive, hydroelectric and dilution purposes, may provide storage reservations for flood protection and may maintain minimum levels for recreation. In view of the diversity of needs, it becomes necessary to seek optimal decisions in the planning, design and operation of the system. The decisions are based on economic, environmental, legal and other requirements and, if implemented, would cause the greatest benefit to the community. For such purposes, LP seems to be a suitable approach, at least, as an initial screening procedure.

A basic requirement in the application of LP is an objective function U which needs to be maximised or minimised. In reservoir management, the decision variables are usually releases R_t from storage during intervals of time $t = 1, 2, 3, \ldots$. The state variables are S_t which are the different states or contents of a reservoir at the end of the time intervals t. Inflows X_t are stochastic, but initially they may be considered to be deterministic. The system will also have constraints such as minimum releases or reservoir capacities. By means of systems analysis an optimum policy is found, conditional to the constraints.

On account of the constraints or inequalities, a strictly analytical solution is generally not feasible, and a problem must be approached through some type of numerical method. If it is possible to define the system through an objective function which is a linear equation and if the constraints are linear functions, then optimisation is possible through LP. In situations where these conditions do not hold, non-linear programming methods should be applied, as subsequently discussed.

8.3.2   Programme formulation

In LP the objective function to be optimised is of the form

$$U = AX \tag{8.1}$$

where $X = [x_1\ x_2\ \ldots\ x_\ell]^T$ is a vector of variables denoting, for example, units of water supplied for domestic uses, irrigation demands and so on; also, $A = [a_1\ a_2\ \ldots\ a_\ell]$ is a vector of constants representing, say, returns per unit of water released and T denotes transpose.

The optimisation is subject to a set of m constraints

$$GX \geqslant H \tag{8.2}$$

in which the sign of inequality may be reversed and where

$$
G = \begin{bmatrix}
g_{11} & \cdot & \cdot & \cdot & g_{1\ell} \\
g_{21} & \cdot & \cdot & & \cdot \\
\cdot & \cdot & \cdot & \cdot & \cdot \\
\cdot & \cdot & \cdot & \cdot & \cdot \\
g_{m1} & \cdot & \cdot & \cdot & g_{m\ell}
\end{bmatrix}
$$

and

$$H = [h_1 \; h_2 \; \ldots \; h_m]^{\mathrm{T}}$$

Also, there are, generally, ℓ non-negativity constraints,

$$X \geqslant 0 \qquad\qquad\qquad (8.3)$$

According to the principle of duality every minimum LP problem (primal) has a corresponding maximum LP problem (dual); here, the words minimum and maximum can be interchanged. Corresponding to equation 8.1 and constraints 8.2 and 8.3, the dual problem is to maximise $B = H^{\mathrm{T}}Y$ conditional to $G^{\mathrm{T}}Y \leqslant A^{\mathrm{T}}$ and $Y \geqslant 0$, where $Y = [y_1 \; y_2 \; \ldots \; y_3]^{\mathrm{T}}$. Note that the optimum solutions obtained from the two methods are the same. It is sometimes more convenient to solve the dual problem than the primal one, as in the application of the simplex method given in subsection 8.3.3, in which the dual variable Y is interpreted[8].

Example 8.1   Towns L, M, N are to be supplied by water from desalination plants costing £50 000 each and boreholes costing £30 000 each. The minimum daily requirements for the three towns are 10, 12 and 23 units of water, respectively. Each desalination plant can supply 9 units of water, and a preliminary design of the distribution system shows that this could be economically distributed in the ratio 6:2:1 for L:M:N. Alternatively, a borehole can supply 8 units of water per day which should be distributed as 1:2:5 for L:M:N. Determine the optimum number of desalination plants and boreholes that are required to satisfy the given constraints.

Primal problem   Minimise $C = 50\,000x_1 + 30\,000x_2$, where x_1 and x_2 are the number of desalination plants and boreholes respectively. The constraints are

$$6x_1 + x_2 \geqslant 10$$
$$2x_1 + 2x_2 \geqslant 12$$
$$x_1 + 5x_2 \geqslant 23$$
$$x_1, x_2 \geqslant 0$$

Dual problem   Maximise $B = 10y_1 + 12y_2 + 23y_3$; where y_1, y_2 and y_3 denote unit prices (£1000) which the towns should pay for capital expenditure from the economic standpoint. The constraints are

$$6y_1 + 2y_2 + y_3 \leqslant 50\,000$$
$$y_1 + 2y_2 + 5y_3 \leqslant 30\,000$$
$$y_1, y_2, y_3 \geqslant 0$$

---

[8] Duality was originated by J. von Neumann. Its main use is in sensitivity analysis and opportunity–cost interpretation; shadow pricing and other economic aspects of duality are given by Baumol (1972) and Hillier and Lieberman (1974, chapter 2). Dantzig (1963) presents the theory including that of the simplex algorithm which he invented: readers may, however, prefer to read the simplified explanations given by Wagner (1975, chapters 4, 5) and Taha (1976, chapter 7); at the other extreme, a mathematical analysis is given by Zoutendijk (1976).

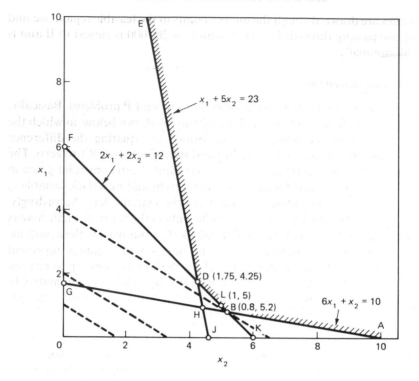

Figure 8.3   Minimum linear programming problem, example 8.1. The straight lines GHBA, FDBK and EDHJ represent the three constraints in given order. The area enclosed by EDBA and the two axes is infeasible for the solution. Broken lines represent isocost lines $C = 50\,000x_1 + 30\,000x_2$; the crucial one is the line $196\,000 = 50\,000x_1 + 30\,000x_2$, which touches the feasible region bounded by EDBA at point B. The optimal point is L(1, 5)

A method of obtaining a graphical solution is shown through figure 8.3. Here, three straight lines GHBA, FDBK and EDHJ are drawn to represent the equations $6x_1 + x_2 = 10$, $2x_1 + 2x_2 = 12$ and $x_1 + 5x_2 = 23$ from the constraints of the primal problem. Note that solutions corresponding to points within the area enclosed by the two axes and the line EDBA are not feasible. If x_1 and x_2 can take non-integer values, we can intuitively suggest that the optimum value of C occurs at one of the points M, D, B and A, where $M \equiv (23, 0)$, D $\equiv (1.75, 4.25)$, B $\equiv (0.8, 5.2)$ and $A \equiv (0, 10)$. Substitution in $C = 50\,000x_1 + 30\,000x_2$ shows that the point B is optimal; hence, $C(\text{optimal}) = 196\,000$. The geometric solution is to draw parallel isocost lines $C = 50\,000x_1 + 30\,000x_2$ outwards from the origin as shown by the broken lines; the one which touches the feasible area represents $190\,000 = 50\,000x_1 + 30\,000x_2$, and the point touched is B. However, x_1 and x_2 can only take integer values. Now, if additional isocost lines are drawn through the integer points in the feasible region, we find that the one passing through L ≡ (1, 5) with $C = 200\,000$ is closest to B and is therefore optimal[9].

8.3.3 Simplex algorithm

The simplex algorithm is an iterative method of solving LP problems. Basically, the approach is to form a simplex tableau initially, as shown below, in which the top row denotes the objective function formed by equating the difference between a variable, say x_0, and the right-hand side of equation 8.1 to zero. The other rows of the tableau represent the m constraints from constraint given in equation 8.2, which are transformed into equations by adding a slack variable s_i, $i = 1, 2, \ldots, m$, correspondingly to each on the extreme left. Accordingly, columns on the left have zero and unit coefficients in the form of a unit matrix because they stand for x_0 and the slack variables. (For this reason, the equations are said to be of the canonical type.) The next set of columns represent respectively the variables in vector X; therefore, the entries from top to bottom in each are the coefficients from vector A, with the signs changed, and matrix G. Finally, a column, designated *Current solution*, is formed from the coefficients from vector H with a zero value added at the top.

Row	x_0	s_1	...	s_i	...	s_m	x_1	x_2	...	x_ℓ	Current solution	basic variable
1	1	0		0		0	$-a_1$	$-a_2$		$-a_\ell$	0	x_0
2	0	1		0		0	g_{11}	g_{12}		$g_{1\ell}$	h_1	s_1
.		.		.		.	.	.		.	.	.
.	.	.		.		.	.	.		.	.	.
$1+i$	0	0		1		0	g_{i1}	g_{i2}		$g_{i\ell}$	h_i	s_i
.	.	.		.		.	.	.		.	.	.
.	.	.		.		.	.	.		.	.	.
$1+m$	0	0		0		1	g_{m1}	g_{m2}		$g_{m\ell}$	h_m	s_m

In the initial tableau, the entries in the *Current solution* column are assigned to x_0 and the slack variables respectively; these solutions are of course suboptimal. The next step is to transform the tableau by elementary row operations so that one of the original variables, say x_2, takes the value given in the *Current solution* column of a slack variable, say, s_i, which is then equated to zero. The second tableau is completed after a column is formed with one coefficient of unity (under x_2 in row i) and zeros elsewhere. More than one revision of the tableau is

---

[9] More complicated situations will require integer programming (Garfinkel and Nemhauser, 1972). Fundamentally, this involves systematic methods of ennumeration or graphical cutting planes.

usually made in the same way, thereby replacing the x_i values and changing the value of x_0, until a terminal tableau is obtained with non-negative coefficients in the top row. Optimum values of the variables and the objective function are given by the terminal tableau, as explained in the following example.

Example 8.2 Find the solution to example 8.1 using the simplex algorithm and the principle of duality.

In the initial simplex tableau which follows, the dual variables y_1, y_2 and y_3 (see the dual problem under example 8.1) are assigned zero values; y_0 is also zero and the slack variables s_1 and s_2 take the values 50 and 30 respectively, in units of £1000, of the dual constraints.

Row	y_0	s_1	s_2	y_1	y_2	y_3	Current solution (£1000 units)	Basic variable
1	1	0	0	-10	-12	-23	0	y_0
2	0	1	0	6	2	1	50	s_1
3	0	0	1	1	2	5	30	s_2

The next step is to replace either s_1 or s_2 in the last column by one of the variables y_1, y_2 and y_3. For this purpose, elementary row operations are made to produce a coefficient of 1 in one of the columns denoting these dual variables; there should also be zeros elsewhere in the column. The variable y_3 which causes a greater change in the objective function than y_1 and y_2 is preferred here. (There is uncertainty, however, regarding the choice of variable that will produce the fastest results; it turns out here that y_2 ought to have been the initial choice.) Also row 3, which makes $y_3 = 6$, from the division of 30 by 5, is chosen. Note that the choice of row 2 will be incorrect because this results in a higher value for y_3 and consequently in a violation of the second or non-negativity constraints. (Obviously, y_1 or y_2 should then be negative to satisfy the second constraint, if $y_3 = 50$.) Therefore, the underlined number 5 under y_3 is taken as the so-called pivot. Row 3 is divided throughout by 5, after which the revised row 3 is subtracted from row 2 and 23 times the revised row 3 is added to row 1. The second tableau is given below.

Row	y_0	s_1	s_2	y_1	y_2	y_3	Current solution (£1000 units)	Basic variable
1	1	0	$23/5$	$-27/5$	$-14/5$	0	138	y_0
2	0	1	$-1/5$	$29/5$	$8/5$	0	44	s_1
3	0	0	$1/5$	$1/5$	$2/5$	1	6	y_3

It is seen that currently $y_3 = 6$, $s_1 = 44$ and y_0 (that is, the objective function) $= 138$; also, it is implied, from the three rows above, that $y_1 = y_2 = s_2 = 0$. To form the third tableau which follows, the underlined number 2/5 under y_2 is chosen as the pivot if we use the same type of reasoning as before. Then row 3 is divided throughout by 2/5, and appropriate operations are made for rows 1 and 2.

Row	y_0	s_1	s_2	y_1	y_2	y_3	Current solution ($£1000$ units)	Basic variable
1	1	0	6	-4	0	7	180	y_0
2	0	1	-1	5	0	-4	20	s_1
3	0	0	1/2	1/2	1	5/2	15	y_2

Note that, because a negative value appears in row 1, the above tableau is not a terminal one. This is obtained by choosing the underlined number 5 under y_1 as the next pivot and by adopting a similar procedure again.

Row	y_0	s_1	s_2	y_1	y_2	y_3	Current solution ($£1000$ units)	Basic variable
1	1	4/5	26/5	0	0	19/5	196	y_0
2	0	1/5	$-1/5$	1	0	$-4/5$	4	y_1
3	0	$-1/10$	6/10	0	1	29/10	13	y_2

Thus unit prices computed on the basis of economic efficiency are $y_1 = 4$, $y_2 = 13$ and $y_3 = 0$ (by implication); on social considerations, however, water costs ought to be divided equitably. Also $y_0 = \max(B) + \min(C) = 196$. Furthermore, the values in row 1 for s_1 and s_2 are in fact the non-integer solutions to the primal problem. However, because these should be integer values, the choice ($x_1 = 1$, $x_2 = 5$) is made as in example 8.1.

The simplex procedure given here is especially useful in multidimensional problems and is easily adaptable for computer programming[10].

8.3.4 Chance-constrained linear programming

When LP is applied to reservoir problems and the like which involve natural time series, deterministic procedures based on historical records have serious limitations. For such practical situations, stochastic LP methods have been

[10] The simplex algorithm and penalty functions are given by Siddall (1972). A listing to solve the dual problem is given by Hassitt (1968).

suggested. A particular form of this, and one which is comparatively straightforward in formulation, is chance-constrained linear programming. The main requirement is to adopt chance constraints in place of deterministic ones, and in this way the probabilities of failure are used in the constraints[11]. When applied to reservoir problems, the operational procedure is known as the linear decision rule (LDR). The method was originated by C. ReVelle and his coworkers and is often quoted in the water resources literature[12]. This is followed here, and an example is given.

If we use the notation of section 8.3.1, the LDR for releases from storage of a reservoir during a time interval t can be expressed in a general form by

$$R_t = uS_{t-1} + vX_t - b_\tau \tag{8.4}$$

in which u and v are two parameters such that $0 \leqslant u, v \leqslant 1$. Also, $b_\tau, \tau = 1, 2, \ldots,$ p, is a periodic set of decision parameters controlling releases. Here, τ corresponds to t in a cycle of p items; for instance, if monthly data are used and the cycle is an annual one, $p = 12$. Thus the LDR means that the release from storage in, say, month t is the sum of a variable fraction of the storage S_{t-1} at the end of the previous month, and a variable fraction of the inflows X_t during the current month less an amount b_τ which is constant for the calendar month τ.

For simplicity, let $u = 1$ and $v = 0$ for all t; the decision rule then takes the form

$$R_t = S_{t-1} - b_\tau \tag{8.5}$$

and

$$S_t = S_{t-1} + X_t - R_t \tag{8.6}$$

which follows from the principle of continuity or mass balance. From equations 8.5 and 8.6, therefore,

$$S_t = b_\tau + X_t \tag{8.7}$$

and at the start of the previous month

$$S_{t-1} = b_{\tau-1} + X_{t-1} \tag{8.8}$$

It follows from equations 8.6, 8.7 and 8.8 that

$$R_t = b_{\tau-1} - b_\tau + X_{t-1} \tag{8.9}$$

If the minimum release required for dilution, river regulation and other purposes during month τ is Q_τ, a necessary prior condition is that $R_t \geqslant Q_\tau$. This means that

$$b_\tau \leqslant b_{\tau-1} + X_{t-1} - Q_\tau \tag{8.10}$$

---

[11] This was originally suggested by Charnes and Cooper (1960). Explicit stochastic methods of a more rigorous kind are described by Williams (1965) and Kall (1976).
[12] See ReVelle et al. (1969) and Eastman and ReVelle (1973).

The decision parameters b_τ can be chosen so that the constraint given in equation 8.10 holds for the observed values of X_{t-1} corresponding to $\tau - 1$. However, as already mentioned, a better practical approach, because of variability and uncertainty, is to express the constraint in equation 8.10 in terms of the probablity that it will hold when a future series of flows is routed through the reservoir. The chance of failure of the system may be minimised by stipulating a probability of exceedance close to unity. It is assumed here that correlations in the X_t values are not significant and that the X_t values are distributed differently in the 12 months of the year. Accordingly, the constraint in equation 8.10 may be formulated so that it holds when X_{t-1} is not less than the value $X^{(\alpha_1)}_{\tau-1}$, which is exceeded in calendar month $\tau - 1$ with probability 1 $- \alpha_1$. In other words, $\Pr\{X_\tau \leqslant X^{(\alpha_1)}_\tau\} = \alpha_1$ for $\tau = 1, 2, \ldots, 12$. Note that, if $\tau = 1, \tau - 1 = 12$. A suitable value for α_1 is 0.05, but the chosen level of probability should depend on the purposes to be served by the reservoir. Hence, the *minimum release constraint* is

$$b_\tau \leqslant b_{\tau-1} + X^{(\alpha_1)}_{\tau-1} - Q_\tau \tag{8.11}$$

Another common requirement in reservoir management is that the storage S_t is not less than a stipulated minimum content S_m which should be provided for recreation and amenities. From equation 8.7, following the probabilistic concepts leading to the constraint in equation 8.11 and using a probability of exceedance $1 - \alpha_2$, we find that S_m should, therefore, be not greater than $b_\tau + X^{(\alpha_2)}_\tau$, for all τ. Hence, the *minimum storage constraint* becomes

$$b_\tau \geqslant S_m - X^{(\alpha_2)}_\tau \tag{8.12}$$

In addition, we may define the LDR so that the reservoir is empty only if the inflow in month τ is less than the value $X^{(\alpha_3)}_\tau$ which is exceeded with probability 1 $- \alpha_3$ (where $\alpha_3 < \alpha_2$). From equation 8.12, therefore, the *storage constraint* becomes

$$b_\tau \geqslant - X^{(\alpha_3)}_\tau \tag{8.13}$$

It may also be necessary to design and operate a reservoir so that flood storage reservations $F_\tau, \tau = 1, 2, \ldots, 12$, estimated from probable high flows within a month, are allowed for within its full capacity C. This means that

$$C - S_t \geqslant F_\tau \tag{8.14}$$

and from equation 8.7

$$C \geqslant b_\tau + X_t + F_\tau \tag{8.15}$$

For this purpose the right tails of the probability density functions of X_t should be examined for each month τ and the chance constraint made to hold for the value $X^{(\alpha_4)}_\tau$, which is exceeded with probability $1 - \alpha_4$. Hence, the *flood storage constraint* takes the form

$$C \geqslant b_\tau + X^{(\alpha_4)}_\tau + F_\tau \tag{8.16}$$

On the other hand, the flood storage requirements F_τ may be foregone and the reservoir capacity C may be chosen so that spillage occurs only if inflows in month τ are higher than the value $X_\tau^{(\alpha_5)}$ which is exceeded with probability $1 - \alpha_5$ (where $\alpha_5 > \alpha_4$). Accordingly, the *overflow constraint* is given by

$$C \geqslant b_\tau + X_\tau^{(\alpha_5)} \tag{8.17}$$

In order to estimate the $X_\tau^{(\alpha_i)}$, where $0 \leqslant \alpha_i$ for all i, it is suggested that the best-fitting probability density function (for example, gamma) is chosen and that its parameters are estimated for each month τ from observed inflow data by following the methods given in chapter 3. Note also that, although the constraints in equations 8.11, 8.12, 8.13, 8.16 and 8.17 may hold for all months τ at the given levels of probability, there could be violations within the monthly intervals. If these are of importance, weekly, pentad or daily data should be used. It will be recalled, from chapter 7, that Gould suggested his empirical refinement because of comparable limitations in Moran's original method.

The decision parameters b_τ should satisfy the constraints in equations 8.11, 8.12 and 8.13 and a reservoir capacity C should be chosen to meet the constraints in equations 8.16 and 8.17. These are conditional to the minimum storage S_m, the minimum releases Q_τ and flood storage requirements F_τ, $\tau = 1, 2, \ldots, 12$, and the non-exceedance probabilities α_i, $i = 1, 2, \ldots, 5$.

It should be noted that C is the minimum effective reservoir capacity to meet the given requirements. Allowances have to be made for accumulation of sediment where necessary, and hydropower commitments will necessitate further constraints with possible increases in capacity. Furthermore, evaporation losses should be accounted for, if significant.

Example 8.3   A reservoir is to be constructed at a site on the River Vyrnwy, where the estimated $\hat{X}_\tau^{(0.01)}$, $\hat{X}_\tau^{(0.05)}$, $\hat{X}_\tau^{(0.95)}$ and $\hat{X}_\tau^{(0.99)}$ monthly flows are tabulated below. The flood storage requirements are given in the last row.

Estimated flow($\times 10^6$ m³)	*Value for month $\tau =$*											
	1	2	3	4	5	6	7	8	9	10	11	12
$\hat{X}_\tau^{(0.01)}$	1.4	1.1	0.8	0.6	0.5	0.3	0.4	0.6	0.7	1.0	1.2	1.5
$\hat{X}_\tau^{(0.05)}$	5.6	4.4	3.2	2.4	2.0	1.2	1.6	2.4	2.8	4.0	4.8	6.0
$\hat{X}_\tau^{(0.95)}$	15.5	12.6	9.2	7.6	5.9	4.2	5.0	7.6	7.6	11.8	14.3	16.0
$\hat{X}_\tau^{(0.99)}$	19.1	15.1	11.1	9.1	7.1	5.1	6.1	9.1	9.1	14.1	17.1	19.1
F_τ	7.8	2.6	0	0	0	0	0	0	2.6	7.8	10.5	10.5

Minimum monthly releases Q_τ of 1.5 units are required to meet minimum acceptable flows in the Vyrnwy from January ($\tau = 1$) to August ($\tau = 8$) and in December ($\tau = 12$), but this should be increased to 3.2 during the 3 autumn months. Also, additional units of 9, 5 and 2 should be released in June, July and August respectively to regulate the River Severn of which the River Vyrnwy is a tributary. If the minimum storage requirement S_m is 5.6 units, obtain a set of decision parameters b_τ and a minimum reservoir capacity C to satisfy the five chance constraints given in equations 8.11, 8.12, 8.13, 8.16 and 8.17 if $\alpha_1 = \alpha_2 = 0.05$, $\alpha_3 = 0.01$, $\alpha_4 = 0.95$ and $\alpha_5 = 0.99$. Hence, draw a set of reservoir rule curves.

From the sums of the 12 constraints given in equation 8.11, it follows that a basic requirement is

$$\sum_{\tau=1}^{12} Q_\tau \leqslant \sum_{\tau=1}^{12} \hat{X}_\tau^{(0.05)} \tag{8.18}$$

The left-hand side and right-hand side are 39.1 and 40.4 respectively, and therefore the above constraint holds. An initial set of parameters b'_τ are obtained as shown in table 8.1 if we assume an initial value of, say, $b'_1 = 0$ and then apply the constraint in equation 8.11 *as an equation*[13]. For example, from rows 1, 2 and 3, $b'_2 = 0 + 5.6 - 1.5 = 4.1$ and $b'_7 = 1.1 + 1.2 - 6.5 = -4.2$; in the same way, b'_1 should be $-3.2 + 6.0 - 1.5 = 1.3$ which is the difference between right-hand side and left-hand side of the constraint in equation 8.18. Because b'_1 ($= 0$) is less than 1.3, the constraint in equation 8.11 will hold. Note that this is always possible if the constraint in equation 8.18 holds. Then the values b_τ of row 6 are obtained by adding to each of the b'_τ values a constant k which is the minimum required to satisfy the constraints in equations 8.12 and 8.13. This is arrived at by comparing the b'_τ values in row 1 of table 8.1 with the values of rows 4 and 5. It is found that the constraint in equation 8.13 is irrelevant in this case. From the column for month 9 (at the end of which the reservoir is at its lowest level), $k = 9.7$. If in a different application the b'_τ values are greater than the right-hand side values of the constraints in equations 8.12 and 8.13 for all τ, then k ought to be the lowest of the 24 differences between the b'_τ values and the right-hand side values; in such a case k is *subtracted* from each of the b'_τ values to obtain the b_τ values. In order to determine the minimum reservoir capacity C, the right-hand side of the constraints in equations 8.16 and 8.17 are evaluated for each month. This means that row 6 should be added separately to rows 7 and 8 and that C is the maximum of the 24 sums. In this example, $C = 33$ which is obtained from month 1 and also from month 12. It is also seen that equation 8.17 is redundant.

In a dry year, with inflows in every month not less than the values that are exceeded with probability 0.95, the reservoir could be maintained at or above the levels given in row 9 of table 8.1. These are also given by the set of points marked 2 in figure 8.4. This follows from equation 8.7, and it is assumed from equation 8.11 that the minimum release is made. On the other hand, if we start from one of these low levels and if the inflow in the following month is as high as the value which is exceeded with probability 0.05, the reservoir will rise at the end of this month to a level given in row 10 after the minimum release is made. These levels are shown by the points marked 3 in figure 8.4.

[13] This was suggested by Eastman and ReVelle (1973).

Table 8.1   Example 8.3, application of LP model with chance constraints

Row	Parameter	Value for month τ =											
		1	2	3	4	5	6	7	8	9	10	11	12
1	$b'_τ$	0	4.1	7.0	8.7	9.6	1.1	−4.2	−6.1	−6.9	−7.3	−6.5	−3.2
2	$\hat{X}_τ^{(0.05)}$	5.6	4.4	3.2	2.4	2.0	1.2	1.6	2.4	2.8	4.0	4.8	6.0
3	$Q_τ$	1.5	1.5	1.5	1.5	1.5	10.5	6.5	3.5	3.2	3.2	3.2	1.5
4	$S_m - \hat{X}_τ^{(0.05)}$	0	1.2	2.4	3.2	3.6	4.4	4.0	3.2	2.8	1.6	0.8	−0.4
5	$-\hat{X}_τ^{(0.01)}$	−1.4	−1.1	−0.8	−0.6	−0.5	−0.3	−0.4	−0.6	−0.7	−1.0	−1.2	−1.5
6	$b_τ$	9.7	13.8	16.7	18.4	19.3	10.8	5.5	3.6	2.8	2.4	3.2	6.5
7	$\hat{X}_τ^{(0.95)} + F_τ$	23.3	15.2	9.2	7.6	5.9	4.2	5.0	7.6	10.2	19.6	24.8	26.5
8	$\hat{X}_τ^{(0.99)}$	19.1	15.1	11.1	9.1	7.1	5.1	6.1	9.1	9.1	14.1	17.1	19.1
9	$b_τ + X_τ^{(0.05)}$	15.3	18.2	19.9	20.8	21.3	12.0	7.1	6.0	5.6	6.4	8.0	12.5
10	$b_τ + X_τ^{(0.95)}$	25.2	26.4	25.9	26.0	25.2	15.0	10.5	11.2	10.4	14.2	17.5	22.5

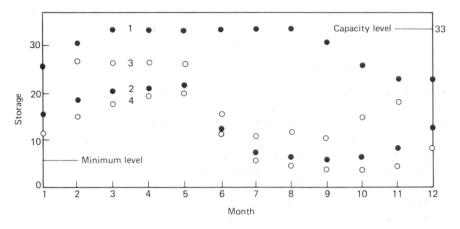

Figure 8.4 Reservoir operation levels for linear decision rule, example 8.3: 1, flood control levels; 2, minimum drawdown levels (probability of inflows equals 0.05); 3, levels with high inflows (probability equals 0.95); 4, levels with very low inflows (probability equals 0.01)

The minimum release could be made if the reservoir level at the end of the previus month is at or above line 2. This is on the assumption that the inflow in the current month is not less than the value which is exceeded with probability 0.95. On the other hand, if the inflows are equal to the values which are exceeded with probability 0.99, then the reservoir level will fall to values given by the differences between rows 6 and 5. The minimum of this is 3.4 (which is below the required minimum of 5.6) at the end of month 10; the levels are shown by the points marked 4 in figure 8.4. Finally, the set of points marked 1 are obtained by subtracting the F_r values from 33, and they represent the flood control line. The reservoir levels should be kept at or below this line in order to accommodate possible high inflows during the following month.

8.3.5 *Limitations of the liner decision rule method*

The LDR method entails some simplifications. It could be argued that the same results are obtainable by more straightforward methods. As already mentioned, serial correlation of inflows is not considered. If this is significant, the joint distribution methods of chapter 7 might be used for determining the reliability of any operational policy. On the other hand, variations of inflows and storage levels within a month may be accounted for at the expense of computational time. The main shortcoming is that the LDR does not provide a global optimum policy for reservoir design and operation; the results are subject to the nature of the rule adopted. Furthermore, proper application of LP methods should entail target releases and target storages, together with economic benefit or penalty functions. Without these, the effectiveness of chance-constrained programming techniques and their information content is restricted[14].

8.3.6   *Other applications of linear programming*

Perhaps the overall simplification of this LP method does not warrant a complicated release rule. Nevertheless, certain modifications to the LDR are feasible. For instance, Loucks and Dorfman (1975) made a comparative study of different operating rules, incorporating storage and release targets in order to judge the individual performances. Also, Luthra and Arora (1976) studied the effects of varying v, $0 \leqslant v \leqslant 1$, in equation 8.4. Amongst others who modified the LDR, ReVelle and Kirby (1970) applied optimisation with various reservoir reliability measures. Elsewhere, Eastman and ReVelle (1973) reduced the number of constraints through a direct solution approach. In addition, weighted present and past inflows have been used in a more general LDR by ReVelle and Gundelach (1975) and Gundelach and ReVelle (1975).

The approach of Eisel (1972), who applied chance-constrained programming for irrigation purposes, is comparable with that of ReVelle *et al.* (1969). The procedure in his sophisticated paper, however, leads to a non-linear separable programming problem; here, the word separable means that several functions are added to form the objective function as shown, for example, by Taha (1976, pp. 572-580). In another adaptation of the LDR, a coefficient A_m used in defining the minimum storage $S_m = A_m C$, where C is the optimum reservoir capacity, is shown by Nayak and Arora (1974) to be independent of the control volume $C - S_m$. Where evaporation losses are significant, further amendments are suggested, for example, in the aforementioned work of ReVelle and Kirby (1970). Applications of the LDR to multireservoir systems have been made by LeClerc and Marks (1973) and by Nayak and Arora (1971). Another advanced chance-constrained model is suggested by Curry *et al.* (1973) for linked multipurpose reservoirs, and this has been adapted by Kos (1975).

Stochastic LP methods in reservoir operation data back to Thomas and Watermeyer (1962). To explain their linear model, let the inflow to the reservoir and releases from storage, at time t, be X_t and R_t respectively. Here, t corresponds to year i, $i = 1, 2, \ldots, n$, and season τ, $\tau = 1, 2, \ldots, p$, that is, $t = (i - 1)p + \tau$. Also, let the target release during season τ be Q_τ, and let f, e and d denote the rates of target benefit, excess and deficit respectively; these are based on the technological, social and economic aspects of systems design. The objective (net benefit) function is given by

$$U(R_t, Q_\tau) = f(Q_\tau) + e(R_t - Q_\tau)^+ - d(Q_\tau - R_t)^+$$

in which the superscripts $+$ signify that the second or third term on the right in parenthesis should be deleted, depending on which one is negative. If $p_{\tau, R, S}$ denotes the probability that the reservoir storage is S at the end of season τ when

---

[14]   See also Loucks (1970), Eisel (1970) and Lane (1973).

R units are released during the season, it is necessary to maximise the expectation

$$E(U) = \sum_{\tau, R, S} U(R_t, Q_\tau) p_{\tau, R, S}$$

This gives an optimum operating policy, conditional to the constraints imposed by the reservoir capacity and minimum storage requirement, and the continuity equation 8.6. The method is in keeping with the broad aims given by figure 8.2.

For other developments of this model such as extension to serially correlated inflows, the work by Buras (1966, references 11, 43) should be consulted. Loucks (1968) following Manne (1960) adopted a LP model for reservoir regulation in which the policy objective was to minimise the squared deviations from the target outflows; transition probabilities in this model represented the net inflows during each of four seasons. Later, Hassitt (1968) extended the work of Loucks to solve the dual problem. Elsewhere, Smith (1973) shows that stochastic LP can play a useful role in irrigation planning.

Simulation has been recognised as a useful tool in operational studies by Joeres *et al.* (1971), who applied LP to the Baltimore multiple-source water supply, and by Jacoby and Loucks (1972) who investigated the Delaware basin in the United States. Amongst others, Loucks and Dorfman (1975) used simulation in the work cited above.

Deterministic LP models were used by Mejía *et al.* (1974) in evaluating the operating rules for the North River system near Montreal, Canada. Elsewhere, various multireservoir operation procedures are discussed by Roefs and Bodin (1970). Amongst other applications, Deininger (1969) showed how LP could be used to estimate the parameters of the unit hydrograph. In addition, Drobny (1971) with an interesting discussion on systems engineering and LP, modelled water quality and quantity. The LP water quality model of Sobel (1965) and the Delaware estuary model of Meta Systems Incorporated (1975) are also of interest.

Another LP algorithm is the zero-one programming method of Balas (1965) in which variables take values of zero and one only; the details of integer programming are given by Garfinkel and Nemhauser (1972).

8.3.7 *Concluding remarks*

As noted, LP was brought about on account of inadequacies in classical methods when applied to large-scale systems, in which constrained problems need to be solved. In practice, however, a linear function and a set of linear constraints can only provide an approximate solution to a problem. Nevertheless, simplicity is its main virtue, and, if treated in the more complicated cases as a preliminary or trial method, LP has great intrinsic value. It has also been recently extended to multiobjective methods. There are innumerable books and papers on the subject[15].

[15] Dantzig (1963) gives 25 pages of references, and many more have been published since then.

8.4 Dynamic programming

Some of the drawbacks in LP led to methods of non-linear programming (which we shall discuss in section 8.5) and to a type of recursive optimisation called dynamic programming (DP). This has the potentiality for providing solutions to a variety of problems in science and industry[16]. Greater flexibility, which means that it is possible to model a complex real world problem with fewer assumptions and the ability which it provides for users to take decisions at every stage are among the main advantages of DP. According to R. Bellman, the sequence of decisions which constitute an optimal policy 'has the property that, whatever the initial state and initial decision are, the remaining decisions must constitute an optimal policy with regard to the state resulting from the first decision'. Bellman's principle of optimality in DP is comparable with the differentiation in calculus (together with the examination of continuity and end conditions).

Basically, the method uses a dynamic recursive relationship

$$f_n(i) = \operatorname*{opt}_k \{u_{n,k} + f_{n-1}(j)\}, \qquad n = 1, 2, \ldots \tag{8.19}$$

Here, $f_n(i)$ is an objective function representing the net cumulative return (or cost) at the end of stage n, given that the system is in state i at the start of this stage. Similarly, $f_{n-1}(j)$ represents the net cumulative return at the end of stage $n-1$ in which the system commences with state j. Variable k denotes a decision made at stage n which results in a net return (or cost) of $u_{n,k}$. The objective is to find the value of k which optimises $f_n(i)$. In the same way, the procedure is repeated successively for other stages. This type of sequential multistage decision making is fundamental to DP.

Note that DP is not restricted to linear objective and constraint functions. Although non-linear programming admits other functions, the policy space bounded by constraints (as shown for a LP application in figure 8.3) need not be convex in DP. It is also possible to build in a form of sensitivity analysis[17]. Functional notation is important in DP, but formulation and algorithms may differ from one case to another. Although the concept seems to be straightforward, application will be difficult if the basic principles are not clearly understood.

8.4.1 *General applications*

Generally, the recursive optimisation in DP is taken backwards in space or time. This means that computations begin with the final stage and proceed towards

---

[16] Bellman (1957) originated DP after outstanding work at the Rand Corporation in the United States during the 1950s; see also Bellman and Dreyfus (1962). The analytical principle of Pontryagin, as for example, used by Nemhauser (1966, pp. 235–9), by Gue and Thomas (1968) or by Rustagi (1976) (also used considerably in control theory) is comparable with DP.

[17] See the general discussion by O'Laoghaire and Himmelblau (1974, chapter 5).

the initial stage. Accordingly, n in equation 8.19 denotes the number of stages remaining, and $f_n(i)$ represents the return or cost at the start of stage n. Alternatively, it is possible to apply forward DP as well[18]. What is sought by these procedures is a set of optimal prior decisions, chosen from several alternatives, that lead to a desirable final state. The fundamental aspects of backward DP can be explained through two examples, the first of which is referred to as the stagecoach problem.

Example 8.4   Figure 8.5 shows the possible routes, with distances in units of 10 km, which a stagecoach can take when travelling from city K to city A. There are 4 stages, and we have to choose between different routes. Through DP, determine the shortest route from K to A.

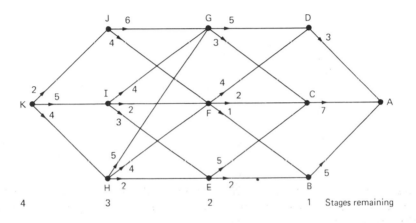

Figure 8.5   Stagecoach problem, example 8.4. Objective is to find the shortest of the prescribed routes from K to A

The problem is worked backwards from A to K, as shown in table 8.2. Because there is only one possible route in the last stage after arrival at B, C or D, stages 1 and 2 are combined in the tabulation. For similar reasons, stage 4 is combined with stage 3. The shortest distance is 12 units through KJFBA as underlined in the table, and this is obtained by following Bellman's rule of optimality[19].

Another case of multistage optimisation is now taken up. Although it would

[18] Forward DP is appropriate to problems of antimissile missiles, aircraft routing and the like as shown, for instance, by Wagner (1975). Note also the examples by Riggs and Inoue (1976, pp. 290, 301). As regards water resource management, see the work of Larson and Keckler (1969).

[19] A similar problem was originally presented by Wagner (1975) at Stanford University. A more general case is that of the travelling salesman (Bellmore and Nemhauser, 1968), who plans to travel by the shortest total distance from city A through n other cities and return to A. This dates back to a seminar talk at Princeton University by Whitney Hassler. Another common trivial example of DP is on choosing a secretary after interviewing several applicants (Wagner, 1975; Norman, 1975).

Table 8.2　Stagecoach problem

Stages remaining	City at start	Route taken (decision)	Distance (benefit or return)	Shortest route (optimal action)	Distance covered by shortest route (benefit)	Distance covered by remaining routes	Total distance to end
2	A	ADG	8	ADG	8	0	8
		ACG	10				
	A	ADF	7				
		ACF	9				
		ABF	6	ABF	6	0	6
	A	ACE	12				
		ABE	7	ACE	7	0	7
4	G	GJK	8	GJK	8	8(ADG)	16
		GIK	9				
		GHK	9				
	F	FJK	6	FJK	6	6(ABF)	12
		FIK	7				
		FHK	8				
	E	EIK	8				
		EHK	6	EHK	6	7(ACE)	13

appear to be a simple one, this practical example is also a useful introduction to the sequential decision making which is basic to DP. As before, the problem is worked backwards in time.

Example 8.5　Formulate a procedure for measuring accurately 2 gallons of water using two tanks of capacity 9 gallons and 5 gallons.

Let L_n and S_n denote the gallons of water in the 9-gallon and 5-gallon tanks respectively when n stages remain to be completed. The L_n and S_n values for $n = 0, 1, 2, \ldots$ are as follows: $L_0 = 0, S_0 = 2; L_1 = 9, S_1 = 2; \underline{L_2 = 6, S_2 = 5}; L_3 = 6, S_3 = 0; \underline{L_4 = 1, S_4 = 5}; L_5 = 1, S_5 = 0; L_6 = 0, S_6 = 1; L_7 = 9, S_7 = 1; \underline{L_8 = 5, S_8 = 5}; L_9 = 5, S_9 = 0; L_{10} = 0, S_{10} = 5.$

Looking backwards in time, the values given to (L_{10}, S_{10}), (L_9, S_9) and (L_8, S_8) mean that the 5-gallon tank is initially full, the contents are then emptied into the 9-gallon tank and the smaller tank is filled again. At the seventh stage (from the terminal one) the 9-gallon tank is filled, without wastage, from the other one, in which 1 gallon will then remain, and at the next stage the large tank is emptied. The rest of the procedure follows. The underlined stages are the more important ones from which the other stages would be obvious[20].

[20] A similar example is given by Nemhauser (1966, pp. 10–14) who based his work on that of Polya (1957, pp. 198–202). For further reading of basic DP formulations, see Shamblin and Stevens (1974, chapter 13), Riggs and Inoue (1976, chapter 10) and also Wagner (1975) whose mammoth book has innumerable 'mind-expanding' problems.

Note that the term stage may mean a point in space or time. However, in the applications of DP to reservoir problems which follow, it exclusively signifies time intervals.

8.4.2 *Application to reservoirs*

Inventory problems constitute an important area where dynamic programming can be applied advantageously. The similarity between reservoir management and inventory theory was recognised in the 1950s. Operation policies can be formulated, by taking into account the probability distribution of inflows, for reservoirs designed for hydropower and other purposes[21].

Further to equation 8.19, a stochastic formulation of DP using discounted benefits or costs is given by

$$f_n(i) = \operatorname*{opt}_{k} \left[E\{u_{n,k} + f_{n-1}(j)/(1+d)\} \right] \tag{8.20}$$

in which E signifies expectation and $f_n(i)$ is the benefit or cost at the start of stage n. Also, $100d$ is the percentage interest rate per unit time and the factor $1 + d$ discounts future benefits (or costs)[22].

When applied to a reservoir of capacity C, say, the states i and j are the levels or storages in the reservoir at the start of stages n and $n - 1$ respectively for $n = 1, 2, 3, \ldots$, the recursive optimisation being made backwards in time. Here, n can be given in quarterly, monthly or other time units. The decision variable k denotes a target release during stage n. The objective is to determine, by using equation 8.20, the optimum release for each stage. For this purpose, it would be necessary to know the seasonal distributions of inflows. However, each of these could be approximated by a set of estimated discrete probabilities $p_{m,x}$, which denote the probability of an inflow x in season m, where m corresponds to n on the time scale, and $x = 1, 2, \ldots, \ell$. This is conditional to $\sum_{x=1}^{\ell} p_{m,x} = 1$. Target releases k are scheduled at the start of each stage n, and the continuity equation $i = j + x - k$ is applied. Note that $0 \leqslant i \leqslant C$ which means that the actual release cannot exceed $j + x$.

An example is given on p. 326 of backward stochastic dynamic programming applied to a conjunctive scheme involving a direct supply reservoir and a borehole supply[23].

---

[21] Little (1955) originally applied the procedure to a hydroelectric system in the Colombia River basin. A similar work is described by Silver *et al.* (1972). There are also publications by W. A. Hall and colleagues concerning deterministic and data generation methods, for example, Hall and Buras (1961), Hall and Howell (1963) and Hall *et al.* (1968).

[22] Thuesen *et al.* (1977, chapter 4), for instance, discuss interest rates.

[23] The formulation and tabulation are similar to the work of Schweig (1968) and Schweig and Cole (1968); the difference is that penalty costs of spills from the reservoir are included and costs of pumping from boreholes is adjusted upwards in winter.

Table 8.3 Example 8.5, backward dynamic programming optimisation

(1)	(2)	(3)	(4)	(5)	(6)	(7)	(8)	(9)	(10)	(11)	(12)	(13)	(14)
Reservoir state i at start of stage 1	Scheduled release from reservoir, $r(R)$	Amount pumped from boreholes, $r(B)$	Cost of releases, $(2)c_r(R)+(3)c_r(B)$	Reservoir In-flow	Proba-bility	Reservoir state $j \leq 3$ at start of stage 0, $j=(1)+(5)-(2)$	Deficits, $\{D(m)-(2)-(3)\}^*+\{(2)-(1)-(5)\}^*$	Expected costs of deficits, $c_d\Sigma(6)\times(8)$	Spills $\{(1)+(5)-(2)-C\}^*$	Expected costs of spills, $c_s\Sigma(6)\times(10)$	Costs from stage 0, $f_0(j)$	Expected costs from stage 0, $(1+d)^{-1}\times\Sigma(6)\times(12)$	Total expected costs, $(4)+(9)+(11)+(13)$
0	0.5	1	20	0.5	0.2	0	1.5	30	0	0	0	0	50
				1	0.5	0.5	1.5		0				
				1.5	0.3	1	1.5		0				
	1	1	24	0.5	0.2	0	1.5	22	0	0	0	0	<u>46</u>
				1	0.5	0	1		0				
				1.5	0.3	0.5	1		0				
	1.5	1	28	0.5	0.2	0	1.5	19	0	0	0	0	47
				1	0.5	0	1		0				
				1.5	0.3	0	0.5		0				
	2	1	32	0.5	0.2	0	1.5	19	0	0	0	0	51
				1	0.5	0	1		0				
				1.5	0.3	0	0.5		0				
1	0.5	1	20	0.5	0.2	1	1.5	30	0	0	0	0	50
				1	0.5	1.5	1.5		0				
				1.5	0.3	2	1.5		0				
	1	1	24	0.5	0.2	0.5	1	20	0	0	0	0	44
				1	0.5	1	1		0				
				1.5	0.3	1.5	1		0				
	1.5	1	28	0.5	0.2	0	0.5	10	0	0	0	0	38
				1	0.5	0.5	0.5						
				1.5	0.3	1	0.5		0				

1	2	3	4	5	6	7	8	9	10	11	12	13	14
2	2	1	32	0.5	0.2	0	0.5	2	0	0	0	0	34
				1	0.5	0	0		0				
				1.5	0.3	0.5	0		0				
	0.5	1	20	0.5	0.2	2	1.5	30	0	0	0	0	50
				1	0.5	2.5	1.5		0				
				1.5	0.3	3	1.5		0				
	1	1	24	0.5	0.2	1.5	1	20	0	0	0	0	44
				1	0.5	2	1		0				
				1.5	0.3	2.5	1		0				
	1.5	1	28	0.5	0.2	1	0.5	10	0	0	0	0	38
				1	0.5	1.5	0.5		0				
				1.5	0.3	2	0.5		0				
	2	1	32	0.5	0.2	0.5	0	0	0	0	0	0	32
				1	0.5	1	0		0				
				1.5	0.3	1.5	0		0				
3	0.5	1	20	0.5	0.2	3	1.5	30	0	5.5	0	0	55.5
				1	0.5	3	1.5		0.5				
				1.5	0.3	3	1.5		1				
	1	1	24	0.5	0.2	2.5	1	20	0	1.5	0	0	45.5
				1	0.5	3	1		0				
				1.5	0.3	3	1		0.5				
	1.5	1	28	0.5	0.2	2	0.5	10	0	0	0	0	38
				1	0.5	2.5	0.5		0				
				1.5	0.3	3	0.5		0				
	2	1	32	0.5	0.2	1.5	0	0	0	0	0	0	32
				1	0.5	2	0		0				
				1.5	0.3	2.5	0		0				

Table represents stage 1, summer (stage 0 is autumn); reservoir capacity $C = 3$; demand $D(m) = 3$. The $f_1(i)$ values are underlined in column 14.

Table 8.4　Example 8.6, backward dynamic programming optimisation

(1)	(2)	(3)	(4)	(5)	(6)	(7)	(8)	(9)	(10)	(11)	(12)	(13)	(14)
Reservoir state i at start of stage 2	Scheduled release from reservoir, $r(R)$	Amount pumped from boreholes, $r(B)$	Cost of releases, $(2)c_r(R) + (3)c_r(B)$	Reservoir In-flow	Reservoir Probability	Reservoir state $j < 3$ at start of stage 1, $j = (1)+(5)-(2)$	Deficits, $\{D(m)-(2)-(3)\}^* + \{(2)-(1)-(5)\}^*$	Expected costs of deficits $c_d \Sigma(6) \times (8)$	Spills $\{(1)+(5)-(2)-C\}^*$	Expected costs of spills, $c_s \Sigma(6) \times (10)$	Costs from stage 1, $f_1(j)$	Expected costs from stage 1 $(1+d)^{-1} \times \Sigma(6) \times (12)$	Total expected costs, $(4)+(9) +(11)+(13)$
0	0.5	1	20	1 1.5 2	0.3 0.4 0.3	0.5 1 1.5	1 1 1	20	0 0 0	0	40 34 33	34.6	74.6
	1	1	24	1 1.5 2	0.3 0.4 0.3	0 0.5 1	0.5 0.5 0.5	10	0 0 0	0	46 40 34	39.0	<u>73.0</u>
	1.5	1	28	1 1.5 2	0.3 0.4 0.3	0 0 0.5	0.5 0 0	3	0 0 0	0	46 46 40	43.1	74.1
	2	0.5	24	1 1.5 2	0.3 0.4 0.3	0 0 0	1 0.5 0	10	0 0 0	0	46 46 46	44.9	78.9
1	0.5	1	20	1 1.5 2	0.3 0.4 0.3	1.5 2 2.5	1 1 1	20	0 0 0	0	33 32 32	31.5	71.5
	1	1	24	1 1.5 2	0.3 0.4 0.3	1 1.5 2	0.5 0.5 0.5	10	0 0 0	0	34 33 32	32.2	76.2
	1.5	1	28	1 1.5 2	0.3 0.4 0.3	0.5 1 1.5	0 0 0	0	0 0 0	0	40 34 33	34.6	<u>62.6</u>

1	2	3	4	5	6	7	8	9	10	11	12	13	14
2	0.5	24	1 / 1.5 / 2	0.3 / 0.4 / 0.3	0 / 0.5 / 1	2.5 / 3 / 3	0 / 0 / 0	0	0 / 0 / 0	0	46 / 40 / 34	39.0	63.0
	1	20	1 / 1.5 / 2	0.3 / 0.4 / 0.3	1 / 1 / 1	2 / 2.5 / 3	0 / 0 / 0	20	0 / 0 / 0.5	.5	32 / 32 / 32	31.2	72.7
	1	24	1 / 1.5 / 2	0.3 / 0.4 / 0.3	0.5 / 0.5 / 0.5	1.5 / 2 / 2.5	0 / 0 / 0	10	0 / 0 / 0	0	32 / 32 / 32	31.2	75.2
	1.5	28	1 / 1.5 / 2	0.3 / 0.4 / 0.3	0 / 0 / 0	1 / 1.5 / 2	0 / 0 / 0	0	0 / 0 / 0	0	33 / 32 / 32	31.5	59.5
	2	24	1 / 1.5 / 2	0.3 / 0.4 / 0.3	0 / 0 / 0	3 / 3 / 3	0 / 0 / 0	0	0 / 0 / 0	0	34 / 33 / 32	32.2	<u>56.2</u>
3	0.5	20	1 / 1.5 / 2	0.3 / 0.4 / 0.3	1 / 1 / 1	3 / 3 / 3	1 / 1 / 1	20	0.5 / 1 / 1.5	10	32 / 32 / 32	31.2	81.2
	1	24	1 / 1.5 / 2	0.3 / 0.4 / 0.3	0.5 / 0.5 / 0.5	2.5 / 3 / 3	0.5 / 0.5 / 0.5	10	0 / 0.5 / 1	5	32 / 32 / 32	31.2	70.2
	1.5	28	1 / 1.5 / 2	0.3 / 0.4 / 0.3	0 / 0 / 0	2 / 2.5 / 3	0 / 0 / 0	0	0 / 0 / 0.5	1.5	32 / 32 / 32	31.2	60.7
	2	24	1 / 1.5 / 2	0.3 / 0.4 / 0.3	0 / 0 / 0	2 / 2.5 / 3	0 / 0 / 0	0	0 / 0 / 0	0	32 / 32 / 32	31.2	<u>55.2</u>

Table represents stage 2, spring (stage 1 is summer); reservoir capacity $C = 3$; demand $D(m) = 2.5$. The $f_2(i)$ values are underlined in column 14.

Table 8.5 Example 8.6, backward dynamic programming optimisation

(1)	(2)	(3)	(4)	(5)	(6)	(7)	(8)	(9)	(10)	(11)	(12)	(13)	(14)
Reservoir state i at start of stage 3	Scheduled release from reservoir, $r(R)$	Amount pumped from boreholes, $r(B)$	Cost of releases, $(2)c_r(R) + (3)c_r(B)$	Reservoir In-flow	Proba-bility	Reservoir state $j < 3$ at start of stage 2, $j = (1)+(5)-(2)$	Deficits, $\{D(m)-(2)-(3)\}^*$ $+\{(2)-(1)-(5)\}^*$	Expected costs of deficits, $c_d\Sigma(6)\times(8)$	Spills, $\{(1)+(5)-(2)-C\}^*$	Expected costs of spills, $c_s\Sigma(6)\times(10)$	Costs from stage 2, $f_2(j)$	Expected costs from stage 2, $(1+d)^{-1}\times\Sigma(6)\times(12)$	Total expected costs, $(4)+(9)+(11)+(13)$
0	0.5	0.5	14	2 2.5 3	0.2 0.3 0.5	1.5 2 2.5	0 0 0	0	0 0 0	0	59.4 56.2 55.7	55.2	69.2
	1	0	8	2 2.5 3	0.2 0.3 0.5	1 1.5 2	0 0 0	0	0 0 0	0	62.6 59.4 56.2	57.0	65.0
1	0.5	0.5	14	2 2.5 3	0.2 0.3 0.5	2.5 3 3	0 0 0	0	0 0 0.5	2.5	55.7 55.2 55.2	54.0	70.5
	1	0	8	2 2.5 3	0.2 0.3 0.5	2 2.5 3	0 0 0	0	0 0 0	0	56.2 55.7 55.2	54.2	62.2
2	0.5	0.5	14	2 2.5 3	0.2 0.3 0.5	3 3 3	0 0 0	0	0.5 1 1.5	11.5	55.2 55.2 55.2	53.9	79.4
	1	0	8	2 2.5 3	0.2 0.3 0.5	3 3 3	0 0 0	0	0 0.5 1	6.5	55.2 55.2 55.2	53.9	68.4

3	0.5	0.5	14	2	0.2	3	0	0	1.5	21.5	55.2	53.9	89.4
				2.5	0.3	3	0		2		55.2		
				3	0.5	3	0		2.5		55.2		
1	0		8	2	0.2	3	0	0	1	16.5	55.2	53.9	78.4
				2.5	0.3	3	0		1.5		55.2		
				3	0.5	3	0		2		55.2		

Table represents stage 3, winter (stage 2 is spring); reservoir capacity $C = 3$; demand $D(m) = 1$. The $f_3(i)$ values are underlined in column 14.

Table 8.6 Example 8.6, backward dynamic programming optimisation

(1)	(2)	(3)	(4)	(5)	(6)	(7)	(8)	(9)	(10)	(11)	(12)	(13)	(14)
Reservoir state i at start of stage 4	Amount released from reservoir, $r(R)$	Amount pumped from boreholes, $r(B)$	Cost of releases, $(2)c_r(R) + (3)c_t(B)$	Reservoir In-flow	Proba-bility	Reservoir state $j < 3$ at start of stage 3, $j = (1) + (5) - (2)$	Deficits, $\{D(m) - (2) - (3)\} + \{(2) - (1) - (5)\}^*$	Expected costs of deficits, $c_d\Sigma(6) \times (8)$	Spills, $\{(1) + (5) - (2) - C\}^*$	Expected costs of spills, $c_s\Sigma(6) \times (10)$	Costs from stage 3, $f_3(j)$	Expected costs from stage 3, $(1 + d)^{-1} \times \Sigma(6) \times (12)$	Total expected costs, $(4) + (9) + (11) + (13)$
0	0.5	1.0	20	1	0.3	0.5	0	0	0	0	63.6	62.3	82.3
				1.5	0.3	1	0		0		62.2		
				2	0.4	1.5	0		0		65.3		
	1	0.5	16	1	0.3	0	0	0	0	0	65.0	61.9	77.9
				1.5	0.3	0.5	0		0		63.6		
				2	0.4	1	0		0		62.2		
	1.5	0	12	1	0.3	0	0.5	3	0	0	65.0	62.9	77.9
				1.5	0.3	0	0		0		65.0		
				2	0.4	0.5	0		0		63.6		
1	0.5	1.0	20	1	0.3	1.5	0	0	0	0	65.3	67.8	87.8
				1.5	0.3	2	0		0		68.4		
				2	0.4	2.5	0		0		73.4		
	1	0.5	16	1	0.3	1	0	0	0	0	62.2	64.0	80.0
				1.5	0.3	1.5	0		0		65.3		
				2	0.4	2	0		0		68.4		
	1.5	0	12	1	0.3	0.5	0	0	0	0	63.6	62.3	74.3
				1.5	0.3	1	0		0		62.2		
				2	0.4	1.5	0		0		65.3		

2	0.5	1.0	20	1	0.3	2.5	0	0	0	2	73.4	75.0	97.0
				1.5	0.3	3	0		0		78.4		
				2	0.4	3	0		0.5		78.4		
	1	0.5	16	1	0.3	2	0	0	0	0	68.4	72.1	88.1
				1.5	0.3	2.5	0		0		73.4		
				2	0.4	3	0		0		78.4		
	1.5	0	12	1	0.3	1.5	0	0	0	0	65.3	67.8	79.8
				1.5	0.3	2	0		0		68.4		
				2	0.4	2.5	0		0		73.5		
3	0.5	1	20	1	0.3	3	0	0	0.5	10.5	78.4	76.5	107
				1.5	0.3	3	0		1		78.4		
				2	0.4	3	0		1.5		78.4		
	1	0.5	16	1	0.3	3	0	0	0	5.5	78.4	76.5	98
				1.5	0.3	3	0		0.5		78.4		
				2	0.4	3	0		1		78.4		
	1.5	0	12	1	0.3	2.5	0	0	0	2	73.4	75.0	89
				1.5	0.3	3	0		0		78.4		
				2	0.4	3	0		0.5		78.4		

Table represents stage 4, autumn (stage 3 is winter); reservoir capacity $C = 3$; demand $D(m) = 1.5$. The $f_4(t)$ values are underlined in column 14.

Example 8.6   Probabilities of seasonal reservoir inflows are tabulated below with seasonal demands $D(m)$. The effective capacity C of the reservoir is 3 units, and the total release $r(R)$ from the reservoir during a season should be one of the following units: 0.5, 1, 1.5, 2. The conjuctive borehole supply has a maximum output $r(B)$ of 1 unit with possibilities of closure or supplying 0.5 unit.

The cost $c_r(R)$ of supplying from the reservoir is 8 in monetary units and that from the borehole $c_r(B)$ is 16 units during spring, summer and autumn and 20 units in winter. The cost c_d of deficits and the penalty c_s for spills are 20 and 10 units respectively. All costs are per unit volume.

Formulate an optimal operating policy given a discount rate of 10% per annum.

Parameter	Value for season, $m =$			
	Summer, 1	Spring, 2	Winter, 3	Autumn, 4
Inflow x	0.5 1.0 1.5	1 1.5 2	2 2.5 3	1 1.5 2
Probability $p_{m, x}$	0.2 0.5 0.3	0.3 0.4 0.3	0.2 0.3 0.5	0.3 0.3 0.4
Demand $D(m)$	3	2.5	1	1.5

The objective is to optimise recursively

$$f_n(i) = \min[p_{m, x}\{r(R)c_r(R) + r(B)c_r(B) + DF c_d + SP c_s$$

$$+ (1 + d)^{-1}f_{n-1}(j)\}] \tag{8.21}$$

in which DF and SP denote deficit (in meeting the demand) and spill from the reservoir respectively during the nth stage.

The procedure can be followed from tables 8.3 to 8.6. Note that, because this is a backward optimisation, n denotes the number of stages remaining. Given a reservoir state i at the start of stage n, the target releases are $k = r(R) + r(B)$ from the reservoir and boreholes respectively; these and costs are given in columns 1, 2, 3 and 4. The release $r(R)$ will not be met if the reservoir inflow x is inadequate. On the other hand, k may be less than the demand $D(m)$. In either case, a deficit DF is incurred as given in column 8; the asterisks signify that the terms within the parentheses should be ignored if their sum is negative. Also, inflows, probabilities and reservoir states at the end of the stage are given in columns 5, 6 and 7 respectively. Again, if $i + x - r(R) > C$, the reservoir spills by an amount given in column 10. In addition, columns 9 and 11 give the expected costs of deficits and spills which are determined by using the probabilities of inflows.

Entries in column 12 need further explanation. First, consider table 8.3 for stage 1. For initial reservoir states $i = 0, 1, 2$ and 3 units, the minimum expected costs $f_1(i) = 46, 34, 32$ and 32 units respectively are underlined in column 14; the corresponding releases in columns 2 and 3, which are optimal, are entered subsequently in table 8.3. Furthermore, the pairs of entries in columns 1 and 14 (underlined) of table 8.3 are used in table 8.4 for stage 2. To understand this, consider columns 7 and 12 in table 8.4. On account of the backward optimisation, column 1 of table 8.3 corresponds to column 7 of table 8.4. Therefore, the first entry 40 in column 12 of table 8.4 which tallies with a reservoir state 0.5 in column 7 is obtained by interpolation from the underlined values 46 and 34 in table 8.3 which correspond to initial states of 0 and 1 respectively. The next entry of 34 in column 12 of table 8.4 follows directly; the third entry of 33, for a reservoir state 1.5, is the result of an interpolation between the values 34 and 32 for initial states of 1 and 3 respectively. The rest of column 12 is obtained in the same way.

By using the discount rate d, entries in column 13 are obtained from the values in columns 6 and 12; here, d is taken as one-quarter of the annual rate. Finally, the cumulative costs are given in column 14. The procedure is repeated in tables 8.5 and 8.6. These optimal policies are shown in table 8.7 for the example given. Note that the given policies are related to the reservoir state at the start of the season. In practice, the procedure should be repeated for additional years of operation, until steady optimal policies are obtained. Under these limiting or stationary conditions, there is a set of optimal releases that minimises costs.

Table 8.7 Example 8.6, optimal policies

Initial state	Releases from reservoir and boreholes = for season, m, D(m) stated							
	$r(R)$ $r(B)$ Summer, 1, 3.0		$r(R)$ $r(B)$ Spring, 2, 2.5		$r(R)$ $r(B)$ Winter, 3, 1.0		$r(R)$ $r(B)$ Autumn, 4, 1.5	
	$r(R)$	$r(B)$	$r(R)$	$r(B)$	$r(R)$	$r(B)$	$r(R)$	$r(B)$
0	1	1	1	1	1	0	1.5	0
1	2	1	1.5	1	1	0	1.5	0
2	2	1	2	0.5	1	0	1.5	0
3	2	1	2	0.5	1	0	1.5	0

The most important information which follows from this analysis is regarding the target releases $r(B)$ from the more costly borehole supply and the releases $r(R)$ from the reservoir in the summer and spring when the initial state is 0.

8.4.3 Dynamic programming with Markov chains

In the previous example, the probabilities of reservoir inflows were used directly in order to obtain the expected values of the objective function. A more logical approach is to weight the recursive dynamic equation with transition probabilities that represent the possible underlying Markov property of the reservoir states (as explained in chapter 7) and hence to replace the unconditional probabilities of reservoir inflows used in the previous example. The objective of these methods is the solution of the steady state problem. For this purpose a matrix of maximum benefits or minimum costs, which gives a set of optimal controls called the policy, is determined[24]. It is assumed that the process is ergodic which means, as noted in chapter 7, that all states communicate and steady state probabilities exist.

In this formulation, the problem considered is one of maximising benefits. Also, backward DP is used. The recursive equation takes the form

$$f_n(i) = \max_k \left\{ b_{n,k} + \sum_{j=0}^{\ell} q_{n,k}(i, j) f_{n-1}(j) \right\} \tag{8.22}$$

in which $f_n(i)$ is the expected benefit at the start of the nth stage under an optimal policy, given that the storage at the start of the stage is i units. Similarly, $f_{n-1}(j)$ denotes the expected benefit, under an optimal policy at the start of the $(n-1)$th stage when the reservoir is in state j. Also, the probability of a storage j in the reservoir at the end of the nth stage, conditional to a storage i at its start is given by $q_{n,k}(i, j)$ in which k denotes the release made during the stage. Furthermore, $b_{n,k}$ is the benefit from releasing k units in stage n. The objective is to find a sequence of optimum target releases by using equation 8.22 and the continuity relationship $j = i + x - k$, in which x denotes the reservoir inflow during the nth stage. The last equation is again conditional to the maximum and minimum limits.

Example 8.7   A reservoir of capacity 3 units is to be constructed to supply variable domestic, industrial and irrigation demands. The benefits or return $b_{m,k}$ in season m when k units of water (1 unit $= 10^6$ m³) are released during the season are given below in monetary units; the variables m (where $m = 1, 2, 3, 4$) correspond respectively to n (where $n = 1, 2, 3, 4, \ldots$) in equation 8.22.

Target release k	Benefits $b_{m,k}$ for season, m =			
	Winter, 1	Autumn, 2	Summer, 3 .	Spring, 4
1	1	1	1	1
2	2	2	4	3
3	2	3	5	4
4	2	3	6	5

[24] The credit for this goes to Howard (1960) who, in an elegant book in which complicated subject matter is made to appear simple, presents the problem of the toymaker and the often-quoted case study of automobile replacements as, for example, used by Norman (1972). His methods have been used in stochastic inventory and similar applications by Nemhauser (1966), Wagner (1975) and others. Also a Markovian decision procedure is applied to a multipurpose reservoir by Hillier and Lieberman (1974, pp. 561–6).

The probabilities of reservoir inflows x are listed below for the 4 seasons.

Inflow x	Probabilities of reservoir inflows for season, $m =$			
	Winter, 1	Autumn, 2	Summer, 3	Spring, 4
0	0	0.1	0.2	0
1	0.2	0.4	0.5	0.3
2	0.3	0.4	0.3	0.4
3	0.5	0.1	0	0.3

Formulate an optimal operational policy for the reservoir so that the storage at the end of winter is at least 2 units. This minimum storage is desirable for the operation of hydroelectric plants and for recreation purposes. The resulting benefits are 4 units.

The computations are given in tables 8.8 to 8.11. On account of the requirement to maintain a level in the reservoir of 2 or 3 units at the start of spring or end of winter, the $f_{n-1}(j)$ values in table 8.8 are equated to 0, 0, 4 and 4 units respectively. (The last two values form part of the given data.) The one-step transition probabilities $q_{n,k}(i,j)$ of reservoir states follow from the tabulated inflow probabilities, the procedure being the same as in example 7.2. For each combination of i and k, the sums of the products in columns 3, 4, 5 and 6 are given in column 7. Benefits from releases during season m (column 8), as given in the data, are then added to give the total benefits in column 9. The optimal release k is underlined in column 2. The values in column 10 of table 8.8 are the benefits at the start of winter under an optimal policy (which is obtained by working backwards, as explained, from the stipulated conditions at the start of spring). This vector of benefits is transposed and entered in columns 3, 4, 5 and 6 of table 8.9 for stage 2 (autumn). These values are then multiplied by the corresponding transition probabilities. The procedure used in table 8.8 is repeated to complete table 8.9, and tables 8.10 and 8.11 are obtained in the same way. On account of the required storage at the end of winter, values of i equal to 2 and 3 only are considered in table 8.11 for stage 4 (spring). Finally, the optimal policies are listed in table 8.12. As in the previous example, these are conditional to initial reservoir states.

A choice of releases is given in some cases because the differences between the corresponding values for total benefits, in column 9 of tables 8.8 to 8.11 are insignificant. The values in parentheses in table 8.12 for spring are hypothetical.

8.4.4 Assumptions and limitations in dynamic programming

A common assumption in the two examples given is that inflows are not serially correlated. This may not be unreasonable for seasonal flows in some rivers. Other problems may necessitate different approaches, and in this respect the

Table 8.8 Example 8.7, backward dynamic programming using Markov chains

(1) Reservoir state at start of stage 1	(2) Amount released in stage 1	(3)	(4)	(5)	(6)	(7) Total expected benefits at start of stage 0, (3)+(4) +(5)+(6)	(8) Benefits from releases in stage 1, $b_{1,k}$	(9) Total expected benefits at start of stage 1, (7)+(8)	(10) Benefits from column 9 with optimal actions, $f_1(i)$
		— Expected benefits at start of stage 0, $q_{1,k}(i,j)f_0(j)$, with reservoir state j at start of stage 0							
		$j=0$	$j=1$	$j=2$	$j=3$				
$i=0$	$k=1$	0.2×0	0.3×0	0.5×4	0×4	2.0	1	3.0	3.0
	$k=2$	0.3×0	0.5×0	0×4	0×4	0	2	2.0	
	$k=3$	0.5×0	0×0	0×4	0×4	0	2	2.0	
	$k=4$	0×0	0×0	0×4	0×4	0	2	2.0	
$i=1$	$k=1$	0×0	0.2×0	0.3×4	0.5×4	3.2	1	4.2	4.2
	$k=2$	0.2×0	0.3×0	0.5×4	0×4	2.0	2	4.0	
	$k=3$	0.3×0	0.5×0	0×4	0×4	0	2	2.0	
	$k=4$	0.5×0	0×0	0×4	0×4	0	2	2.0	
$i=2$	$k=1$	0×0	0×0	0.2×4	0.8×4	4.0	1	5.0	5.2
	$k=2$	0×0	0.2×0	0.3×4	0.5×4	3.2	2	5.2	
	$k=3$	0.2×0	0.3×0	0.5×4	0×4	2.0	2	4.0	
	$k=4$	0.3×0	0×0	0×4	0×4	0	2	2.0	
$i=3$	$k=1$	0×0	0×0	0.0×4	1.0×4	4.0	1	5.0	6.0
	$k=2$	0×0	0×0	0.2×4	0.8×4	4.0	2	6.0	
	$k=3$	0×0	0.2×0	0.3×4	0.5×4	3.2	2	5.2	
	$k=4$	0.2×0	0.3×0	0.5×4	0×4	2.0	2	4.0	

Table represents stage 1, winter (stage 0 is spring).

Table 8.9 Example 8.7, backward dynamic programming using Markov chains

(1)	(2)	(3)	(4)	(5)	(6)	(7)	(8)	(9)	(10)
Reservoir state at start of stage 2	Amount released in stage 2	Expected benefits at start of stage 1, $q_{2,k}(i,j)f_1(j)$, with reservoir state j at start of stage 1				Total expected benefits at start of stage 1, (3)+(4)+(5)+(6)	Benefits from releases in stage 2, $b_{2,k}$	Total expected benefits at start of stage 2, (7)+(8)	Benefits from column 9 with optimal actions, $f_2(i)$
		$j=0$	$j=1$	$j=2$	$j=3$				
$i=0$	$k=1$	0.4×3	0.4×4.2	0.1×5.2	0×6	3.40	1	4.40	4.40
	$k=2$	0.4×3	0.1×4.2	0×5.2	0×6	1.62	2	3.62	
	$k=3$	0.1×3	0×4.2	0×5.2	0×6	0.30	3	3.30	
$i=1$	$k=1$	0.1×3	0.4×4.2	0.4×5.2	0.1×6	4.66	1	5.66	5.66
	$k=2$	0.4×3	0.4×4.2	0.1×5.2	0×6	3.40	2	5.40	
	$k=3$	0.4×3	0.1×4.2	0×5.2	0×6	1.62	3	4.62	
	$k=4$	0.1×3	0×4.2	0×5.2	0×6	0.30	3	3.30	
$i=2$	$k=1$	0×3	0.1×4.2	0.4×5.2	0.5×6	5.50	1	6.50	6.66
	$k=2$	0.1×3	0.4×4.2	0.4×5.2	0.1×6	4.66	2	6.66	
	$k=3$	0.4×3	0.4×4.2	0.1×5.2	0×6	3.40	3	6.40	
	$k=4$	0.4×3	0.1×4.2	0×5.2	0×6	1.62	3	4.62	
$i=3$	$k=1$	0×3	0×4.2	0.1×5.2	0.9×6	5.92	1	6.92	7.66
	$k=2$	0×3	0.1×4.2	0.4×5.2	0.5×6	5.50	2	7.50	
	$k=3$	0.1×3	0.4×4.2	0.4×5.2	0.1×6	4.66	3	7.66	
	$k=4$	0.4×3	0.4×4.2	0.1×5.2	0×6	3.40	3	6.40	

Table represents stage 2, autumn (stage 1 is winter).

Table 8.10   Example 8.7, backward dynamic programming using Markov chains

(1)	(2)	(3)	(4)	(5)	(6)	(7)	(8)	(9)	(10)
Reservoir state at start of stage 3	Amount released in state 3	Expected benefits at start of stage 2, $q_{3,k}(i,j)f_2(j)$, with reservoir stage j at start of stage 2				Total expected benefits at start of stage 2, (3)+(4)+(5)+(6)	Benefits from releases in stage 3, $b_{3,k}$	Total expected benefits at start of stage 3, (7)+(8)	Benefits from column 9 with optimal actions, $f_3(i)$
		$j=0$	$j=1$	$j=2$	$j=3$				
$i=0$	$k=1$	0.5×4.40	0.3×5.66	0×6.66	0×7.66	3.90	1	4.90	5.32
	$k=2$	0.3×4.40	0×5.66	0×6.66	0×7.66	1.32	4	5.32	
$i=1$	$k=1$	0.2×4.40	0.5×5.66	0.3×6.66	0×7.66	5.71	1	6.71	7.90
	$k=2$	0.5×4.40	0.3×5.66	0×6.66	0×7.66	3.90	4	7.90	
	$k=3$	0.3×4.40	0×5.66	0×6.66	0×7.66	1.32	5	6.32	
	$k=4$	0×4.40	0×5.66	0×6.66	0×7.66	0	6		
$i=2$	$k=1$	0×4.40	0.2×5.66	0.5×6.66	0.3×7.66	6.76	1	7.76	9.71
	$k=2$	0.2×4.40	0.5×5.66	0.3×6.66	0×7.66	5.71	4	9.71	
	$k=3$	0.5×4.40	0.3×5.66	0×6.66	0×7.66	3.90	5	8.90	
	$k=4$	0.3×4.40	0×5.66	0×6.66	0×7.66	1.32	6	7.32	
$i=3$	$k=1$	0×4.40	0×5.66	0.2×6.66	0.8×7.66	7.46	1	8.46	10.76
	$k=2$	0×4.40	0.2×5.66	0.5×6.66	0.3×7.66	6.76	4	10.76	
	$k=3$	0.2×4.40	0.5×5.66	0.3×6.66	0×7.66	5.71	5	10.71	
	$k=4$	0.5×4.40	0.3×5.66	0×6.66	0×7.66	3.90	6	9.90	

Table represents stage 3, summer (stage 2 is autumn).

Table 8.11 Example 8.7, backward dynamic programming using Markov chains

(1) Reservoir state at start of stage 4	(2) Amount released in stage 4	(3)	(4)	(5)	(6)	(7) Total expected benefits at start of stage 3, (3)+(4)+(5)+(6)	(8) Benefits from releases in stage 4, $b_{4,k}$	(9) Total expected benefits at start of stage 4, (7)+(8)	(10) Benefits from column 9 with optimal actions, $f_4(i)$
		Expected benefits at start of stage 3, $q_{4,k}(i,j)f_3(j)$, with reservoir state j at start of stage 3							
		$j=0$	$j=1$	$j=2$	$j=3$				
$i=2$	$k=1$	0×5.32	0×7.90	0.3×9.71	0.7×10.76	10.45	1	11.45	12.48
	$k=2$	0×5.32	0.3×7.90	0.4×9.71	0.3×10.76	9.48	3	12.48	
	$k=3$	0.3×5.32	0.4×7.90	0.3×9.71	0×10.76	7.67	4	11.67	
	$k=4$	0.4×5.32	0.3×7.90	0×9.71	0×10.76	4.50	5	9.50	
$i=3$	$k=1$	0×5.32	0×7.90	0×9.71	1.0×10.76	10.76	1	11.76	13.48
	$k=2$	0×5.32	0×7.90	0.3×9.71	0.7×10.76	10.45	3	13.45	
	$k=3$	0×5.32	0.3×7.90	0.4×9.71	0.3×10.76	9.48	4	13.48	
	$k=4$	0.3×5.32	0.4×7.90	0.3×9.71	0×10.76	7.67	5	12.67	

Table represents stage 4, spring (stage 3 is summer).

Table 8.12   Example 8.7, target releases under an optimal policy

Initial state	Target release for season =			
	Winter	Autumn	Summer	Spring
0	1	1	2	(0)
1	1	1	2	(1)
2	2	2	2	2
3	2	3	2 or 3	2 or 3

flexibility of DP techniques is a great advantage. However, difficulties may arise in assessing costs, benefits, utilities and the like. In the examples given, the number of reservoir states and discrete inflow probabilities are reduced to a minimum so that the numerical solutions given could be followed. Elsewhere, the dimensions should be increased to suit practical purposes. It would also be necessary to formulate computer programmes[25].

One possible deterrent in DP methods is the large amount of computer time required, which increases drastically when problem dimensions are increased[26]. Even if solutions which are obviously non-optimal are excluded, DP evaluations could take considerable time. Another prohibitive requirement might be excessive storage space or memory; for example, given 10 states and 10 decisions, a storage of $(10^{10})^{10}$ may be required. In this context the methods developed by Larson (1968) for high-dimensional problems are of importance.

8.4.5   Further developments

The significance of Howard's value iteration backward recurrence relationship has been noted. Mawer and Thorn (1974) applied the procedure to water resource systems including desalination plants and pumped storage reservoirs. They also used simulation procedures and discussed the effects of errors due to neglecting serial correlation of inflows. Markov chain transition probabilities were used by Dudley and Burt (1973) in the management of an irrigation reservoir; here, acreages irrigated and the distribution system are variable; so too are reservoir capacities. Other examples of Howard's stochastic approach to DP, as applied to a hydroelectric scheme, are given by Jovanovic (1967), and in a less mathematical paper by Butcher (1971). The operational policy is such that the long average reward of the system is maximised.

At an elementary and instructive level, Meredith et al. (1973, pp. 309–25) give two examples of DP: one concerns an irrigation distribution system, and the

[25] See, for example, Kuester and Mize (1973), who include LP and non-linear programming methods, and Himmelblau (1972).
[26] For example, in the travelling salesman problem, if 16 cities are to be visited Nemhauser (1966) reckons that a high-speed computer will take 20 years to enumerate all solutions!

other is a reservoir operation problem. Elsewhere, several studies on the conjunctive use of ground- and surface-water sources have been made. In addition to the work already cited by Schweig and Cole (1968) and Buras (1966), the optimisation of combined resources in a part of California was investigated by Aron and Scott (1971). Again, there is the original Monte Carlo DP procedure of Young (1967) in which he found reservoir operating rules using data generation.

There have been numerous applications with regard to water quality. A DP approach to meeting dissolved oxygen standards in a stream is presented by Liebman and Lynn (1966); a comparable water quality improvement LP model is applied to water quality control by Sobel (1965). Again in the same field, Orlob and Dendy (1973) made a more general study on the systems approach to water quality management. However, because of the nature of the parameters involved, applications are comparatively difficult.

A reliability constraint in DP was introduced by Askew (1974); this was called chance-constrained dynamic programming, but it admittedly lacked the elegance of that used in LP. Reliability constraints pertaining to system performance are generally based either on the number of failures during a given period (for example, the number of years in which the supply cannot meet the target or scheduled release) or on the probability of one or more failures. Askew applied the technique to annual data using an algorithm similar to the one in example 8.5, and the average number of failures was counted for each of 36 systems after simulation. However, the various penalties that were added whenever the constraints were violated do not necessarily indicate optimum operating policies; Sniedovich and Davis (1975) thought that the imposition of a penalty function leads to suboptimal solutions. Klemeš (1975) suggested the use of an 'optimum reliability' as a decision parameter and direct methods (as in chapter 7) for calculating the probability of failure over a specified period. Askew (1975) also tried variable discount factors in place of penalties. In the same area, Rossman (1977) reformulated the problem using Lagrange functions and dual variables. More recently, Sniedovich (1978) studied five types of reliability constraints; although probabilistic constraints were feasible within a DP framework, he advocated caution when dealing with the expectation of the total number of failures or the probability of one or more failures.

Multiple-reservoir systems are optimised by Becker and Yeh (1974) who combined LP and DP in the application to the Shasta–Trinity system in California's Central Valley project; earlier work on this is explained by Fults and Hancock (1972). Also, Liu and Tedrow (1973) investigated the operation of eight major lakes and a canal in the Oswego River system of New York state. Garcia (1974) examines a three-reservoir system. Amongst the most instructive, in spite of its simplifications, is the paper by Larson and Keckler (1969) who applied DP to a pumped storage scheme, a four-reservoir system, 1-year management of a reservoir with stochastic variations of inflows and an optimal 30-year plan for a system that involves interest rates. Case studies with numerical solutions are also presented by Butcher et al. (1969). These authors include discount rates in their DP formulation in common with Hall and Howell (1963), who had also suggested a combination of DP and data generation, and with others.

8.5 Other methods of systems engineering

Other methods of system engineering are considered here. On account of limitations in space, the treatment given is brief. For detailed explanations and examples, reference should be made to some of the publications cited.

Non-linear programming methods deal with functions and constraints that are not linear. One of the well-known methods of solving non-linear problems is through gradient methods. By referring to figure 8.1, the basic idea here is to commence with a starting point and to obtain a series of points which are successively on the steepest gradients on a path to the maximum point. Although we expect non-linear models to be more representative than their linear counterparts, computational problems may limit their use[27].

Quadratic programming (QP) is a general programming method, applicable to many optimisation problems, of which LP is a special case. The objective function is non-linear and, with the notation of equation 8.1, it takes the form

$$U = AX + X^T BX \tag{8.23}$$

in which

$$B = \begin{bmatrix} b_{11} & \cdot & \cdot & \cdot & b_{1\ell} \\ \cdot & \cdot & \cdot & \cdot & \cdot \\ \cdot & \cdot & \cdot & \cdot & \cdot \\ \cdot & \cdot & \cdot & \cdot & \cdot \\ b_{\ell 1} & \cdot & \cdot & \cdot & b_{\ell\ell} \end{bmatrix} \tag{8.24}$$

A practical problem is solved iteratively by assuming different forms of the quadratic objective function. The constraints are, however, linear as in LP.

Geometric programming (GP) is a comparatively modern method of non-linear optimisation. In this case, the function to be optimised has a form similar to $\sum_{i=1}^{m} a_i \sum_{j=1}^{m} x_j^{k_{ij}}$ with non-linear constraints. The dual problem is solved here; the reasoning behind it is that because, for example, the mean of two numbers is

[27] Lee and Waziruddin (1970) make a comparative study of non-linear methods in their application to a three-reservoir system; see also O'Laoghaire and Himmelblau (1974). Non-linear programming methods are explained, for example, by Churchman et al. (1957), by Himmelblau (1972), by Taha (1976) and by Cooper and Steinberg (1970). For practical cases with non-linear constraints and objective functions in water resources engineering with economic considerations, see Dorfman (1962).

greater than (or equal to) their geometric mean it is convenient to transform a primal problem with non-linear constraints to a dual problem with linear constraints; the procedure is called geometric programming for the same reason[28]. However, the method has not yet found favour in water resources engineering but has been used, for example, in structural applications such as for the optimisation of industrial buildings.

Another field which has not been fully explored for application to water resource problems is the theory of games. This has been developed to optimise strategies when there is a conflict of interests and a choice for action, but information may be incomplete. To explain a simple case, in a two-person zero-sum game between players A and B (who may be, for example, countries) amounts to be paid by B to A are entered in a matrix with negative values, indicating that payment is from A to B. Each play ends when a row and column are chosen by A and B respectively; the resulting payment is given by the entry which is common to both. Here, zero sum signifies that the net sum of payments between A and B is zero. When the minimum of the maximum entries in the columns (which is the basis of von Neumann's minimax theorem) coincides with the maximum of the minimum entries in the rows a saddle point occurs. This shows the optimum strategy for A and B. If such a condition does not hold, the game is said to be non-strictly determined; A and B should then play the rows and columns on a chosen probability basis to maximise returns[29].

With the advances and expansions during the second half of this century, large-scale systems are being planned and designed. There is, consequently, a greater need for taking account of political, sociological, technological and environmental aspects, in addition to economic considerations. For such purposes, multiobjective and multipurpose methods in planning and management are required. The approach involves a vector of objective functions (representing, for example, target yields, reliabilities, capital expenditure, operation costs and so on) rather than a simplified single function. A new

[28] Duffin et al. (1967) were the pioneers. According to Wilde and Beightler (1967) 'geometric programming is one of the most refreshing developments in optimisation theory since the invention of the calculus'. Details of QP and GP are given by Gue and Thomas (1968), by Siddall (1972), by Gottfried and Weisman (1973) and by White et al. (1974). The problems given by Taha (1976, chapter 6) are particularly instructive. Computer programmes given, for example, by Kuester and Mize (1973) are an essential requirement.

[29] See, for example, the elementary text by Carlson and Misshauk (1972), the explanations given in the Encyclopaedia Brittanica (1977) and the hilarious games of Williams (1966). Other references are Churchman et al. (1957), Nemhauser (1966) and Maki and Thompson (1973). A game theory approach with LP is given by Rogers (1969) for cooperative action between India and Bangladesh, in the lower Ganges and Brahmaputra; see also Meta Systems Incorporated (1975). A metagame is a further development in which the likely reactions of a player to the other player's choice of strategies is investigated by a non-numerical method; Hipel et al. (1974) present methods for resolving (a) water quality conflicts amongst adjoining cities and (b) water allocation disputes between neighbouring countries. On the other hand, economists Tintner and Sengupta (1972, p. 11) are sceptical about the practicability of game theory.

method of finding an optimum policy here is the so-called surrogate worth trade-off (SWT) in which the interaction between executives and system analysts is minimised. In this method the trade-off values of marginal losses and gains between pairs of objectives are assessed whilst collectively enumerating all the objective functions[30].

Finally, it is appropriate here to return to simulation methods which have gained acceptance in water resource engineering. These could supplement optimisation techniques, they could provide information on systems behaviour or they could serve as a form of verification of system models. As mentioned, it is mainly on account of the difficulties in finding analytical solutions that simulation has been used in planning and design[31].

8.6 General comments

The treatment and examples in this chapter have been simplified to serve introductory purposes. However, in several real world applications, systems analysis can indeed be a very powerful tool. If used with care and judgement and without oversimplification, the systems approach should provide results that are justifiable on economic and other grounds.

On the other hand, it appears that the needs of practising engineers with regard to the usefulness and practicability of systems engineering have not received adequate attention. Costly, time-consuming and hypothetical data studies are of little value regardless of (or perhaps on account of) sophistications. They may, on the contrary, provide misleading answers and may even discourage potential users.

Furthermore, the use of systems techniques may be constrained on account of limited man power, funds and computer time. Besides, lack of data would discourage potential users[32].

For these reasons, more attention should be paid to the training of staff and to

---

[30] See Haimes et al. (1975) on SWT, the survey paper on muliobjective planning by Bishop et al. (1976) and by Cohon and Marks (1973) on multiobjective LP methods. Haimes (1977) has written a comprehensive book on the modelling and optimisation of water resources systems.

[31] Johnson (1972) finds that simulation is the most common technique used in practice. In addition to the work already cited, simulation methods are used or described by Dorfman (1965), by Hufschmidt (1962, 1965), by Moran (1970), by Cole (1975) and by Fiering (1965). Fiering dealt with the problem of water lagging and salinity of agricultural lands in west Pakistan. James (1972) gives a rationale for developing simulation models. Also, the books by McMillan and Gonzalez (1973, chapter 2), by White et al. (1974, chapter 5) and by Meta Systems Incorporated (1975, section D) may be useful.

[32] The report of Johnson (1972), based on answers required to a questionnaire sent to various professionals in public and private organisations, focuses attention on various needs and shortcomings. Limitations are also investigated by de Neufville and Marks (1974, chapter 4) with regard to additions to New York city's water supply system; see also Beard (1973) and the comments of Martin and Denison (1971).

increased efficiency in the problem-oriented use of men, machines and data. Also, the greatest value ought to be attached in future to applied research conducted by those at the supervisory and managerial levels. At the same time, emphasis should be placed on multidisciplinary procedures as the originators of the systems approach intended, on account of the multiobjective nature of decision making.

References

Aron, G., and Scott, V. H. (1971). Dynamic programming for conjunctive water use. *J. Hydraul. Div., Am. Soc. Civ. Eng.*, **97** (HY5), 705–21

Askew, A. J. (1974). Optimum reservoir operating policies and the imposition of a reliability constraint. *Water Resour. Res.*, **10**, 51–6

—— (1975). Use of risk premiums in chance-constrained dynamic programming. *Water Resour. Res.*, **11**, 862–6

Balas, E. (1965). An additional algorithm for solving linear programs with zero-one variables. *Oper. Res.*, **13**, 517–46

Baumol, W. J. (1972). *Economic Theory and Operations Analysis*, 3rd edn, Prentice-Hall, Englewood Cliffs, New Jersey

Beard, L. R. (1973). Status of water resource systems analysis. *J. Hydraul. Div., Am. Soc. Civ. Eng.*, **99** (HY4), 559–65

Becker, L., and Yeh, W. W. C. (1974). Optimization of real time operation of a multiple-reservoir system. *Water Resour. Res.*, **10**, 1107–12

Bellman, R. E. (1957). *Dynamic Programming*, Princeton University Press, Princeton, New Jersey

Bellman, R. E., and Dreyfus, S. E. (1962). *Applied Dynamic Programming*, Princeton University Press, Princeton, New Jersey

Bellmore, M., and Nemhauser, G. L. (1968). The travelling salesman problem: a survey. *Oper. Res.*, **16**, 538–58

Bishop, A. B., McKee, M., Morgan, T. W., and Narayanan, R. (1976). Multiobjective planning: concepts and methods. *J. Water Resour. Plan. Manage. Div., Am. Soc. Civ. Eng.*, **102** (WR2), 239–53

Buras, N. (1966). Dynamic programming in water resources development. *Adv. Hydrosci.*, **3**, 367–412

Butcher, W. S. (1971). Stochastic dynamic programming for optimum reservoir operation. *Water Resour. Bull.*, **7**, 115–23

Butcher, W. S., Haimes, Y. Y., and Hall, W. A. (1969). Dynamic programming for the optimal sequencing of water supply projects. *Water Resour. Res.*, **5**, 1196–204

Carlson, J. G. H., and Misshauk, M. J. (1972). *Introduction to Gaming: Management Decision Simulations*, Wiley, New York

Charnes, A., and Cooper, W. W. (1960). Chance-constrained programming. *Manage. Sci.*, **6**, 73–9

Checkland, P. B. (1970). Systems and science, industry and innovation. *J. Syst. Eng.*, **1**, No. 2, 3–17

Churchman, C. W., Ackoff, R. L., and Arnoff, E. L. (1957). *Introduction to Operations Research*, Wiley, New York

Cohon, J. L., and Marks, D. H. (1973). Multiobjective screening models and water resource investment. *Water Resour. Res.*, **9,** 826–36

Cole, J. A. (1975). Assessment of surface water sources. *Proceedings of the Conference of Engineering Hydrology Today*, Institution of Civil Engineers, London, pp. 113–25

Cooper, L., and Steinberg, D. (1970). *Introduction to Methods of Optimization*, Saunders, Philadelphia, Pennsylvania

Croley, T. E., II (1974). Sequential stochastic optimization for reservoir system. *J. Hydraul. Div., Am. Soc. Civ. Eng.*, **100** (HY1), 201–19

Curry, G. L., Helm, J. C., and Clark, R. A. (1973). Chance-constrained model of system of reservoirs. *J. Hydraul. Div., Am. Soc. Civ. Eng.*, **99** (HY12), 2353–66

Dantzig, G. B. (1963). *Linear Programming and Extensions*, Princeton University Press, Princeton, New Jersey

Deininger, R. A. (1969). Linear programming for hydrologic analyses. *Water Resour. Res.*, **5,** 1105–9

Dorfman, R. (1962). Mathematical models: the multistructure approach. *Design of Water Resources Systems* (eds A. Maass *et al.*), Harvard University Press, Cambridge, Massachusetts, chapter 13, pp. 494–539

—— (1965). Formal models in the design of water resource systems. *Water Resour. Res.*, **1,** 329–36

Drobny, N. L. (1971). Linear programming applications in water resources. *Water Resour. Bull.*, **7,** 1180–93

Dudley, N. J., and Burt, O. R. (1973). Stochastic reservoir management and system design for irrigation. *Water Resour. Res.*, **9,** 507–22

Duffin, R. J., Peterson, E. L., and Zener, C. (1967). *Geometric Programming*, Wiley, New York

Eastman, J., and ReVelle, C. (1973). Linear decision rule in reservoir management and design, 3, direct capacity determination and intraseasonal constraints. *Water Resour. Res.*, **9,** 29–42

Eisel, L. M. (1970). Comments on 'The linear decision rule in reservoir management and design' by C. ReVelle, E. Joeres and W. Kirby. *Water Resour. Res.*, **6,** 1239–41

—— (1972). Chance constrained reservoir model. *Water Resour. Res.*, **8,** 339–47

Encyclopaedia Britannica (1977), vol. 12, 15th edn, William Benton, Chicago, Illinois, p. 1067

Fiering, M. B. (1965). Revitalizing a fertile plan. *Water Resour. Res.*, **1,** 41–61

Fults, D. M., and Hancock, L. F. (1972). Optimum operations model for Shasta–Trinity system. *J. Hydraul. Div., Am. Soc. Civ. Eng.*, **98** (HY9), 1497–514

Gablinger, M., and Loucks, D. P. (1970). Markov models for flow regulation. *J. Hydraul. Div., Am. Soc. Civ. Eng.*, **96** (HY1), 165–81

Garcia, L. L. (1974). Optimization of a three reservoir system by dynamic programming. *Proceedings of the 1971 Warsaw Symposium on Mathematical Models in Hydrology*, vol. 2, International Association of Scientific Hydrology, Paris, pp. 936–41

Garfinkel, R. S., and Nemhauser, G. L. (1972). *Integer Programming*, Wiley, New York

Gottfried, B. S., and Weisman, J. (1973). *Introduction of Optimization Theory*, Prentice Hall, Englewood Cliffs, New Jersey

Gue, R. L., and Thomas, M. E. (1968). *Mathematical Methods in Operations Research*, Macmillan, New York

Gundelach, J., and ReVelle, C. (1975). Linear decision rule in reservoir management and design, 5, a general algorithm. *Water Resour. Res.*, **11**, 204–7

Haimes, Y. Y. (1977). *Hierarchical Analyses of Water Resources Systems*, McGraw-Hill, New York

Haimes, Y. Y., Hall, W. A., and Freedman, H. T. (1975). *Multiobjective Optimization in Water Resources Systems*, Elsevier, Amsterdam

Hall, W. A., and Buras, N. (1961). The dynamic programming approach to water resources development. *J. Geophys. Res.*, **66**, 517–20

Hall, W. A., Butcher, W. S., and Esogbue, A. (1968). Optimization of the operation of a multi-purpose reservoir. *Water Resour. Res.*, **4**, 471–477

Hall, W. A., and Dracup, J. A. (1970). *Water Resources Systems Engineering*, McGraw-Hill, New York

Hall, W. A., and Howell, D. T. (1963). The optimization of single purpose reservoir design with the application of dynamic programming to synthetic hydrology samples. *J. Hydrol.*, **1**, 355–63

Hassitt, A. (1968). Solution of the stochastic programming model of reservoir regulation. *IBM Washington Sci. Cent.*, Wheaton, Md., Rep., No. 320-3506

Hillier, F. S., and Lieberman, G. J. (1974). Operations Research, 2nd edn, Holden Day, San Francisco, California

Himmelblau, D. M. (1972). *Applied Nonlinear Programming*, McGraw-Hill, New York

Hipel, K. W., Ragade, R. K., and Unny, T. C. (1974). Metagame analysis of water resources conflicts. *J. Hydraul. Div., Am. Soc. Civ. Eng.*, **100** (HY10), 1437–55

Howard, R. A. (1960). *Dynamic Programming and Markov Processes*, Massachusetts Institute of Technology Press, Cambridge, Massachusetts; Wiley, New York

Hufschmidt, M. M. (1962). Analysis by simulation: examination of response surface. *Design of Water Resources Systems* (eds A. Maass *et al.*), Harvard University Press, Cambridge, Massachusetts, chapter 10, pp. 391–442

—— (1965). Field level planning of water resource systems. *Water Resour. Res.*, **1**, 147 63

Jacoby, H. D., and Loucks, D. P. (1972). Combined use of optimization and simulation models in river basin planning. *Water Resour. Res.*, **8**, 1401–14

James, W. (1972). Developing simulation models. *Water Resour. Res.*, **8**, 1590–2

Joeres, E. F., Liebman, J. C., and ReVelle, C. S. (1971). Operating rules for joint operation of raw water sources. *Water Resour. Res.*, **7**, 225–35

Johnson, W. K. (1972). Use of systems analysis in water resource planning. *J. Hydraul. Div., Am. Soc. Civ. Eng.*, **98** (HY9), 1543–56

Jovanovic, S. (1967). Optimization of the long-term operation of a single-purpose reservoir. *Proceedings of the International Hydrology Symposium*, vol. 1, *Fort Collins, Colorado*, pp. 422–9

Kall, P. (1976). *Stochastic Linear Programming*, Springer, Berlin

Klemeš, V. (1975). Comments on 'Optimum reservoir operating policies and the imposition of a reliability constraint' by A. J. Askew. *Water Resour. Res.*, **11**, 365–8

Kos, Z. (1975). Chance constrained model of water resources systems. *Proceedings of International Symposium and Workshops on the Application of Mathematical Models in Hydrology and Water Resource Systems*, International Association of Scientific Hydrology, Bratislava, preprints

Kramer, N. J. T. A., and de Smit, J. (1977). *Systems Thinking*, Martinus Nijhoff Social Sciences Division, Leiden

Kuester, J. L., and Mize, J. H. (1973). *Optimization Techniques with FORTRAN*, McGraw-Hill, New York

Lane, M. (1973). Conditional chance-constrained model for reservoir control. *Water Resour. Res.*, **9**, 937–48

Larson, R. E. (1968). *State Increment Dynamic Programming*, American Elsevier, New York

Larson, R. E., and Keckler, W. G. (1969). Applications of dynamic programming to the control of water resource systems. *Automatica*, **5**, 15–26

LeClerc, G., and Marks, D. H. (1973). Determination of the discharge policy for existing reservoir networks under differing objectives. *Water Resour. Res.*, **9**, 1155–65

Lee, E. S., and Waziruddin, S. (1970). Applying gradient projection and conjugate gradient to the optimum operation of reservoirs. *Water Resour. Bull.*, **6**, 713–24

Liebman, J. C., and Lynn, W. R. (1966). Optional allocation of stream dissolved oxygen. *Water Resour. Res.*, **2**, 581–91

Little, J. D. C. (1955). The use of storage water in a hydroelectric system. *J. Oper. Res. Soc. Am.*, **3**, 187–97

Liu, C., and Tedrow, A. C. (1973). Multilake river system operation rules. *J. Hydraul. Div., Am. Soc. Civ. Eng.*, **99** (HY9), 1369–81

Loucks, D. P. (1968). Computer models for reservoir regulation. *J. Sanit. Eng. Div., Am. Soc. Civ. Eng.*, **94** (SA4), 657–69

—— (1970). Some comments on linear decision rules and chance constraints. *Water Resour. Res.*, **6**, 668–71

Loucks, D. P., and Dorfman, P. J. (1975). An evaluation of some linear decision rules in chance-constrained models for reservoir planning and operation. *Water Resour. Res.*, **11**, 777–82

Luthra, S. S., and Arora, S. R. (1976). Optimal design of single reservoir system using δ release policy. *Water Resour. Res.*, **12**, 606–12

Maki, D. P., and Thompson, M. (1973). *Mathematical Models and Applications*, Prentice-Hall, Englewood Cliffs, New Jersey

Manne, A. S. (1960). Linear programming and sequential decisions. *Manage. Sci.*, **6**, 259–67

Martin, M. J. C., and Denison, R. A. (eds) (1971). *Case Exercises in Operations Research*, Interscience, Wiley, Chichester, Sussex

Mawer, P. A., and Thorn, D. (1974). Improved dynamic programming procedures and their practical application to water resource systems. *Water Resour. Res.*, **10**, 183–90

McMillan, C., and Gonzalez, R. F. (1973). *Systems Analysis, A Computer Approach to Decision Models*, 3rd edn, Irwin, Homewood, Illinois

Mejia, J. M., Egli, P., and LeClerc, A. (1974). Evaluating multireservoir operating rules. *Water Resour. Res.*, **10**, 1090–8

Meredith, D. D., Wong, K. W., Woodhead, R. W., and Workman, R. H. (1973). *Design and Planning of Engineering Systems*, Prentice-Hall, Englewood Cliffs, New Jersey

Meta Systems Incorporated (1975). Systems analysis in water resources planning. *Water Inform. Cent., Port Washington, N.Y., Publ.*

Moran, P. A. P. (1970). Simulation and evaluation of complex water systems operations. *Water Resour. Res.*, **6**, 1737–42

Nayak, S. C., and Arora, S. R. (1971). Optimal capacities for a multireservoir system using the linear decision rule. *Water Resour. Res.*, **7**, 485–98

—— (1974). Linear decision rule: a note on control volume being constant. *Water Resour. Res.*, **10**, 637–42

Nemhauser, G. L. (1966). *Introduction to Dynamic Programming*, Wiley, New York

de Neufville, R., and Marks, D. H. (eds) (1974). *Systems Planning and Design, Case Studies in Modelling, Optimization and Evaluation*, Prentice-Hall, Englewood Cliffs, New Jersey

Norman, J. M. (1972). *Heuristic Procedures in Dynamic Programming*, Manchester University Press, Manchester

——(1975). *Elementary Dynamic Programming*, Edward Arnold, London

O'Laoghaire, D. T., and Himmelblau, D. M. (1974). *Optimal Expansion of a Water Resources System*, Academic Press, New York

Orlob, G. T., and Dendy, B. B. (1973). Systems approach to water quality management. *J. Hydraul. Div., Am. Soc. Civ. Eng.*, **99** (HY4), 573–87

Polya, G. (1957). *How to Solve it*, Doubleday, New York

ReVelle, C., and Gundelach, J. (1975). Linear decision rule in reservoir management and design, 4, a rule that minimizes output variance. *Water Resour. Res.*, **11**, 197–203

ReVelle, C., Joeres, E., and Kirby, W. (1969). The linear decision rule in reservoir management and design, 1, development of the stochastic model. *Water Resour. Res.*, **5**, 776–7

ReVelle, C., and Kirby, W. (1970). Linear decision rule in reservoir management and design, 2, performance optimization. *Water Resour. Res.*, **6**, 1033–44

Riggs, J. L., and Inoue, M. S. (1976). *Introduction to Operations Research and Management Science*, McGraw-Hill, New York

Roefs, T. G. (1968). Reservoir management: the state of the art. *IBM Washington Sci. Cent., Wheaton, Md., Rep.*, No. 320-3508

Roefs, T. G., and Bodin, L. D. (1970). Multireservoir operation studies. *Water Resour. Res.*, **6**, 410–20

Rogers, P. (1969). A game theory approach to the problems of international river basins. *Water Resour. Res.*, **5**, 749–60

Rossman, L. A. (1977). Reliability-constrained dynamic programming and randomized release rules in reservoir management. *Water Resour. Res.*, **13**, 247–55

Rustagi, J. S. (1976). *Variational Methods in Statistics*, Academic Press, New York

Schweig, Z. (1968). Reservoir yield, III, optimization of control rules for water storage systems by dynamic programming. *Water Res. Assoc., Medmenham, Tech. Paper*, No. TP. 61

Schweig, Z., and Cole, J. A. (1968). Optimal control of linked reservoirs. *Water Resour. Res.*, **4**, 479–97

Shamblin, J. E., and Stevens, G. T., Jr. (1974). *Operations Research, A Fundamental Approach*, McGraw-Hill, New York

Siddall, J. N. (1972). *Analytical Decision Making in Engineering Design*, Prentice-Hall, Englewood Cliffs, New Jersey

Silver, R. J., Okun, M. H., and Russell, S. O. (1972). Dynamic programming in a hydroelectric system. *Modelling of Water Resources Systems*, vol. 2 (ed. A. K. Biswas), Harvest House, Montreal, pp. 623–36

Smith, D. V. (1973). Systems analysis and irrigation planning. *J. Irrig. Div., Am. Soc. Civ. Eng.*, **99** (IR1), 89–107

Sniedovich, M. (1978). On the reliability of reliability constraints. *Proceedings of the International Symposium on Risk and Reliability in Water Resources, Waterloo, Canada, 26–28 June* 1978, preprints

Sniedovich, M., and Davis, D. R. (1975). Comment on 'Chance-constrained dynamic programming and optimization of water resource systems' by A. J. Askew. *Water Resour. Res.*, **11**, 1037–8

Sobel, M. J. (1965). Water quality improvement programming problems. *Water Resour. Res.*, **1**, 477–87

Taha, H. A. (1976). *Operations Research*, 2nd edn, Macmillan, New York

Thomas, H. A., Jr., and Watermeyer, P. (1962). Mathematical models: a stochastic sequential approach. *Design of Water Resources Systems* (eds A. Maass *et al.*), Harvard University Press, Cambridge, Massachusetts, chapter 14, pp. 540–61

Thuesen, H. G., Fabrycky, W. J., and Thuesen, G. J. (1977). *Engineering Economy*, 5th edn, Prentice-Hall, Englewood Cliffs, New Jersey

Tintner, G., and Sengupta, J. K. (1972). *Stochastic Economics*, Academic Press, New York

Wagner, H. M. (1975). *Principles of Operations Research*, 2nd edn, Prentice-Hall, New York

White, D., Donaldson, W., and Lawrie, N. (1974). *Operation Research Techniques*, vol. 2, Business Books, London

Wilde, D. J., and Beightler, C. S. (1967). *Foundations of Optimization*, Prentice-Hall, Englewood Cliffs, New Jersey

Williams, A. C. (1965). On stochastic linear programming. *J. Soc. Ind. Appl. Math.*, **13**, 927–40

Williams, J. D. (1966). *The Compleat Strategyst*, revised edn, McGraw-Hill, New York

Young, G. K. (1967). Finding reservoir operating rules. *J. Hydraul. Div.*, *Am. Soc. Civ. Eng.*, **93** (HY6), 297–321

Zoutendijk, G. (1976). *Mathematical Programming Methods*, North-Holland, Amsterdam

9 Applied decision theory

The design and operation of water resource systems are affected to a great extent by the uncertainty of future events, as stressed throughout this text. In spite of the immense variability in the states of nature which have to be coped with and the limited information available, the engineer is called upon to make decisions and to take appropriate actions. Decision theory attempts to provide, for a large body of applied scientists and managers, a systematic approach to the statistical problems involved.

Basically, the procedure is to reduce the problem to two or more alternatives and then to choose the alternative which is expected to have the highest value, on the basis of all the available information; there is, of course, no guarantee that the outcome will be up to expectations. The subject is related to the programming methods in chapter 8; the difference is that, whereas in dynamic programming, for example, the operational ordering of policies is considered, here the preference is between terminal decisions.

As a first step, statistical parameters need to be known and estimates of these parameters may be crucial to the decision process. For such inferential purposes, bayesian analysis can be a useful practical tool to the decision maker; the approach has, however, aroused a great deal of controversy. In the application of decision theory, bayesian probabilities are used to weight the utilities of feasible actions. This leads to a choice for action, the so-called Bayes solution, based on optimum expected utility.

All these aspects are taken up here. Also included in this chapter is the worth of additional data, depending on which a decision could be postponed. In addition, non-bayesian methods of decision making are explained. Introductory notes on decisions, utilities and uncertainties with historical background are found in sections 9.1 and 9.2. These and also the reviews of applications in different areas and suggestions for further reading, given in sections 9.3 and 9.4, should be of benefit particularly to research workers[1].

---

[1] Benefit–cost, sensitivity and other types of economic analysis as, for example, used by Thuesen *et al.* (1977) or by Kuiper (1971) are outside the scope of this book; it is

9.1   Introduction with historical background

In a non-mathematical discussion, Bross (1953) notes that decision problems started with the beginning of life when survival depended on the nature of actions taken. Indeed, the models of the real world might have originated from devil theory which arose from the primitive methods of witchcraft and the like. With the progress of civilisation came reason and the scientific method, but the decision maker had to cope with uncertainty which Aitchison (1970) finds 'is one of the disturbing and at the same time fascinating features of human existence'. This led to the development of statistical methods for problem solving.

Modern decision theory, specifically the operations research technique of game theory, may be traced back to Blaise Pascal, the seventeenth-century French mathematician (who is well known for his triangle of binomial coefficients), philosopher and devoted Christian. His arguments which had a strong religious basis have been reconstructed in recent times with monetary values. Incidentally, Pascal is credited with the initial development of probability as an independent science, although problems associated with games of chance had been dealt with before his time[2].

9.1.1   Utilities

The principles of operations research including game theory were discussed in chapter 8. In a two-person game, each player aims to maximise gains or to minimise losses at the expense of the other, whereas in decision theory nature, who could be regarded as the other player, does not try to win. In this case the statistician attempts to find the true state of nature by sampling or through experiments.

When gambling, most people seem to prefer a small prize with a good chance of success to a large reward with a high risk. Studies of such behaviour led to the St Petersburg paradox and the hypothesis of expected utility. The pioneer was Daniel Bernoulli, one of the famous family of eighteenth-century Swiss mathematicians and applied scientists[3]. He regarded utilities as numbers which a person assigns to the consequences of an action; the preference for a particular action is shown by its expected utility.

Consider a particular coin-tossing game, to join which a fixed charge is made to each player. The procedure here is to toss a coin until a head appears for the first time. The probability of this happening is $\frac{1}{2}$ after one attempt, and, in general, it is $(\frac{1}{2})^n$ if n tosses are required. Correspondingly, the player receives 2

---

interesting to note that subjectivity is involved in all such assessments, as in the bayesian methods introduced in the following sections.

[2] Maistrov (1974) gives an interesting historical sketch on probability; see also the hypothetical letters quoted by Rényi (1972) concerning Pascall.

[3] St Petersburg is the name of the journal in which Bernoulli's paper was published. It is also the former name of Leningrad, where he once taught.

dollars, say, when a head appears on the first attempt or 2^n dollars if n tosses need to be made. It follows that the expected monetary gain from this game is $\sum_{n=1}^{\infty} (1/2)^n 2^n$, when summed over all possible trials. Because this is infinite, it appears that a person should be willing to pay a large sum of money to play the game; in other words, regardless of the entrance fee, it seems worthwhile to enter. However, in practice there is a limit beyond which a person will not pay. This limit depends on the individual's utility function. Here, it is important to note that the face value of a person's wealth is not what it is really worth to that person. For instance, 10 dollars is of great importance to a poor man but is comparatively worthless to a millionaire; likewise, there would be a larger difference in utilities associated by a rich man with, say, \$1 000 000 and \$100 000 than what is evidenced from a pauper's utility function. This means that a graph of utility against monetary worth is not linear. For instance, a risk avoider's curve, which is more common, is concave downwards, and this is in direct contrast with the curve of a risk seeker, as shown in figure 9.1. The situation in the St Petersburg case, therefore, is not really paradoxical unless the game is played to infinity.

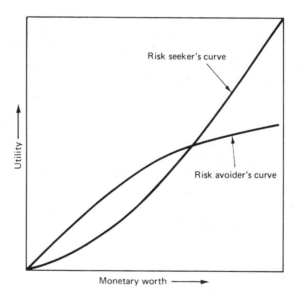

Figure 9.1   Two contrasting utility functions

Utility theory which embodies indifference curves, values and preferences is the important contribution made by economists in finding solutions to uncertainty and risk. Note that utility conveys the same meaning as preferability. It is a measure of the worth of various outcomes and forms part of an individual's non-linear psychological variables. However, it is not an easy matter to determine the form of a person's utility curve, and it is easier to use utilities than to find them[4].

With the advancement of economic theory, most of which has evolved during this century, came the acceptance of insurance against various forms of risk. On the other hand, rapid technological advancements necessitated continuous decisions, and, because natural and man-induced events seem to occur in unaccountable ways, there was an urgent need to quantify uncertainty.

9.1.2 Probabilistic approaches to decision making

A practical way in which uncertainty could be quantified is through probabilities. However, the subject has aroused a great deal of controversy, particularly during the past half-century, and it now appears that there is no generally accepted way of defining probability. James Bernoulli seems to be the first to treat probability, in his seventeenth-century 'Ars conjectandi' (the art of conjecturing), as the degree of confidence which a rational individual has, according to the information available, on the outcome of an uncertain event. This is the subjective definition of probability, and its value which is an educated guess, therefore, varies between individuals[5]. In other philosophical writings prior to the twentieth century, it appears that De Morgan and Laplace (the French mathematician), who stated that probability is an 'expression of ignorance', shared the same subjective or personal beliefs about probability. The values which a subjectivist assigns to probability are, unfortunately, not amenable to verification.

The opposing classical treatment of probability, as a limiting or long-run relative frequency in identically conducted repetitive trials, was initiated by the French physicist Poisson; the British logician Venn was also an important contributor in the nineteenth century. This so-called frequentist's or objective concept is thought by some to go back to the days of Aristotle[6]. It was developed for inferential purposes in the eighteenth century by Bayes, by Laplace and by Gauss and more recently by Galton and by Karl Pearson. The current

[4] The work of Good (1962) and of Riggs (1968), who discusses present worth, future worth, utility functions and decision trees at an elementary level, are relevant here. The development of modern utility theory owes a great deal to von Neumann and Morgenstern (1953) who present axioms on the choice of probability distributions for maximising utility, in their pioneering (comparatively advanced) text on game theory and economic behaviour; see also Arrow (1970) and Coombs and Beardslee (1954). Further illustrations of utility curves are given by Rose (1976) and by Lee and Moore (1975).
[5] Modern writers follow Keynes (1921, 1973) in referring to it as the degree of belief approach, and de Finetti (Kyburg and Smokler, 1964) has linked this to the betting odds that would be placed on a chance event.
[6] Kendall (1949) attempts, in a non-mathematical paper, to reconcile these conflicting theories. Further details of the various interpretations of probability are given by Good (1959), by Kyburg (1966) and by Gnedenko (1968); also lucid explanations are found in the Encyclopaedia Brittanica (1977).

frequentist approach to statistical inference is due to Fisher and also to Neyman and to E. S. Pearson, famous for their work on testing hypotheses.

In fact, during the early part of this century it seemed that there were no other acceptable methods. However, towards the mid-twentieth century, inferences based on subjective probabilities began to be recognised in application to decision theory[7]. It is important to note that decision theory deals with optimal actions, based on past and current information, in addition to inferences and conclusions. In its application, we have to deal with possible states of nature and choose between different possible actions. The flow chart given in figure 9.2 outlines the steps involved in decision making.

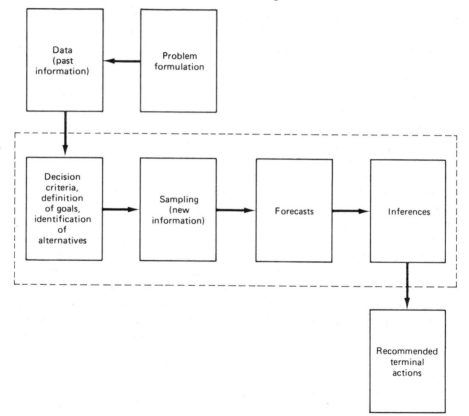

Figure 9.2   Flow chart for decision making. Decision making under *uncertainty* is based on subjective (unknown) probabilities, typically in a bayesian framework. If objective (known) probabilities are used, the procedure is termed decision making under *risk*

---

[7] In this context Savage (1954, 1962), in particular, should be given credit. Amongst other notable contributers to modern decision theory from the same school are de Finetti (1972), Kyburg and Smokler (1964), Good (1950) and Jeffreys (1961). The broader aspects of statistical decision theory were formulated by Wald (1950), whose book though mathematical has a general appeal in parts.

To summarise, the main argument for justifying decision making of this type is that, in most practical situations, a knowledge of probabilities is incomplete. For instance, in contrast with games of chance and lotteries, the probability that a horse wins a race is subjective, that is, it depends on personal knowledge or, as Kyburg (1966) puts it, it 'embodies epistemological uncertainty'. Unlike in classical decision theory, subjective probabilities quantifying personal knowledge could be incorporated in bayesian decision theory. Because of the inclusion of the subjective element, the approach is often referred to as *decision making under uncertainty*[8]. On the other hand, by the same definition, *decisions made under risk* are based on objective probabilities.

9.1.3 *Bayes' theorem and its use*

This theorem is named after Thomas Bayes, an eighteenth-century Presbyterian minister and philosopher from Tunbridge Wells in England, whose 'Essay towards solving a problem in the doctrine of chances' was published after his death by a friend named Price. It is derived, in fact, from a basic law of probability theory and is regarded by a growing number of statisticians as being fundamental to the revision of probability through evidence. The procedures involved in the application of the theorem have, however, advanced a great deal from the initial concept[9].

Bayes' theorem, which follows from the definition of conditional probability, involves a prior (or *a priori*) distribution which may be based on previous data samples, on theoretical considerations or on the investigator's own beliefs about the possible states of nature. This distribution describes all the relevant information prior to the receipt of (an additional) sample of data. Given the prior distribution and a new set of data or observations, by compounding these, the posterior (or *a posteriori*) distribution could be evaluated.

To explain the derivation, let θ_i, $i = 1, 2, \ldots, k$, denote all possible states of nature which may refer to the state of weather, the water level in a reservoir or any other variable or parameter which is subject to uncertainty. Also, let x represent a sample of data such as a forecast or an estimate of inflows. Accordingly, the prior probabilities estimated before receipt of the data are expressed by $P_0(\theta_i)$ and the conditional probabilities of the sample x subject to the states of nature θ_i are denoted by $\Pr(x|\theta_i)$. Also, let the posterior probabilities $P_1(\theta_i|x)$ represent the probabilities of the states θ_i of nature, given the sample x. If $\Pr(\theta_i, x)$ denotes the joint probability of θ_i and x, by using conditional probabilities, we can state that

$$\Pr(\theta_i, x) = P_0(\theta_i)\,\Pr(x|\theta_i)$$

$$= \Pr(x)\,P_1(\theta_i|x)$$

[8] See, for example, Like and Raiffa (1957), Siddall (1972) or Bradley (1976).
[9] The essay was also reprinted later under a revised title (Barnard, 1970). However, the formula currently known as Bayes' theorem (see equation 9.2) is not found in the original work; it appears that the name was given by the renowned Frenchman Laplace.

As given by equation 7.7, the marginal probability of x is

$$\Pr(x) = \sum_{i=1}^{k} P_0(\theta_i)\Pr(x|\theta_i) \qquad (9.1)$$

which leads to the following theorem named after Bayes.

$$P_1(\theta_i|x) = P_0(\theta_i)\Pr(x|\theta_i) \Big/ \sum_{i=1}^{k} P_0(\theta_i)\Pr(x|\theta_i) \qquad (9.2)$$

Bayes' theorem states, therefore, that the posterior probability of a state θ_i, conditional to a sample x, is the joint probability of θ_i and x (that is, the product of the prior probability of θ_i and the probability of x conditional to θ_i) divided by the marginal probability of x which is, in fact, the sum of joint probabilities, for all i. The divisor, which should of course be non-zero, makes the sum of the posterior probabilities, for all i, equal to unity. Note that it should be changed to integral form for continuous states and probability density functions (see example 9.3).

The posterior distribution obtained enables us to make inferences on the state of nature through some parameter specifying it. The inference depends, of course, on the assumptions made regarding the probability model just as in other types of statistical analysis. In other words, given that states of nature, models and parameters embody forms of uncertainty, ensuing decisions will depend on the probability distributions of the variables. Ideally, the parameters of the distribution should also be treated as random variables.

It is thought that a rational individual behaves, when making a decision, as though he has a prior distribution in mind, in addition to, as commonly expected, a form of utility function[10]. However, psychological studies show that he may not always revise probabilities intuitively; for this reason, the bayesian method is suggested. The alternative, if the prior information appears to be vague, is to consult the expert. For example, in drilling for water or oil, the geologist can be consulted and will base prior probabilities or odds on the evidence presented and on personal experience. It appears that, in the same way, all scientific activities are strongly influenced by the subjective element[11].

The mathematical soundness of the bayesian approach has been widely accepted; the present controversy is with regard to application, the choice of prior distribution in particular. The main objection to the use of Bayes' theorem is that prior distributions are unknown or not easily obtained. The bayesian extremists use the theorem even when the prior probability is assumed to be within wide intervals or, in other words, has a limiting uniform density. They admit in this case, though, its lack of effectiveness. This is said to be an

---

[10] Strong arguments for the use of prior probabilities are presented by Savage (1954) and Ramsey (1931, 1966); see also Jeffreys (1961) who, according to Savage, is a firm believer in Bayes' theorem, though not a subjectivist. Again, Ferguson (1967) notes that practical decision rules are generally bayesian.
[11] See, for example, Broadbent (1973).

application of the principle of insufficient reason or Bayes' postulate. The arbitrariness of results so obtained suggest that the prudent applicant should use bayesian theory only when the prior probabilities can be expressed more specifically.

In the 200 years since Bayes' paper was first published, the theorem has been applied without any serious challenge during the first 100 years. Thereafter, it became less acceptable owing to problems in assessing prior probabilities. Perhaps the greatest blow came from Fisher (1966) who in a three-pronged attack rejected the theory of inverse probability which, according to him, underlies Bayes' axiom. He also thought that Bayes withheld publication because he had doubts on the validity of his treatise. In various writings, Fisher opposed the view that statistics could be reduced to a utilitarian basis. There have been other criticisms of the technique mainly on account of dubious applications. Nevertheless, the decision-oriented efforts of L. J. Savage and others brought about a revival in the 1960s. This has been strengthened by the beliefs of many scientists and engineers that bayesian decision theory could play a useful role in practical situations where uncertainties could only be quantified through experience and professional expertise. Several of the problems in the planning and management of water resources are understandably in this class.

9.1.4 *Basic application of Bayes' theorem*

Bayes' theorem could be applied to modify the forecasts from a meteorological station. Here, previously enumerated probabilities are updated in the light of current information[12].

Example 9.1   Let θ_1 (rain) and θ_2 (dry weather) be two states of nature in a certain region, that is, state $S = (\theta_1, \theta_2)$. Meteorological evidence suggests that the prior probabilities of these states are $P_0(\theta_1) = 0.3$ and $P_0(\theta_2) = 1 - P_0(\theta_1) = 0.7$.

Also, let x_1 and x_2 represent 24-hour forecasts of rain and dry weather respectively from currently available meteorological data. From previous forecasts, the estimated conditional probabilities of success of these forecasts are $\Pr(x_1|\theta_1) = 0.75$ and $\Pr(x_2|\theta_2) = 0.65$. It follows that the probabilities of failure are $\Pr(x_2|\theta_1) = 1 - \Pr(x_1|\theta_1) = 0.25$ and $\Pr(x_1|\theta_2) = 1 - \Pr(x_2|\theta_2) = 0.35$. By using equation 9.2, the posterior probability of rain when it is forecasted is given by

$$P_1(\theta_1|x_1) = P_0(\theta_1)\Pr(x_1|\theta_1)/\{P_0(\theta_1)\Pr(x_1|\theta_1) + P_0(\theta_2)\Pr(x_1|\theta_2)\}$$

$$= 0.3 \times 0.75/(0.3 \times 0.75 + 0.7 \times 0.35)$$

$$= 0.4787$$

---

[12] Other applications of bayesian methods in meteorology are given, for example, by Epstein (1962), by Glahn (1964), by Halter and Dean (1971), by de Neufville and Stafford (1971), by Wonnacott and Wonnacott (1977) and by Hillier and Lieberman (1974). The general paper on Bayes' theorem by Cornfield (1967) is excellent as an introduction at a low mathematical level.

It follows that

$$P_1(\theta_2|x_1) = 1 - 0.4787$$

$$= 0.5213$$

The posterior probability of dry weather, when this is forecasted, is

$$P_1(\theta_2|x_2) = P_0(\theta_2)\Pr(x_2|\theta_2)/\{P_0(\theta_2)\Pr(x_2|\theta_2) + P_0(\theta_1)\Pr(x_2|\theta_1)\}$$

$$= 0.7 \times 0.65/(0.7 \times 0.65 + 0.3 \times 0.25)$$

$$= 0.8585$$

Therefore,

$$P_1(\theta_1|x_2) = 1 - 0.8585$$

$$= 0.1415$$

The procedure is shown diagrammatically in figure 9.3.

From the foregoing it is noted that, after reassessment, we could expect that, out of 100 forecasts of dry weather, 86 are correct. Predictions of rain, however, have only an approximately even chance of success.

Now consider a case when prior information is vague and the prior distribution is assumed to be uniform, that is, $\Pr(\theta_1) = \Pr(\theta_2) = 0.5$. If the conditional probabilities are the same, it follows that $P_1(\theta_1|x_1) = 0.6818$ and $P_1(\theta_2|x_1) = 1 - 0.6818 = 0.3182$ and also that $P_1(\theta_2|x_2) = 0.7222$ from which $P_1(\theta_1|x_2) = 1 - 0.7222 = 0.2778$. It is seen that, on account of the diffused prior information, the posterior probabilities are close to the original conditional probabilities. We may question whether the procedure is really necessary, even with the more definite prior information given initially. The answer is that the estimated probabilities are not quite reliable because these are based on a limited number of observations. Hence, there is justification for the combination of prior and current information.

If the prior information is highly subjective or in other words is based on insufficient knowledge and if it is thought that, on the other hand, the conditional probabilities are close to their 'long run', that is, to their classically defined values, the validity of the method is in doubt. However, the length of a so-called long run is uncertain, and it does not seem to be practically meaningful[13].

Finally, consider the extreme situation when $P_0(\theta_1) = 0.1$ and $P_0(\theta_2) = 0.9$ with the same conditional probabilities as before. This is merely given for the sake of comparison because, in this case, weather forecasts are not really needed. It is found that $P_1(\theta_1|x_1) = 0.1923$ and $P_1(\theta_2|x_2) = 0.959$. In this case the more definite prior information has a strong influence on the posterior probabilities.

[13] As Keynes (1929, 1973) (the economist about whom several books have been written) put it, 'In the long run we shall all be dead.'

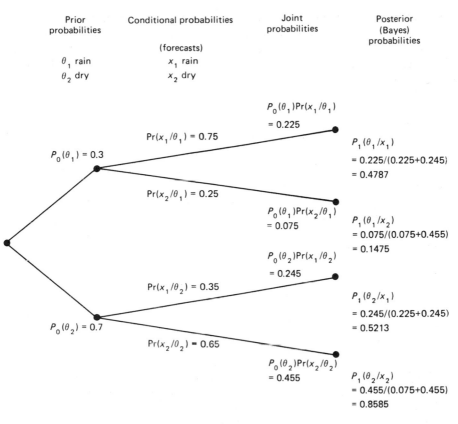

Figure 9.3 Revising probabilities of wet and dry weather, example 9.1. A simple application of Bayes' theorem

It should be noted, however, that such clearly defined prior knowledge is rarely available; usually prior information is diffuse relative to that in the sample data. Zellner (1971) distinguishes between two types of prior probabilities: (1) those obtained from past samples of data are termed *data based*; (2) if personal or theoretical considerations are taken into account, the probabilities are *non-data based*. As increasing amounts of sampling information become available, the influence of the prior probabilities on the posterior probabilities becomes less.

9.2 Bayesian decision making

The bayesian decision rule requires estimation of the optimum expected utility which is commonly referred to as the Bayes estimator or the Bayes risk[14]. The

[14] See Tiao and Box (1973).

procedure is to assign numbers or utilities (which could be in the form of gains or losses) to the possible actions and to weight these by the posterior probabilities. The optimum action is then found by comparing the expected utilities as shown in the next example. The corresponding expected utility is the Bayes risk.

9.2. *Use of discrete probabilities*

The simplified application of bayesian decision making which follows is based on discrete probabilities. It concerns a reservoir designed for irrigation purposes. Forecasts of reservoir inflows are made and optimal actions are planned, ahead of the irrigation season[15].

Example 9.2   The prior probabilities $P_0(\theta_i)$, $i = 1, 2, 3, \ldots$, of the yield θ_1 of a reservoir are given below. Here, θ_1, θ_2 and θ_3 are units of water respectively. The probabilities are estimated from precipitation, run-off, temperature and other regional data as follows.

$$P_0(\theta_1) = 0.25$$

$$P_0(\theta_2) = 0.50$$

$$P_0(\theta_3) = 0.25$$

Each year a hydrologist makes a forecast $x_j, j = 1, 2, 3$, of the amount of water available during the ensuing season prior to release for irrigation. The forecasts are made on the basis of current hydrological information on the catchment and the reservoir storage at the start of the season. The conditional probabilities or likelihoods $\Pr(x_j|\theta_i)$ of each of the 3 forecasts relative to a given future state θ_i, $i = 1, 2, 3$, of nature (yield) are as follows.

State of nature (reservoir yield)	Conditional probability for forecast =			
	x_1	x_2	x_3	*Total*
θ_1	0.70	0.20	0.10	1.0
θ_2	0.10	0.80	0.10	1.0
θ_3	0.10	0.15	0.75	1.0

From these values, evaluate the *a posteriori* probabilities $\Pr(|\theta_i|x_j|)$ of the true states of nature given each of the forecasts x_j, using Bayes' theorem.

Early in the year, the controller of irrigation has to take a prior action $A_i, i = 1, 2, 3$, based on the forecasts made. Alternative actions are the preparation of a variable extent of land for farming and decisions on the types of crops to be

[15] A case study of this type is given by Anderson *et al.* (1971) with correction by Cavadias (1972).

grown and whether to import or export water. These are reduced to three (as in the case of the prior probabilities) in this example, which is a simplification for the purpose of illustration. The annual assessed net benefits, in units of money, from farming for each of the three types of action A_i and each of the yields θ_i, $i = 1, 2, 3$, are given below.

State of nature (reservoir yield)	Annual assessed net benefit for action =		
	A_1	A_2	A_3
θ_1	100	80	60
θ_2	120	180	140
θ_3	150	200	250

(a) If the controller acts on the Bayes solutions, arising from the forecasts, what is the expected annual income from irrigation?

(b) Determine the expected annual income in the two limiting cases: (i) when the forecasts are 100% accurate; (ii) when the forecasts are totally unreliable and actions are taken solely on the prior probabilities.

(a) First compute the joint probabilities $P_0(\theta_i)\Pr(x_j \mid \theta_i)$.

State of nature (reservoir yield)	Joint probability for forecast =		
	x_1	x_2	x_3
θ_1	$0.25 \times 0.7 = 0.175$	$0.25 \times 0.2 = 0.05$	$0.25 \times 0.1 = 0.025$
θ_2	$0.50 \times 0.1 = 0.050$	$0.50 \times 0.8 = 0.40$	$0.50 \times 0.1 = 0.05$
θ_3	$0.25 \times 0.1 = 0.025$	$0.25 \times 0.15 = 0.0375$	$0.25 \times 0.75 = 0.1875$
Marginal probabilities	0.25	0.4875	0.2625

The posterior probabilities $\Pr(\theta_i \mid x_j)$ given below are obtained by dividing the joint probabilities by the marginal probabilities, the sum of which is 1.0.

State of nature (reservoir yield)	Posterior probability for forecast =		
	x_1	x_2	x_3
θ_1	0.7	0.103	0.095
θ_2	0.2	0.820	0.190
θ_3	0.1	0.077	0.715
Total	1.0	1.0	1.0

Given each forecast x_i, $i = 1, 2, 3$, one of three actions A_j, $j = 1, 2, 3$, is possible. In order to choose the action that will be given the highest expected return, the annual assessed returns of net income are weighted by the corresponding posterior probabilities and are then added for each pair of x_i and A_j as follows.

The expected returns from actions taken are given in the following table.

Forecast	Expected return for action =					
	A_1		A_2		A_3	
x_1	$0.7 \times 100 = 70$ $0.2 \times 120 = 24$ $0.1 \times 150 = 15$	109	$0.7 \times 80 = 56$ $0.2 \times 180 = 36$ $0.1 \times 200 = 20$	112	$0.7 \times 60 = 42$ $0.2 \times 140 = 28$ $0.1 \times 250 = 25$	95
x_2	$0.103 \times 100 = 10$ $0.820 \times 120 = 98$ $0.077 \times 150 = 12$	120	$0.103 \times 80 = 8$ $0.820 \times 180 = 148$ $0.077 \times 200 = 15$	171	$0.103 \times 60 = 6$ $0.820 \times 140 = 115$ $0.077 \times 250 = 19$	140
x_3	$0.095 \times 100 = 9$ $0.190 \times 120 = 23$ $0.715 \times 150 = 107$	139	$0.095 \times 80 = 8$ $0.190 \times 180 = 34$ $0.715 \times 200 = 143$	185	$0.095 \times 60 = 6$ $0.190 \times 140 = 27$ $0.715 \times 250 = 179$	212

Given the forecasts x_1, x_2 and x_3, the bayesian solution is that optimal actions A_1, A_2 and A_3 should be taken with maximum expected incomes of 112, 171 and 212 respectively.

In order to determine the expected (that is, the long-average) annual income from these optimum actions, the maximum expected incomes are multiplied by the marginal probabilities of the respective forecasts. This is, of course, because the forecasts are different from year to year. Therefore, the expected annual income is $112 \times 0.25 + 171 \times 0.4875 + 212 \times 0.2625 = 28 + 83 + 56 = 167$.

(b) If the forecasts are 100% accurate, the conditional probabilities $P(x_j|\theta_i)$ are as follows.

State of nature (reservoir yield)	Conditional probability for forecast =		
	x_1	x_2	x_3
θ_1	1.0	0	0
θ_2	0	1.0	0
θ_3	0	0	1.0

These are also the posterior probabilities $P(\theta_i|x_j)$. The marginal probabilities of the forecasts are equal to the corresponding prior probabilities.

The expected returns from actions taken are as follows.

Forecast	Expected return for action =		
	A_1	A_2	A_3
x_1	100	80	60
x_2	120	180	140
x_3	150	200	250

Note that these values are the same as in the second table. The expected annual income is $100 \times 0.25 + 180 \times 0.50 + 250 \times 0.25 = 177.5$.

(c) If only the prior probabilities are known, the expected returns from actions are given below.

State of nature (reservoir yield)	Expected return for action =		
	A_1	A_2	A_3
θ_1	$100 \times 0.25 = 25$	$80 \times 0.25 = 20$	$60 \times 0.25 = 15$
θ_2	$120 \times 0.50 = 60$	$180 \times 0.50 = 90$	$140 \times 0.50 = 70$
θ_3	$150 \times 0.25 = 37.5$	$200 \times 0.25 = 50$	$250 \times 0.25 = 62.5$
Total	122.5	160	147.5

This suggests that action A_2 should be taken invariably each year, in which case expected annual income is 160.

In summary, the expected annual incomes are as follows: given the forecasts, from sampling information it is 167; if forecasts are perfect, it is 177.5; given only the prior information, it is 160. Thus it follows that the expected value of sample data on which forecasts are made is $167 - 160 = 7$, and the expected value of perfect information is $177.5 - 160 = 17.5$.

It appears that the expected value of the forecasting services is very low. This is, of course, highly dependent on the estimated benefits and a sensitivity analysis should be useful in such an application[16]. The limitations in such procedures are due to likely errors in the assessment of benefits or costs of action and in the estimation of prior and conditional probabilities.

9.2.2   Use of probability functions

In examples 9.1 and 9.2, the revision of probabilities through Bayes' theorem was made on the assumption that the states of nature could be represented by a few discrete values. As the number of values of the variable state becomes

[16] Elsewhere, Cavadias (1967) used Bayes' theorem and decision theory in a flood-forecasting problem to determine whether it pays to employ a consultant.

necessarily large it will be increasingly difficult to assign probabilities to these values. If so, the technique can only be applied through mathematical functions which define probability densities of discrete or continuous variables. Specifically, the beta and binomial functions have been used in the application of Bayes' theorem, for instance, when flood events are involved[17]. It will be noted, however, that the use of mathematical functions necessitates certain assumptions[18].

Another point is that, in the previous example, gains or benefits are maximised when applying the decision rule. However, it is now a more common practice in bayesian procedures to measure the consequences of actions taken through losses rather than through gains.

A case study is presented here, in which the work of Davis (1971) is adapted. The problem concerns the economic feasibility of constructing a dam for flood prevention over a s-year period of effectiveness. There are three possible alternative actions; in each case a cost $C(A)$ is involved.

The first alternative action A_1 is to construct a dam in which case the costs are directly related to the cost D of the dam and the annual maintenance costs M, that is, $C(A_1) = D + Ms$.

The second course of action A_2 is not to construct the dam. The damage caused by floods during the s-year period depends on the number and magnitudes of floods. Some simplifying assumptions are made here. A flood is defined as a high flow which exceeds a certain magnitude with unknown probability θ. Not more than one such flood occurs in a single year, and the probability of occurrence of a flood in any year is independent of that in any other year. It is also assumed that high flows which do not exceed the defined flood magnitude cause no damage and that the cost of damages due to any such flood, regardless of its magnitude, is F. Therefore, if n floods occur in s years, $C(A_2) = Fn$.

The third alternative is to construct a system of dikes as a protection against floods except the extreme ones. In this case, however, some damage is caused during this period of s years by $n'(<n)$ floods; the unknown probability of exceedence of the higher flood level here is $\theta'(<\theta)$. The cost of action $C(A_3) = M's + F'n'$, where M' and F' are the annual costs of the protection scheme and the reduced cost of damage per flood respectively; capital costs are included in M'.

Let the likelihood of having n floods in s years be $\ell(n|s, \theta)$, where θ is the probability of exceedance. Subject to the assumptions made, this could be

---

[17] See, for example, Thomas (1948), McGilchrist et al. (1970), Benjamin and Cornell (1970) and Paintal (1972).

[18] Since the early 1970s many examples of bayesian decision theory, formulated on a mathematical basis, have been published. These works have been greatly influenced by the research of Raiffa and Schlaifer (1961). Some of the illustrative case studies in water resources originated at the University of Arizona and the state of the art prior to 1971 is given by Davis (1971); see also Davis et al. (1972b) for further details of bayesian procedures.

modelled by the Bernoulli likelihood function

$$\ell(n|s, \theta) = \binom{s}{n} \theta^n (1 - \theta)^{s-n} \tag{9.3}$$

Multiplying $\ell(n|s, \theta)$, $n = 0, 1, 2, \ldots, s$, by the costs of action $C(A)$, the loss function, we obtain

$$L(A) = \sum_{n=0}^{s} C(A)\ell(n|s, \theta) \tag{9.4}$$

is obtained. The objective is to choose the action which minimises $L(A)$ by substituting in equation 9.4 the values for $C(A_1)$ and $C(A_2)$. For action A_1, therefore,

$$L(A_1) = (D + Ms) \sum_{n=1}^{s} \binom{s}{n} \theta^n (1 - \theta)^{s-n}$$

$$= D + Ms \tag{9.5}$$

This follows because the summand on the right-hand side is unity by the definition of probability functions. Again, for action A_2, the loss function is

$$L(A_2) = F \sum_{n=0}^{s} n \binom{s}{n} \theta^n (1 - \theta)^{s-n}$$

$$= Fs\theta \tag{9.6}$$

This is based on the expected number of floods in s years which, as obtained[19] from the summand on the righ-hand side, is $s\theta$. Finally, for action A_3, the loss function is

$$L(A_3) = M's + F's\theta' \tag{9.7}$$

There is uncertainty about the random variable θ, which is the probability that in any year the flow in the river will exceed a certain magnitude. However, some prior information about θ is often available; for example, m floods exceeding the specified magnitude may have occurred during the past r years. The prior distribution in this case may be modelled by the two-parameter beta distribution explained in chapter 3, in which the variable, like the probability θ, has limits of 0 and 1. (The random variable θ' can be similarly treated.) Accordingly, the probability density function of θ is

$$f(\theta) = \theta^{m-1}(1 - \theta)^{r-m-1}/B(m, r - m), \qquad 0 \le \theta \le 1 \tag{9.8}$$

and

$$B(m, r - m), = \int_0^1 \theta^{m-1}(1 - \theta)^{r-m-1} \, d\theta$$

---

[19] If we substitute $k = n - 1$ and divide by $s\theta$, the summand is equal to the binomial expansion of $\{\theta + (1 - \theta)\}^{s-1}$ which sums to unity.

is the complete beta function. Here, the beta is regarded as the conjugate prior of the Bernoulli distribution[20]. A distribution and its conjugate when compounded can be integrated without difficulty; that is, there is no need to resort to numerical methods or computer algorithms. When sampling from a Bernoulli process the beta distribution may not fit the prior information in every case. However, because of the versatility of the beta family this is perhaps exceptional[21].

$L(A_1)$ is independent of θ, and, therefore, its expectation $E\{L(A_1)\} = D + Ms$. The expectation of $L(A_2)$ is

$$E\{L(A_2)\} = \int_0^1 Fs\theta\theta^{m-1}(1-\theta)^{r-m-1}d\theta/B(m, r-m)$$

$$= FsB(m+1, r-m)/B(m, r-m)$$

$$= Fsm!(r-m-1)!(r-1)!/r!(m-1)!(r-m-1)!$$

$$= Fsm/r$$

This result is intuitively expected when the prior distribution of θ is assumed to be of the beta type[22]. Similarly, the expectation $E\{L(A_3)\} = M's + F'sm'/r$ given that m' floods exceeding the specified (higher) magnitude may have occurred in r years. The Bayes risk $R(A)$ is defined as $\min_A[E\{L(A)\}]$. This means that $R(A)$ is the minimum value of expected loss which is found by varying the actions A. Therefore,

$$R(A) = \min(D + Ms;\ Fsm/r;\ M's + F'sm'/r) \tag{9.9}$$

Example 9.3   A reservoir is to be constructed across a stream at a cost of $150\,000\,(= D)$ units of money in order to prevent flooding during the next 50 $(= s)$ years. The cost of maintenance of the dam is $1000\,(= M)$ units per year. Prior to the construction, $3\,(= m)$ flood flows which exceed a critical magnitude have occurred during 3 of the past $5\,(= r)$ years, causing an annual damage of $8000\,(= F)$ units to a community below the reservoir site. On the other hand, if dikes are constructed, the annual costs of maintenance and flood damage are $2000\,(= M')$ and $6000\,(= F')$ units respectively; the reduced flood damage is caused by floods which exceed a critical higher magnitude, and it is recorded that $2\,(= m')$ such events have occurred during the past $5\,(= r)$ years. Determine the Bayes risk and the optimal action.

$$R(A) = \min(150\,000 + 1000 \times 50;\ 8000 \times 50 \times 3/5;$$

$$2000 \times 50 + 6000 \times 50 \times 2/5)$$

$$= \min(200\,000;\ 240\,000;\ 220\,000)$$

[20] These so-called conjugate distributions were originally studied by Raiffa and Schlaifer (1961).
[21] See, for example, Winkler (1972).
[22] Empirical Bayes' methods (Maritz, 1970) provide a sophisticated approach to parameter estimation.

The action which gives the minimum expected loss or the Bayes risk is A_1, the construction of the dam[23].

9.2.3 *Opportunity loss*

The problem could be reformulated by using the concept of opportunity loss (OL). OL is the difference between (a) the cost of action taken and (b) the lesser cost of the action which should be taken if the state of nature θ is known.

For the sake of simplicity, the non-optimal action A_3 will not be considered in this enumeration[24]. Theoretically, OL is a measure of the value of perfect information. Because the true value of θ is not known, the following procedure is adopted. The values $OL(A_1, \theta)$ and $OL(A_2, \theta)$ which are non-negative by definition, are expressed by

$$OL(A_1, \theta) = (D + Ms) - Fs\theta, \qquad 1 \geqslant t \geqslant \theta \geqslant 0$$

and

$$OL(A_2, \theta) = Fs\theta - (D + Ms), \qquad 1 \geqslant \theta \geqslant t \geqslant 0$$

where $t = (D + Ms)/Fs$ is based on estimates of D, M and F. Note that the two sets of constraints merely exclude negative values of OL, which are not permissible, whilst keeping θ within or at the limits 0 and 1.

These two values of OL are functional to θ, the unknown state of nature, but, with the prior information represented by $f(\theta)$, the mean value or expected opportunity loss (EOL) could be evaluated in each case. Substituting from equation 9.8 in the above, we obtain

$$EOL(A_1) = \{B(m, r - m)\}^{-1} \int_0^t (D + Ms - Fs\theta)\theta^{m-1}$$
$$\times (1 - \theta)^{r-m-1} \, d\theta \qquad (9.10)$$

and

$$EOL(A_2) = \{B(m, r - m)\}^{-1} \int_t^1 \{Fs\theta - (D + Ms)\}\theta^{m-1}$$
$$\times (1 - \theta)^{r-m-1} \, d\theta \qquad (9.11)$$

According to bayesian decision theory, the action which causes the minimum expected opportunity loss and that which corresponds with the Bayes risk are the same[25].

Example 9.4 For the data given in example 9.3, determine the expected opportunity loss for each of the actions.

---

[23] In a practical situation the decision maker may need to take into account social, technological and other environmental factors.
[24] The work of Davis (1971) is followed more closely here.
[25] See Raiffa and Schlaifer (1961, p. 83).

From equations 9.10 and 9.11,

$$B(m, r - m) = 2!1!/4!$$

$$= 1/12$$

$$t = (150\,000 + 50\,000)/400\,000$$

$$= 1/2$$

$$\int_0^{\frac{1}{2}} \theta^2(1 - \theta)\, d\theta = 5/192$$

$$\int_0^{\frac{1}{2}} \theta^3(1 - \theta)\, d\theta = 3/320$$

$$\int_{\frac{1}{2}}^1 \theta^2(1 - \theta)\, d\theta = 11/192$$

$$\int_{\frac{1}{2}}^1 \theta^3(1 - \theta)\, d\theta = 13/320$$

It follows that

$$EOL(A_1) = 12(200\,000 \times 5/192 - 400\,000 \times 3/320)$$

$$= 17\,500$$

$$EOL(A_2) = 12(400\,000 \times 13/320 - 200\,000 \times 11/192)$$

$$= 57\,500$$

As seen from example 9.3, the optimal action is to build the dam (action A_1).

9.2.4 Worth of additional data

On the evidence presented, the optimal decision is to build the dam. However, the conclusion is made only from a small sample of data, and therefore it is worth considering whether to postpone the decision by 1 year, after which period additional data will be available. This reconsideration does not, of course, arise if the optimal action is not to commence work on the dam. Therefore, the condition $Fsm/r < D + Ms$ is excluded from the following assessment. To simplify the analysis, action A_3 is not considered.

Let $x = 1$ represent the occurrence of a flood next year, greater than the value which is exceeded with probability θ, and $x = 0$ signify that there is no such flood next year. The likelihood of x (conditional to θ) is

$$\ell(x|\theta) = \theta^x(1 - \theta)^{1 - x} \tag{9.12}$$

and this result tallies with that given by equation 9.3 if we assume that x can only take one of two values. The integral of the product of $\ell(x|\theta)$ and the prior distribution $f(\theta)$, given by equation 9.8, is the bayesian or predictive distribution[26] of x. It is, in fact, the denominator in Bayes' theorem, the discrete form of which is given by equation 9.2. Hence,

$$\ell(x) = \int_0^1 \ell(x|\theta) f(\theta)\, d\theta$$

$$= \int_0^1 \theta^{m+x-1}(1-\theta)^{r-m-x}\, d\theta / B(m, r-m) \tag{9.13}$$

It should be noted that the posterior probability density $f(\theta|x)$ like the prior probability density $f(\theta)$ also belongs to the beta family. For the decision process, however, the unconditional distribution $\ell(x)$ is required. It follows from the evaluation of the beta integral shown in chapter 3 that

$$\ell(x) = B(m+x, r-m-x+1)/B(m, r-m)$$

$$= \{(m+x-1)!\,(r-m-x)!/r!\}\,(r-1)!/(m-1)!\,(r-m-1)!$$

in which all the functional terms are non-negative. Hence,

$$\ell(0) = (r-m)/r$$

$$\ell(1) = m/r \tag{9.14}$$

By using equation 9.9, the Bayes risk conditional to $x = 0$, after collecting $r+1$ years of data, is

$$R'(A|x = 0) = \min\{D + Ms,\ Fsm/(r+1)\} \tag{9.15}$$

The difference between the Bayes risk $R(A) = D + Ms$ with r years of data and the Bayes risk $R'(A|x = 0)$ with $r+1$ years of data, as given by equations 9.9 and 9.15 respectively, amounts to

$$D + Ms - Fsm/(r+1), \qquad D + Ms > Fsm/(r+1)$$

On the other hand, if the last constraint is reversed, the difference in the Bayes risks is obviously zero.

The expected value of sample information (EVSI) is equal to the product of this difference in the Bayes risks and $\ell(x)$ given by equation 9.14[27]. For $x = 0$, therefore,

$$\text{EVSI} = \{(D + Ms) - Fsm/(r+1)\}\,(r-m)/r$$

If a flood occurs in the following year (that is, $x = 1$), m is changed to $m+1$ and

$$R'(A|x = 1) = \min\{D + Ms,\ Fs(m+1)/(r+1)\} \tag{9.16}$$

---

[26] This is given by Benjamin and Cornell (1970, chapter 6) as $\ell(x)$; see also Winkler (1972, chapter 4) and Horowitz (1972, chapter 4).
[27] See Raiffa and Schlaifer (1961, chapter 4)

It is known that $Fs(m+1)/(r+1) > Fsm/r$ because $m < r$. (This follows from the theorem that the addition of equal numbers to the numerator and denominator of a fraction less than unity makes the fraction larger, that is, closer to unity.) Also, this assessment is conditional to the constraint $Fsm/r > D + Ms$. Therefore, for the case $x = 1$, the difference in the Bayes risks given by equations 9.9 and 9.16 is zero. For this reason, equation 9.16 is not considered.

For comparison, the expected cost of additional sampling (ECS) is computed. This is the expected annual cost of flood damage less the cost of the reservoir for 1 year of operation. It is found from the difference in the expected losses, given by $E\{L(A_1)\} - E\{L(A_2)\}$, computed before, divided by the design period s, that is,

$$\text{ECS} = Fm/r - (D + Ms)/s$$

Example 9.5   For the optimal action from example 9.3, determine whether action should be delayed by 1 year. By substituting,

$$\text{EVSI} = \{200\,000 - 400\,000 \times 3/6\} \times 2/5$$

$$= 0$$

and

$$\text{ECS} = 8000 \times 3/5 - 200\,000/50$$

$$= 800$$

The expected cost of additional sampling is more than the expected value of sample information. Therefore, the Bayes solution shows that in this case it does not pay, on average, to delay the construction of the dam by 1 year in order to reconsider the decision after collecting additional data.

In this simplified example, decisions are based on 5 years of data. When larger samples become available, the worth of an additional year's data will obviously decrease.

9.3   Further applications of bayesian theory and general comments

Numerous methods of using bayesian theory have been suggested in the 1970s. Several of these are reviewed here. This is followed by a discussion on the advantages and limitations of bayesian decision theory.

9.3.1   *Review of applications in flood estimation*

In example 9.3 it is assumed that not more than one flood flow occurs in a year. In practice, more than one such event can occur in a single year. If these are serially independent events, the likelihood of n floods in T years, given a state of nature θ (where θ is the average number of floods per year), can be represented by the Poisson function

$$\ell(n \mid T, \theta) = (\theta T)^n e^{-\theta T}/n! \tag{9.17}$$

However, a linear loss function is not applicable in this case. Duckstein and Davis (Shen, 1976) give two types of non-linear loss functions and show the sensitivity of these to the Bayes solutions.

The Poisson density function has also been used in a simple bayesian application by Benjamin and Cornell (1970) to model the arrival of rare hurricane events in designing a barrier for a small harbour. Elsewhere, Davis *et al.* (1972a) apply the function to the number of thunderstorms per season and Wood (1973) assumes that floods above a threshold value are Poisson distributed. In all these, conjugate distributions given by Raiffa and Schlaifer (1961, chapter 3) are used to determine the posterior distributions.

Paintal (1972) assumes that the damage y caused by flood events has a negative exponential density $f(y) = \lambda^{-1}e^{-y/\lambda}$, where λ is the average damage per flood. By convolution, the total flood damage is shown to have a gamma density. Elsewhere, in a pioneering work, Bernier (1967) estimated prior probabilities of flows of the Seine and Marne in France using a regression model, for run-off and rainfall, and then found posterior distributions through Bayes' theorem. Also in the same area, prior probabilities are estimated by using the beta distribution from regional data in New South Wales by McGilchrist *et al.* (1970), and return intervals of river flows are evaluated through Bayes' theorem by using sample data. A similar study using objective prior probabilities is made by Schane and Gaver (1970) based on 38 stations in the southwestern United States. Again, the frequency of annual maximum floods are estimated by Cunnane and Nash (1974) using Bayes' theorem to compound the information in regional flood data, expressed by regression equations, and sample data to which the Gumbel distribution (explained in chapter 6) is applied.

One of the first hydrological studies on the evaluation of the worth of additional data was made by Davis and Dvoranchik (1971). The decision problem concerned the depth of piles for the construction of a bridge. Subsequently, Davis *et al.* (1972b) applied bayesian decision theory to the construction of dikes for flood protection on the Rillito Creek in Arizona. They used numerical methods for solving the decision problems in which the normal gamma function (the simple explanation by Schmitt (1969, chapter 6) should be referred to) represents the bivariate distribution of the parameters in the lognormal prior model for flood frequencies. An extension of this work using different probability functions has been made by Bodo and Unny (1976).

Yakowitz *et al.* (1974) have fitted the gamma family to winter rainfall at Tucson. Return periods and heights of flood levels are obtained numerically by using bayesian analysis. A conjugate family for the gamma law is derived. The discussions on the practical aspects of finding conjugate distributions and the numerical methods used, following Raiffa and Schlaifer (1961) and DeGroot (1970), make this a useful contribution.

9.3.2   *Summary of additional bayesian water resource methods*

Applications of decision theory to reservoir operation did not receive much attention prior to the mid-1970s. Russell (1974) presents a procedure for the derivation of rule curves required to operate a Canadian lake. He incorporates an engineer's subjective probabilities with maximum and minimum expected utility curves in the decision analysis. Elsewhere, a bayesian method for designing a reservoir under a stochastic sediment load is given by Duckstein *et al.* (1977).

Bayesian theory could be effectively applied to water quality and associated problems. An elementary case in flow measurement is given by Benjamin and Cornell (1970, p. 568) using an exponential utility function, subjective prior probabilities and sample likelihoods based on flow-gauging relationships.

Bayesian inference in a biological examination of water supplies is treated at a more advanced level by von Mises (1942), the German scientist and applied mathematician who was a renowned critique of classical methods. In this application, n samples are taken from a water supply, and biological tests are made to determine the possibility of contamination by bacteria. Here, the main interest is in whether each sample contains at least one bacterium of a particular kind, the probability associated with such an occurrence being θ; also, it is assumed that, if λ is the average number of bacteria per sample, $\theta = 1 - e^{-\lambda}$. For a·given value of θ the likelihood of x positive tests out of n is expressed by the Bernoulli function

$$\ell(x \mid n,\theta) = \binom{n}{x} \theta^x (1 - \theta)^{n-x} \tag{9.18}$$

If $g(\theta)$ denotes the prior density function of θ with regard to its variation over repetitions of the same procedure, the marginal distribution of x positive results is given by

$$P(X = x) = \int_{\theta_1}^{\theta_2} \binom{n}{x} \theta^x (1 - \theta)^{n-x} g(\theta) \, d\theta \tag{9.19}$$

von Mises has proved that as n increases the final probability becomes, as we expect, less dependent on the prior distribution. He showed the correct use of Bayes' theorem to determine the probabilities of a λ value between 0 and 1 and other intervals for given values of x. The example is based on results from 3420 examinations carried out in Massachusetts during the 1930s.

Algal counts x_i taken at time t_i from a sample of size v_i for monitoring the quality of lake water are assumed to have a Poisson distribution with an expected value $\alpha v_i e^{\beta t_i}$ by Behnken and Watts (1972). This leads to a likelihood function for parameters α, the theoretical algal density at the start of tests and β, the growth rate. For the non-informative prior distributions of the parameters α and β, the theory of invariance by Jeffreys (1961) is used. In this way, the bayesian posterior densities are obtained. However, the relative flatness of the prior densities does not make this a particularly useful practical application.

Elsewhere, Moore and Brewer (1972) show that bayesian methods can provide methodologies to deal with uncertainties in environmental systems.

Another area in which the bayesian approach has recently been applied is in the estimation of parameters to be used in producing synthetic data sets for water resource planning. Methods of dealing with estimation problems in the application of the first-order autoregressive models are suggested by Conover (1971), by Lenton *et al.* (1974) and by Vicens *et al.* (1975); an introduction is given by Box and Jenkins (1976, pp. 250–8). Such procedures can be beneficial when annual data are generated by using short historical samples.

Furthermore, a comprehensive review of decision making which embodies uncertainty in water resource systems is given by Duckstein and Davis (Shen, 1976, chapter 14).

An alternative non-bayesian approach to the worth of additional data is presented by Dawdy *et al.* (1970) using estimates of parameters from a long historical record. Increases in net benefits are found from a long historical record. Increases in net benefits are found from synthetic samples of different lengths and are compared with those from the historical data. The more rational bayesian method of estimating the distribution of the parameters conditional to the sample is indicated by Davis *et al.* (1972c).

9.3.3. *Potentialities and limitations of bayesian decision theory*

Since its revival in the second half of the twentieth century, it is apparent that bayesian theory is gaining acceptance as a practical tool for decision making in diverse fields. As shown here it could be beneficial to the water resource engineer in many situations. Elsewhere, considerable use has been made in kidney transplants, cancer research, medical diagnosis, space exploration, electrical power systems and other areas. This does not, on the other hand, justify indiscriminate application of bayesian decision theory; to express it differently, we should not bend a problem to suit the bayesian method.

If prior probabilities could be formulated on a rational basis or could be estimated from previous data sets or from outside evidence, we could reasonably update the probabilities after acquiring new information. It should be noted, though, that the mathematical functions used need scrutiny with respect to the assumptions made and the acceptable margins of error. The decision rule, of course, necessitates appraisal of loss or benefit functions or their discrete approximations. The effects of subjectivity in such valuations could only be assessed through sensitivity analyses.

There are those who argue vehemently against bayesian theory. The main argument seems to be about subjective prior probabilities. They find that experts could be irrational[28]. Against this, bayesian statisticians show that prior probabilities have little effect as data samples increase in length. They also say that the antagonists cannot produce a viable alternative.

[28] For instance, Hartley (1963) casts doubts on the concept of subjective probabilities when narrating a hypothetical story of happenings in the consulting room of a Dr Bayes.

By tradition, engineers do not often get involved in basic philosophies. To them quick practical solutions are of primary importance. If it is accepted that a decision maker has to rely to a certain extent on personal experience, judgement and preferences, a view which is obviously enhanced when considering nature's complexities, then a logical solution is attainable through the bayesian approach, provided it is used with discretion.

9.4   Other methods of decision theory and further reading

Apart from the bayesian approach there are several other techniques available to the decision maker. In general, the methods concern decision under risk because probabilities are assumed to be known. The Laplace, maximin, maximax, minimax and Hurwicz criteria constitute some of the older methods; these are explained in the following example.

Example 9.6   Consider the net benefit matrix shown in example 9.2.

State of nature (reservoir yield)	Net benefit for action =		
	A_1	A_2	A_3
θ_1	100	80	60
θ_2	120	180	140
θ_3	150	200	250

The Laplace criterion follows the principle of insufficient reason by assigning equal probabilities to each of the states of nature (under each action). Hence, the expected benefits are 123, 153 and 150 respectively for the three actions. By this method, therefore, action 2 is optimal because it gives the maximum expected benefit.

Again, it is seen that, under each of the actions, the minimum benefits are 100, 80 and 60 units. (These minima could occur in more than one row in other applications.) By the maximin criterion, action A_1 which gives the maximum benefits is chosen. In contrast with this pessimistic approach, if the maximum benefits are chosen for each action as given in the third row in this case, the maximax rule will lead to action A_3. These two methods are based on extreme utility functions and may result in unreasonable decisions in practical situations.

In von Neumann's minimax approach the matrix of benefits is converted to a loss, regret or OL matrix (von Neumann and Morgenstern, 1953). This is obtained by subtracting the highest value in a row from the values in that row. The row maxima are 100, 180 and 250; hence, the following regrets are obtained.

State of nature	Loss for action =		
	A_1	A_2	A_3
θ_1	0	20	40
θ_2	60	0	20
θ_3	100	50	0

For each of the actions the highest losses are 100, 50 and 40 units. The minimax solution is to find the minimum of these; hence, the decision is A_3. The shortcoming in this method is that differences in regrets may be linearly disproportionate to differences in benefits. Nevertheless, an adequately defined regret matrix may lead to useful design solutions. For example, Duckstein and Bogardi (1975) have suggested that the minimax method could be used in the design of large dams.

In another method named after the econometrician Hurwicz, a compromise solution is found by using the maximin and maximax criteria. The procedure, which is subjective, is to weight the minimum benefits under each action by α and the maximum benefits by $1 - \alpha$ and then to add the two values in each column to find the action giving the maximum benefits. For example, if $\alpha = 0.6$, totals of 120, 128 and 136 are obtained for each of the actions from the benefits matrix in example 9.2, this suggests that action A_3 is optimal. On the other hand, if $\alpha > 0.7$, which is a more conservative approach, the decision will be reversed.

Compared with decision theory under uncertainty involving Bayes' theorem and expected utilities which takes account of uncertainty in nature, the scope of these methods is restricted. Nevertheless, there are situations in which they can play a useful role. Tutorial type expositions, examples and critical appraisals of various decision criteria including these and others such as Laplace's principle of insufficient reason are found in Fishburn (1966), in Riggs (1968), in Halter and Dean (1971), in de Neufville and Stafford (1971) and in Luce and Raiffa (1957) (numerous references are also given by Luce and Raiffa). Also Sobel (1975) discusses stochastic minimax reservoir capacity.

As a general introductory text on decision theory, the book by Tribus (1969) should be of value to engineers; Siddall (1972) and Meredith et al. (1973) may also be referred to. The mathematical treatment of bayesian inference and decision in Winkler (1972) is simple, and, on the same subject, Schmitt (1969) provides an elementary introduction. The advanced work of Raiffa and Schlaifer (1961) on applied decision theory has already been cited. Readers who are discouraged by the rigorous notation will find the other books written by these authors more to their liking; for example, the lucid work on games and decisions by Luce and Raiffa (1957) needs hardly any mathematical background, and Schlaifer (1971) gives some basic computer programmes. For a modern philosophical background, the work of Levi (1967) should be useful. This is also at a lower mathematical level like the book on decision making by

Lindley (1970) and the book edited by Edwards and Tversky (1957) which provides notable contributions by several well-known authors on decisions, utilities and subjective probabilities. In addition, readers may find that the book on applications of bayesian methods in economics edited by Aykac and Brumat (1977) is informative. Finally, for an instructive though sophisticated text on subjective probabilities and non-bayesian decision making, White (1976) may be consulted.

References

Aitchison, J. (1970). *Choice Against Chance*, Addison-Wesley, Reading, Massachusetts

Anderson, J. C., Hiskey, H. H., and Lackawathana, S. (1971). Application of statistical decision theory to water use analysis in Sevier County, Utah. *Water Resour. Res.*, **7**, 443–52

Arrow, K. J. (1970). *Essays in the Theory of Risk-Bearing*, North-Holland, Amsterdam

Aykaç, A., and Brumat, C. (eds) (1977). *New Developments in the Applications of Bayesian Methods*, North-Holland, Amsterdam

Barnard, G. A. (1970). Essay towards solving a problem in the doctrine of chances by Thomas Bayes. *Studies in the History of Statistics and Probability* (eds E. S. Pearson and M. G. Kendall), Griffin, London, pp. 131–53; *Biometrika*, **45** (1958), 296–315

Behnken, D. W., and Watts, D. G. (1972). Bayesian estimation and design of experiments for growth rates, with applications to measuring water quality. *Proceedings of the International Symposium on Uncertainties in Hydrologic and Water Resource Systems*, vol. 1, *University of Arizona, Tucson, 11–14 December 1972, pp. 2–15*

Benjamin, J. R., and Cornell, C. (1970). *Probability, Statistics and Decision for Civil Engineers*, McGraw-Hill, New York

Bernier, J. (1967). Les methodes bayesiennes en hydrologie statistique. *Proceedings of the 1st International Hydrology Symposium*, vol. 1, *Fort Collins, Colorado*, pp. 459–70

Bodo, B., and Unny, T. E. (1976). Model uncertainty in flood frequency analysis and frequency-based design. *Water Resour. Res.*, **12**, 1109–17

Box, G. E., and Jenkins, G. M. (1976). *Time Series Analysis: Forecasting and Control*, revised edn, Holden Day, San Francisco, California

Bradley, J. V. (1976). *Probability; Decision; Statistics*, Prentice-Hall, Englewood Cliffs, New Jersey

Broadbent, D. E. (1973). *In Defence of Empirical Psychology*, Methuen, London

Bross, I. D. J. (1953). *Design for Decision*, The Macmillan Company, New York

Cavadias, G. (1967). Decision on basic statistical concepts. *Proceedings of the 5th Hydrology Symposium, McGill University*, 1966, Queen's Printer, Ottawa, pp. 29–34

—— (1972). Comments on 'Applications of statistical decision theory to water use analysis in Sevier County, Utah' by J. C. Anderson, H. H. Hiskey and S. Lackawathana. *Water Resour. Res.*, **8**, 746

Conover, W. J. (1971). Introduction to bayesian methods using the Thomas–Fiering model. *Water Resour. Res.*, **7**, 406–9

Coombs, C. H., and Beardslee, D. (1954). On decision making under uncertainty. *Decision Processes* (eds R. M. Thrall, C. H. Coombs and R. L. Davis), Wiley, New York, chapter 17

Cornfield, J. (1967). Bayes theorem. *Rev. Int. Statist. Inst.*, **35**, 34–49

Cunnane, C., and Nash, J. E. (1974). Bayesian estimation of frequency of hydrologic events. *Proceedings of the 1971 Warsaw Symposium on Mathematical Models in Hydrology*, vol. 1, International Association of Scientific Hydrology, Paris, pp. 47–55

Davis, D. R. (1971). Decision making under uncertainty in systems hydrology. *Univ. Arizona, Tucson, Arizona., Tech. Rep.*, No. 2

Davis, D. R., Duckstein, L., and Kisiel, C. C. (1972c). Comments on 'Value of streamflow data for project design—a pilot study' by D. R. Dawdy, H. E. Hubik and E. R. Close. *Water Resour. Res.*, **8**, 173

Davis, D. R., Duckstein, L., Kisiel, C. C., and Fogel, M. (1972a). Uncertainty in the return period of maximum events: a bayesian approach. *Proceedings of the International Symposium on Uncertainties in Hydrologic and Water Resource Systems*, vol. 2, 11–14 *December* 1972, *University of Arizona, Tucson*, pp. 853–62

Davis, D. R., and Dvoranchik, W. M. (1971), Evaluation of the worth of additional data. *Water Resour. Bull.*, **7**, 700–7

Davis, D. R., Kisiel, C. C., and Duckstein, L. (1972b). Bayesian decision theory applied to design in hydrology. *Water Resour. Res.*, **8**, 33–41

Dawdy, D. R., Kubik, H. E., and Close, E. R. (1970). Value of streamflow data for project design—a pilot study. *Water Resour. Res.*, **6**, 1045–50

DeGroot, M. H. (1970). *Optimal Statistical Decisions*, McGraw-Hill, New York

Duckstein, L., and Bogárdi, I. (1975). Discussion on 'Use of decision theory in reservoir operation' by S. Russell. *J. Hydraul. Div., Am. Soc. Civ. Eng.*, **101** (HY3), 558–60

Duckstein, L., Szidarovszky, F., and Yakowitz, S. (1977). Bayes design of a reservoir under random sediment yield. *Water Resour. Res.*, **13**, 713–19

Edwards, W., and Tversky, A. (eds) (1967). *Decision Making*, Penguin Books, Harmondsworth, Middlesex

Encyclopaedia Britannica (1977), vol. 11, 15th edn, William Benton, Chicago, pp. 666–70

Epstein, E. S. (1962). A bayesian approach to decision making in applied meteorology. *J. Appl. Meteorol.*, **1**, 169–77

Ferguson, T. (1967). *Mathematical Statistics: A Decision Theoretic Approach*, Academic Press, New York

de Finetti, B. (1972). *Probability, Induction and Statistics*, Wiley, London

Fishburn, P. C. (1966). Decision under uncertainty: an introductory exposition. *J. Ind. Eng.*, **17**, 341–53

Fisher, R. A. (1966). *The Design of Experiments*, 8th edn, Oliver and Boyd, Edinburgh

Glahn, H. R. (1964). The use of decision theory in meteorology. *Mon. Weath. Rev.*, **92**, 383–8

Gnedenko, B. V. (1968). *The Theory of Probability* (translated from Russian by B. D. Seckler), 4th edn, Chelsea, New York

Good, I. J. (1950). *Probability and the Weighting of Evidence*, Griffin, London.
—— (1959). Kinds of probability. *Science*, **129**, 443–7
—— (1962). *The Scientist Speculates*, Heineman, London

Halter, A., and Dean, C. (1971). *Decisions under Uncertainty with Research Applications*, Southwestern Publishing, Cincinnati, Ohio

Hartley, H. O. (1963). In Dr Bayes' consulting room. *Am. Statist.*, **17**, 22–4

Hillier, F. S., and Lieberman, G. J. (1974). *Operations Research*, 2nd edn, Holden Day, San Francisco, California

Horowitz, I. (1972). *An Introduction to Quantitative Business Analysis*, 2nd edn, McGraw-Hill, New York

Jeffreys, H. (1961). *Theory of Probability*, 3rd edn, Clarendon Press, Oxford

Kendall, M. G. (1949). On the reconcilation of theories of probability. *Biometrika*, **36**, 101–16

Keynes, J. M. (1921). *A Treatise on Probability*, Macmillan, London
—— (1973). A treatise on probability (with minor corrections) by The Royal Economics Society. *The Collected Works of John Maynard Keynes*, vol. 8, Macmillan, London

Kuiper, E. (1971). *Water Resources Project Economics*, Butterworth, London

Kyburg, H. E., Jr. (1966). Probability and decision. *Philos. Sci.*, **33**, 250–61

Kyburg, H. E., Jr., and Smokler, H. E. (eds) (1964). *Studies in Subjective Probability*, Wiley, New York

Lee, S. M. and Moore, L. J. (1975). *Introduction to Decision Science*, Petrocelli–Charter, New York

Lenton, R. L., Rodríguez-Iturbe, I., and Schaake, J. C., Jr. (1974). The estimation of ρ in the first order autoregressive model: a bayesian approach. *Water Resour. Res.*, **10**, 227–41

Levi, I. (1967). *Gambling with Truth*, Massachusetts Institute of Technology Press, Cambridge, Massachusetts

Lindley, D. V. (1970). *Making Decisions*, Wiley, New York

Luce, R. D., and Raiffa, H. (1957). *Games and Decisions*, Wiley, New York

McGilchrist, C. A., Chapman, T. G., and Woodyer, K. D. (1970). Recurrence intervals between exceedances of selected river levels, 3, estimation and use of prior distribution. *Water Resour. Res.*, **6**, 499–504

Maistrov, L. E. (1974). *Probability Theory—A Historical Sketch* (translated and edited by S. Kotz), Academic Press, New York

Maritz, J. S. (1970). *Empirical Bayes Methods*, Methuen, London

Meredith, D. D., Wong, K. W., Woodhead, R. W., and Workman, R. H.

(1973). *Design and Planning of Engineering Systems*, Prentice-Hall, Englewood Cliffs, New Jersey

von Mises, R. (1942). On the correct use of Bays' formula. *Ann. Math. Statis.*, **13**, 156–65

Moore, S. F., and Brewer, J. W. (1972). Environmental control systems: treatment of uncertainty in models and data. *Proceedings of the International Symposium on Uncertainties in Hydrologic and Water Resource Systems*, vol. 1, 11–14 December 1972, *University of Arizona, Tucson*, pp. 16–30

de Neufville, R., and Stafford, J. H. (1971). *Systems Analysis for Engineers and Managers*, McGraw-Hill, New York

von Neumann, J., and Morgenstern, O. (1953). *Theory of Games and Economic Behaviour*, 3rd edn, Princeton University Press, Princeton, New Jersey

Paintal, A. S. (1972). Stochastic model of flood risk evaluation. *Floods and Droughts. Proceedings of the 2nd International Hydrology Symposium, Fort Collins, Colorado*, pp. 343—8

Raiffa, H., and Schlaifer, R. (1961). *Applied Statistical Decision Theory*, Harvard University Press, Boston, Massachusetts

Ramsey, F. P. (1931). Truth and probability. *The Foundations of Mathematics and Other Logical Essays by F. P. Ramsey*, Harcourt, New York

——(1966). Truth and probability. *Studies in Subjective Probability* (eds H. E. Kyburg, Jr., and H. E. Smokler), Wiley, New York, chapter 3

Rényi, A. (1972). *Letters on Probability*, Wayne State University Press, Detroit, Michigan

Riggs, J. L. (1968). *Economic Decision Models for Engineers and Managers*, McGraw-Hill, New York

Rose, L. M. (1976). *Engineering Investment Decisions, Planning under Uncertainty*, Elsevier, Amsterdam

Russell, S. O. (1974). Use of decision theory in reservoir operation. *J. Hydraul. Div., Am. Soc. Civ. Eng.*, **100** (HY6), 809–17

Savage, L. J. (1954). *The Foundations of Statistics*, Wiley, New York

Savage, L. J., *et al.* (1962). *The Foundations of Statistical Inference*, Methuen, London

Schane, R. M., and Gaver, D. P. (1970). Statistical decision theory techniques for the revision of mean flood flow regression estimates. *Water Resour. Res.*, **6**, 1649–54

Schlaifer, R. (1971). *Computer Programs for Elementary Decision Analysis*, Harvard University Press, Boston, Massachusetts

Schmitt, S. A. (1969). *Measuring Uncertainty, An Elementary Introduction to Bayesian Statistics*, Addision-Wesley, Reading, Massachusetts

Shen, S. W. (ed.) (1976). *Stochastic Approaches to Water Resources*, Water Resources Publications, Fort Collins, Colorado

Siddall, J. N. (1972). *Analytical Decision-Making in Engineering Design*, Prentice-Hall, Englewood Cliffs, New Jersey

Sobel, M. J. (1975). Reservoir management models. *Water Resour. Res.*, **11**, 767–76

Thomas, H. A., Jr. (1948). Frequency of minor floods. *J. Boston Soc. Civ. Eng.*, **35**, 425–42

Tiao, G. C., and Box, G. E. P. (1973). Some comments on 'Bayes' estimators. *Am. Statist.*, **27**, 12–14

Thuesen, H. G., Fabrycky, W. J., and Thuesen, G. J. (1977). *Engineering Economy*, 5th edn, Prentice-Hall, Englewood Cliffs, New Jersey

Tribus, M. (1969). *Rational Descriptions, Decisions and Designs*, Pergamon, New York

Vicens, G. J., Rodríguez-Iturbe, I., and Schaake, J. C., Jr. (1975). Bayesian generation of synthetic streamflows. *Water Resour. Res.*, **11**, 827–38

Wald, A. (1950). *Statistical Decision Functions*, Wiley, New York

White, D. J. (1976). *Fundamentals of Decision Theory*, North-Holland, New York

Winkler, R. A. (1972). *An Introduction to Bayesian Inference and Decision*, Holt, Rinehart and Winston, New York

Wonnacott, T. H., and Wonnacott, R. J. (1972). *Introductory Statistics for Business and Economics*, 2nd edn, Wiley, New York

Wood, E. F. (1973). Flood control design with limited data—comparison of classical and bayesian approaches. *Design of Water Resources Projects with Inadequate Data, Symposium, Madrid, Int. Assoc. Sci. Hydrol, Publ.*, No. 108 1974, vol. 1, pp. 31–46.

Yakowitz, S., Duckstein, L., and Kisiel, C. (1974). Decision analysis of a gamma hydrologic variate. *Water Resour. Res.*, **10**, 695–704

Zellner, A. (1971). *An Introduction to Bayesian Inference in Econometrics*, Wiley, New York

Index

* (f) denotes the footnote on the appropriate
page.

THE MINISTER is a richly
of twenty-five ve
Protestant m

by-ste
ing his
the challenge

The scope of
esty Charles Mercer rec
dramatically and wh
of two deeply committed
Martin Judson and his son-in-la
Murchison, who is very much of the so
school of social action. Though they se
their calling differently, they both confront the common problems and quoti-
dian details of the minister's life: the
difficulties of living on a minister's
salary in today's affluent society, the
politics of a deacon's meeting, the need
to keep a minister's wife slightly less
well dressed than the wives of congregational leaders, the constant pressure t
increase membership, interviews w
pulpit-hiring committees, the pre
of unchristian bigotry in the

Christians,
for any mi
age of forty.

Martin's pers
complex. He ha
his years as a mi
year post to a pos
a foundation missi
during the Korean
of a crumbling ba
church. But always
lenge, the sense of
Martin finds himself
where he belongs in the

Like such best-selling
Cardinal, The Rabbi, and
Douglas' novels, THE MINI
a picture of the religious
frustrations—of the reward
THE MINISTER is a superb novel not only
because Charles Mercer is a seasoned
novelist with eleven highly acclaimed
books to his credit, but also because he
knows the story of a Christian minister—he has lived it. His father is a
prominent Baptist clergyman, and THE
MINISTER is the novel Charles Mercer
has been wanting to write all his life.

(Continued on back fla

today.

THE MINISTER

Novels by Charles Mercer

THE NARROW LEDGE

THERE COMES A TIME

RACHEL CADE

THE DRUMMOND TRADITION

ENOUGH GOOD MEN

THE RECKONING

GIFT OF LIFE

BEYOND BOJADOR

PILGRIM STRANGERS

THE TRESPASSERS

PROMISE MORNING

THE MINISTER

THE
MINISTER

BY

Charles Mercer

G. P. Putnam's Sons
New York

To
Alma, my wife

—

Walter J. Minton

—

The memory of my mother,
Alma Hoover Mercer

—

My father,
the Reverend Alfred T. Mercer

THE MINISTER

 One

IN later years, when they would say there were few certainties, they would remark that there nevertheless was one: On whatever day they moved themselves and their belongings from one place to another it would rain.

It was so on their first move from Davidson in New York State to Upton, a small city in Pennsylvania. Even if the rain had not been pouring down on that late afternoon in September, Upton would have appeared depressing. They approached it from the north along a highway lined by auto graveyards and secondhand car lots; then a trolley line began among billboards and rushed down a hill into rain, smoke, and heavy traffic. Though they knew their destination, they had no idea how to get there.

Jane said, "Why don't we ask directions?"

"There's plenty of time to case this city." Martin sounded dispirited. "Looks dismal, doesn't it? I wouldn't mind driving straight on through it. All the way to Florida. We've never been there. After all, we have a hundred and fifty bucks. I qualify as a short-order cook. You qualify as a teacher of fifth-grade primates. I'll walk the beach with you, and that is all we'll ever do."

She cast him a look of amusement rather than alarm. Then the baby, Kathy, trussed securely in the back seat of the Model A, began to talk in her private language, reminding him that he was a father, as well as a short-order cook and lover. If the child would wail and the wife be alarmed, he could drive straight through this lousy place, on to Florida or bust.

Somewhere beyond a dingy railroad station, among bleak buildings where possibly things like floor wax and cardboard boxes were manufactured, he drew up beside a man who stood solemnly in the rain for no discernible reason.

Rolling down the window, Martin asked him, "Can you tell me how to find the First Baptist Church?"

The man said, "You got me, Mac."

"You got me, Mac." Martin never forgot the words. Somehow they fixed the date: 1940.

By the time they found the church, all the joyful anticipation of the past month had drained from him. The church was a monstrosity—an aged, angular spinster of a building, corseted frigidly in dirty yellow brick, with a tall spire which probed the smog like a dirty plume. He had curbed his undergraduate habit of cursing when under emotional stress, so he merely said, "Good gosh!"

Jane said, "But it has a nice big porch."

He realized she was gazing at the parsonage, which looked like the squatting cousin of the old maid church. On the other side of the church from the parsonage was a large lot gone to brush and surreptitiously dumped refuse. ("We have plenty of room for expansion," the churchman of the pulpit committee had told him by telephone.) Up and down the street dull clapboard houses crowded heaving slate sidewalks and dying swamp maples.

Jane said, "How did the movers get here before we did?"

Martin saw, then, the small van on the cinder driveway. He was taking in things too slowly. He said, "We must have spent too much time picnicking at Watkins Glen."

Leaving Kathy in the car, he and Jane walked up the brick

path toward the long front porch and gaping front door as the mover, a spidery old man, and his young helper came out.

"You finally got here," the spider said accusingly. "All the stuff's inside. We got to get on our way. Here's the bill."

"Well," Jane said, "we'll just see first if all the stuff *is* inside."

Martin paused in starting to grope for his wallet. He wanted to get rid of the spider, but Jane was right. He took the bill, holding it from him as if it were a bit of dead fish, then followed Jane. Ninety-eight dollars. It was the amount he and the mover had agreed on, and the pulpit committee chairman had said the church would pay the bill.

"I should have followed Father's advice," he said to Jane. "He told me always to look over the charge before accepting the call."

But he had not had a chance. He had been making money that summer teaching a philosophy course in Ohio. The Upton pulpit committee had heard him preach in Davidson last June, and he had forgotten about them until the telephone call a month ago, when they presumably had decided that green though he was, he was the best they could get for thirty-six hundred a year and parsonage.

"Reverend Judson, Mrs Judson. Welcome to Upton."

The speaker was a tall, drably dressed woman with a Gothic face, in which pity for them was mixed with uncertainty about herself. Or so Martin thought. His thinking was convulsed. The woman standing there reminded him of a thousand he had known in his youth as a Congregational preacher's son. She couldn't put anything over on him—*them*—because he was the preacher's crafty kid who knew every angle of the sport and several more besides when it came to sparring against pity, uncertainty, patrimony. *She* of the Gothic face looking down at him was why he had vowed in youth never to be a preacher: The organized church was passive, woman-dominated, ineffective with the young.

"Well," Jane said, "it's good to be here."

Well, indeed, he was *here*, a preacher himself who retained many of the misgivings of the preacher's crafty son. He wreathed a smile on her Gothic face and got her name at once, Mrs. McDonald, without the *a,* and saw beyond her a happier female face mounted on a portlier frame. *Her* name was Mrs. Tabor, with an *o,* and everyone was glad to meet.

The interior of the parsonage was the cavernous place he expected it to be. A large center hall with stairs ascending into gloom. To the right a large, wide-windowed room, which inevitably would be his study; Mrs. McDonald and Mrs. Tabor had known that, for they had directed the movers to place his desk and cartons of books there—all looking small and lost in the infinite spaces. To the left a smaller room, where their rug and two easy chairs had been placed. And behind that, heaven help the Judsons, another room, vacant, and to the right of *that* a large dining room, where their little Woolworth's dinette set was spread in forlorn embarrassment. And behind everything a kitchen big enough to feed the inmates of a county jail.

"Well," Martin said, "I see we have plenty of room for boarders."

Mrs. M. and Mrs. T. tittered nervously.

"Oh, look!" Jane exclaimed. "What a *beautiful* refrigerator!"

It was a big one all right, much larger than the one they had used in their two-room apartment in Davidson. Happiness came to the women as Jane kept opening and closing the refrigerator door. "It's almost brand-new," said Mrs. McDonald.

The mover, who had been following in their wake, whined again that he had to get going. "We had him put your bed in the front room upstairs," said Mrs. Tabor, "if that's all right."

Martin took five twenty-dollar bills from his wallet and said, "Keep the change." The mover looked at him with loathing. "And receipt the bill." The mover did so and left silently.

Mrs. McDonald, looking worriedly at the receipted bill on the drainboard, said, "Mr. Ingham should be along any minute." Ingham, chairman of the pulpit committee, obviously was the Mr. Big of the First Baptist Church of Upton.

When Ingham arrived, Martin was in the cellar staring with

consternation at the furnace. He had observed that the parsonage had a hot-water heating system—a coal saver, but hot water
could be tricky. From his youngest days in cold country parsonages in Maine, New Hampshire, Vermont, and Massachusetts
he had helped his father struggle with a variety of heating
systems; indeed, he considered himself something of a furnace
expert. But this furnace he stared at in the dim light of a fifty-
watt bulb defied his knowledge; it was festooned with valves
which made utterly no sense. Worse yet, the cellar, only half
paved, bore signs of periodic flooding.

And then Jane called down the stairs, "Dear, Mr. Ingham
and the other men are here."

"Yes, *dear*." He did not mean to sound sarcastic.

There were four men, and Martin recognized Ingham at once
—even before he said, "John Ingham, Pastor." He had the
strong, stocky body, the balding, brave skull, the fleshy jaw, and
shrewd blue eyes of those men who follow the bidding of
empire builders.

"And you probably remember Mr. Warren, chairman of the
board of deacons, from our talk after church in Davidson last
June." Warren was old and withering, a relic of the McKinley
administration, complete with stiff collar.

"And Harcourt Prescott of the board of trustees." Tall,
ascetic, ineffectual somehow, he sparked a foolish prejudice in
Martin. Harcourt Prescott? Why not Prescott Harcourt? Men
with interchangeable names so often were interchangeable on
any issue. Strike that from the record. After all, why not Judson Martin?

"And this is Bill Powers, the youngest member of the board
of trustees." Martin liked him at once, perhaps because he was
guilty of being under thirty. He had the cheerful countenance
and compact body of a high school athlete. Martin knew that
Powers sized him up swiftly, liked him immediately, and then
his expression changed, and he cast him a warning: Look out
for what's coming, buddy. Or did Martin only imagine it?

There were eight of them now and only seven chairs, even

counting the desk chair in the study. But that was all right, for Ingham glanced a dismissal at Mrs. M. and Mrs. T., who suddenly seemed relieved to go. Jane went to the door with them, and Ingham said to Martin, "Is everything all right?"

"Why, yes, I guess so, Mr. Ingham. The furnace looks a bit baffling. Has there been trouble with it?"

Prescott and Powers sat tensely, but Warren hooked a creaking knee over the other relaxedly and said, "I've got her working fine now, Pastor. Fixed it myself last March. I was in the plumbing business till my son-in-law took it over and I retired last year. You know, it's fine you made such a good record at Davidson Theological Seminary, but the thing I liked best when we checked up on your background is that you're a *Yankee*. My folks came from Connecticut two generations back, but before then, why—"

"Yes," said Ingham as Jane, carrying Kathy, sat down and only Powers made a move to rise. "Yes." Ingham looked at Kathy doubtfully; she questioned Martin with a glance asking whether she should stay there, and his eyes told her firmly, yes.

"Well," Ingham said, "we might as well come to the point. We have bad news."

Martin looked at him.

"We've found the church is in a bad budget situation. Of course we've been without a pastor since Dewey ran out on us last April. The economy here in Upton has been on the slide for the past year, too. Triller's and a couple of other plants are laying off. Between the New Deal and the war in Europe and everything, nobody knows what's going to happen. Anyway, church contributions have fallen 'way off. We're in a bind. Frankly, Mr. Judson, we can't meet that salary figure of thirty-six hundred. I mean we'll have to work *back* to it. We'll have to start you in at twenty-eight."

Martin felt himself flushing. He remembered one other bit of advice from his father: "Martin, if you're going to preach, you'll just have to forget you have a temper."

Warren leaned toward him eagerly. "You see what we mean, Pastor?"

Ignoring him, Martin said to Ingham, "When did you find this out? Last night?"

Ingham stirred. "The trustees met on Monday night, two days ago."

Warren said, "Twenty-eight hundred and house to boot is mighty good for a young fellow of twenty-five like you with no experience. My grandson—he's twenty-four—you know what he's making as a salesman out in Pittsburgh?"

"Pipe down, Tom," Ingham told him. "Let Mr. Judson have his say."

"Are you a businessman, Mr. Ingham?"

Ingham looked mildly surprised that he did not know. "I'm treasurer of Makinson Tool and Die."

Martin said, "A college teacher of mine—"

"Excuse me," Prescott said, "but I can't remember what college you attended."

"Brown."

"A good little college, Brown."

"Well, thanks."

"Harcourt went to *Yale*." Was Warren bragging or complaining?

Martin continued doggedly. "This college teacher—I respected him greatly—was fond of saying that the two most immoral professions in the world are teaching and the clergy. And the most moral, he said, is business. That's because business understands and abides by what *contract* means. But my friend said that in the main preachers and teachers have no sense of the obligation of contract."

Ingham was looking at him with a hint of a smile. "Then why didn't you go into business?"

"Maybe because I couldn't find a job that seemed interesting and worthwhile."

Prescott said, "But we didn't *sign* anything with you."

"That has nothing to do with it," Powers said. "There was an understanding, a verbal contract."

Ingham said, "Bill wanted to come along to express his personal exception to what we have to do in the light of the sad facts of the budget."

Warren said, "Bill is a *teacher*. Over the hill at Gannon College."

Bill Powers said, "I teach *business* administration."

Ingham said, "I like the way you talk, Mr. Judson. I mean that honestly, no sarcasm. I believe what the dean of Davidson Theological wrote us—that you have the makings of an outstanding minister. But now we're all up against a reality—a fact of life. What are you going to do?"

To Martin's surprise his anger was ebbing. Perhaps just to *talk* and sound wise was the chief compensation he sought. And yet he knew that was not true. They had conned him into coming here, and now he had no choice but to stay. He cooled himself further with two bits worth of rhetoric, the only coin available to him under the circumstances: Take it gracefully, Buster, and never wash yourself down the drain of revenge.

Thinking of something moderately graceful to say, he got to his feet. "I guess the lecture period is over. Let's get down to the lab work. When can I have a telephone installed?"

Ingham's face relaxed in a smile. "Tomorrow. I'll see to it. We agreed to pay your moving expenses. Do you have the bill?"

Martin started going through his pockets, and Jane said, "It's on the kitchen drainboard. I'll get it."

"You're pretty short of furniture here," Warren said. "The wife and I have some things stored in her sister's place that you can—"

"No," Martin said.

"But—"

"No," Ingham said.

"But I'm just trying to—"

"*No*, Tom," Ingham said.

A letter came from Tubby Larsen one golden Saturday morning late in October. "Hey, Marty" it began, in the way Tubby nearly always addressed him, reminding Martin of such golden fall days as this back in 1933, when both were freshmen at Brown and living in upper cubicles of Hope College.

Now the Reverend Robert B. (for Browning) Larsen reported under the letter head of the First Baptist Church of Thornton, Massachusetts, that last Saturday he had developed laryngitis cheering another failing Brown team at the Dartmouth game and on Sunday morning, it being too late to find a supply preacher, had conducted a musical service of worship. "My people are downcast over me. They view me with alarm and doubt. How can such a strapping fellow suddenly lose his voice?"

Martin, smiling, wandered to the kitchen, where Jane was mixing a cake. "You know," he said, "Tubby's lonely. He ought to get married."

"Do you think you have a profound solution to his problem?" Jane asked. "He could have married any girl we introduced him to in Davidson. He's just too shy."

"He's not really," Martin said, continuing to read the letter. "Do you want me to stir that cake for you?"

"No, thanks. You work your side of the street; I'll work mine. You must have something more important to do."

He ambled back to his study. His Sunday sermon was prepared. Usually he had a sermon in hand by Wednesday or Thursday; the preparation was the most interesting thing he did.

He read the end of Tubby's letter: "You remember Colonel Birdwell—the Barber Pole Affair. At the game on Saturday I was talking to Dan McIntyre, who kept track of the colonel. It seems that almost a year ago Birdwell joined the RAF. And on October first he was shot down and killed while fighting in the Battle of Britain. It sets you to thinking, Marty, about who and what is worthy. . . ."

Martin's pleasure in the letter ebbed into disquiet. Through college and seminary both Tubby and he had displayed schizoid emotions about world affairs: on the one hand, alarm at the increase of totalitarian power; on the other, a vociferous pacifism. Now, to them both, the cause of Britain was indubitably right. Now they, as clergymen, were *safe* from war while Laurence Birdwell. . . . Now he had offered to help his wife stir a cake while Birdwell in a final ecstasy of fear and pleasure high over Britain. . . .

"Hey, Tubby—"

He wrote the salutation to the letter on his typewriter but did not know how to begin.

Tubby was not short and stout, as the name implied. He was, rather, round and strong and durable, like one of those indestructible hickory tubs in which rural citizens of New England used to catch runoff rainwater for the weekly wash. Most people called him Bob; only a few close friends, of whom Martin became the most intimate, knew him as Tubby.

As freshmen at Brown they had eyed each other warily at first. Tubby immediately joined the Brown Christian Association while Martin was in a phase of militant agnosticism. Mutual respect began to grow, however, when both made the freshman hockey team. Tubby was to become one of the greatest goalies Brown ever had. Martin was a flashy skirmisher. Each loved the game. Each was a serious student, too; Martin made Phi Beta in his junior year, Tubby when a senior. Martin became managing editor of the *Daily Herald* and wrote passionate editorials about nearly everything while Tubby (who was caged for twenty minutes for assaulting the captain of the Harvard team in the '37 game) plugged for God and pacifism in the Christian Association.

The first tie to bind them, even more than hockey, was poverty. Five hundred dollars a year was the most the Reverend David Judson could put toward Martin's higher education. Martin had to earn the rest by winning scholarships, waiting on tables, and working as a cook summers in New England resorts.

Tubby, whose father had gone broke in the failure of a Fall River textile mill, had to work as hard as Martin.

The Barber Pole Affair occurred early in their sophomore year. It began with a yearning on the part of the classmate called Colonel Birdwell, who hailed from South Carolina and whose speech and manner seemed such a caricature of Southern colonelism that some suspected he actually came from Iowa or Illinois. The colonel, who smoked cigars and consumed large quantities of bourbon, boasted of expertise in horseflesh and womenflesh, in pinochle and hunting dogs. His days at Brown were numbered. "By my own hand, my own indolence," he was fond of saying with a measure of regret.

On a beautiful October morning in 1934 he was hanging out a window of Slater Hall and talking to Martin and Tubby on the ground below. "Gentlemen, before I leave these ivied halls [he really talked that way], I would like to do *some one thing*. Something the gentlemen here would always remember. Something I, down there on the old plantation, would always remember with pride."

"Such as what, Colonel?" Martin asked him.

"I don't rightly *know*. Last night I dreamed of barber poles. I know it was a phallic dream. I awoke with a two-foot erection and no female handy. But this morning I've been thinking of barber poles. It would be mighty fine if I could acquire every barber pole in downtown Providence before I leave."

Martin had a slight inspiration. He would refine it later, but he had the beginning of a plan. "Colonel, you have money?"

"Pots of it, Marty my boy. I could *buy* every barber pole in downtown Providence. But there'd be no *distinction* in that."

"Here's what you do right now," Martin told him. "Go downtown. Get the location of every barber pole between the foot of College Hill and where Elm Street begins to rise and between Pearl Street and Union Station. I'll be in the *Herald* office at four o'clock this afternoon. Bring me the list."

"Well, now," the colonel said, "I can't go downtown after dark. I—"

"This is broad daylight," Tubby said.

"I know, but I'm anticipatin' you gentlemen. After what happened to me at the Old France and that business with the two dames at the Biltmore, the police captain, he said—and Dean Arnold, he said—I—Not after dark." He brightened. "But I know you as intelligent gentlemen. I'll just hie me downtown *right now*. I'll take a little stroll."

When Martin described the germ of his plan, Tubby hailed his genius. "It will take great organization, Marty. I'll get to work on it right away."

The colonel came to the *Herald* office at four o'clock, his usually sleepy countenance almost animated. "There's forty-*three* of them there poles in the prescribed area. I've marked 'em on this map. But the one in the basement of the Biltmore is see-mented in. Now what? I can't go *downtown* after dark."

"Establish your headquarters in Slater Hall, Colonel. The troops will be deployed. Give me seventy-five bucks."

Unhesitatingly Colonel Birdwell peeled the amount from a roll in a pocket, and a few minutes later Martin and Tubby hurried down College Hill. They selected a barbershop on the far side of the downtown area from the campus, and by agreement Tubby, because he exuded the sincerity of a good Christian youth, addressed the Italian shopowner: They were boys from Brown who had been delegated to buy a barber pole for a fraternity initiation. How much? After some dickering they agreed, surprisingly, on a price of seventy-five dollars. Then Martin explained that they couldn't pick up the pole until seven o'clock, after closing time. They must have a bill of sale. Furthermore, they must have the owner's home phone number so that if the police should think they were stealing the pole, its sale could be verified. The barber agreed.

When they went to Slater and revealed the extent of the plan, the colonel's eyes moistened with pleasure. He poured himself half a tumbler of bourbon and chided them gently for being teetotalers. "I'll have an adjutant commandeer the dormitory phone. Phase one of the operation is under way." And then he had to say a few words about his great-grandfather, who allegedly had ridden with Jeb Stuart.

At seven o'clock, after darkness had fallen, Martin and Tubby arrived at the barbershop. Acting as furtively as thieves, they worked with screwdrivers and a wrench at the pole fittings. The pole was almost loosened when a police squad car drew up and there was the inevitable encounter. The police, believing the bill of sale a fraud, took them to precinct headquarters. The desk sergeant there, like most desk sergeants in New England in those days, was Irish, and like nearly every desk sergeant in Providence, Rhode Island, in those days, he hated Brown undergraduates as a gang of dirty, tormenting Protestants and Jews. To Tubby's scarcely concealed amazement, Martin identified him by the name of the religion department chairman at Brown and himself by the name of the philosophy department chairman. (It was a sudden improvisation in the original plan.) Martin insisted that the sergeant phone the barbershop owner, who verified their story. Though still suspicious, the sergeant knew the penalty for false arrest and let them go.

They resumed work on the barber pole. After they had released it, they carried it off in the most furtive manner possible. They had gone less than two blocks when a foot patrolman arrested them.

Upon seeing them again, the desk sergeant yelled, "Get those young bastards the hell out of here!"

Leaving the precinct headquarters again, they carried the pole stealthily down the street. They had gone some distance and were beginning to fear their mission had failed when another patrol car stopped them and took them back to the precinct station.

The sergeant was enraged. These young bastards were making fools of the Providence police force. He ordered a message put on the printer to all precincts, for forwarding to all cars: Two Brown students—he slightly misspelled the names of the department chairmen of religion and philosophy—had bought a barber pole and were carrying it back to the campus. Pay no attention to them. "Now get the hell out of here!"

They stopped at the first telephone booth, and Martin called the colonel's adjutant. "Deploy the troops for phase two." Each team, if questioned, was to identify themselves as—

By ten o'clock that evening there were thirty-seven barber poles in Colonel Birdwell's room. The DU's, Dekes, and Alpha Delts each kept one as compensation for their efforts. The colonel didn't care. He never had been so happy—and possibly never would be so happy again. He had his picture taken with the barber poles for future verification of his greatest undergraduate accomplishment.

A few days later, before he departed from Brown, the colonel told Martin of his final interview with the dean: "The dean he said to me, 'Birdwell, you have steadfastly maintained that the affair was entirely your idea, not the result of a mastermind or a committee of masterminds!' Honest, Marty, I wanted to give you credit, but I had to protect my *friends*. And the dean says, 'Birdwell, in the light of everything else that's happened, I have to send you away. But as man to man, if the Barber Pole Affair really *was* your idea, I must commend your creative thinking and organizational ability. It indicates you'll go far in one of the only two fields in which Americans really excel— business and politics.' How about that, Marty? In a few years when you and Bob Larsen are in the Senate or chairman of the board of U.S. Steel you'll know that the old colonel is down there on the plantation cheerin' you on. . . ."

Now Tubby and he were the pastors of small, inconsequential churches while the colonel had fought and died gloriously in a war that was, in the great Augustinian tradition, truly just.

Martin stepped to the big front window and looked out. In the mellow October sunlight the dying swamp maples along Congress Street expressed a menopausal yearning to look golden. A two-door Oldsmobile came slowly along the street and stopped in front of the parsonage. The man who climbed out surely was a clergyman. How did you spot one? Martin sometimes had pondered the question. Dark suit and benign visage, yes. But there was some other quality difficult to define. Could it be a hasty pace that disguised subconsciously a man with infinite time to kill? Or could it be the carefully pressed clothing and cautious haberdashery that reflected a parsimonious wardrobe?

Martin answered the doorbell. "Martin Judson? . . . Harold Engel, pastor of Brick Presbyterian." They shook hands, and Martin led him into the study. "Missed meeting you at the ministerial fellowship luncheon last week. Couldn't make it. Had a funeral."

Engel was a well-preserved sixty or so. He had a knowledgeable air; perhaps it was the way he took in Martin and his scantly furnished study without obvious staring. The index and middle fingers of his right hand were stained with cigarette tar, so Martin moved the ashtray from his desk to the little table beside Engel's chair.

"Thanks." Engel relieved himself of a smile. "I'm an inveterate smoker." He took out a pack of Camels. "Have one?"

"No, thanks."

"Saw you staring out your window as I was passing. Having trouble with tomorrow's sermon?"

"No. Just daydreaming, I guess. I *think* my sermon was wound up day before yesterday."

"Mine, too. It usually is. Saturday is the worst day of the week for a minister. The tardy ones are thrashing about wildly for an idea. The earlies, like you and me, don't know exactly what to do with themselves."

Without subtlety Engel grilled him on his background. Martin had gathered that Brick Presbyterian and Grace Episcopal were the strongest churches in Upton, meaning their memberships included many wealthy and socially prominent citizens. Engel bluntly stated what Martin already had learned: The membership of the First Baptist Church was largely middle and lower middle class with some from the upper lower. These sociological distinctions, expressed so badly, made Martin uncomfortable, even though Engel hastened to add that he simply meant to be *helpful*. That is, he meant Martin and his wife faced the social repressions that the American middle classes typically inflicted on their clergy. A real smart guy, Engel, a real snob.

In an effort to divert him, Martin called Jane in and introduced her.

"Your wife is very attractive," Engel said after she had gone. "Too attractive to meet many people's ideas of a minister's wife."

Martin looked at him blankly and said, "As long as she's my idea of a wife, I don't care what other people think."

Engel retreated and then cautiously began a flanking movement. "Do you have any hobbies?"

Martin shook his head.

"You need some hobby other than God if you're going to be credible to people. D'you like any sports?"

"Hockey."

"Hockey? *Hockey!* No good."

"I enjoy skiing, swimming, hiking."

"Unh-unh." Engel shook his head. "Too solitary. Rich men's pastimes. You should take up golf."

"The couple of times I tried to play it I hated it."

"Nobody really likes golf. It's a form of masochism—an atonement for sins real or imagined. But you learn to play it, and play it well. Never join a club, even if you can afford it someday. Let the rich men invite you to *their* clubs, and beat them at their detestable game. Have a drink in the locker room afterward—*one* drink. The point of all this is to demonstrate that while you're a minister, you're nevertheless a man."

Martin began to be amused by Engel's cynical pragmatism about the nature of their profession.

"Join a service club. Speak anywhere—everywhere—about commonplace things—not about religion. To be a truly effective minister, my young friend, you have to learn the con game."

Then was life just one grand Barber Pole Affair?

"I know you're young and idealistic and probably think I'm cynical. But I'm giving you good advice I had to learn the hard way over the course of forty years. Why did you become a clergyman?"

"I'm not sure." Martin weighed his words slowly, knowing there was no use in talking about *belief* since that was implicit. Engel, like most shrewd and successful men, was concerned chiefly with means and kept ends somewhat vague on the gambler's chance they might turn out to lack abiding satisfaction. (In the Barber Pole Affair the fun had been in *getting* those poles rather than *having* them stacked in Colonel Birdwell's room.) "My father was a minister, so I know something about the life. I had to work most of my way through college. I thought about going to law school, but I wasn't eager for three more years of grinding labor. My father couldn't give me any more money. I majored in philosophy in college. I went through a . . . development, you might call it, a . . . *thing*. The *reason* in Christianity coincided with the . . . development of my thinking. But I didn't have to make it a full-time profession. I might not have if some company had offered me an interesting job at a living wage. But no one did. Most of my classmates graduated into careers of job hunting. My closest friend was going to Davidson Theological. And then the seminary offered me a full scholarship, plus a well-paid job in the library, where I could read most of the time. So—here I am."

"Good." Engel smiled at him warmly. "The best answer I've yet heard to all the gratuitous advice I'm always giving young ministers. Absolute honesty. Absolute recognition of the role of the buck in every man's life. You may not last the course. An awful lot go down the pipe. But you show possibilities for it."

In some respects an individual is like a boat. (That was, at least, the imagery Martin chose.) One has specific dimensions, a definite capacity, a means of locomotion, a cruising range.

A few weeks after Martin came to Upton he employed the

imagery in the most acclaimed sermon he had yet preached. As with every art, his preaching was self-taught. He had, of course, studied homiletics in the seminary: the how to do it; where to find it; when to try it. But when it came to actually preaching, he found homiletics as little useful as a practicing novelist would find a course in creative writing. That sermon, which he entitled "The Same Boat?" on the church bulletin board and in the weekly calendar, became a significant guidepost to him in the course of his preaching. He stumbled on the concept accidentally and tried, despite the interest it aroused, not to preach precisely the same kind of sermon repeatedly.

The concept was not a rousing preachment of faith; rather, it offered listeners the *implication* of faith. From it Martin began to learn it is better to suggest than to affirm. In preparing it, he began to analyze great preaching—how it is developed, why it rarely is achieved. A good sermon, he began to see, is different from a good essay. Though it is not histrionics, it is like a moving theatrical experience in that it is human experience realized.

It would be easy for him to preach *down* to the people of First Baptist. But that would be fatal—if not to them, to him personally, for he would lose all interest in preaching and therefore all self-respect. So he would try to pretend that things were a bit better than they actually were, his audience a bit more sophisticated than it appeared to be.

"So let's imagine a person being like a boat," he told the congregation. "We usually think of a boat as something that never changes. Can a slow old barge become a swift racing sloop? One thinks not. And in the same way many of us believe a person cannot change. Yet I want to tell you about a boat that used to ply out of Bristol, Rhode Island. She was called the *Lazy Susan,* a stout old sailing tub which once carried fresh vegetables to the Providence market. Slow, but her timber was the finest."

One day, Martin continued, a plank was removed from the *Lazy Susan* and an aluminum strip fitted in its place. As time went on, there were other replacements until the boat finally was dry-docked and completely refitted and refurbished.

"Was it the same boat? She still was called the *Lazy Susan,* but was she another boat? Meanwhile, a boatbuilder had been collecting the fine timber of the original boat as it was discarded. From it he built a fine racing sloop, which won more than one racing cup off Newport. Though he called it the *Lazy Susan* for sentiment's sake, he considered it a new boat. But was it? Or was it the original boat? Which was the new, which the old, or were *both* the same boat?"

Martin did not attempt to answer the question. Instead, he led his listeners into pondering the identity of the self—of the seemingly unchangeable giving birth to something new, of the seemingly new really being something old. And then he related the curious nature of personal identity to religious faith. One's personality was strengthened, he said, by belief in God.

He was surprised at how many people expressed satisfaction with the sermon.

The most surprising reaction came from Tom Warren, who rang the parsonage doorbell at eight o'clock on Monday morning and came in bearing a new toilet box fitting.

"Doggone it, Pastor, I tossed and turned all night thinking about that boat—boats. Was it—they—one or two? What's the answer?"

"As with nearly everything, Tom, there's more than one way of looking at it."

"I know that. I got your point. Sometimes I get too set in my ideas. But—" He grinned feebly. "Since I'm here I'm going to put a new plunger in your toilet. Noticed she was about to go the last time I was here. In my time I've put in and taken out so many parts on that toilet it may be three different ones by now—or is it still the same?"

Following Engel's suggestion, Martin joined Rotary upon an invitation instigated by John Ingham and spoke at two high schools about "Finding a Career." (So many blank young faces headed for the draft.)

But in many respects he was his own best adviser.

One day at a Rotary luncheon a couple of members gibed him unmercifully about a minister's easy life—getting up whenever you felt like it in the morning, accountable to no one for the hours you kept. He pondered their remarks on the way home and had an inspiration when he turned into the drive.

Jane found him folding back the curtains she had hung at the front bay window of his study and asked what he was doing. In reply he asked if the curtains could be tied back.

"Not those curtains," she said. "But if you want tieback curtains, I can hang them."

"Please do," he told her. And then he asked her to help him move his desk and place it in front of the window.

She got his point and grimaced. "Marty, isn't that being hypocritical?"

"Not at all. I'm up earlier every morning than most members of the church. Most days I'm working at my desk between four and six after I come home from calling and before we have dinner. I want to know how they live and work, so why not let them see how we live and work?"

People could not help seeing him as they passed to and from work along the street.

Jane was a first-rate adviser, too.

One morning he was in the study tinkering with a sermon when she came in to dust the books. Watching her was a delightful distraction. She was slender, well formed, just one month younger than he. No man ever could describe how his wife looked, but Martin sometimes tried to describe Jane to himself. To call her hair brown was not to describe its fine texture. To call her eyes blue failed to describe how her lids seemed to veil seductively when she looked at him. His first attraction to her had been utterly physical, and it was with some astonishment that he had discovered she was intelligent and principled.

Now, as she leaned over to dust the books on a lower shelf, he reached out and stroked her behind.

"Sexpot," she said.

"You're the sexpot," he said.

"I shouldn't come in here when you're working, but I haven't had a chance to dust these books in two weeks. I can't do it this afternoon because I'm going calling with you."

"Oh?" Five afternoons a week he had been making five or six calls on church members after first telephoning to inquire if they would be home. He was working his way methodically, occasionally desperately, through the entire membership. "What are you going to do with Kathy?"

"Mrs. Tabor is coming to stay with her while we're out."

"And who are we calling on, sexpot?"

"Mrs. Moffat, Mrs. Neislinger, and Miss Thomas. You're going to interrupt your devotions with that typewriter right now, old skipper, and phone them and say that Mrs. Judson and you would like to drop by for a brief call if convenient."

He looked at her with wonder. "Why am I going to do that?"

"Because Mrs. Tabor thinks we should. And she's convinced me we should. We can't call on Mrs. Davis because you called on her yesterday all by your little self."

He still was mystified—and showed it.

"Look, sweetheart"—she placed an index finger on his nose —"and don't get mad. *I* know it's silly and *you* know it's silly, but Mrs. Tabor dropped by yesterday afternoon and just happened to mention one of the rules of the road we never thought about. What do the women I've mentioned have in common?"

"So help me, Jane, you've got me."

"They're *attractive*."

When he thought about it, that was true. "Except that Miss Thomas has a long nose and her hair is graying."

"That has nothing to do with it. By the way she walks, you can tell her mind is on her crotch. And that makes her attractive to men—and maybe some women, too."

He started to get mad. But then, instead, he laughed. "Did Mrs. Tabor use the word 'crotch'? I'd give a week's pay to hear it."

"No, she didn't. *I* did. It's something I noticed about some women long before I ever heard of Upton. Mrs. Tabor isn't a dirty old gossip. She's the herald who speaks for the court. It seems that what's his name—Dewey, the poor chap who was here before you—set tongues to wagging by the amount of time he spent calling all by himself on Mrs. Neislinger and Miss Thomas. I guess it snowballed on him. He and his wife—a poor little mouse, Mrs. Tabor called her—sort of scuttled out of here in a hurry. I don't really give a darn about any of this, Marty. But I know you want to do a good job here. And that means having the total confidence of the people. And I want to help you."

For an instant he thought his eyes would fill with tears. Getting to his feet, he brushed his lips across her forehead. Then he took the membership list from the top drawer of his desk and turned to the telephone.

Mrs. Moffat, Mrs. Neislinger, Miss Thomas—each acted pleased to have them call. As they talked about this and that, Martin had some difficulty in keeping his thoughts pure. He tended to become speculative about each woman. He saw what Jane meant. He even saw what possibly poor Dewey had meant. Heaven forbid it ever should happen to him. Yet how could it?

As they were driving home, he said to Jane, "I forgot to tell you a pretty good story I heard yesterday. There was a group of clergymen in a town like Upton who became good friends and got together regularly to discuss church problems. They were a Catholic priest, a rabbi, an Episcopalian, and a Baptist. One day they got in a confessional mood, and the Baptist suggested they talk about their *personal* problems. The priest confessed he was a compulsive gambler, and sometimes, when he was behind on payments to his bookie, he had to dip into the poor box. The rabbi admitted he had a compulsion toward attractive women, and sometimes, when he called on a pretty member of his congregation, he got between the sheets with her for a piece of flesh. The Episcopalian confessed his communion service had become such a bore to him that he filled his communion cup with straight bourbon. Then all of them asked the Baptist what was *his* problem. 'Well,' said the Baptist, 'I'm a compulsive gossip, and I can't wait to get out of here!' "

Jane laughed heartily. Laughter always cast her into a bright glow that was apparent to everyone. It was apparent, at least, to Mrs. Tabor when they went into the parsonage. The old duenna left, clucking happily. Apparently she felt by teaching them that both always must call on an attractive female of the congregation something had been saved, something preserved. It was ridiculous. But it also was the year of our Lord 1940 in the city of Upton, Pennsylvania, where he had come to preach salvation on earth and the hope of eternal life in the hereafter.

After dinner they had a second cup of coffee while they listened to Lowell Thomas on their little radio. Hitler still appeared to be mounting an offensive against Britain. The long night for Europe's millions of Jews was growing darker. At some place called Benning in Georgia young draftees would have to drill with sticks because the Army lacked rifles.

Martin listened uneasily. On October 16 he had registered for the draft along with millions of other young Americans. He would be classified 3A because he had a wife and a child. And later, if the services began to take married men, he would be reclassified again in a safe preserve of clergymen and divinity students. Safe! He did not like it. What was the proper role of a man in these times? He never could bring himself to kill anyone. Yet he gladly would perform any arduous and dangerous service that would support men who were willing to kill in order to destroy totalitarian governments. At the same time he doubted the role of chaplain was worthy, for he could not quite believe in trying to bring faith in the divinity of a benign God to men who were launched on a killing spree.

The phone rang as Lowell Thomas was signing off his

broadcast. A woman identified herself as Dorothy Barton; he recalled seeing the name on the church rolls. She would like to "consult" him, this evening if possible. That would be fine —eight o'clock in his study.

"It seems to be ladies' day at the ball park," he said when he went out to the kitchen, where Jane was stacking the dishes.

Though they had not realized that both were expected to make pastoral calls on attractive females, they understood the procedure involved in "pastoral consultations" with women. Jane would answer the door and usher her into Martin's study, then close the door behind her and remain in the living room across the hall until the woman left. She must play the role that a secretary would in the unlikely event he ever had a pastorate big enough to involve a church office and paid help. Or, as a teacher in the seminary had put it dryly: "If not exactly the nurse to the gynecologist, the wife or secretary must be within screaming distance to forestall scandal or slander."

Dorothy Barton was a comely blonde in her early twenties. She was extremely tense. Martin's offer of a cigarette seemed to surprise her agreeably. (His experience with Engel had cued him to keep two ashtrays and a pack of cigarettes in the study.) He hoped that his taking the cigarettes out of a desk drawer and lighting hers and one for himself would help put her at ease. But soon, a hand clenched tightly, she blurted:

"I don't know who to talk to. I haven't been to church in a year, but Susy Mitchell says you seem like a sensible guy, easy to talk to—Excuse me, but I mean, when my parents and I used to go to church, they always said you should be able to take your problems to the minister. But they never did. I mean they don't seem to have any they want to talk about. But I do. I mean I—I'm—involved with a guy. He's my boss and—"

"Excuse me," Martin interrupted her, "but unless there's some reason—which may develop later—wouldn't it be wise not to mention names? Just circumstances, the . . . situation. Afterward you might worry—unnecessarily."

She absorbed his thought and smiled wanly. "Yes, Reverend
. . . Judson. I see what you mean."

Probably her story was commonplace, but it was the most
important event of her life to that time. It was the sort of happening that people described in letters to a syndicated col-
umnist in the Upton *Daily Chronicle* named Mary Haworth,
a sensible-sounding woman who dispensed advice with cool
omniscience. (Why, indeed, had not Dorothy Barton consulted
Mary Haworth by letter rather than coming to him? Was it because of fear of the written word? Or was it because of an
instinctive, almost forgotten feeling that she should seek the
advice of *the minister* in time of trouble?)

The man, her boss, was married and had two children. He
had made a play for her, and she had succumbed. He claimed
that he loved her. He said he was going to divorce his wife. But
he had been saying that for some time, and Dorothy knew it
was not true. She wanted to break it up; she knew he was conning her. But every time she tried, he kept at her. She was *there*
in that office with him, feeling miserable about it, but unable
to change the way things were. What should she do?

It was the first time anyone had sought Martin's advice on a
problem of this nature. He knew what his father would have
said: " 'Thou shalt not commit adultery.' There is the com-
mandment, and that is it, young lady. Get yourself back into
God's grace or perish." Period. That was the answer of his
father's generation. But it was no answer for Dorothy Barton.
She would scorn him and walk out if he told her that the Bible
called what she was doing adultery and fornication, that she
was being a sinner and had better stop it. Then what strategy
could he use with her?

He was agonizingly slow in speaking. "Why do you think
you're half a woman?"

She bridled. "What do you mean, half a woman?"

Martin said, "If you were a full woman, you'd be able to get
a man who would commit himself all the way to you in public.

But as it is, you're willing to settle for half of what you could settle for—or even less than half."

His meaning dawned on her slowly; when she finally understood him, she did not know what to say.

"To put it another way, Dorothy, I'm asking you: What are you really interested in? What's really going to work to make your life full and content?"

She groped in her bag for a cigarette, and he lighted it for her. She said, "I want to marry—I don't know exactly *who*. I want to marry and have babies. I like to work, too. I'm a good secretary. I type a hundred and ten a minute. I have a good job. I'm making thirty a week. But I shouldn't go back *there*."

"Then don't."

She looked pained. "Mr. Judson, do you know how hard it is to find a job around this city now? My father has been cut to fifty a week. I'll be honest with you, the reason they quit going to church is they're *embarrassed* to. Everybody knows he's been cut, and paying even a dollar a week to the church hurts now. I can't quit work. They need the fifteen I bring in every week."

Did absolutely everything have to be measured by the buck?

"You honestly want to break this up?" he asked her.

She looked at him levelly. "Yes—yes, I do. That's why I came to you. You make sense. But."

But period. He said, "Then at least don't go back there tomorrow. Phone me at noon. I'll let you know if I can turn up another better place."

In the hall she said good night to Jane and him. Then she turned in the doorway, looked at him oddly, and said, "Thanks."

Returning to the study, he telephoned John Ingham and asked if he could speak to him for a couple of minutes.

"Beatrice has gone to bed with a headache, and I'm just walking out the dog," Ingham said. "I'll come along Edwards Street and down Congress."

"I'll meet you on the way," Martin said.

Ingham plodded down Congress Street, smoking a White

Owl and leashed to his collie, an ill-tempered old bitch that he had named Lady. As Lady paused to relieve herself under a streetlight, Ingham made out Martin and asked, "Problems?"

"Nothing personal. I want you to help me find a job for a young woman."

"Who is she?"

"Dorothy Barton."

"She and her folks haven't been to church in more than a year."

"So I understand."

"She has a job. Why do you want to get her another?"

"Frankly, John"—it was the first time he had called Ingham by his first name—"that doesn't concern you. She came to me for . . . help. And I want to help her in a practical way. I hoped you might know of someone—someplace. She's earning thirty a week. She says she types a hundred and ten a minute."

Ingham held his cigar away from Lady and slowly tapped off its ash. "Tell her to phone Dana Chandler at Makinson Tool and Die tomorrow. Have her tell him that I—No, that *you* said she was to call him."

"Thanks," Martin said.

Lady tugged at the leash, and John Ingham turned back toward home. He said, "Good night—Martin."

When Martin reached home, Jane was still seated in the living room. He said, "Dorothy Barton wants a new job. I hope John Ingham can help her find it."

Probably she knew he was speaking a half-truth. If she did, she did not show it. And if she did, he hoped she understood why he always must speak to her in half-truths about matters of this nature.

Jane's mother died early in January, and Jane, taking Kathy, went to Davidson by train for the funeral. She wanted to drive, but Martin insisted the winter roads were too dangerous. He thought he should go with her, but she insisted that he not; it would mean his finding a Sunday supply preacher at his own expense, and they already were three hundred dollars in hock to the Citizens Bank for furniture. Furthermore, he had not been close to her mother—or father either. She had not been able to make him understand that no one—not even she herself—ever had been close to Doris and Edward Williams. Their manner (was it shyness or a purposeful wall they had built around themselves?) had convinced Martin they did not approve of the marriage—which, in truth, they had not.

Jane thought about it on the tedious train trip with Kathy. Almost no one had approved of their marriage about two years ago, when Martin was a second-year student in the seminary. She never would forget the first time she met him. Merely thinking about it brought tears to her eyes. It was ridiculous— and rather sad under the circumstances: She was ashamed that she had not shed a tear when her father phoned and said in a stunned tone that her mother had died suddenly of a cerebral hemorrhage.

Marty had a wonderful baritone voice, which bore a trace of Yankee accent, especially if he became excited. Jane heard it first on a Friday evening in October, 1938, inquiring by telephone if her father was home. Fortunately, he was not.

Though Edward Williams was neither scholarly nor devout, he was the librarian of Davidson Theological Seminary. He had a passion for order and detail, a wish for quiet, a subdued sense of helpfulness that made him ideally suited to his job.

That night the voice explained he was Martin Judson, who worked in the library for her father. It went on good-humoredly: "I didn't know Mr. Williams had a daughter. I don't suppose he's ever told you the exact location of the *George Cross Correspondence on the Social Gospel?*" No, he had not. But the voice did not go away. It said: "I hear music in your background. Cole Porter." She explained that some friends and she were listening to records and drinking cider, but she did not yield to the impulse to invite him around because Joe Stammler, to whom she was engaged, was due at any moment.

Half an hour later Martin Judson rang the doorbell. (Afterward he explained: "Your voice made me curious.") Fortunately, her father and mother had still not returned from the movies. Fortunately, too, Joe did not appear all evening; he phoned to explain that he had a hot prospect and couldn't make it. (He was a customer's man for a brokerage house, bright, ambitious, really quite dull.)

When Edward Williams came home, he was upset to find that Martin had deserted his night post in the library, even though the library had long since closed and Martin explained that Tubby Larsen had filled in for him during the final half hour. Any fool should have known where the *Cross Correspondence* was, Williams said.

Jane and her friends had difficulty in believing Martin was a divinity student. Ignoring her girlfriends, he danced with Jane all evening. He was not a good dancer, but at least he kept in time to the music as they shuffled around the dining room, and he held her too tightly for a proper divinity student. In conversation she could think of little to commend herself to him: She had been graduated from Oberlin a year previously and, failing to find gainful employment, had qualified as a public school teacher—fifth grade, on the west side of town. He didn't seem to take her seriously when she said that teaching fifth-graders was fun. Nor did he seem to take it seriously when a friend untactfully pointed out that she was engaged to Joe Stammler. The next day he invited her to the movies, and one month later she gave the ring back to Joe.

Her parents were deeply disturbed. Edward Williams attended a Methodist church occasionally, Doris rarely, and Jane not at all in a number of years. Did she have any idea of the life she would lead as a clergyman's wife? She started attending church regularly, and though much of the service bored her, she persevered in her attempt to learn just what it was that made Martin want to be a minister. Sometimes she thought she understood, sometimes not. Martin did not consciously try to be of help to her. He did not discuss "religion" with her, and it was one of the perpetual wonders of her life that he never did. Apparently he assumed that she shared his belief in the divinity of God and the life of Jesus Christ as representing His life on earth. Once she asked him if he believed in the Virgin Birth, and he replied that he did not personally but considered the question of no consequence in the pursuit of Christian faith. Gradually she came to understand that he saw such matters as baptism and communion as helpful ceremonies and symbols not to be taken literally. Because he assumed she shared his beliefs and doubts, she came actually to share them.

But "religion" in the sense of who believed what and why one did believe had little relevance to their life together. They simply met and fell in love. They had one resounding quarrel brought on by their sexual tensions: They wanted to go to bed together, but neither would because (and she thought in later years that you could take your pick of the reasons) either they were scared to, or they had persuaded themselves it would be immoral, or each felt it would be unfair and damaging to the self-respect of the other. They patched up their quarrel by deciding to get married—not to wait, but to marry *in one month*.

Martin's father, a peppery fellow of sixty-five, came from Vermont and married them. He grumbled just once that they didn't know what they were letting themselves in for, and then he became cheerful about it. Martin's mother was dead. He had a much older sister, Bess, living in California, who sent them a silver vase, and a mysterious older brother, Nathaniel, who long ago had quarreled with his father and disappeared but who somehow had kept track of Martin and each Christmas wrote him a humorous letter from outlandish places such as New Mexico and Saskatchewan. Jane, an only child, envied Martin his siblings, remote and vague though they were. It was her wish, which she did not confide in Martin, to have seven or eight children and *love* them in a way she felt her parents never had loved her.

Her parents' deep misgivings and dire warnings turned out

to be ridiculous. She and Martin were ecstatically happy in the two-room apartment which she supported on her teacher's salary. They had good friends and exciting times, skating, skiing, swimming—and forever loving. Jane especially liked Tubby Larsen, a rock of Gibraltar. She also liked another friend of Martin's at the seminary, Lance Bishop. Lance came from some place in the Middle West called Freeport and was often called the Freeport Flash. He was fond of saying he had decided to become a Baptist rather than a Methodist clergyman because he never could bear to be called Bishop Bishop. After graduation, when Lance became the assistant pastor of a large church in New York, Jane secretly could not understand why the church should have picked him instead of Martin.

During the last month of her pregnancy, before Kathy was born in June, Martin had been in a sweat about a job. It seemed that no church wanted a minister green from the seminary—though neither did any church seem to want a minister over thirty-five. Martin had been thinking about staying on as a teacher in Ohio when the call had come from Upton. There had been times (which she guarded closely to herself) when she wished he had stayed in Ohio. Curiously, she did not truly appreciate Upton until she went back to Davidson for her mother's funeral.

She could not bring a sense of reality to what she found in Davidson. The poverty of emotion there—her father's over her mother's death, her own toward both—made life in Upton seem like the Golden City. She was gone six days, which seemed like six years, and planned to stay longer until she realized her father would welcome her leaving: Kathy got on his nerves; long before her mother's death he had grown fond of cooking the meals; he could scarcely wait for the end of the decent interval of mourning so that he could return to the comfortable routine of the library. The day before she left she learned that her mother, leaving a small inherited estate to her father, had also bequeathed her five hundred dollars.

She had been back in Upton the Golden (what a joyous re-union!) a day and a night before she thought to mention it to Martin.

He looked surprised. Then he said, "There's the chance for you to do what I haven't been able to. Get yourself a Persian lamb coat."

Jane felt that would be spendthrift. Yet she always had wanted a Persian lamb, and eventually went shopping for one upon Martin's insistence. In a shop on Front Street she finally found an acceptable one for three hundred and thirty dollars. With the remainder of her inheritance she bought Martin a double-breasted Oxford gray suit and put the difference toward their debt for furniture.

The following Sunday she wore her new coat to church happily. Beatrice Ingham had a Persian lamb. So did Gertrude Prescott. Jane anticipated their passing some pleasantry about hers. But to her surprise they ignored her coat; indeed, they totally ignored her after the service.

A few weeks passed before she understood the cause of their coolness. And even then she might not have understood if she had not overheard Harcourt Prescott speaking to Martin.

"John Ingham brought up the matter of giving you a raise." Harcourt told him. "It was voted down. We gather you don't need it at this time."

"How did you gather that?" Martin asked.

"We gather Mrs. Judson came into an inheritance when her mother died. After all, the Persian lamb coat, you know."

How, Jane wondered, could she have been so obtuse? A Persian lamb, which she admired as a thing of warmth and beauty, was a symbol of wealth, privilege, power to Beatrice Ingham and Gertrude Prescott. It was a symbol not to be shared with the preacher's wife. When would she learn all the tricks of this incredible clergyman's trade?

In February Martin wrote Tubby:

The monthly deacons' meeting at the parsonage tonight for the usual discussion of the 'spiritual' life of the church. Are your deacons the trial that mine are? When they can't find anything else to quarrel about they pick on the board of trustees. They seem to resent the fact the trustees are responsible for all those secular matters of the church involving money, money, money. No wonder that Father Ryan, a Roman Catholic priest here with whom I've become friendly, says that our congregational area of Protestantism with final authority of church government vested in the congregation is just plain religious anarchy. . . .

The anarchist deacons assembled at eight o'clock that evening in the parsonage. As usual, Tom Warren, chairman of the board, delivered a brief opening prayer. Then he made a remark that had become habitual with him: "Pastor, it's time we trim out the deadwood and cut the church membership rolls."

Martin replied with a remark that was becoming equally habitual: "Well, Tom, let's first make sure what wood is really dead."

There were five hundred and twelve names on the rolls of the church. Of these, fewer than three hundred attended services or participated in church activities when Martin came to Upton. But gradually, as he worked, a little green began to come to the so-called deadwood. An example was the Barton family. After Martin found a new job for Dorothy, she began to attend church and soon was singing in the choir and enjoying what was called the Fellowship Club, a growing group of young marrieds and singles, who, sparked by Martin and Jane, met once a fortnight for games, refreshments, and discussion of matters related to such matters as jobs, home, church. Not long after Dorothy began coming to church again, her parents resumed attending, too. Subtly Martin made it clear to her father that the amount one paid to the church was of no consequence, and before long Evan Barton was contributing two dollars a week and pleased to be an usher.

Tom rambled on at length about the deadwood that was ripe for burning until he was finally interrupted by old Luther Balch, chairman of the stewardship committee and a supply sergeant of sorts.

"Tom, you're taking up the whole evening. I have my report to make."

Tom glowered at him and said, "All right, Luther, make it snappy."

Luther said, "Report of the stewardship committee," unfolded a sheet of paper, and gravely recited the cost of the grape juice, which was served as wine at the monthly communion service, and the cost of the bread, representing Christ's broken body, which Luther bought cut-rate, day-old at the A&P for the service. "One further matter," he said. "I'm glad to report that I got the leak in the pastor's baptismal boots repaired for two dollars and ninety-five cents. Nason's wanted *five dollars,* but I took it to Fred Grinnell. You know he—"

"All right," Tom said. "As usual, the next order of business concerns the needy. Will?"

Will Swain uttered a rumbling sound which finally took the form of words. "The fellowship committee give—gave ten dollars to old Mrs. Post last Friday from the fellowship fund, which now"—he searched for a slip of paper—"totals three hundred and sixty-eight dollars. Mrs. Post has been poorly and—"

"But does she *need* it?" demanded Luther Balch. "Harry Post told me before he died—"

"Listen," Will said, "I know for a fact that Harry could have got work in Sayre if. . . ."

How reluctantly the deacons let crumbs fall to the destitute of the congregation—widows, broken or whole families that had become hopeless derelicts for reasons either personal or as a result of the deadly Sargasso of the Depression.

At last Martin said, "Well, let's at least admit there was a Depression."

"Yes, sir, there sure was, and it's still going on," Tom said.

"But it would have ended if Roosevelt had *let things work out* and not. . . ."

They went on in a tedious lament for some golden past time that might or might not actually have existed. Tom finally ended it by blurting, "Consideration of new members. Any candidates, Pastor?"

"Five." Martin recited the names and identified them while all leaned forward attentively.

J. B. Stokes, an undertaker for forty-seven years, said, "I know that young woman Grace Peterson, Mr. Judson. And from where I sit I'm sure of one thing: She don't believe in predestination to grace and glory."

Will Swain literally writhed. "Who does, J. B.?"

"You'd better!" His voice rose harshly. "How can you be a church member if you don't believe in predestination and reprobation? Of course, God inflicts everlasting damnation on those He foresees will die in the state of grave sin. . . ."

Predestination or reprobation was not the basic source of bitterness between Will and J. B. It had something to do with J. B.'s being a well-off man who gave one dollar a week to the church while Will, despite financial straits, gave two.

Tom cried above the hubbub of many voices in argument, "At least she believes in total immersion. I move—"

"We *all* believe in total immersion!" cried Luther. "Is there one of us has any use for a little Papist sprinkling? You've got to go *all* the way under to be born again."

"Well now, Luther," said Ray Pyle, a retired farmer, "my daughter went Methodist and I'd still say that Mae is one of the finest girls ever born. . . ."

As the arguments grew more vociferous, Martin glanced at his watch and saw it was past ten o'clock. He smelled coffee from the kitchen and knew that Jane was ready to serve refreshments.

"Gentlemen," he said, and was surprised at how quickly they grew quiet. "Is there need of further discussion on the qualifications of these candidates for church membership?"

"No," Tom said. "I move. . . ."

The cake, ice cream, and coffee Jane served them quieted the beasts of contention within them, and they left about eleven o'clock. Patience and self-control had enabled Martin to weather another deacon's meeting.

Yet there was an end to patience, if not to self-control. As Engel had said, sometimes you had to be a con artist.

It had been a cold winter in Upton, one of the worst. The old furnace did not work well; often it did not seem to work at all. They were cold much of the time. By the first of March their coal bill totaled one hundred and ninety-seven dollars. Tom Warren came two or three times a week and tinkered with the furnace, always assuring them that everything was all right now. Three times Martin asked John Ingham for a new furnace, but John always replied that Tom had assured him everything had been put in working order. Around the first of March the temperature dropped again, and both Jane and Kathy had colds.

The March deacons' meeting at the parsonage fell on the fifth. In the afternoon Martin told Jane what he intended to do and warned her that if it worked, they would have to stay for a few days at some parishioner's home.

She said, "Are you sure you want to try it? Spring is almost here."

"So's fall," he replied. "And in the fall it will be the same old furnace."

Jane did not smile; she grinned, an expression she could manage sometimes. *"Let's!"*

Late in the afternoon Martin damped down the furnace. Then he drained the boiler of thirty-six buckets of water, leaving only a bit. Next, he cut off the water gauge, uncapped it, filled it well above the safety level, and then recapped it. Finally, he followed the water intake from the furnace to a remote corner of the cellar, turned it off, and removed and hid the spigot so that it could not be turned on. Just before meeting time he drained the remainder of the water from the boiler.

When the deacons arrived, the thermometer in the study registered thirty-five degrees. They agreed with Martin that the house was very chilly; in fact, all except Tom Warren kept overcoats on. Tom hustled down to the cellar, where he made a great deal of noise.

He came upstairs smiling. "Pastor, I know you weren't trained to be an engineer, but you just plain let the fire die. It's always happening. I've got her going now. We'll be comfortable in a few minutes. Now I'll lead us in the opening prayer. Almighty God. . . ."

When he had finished praying, Martin asked him, "Tom, are you sure the water level's all right?"

"She's fine. Absolutely okay."

Martin, uncertain over what might happen, had told Jane to take Kathy to the second floor and stay there. As time passed and nothing happened, he was increasingly uneasy. When the house failed to grow warmer, Luther Balch finally ventured to complain. Tom insisted it *was* getting warmer and launched into a discussion of why the church should cut off further aid to the Hodgins family.

He had reached his peroration when there was a resounding *whoomp!* in the cellar. Crying, "Jesus!" Tom raced from the study.

In the cellar was a cloud of smoke, a smell of fire, broken dials, bits of metal. Someone phoned for the fire department, which was not necessary but enhanced the drama.

Jane, Kathy, and Martin stayed for three days and nights with the Inghams, who were greatly upset by what had happened. By that time workmen had installed a new furnace, which kept the parsonage warm as long as the Judsons lived in Upton.

Jane, loving Martin, knew how much he loved her. Above all, she wished to make him happy. And like most intelligent women, she learned that was not simple—or was it simple and did she try to make it seem complex? Their loving was unrestrained. She must guard against acting officiously, but sometimes—really! He was indifferent about his clothing; in his wish not to look like a straitlaced preacher, he was inclined to dress like an unbuttoned college sophomore. Then she would say sharply, "Time to put on your hair shirt, Jeremiah," or, "Martin Judson, you can't wear that sports shirt to school another day." And he was impossible about food. She liked to cook the best food they could afford. But his appetite was sparing, his tastes simple. He liked oatmeal, apples, milk, poached eggs, fresh vegetables in season, fish, a little meat well done—and ice cream. His notion of a gourmet feast was to drive Kathy and her out to Fowler's Dairy Farm on a spring evening, there to sit under an apple tree and stare at the green with a transfixed expression while he slowly ate a pint of chocolate ice cream. Too, he was careless about his drinking. The only time he expressed a wish for anything stronger than coffee was after he finished mowing the lawn on a hot day; then he would carry a bottle of cold beer from the icebox to the front or back steps— which place seemed to make no difference; both were equally exposed to cynical public view—and sit there while he slowly drank his beer. The first time she caught him at it, she suggested as tactfully as possible that it might be wise for him to do his tippling in privacy. He simply looked at her, silent and unmoving, his gaze telling her that man always had drunk his beer on his doorstep after mowing his lawn, until she went away. She never mentioned it again. After that, perhaps for variety, he sometimes sprawled with his beer on the side lawn where the fresh-mown grass smelled sweet.

In her wish to make him happy, she tried to be secretive about matters that might worry him. She did not reveal her desire to have many children because it appeared they could not afford them. Nevertheless, her desire persisted; instinctively she would have liked to enclose Martin and herself behind walls of loving babies, a castle whose minarets would be strung with diapers. She tried, too, not to reveal her dislike of certain church members with whom Martin had to work.

But she failed to disguise her dislike of the rural life that Martin relished. They had the month of August for vacation, but they could not afford to do anything except spend a few days with her father in Davidson and then go on to the backwoods acreage in southern Vermont which Martin's father called "my farm." David Judson, who had taken his vacation in July, had generously offered the run-down place to them in August. Yes, the views were lovely, and there was good swimming and fishing in a small lake nearby. But they had to drive four miles for ice, milk, and everything else except the perch Martin caught and the berries he picked. Martin thoroughly enjoyed being Huck Finn in the country, and she tried to find joy in his enjoyment. She had thought the lack of society following too much society in Upton would be wonderful, but after a week the solitude began to depress her. The multifarious life of meadows, woods, and water which Martin found so fascinating was boring and finally repellent to her. She tried not to show it, and then, to her dismay, one day she had a fit of crying. She blamed it on her menstrual cycle, but Martin was not taken in by that subterfuge. They went back to Upton several days earlier than planned.

One happy result of the Vermont vacation was that she thought she had become pregnant. When Martin learned about it, he looked worried. Money again, she knew. About a week later, when John Ingham dropped by to see Martin about a church matter, she overheard their parting exchange at the front door.

"John, is it possible now for me to get a raise?"

"No, Martin, not yet."

A couple of weeks after that Martin brought a letter to her in the kitchen. It was from Lance Bishop, the Freeport Flash. He had started a series of Sunday morning sermons from New York on radio network; it was going very well, but sometimes, ha-ha, the pump needed priming; remembering Martin's facility with pulpit ideas, Lance wondered if by some remote chance he'd be interested in sending him sermons at twenty bucks per—and keep 'em down to twelve minutes' running time, buddy.

"What a phony he is!" Jane said.

Martin looked reflective. "But what an opportunity!"

"He wants to cheat you. I'll bet the radio people are paying him fifty a week."

"Lance isn't a cheat. I doubt if he's receiving anything from the radio. That sort of thing is just great prestige for a young man. He has some money—income from a funeral parlor or something in Freeport. Lance wants . . . eminence. I want . . . money. I might have some ideas he could use."

Before long Martin was receiving a check for twenty dollars nearly every week from Lance. Occasionally he turned on the radio at nine o'clock on a Sunday morning to hear Lance read the sermon he had written. It seemed to amuse him, but it irked Jane.

She was thoroughly annoyed when, one Sunday after morning service as Martin greeted people in the vestibule, old Mrs. Rowley spoke up: "Pastor Judson, your sermons sound more and more like those of Reverend Bishop on the radio. He's very good. You must get a lot of your ideas from him."

Martin smiled bravely. "I'll have to listen to him some time, Mrs. Rowley."

Jane *was* pregnant, thank heaven. It seemed to her that she had her most fertile ideas when pregnant. The wonderful new idea came to her when she awakened at two o'clock one morning. She wakened Martin and started to tell him about it, but he simply said, "Uh," and fell asleep again. So she went down to the kitchen and ate sliced bananas and milk and thought about her idea.

Each fall the women's guild of First Baptist held a two-day rummage sale in a vacant store downtown and made five hundred to six hundred dollars. The few things left over were picked up by secondhand merchants for a song. Why not hold a *perpetual* rummage sale, including all sorts of articles besides clothing? On the one hand, most of the people in Upton

were always hunting for bargains. On the other, the attics of
Upton seemed to be stuffed with unused things. First Baptist
could not run such a shop alone but could manage it one day a
week. And the local chapter of the American Association of
University Women, the only organization apart from the church
in which Jane was active, was always questing about for a means
of raising money. It could run such a shop another day a
week. . . .

It was one of those rare ideas that seemed as good at eight
o'clock in the morning as it had at two o'clock. Indeed, at eight
o'clock Jane was struck by a positively magnificent name for the
secondhand store. They would call it the Nearly New Shop!

The women's guild took to the idea enthusiastically. Attics
and closets cleaned out, money for the church, pleasant so-
cializing once a week—the combination was irresistible. The
AAUW joined in, too. Jane spent days in obtaining three more
weekly cosponsors, and then more days in politicking the First
Baptist guild into accepting Catholic Charities, the Seventh-
day Adventists, the Jewish Fund.

When they finally got under way in a small store on Front
Street, no one was more astonished than Jane at the popularity of the Nearly New Shop. In the first week First Baptist
alone cleared more than one hundred dollars. The amounts
grew larger in the weeks before Christmas. The catastrophic
news of Pearl Harbor and the start of war seemed to send
people into a frenzy of buying anything they could get their
hands on. Jane thought that First Baptist was growing fan-
tastically rich. Perhaps the church would decide it now could
afford to give Martin a raise; perhaps it would be done at
Christmas, and then Martin could stop writing sermons for the
Freeport Flash and stop calling himself the Baptist Holy Ghost
Writer. But at Christmas the church gave Martin an unabridged
Webster's Dictionary and Jane a glass punch bowl with twenty-
four cups.

Her doctor had told her repeatedly that she must get more
rest, but the Nearly New Shop took increasing time and en-

ergy. Then, one day in January, she collapsed at the shop, and the next day she lost their child.

Martin's sermon on December 7, 1941, had a hackneyed theme that most clergymen employ at one time or another. It was one of those "rendering unto Caesar" subjects in which he reminded Christians of their duties as citizens. It gave him the opportunity to discuss the critical state of affairs in Europe, which he believed inseparable from the eventual welfare of Americans. He did not expect it to be popularly received; no one liked to hear unpleasant, opinionated statements from the pulpit. But he was surprised by the vehemence with which Harcourt Prescott refuted him in the vestibule after the service.

Harcourt, an American Firster, declared, "You don't know what you're talking about. You shouldn't pass on your half-baked ideas as *sermons*. Nobody is ever going to attack the United States. What we should do is mind our own business and live in peace."

That afternoon the radio report of the Japanese attack on Pearl Harbor refuted Harcourt. (He never mentioned to Martin the irony of his and the Japanese having engaged in an outburst simultaneously. Indeed, he became renowned for his patriotism by hawking war bonds.) Martin's delivering that particular sermon on that particular day was, of course, sheer happenstance. He was embarrassed that it brought from the congregation a kind of awe of him, as if he were a seer who had prophesied the approach of the Japanese planes.

But the happenstance was superficial to the hard fact of Pearl Harbor. Now what was the duty of the preacher who advocated tough resistance to totalitarianism? Should he sit safely while young men of his age left the comforts of home and went away to fight? Like most American males who had an instinct for service, he was concerned about the welfare of his family. But that question was easily answered: Presumably, as a healthy clergyman, he could obtain a first lieutenant's commission as a chaplain; it would mean Jane would be better off than the wives of most men in service.

After Jane's miscarriage, he no longer had the excuse of postponing a decision until the child was born.

One Tuesday afternoon in February he came home from pastoral calling and heard familiar voices in the living room.

"Am I hallucinating?" he called out.

"No," Tubby replied.

"Not at all," said Lance.

Martin stepped into the living room, where they had been talking to Jane, and looked at them dazedly. Tubby wore the uniform of a first lieutenant of chaplains in the Army of the United States. Lance wore, besides a well-tailored Oxford gray suit, a worried expression.

"You *did* it!" Martin exclaimed as he gripped Tubby's hand.

Tubby was on travel time between Camp Dix and a camp in South Carolina. Lance was on his way to a church convention in Pittsburgh. They had met by agreement in Philadelphia and decided to detour to Upton and see Martin and Jane for a few hours.

"The noble pacifist is badly shaken," Lance said.

"I sure am." Tubby rubbed the top of his head. "I've been sitting around Dix for two weeks doing absolutely nothing. I've been so depressed I couldn't even write you and tell you I've committed suicide."

"He thinks," Lance said, "that maybe he did it because he was the most bored bachelor in Thornton, Massachusetts."

"There's more to it," Tubby said. "It is a . . . *just* war. Haven't we all been preaching that?"

Yes, all had.

"You made the right decision," Martin told him. "I'm going to do the same."

"No, you're not," Tubby replied sharply. "I was afraid you might when you heard. And I came out of my way to *tell you*

not to! You have Jane and Kathy to think of. I don't have anyone."

"Neither do I," Lance said. "So I'm going to try to do something about getting into service. But you mustn't, Marty. I told
Tubby about your—ghosting radio sermons for me. And I have
to confess something. I've been planning to write and tell you
we should, uh"—Lance grimaced—"bear down a little harder
on the patriotism theme. But now, in the light of what Tubby
has done, I think that idea reeks of hypocrisy. In fact, I think
the whole radio sermon deal is beginning to reek. So I'm going
to give it up. . . ."

April came sourly: winds, heavy rain, an almost constant
sense of depression. Martin had an annoying diarrhea that Sunday, but somehow he got through the morning service. Then,
instead of going to the vestibule to greet people, he hurried to
the dingy men's room in the basement and enclosed himself in
a stall.

Someone came in and stood at the urinal. In a moment John
Ingham entered and greeted Luther Balch: "Are you going to
stand there all day, Luther?"

"I just might," Luther replied. "You don't know what it's
like to have trouble passing your water. That was a poor sermon
today, wasn't it?"

"I wouldn't say that." John's tone sounded guarded.

Luther said, "Sometimes Martin can be downright senseless
in the pulpit. Young preachers are something. About all they
seem to know how to do is unsheathe the sword and get their
wives pregnant."

John said, "Luther, you're talking like a horse's ass," and
left, slamming the door behind him.

Martin nearly cried out in rage. But he sat, doubled in cramp,
almost strangling in his effort of silence. He left the toilet soon
after Luther and hurried up the stairs. John was standing at
the head of the stairs, looking at him strangely. He said something, but Martin, staring through him, hurried out the side
door and across the drive to the parsonage.

Being a chaplain might seem a futile, empty occupation, but it could not be more futile and empty than being pastor of the First Baptist Church of Upton. The Army was at least an opportunity to minister to the living before they became the dead. What better thing could a clergyman do than to go where men were living under stress and possibly be of some help there?

When Jane came from the church, he was at his typewriter, beginning a letter requesting Army duty as a chaplain. Kathy, who during the service had been cared for in the church nursery (an innovation Jane had suggested), toddled after her.

Martin said, "I'm doing it."

Kathy said, "I big girl." Jane stood in the doorway looking stricken. Kathy said, "Daddy, I big girl."

Suddenly Martin thought he could not go through with it. What insanity could make him think he must leave them and go off to do—what? Tears came to his eyes. Then he found he had drawn Jane to him, and they were clinging tightly to each other, as if some powerful force was trying to sunder them forever. She spoke through tears: "I know how you feel, my darling. Maybe Kathy and I can stay here till you find a place for us to be with you."

The telephone rang. Martin said, "I'm sick in bed."

Jane said, "I don't want to talk to any of them just now either." But then she answered the phone and said he was ill. "John Ingham," she told him after she hung up. "I'll start the beef stew heating."

They were about to sit down to the table when the doorbell rang. She went to the door, and he heard John speaking in an insistent tone. He went into the hall and faced him silently.

"I know you've got the trouble that's going the rounds," John said, "and I won't keep you, Martin. I just wanted you to know that tomorrow night the trustees will approve an eight hundred raise—the figure we offered you to come here."

"Don't waste your money, John. I'm applying for an Army chaplaincy."

"Don't waste your life," John Ingham replied. "You're doing a good job here. You've brought new strength to the church, and it's growing—no matter what some of us old farts say once in a while. I spent almost a year in the Army in the last war, Martin. Saw a lot of chaplains. We all wasted our time there, but the chaplains most of all."

"I'm twenty-six years old," Martin said. "I can't preach the way I have and then hide in the cellar. I've made up my mind."

John gazed at him blankly.

"You have time to start looking for another preacher. It may be a while before they call me in. Sometimes these things take a couple of months."

"Sometimes longer," John said.

"Until you get a new man, may Jane and Kathy stay here? Maybe until I can find a place for them to live near me—before I'm shipped overseas."

"Of course. They can stay as long as they want to. Just one thing. Let's keep your decision strictly between you and me— and Jane. If word gets out, it won't do morale around here one bit of good."

On Wednesday Martin received formal notice from Harcourt Prescott, as secretary of the board of trustees, that his monthly salary had been increased to three hundred dollars. He was not as pleased as he thought he should be.

His correspondence with the Army dragged on in the immemorial way of correspondence with all armies. He toiled as conscientiously as ever at First Baptist. Each day with Jane and Kathy became more precious. His anticipation of Army life was not whetted by the letters he received from Tubby, who, never a griper, now was griping as eloquently as any draftee from a camp in South Carolina.

At last the fateful notice came. He would report for a physical in Harrisburg at the end of July; if he passed it, his mobilization date would be assigned. The parting with Jane and Kathy, when he boarded a bus for Harrisburg, was the saddest moment of his life.

In the Harrisburg reception center he fettered himself stoically to the chain gang. Slowly he crept forward, nude, in the long line of nude and complaining men.

At last he handed his form to an aging physician, who told him to turn all the way around slowly. Then the physician stamped the form and said, "You're rejected."

Martin gaped at him. "What's the matter? I'm in perfect health."

"You're a healthy-looking specimen all right," the physician said. "But you have a hernia."

Martin said he did not, but the physician insisted that he did and rejected him.

Later he learned that he—not the physician—was correct. But by that time he had decided not to try to argue further with the Army of the United States.

Following a friendly tip from Engel, Martin took a copy of his sermon each Friday afternoon to Miss Genevieve Bonwell, the "religion reporter" for the *Daily Chronicle*. During his first year in Upton he found that sometimes Miss Genevieve, as everyone called her, would run a brief story in the Saturday afternoon edition on the next day's service at First Baptist— and sometimes would not. Sometimes there was a story in Monday's edition on the Sunday sermon—but more often not. Often, too, she missed the point of a sermon entirely.

One Friday afternoon, when Martin took his copy to Miss Genevieve in the city room, she was frowning and working her lips while blacking out much of her copy. Observing her having the same difficulties in ensuing weeks, Martin came to a conclusion. Like a surprisingly large number of people who worked for newspapers, Miss Genevieve did not write well and did not really like to write at all; she simply loved the distinction of being known as a reporter.

The next Friday Martin did not take her a copy of his sermon. Instead, he went to the city room with two competently written news stories—one for the Saturday edition on what he *would* preach about on Sunday, and the other for the Monday edition on what he *had* preached.

"Miss Genevieve," he told her, "I've noticed recently that you're terribly overworked, so I thought I'd try to help out. You can change these stories around, but at least you won't have to read the sermon."

She laughed nervously. "Well," she said, "they do keep me awfully busy here— Thanks, Mr. Judson."

On Saturday and Monday the stories ran exactly as Martin had written them.

On the following Friday, Martin took her two more news stories, and she said, "Mr. Judson, you have real reportorial ability."

"Thank you, Miss Genevieve. But you give them the professional touch."

After that she always sent his stories to the copy desk just as he had written them. In time he began to add a small feature story on something that was happening at First Baptist. Martin's stories rarely ended in the overset.

Engel cornered him one day after a ministers' fellowship luncheon and asked, "What have you done to charm Miss Genevieve?"

At first Martin feigned surprise.

"Really, Martin," Engel said, "every Saturday and Monday afternoon, when I open the *Chronicle,* it reads to me as if First Baptist is the biggest and almost the only church in town. How do you do it?"

Harold Engel had tried to be friendly and helpful, so Martin told him his method with Miss Genevieve.

"Well!" Engel exclaimed. "You're really learning."

"No, Harold." Martin winked at him. "*You* are. . . ."

Martin had no way of knowing whether the publicity in the *Daily Chronicle* resulted in increasing Sunday attendance or helped the church grow. He simply knew that the church was filled almost to capacity nearly every Sunday and the membership was growing larger.

John Ingham traced the growth to the strengthening of the Sunday school. In a rare compliment to Martin, he said, "I *see* what you're doing." He smiled. "Keep it up."

Though John recognized his strategy, many others did not.

When he first came to Upton, Martin spent consecutive Sundays in each of the school classes which were held after church.

"The same old story," he told Jane. "When I was a kid I hated Sunday school. Most of my teachers were well-intentioned ladies who had no real idea of what they were trying to do. Things haven't changed."

From his observation of the various classes he drew up a list of eight teachers who must be relieved. All were aging women who had taught Sunday school for years.

"They all have one thing in common," he said to Jane. "Basically they don't like children. And the single basic requirement of a Sunday-school teacher is a fondness for and understanding of children. All of them are living back in the days of the little red schoolhouse. Memorizing facts from the Bible. Gold stars for this and gold stars for that. The kids are bored wall-eyed."

On a Friday evening he called the eight women together at the parsonage for what he called "a dessert discussion." Jane filled them with pie, ice cream, and coffee. Then Martin began to talk.

"I guess all of you know why you're here." Miss Victoria Ridge looked at him with anguish. Was she going to be fired after all these years of loyal service? "By looking around you," Martin continued, "you can see that you're the most experienced—the, uh, best of our teachers." Smiles of relief and gratification everywhere.

"So it seems to me it's time all of you are *elevated* to a position of greater honor. I propose to form what we'll call the Sunday school advisory board of directors. . . ." The idea delighted them. Even when they finally understood that they would withdraw gradually from active teaching, they remained pleased. For, as Martin realized, most of them had been teaching all these years through a sense of duty rather than satisfaction.

The next week he called together eight younger women and men who had expressed an interest in teaching.

"I'm going to help each of you individually with the class age levels in which you've expressed interest," he told them. "But there's one generality I want to express to all of you. The Bible is not an abstract document. Its sacredness can't be enhanced by insisting that children learn some of its statements and then parrot them back. Above all, the Bible is a kind of wonderful library of interesting stories that tells truths about the nature of people in Upton at this very moment. . . ."

After a while Janet Tate smiled at him drolly and asked, "Mr. Judson, suppose the advisory board of directors doesn't approve of some of us and our different methods?"

"Oh, they will approve, Janet, they will."

And they did. They even approved when Martin moved the Sunday-school hour from noon—following church service—to ten o'clock, preceding it. They argued a bit but gave in to his sensible statements: Around noon everyone wanted to get home for Sunday dinner, and at ten o'clock on a Sunday morning many parents were glad to get noisy children out of the house.

He must have been right, for by the end of his third year Sunday-school attendance had trebled and the church had to rent additional space for classes in an empty store down Congress Street. His wish to build an addition to the church on its adjoining empty lot was approved by everyone; it was frustrated only by wartime restrictions on building materials.

The war seldom was far from Martin's thoughts. Sometimes he pondered what he had missed by not having military service.

Correspondence with Lance indicated he had missed an interesting and good time.

"Trust Lance to cover the iron spikes with a mattress," he remarked to Jane. He was neither sarcastic nor envious; he simply was describing Lance's talent for winning friends, influencing people, and making a good life when things were at their worst.

Lance had become a Navy chaplain. "Tubby simply scared me out of the Army," he wrote from Norfolk. "Am being sent to the Pentagon in Washington next week for TDY."

"What's a Navy chaplain doing in the Pentagon?" asked Jane.

"Maybe converting generals into good Navy men," Martin said. "If anybody could do it, Lance could."

They heard from him next in Pearl Harbor. "Expect to shove on soon into the far fighting zones," he wrote. "Adieu, adieu, dear friends." Somehow, without coming right out and saying it, Lance conveyed a picture of himelf going down with his ship in some great battle, praying with his faithful men gathered about him, and all singing "Nearer My God to Thee" as the sea closed over them. "Am probably shoving off next week. . . ."

But he didn't shove. The next they heard he had been promoted to lieutenant commander. "All is temporary in war, of course, but at present have been assigned to CINCPAC. . . ." As time passed, Lance gave the impression in his letters that his assignment was the welfare of the souls of several admirals. Though he referred to Admiral Nimitz only as the Skipper, Martin wondered if he might not talk to him personally as Chet. Certainly he was the only person Martin ever knew who always referred to Admiral William F. Halsey, Jr., as Bill.

Martin's brother, Nathaniel, wrote him of a quite different war in the Pacific. Nathaniel was a Seabee on an anonymous atoll.

"The sun rises and the sun goes down," Nathaniel said. "Between times you push your bulldozer and eat your chow and, if you're lucky, have a warm can of beer before supper."

He wrote Nathaniel frequently and received frequent replies. It was not an easy correspondence because they did not really know each other. The only clue to Nathaniel's interests was his wish to have some paperback mysteries sent him.

Correspondence with Tubby was far more satisfying. Once Tubby was freed of the Carolina pine barrens and landed in North Africa, his letters became spirited. Since he was one of the regimental censor officers, he wrote with candor.

"One thing that impresses me above all, Marty, is man's capacity to endure," he wrote after the confusion at Kasserine Pass. "We came here expecting heat, and what we have is extreme cold. We came dreading death and have found we dread most the creeping monotony of days of waiting for the unexpected. The griping is eloquent, but few funk out. Nearly all go on stoically. . . ."

From Sicily:

> What is there about some clergymen that makes them dislike to get their feet wet? Our chief of chaplains is such a man. An Episcopalian from Los Angeles in civilian life. Not a coward. Really a nice guy. But he's convinced that a chaplain's role is to give the guys a good service in a rear area and let 'em go. He says, "A chaplain is just a nuisance up forward. . . ."

From Salerno:

> Maybe the chief of chaplains is right. Take my word for it, foxholes are infested with atheists. They're some of the best soldiers we have. But they're beginning to accept me, despite my eccentricity of being a Christian. I have a lot of luck, and some are beginning to think I bring them luck. Can't cite any conversions in the forward area. But some are beginning to call me Rabbit's foot, which is the greatest compliment a chaplain can receive. . . .

Months passed when they did not hear from Tubby, and they grew deeply concerned. Then he wrote from England, where he had been hospitalized for some time, though he did not say why.

> Children, old Daddy is in love. Her name is Eunice Caldwell, a lieutenant of nurses at this base hospital, from Horn Wolf

(no kidding), Idaho. She is blond (natural), beautiful, smart, gentle. Everybody is in love with Eunice. But the news is that Eunice is in love with me. We're engaged and will marry as soon as the current unpleasantness is ended. She was raised a Mennonite, but she says she's willing to be a Baptist preacher's wife. I'm shoving out of here soon. . . .

They received a letter from Eunice about a month later. Tubby was with Patton's Third Army in France and asked her to pass the word that he would write them when he could.

> Tubby—I finally understand why those close to him call him that—may not have told you he was badly shot up in Italy. It would be like him not to mention it. Thank heaven he was sent to England. He received the Silver Star for doing something brave and foolish. Though he could have gone Stateside from here, he preferred France. . . .

One evening late in October, 1945, they received a telephone call from New York. Major and Mrs. Robert Browning Larsen had arrived home on terminal leave and were staying at the Astor.

"Get down here!" Martin cried. "Bus is fastest. Now let me talk to Eunice, and then Jane wants to talk to her. . . ."

They arrived the next afternoon. When Jane saw them at a distance, she exclaimed, "Such beautiful people!" and burst into tears.

Martin said, "My gosh, Tubby, you look like Omar Bradley with a good head of hair."

Both still were in uniform. Though Tubby, like Martin, had disdained ever wearing his Phi Beta Kappa key, he wore his service ribbons proudly—Silver Star, Bronze Star, the Purple Heart twice, eight battle stars.

"It's my last chance for glory," he said wryly. "Next month I'm going back to pacifism."

They talked from early morning till late at night. Eunice

wanted to learn everything she possibly could from Jane about being a minister's wife.

"It's impossible to summarize," Jane said. "It's like being a colonist on the moon. You have to adapt to absolutely everything as you go along."

"I want to go back to Thornton," Tubby told Martin. "Yet I don't want to. I look forward to it, but I dread it."

"What do you dread the most, Tubby?"

"The formlessness of the life. With all its innumerable faults, Army life gives a form to the days. You work within specific limitations. But thinking back to civilian preaching, I remember it as so—limitless. Where to begin and when to quit?"

Martin agreed with him. "For most of these first six years I've been haunted by the feeling that when I'm doing one thing, I should be doing something else."

"And something else ambles on to still another thing," Tubby said.

Martin kept trying to lead him into talking about Army life, but Tubby kept switching back to the ministry.

"In Thornton I drew up a weekly schedule. Most elaborate, ironclad thing you ever saw. Within a week I threw it out as sheer fiction."

"I know. I tried the same here in Upton. It won't work. For instance, study period from four to six P.M.—"

"Hey!" Tubby grinned. "I see where you located your desk with those tieback curtains. Pretty clever, old boy. I'm going to take your tip when we get back to Thornton."

"I remember just one instance," Martin said. "Around four thirty there was a call from the hospital. Mrs. Bronson on the critical list, and the family wanted me there right away. On the way out I ran into a fellow I knew who had been having a drinking problem. He was fighting it, trying to work his way through the sundown blues without a drink. I knew it, and he knew that I knew it. So I took him bowling and plied him with hot dogs and Cokes till about seven thirty. He had licked the sundown blues one more day. I can't *cure* 'em, of course.

I'm not Menninger. But one more day. So I hurried home and had a bite of the supper Jane had prepared for six—and was late for an eight o'clock meeting. You just can't *schedule* it."

"I want Eunice to hear that story," Tubby said. "She keeps wondering what it's *like*. Marty, your mentioning the psychiatrist Menninger reminded me of Joe Menninger. Remember him in our class at Brown? Well, one day in Casablanca. . . ."

Thus they talked for four days and nights. Only after Tubby and Eunice had been gone for some time did it occur to Martin that not once had Tubby and he discussed God or religious faith.

❧ *Two* ❧

ONCE Jane asked Martin, "How does a minister get a new church?"

"Restless?"

"No. I was just wondering. I'll put it the other way around. In a denomination like the Baptist or Congregational—where every church is independent and there is no hierarchy—how does a church get a new minister?"

"By guess and by God."

"Seriously, Marty."

"Seriously. Well, they can write to denominational headquarters for suggestions and then follow up prospects on their own. Or they can write a seminary like Davidson and do the same thing. That's the way we came here. I guess it's the way we'd get a crack at some other church."

It was the way whereby Martin received a letter one day in May, 1946, from Norman Street, president of the Street Paper Company of Sylvia, Illinois, stating that he was the chairman of the pulpit committee of Central Baptist Church of Sylvia. The church was looking about for a new minister since its pastor was leaving, and Martin's name had been suggested by the dean of Davidson Theological and Mallory Swayne, an official of the

American Baptist Convention. Was Martin planning to preach in his pulpit a week from the following Sunday, and would it be agreeable for a delegation from Central to hear him?

"Jane!" he cried.

She came quickly. Her first question after she read the letter did not sound very sensible to him. "Who is Mallory Swayne?"

"I haven't the vaguest idea."

"But how could a high official of the convention know about you?"

"Hadn't you heard? The Pope spies on all us priests. Seriously, the important question is what is Sylvia?"

"I've heard of Sylvia, Illinois," Jane said.

"So have I, vaguely. But where is it?"

He phoned his friend Miss Crofts at the public library, and she quickly informed him that Sylvia was a city of about eighty thousand population in the greater Chicago area of northern Illinois. It had a college, a number of Class A manufacturing plants, and one of the best public school systems in the country.

"One of the best public school systems in the country," Jane repeated. "Isn't that wonderful?"

"I suppose so." He decided to shoot a couple of bucks on a phone call to Bud Bennett, the dean of Davidson. Bud's reply to his questions astonished him.

"Central of Sylvia is one of the dozen or so strongest churches in the denomination, Marty. By strong I mean big, rich, influential at the top—all that. Rather difficult, too, I gather. All big churches are, you know. . . . Oh, stop sounding modest. Word gets around. You've done a fine job at Upton. It isn't necessary for a bishop or superintendent to keep his eye on a minister for other people to learn how he's doing. I think you have the resilience and administrative ability to handle Central. How much are you making?"

"Four thousand. Parsonage, too. And this year they've started giving me three hundred extra for auto upkeep."

"That's big of them," Bud said. "Central will pay ten to start, and parsonage, and fringe benefits."

Martin could not believe he had heard correctly, but Bud assured him that he had.

"Ten thousand dollars a year!" Jane sank back in her chair. "We wouldn't know what to do with it!"

"We haven't been offered it yet," Martin said. "And if we were, I'm not sure I'd want to go there."

"Neither am I," Jane said. "During the first months here I'd have given anything to go anywhere. But now—I don't know."

Martin hesitated. "Or am I being hypocritical? You know, I— Well, I know I display many of the symptoms of what has been called the American success syndrome."

"Is that bad?" asked Jane.

"The wiseacres say it is. But I know scarcely any man who doesn't have it. The belief in growth—in making small things become larger as a virtue in itself. I want the community to esteem me so it will be a help in my influencing others to share —you know. I want to make more money. Not to hoard it. But to make things more pleasant for you and Kathy—and me. You know these things are counter to the teachings of Jesus, to the fulfillment of the kingdom of heaven on earth."

Jane cast a look that asked, "How did He get into this discussion?"

"But I can't help those tendencies," Martin said. "They were bred into me like the size of my bones and the color of my eyes. They seem to have been bred into just about everybody I know."

So he wrote Norman Street a courteous note. He decided to preach that Sunday on the theme that worldly success need not spoil human virtue. He rehearsed his sermon while he polished his shoes with great vigor. He fussed about the appearance of their furniture.

From the pulpit on Sunday he immediately spotted the Central pulpit committee, two men and two women. Others spotted them, too, and guessed who they were. The resentful gaze that Harcourt Prescott cast up from his pew was amusing; Harcourt would have been delighted if he stammered and fumbled through his sermon. (But Jane told him later that he preached well.) He guessed correctly that the man of Socratic dome was Norman Street; he was a bigger, richer, presumably more powerful John Ingham.

After the service Norman Street introduced himself and the others: Mrs. Thornton was a tall, expensive-looking woman with a shrewd smile. Dana Halpern was about Martin's age, vigorous-acting, deeply tanned. His wife was small, pretty, with a merry manner. Martin introduced Jane, who invited them to the parsonage.

Conversation flowed more spontaneously than Martin had anticipated. Only one thing hung him up momentarily: Halpern said they had flown in that morning from Chicago in his company's plane. Martin couldn't quite get over it. They must have had to leave awfully early, and flying all that distance just to listen to Martin Judson!

"Suppose the airport had been socked in?" he asked.

Halpern shrugged. "Then we'd have to try another Sunday. It was a nice flight. We played bridge all the way."

Martin said, "Then your morning wasn't completely wasted."

Kathy, who was passing through a cute phase, had decided to act with decorum. Presently Mrs. Tabor arrived to take Kathy home with her, following the arrangements made by Jane, who wafted them both to the door after introducing a wide-eyed Mrs. Tabor to the four from Sylvia. Martin explained that Jane and he wished them to go to dinner at the Iron Kettle Inn.

Street almost looked surprised and muttered about taking *them*. Then he did show surprise—and a kind of relief—as Martin continued: "Pennsylvania blue laws prohibit buying drinks on Sunday. Would you like a sherry before we go? Jane also has coffee."

Jane had demurred about his offering sherry, but he had insisted. If they moved from Upton, it would be to a place of freer social manners. (John Ingham and a few others drank their bourbon like secretive soaks, never offering a sip to Martin, who didn't want it anyway.) Each of the four took a sherry—and then another before they went to the Iron Kettle for dinner.

Street said, "Churches don't have a buyer's market in clergymen these days. A lot of those in seminaries during the war were just draft dodgers. A lot of those who became chaplains don't want to go back to working for a living."

Jane said something Martin didn't think necessary: "Martin tried to get in, but the Army rejected him because they said—mistakenly—he had a hernia."

"I know," Street said.

Martin showed his surprise. "How did you know that? I never told anybody—hardly anybody."

Street smiled at Halpern. "Shall we tell him?"

Halpern smiled, too. "Why not?"

"Curtiss Welch, one of our trustees—you've probably heard of him, Welch Cosmetics—uses an investigative agency before hiring new key employees—"

"A lot of companies do that now," Halpern said.

"So Curt has had his agency check on you—and other prospects."

Martin, angry suddenly, said, "That Pinkerton business hardly seems sporting to me. But then I suppose you view bridge and golf as sporting. And business and Central Baptist aren't sporting ventures."

Obviously what he often had heard was true: Pulpit committees spoke and acted autocratically.

After the four from Sylvia had driven off to the airport in their rented car, Martin told Jane, "Let's forget about it for the time being."

But Norman Street telephoned him on Tuesday evening.

"Mr. Judson, we're seriously interested. If you're seriously interested, too, I know you'll want to look over our spread—check out the plant. How about you and Mrs. Judson flying out here a week from today and flying back Thursday. Dana's company plane is leaving New York early Tuesday morning. They'll pick you up about ten o'clock in the morning. Take you back, too, of course. You'll stay with Verna and me. There's an affair at Roaring Brook Country Club we'd like you both to attend Wednesday evening. Black tie. And bring along the little girl. She's a charmer."

The airplane trip was exciting. While two sales executives from New York played gin rummy and kidded Kathy, the wonderful land stretched out below them.

They were met at the Chicago airport by Georgia Thornton, Rita Halpern, and Verna Street with a large station wagon. Verna Street was older than she wished to be and had a stubborn jaw. Since Jane wore a sweater and tweed suit similar to those of the other women, everyone was happy.

At first glance the area of Sylvia through which they drove made it appear to be one vast suburban complex. Its manufacturing plants were hidden. Its streets were called drives, lanes, roads—anything but streets. In Upton there were only a few streets of substantial houses set in large grounds compared to scores of such streets in Sylvia. The spring air smelled of lilacs and prosperity.

The Streets lived in a big Colonial imitation, where Kathy was tendered to the care of a friendly servant woman. Verna Street's children having grown up and left her, she had found a five-year-old boy someplace for Kathy to play with. When Kathy put her arms about him and kissed him, everyone was delighted.

Dana Halpern was in Milwaukee, but planned to be back that afternoon; Bill Thornton was in Dallas. Norman Street came home for lunch, however, bringing with him Curtiss Welch, a big, bespectacled man of about sixty with a booming voice he constantly tried to modulate.

After meeting Jane and Martin, Welch boomed to Street: "What a morning I put in. I need—I may not need, but I want [*sotto voce*] a martini."

After lunch Street and Welch said they would take Martin to the church to look it over. On the way Street asked him if there was anything else he wanted to see.

"The whole town," Martin said. "And I'd like to meet your present minister—I don't know his name."

"Manter," Welch said. "He's away at the Mayo Clinic for a checkup. His wife went with him. The girls are taking Mrs. Judson by the parsonage. We'll meet 'em there later. Manter is a good guy, but he's getting almost as old as me, and he's tiring. He's found himself a nice quiet little place up in Wisconsin. Our assistant minister, Jay Holmes, is at the church office. At least he'd *better* be."

As they drove up to Central Baptist Church, Martin was impressed to the point of silence. It was large (huge, he thought), of gray stone, sensibly designed, fronting on a beautiful park, with a big, newer building complex at a rear side, where the office was located. The pastor's study was large, handsomely appointed. The secretary, Mary Boyce, was plain, middle-aged, with an air of great efficiency. And then young Jay Holmes came in. He started nervously each time Welch boomed; his desire to please was painful; his reply when Martin asked his duties was vague and rambling. Martin thought: *Holmes must go—* and then regretted his snap judgment.

He inspected the complex of classrooms, recreation rooms, a kitchen which could serve five hundred. Most impressive of all was the auditorium, which seated eight hundred, Street said.

"What's your average attendance?" Martin asked.

Street hesitated, and Welch said, "I had my accounting department do an averaging. Three forty so far this year. Three sixty-eight last year. Three eighty-eight year before. We're"— he turned to Holmes—"Jay, thanks for showing us around. See you later."

Holmes extended a damp hand to Martin and then fled. Welch said, "We're going down. Do you want my opinion why?" Martin nodded. "Manter is angry at us, and we can't figure why.

When he gets up here in the pulpit, he lays it on us with whips. We're far from perfect. What people are? And I don't mind being given a little hell sometimes. But it gets . . . tiresome. Have you ever heard of anything like that before?"

"Yes. It's not unusual." Martin cited a couple of examples. "It seems to happen with older men. Some of the seminaries are trying to work at the problem. It seems to begin with too much submissiveness in a young preacher—feeling he must be subservient and kowtow to everyone. I know a young minister in a town near Upton who drives twenty miles to buy a pack of beer, and then he and his wife drink it in the cellar because they're scared of what the congregation will think. You know what that sort of thing does. Builds resentment in a man. And if he doesn't watch out, he'll turn into an angry old preacher."

Street and Welch gazed at him thoughtfully, then glanced at each other. Street asked, "Have you any criticism of the layout here?"

"It looks excellent to me."

They spent the next hour driving about town. Both men were proud of Sylvia—of its college, its public buildings, its light skilled industries. But Sylvia also had a depressed area, and Martin asked them to drive them through it.

"It's the same old story," Street said. "People want cheap help, and so Negroes pour up from the South. You see them here. It's pretty bad, but they don't seem to care much about trying to help themselves."

Martin asked if Central participated in any community activities, and they answered him vaguely; apparently there didn't seem to be anything in which the churches needed to cooperate.

At last they arrived at the parsonage, which was two blocks from the church. It was an English-style stucco and shingle with fine yard space. Jane and the other women had been there for some time. Martin knew at once by Jane's expression that she loved the place. Despite his and Jane's reluctance to nose about the parsonage while the Manters were absent, the others insisted that he inspect its rooms and Jane look at them again. He, like Jane, never had lived in such a fine house.

When they reached their bedroom at the Streets', Martin asked Jane, "What do you think?"

"Oh, Marty, I don't know what to think. I've never been so . . . wowed in my life. Or so scared. Have they *said* anything to you?"

"Not yet. But I smell it coming. It scares me a bit, too. But if we start running scared at thirty-one, where will we be at forty? In Upton, I suppose. And always wondering if maybe— The point is, do you *like* it?"

"I *love* it. Too much for my own good, I'm afraid. But it . . . *challenges* me. And that's where all the fun is, isn't it?"

"Yes. But I'm not sure it's the *right* kind of challenge. And when I say that, I don't know exactly what I mean. Maybe I mean these people make me vaguely uncomfortable. Which is another way of saying I'm scared of 'em. And I don't want to be scared of anything. Well, they may not make an offer."

But they did.

Dinner that evening was at Curtiss Welch's house, which was even larger and grander than the Streets'. Welch's wife, Alice, was away. The guests included the Streets, Georgia Thornton, Harold West Brown, a bachelor who was chairman of the history department at the college and chairman of the Central board of deacons, and Mrs. Whitney Thayer, a widow who was a church trustee and the director of social service agencies in Sylvia.

The five-course dinner and the formality of its serving seemed unnecessarily pretentious to Martin. And they watched him too closely. Did they think he would be confused by the array of silverware?

At last the meal was over, and the males separated from the females, as in an English novel. In the game room there were cigars and liqueurs. Martin wanted neither; he was suffering from indigestion. Soon Mrs. Thayer appeared in the library, and Welch in effect called the meeting to order.

"Mr. Judson—may we call you Martin—this has been a fascinating afternoon for Norm and me, and it would have been for the others if they had been along. As you can imagine, we were on the phone talking to many people before dinner. It's the unanimous consensus of the committee we want you for pastor of Central. We thought it might take longer to come to a decision, but it didn't. Are you interested?"

Martin wondered what to do with his hands. "Yes, I'm interested."

"Let me state our proposition. Eleven thousand a year, parsonage, five hundred allowance on a car, the church carries your pension fund, plus hospitalization and surgery insurance on the entire family. Does that sound reasonable to you?"

Martin crossed his hands.

Brown asked, "What are you making in Upton, Mr. Judson?"

"Forty-two thousand a year."

There was silence, then laughter.

Martin said, "I don't mean to be a wise guy, Mr. Brown, but you must know what I'm earning. I have been . . . investigated. No one needs to remind me that your offer is generous and far better than what I'm earning. But I have a few misgivings. You must, too, in taking an unknown quantity and tripling his salary. I'm not sure what you want here—and I wonder if you are sure yourselves. Do you want a first-rate administrator? A great pastor? An outstanding preacher?"

Welch took his time in lighting a cigar. "We believe you're capable in all these fields."

Brown said, "Central needs a strong preacher."

"But what is that?" Martin asked. "I like to preach. But my style is plain, informal. I'm no John Barrymore. Oration makes me . . . embarrassed."

Dana Halpern said, "Let me ask you a question . . . Martin. This deals, I suppose, with administrative aspects of the pastorate. Norm says you met Jay Holmes this afternoon. What is your candid opinion of him?"

Martin hesitated briefly. "I think your new pastor should

pick his own assistant, preferably a man fresh out of seminary, and train him himself."

Mrs. Thayer asked, "Mr. Judson, what is a great pastor?"

"Certainly not one who coddles parishioners and holds their hands. Maybe a great pastor is created by a great church rather than the other way around. And by a great church I mean one for *all* people. Among the worldly aims of the church I think just about the most important one is tolerance."

They agreed with him. Curtiss Welch said fervently, "That's exactly what we want to be—a church for *all* people."

The next day Martin accepted the invitation to become the pastor of Central Baptist Church of Sylvia.

Jane divided eleven thousand dollars, Martin's salary, by twelve, the number of months in the year, but she couldn't make the resulting figure meaningful. Like Mount Everest, it was *there,* but like Everest becoming wrapped in clouds, it disappeared fast.

There were eight rooms in the new parsonage; when they arrived, they could furnish only five properly. They needed a new dining-room set, three new rugs, a divan for the living room, a new set of china, several silver pieces, furniture for a guest room. To Jane's growing consternation, the cost of these new things came to nearly twenty-five hundred dollars. They paid on time.

Jane began to realize that while it might be said they were "living better" in Sylvia than they had in Upton, they did not actually have more money—and they had little prospects of saving it. Life in Sylvia merely was a slight revision of life in Upton. They must still live neither "up" nor "down" to the people of the congregation. Socially they must appear to be on a par with the most influential people of the church. But *economically* there was a general wish on the part of the flock that the shepherd not earn as much as they. After all, who produced the wool? It had been true in Upton. It was true in Sylvia. And doubtless it was true everywhere.

One morning Georgia Thornton dropped into the parsonage. Jane sensed there was some purpose to her call, and it came out soon.

"The winters get very cold here," Georgia said. "You're going to need something warmer than your Persian lamb. I'd suggest a mink-dyed muskrat." Georgia wore a full-length genuine mink herself. "Come shopping with me tomorrow, Jane. I know a place where you can get a good one for under five hundred."

Jane agreed reluctantly. No coat was warmer than Persian lamb. And she disliked mink-dyed muskrat as being a phony article. Yet she must try to view the question of the mink-dyed muskrat—like so many other things—as a challenge rather than a problem.

"I don't want a mink-dyed muskrat," she told Martin.

"Then don't get one," he replied.

"No, I'm going to get it. I went through enough *coat* trouble in Upton. My instinctive reaction to Georgia's suggestion isn't kind. I think she feels a Persian lamb doesn't look quite *rich* enough for the pastor's wife. Every woman recognizes a phony mink. Georgia knows that and wants me to seem to *aspire* to it."

"Then don't get one," he repeated.

"No, I'm going to get it. I'm going to ignore my instinctive reaction to Georgia. I'm going to play it that her thought is *kind*. Marty, we have to have some self-deceptions. I mean we have to make things seem a bit better than they really are."

He grimaced. "You mean, 'Be of good cheer,' said the Apostle Paul, barefoot and in jail."

"I mean, we not only must *do*. We must *like* what we do. Otherwise, we'll fall into self-pity and resentment, and then you never could minister effectively."

The next day she went shopping with Georgia and bought a mink-dyed muskrat. It cost four hundred and seventy-five dollars, and they would pay for it on time.

"Isn't it a beauty?" she said to Martin when she brought it home and tried it on for him.

"Very nice," he said. "A real beauty."

About a week later a loyal member named Mrs. Fredericks called at the parsonage in the afternoon. She came to the point faster than Georgia had.

"I know you and Mr. Judson have heard about the fine work the Luke Boys Farm is doing for homeless youngsters. . . ."

Here it came again, Jane thought. Charity could not begin at home in a minister's family. It began with everyone else's charitable interests, and seemingly these knew no bounds. Whatever a person's favorite charity, he seemed to fasten first on the pastor and wife as the most charitable. After all, didn't the charity-minded ones give to *their* favorite charity—Central Baptist?

"When I gave her five dollars," Jane told Martin that evening, "she acted disappointed. And we're away above the amount I budgeted for charitable giving."

"Did you write her a check?" Martin asked.

"Of course." Suddenly she was angry with him. "But where do you think the checks come from?"

"From the church," he said, "on the first of the month."

Oh, he could be impossible sometimes! Her voice rose: "So much magic from so little. Just like the two loaves and five fishes, I suppose."

"Jane, honey, you got it the wrong way around. It's five loaves and *two* fishes."

She started to laugh, she could not help herself, and he joined with her. . . .

They tried to take pleasure in entertaining members of the church, and both felt they succeeded pretty well.

Then, one evening in September, 1947, after they had had four at dinner, they were utterly weary of entertaining. But they kept on doing it.

Jane wondered sometimes if their social tolerance would have

remained stronger if they had not become friends with Abe
and Rachel Lamber. She met Rachel, a darkly beautiful woman
with a mordant wit, on a committee of the AAUW, and they
took to each other at once. She did not know the occupation
of Rachel's husband, and Rachel did not know Jane was a
clergyman's wife; one never asked such things; there was a
pleasing anonymity within the organization that Jane, always
the pastor's wife in Central Baptist activities, enjoyed for a
change.

One hot day Martin came home in midafternoon with a
short, stout, pleasant man whom he introduced as Rabbi Abraham Lamber. It developed that Rachel was his wife. Abraham
and Martin sat in the backyard for the rest of the afternoon,
drinking iced tea and talking. Abraham was the rabbi of the
Reformed congregation in Sylvia. Martin had never met him
until that afternoon while making hospital calls.

The four became close friends. Jane enjoyed Rachel; they
had similar interests in music and books, and, above all, they
shared a wry sense of humor. It was quickly obvious, too, that
Martin liked Abe better than any Christian clergyman he knew
in the area—even better than Rob Daniels, the young graduate
of Union Theological whom he had chosen to be his assistant.
In time Abe became his closest friend in Sylvia.

Through Abe and Rachel they learned that the Jewish community in Sylvia had its own ghetto—a fairly comfortable one
embracing shaded streets, as well as flats over storefronts, but
nevertheless a ghetto. It was created by restrictive clauses in the
sales of property. Martin was indignant when he heard about
it.

"Oh, stop sounding like a *Christian*," Abe said mildly. "Do
you want a Jew to move next door? Do you want your daughter
to marry a Jew?"

When Martin looked hurt, Abe touched him on an arm and
said, "I'm kidding you, Marty. I honestly don't think most of
the Jews in town mind the property restrictions. Some care—

very much. But most Jews have been living in ghettos for so many centuries they wouldn't know what to do without 'em."

Martin said, "Now *you* sound like a Christian."

"Now *you* are kidding," Abe replied. "I'm a Jew of the most objectionable kind from the Gentile viewpoint. I protest vehemently these real estate covenants. We may not be the chosen race, but neither are we second-class citizens. Didn't we set the Western world on its ear with three of our smartest Jews—Jesus, Freud, and Marx? If it weren't for us, you Gentiles still would be wearing animal skins. So you see I'm the objectionable kind of Jew—one who believes in fighting for his rights. I'd like to see Jew living beside Gentile along every street in Sylvia."

"So would I," said Martin. And Jane knew that he meant it.

Inevitably people in Central Baptist learned of the friendship between the Judsons and the Lambers. At first they seemed to be amused. But their attitude changed following a night in February, 1948. Long in advance Jane and Martin, Abe and Rachel had bought tickets to a symphony in Chicago. Then Verna Street phoned Jane and invited Martin and her to dinner and a play by the Sylvia Sock and Buskin Players on the same evening. Jane replied that they had a previous engagement in Chicago; she did not say they were going with the Lambers.

The four took a late afternoon train to Chicago, had dinner, enjoyed the concert, and returned to Sylvia after midnight. At some place they were observed by someone who spread the information that reached the Streets—who were furious.

In early spring Jane sharply reduced her church and social activities. She was pregnant. She had had two miscarriages, and after the second, an obstetrician had advised her not to become pregnant again. But happily, she *was* pregnant again—and determined this time to bear their child. This time she went into a kind of Victorian confinement and found herself enjoying it thoroughly. Church affairs receded to a comfortable distance; she kept informed about them largely through Martin, who suddenly had become a kind of pampering Victorian husband.

She was present one afternoon when Abe, Martin, and Rob Daniels decided it would be a fine idea if some Saturday and Sunday their congregations held interfaith services—Saturday at the temple and Sunday at the church. Martin brought up the matter. "Would your people go along with it, Abe?"

"Of course. They'd like to have diplomatic relations with the *shkotzim*. The question is whether *your* people would go along with the idea."

"I don't know why they shouldn't. They seem to listen to what I preach to them on Sundays. So they should understand the importance of this."

"Well"—Abe sounded skeptical—"I guess you know your people better than I do. But I won't kid you on one thing, Marty. I'm not going to bring up the question to my people till you've settled it with yours. If I built them up to it and then you people let us down, it wouldn't make Sylvia a better place to us Jews."

Martin said he would propose the matter a week later, when there would be a joint meeting of the deacons and trustees.

When Martin brought up the matter, he was surprised at the vehemence of Norman Street's reaction.

"Give the Jews an inch," Norman cried, "and they'll take a mile! All they really want to do is break down property covenants in town. Once they do that we'll have every Jew pawnbroker in Chicago commuting up here. This town will become Jerusalem, and they'll chase all of us to the north woods."

Martin's surprise turned into an anger which he tried to control. "Norman, I thought the subject under discussion concerned humanity—not property."

"That shows how naïve you are," Norman replied.

A deacon named Bill Morris said, "Norman, I'd suggest you retract that statement.

"Well," Norman said, "what I mean is that this is the first time I've seen Martin acting naïve."

"Just a minute!" Rob Daniels was almost shouting. "I want to tell you people something. None of you appreciates what a great minister you have in Martin. His preaching and pastoral work have brought church attendance to well over six hundred. He gives of himself unstintingly in more activities than you can name. He'll rise from sleep at any hour of the night or turn from anything during the day to help anyone in trouble. Above all, his *faith*—which he never wears on his sleeve—is with him always. What's the matter with you? *You should agree to this just because he says so.*"

There was silence for a moment; then someone said, "Vote!"

Seventeen were against Martin's proposal—and seven for it.

"I quit!" Rob cried.

"Knock it off, Rob," Martin said. He was still angry, but his tone was under control. "We have heard the vote, and we know the decision of the board. Let's take up the next matter of business."

But Rob—who was not married and wanted to take further work at Yale—did resign, declaring he had no intention of being a missionary to the Yahoos of Sylvia. Besides, he was infatuated with the polemic he had composed as a letter of resignation and wanted it to have wide readership.

Abe and Rachel took the defeat philosophically. Perhaps, Martin thought, an advantage in being a Jew was that you never were surprised by defeat while Anglo-Saxons were reared on the myth of continual victories. A couple of months later, they left Sylvia and moved to a synagogue in Washington. Martin and Jane felt they had lost their closest friends in town.

As time passed, Martin became somewhat resigned to the bigotry of Norman Street and those who felt as he did. But he was not resigned to the mental and emotional frame that prompted it and did all he could to struggle against it.

Early in June the troubles of Gentiles and Jews became of

little importance to Martin and Jane. All that mattered was
the fact she went into labor prematurely. It appeared that she
would lose a child again. But a boy was born to them—and
lived. They named him Abraham. . . .

Mrs. Vernon Rankin died of a heart block in the Farrar
Nursing Home about ten o'clock on the evening of September
26, 1948. Shortly before nine o'clock her husband phoned Martin, who hurried to the nursing home at once. The head nurse
there had been trying to reach Mrs. Rankin's doctor since five
o'clock in the afternoon; then she had tried to find *any* doctor; and finally, realizing there was nothing a physician could
do to prevent Mrs. Rankin from dying, she had given up. She
waited by the bedside with Mr. Rankin and Martin.

"The Lord is my shepherd. . . . I am the resurrection and
the life. . . ."

Martin recited the familiar passages in a low tone while Mr.
Rankin wept. He repeated them again and again at Mr. Rankin's insistence. He doubted that Mrs. Rankin understood or
even heard him. She was in great pain, her entire being absorbed in the futile struggle for life. In moments when she
had the strength she whispered, "Vern, get the doctor. . . .
Vern, where is the doctor? . . . I want the doctor. . . ." Mr.
Rankin cursed the doctor for not coming. The nurse said there
was nothing a physician could do, making Mr. Rankin only
more angry. Then his anger was drowned by grief again, and
he asked Martin to pray once more.

A few minutes after Mrs. Rankin died, her doctor arrived.
Mr. Rankin cursed him and fled. The doctor told Martin it
was his day off, and somehow the exchange had balled up all
his calls. Martin, unable to find Mr. Rankin, phoned an undertaker and arranged to have the body taken away. Then, feeling depressed, he went out into the raw, foggy night.

Death was the great misunderstanding. The one dying
rarely could understand it was inevitable. Those who loved the
one dying could not believe it was happening. All labored under

the misconception that the physician could perform some feat of magic to prevent death. Some, though not all, hoped that the clergyman could ameliorate the repulsive fact of life ending. But how could he as long as people continued to misunderstand? Was the subject worthy of development in a sermon?

Absorbed in these thoughts, Martin turned onto Lincoln Avenue, the main route north through Sylvia, and braked his car to a stop at a traffic light. A moment later there was a loud crump, and he was thrown against the wheel.

He got out and walked to the rear of his car. The back bumper appeared to have absorbed the shock and prevented much damage. But the front of the car which had struck his had been staved in; its radiator was cracked and erupting steam.

"Kee-rist Almighty!" a man cried. He stood beside Martin, gaunt and shabbily dressed. "That does it. But I didn't go to do it."

"I know you didn't," Martin said. "Everybody all right in your car?"

"Ma was flunged agin' the windshield, but I reckon she's all right. But *this* does it! Fifty-dollar job there. No insurance."

A husky young man climbed out of the back seat and accused Martin of stopping suddenly. The older man told him to shut up. Then, with Martin's help, they pushed the car to the curb.

The driver, Matt Pennington, had a West Virginia driver's license. His wife was thin, small, probably not as old as she appeared to be; she looked at the damaged car with a fierce determination not to cry. Their daughter was a pregnant, indistinct figure in the misty glow of a streetlight.

They stood together while Martin talked with the policemen who arrived in a patrol car. One of the policemen, recognizing Martin, accepted his word that there was no need of action. The car, which would not start, could be left at the curb overnight.

After the police left, Pennington told Martin that he and

his family had left Chicago that morning, bound for Milwaukee. His account was not coherent. They had been plagued by
car trouble all day. His son had decided to stay in Chicago. He
and Jim had heard there were jobs in Milwaukee. Chicago was
no good. They'd come there from West Virginia eight, ten
months ago—he couldn't remember exactly when. West Virginia was no good now either. A man needed land, and for
some unexplained reason the land had failed them. "I'll tell
you what's a fact, mister, amongst the all of us we got about
seven dollars left. We'll sleep hit out here in the car."

Martin, unable to think of any place for them to spend the
night, decided to take them home. They did not protest. They
brought an old valise, a guitar, and several paper packages into
his car with them.

When they filed into the parsonage, the four acted dumb-
founded. Matt Pennington, recovering first, said to Jane,
"Ma'am, it's mighty decent of you to take us in this way."

Jim grinned and said, "Yeh, look what the cat dragged in."
His wife, a drab girl in her teens, whose name was Viola, looked
at him reproachfully, and he grew abashed.

Jane, undismayed, said the Penningtons would have their
room and the McFarlands the guest room; Martin knew that
she and he would sleep on the rollaway cots. Then she asked
if they were hungry.

Mary Pennington spoke for the first time. "Miz Judson,
we ain't eat since noon."

She and her daughter went to the kitchen with Jane while
Matt sat, hands curled on his knees, and delivered a rambling
monologue on their bad luck since leaving West Virginia.
When Martin asked why they had left, Matt replied, "The
land was played out. Tim Henderson come back from Chicago
and says jobs was plentiful there. But I notice he don't come
back to Chicago." What sort of work had he and Jim found in
Chicago? "Nothin' much. And we can do anything. We're
handy with machinery."

The men's eyes lighted when they saw the dining-room

table: fried ham, eggs, potatoes, bread, preserves, milk, coffee. Matt stood behind his chair and asked a lengthy blessing, thinking apparently that Martin would neglect to do so. Though Martin knew they must be ravenous, each took care not to show it; they began to eat slowly, watchfully, with dignity.

At last Matt said, "Mr. Judson, what's your line o' work?"

"I'm a minister."

Matt laid down his knife and fork and joined the others in staring at him. "What church?"

"Matt," his wife said, "you ask too many questions. It's not good manners. I knew Mr. and Miss Judson was a God-given gentleman and lady, but—" She looked about the dining room wonderingly.

"Baptist," Martin said.

"Well, I'll be! We's Baptist!"

"Well, I'll be!" Mary said. "The Lord is with us tonight." Her eldest sister's husband was a Baptist preacher near Clarksburg. Once she started talking, she would not stop. . . .

As Martin and Jane were undressing for bed, she asked him, "Can you do anything for them?"

He shrugged. There was a predictable thing he could do: At his disposal was the church stewardship fund for use in situations such as this; in the morning he could have Matt Pennington's car repaired and then give him money to take them on to Milwaukee. But what then? Matt, fleeing a vaguely explained situation in Chicago, was equally vague about what he hoped to find in Milwaukee. What would he and his people do after they decided to flee Milwaukee? To help them on their way might sound charitable, but it would not truly be charity. From Martin's experience with poverty he could make one generality about its causes: Usually it was a result of one's failure to dig in and struggle hard enough over a particular issue. While habitual poverty often caused flight, it was equally true that habitual flight could not bring an end to poverty.

In the morning Matt's chief concern was to have his car repaired. Martin's serviceman, Jake Donahue, said it would cost eighty-five dollars—and the car wasn't worth it. Since Matt was as frightened at the prospect of losing his car as a bird with a broken wing, Martin told Jake to go ahead and fix it. While Jim watched and offered gratuitous advice about its repair, Martin talked with Matt. He learned that Matt did not truly want to go to Milwaukee. Above all, he wanted to work with *land,* and Jim, above all, wanted to work in a *gaa-rage.*

After Matt's car had been repaired, Martin took Jake aside and made a proposition: If he could use another man and would hire Jim for one week on trial, a church fund would reimburse him for the week's salary Jim received. "From there on, it's up to you, Jake. And Jim's never to know where the week's salary came from."

Jake looked at him oddly. "These people mean something to you, Doc?"

They *did,* but he was not about to try to describe his motives to Jake. "That's not the point. Can you use another man?"

"A *good* one, yes. Not just a grease monkey. Okay, Doc. I begin 'em at fifty a week and see how they pan out."

Jim was elated, but Matt, crestfallen, asked, "What can I do in this place?"

Martin telephoned Peter Kreuger, a church member who operated a large nursery on the western limits of town, and made a proposal like that he had made to Jake Donahue. Then, while Jim began work at once, Martin drove Matt to the nursery to meet Kreuger. When Matt saw what the work entailed for fifty a week, he reckoned he'd give it a try.

The next morning Jake Donahue phoned Martin and told him Jim was a proficient, hardworking mechanic; the church would not have to pay the week's salary, for Jake was glad he had hired him. In the afternoon there came a similar call from Peter Kreuger about Matt. Martin and Jane helped the four find two furnished rooms with kitchenette and bath over a drugstore, and Jane arranged an appointment for Viola with the obstetrician who had delivered Abe.

"I didn't think what you set out to do would work," Jane told Martin. "But it has. You knew what you were doing."

Not really, he thought. He possessed no grand schemes and panaceas for solving human problems. He was largely an improviser, playing it by ear and instinct. For a time he had made cryptic notes of the "problems" presented to him as a pastor and had found he offered a lasting solution only to about one in ten. Once he remarked on it in a letter to Tubby, who had become the pastor of a large Congregational church in Boston, and he was interested by Tubby's reply: "That's a high batting average in the ministry, Marty."

He had not thought consciously about the Penningtons and McFarlands attending Central Baptist; after listening to Matt and Mary carry on about the sanctifying virtues of total immersion, he had believed they would not care for his liberal brand of theology. So he was surprised a couple of weeks after they had arrived in Sylvia to see them in the congregation on Sunday morning. All had bought new clothing, but it was not right somehow. Martin's observation troubled him; as he led the congregation in the Lord's Prayer, he thought: *What's come over me that I think one must wear the* right *clothing to worship God? What's become of my wish to have this a church for all* people?

He had learned in the pulpit that a self-conscious worshiper was as obvious as a purple hat. It was an intuitive thing, hard to explain. The self-conscious one had a rigidity of bearing and a jerkiness of movement, like an agnostic who had mistakenly wandered into a Roman Catholic mass. The Penningtons and the McFarlands were self-conscious now—not, Martin thought, because they had yet been exposed to an obnoxious theology but because they knew their clothing was not *right*. This economic and social pecking order was a dismal, impossible approach to the worship of God, yet how could it be changed without a fundamental change in human nature?

The service went on, and so did Martin's thoughts counter to it. The excellent choir and organ joined in an anthem he

liked, "This Is the Day," an anonymous sixteenth-century composition with the words taken from Psalm 118. But he did not
listen to it as he watched Matt, anticipating the offering, cast
his eyes this way and that in an effort to learn what others were
giving. He recalled a passage from II Kings: "The money for
the trespass-offerings and the money for the sin-offerings was
not brought into the house of Jehovah: It was the priests'."
Matt wanted to give a proper offering to the priest who had
succored him; God was somewhere back in West Virginia.
The motive of the priest Martin Judson had been simply to
do something good. But Moses' father-in-law, Jethro, had had
something to say about that in Exodus. When Moses claimed he
did a good thing by telling the people God's thoughts, Jethro
replied, "The thing that thou doest is not good. Thou wilt
surely wear away, both thou and this people that is with thee;
for the thing is too heavy for thee; thou art not able to perform
it thyself alone."

"Thyself alone. . . ." He delivered his sermon heavily. The
subject was "The Great Misunderstanding" about death, a
development of the thoughts that had occurred to him on the
night Mrs. Rankin died. He started to preach it to Matt and
Mary Pennington until he no longer could bear their expressions of surprised incredulity. He was not preaching over their
heads; he was preaching *below* them. They understood the
inevitability of death and accepted it. They were asking themselves, What was he talking about? Didn't these people in the
congregation who were so much better off than they understand it, too? Whence came their prosperity, if not from God?

After the service Matt and Mary shook his hand limply. They
said something nice about his sermon. Then they left, puzzled
and confused. He knew they would not attend his services
again.

They did not. But he continued to think about them, as did
Jane. After Viola bore a son, Jane went often to the apartment
and helped Mary Pennington assemble a layette. Each time Martin took his car to Jake's for servicing, he talked with Jim. Once

he came upon Matt downtown; though they had a long conversation, there was something reproachful in Matt's manner
that made Martin ponder how he had failed him.

One evening in the week before Christmas Martin and
Jane drove Kathy downtown to the leading department store
to see Santa Claus, and they took Abe with them. Since Kathy
no longer believed in Santa Claus and Abe was too young to
care, there was not much point to the trip. It was simply another of those outings they frequently enjoyed as a family, but
this time Kathy was as bored with the commercial folderol as
Martin himself.

"Not yet nine and already too sophisticated for Christmas."
Jane sounded cross. "Isn't there *anything* you'd like to do,
Katherine?"

Kathy made a sucking sound with her teeth brace. "I'd like
to go to Bethlehem and stay there through Christmas."

Martin, who was carrying Abe, said, "We can't get back in
time. I have to preach on Sunday."

Kathy said, "What about the people from West Virginia who
visited us? The ones with the new baby. Why don't we go see
them, their having a new baby and Christmas and all?"

Jane and Martin looked at each other, and then they went to
visit the Penningtons and McFarlands.

They were received warmly, with surprise—and some embarrassment. Martin saw that their cause of embarrassment was
Jim, who strummed his guitar beside a table on which there
was a tumbler and a pint of cheap bourbon. He nodded to
them gravely but did not rise. He was not drunk; he simply
was sad.

The tunes he plucked from his guitar and the words he sang
in a husky voice were so sad they made Kathy cry. She listened
raptly, saying the songs were good, while tears streamed down
her cheeks. She especially liked one song that Jim had made up
himself:

> I am so lonely,
> Lonely am I—

I am so lonely,
I'm fit to die. . . .

When they reached home, Martin told Jane, "In thinking
about them, I overlooked a simple, obvious thing. You think
about all the windy generalities in connection with them—
education, job opportunities, soil depletion, all that stuff. But
you forget how much they're driven by a sense of loneliness in
their wanderings. The trouble with them here, the reason they
look so reproachful is that they can't find friends of similar experience."

"Is there something more we can do?" Jane asked.

"I don't know what. We never meant to patronize them, but
somehow everything we do comes out that way. Matt and I
can't even come to terms on a topic of conversation. He always wants to talk about the importance of total immersion.
And I want to learn what really happened back in West Virginia."

One day after Christmas, when Martin came home from the
church study, Jane said, "Jim has gone. I dropped by to see
Mary and Viola this afternoon, and they told me he left a
couple of days ago."

Martin was astonished. "Where did he go?"

"They don't know. He didn't say. I don't think he and Viola
have been getting along too well since the baby came. But
they didn't seem much upset. They just said they guessed he'd
gone back home to see his folks."

The following week Martin went to call on them, but no one
answered the door. Then the druggist downstairs, who was
their landlord, said they had moved out the previous morning
and not told him where they were going.

Martin and Jane never saw or heard from them again.

One Sunday in May, 1949, two middle-aged Negro couples
came to church at Central Baptist. An usher, wishing to act
with discretion, seated them near the rear. Old Mrs. Staples,

wishing to act like a Christian, shared her hymnbook with one of the Negro women. There were many sidelong glances in the congregation; heads inclined toward one another like drooping lilies.

Observing the Negroes from the pulpit that Sunday, Martin saw that they were not at all self-conscious, as the Penningtons and McFarlands had been. They wore—forgive us, Lord—the *right* clothing; they sang with spirit; they bowed their heads in prayer; they were not frightened by the collection plate. In every respect they acted like practicing Central Baptists. Except, of course, that their skins were black.

After the service Martin shook hands with the four and was impressed by their manner: They seemed undisturbed by the color of their skin in the midst of so many pale faces. That afternoon Martin's new assistant, Mark Walworth, phoned him at home and said the four had filled in the cards, which were always available in the back of each church pew, requesting a visit by a clergyman. There was a tremor of excitement in Mark's voice. It was his duty to pay such requested calls, and he undertook this particular detail joyfully the very next afternoon.

During the three months Mark had been in Sylvia, he had become close to Martin. Though Mark was yoked to a neurotic wife and saddled with a retarded son, he was the most cheerful, optimistic young clergyman Martin had met.

On Monday afternoon he strode into Martin's study, grinning happily. "They're *interested!*" he exclaimed.

They were Dr. Gordon Grant, his wife, Marjorie, and their friends, Mr. and Mrs. George Edwards. The Grants had two young children, the Edwardses three. Dr. Grant was the only pediatrician in the Negro ghetto of Sylvia. He was a graduate of Howard University and Fisk Medical; his wife had taken two years at Northwestern, then had dropped out for financial reasons and worked for a social service agency in South Chicago. George Edwards ran the largest hardware store in the ghetto. He and his wife were high school graduates. The

Edwardses had been in town three years, the Grants two. All had attended occasionally the Free Abyssinian Baptist Church, which had an all-Negro membership, but they did not find the people there congenial or the sermons even comprehensible. In the towns and cities of the North, where they had grown up, all had attended congenial Negro Baptist churches, but the Free Abyssinian of Sylvia was impossible to them. They had simply stopped going to church. But then they had begun to worry about a lack of religious life for their children. In the public schools of Sylvia their children received the best of educations, but they deserved the right to be exposed to the good church life the parents had enjoyed—and the Free Abyssinian Sunday school was an impossible inferno of *darky* (yes, that was the word Marjorie Grant had used) superstitions.

"Martin"—Mark looked at him radiantly—"this is a great opportunity for us at Central."

"Tell me, Mark, do the Grants and Edwardses seem to have any . . . fears about how they might be accepted here?"

Mark looked surprised. "Of course they do. They aren't naïve. They don't have white friends. They're mainly interested in the welfare of their children. The children go to schools that are largely white, and they have practically no difficulty. You know how it is with kids. They're never racially prejudiced till their parents contaminate 'em. I think it took a long time for the four parents to get up the nerve to come here to church."

They must be remarkable people, Martin thought, for they positively had not acted self-consciously on Sunday. Yes, it could be a wonderful opportunity—or disastrous for them.

The point was that they wanted their children to attend Central Baptist Sunday school. So the children should come the very next Sunday. Martin told Mark to select the proper classes and inform the teachers in advance. "You and I will take them to their classes. Have them come here to my study shortly before ten o'clock."

The children appeared well before ten on the following Sunday. They were bright, pleasant, a bit scared by the new experience. But their teachers received them warmly, and the white children appeared only mildly interested that they were Negroes.

Before the eleven o'clock morning service began, Martin sat in his study, scanning his sermon, as was his custom. Suddenly he realized he was not concentrating on the text. He was thinking about the Grants and Edwardses and wishing—God help his soul!—that they would not come to church today. *The Sunday school can absorb the children, but the church won't absorb the parents. Somebody is going to get hurt, and I am a coward.*

When he and Mark stepped onto the platform, the Grants and the Edwardses were seated in the congregation.

That afternoon he talked candidly to Jane about how he felt. "People were polite to them again today. But I could feel a coldness like the Greenland ice cap. They must have felt it, too."

"I'm sure they did," she said. "But I'm sure they feel as I would if I were in their spot. They hope that if they keep coming, people will become accustomed to them and take them for granted. Don't you think that might happen?"

"I wish it would. But I don't know, Jane."

In the following month the Grants and Edwardses attended church three times. Martin had judged correctly that the Sunday school could absorb the children, but a marked coldness continued on the part of most adults toward the parents.

Then it was summer; church attendance dropped, and the Sunday school was closed. The Grants and Edwardses did not appear. Mark had the month of July for vacation, and Martin and Jane took the children to Vermont in August.

On the first Sunday after Labor Day the Grants and Edwardses appeared in church again.

At dinner early that afternoon Jane said, "Mrs. Grant spoke to me after church. She wishes you would call. She wishes it could be in the evening when Dr. Grant and Mr. Edwards could be there."

"I'll phone and see how they're set for Thursday," Martin said.

"Fine. I'm going with you. I was looking at them during the service today. I don't think there were any people in the congregation who were more attentive."

She went with him to the Grants' home on Thursday evening. They lived in an old house which had been repainted and refurbished; half of the first floor served as Dr. Grant's office. George Edwards and his wife, who lived across the street, were in the Grants' living room when Jane and Martin arrived. They seemed tense, but Gordon and Marjorie Grant were at ease and marshaled the conversation along uncontroversial byways: the weather, children, a balky automobile. There was no need for them to fear controversy, Martin thought, and at the same time heard himself going on about the uncontroversial beauty of Vermont.

He knew why they had wanted him to call: They had hoped he would invite them to become members of Central Baptist. Knowing the prejudices confronting them, they would not ask to join the church; they only hoped for an invitation. What a travesty of Christianity! And yet what a fact of church life! He would ask them to join, though not tonight. It would be done because it *had* to be—otherwise, he had better quit the ministry. But it had to be done by due process of church law. A pastor nominated a person for church membership to the board of deacons, which automatically approved his recommendation. In the case of the Grants and the Edwardses, however, there would not be automatic approval. There would be a struggle, which he hoped he would win eventually. The prospect was dismal: All those banal emotions people had displayed over a temporary joint worship of God with Jews would be even stormier at the idea of permanent joint worship with Negroes. But he would begin tomorrow by talking with deacons individually and preparing the way for his recommendation at the board meeting next Tuesday.

Now the Grants were talking cautiously about how much their children enjoyed Sunday school and they enjoyed church. (A really controversial subject, this matter of worshiping God in twentieth-century America!)

Martin asked, "Weren't you a bit scared to come to Central?"

Even Jane looked surprised. Gordon Grant, the first willing to face the unpleasantly controversial fact, spoke slowly, "Should we have been?"

"Not as far as *I* am concerned or Jane or Mark Walworth or lots of others. But we all know that not everybody in Sylvia agrees."

"Well," Gordon said, "I'll tell you. The *second* time was worse than the first."

George Edwards grinned. "Well, *I'll* tell you. The *first* time was pretty hard, too."

"None of you showed it."

Now everyone was smiling. Their mood was almost ebullient, as if they had reached a happy ending without further struggle.

George said, "Gordon trained us."

Gordon said, "Oh, cut it out, George."

But George's thoughts had arrived at that happy ending, and now he was looking back humorously at his past uncertainty. He was going too fast, but no one could stop him. "Gordon he says to us, 'If you wants your kids like ours to have a decent Christian education, you can't *crawl* into that church. Suppose Congressman Rankin is there'—that's what Gordon says—'and the Congressman says, "Boo to you!" '—this is what Gordon says—'Are you gonna cut and run? No, sir. . . .' "

How, Martin thought, *could a Negro help being an actor since his life was an endless drama?* A tragic drama, therefore requiring comic relief. And now George found wild comedy at the heart of his past despair. With abandon—and doubtless some exaggeration—he acted out now what had happened then: Gordon Grant *had* drilled them—and himself—to act without self-consciousness when they invaded the white man's church.

George's comic charade alarmed the Grants. Probably they thought he burlesqued both the church and their own sincere wish by carrying on in this crazy fashion. But Martin did not think so. In his opinion George was simply being completely honest, the essence of both Christianity and good comedy.

Something similar to what he was acting out must have happened before the four started attending church, and the way he told it was very funny. Martin and Jane started laughing—not at George, but at the absurdity of the ways people felt they must appear in church. Then the Grants began to laugh, too.

Marjorie Grant served punch and layer cake, and Martin and Jane went home about eleven o'clock.

He was awakened shortly after three o'clock in the morning by the clamor of the bedside telephone. It shattered a pleasant dream with the thought of death. The caller was Mrs. Scheer, who had served as his father's housekeeper for several years in the hamlet of Winbeam.

"Mr. Judson, your father's had a heart attack and been taken to the Middlebury hospital. The doctor says you should come right away."

He left before seven o'clock on Friday morning, taking a train to Chicago and then flying to New York. Middlebury was difficult to reach; he finally located an air service to Rutland and made the last leg of the journey by rented auto. It was almost midnight when he reached the hospital in Middlebury. His father had died late that afternoon.

It was months since he had heard from his brother, Nathaniel, in Colorado; he sent a telegram, but no reply came. He telephoned his sister, Bess, in California and learned that she and her husband were vacationing in Hawaii. The frailty of family ties was more depressing to him than the fact of his father's death: He had not seen Bess in five years or Nathaniel since his freshman year at Brown. David Judson, dead at seventy-five, must have pondered sometimes why two of his three children had deserted him.

Summer was dying under a gentle September rain as he sat in his father's house in Winbeam the following afternoon and looked through the contents of an old cowhide suitcase which Mrs. Scheer said David Judson had left for him. On the top of a pile was a brief note written two years previously.

> DEAR MARTIN,
> Do with these things as you wish. I am leaving them to you. I am happy that you have done what you have with your life. I am proud of you.
>
> > Love,
> > FATHER

Love? It was the first time Martin remembered his father having used the word in connection with him. Always the emotion had remained implicit. Only his mother sometimes had said when he was young, "Martin, I love you." It was the first time, too, that his father ever had said he was proud of him.

There was David Judson's diploma from Dartmouth College in 1894 and some yellowed reports on his grades. They revealed that he had been excellent at mathematics, but only fair at English literature and philosophy. Another diploma testified he had received the degree of Bachelor of Divinity from Crozier in 1898. A birth certificate proved that he had been born in East Sutton, New Hampshire. But these were merely facts. Where was a significant clue to his nature?

Perhaps there was one in a faded photograph of his grandfather's New Hampshire farmhouse taken by a traveling country photographer late in the last century. Martin's grandfather and a hired man were lined up with two sturdy teams of horses, and there was a cluster of women on the porch. On the cardboard frame David Judson had written, "Looks nice, but a hard

life." Had he become a preacher because, like old Lyman
Beecher, he could not plow a straight furrow?

There were many photographs of Martin's mother, taken in
places like Pittsfield and Bangor. There were photos, too, of Nathaniel, Bess, and himself when they were young and roughing
it on vacation at Memphremagog. In all the snapshots his
mother, Mildred, looked tired. She had been forty-three years
old when she bore him and had died when he was a senior in
high school. Always a hard life. David Judson had chosen the
scrabble of the north country. He loved it. There was a bit of
spruce bough, crumbling to dust in the suitcase, whose exact
significance Martin could not fathom. A memento to some moment of tenderness that Father had not seen fit to explain.

But here was something. A letter written to Martin in 1940,
with a note at the top in a shakier hand.

Never sent you this. Seemed sort of preachy at the time. When
I die you'll understand it better. FATHER

The letter:

DEAR MARTIN·

I'm very pleased you've got yourself a church. Now you're
going to come up against some hard things—and that's what
makes life worth living. I'd like to tell you just a bit about one
aspect of my ministry. You'll learn in time that preachers never
talk much among themselves about the things that count most.

I think the main problem of a church in meeting its people's
needs consists of its being more than a reflection of their daily
social desires. Does a church—or its minister—prepare a person
any better for the roughest thing of all: death? The hardest task
I have is trying to bring comfort to the dying. You might be
surprised to learn that praying never has come easy for me. I
don't know just what to say in the face of death. Maybe it's
better to shut up.

But there is the person, eyes straining for *something*. And
there are his loved ones, weeping for *something*. The most
helpful words I've found are the old, powerful ones. You
know—'I am the resurrection. . . .' I think if those words can

be meaningful to a person at the approach of death, then he
has *something*. Basically, to my mind, the chief duty of the
church—and its minister—is to prepare a person to face death
with some serenity. No pie in the sky, mind you. No promises of
pearly gates and all that.

But it's hard to do because people go through life taking no
account of the idea of God when they face important decisions.
Adultery, for instance. Or slander, theft, cheating. They don't
want God around spoiling their fun. It's easy to entertain them
with the *mechanics* of the church—all the taffy-pulling, sleigh-
riding, logrolling, budgeting, Moses-in-the-bulrushes Sunday
schooling. You'll spend most of your ministry working at the
mechanics of it. But understand that is only the priestly
trickery—old as mythology. Entertain them while you try to
lead them into at least an idea of the role of God in the life—
and the death—of man.

All good to you,
FATHER

Martin's eyes were moist when he finished the letter and put
it in a pocket. Did Father understand death now?

David Judson's funeral service was held in the small Winbeam Congregational Church, which had been his pastorate for
many years until he retired only six months previously. The
rural church had no pastor now; at the request of aged friends
of his father, Martin conducted the service.

It was the hardest assignment of his life. The old folk,
deeply fond of his father, expected an emotional eulogy. He
eulogized him gladly, because he deserved it—as had his
mother. But reciting the plain hard facts of their lives when
Martin was under such emotional tension brought him close to
pity for them—which they never had wanted and did not really
deserve. He ended his eulogy by reading the letter his father
had written and never sent to him.

A lawyer in Middlebury sent word for him to come to his office on Monday afternoon. David Judson had left a will: one

fourth of his estate each to Martin, Bess, Mrs. Scheer—and Nathaniel.

Nathaniel, too! For whatever reasons Nathaniel had scorned his father—and Martin did not know why—his father had forgiven him and possibly blamed himself. The lawyer said there was one other matter: As best he could determine, the cash value of David Judson's estate after funeral and other expenses was less than nine hundred dollars. Martin assigned his share of the estate to Mrs. Scheer and then drove away from Middlebury in a heavy rainstorm.

His plane from New York was due to arrive in Chicago at five o'clock on Tuesday afternoon, but the airport there was fogged in, and the flight was directed to Milwaukee. It was one o'clock on Wednesday morning when he finally reached home.

"I'm dead beat," he told Jane, whom he had awakened. "Everything okay with you and the kids?"

"Yes, fine. I'll get you something to eat."

"Not hungry, sweetheart. Just want to *sleep*. Everything else all right around here?"

"Yes. I'm turning off the bedside phone. Sleep till noon if you can."

The muted ringing of the downstairs telephone awakened him shortly after nine o'clock. His head throbbed; he felt as must men who went on colossal benders. Going downstairs, he sat at the kitchen table with Jane and began to tell her about the trip. Then the front doorbell rang.

Jane said, "I'm not answering it."

"Suits me. I'm going to get that old suitcase of Father's and show you—"

There were footsteps on the back steps, and then Mark Walworth tapped on the window of the back door and peered in at them with a faltering smile. Jane let him in.

"Glad you're back, Martin," he said. "Has Jane told you?"

"Has she told me what?"

"I sort of kicked up a ruckus at the deacons' meeting last night. I phoned and told her about it around midnight."

The telephone rang, and Martin said, "Don't answer it, Jane. Please pour me some more coffee, and give Mark a cup, too. Sit down, Mark. No, Jane hasn't told me. I guess she figured I was too pooped to hear bad news. What was the ruckus about?"

"I told the deacons I'd invited the Grants and Edwardses to join the church."

Incredibly Martin wanted a cigarette. Though he smoked rarely, he might be about to begin the habit.

He said, "Let me get this straight. You told the deacons that you recommended—"

"No, I told them I'd *invited* them. And I did, on Monday night. They accepted—happily. I know how you feel about it. I know you and Jane called on them last Thursday. They told me what a fine time ever) ody had. Marty, I figured it was time for *action*. I presented it as . . . an accomplished fact. I thought it would stifle opposition, but—"

"You jerk," Martin said. "You're my friend, Mark, but you acted like a stupid jerk." Mark looked offended, and Martin said, "Don't look hurt. I'm simply telling you that you really booted this one."

"Isn't it my right as assistant minister to propose members?"

"Of course."

"Aren't you in favor of their becoming members?"

"Of course again. But why did you act while I was away? Wasn't it because you feared I didn't have the guts to see the thing through? Wasn't it because you fear I'm a bit soft around the edges and prone to go along with the . . . Establishment?"

Mark lowered his head, then lifted it and said, "Yes. You can have my resignation."

"Oh, for—" Martin felt his anger flooding into his face. "No! You're sticking, Buster, and fighting this thing along with me. But you've got us off to a bad start through an error of judgment. Do you understand the phrase 'Due process'?"

"Of course!" Mark was angry now, too. "You don't have to treat me like an adolescent. But when it comes to something like this, when such a basic principle is involved, when you know how the Grants and Edwardses feel—"

"You start with due process," Martin said. "By throwing weight—by trying to pull a fast one is what people think— Well, it's done. You *told* the deacons you had invited these people when the normal process is to *ask* their agreement to invite them. Well—let's get organized. Who was with us and who against?"

Mark told him. Eight were opposed, four in favor. One of those in favor, to Martin's surprise, was Harold Brown. But there were no other surprises on Mark's scorecard.

The telephone rang again, and Jane said, "I won't answer it." "I will." Martin went to the phone.

Norman Street offered condolences on his father's death. He went on at length about how sorry he had been to hear of it. Then he said, "Martin, a bomb was thrown at the deacons' meeting last night."

"I'd like to hear about it," Martin replied. "Norman, I owe you a lunch. How about joining me at the Downtown Club today? . . ."

A few days later Mark told Martin, "Let the church *split* over this. You're too conservative."

"I thought I was a liberal," Martin replied.

"If you're a liberal, then I'm a radical."

Martin shrugged. "While we're slinging epithets around, I'd say that a liberal is somebody who thinks other people need help. A radical is somebody who feels he needs help himself. I feel I need help. So what does that make me?"

"You're always a good phrasemaker, Martin." Mark smiled when he said it, but it was a veiled rebuke. Mark was dissatisfied with Martin's slow, cautious handling of the situation.

Mark did not know that Norman Street, the leader of the opposition, wanted his scalp; fire that crazy Walworth, and of course, bar the damn niggers—that, in effect, was the way Norman would restore serenity to Central Baptist. Neither did Mark know Martin's reply to Norman: "The day you fire Walworth is the day you fire me. Because a young man acted in foolish haste is no reason, Norman, for a man of your age and wisdom to act the same."

Among Martin's difficult tasks was to discuss the matter with the Grants and Edwardses. Jane went with him to call on them. After he described the situation, Gordon Grant shook his head and said, "We'll drop it. We didn't intend to—start a revolution."

"You *can't* drop it," Martin replied. "Well, I suppose you could, but I hope you won't. It's going to take a lot of courage, but there are many people for you. I believe the day can come when Negroes and whites worship together. But you know what it takes to bring that day about."

He urged them to be patient, to keep their children in the Sunday school, and suggested that they absent themselves from church for a few Sundays.

Meanwhile, he worked hard to persuade the opposition and began to find fresh allies.

One evening late in September Curtiss and Alice Welch called at the parsonage. Curtiss came to the point quickly.

"Martin, you haven't broached me yet about the, uh, current unpleasantness."

"Well, Curt, I didn't think there was much point. I think I know where you . . . stand."

Curtiss smiled. "Oh, do you now? Since I was against the Jews, I'm against the Negroes, too. And such a rockhead I won't yield an inch. That's what you've been thinking. I'll confess something I haven't been man enough to admit to you before. But I admit it every Sunday in the silent prayer of confession. That confessional prayer you started is a good idea, Martin. Anyway, I think every Sunday, 'Dear Lord, I'm a Jew-baiting bastard and—' "

"Curt!" Alice exclaimed. "You can't use such language in prayer!"

"Why can't I? I can use any kind of language I want to in talking to the good Lord who made me and He knows exactly what I mean. Anyway, I'm sorry about that thing last year—the way I acted. This is a cornball thing to say, but it's honestly true: Some of my best friends are Jews. I do business with 'em, fight with 'em, drink and play poker with 'em. There are four guys in Chicago I particularly fight with and am friendly with. We get together every month or so. They're all Jews. Last spring that thing I did was bothering me more and more. So one night, after we'd had a few drinks, I confessed to 'em what I'd done. They just looked at me, and then one said, 'We know about it, Curt.' *Knew* about it! One had heard somewhere, and so they all knew. I said they must hate my guts. One said, 'Sure we hate you, Curt, but now that you've admitted it, we don't hate you quite so much.' He was kidding, you know what I mean. I felt better about it and said I was going to suggest to you that we try an interfaith service again. And then one of the guys—a guy who doesn't live in Sylvia, mind you—says, 'There's no point in trying, Curt, because the new rabbi won't go for it.' I said, 'You bastards'—Excuse me, Jane— I said, 'You fellas always have to have the inside track!' Then we all laughed. We've been better friends ever since. Is there any point in trying your idea again, Martin?"

"Afraid not. Your friend is right. Rabbi Goldstein is much more—*choosy* than Abe Lamber about the religious company he keeps."

Curtiss said, "Now about these Negroes who want to join the church. I don't hate them. I'm tired of worrying about property values in Sylvia. And that's really what's needling Norm Street and the others. Only they don't put it that way. Honestly, sometimes Norm worries me—his mind, I mean. Since his kids are grown up and married to whites, he's going around asking people, 'Would you want your *grandchild* to marry a Negro?' And he thinks he's speaking a thought-provoking non-cliché. It's a good thing the paper business isn't a changing industry like cosmetics, or Norm would go broke. Thinking the way he does, I mean. Anyway, you've been telling people that these Negroes are fine, decent people who want to worship with us because they find the holy rollers at Abyssinian silly. Is that true?"

"Yes."

"Okay," Curtiss said, "then I'm all for having these people join our church. When you say it's right, I know it's right. Alice and I are all with you. There's going to be plenty of trouble next Thursday."

The annual business meeting of the church was held on the first Thursday in October. Usually it was not a well-attended affair, for relatively few cared to listen to the representatives of various church organizations deliver reports which would be digested later in the weekly bulletin. But on that Thursday in 1949 nearly two hundred people appeared for the supper preceding the business session, and a hundred more flocked in later.

Martin, as usual, served as moderator. After the reports were finished, he said, "This concludes the regular business. But there's a special matter I wish to present from the floor, and so I'm handing over the post of moderator to our assistant pastor, Mark Walworth."

Norman Street rose and said, "Objection."

Martin was surprised. "Objection to what?"

"To the *Reverend* Walworth serving as moderator in the matter coming before us. He's biased. I nominate Dana Halpern."

"Second the motion," someone called out.

Martin hesitated. Then he said, "All those in favor will say, 'Aye.'"

There was loud approval.

"Opposed?"

The disapproval sounded equally loud, but Martin said, "The ayes have it. I'll turn over the chair to Dana Halpern with the request that he recognize me from the floor."

Dana Halpern's face was pale, his expression blank as he stepped onto the platform.

Martin, standing below the rostrum, said, "Mr. Chairman."

Norman Street, standing, too, said, "Mr. Chairman."

Dana Halpern, looking at Norman, said, "The chair recognizes Mr. Street."

"I'll be a son of a bitch," said Curtiss Welch in a voice loud enough to be heard almost everywhere. There was a rising hubbub of voices. People rose, shouting, and others cried at them to sit down.

Martin, his face flushed, his head lowered between his strong shoulders, shouted, "Be quiet, everyone! Norman Street has the floor!" His voice sounded thunderous, authoritative. The people grew quiet, and everyone but Norman Street sank down.

"Mr. Chairman, fellow members of Central Baptist." Norman's voice quavered and then grew stronger. "The special matter before us this evening concerns the wish of our clergy to take into the membership some people that most of us find undesirable. This *wish* by the clergy has become a *demand* that violates the principles of our democratic church government. I won't say anything more about these people. We all know who they are. But I wish now to read to our clergy a list of one hundred and sixty-eight church members who have signed a statement as good Christians and citizens of our free society objecting to the high-handedness of our clergy."

Norman hesitated as Mark Walworth got to his feet and walked to Martin and stood quietly beside him, gazing inscrutably at the people. A murmur grew and then died away.

Norman read the list slowly. Some were rich and powerful; many were weak and hysterical by nature. After Norman had finished reading the names, he said, "The statement we people have signed consists of only one sentence. I read it, 'If the effort persists to bring undesirable people into our church, we, the undersigned, shall withdraw our membership from Central Baptist.' "

The ensuing silence was broken by the cry, "Then get out!"

Dana Halpern said, "The chair recognizes the Reverend Mr. Judson."

Martin faced them silently until some began to stir uneasily. "Fellow *Christians!*" He fell silent again for a moment. "It was my intention this evening to present the names of four persons for membership in Central Baptist. I wanted us to talk candidly together about them. I consider them the finest of people, the best of Christians. I felt they could gain much from the life of our church and contribute much to it. But I see this is not true. I won't present their names. I'll inform them they wouldn't be welcome here."

"Oh, *why?*" exclaimed Alice Welch.

"Because," Curtiss said, "he *has* to. He can't do anything else."

Mark said, "Mr. Chairman!"

Dana said, "The chair recognizes the Reverend Mr. Walworth."

Mark spoke resonantly. "Under the circumstances I find it impossible to try to minister longer to the people of Central Baptist Church. I hereby resign as assistant pastor." Turning, he strode toward a side door.

Dana Halpern said quickly, "The meeting is adjourned." He leaned over the lectern. "Martin—"

But Martin was walking toward the doorway through which Mark had disappeared. Jane hurried after him while Norman Street called, "Martin! Jane!"

She caught up with Martin on the side path and asked, "Where are you going?"

"Home."

"So am I." She hooked a hand under his arm.

They were almost there when he asked, "How much money have we in the bank?"

"Over nineteen hundred."

He closed his hand over hers. "We don't have much more going than we had coming, do we?"

"Where are we going, Marty?"

"I don't know yet. I only know we're going."

 Three

"WHEELS within wheels," said Dr. Alex Carpenter. "Towers on top of towers."

He was talking about foundations, on which he was something of an expert, for he was the executive director of the Honeywell Foundation. Martin had come to New York from Sylvia to see him about a job that day in November, 1949.

"There are all kinds of foundations," Carpenter said. "Ours is nothing like the Ford or the Carnegie. By the way, the Honeywell has no relationship to the well-known corporation of that name. It was established early in the century by Miss Naomi Honeywell."

He gestured toward her portrait on a wall of his office. She was a firm-chinned woman, who returned his gaze with an inscrutable expression.

"Miss Naomi was a spinster secretly ashamed of the ways in which her father amassed a fortune. She wanted all those millions of dollars to go to *Christian*—meaning *Protestant*—ends. But she mistrusted the good sense of the various boards, committees, and so forth that run the various large Protestant denominations. She refused to hand over all her inherited wealth without strings attached. This foundation is the agency she and her lawyers devised to hold the strings. The denominations can ask for money. But the foundation decides whether a gift is worthy. Wheels and towers again. Our operation is much like that of the executive headquarters of various denominations. The cream and the cat's tongue are indistinguishable."

Martin liked Carpenter immediately. His doctorate was in divinity—earned, not honorary. Friends had told Martin something of his background: He had held a pastorate for only two years, then had turned to teaching and become the dean of a divinity school. Finally, he had come to the Honeywell as assistant to the executive director, a septuagenarian who had been eased out to green pastures only last year. As was to be expected, Carpenter had learned more about Martin than Martin had about him.

"So you've decided you want no more of the pulpit and parish."

Yes, that was the general idea.

"I don't blame you," Carpenter said. "You lasted a lot longer at it than I did. I didn't like it. I don't enjoy being a *housekeeper*."

The foundation, Carpenter said, was concerned with the well-being of the underprivileged in many areas of the world. It had become disillusioned with aspects of the missionary movement which emphasized only Christianizing to the neglect of a people's physical welfare. Now the foundation was interested only in areas of effort where there was a fighting chance of significant solutions.

"Our concern in this office is not with raising money," he said. "That's the job of the trustees, who have a nose for money such as you and I couldn't smell out in a million years. Our job is deciding how to spend it wisely in various Protestant efforts. We can only *recommend* how to spend it. The trustees must make the final decision."

He paused, lighted a cigarette, and stared out a window for several seconds. "The founder provided that two-thirds of our personnel, exclusive of trustees and clerical employees, must

be ordained clergymen. Frankly, it's an unfortunate provision
—one we never found any legal means of circumventing. By
unfortunate I mean, how many of us who have been clergymen
are adapted to—say, for example—immersing ourselves in the
agricultural problems of some area of the Philippines, sweating
around there on location, figuring out a program that will tie
religion even tenuously to an agricultural project, and then
convincing the trustees of its worth? Remember, by the very
nature of the foundation, all allotments of funds must have a
Christian purpose, meaning in our terms the *Protestant* faith
pitted against more firmly established religions in many lands
—Roman Catholic, Buddhist, Moslem, and others. If we could
just go out and create a neat slum-clearance project with no
hint of religious purpose involved, it would be easy. But we
can't. What I'm saying is that this would be a far easier organization to run if we could hire one clergyman to ten experts in
agriculture, housing, transportation, sociology—many other
things. But we *can't*."

He flicked his ash and missed the large tray on his desk by
several inches.

"We clergymen drop out of active pastorates for many reasons, Judson. Some merely seek greater security. The Honeywell is a secure place. It offers its employees a good salary, all
the well-known social securities, including a pension. No one
above the clerical level has been fired from here in three years.
So working here can be pretty soft. That's the worst thing about
it. I mean the effects of softness are the worst thing. Well, I'd
like you to come with us. I've made inquiries about you and
like what I hear. Are you still interested?"

"Yes."

"Would you object to foreign travel? There might be periods
when you'd be away from your family for some time."

"I wouldn't object if the travel was to good purpose."

"*Why*, basically, do you want to come here?"

"I'm . . . disenchanted with my present church. But not
with the . . . ideas that took me into the ministry. I've begun

to wonder whether the parish church is the . . . most significant place for me to work. I like what you've told me about the Honeywell. I think I'd find satisfaction in a job here."

Carpenter stared at him thoughtfully for a time. "When can you start?"

"January first."

"You haven't asked about your salary."

"You haven't told me yet. I assume it will be . . . appropriate."

Carpenter grimaced. "You're the first hand I've hired who hasn't asked me before I could bring it up. There isn't a rigid salary system here. Is fifteen satisfactory to start?"

"Yes."

"Better make it sixteen. The price indices are rising. Let's see, you have a daughter, nine, and a son going on two. Do you want to get a house in the suburbs or an apartment in town?"

"I think we'd better start with an apartment."

"That's probably wise. In case you don't like it here. Do you want to talk this over with your wife?"

"I don't need to. She knows I came here hoping for a job. She's all for it."

"We have a kind of housekeeper here at the Honeywell, Mrs. Taylor. She takes care of everything, right down to pencil sharpeners, I guess. She can help you find an apartment. I'll introduce you to her in a minute. You have to fill out a lot of forms—Social Security and all that. Do you have any idea what size apartment to rent?"

Martin hesitated.

"Of course you don't!" Carpenter sounded triumphant. "Judson, take my advice and phone your wife. You can use a telephone in Mrs. Taylor's office. Come on and meet her. Can you join me for lunch? . . . I'll pick you up in her office a little after noon."

The apartment which they subleased was on the twelfth floor of a new building on Murray Hill. It included three bedrooms, an inadequate kitchen, and a large living room affording a view of a stretch of the East River. Perhaps it was too expensive, but Jane adored it.

For the first time since their marriage they were living, she thought, "like other people." Five mornings a week Martin walked twenty-six blocks to his office, whatever the weather. At five o'clock he walked twenty blocks home, a shorter distance because in the morning he accompanied Kathy to her public school. They sold their car, for it did not make sense to keep one in Manhattan.

Jane did not know anyone in New York; the telephone never rang; there were no meetings to attend. She felt as free and perky as a jaybird, especially after she discovered that Abe was a precocious walker. Together they walked or took subways or buses to all sorts of interesting places; Abe was particularly fond of the labyrinths of Macy's and Gimbels with all those bright lights and blond-haired women. For the first time in years Jane had leisure to read as much as she wished. She tried Proust, Stendhal, Faulkner.

It was a happy time that winter and early spring. The uninterrupted hours of evening after Martin came home were the best. He was an exceptional father, she knew, in that he truly liked to play with his children.

Each Saturday, when weather permitted, they would take Kathy and Abe on an odyssey to a museum or places such as the Statue of Liberty and the top of the Empire State.

One Saturday Kathy announced a wish to go skating, and so they went to the rink in Rockefeller Center. Jane sat in the English Grill with Abe and drank tea while she watched Kathy and Martin. They had started Kathy on ice skates when she was five, and she was a proficient skater. Martin danced with her for a time; then she let him go. He did swift swoops around the small rink until an attendant told him to slow down. He was extraordinarily graceful; he needed five miles of open lake ice on which to expend his energy. His skill was apparent to an equally graceful blonde on the windward side of thirty who had been doing school figures at the far end of the rink. She was a lovely creature; each time she raised a long leg on her S-turns, she drew whistles from the crowd watching at the upper balustrades. As Martin passed near her, she said something to him that made him smile. He braked, skated backward around her, and said something that made *her* smile. Then he introduced Kathy, and the three promenaded gravely around the rink, the blonde talking animatedly. When the music changed to a Viennese waltz, she invited Martin to dance. What beautiful people they were, the blonde's face aglow with the promise of the music. Jane realized that her tea had grown cold. She told Abe to stop sucking air through the straw in his Coke glass and thought, *Dear heaven, I'm jealous!* How many beautiful women romanced him at his office? He didn't tell her much about his work; she lived in isolation with the children. Now that he had quit the ministry, might there not be a total change in his character? "Abe, *stop* that!" Martin and Kathy and the lovely creature were leaving the rink and treading the rubber matting into the grill. Martin said to the blonde, "This is my wife and son. I—" He didn't know her name.

The blonde looked at Jane. "How d'you do," she murmured and fled.

Martin sat down at the table, saying, "She's pretty good, isn't she? A couple of times I thought I was going on my prat. Where would you like to go now?" Jane just looked at him wonderingly.

Kathy said, "Mom, the lady said Daddy should be in the Ice Capades."

"Oh," Jane said, "I think they like much younger men for that." Martin looked at her, his mouth open, and then he threw back his head and laughed. The maître d' came and told him he wasn't supposed to wear skates into the grill, so he left for the dressing room with Kathy, still grinning.

On their first Sunday in New York they had been so busy unpacking and arranging furniture that they decided to skip going to church. On the following Sunday there was still much to do in the apartment. But at breakfast on the third Sunday morning Martin suggested they try a nondenominational church in the neighborhood. There the children were sent to appropriate age wards while Jane and Martin sat through a lecture based on a current book that did not interest them. Afterward Kathy said, "I might as well have stood home. All I did was draw pictures."

The next Sunday they went to a large Baptist church where the clergyman delivered himself of a hackneyed theme about the love of God complete with oratorical gestures. The Sunday after that they stayed home, and when the day began to seem long, Kathy asked, "Have we stopped going to *church?*" So the following Sunday they took a subway for uptown to the large, well-known nondenominational church which some Protestants called the Cathedral. The sermon was excellent, the atmosphere of worship in the beautiful church moving to them both. Though the trip from home took an hour, they agreed it was worthwhile. A week later, however, there was a heavy storm, so they stayed home and Martin told Kathy stories from Genesis. They went to the Cathedral a second time, then tried church after church nearer the apartment.

"I don't like this being on the fringe," Martin told Jane. "We must be too critical. We should dig in somewhere, but I can't find the place."

"On the fringe." Jane thought of the phrase often as time passed. At first she had been glad that the telephone never rang, but then she began to wish it would. Every two or three weeks she left the children with a sitter for the evening, and she and Martin went to the theater or a concert at Carnegie Hall; she joined the AAUW and attended teas and lectures, where she made acquaintances but no close friends. She kept busy and was happy, but she no longer was closely involved with the lives of other people.

In February Martin brought Lance Bishop home to dinner.

"Jane!" He hugged her, ever the ebullient Freeport Flash. "You're more beautiful than ever."

She told him he was pretty, too. He was the pastor now of a large Presbyterian church on the Philadelphia Main Line, married to a socially prominent woman, childless.

"I'm impressed by your move to the Honeywell," Lance told Martin. "That's a terrific organization. Tell me about it."

But Martin was more interested in hearing about Lance's pastoral work.

During dinner Lance said to Jane, "My wife, Esther, would love to live in New York. It must be a wonderful release from being a preacher's wife."

"I like it," Jane said. "We're having a grand time. But sometimes I feel I'm on the fringe. I'm not . . . involved with people the way I was when Marty had a pastorate. But you understand I like it very much."

Was she trying to convince herself, as well as him?

In March she and Martin attended a tea which the foundation gave at the Plaza, an annual event on the anniversary of the founder's birthday. It was a painfully formal affair, empty of feeling; all appeared with spouse because they were expected to be there. Jane met names, some that Martin had mentioned, but personalities failed to emerge. The only exceptions were Alex Carpenter, whom Martin obviously liked, and his wife. Mrs. Carpenter told Jane, "My dear, I hope you're enjoying New York. Alex is very fond of your husband." So Jane remembered her pleasantly. Perhaps, however, she said the same thing to all the wives.

On Martin's first day at the Honeywell, Carpenter assigned him to the North America section and introduced him to the aging chief of section, Ross Partridge. He was given an office with a carpet and a window and one-third share in a young, bored secretary. After introducing him to a half-dozen other people and giving him a general idea of the filing systems, Partridge said, "The only way to learn what we do here is by osmosis. I'm going to have Charlie Smith run over a project of his with you. Charlie's a bit late this morning. I'll pick you up for lunch at twelve-thirty."

Charlie, stout and around sixty, came into Martin's office about ten o'clock. He was short of breath, complaining about service on the Hudson Tubes from New Jersey, and very glad to meet Martin. He, too, had been a Baptist clergyman for a number of years until, as he explained, he grew tired of starving and had vaulted into the Honeywell.

"Martin," Charlie said, "you're going to like life here at the top."

"At the top?" Martin asked.

"That's what it is, the cream at the top of the bottle. Even if this is a private foundation, it's the way life is at the top level of all denominations. Nobody pushing you around anymore. You do your job and go home, and there won't be some complaining member of the congregation calling you about her ingrown toenail."

Charlie went on to explain in minute detail the provisions of the foundation's retirement, life insurance, and sick benefit plans. "For instance, I have four years to go to retirement at sixty-five, and I've already been here twelve years. That's sixteen years. Suppose my average salary is ten thousand a year. You divide that total gross by. . . . That plus Social Security at sixty-five. . . . My wife and I have bought a little place up near the Delaware Water Gap and— Well, as my oldest son says, 'Just sweat it out, Pop, just sweat it out. . . .' Do you have a date for lunch?"

"Ross Partridge asked me."

"Oh." Charlie got up, closed the door quietly, and came back to Martin's desk. "Let me give you a tip, Martin. Watch out what you say to Partridge. They say in the mail room, 'Beware of the Partridge in the pear tree.' He's *consumed* by ambition. At his age, mind you! He toadies to Carpenter. He has a PhD in agronomy. Soil management! He detests everyone who's been a minister. Doesn't even go to church. He'll knife you if he can.

I'm glad I have a good friend among the trustees. Partridge came here when old Dr. Bevan was executive secretary. Dr. Bevan made everyone's salary a personal, confidential matter, and Carpenter has continued the same practice. Partridge thinks he should know what everybody is earning and run the department as if it's a budgeted operation. He wants to build an empire. I'll bet he's making sixteen, *seventeen* thousand a year. But it kills him that he can't learn what everybody else is making. . . ."

About half past ten Martin reminded Charlie that they were supposed to review a project of his. Charlie returned after a time with a stack of folders and envelopes, which he spread out on Martin's desk.

The project, proposed by the mission board of a large denomination, involved the problem of a few hundred Eskimos on the Arctic coast of the Yukon Territory whose hunting and fishing resources were dissipating for a complexity of reasons. Within a few years they would face starvation unless they moved to better hunting and fishing grounds. Such an area, sparsely populated by Eskimos, existed several hundred miles to the east. The Canadian government, concerned by the problem, had recommended the move but had not been able to finance it. The move was also strongly recommended by the two capable missionaries of the denomination who served the group of Eskimos. Indeed, these two men, one a physician, intended to go with their people (who, Charlie said, were "more or less Christianized").

It took Martin awhile to comprehend the situation. Charlie had been assigned the project last August and had flown to the Arctic. The travelogue he delivered was enthusiastic, and he kept passing Martin photographs the missionaries had taken of him grinning widely with various groups of grinning Eskimos. But that had occurred last August, and this was January. What had happened meanwhile?

Well, Charlie explained, Martin would learn that you shouldn't work too fast at foundation projects. Quick solutions to problems had a way of turning out to be no solutions at all. He had turned in his preliminary report, but he had not yet "finalized" his summary presentation for Carpenter. Because there was a hooker in the plans that seemingly could not be resolved.

"Those Eskimos *don't want to move*." Charlie shook his head. "In that country one place looks just like another. But where those people live is *home* to them, and they don't want to budge despite what the missionaries and the Canadian experts tell them and what they themselves see is happening. They have no faith in there being more game or fish over east. And it's a basic rule that we won't assign funds to any project unless the people who would benefit are enthusiastically for it. No ramming *improvement* down people's throats. That's only sensible. I think this is a very worthwhile project, but I've slowed down on it in the hope the missionaries can change their people's minds before I have to shelve the whole thing."

The cost of moving the people, which the foundation had been asked to underwrite, was approximately fifty thousand dollars.

A thought occurred to Martin. "These people must have recognized headmen, the smartest hunters and fishermen. What would happen, Charlie, if you allotted a small amount of money to fly these leaders over east and let them see for themselves what the country offers?"

Charlie stood up and then sat down, looking at Martin oddly. "I'd thought of that. I don't know whether Carpenter would agree to a small provisional grant. I'd thought of it. . . ."

Had he really? It seemed an obvious suggestion, but how much was obvious to Charlie Smith while he served out his time at the Honeywell? Apparently Alex Carpenter had problems. Charlie still was talking when Ross Partridge took Martin to lunch at half past twelve.

Partridge was an extraordinarily gloomy man. His mood of bitterness was deeply seated, not caused by something that had happened just that morning. He sat across the table from Martin in Schrafft's, sipping a Bloody Mary and complaining about the slow service of an overworked waitress. Did his bitterness stem from the fact he found people less manageable than soil?

His cross-examination of Martin began when they were served coffee. "Is your salary satisfactory?" It was. "There's a wide range of salaries in the organization. They seem to pay by whim. It doesn't make any sense. A man doesn't know what to expect. There should be regular graded levels. But a man can go on for years without a raise. What do you think Charlie Smith earns?" Martin had no idea. "But you say your salary is satisfactory?" Yes. "What did Carpenter start you at?"

"He said salaries are a confidential matter at the foundation." Carpenter had not said that, but he was following Charlie's tip. Then he saw that his answer to the question had not endeared him to this bitter old man who was his boss.

Partridge picked up the luncheon check and frowned. He did not protest when Martin suggested they split it.

That afternoon Carpenter called Martin to his office and explained something trivial about the employees' insurance plan. Then, casually: "I think I forgot to mention to you that salaries are confidential here. Has Partridge asked you any questions?"

"I lied," Martin said. "I said you had told me it was confidential."

Carpenter smiled. "Good. Lie all you want to the nosy old men. Just keep *thinking* fast, and things will work fine."

But in the ensuing days Martin felt things were not going at all well. He was not given anything to do. He became tense and restless. Presumably he had offended Partridge and was being punished with solitary confinement.

At last the interoffice mail brought a Partridge dropping. To a file of letters Partridge had clipped a scrawled note: "How would you handle this one?"

The covering letter of the file was from the Reverend T. T. Bonham of Ardsley, Tennessee, president of the Only True Evangelical Church of God, and began with a quotation from Luke: "Go thou and publish abroad the kingdom of God."

Bonham said he had been engaged in an evangelist's ministry in Tennessee, Kentucky, and the Carolinas for more than ten years and had brought about the conversion of nearly ten thousand persons (notarized affidavit of the membership rolls enclosed). Now he had heard the call to preach to the millworkers of New England, who were woefully irreligious (statistics from an unnamed source enclosed to prove his point). Salvation would improve the economic well-being of the millworkers; he cited several passages from Scripture as demonstration. In order to carry out his mission, Bonham must have a large tent, collapsible benches, a truck, two new trailers (costs itemized). His church could defray all but five thousand dollars of the costs. . . .

Martin, reading Bonham's letter and its supporting documents, believed him sincere and honest. Personally, however, he had always had grave doubts about the lasting effects of the emotional sort of evangelism that Bonham obviously practiced. Assuming from what he had learned of the foundation's policies that it shared his viewpoint, he drafted a courteous reply to Bonham stating that the Honeywell did not allot funds to purely evangelistic efforts, then sent the draft to Partridge.

Late in the morning Partridge appeared, frowning, waving the draft of the letter, and saying, "You can't kiss it off this easily."

Martin was surprised. "Do you mean we'd be interested in this project?"

"Of course not. But you can't kiss it off this easily. You have to *refute* him."

"I would suggest," Martin said, "that you can't *refute* a man like T. T. Bonham."

"And *I* would suggest," Partridge said loudly, "that you learn how we operate here and get with it. What's the weakest link in his argument?" Martin was at a loss since the entire proposal sounded flimsy to him. "Come now, *Mr.* Judson, we can't attack evangelism, and no matter how we feel, we can't put it in writing that salvation does not necessarily mean another pork chop on every plate. So our point of refutation is that the millworkers of New England *are* religious. That's why we have a research department. We turn the question over to research and ask them to supply the data to demonstrate our contention. Do you follow me?"

Martin looked at him wonderingly. "Yes, I follow you, Mr. Partridge."

"And what do you think?"

Martin got to his feet. "As I take this request to research, I can't help thinking chickenshit."

Partridge's face flushed; then he turned and strode away. As Martin began to prepare a research department request form, Charlie Smith slipped in, convulsed with silent laughter. "Chickenshit!" he whispered. "I overheard it. Wonderful! But you're in hot water. Partridge will go straight to Carpenter, tell on you, and demand that you apologize."

Partridge remained aloof for a long time. Martin anticipated a reprimand from Carpenter, then forgot about it until the following week, when Carpenter invited him to lunch at the Century Club.

Carpenter looked tired as they walked to his club. "What a morning! Trustees!" He decided he wanted a Beefeater martini straight up. Martin, who had passed most of the morning reading the *Times* in his office, suddenly felt tired, too, and joined him in a martini.

When the waiter brought their menus, Carpenter said, "The beef pie is pretty good. But so is everything." He grinned suddenly. "You'll look a long time without finding any chickenshit." And that was all he ever said about it.

More than two weeks passed before the research department sent Martin data demonstrating that the millworkers of New England *were* religious. Martin wrote T.T. Bonham, who fired back a letter with evidence that they were *not*. The pointless argument dragged on for weeks until Carpenter sent Martin a curt note telling him to reject Bonham's application for funds *at once*. By that time Martin had developed a liking for the

stubborn Bonham, who was no charlatan. (Indeed, Martin felt
that he himself was the charlatan for seeming to lead Bonham
on by prolonging the wasteful argument.) His letter of rejection was not the end of the correspondence, however. Bonham
immediately replied that while he realized Martin was personally antagonistic to him, he nevertheless would pray for God
to forgive his meanness of spirit. And Martin thought, *Brother,
I can use your prayers.*

As the weeks passed, he grew increasingly discouraged. But
he took pains not to let Jane know it. She was happy, and he did
not want to spoil her enjoyment of life in New York. Perhaps
this was the way most men felt about their jobs. Perhaps things
would take a turn for the better.

But he saw little hope of improvement the better acquainted
he became with men and events in the Honeywell and the governing groups of the denominations that sought its aid. Nearly
everywhere there was a tendency to confuse motion with progress; men who wanted to go up or feared being dropped were
constantly moving sideways. Nearly everywhere, too, Martin
saw a penchant for playing politics—sometimes just for the
sake of the game rather than to try to serve some useful purpose. If this was life at the top, which it certainly was from the
viewpoint of power structure, then he would take the dregs.
And do what down there?

On the first morning of spring Carpenter asked him how he
would like to work for the Asia section. Martin was delighted.

"Then I'll send you to Larry Sprague. He operates differently from Partridge. You can follow his, uh, directions with
confidence. If Larry told me to jump out the window, I'd seriously think he had some good reason for suggesting it."

Lawrence Sprague was the outstanding scholar at the Honeywell. His variety of experience as a writer, editor, teacher, and
Washington bureaucrat made him indifferent to the prestige
or security that many other men cherished at the Honeywell.
Indeed, he had a bit of intramural fame for having coined a
phrase: "If not the Honeywell, then what the hell."

Sprague was a liberal, a humanitarian, an internationalist in the tradition of most Westerners who wished to bring enlightenment to the East. Thus he favored industrialization, a moderate Socialism, programs of birth control above all. At the same time he was pessimistic about overcoming the corruptiveness of Asian ruling classes and such deep-seated superstitions as those damned sacred cows of India. Nevertheless, he had the humanitarian's determination to try.

Giving Martin a long list of books, he said, "Don't do anything but read for a couple of weeks. No point in hanging around the office. Go up to the New York Society Library, where the foundation has a membership, and get yourself one of those cubicles. Don't make notes except for any questions that puzzle you."

The following two weeks were the most pleasant Martin had spent in New York. Then Sprague asked him to concentrate on Korea for a week. Finally, he presented him with a project.

For two years the Honeywell had been giving substantial grants to a large denomination for its missionary program in South Korea. Sprague was dubious that grants should be renewed for another year.

"I'm not positive," he said. "I just have a feeling that things on the spot are not going exactly the way we think they are. Your job will be to investigate and report. Plan to fly to Korea around the middle of June. Figure on being gone about a month."

 *Four*

ON SUNDAY morning, June 26, 1950, Martin jounced in a Jeep along a cart track a long distance northeast of Seoul. His guide and interpreter, the Reverend Kim Suh, bounced beside him in the back seat, shouting occasionally at their driver to slow down.

They had left Seoul early on Saturday morning. The American missionary who was to have accompanied them had been confined to bed with something like the flu. They had ridden far east to a remote mountain village where the denomination maintained a Christian school. The afternoon and evening Martin spent there had depressed him, especially when the children sang "My country 'tis of thee" in English for him. The subjects the children studied had slight relationship to the predictable courses of their lives. Like their parents, nearly all would be farmers or farmer's wives and fall under the serfdom of usurers who charged interest rates of about 100 percent. "Sweet land of liberty!" the children shrilled. . . .

After passing Saturday night in the principal's house, Kim and Martin rode toward a village called Yi, where, said Kim, there was "a typical rural church." Martin was uncertain of their direction, for the summer monsoons were beginning and the sun was lost to view, but Kim said they were going north and west. Rain had fallen during much of Saturday, and though it now had ceased, they occasionally heard a rumbling in the north. Thunder, Kim said.

As they bounced along the cart track that morning, the land was bathed in lemon light. Though Martin had been in Korea only a week, he had decided that one place looked much like another. This road of gravel and loess earth, curving along the base of a mountain, was hauntingly familiar. He was positive that beyond its farthest turning he would find mountains which appeared to be formed of concrete and a few white plantains blooming. The Jeep bounced, his guts growled, and he wished he had not packed his diarrhea medicine in his B-4 bag.

They passed around the mountain shoulder, and at first Martin had an impression of a land as devoid of life as some lunar scape. But he was mistaken. There was a stream, a row of poplars, paddies, fields, a broken stone tablet, thatched roofs. "This is Yi," Kim said.

The driver slammed them to a halt in the midst of a clutter of houses which seemed to have been piled one against another. The silence was startling. Only the smell of excrement indicated human habitation. Otherwise, Yi appeared to be a ruin, buried in oblivion.

"Where is everybody?" Martin's voice sounded loud in the silence.

Kim did not answer his question. He said, "The Reverend Li Bum has finished building his church. I sent word we would be here today."

A distant rumbling sound was echoed by Martin's bowels, and he said he had to relieve himself again. Swinging out of the Jeep, he looked about with Occidental modesty. Then he hurried up a rutted lane between two huts, crossed a terraced garden, and clambered behind a rock pile. Gradually he became aware of a rising din that sounded like trucks. And then, suddenly, he saw a small boy sitting a dozen feet from him, pondering with wonder his human function, his American toilet paper, the similarity of man.

Now that his bowels were momentarily at peace, Martin realized he had climbed to a vantage point overlooking the mysteriously dead village. Then a movement on the distant curving of the road to the north caught his attention and startled him.

A tank rumbled toward the village, slowing down and then speeding up, like some enormous land turtle. Behind the tank came three, four, five trucks filled with soldiers. Army maneuvers, Martin thought at first. But then he recalled that the Republic of Korea Army did not have tanks.

His disbelief grew as the tiny figures of three men detached themselves from the shelter of a stone wall by the roadside and raced toward the oncoming tank. One carried a long bamboo pole with something, perhaps a crude satchel charge, weighting its tip. As the man tried to thrust the tip of the pole into the treads of the tank, there was a rattle of small-arms fire, and he fell. An instant later the other two men sprawled near him. The satchel charge, if that it was, did not explode. The tank halted; its gun belched flame. Something jarred the ground not far from Martin, and a house in Yi disintegrated.

Down on the road the driver swung the Jeep around jerkily. Martin, shouting, ran toward it. When he reached the spot where it had been, it was racing away to the south. He saw Kim look back at him, then duck his head, as if expecting Martin's shouts and gesticulations to destroy him. Still Martin ran as the Jeep sped faster and disappeared around the curving of the road. At last he halted, gasping for breath, his heart knocking in panic.

Looking around at the sound of a shrill squealing, he saw the little boy who had been at the rock pile racing toward him. Legs flailing below his long straw shirt, the boy beckoned to Martin as he turned off the track. Martin ran after him. Splashing through the shallow stream, they crossed a paddy, stumbled over a low dike, and pitched into another paddy, which was flooded to the depth of about one foot. The boy, shouting something incomprehensible, belly flopped into the water, then flung himself about and rested his chin on the top of the dike. Martin followed his example.

His view of Yi was like that of a stage from an orchestra pit. As if by direction, sunlight began to filter through the cloud rack, playing on Yi as on an ancient parchment print. It shone on the black-tiled roofs of the village's two landowners, it wrought a yellow sheen on the thatched roofs of the farmers' houses, yet it did not seem to touch the jumble of huts belonging to the landowners where the poorest lived in serfdom. A poplar leaf fluttered toward earth. And then, again as if by a director's order, life exploded from the village in every direction. Men, women, and children ran along the track, some with upraised hands toward the tank and trucks from which soldiers deployed in skirmish lines. Others fled in the opposite direction. Still others scrambled up the mountainside or scurried across the valley fields. A white ox tossed its head, uncertain where to go, while dogs ran, barking, this way and that.

Rifles blazed in staccato, and many hurrying toward the soldiers with upraised hands wilted and fell. The rest turned and ran in the opposite direction, but not many reached the village as the soldiers continued to fire. The tank gun crumped, and one of the black-tiled roofs of a landowner collapsed. The gun crumped again, and the house of the other village landowner became rubble. It was calculated; it was—alas—neatly executed. Two, three fires began to blaze in the village, where poultry and pigs cried in terror.

The tank came on slowly, the skirmish lines of soldiers winging from it into the valley and up the mountainside. They held their fire and fixed bayonets to their rifles, doubtless realizing by this time that the village was undefended, that the insane attempt to detread the tank had been the work of fools who would be heroes. A dog scampered toward the skirmish line, and a child ran after it. The dog pranced between a couple of soldiers, who paid no attention to it, while the child clutched for it with outstretched hands. Suddenly one of the soldiers swung his rifle with a pitchfork motion, skewering the child's breast with his bayonet and lifting him high into the air. Distant though Martin was, the child's scream rang above all sounds of panic in Yi.

He closed his eyes and retched. Now he was aware of the alluvial slime in which he lay, a stench compounded of excrement, prehistoric earth, and—there was no doubt about it—death. Terror for his own life sprang from the horror he had just observed. He glanced around but saw no better hiding place; the valley and hills beyond it were like a paring of cheese. . . . "Thy will be done, on earth as. . . ." The boy turned his coallike eyes toward Martin, then settled his chin on his fists for a rapt view of the destruction of Yi.

Now the tank picked up speed and disappeared into the burning village, while the following trucks halted at its farther limits and the soldiers on foot enfiladed at a trot and drew a skein about it. An old woman hopped out of the village southward along the track while the roaring of the tank rose behind her. It flashed into view, and the old woman uttered no audible sound as a tread ground her into the road. The tank halted and spun as smartly as a mechanical toy. Its lid was flipped back, and the head that popped up appeared to be wearing an American football helmet while the bare arms that rested relaxedly on the conning were like those of an athlete who was enjoying a victory.

Yi burned, and from its smoke and flames rushed pigs, chickens, geese, the white ox. With them came men, women, children until it seemed impossible that so many people had stayed hidden there. The soldiers, shouting hoarsely, took or spared as they pleased. Some bayoneted pigs; others chased chickens. Four beat an old man to death with their rifle butts. One knocked a girl to the ground and stood on her shoulders while another tore off her clothing and fell on her. The boy whistled between his teeth, and Martin sank back into the paddy slime with only his face exposed to the fitful sunlight. He was ready—indeed, almost eager—to die.

While he waited for the soldiers to find and kill him, he thought, *Jane, I love you so.* He carried an insurance policy of fifteen thousand on his life, and at the Honeywell he had acquired twenty-five thousand more. Jane could return to teaching. . . . He could not control his diarrhea; the toilet paper in his pocket was a sodden ruin. It was not the way to die, but how could he avoid its indignity? . . .

The boy touched his shoulder with a foot, and he presumed that soldiers were approaching. He sat up. He must be shot or bayoneted standing, not shriveling in the slime. Some gesture of—what? Not courage, for he did not have it; he was shaking with fear. Then he heard whistles blowing shrilly and was ashamed of his quaking cowardice, compared to the coolness of the boy who watched death approach with chin propped on clenched hands. Martin slithered up beside him and looked at the village.

The trucks had assembled in line behind the tank, and the soldiers were climbing into them. They pulled in slaughtered pigs and live chickens and a couple of girls, who seemed willing to go. The tank moved ahead briskly, and the trucks followed. Soon they had disappeared around the mountain shoulder to the south.

Far up on the mountainside there rose the mournful notes of a bamboo pipe. Figures moved up there, and soon other figures began to move in the valley. Martin heard a sound like the buzzing of mosquitoes that grew louder gradually. The boy sat up on the dike, weeping, and Martin realized that the sound he heard was of wailing from the surviving villagers who had returned to Yi.

He got to his feet, feeling dizzy, pressing a hand against the grinding pain in his intestines. Though death had passed him this once, he still believed it imminent and felt powerless to resist it. He had stumbled onto what looked like the start of a

war between North and South Korea. Could he somehow make
his way on foot to Seoul? At the moment he thought he barely
could totter to the ruins of the village.

When he came to the stream, he lay in its cool, running water
for several minutes and tried to cleanse himself of filth. As he
got to his feet, he heard a bell begin to ring with a tinny sound
someplace in the rubble of Yi. He found himself walking toward it while the boy, who was still crying, followed closely at
his heels.

He picked his way slowly into the smoking, acrid-smelling
ruins, taking care not to look at the bodies he passed. After a
while he found himself in a cleared space which must have
been a kind of town square, where people, weeping and wailing, slowly gathered. A frail-looking old man who wore the
straw clothing of a peasant came toward Martin. His face was
deeply lined, his head completely bald when he took off his
straw-plate hat. Unlike the others, he was not weeping as he
fixed his dark eyes on Martin.

Bowing and placing a withered hand on his chest, he said,
"Li Bum. No English."

Martin bowed with less dignity "Martin Judson." Then he
extended his right hand, which Li Bum took in a strong grasp.
"No Korean."

Li led him to a smoky corner of the square, where he picked
up the bell Martin had heard. It was a small, cheap bell such as
those teachers once used in American rural schools. Swinging it
in a graceful arc, Li shook a vaguely sweet music from its tinny
clamor until a score of women and children and a couple of
men had gathered about him. Then he put down the bell and
knelt, eyes closed and hands clasped on his breast. Most of those
about him knelt, too, as Li began to pray.

Martin finally knelt also, only half listening to Li's high
voice speaking incomprehensible words. At last Li finished his
prayer and, still kneeling, said, "Mar-teh."

Martin licked his dry lips and began in English: "The Lord
is my shepherd. . . ." His voice gathered strength as he con-

tinued until he realized he sounded calm, almost cheerful—
not at all like the quaking coward that he was.

Li Bum led Martin out of the rubble and up the mountain a
little way to the small hut where he lived alone.

There they sat down together and began to try to communicate. It was not as difficult as Martin had believed, for both
were intelligent. Martin realized there was no sense in his trying to make Li comprehend his plight: how he was bereft of all
the things he always had found necessary to sustaining life, or
at least self-respect—a change of clothing, a clean towel, soap,
razor, toothbrush, pure drinking water, gentle toilet paper, the
health medicines which responded to the crotchets of his Occi-
dentalized flesh. But he did make Li understand that he was
suffering from dysentery.

Li, sympathetic, immediately brewed him scorched rice tea.
He stirred boiling water into the bottom of a pot in which he
had cooked his breakfast rice, then poured the faintly colored
liquid into a drinking bowl which he passed to Martin. The
taste, like the color, was indistinct, yet it was soothing to his
stomach and left a delicious, faintly bitter taste on his palate.
Now the sun had come out full, and Li, mindful of the healing
qualities of its light, led Martin into the small garden behind
his hut. There he made him understand it would be sensible
to dry his only possessions on the rocks and let his body benefit
from the warmth of the sun. Having spread sodden suntan
shirt, trousers, underwear, socks, handkerchief, and durable
GI boots on the rocks, Martin sat on a stool, as naked as Adam
before his fall, and sipped the scorched rice tea with which Li
refilled his bowl. As the tumult of his bowels quieted, he
began to feel calmer.

They were silent for a time in sun-drenched meditation.
Then Martin picked up a stick, smoothed a patch of dirt, and
drew a crude map showing the approximate positions of Yi
and Seoul. Then he traced a line from Yi to Seoul and pointed
to the sun. Li, understanding, raised the curled fingers of his

right hand and the thumb of his left: a six-day walk to Seoul.
Then, shaking his head vehemently, he dusted out Martin's
line and traced another straight south from Yi.

They gazed intently at each other. Martin, having read books
on warfare, had some theoretical knowledge of tactics and
strategy. Li, possibly having read none, nevertheless understood their elements instinctively. Of course the North Koreans,
in their surprise attack, would converge on Seoul. Whether or
not they could capture it, they already had interposed themselves between it and Yi. The tiny force which had come
through Yi and its valley must be only an infinitesimal part of
the powerful host sweeping down many routes on the capital.

Then Li kindled Martin's hopes for the first time. Gesturing
eloquently, he caused him to understand that he and several
villagers would start a trek south in the morning, that Martin
must accompany them. Perhaps they were leaving because the
destruction of houses, implements, and livestock made survival
impossible there. Or perhaps Li thought that Christianity
would be obliterated behind the Communist lines. In any
event, they were going.

They numbered forty-seven Koreans in all, including four
infants who were carried. Only nine were men, of whom only
two appeared to be as young as Martin. There were twelve children who walked but did not carry substantial burdens. The
rest, totaling twenty-two, were women ranging from young
maidens to a couple who appeared close to feeble age. A breeze
brought back to Martin, at the tail of the column, the strong
smell of their sweat.

Li had provided him with a long straw coat and a wide-
brimmed straw hat, which failed to keep him dry in the frequent torrential rains. Li also had given him an ash staff and a
shorter shoulder stick on which were lashed a straw blanket, a
pair of sandals, and a large clay pot. In the pot were a drinking
bowl, a wooden spoon, dried rice, and some bits of cooked meat,
which Martin suspected of being boiled dog flesh.

The first day of the trek was a nightmare ordeal to him. He had to fall out frequently because of his diarrhea, and sometimes he thought he could not possibly summon the strength to catch up with the column that wound into an eerie yellowish fog. But he always did catch up. And the next morning he felt stronger.

Every man and woman was bent under the weight of belongings carried on a *chige*. Americans called the wooden *chige* an A-frame, for it was tree branches in the shape of the letter *A*. It was, Martin began to see, a wonderful implement, containing not a single nail, with even the stick which supported the frame being cut from a Y-shaped branch. Thus it contained the strength of a tree itself, rather than the weakness of man-made nails. It was capable of bearing whatever weight one could support on his back; at the top of one huge A-frame burden on a young man's back there even swayed a wrapped and sleeping child, like a bird in a safe, high nest. The A-frame was a consoling companion, as well as an implement, Martin observed: Now that the going was easier, several began to tap the legs of their frames with sticks and chant a low, rhythmic song. When Li stopped them for a rest, no one released himself from his *chige* but simply lay down on its comfortable support, and when it was time to go on, one rolled onto all fours and raised oneself. Thus, Martin thought, the balance of life—supporting the burden, and letting the burden support him.

One old woman, bent nearly double under the weight of her A-frame, fell farther back as the morning progressed till she was tottering along just in front of Martin when Li called the noon break. Martin was light-headed from hunger; his thirst had become a burning in his mouth, his throat, his very lungs, but there was no water. He found strength and the will to endure, however, in the happy fact that his diarrhea had ceased and his body no longer ached.

He spoke to the old woman, indicating he would carry her burden for a time when the march resumed. She replied angrily, raising such a fuss that others joined in the argument.

Li strolled to them. When he understood the trouble, he looked dubious and indicated to Martin that he lacked the strength. He made him understand, too, that each was supposed to carry his own burden and that the woman thought her belongings would become Martin's if he carried them. But Martin insisted on trying.

People watched interestedly as he crouched on all fours and then got awkwardly to his feet. The load was not nearly as heavy as he had expected. As the afternoon wore on, it seemed to grow heavier, of course, yet it was not intolerable, perhaps because it gave a greater purpose to marching on. No longer a freak, he walked now in a place of greater honor near the head of the column. The old woman, whose name was Lee Bang, trod at his heels with his light stick bundle over her shoulder. He and the boy who had led him to safety on Sunday had found each other again. The boy called him Mar-teh, and Martin learned the boy's name was Yangseng. They walked side by side, with Yangseng carrying an infant on his back. Soon Yangseng began to tap rhythmically on the leg of Martin's A-frame with a little stick and chant a song that sounded spirited and yet sad.

Li was leading them toward Taejon, where his church maintained a large school. But their progress was slower each day as troubles beset them.

One morning an old woman failed to rise from sleep; she was dead, and they passed half the morning in giving her a Christian burial. The next morning it was discovered that one of the younger men had disappeared with one of the young maidens, leaving his wife and child behind. Li, as wrathful as Moses, halted the march to deliver a two-hour sermon against adultery and fornication. That was the day, too, when sickness came to them. So many were sick that they had to halt in mid-afternoon. Martin, weak from retching and fever, was sure that at last he would die. Only Li, Lee Bang, and a few of the old people were immune; they dug arrowroot which they mixed with a flowering herb and served the bitter brew to the ailing.

The second morning after that, Martin felt better, but two infants and a little girl were dead, their faces marked with purple splotches.

Almost as distressing to Martin as his illness was the fact that he was infested with lice. His hands and arms were as dark from sun and dirt as his shaggy beard. A boil plagued his left forearm; he was walking his foot blisters into calluses. His gaunt body stank, and no amount of plunging about in streams would cleanse it or rid his hair of lice. He realized vaguely that the strain was resulting in strange mental crotchets. One night he dreamed vividly of Jane standing at a marriage altar with a stranger, and then he awakened, confused and frightened. How long had he actually been missing? There was something called an Enoch Arden law, but how long was it before he would be declared legally dead and Jane could remarry? The sun was burning through the morning mist before he could try to laugh at himself.

He lost track of the days as they wended through a country of sparsely cultivated valleys and deserted conical hills—one hill like another, one day like another. Intolerable heat and rains only made the land steam and shimmer like some huge basin of boiling water.

In the steaming shimmer of a breathless afternoon Martin, walking in the lead with Li, saw a form—a color—that made him think at first he was hallucinating. On a rock above the road sat a Negro, wearing stained GI fatigues and a helmet liner, his feet bare, his boots tied about his neck, a rifle across his knees.

"Hey, there!" The Negro's voice came down to them gently. "You, Jesus, with the shepherd's crook—speak English?"

Li halted and smiled at Martin, who cried, "Yes!"

The Negro shifted his rifle, resting the butt on the rock and pressing the trigger. The resulting crash caused everyone but Li and Martin to fall prone. The Negro laughed and called to Martin, "What outfit?"

At first Martin did not understand. He watched the hillside stir with life and counted fourteen men converging toward them. Most bore rifles, but two carried only heavy barracks bags. The man swinging agilely in the lead was heavily armed: crossed bandoliers, grenades festooning his belt like dwarf pineapples, a .45, a carbine in one hand, and a rifle slung over his shoulder. His face was young, blank, his body like a broad slab of dirty granite. One sleeve was in tatters, but on the other Martin made out the rockers of a master sergeant.

"What outfit?" the sergeant asked him.

"I'm not in the Army."

"Then what the hell you doing here?"

"Trying to escape. I was up near the parallel when . . . it happened."

"You a doctor by any chance?"

"No."

"Savelson needs a doctor. The sulfa's no good. What are you?"

"I'm— My name is Martin Judson. I was in Korea on business. I'm with a foundation—the Honeywell Foundation."

"My name is Trask—Joe Trask. Master sergeant." He named his outfit. "The Sasebo clam diggers. We've been in Korea less than a week—I think. What day is it?"

"I don't remember."

"Neither do I. They put us into something called a task force. And as far as I can see, about all that's left is this *Trask* force. Some joke, eh, boss? We went into action near Osan on the fifth, and they beat the hell out of us. They had T-thirty-four tanks. We had bazookas—two point thirty-sixes. They told us once in Japan if you fire a bazooka into the tail of a T-thirty-four, he'll blow up. Well, I fired *fourteen* rounds into the tail nearest mine, and nothing happened. We had some recoilless rifles—seventy-fives. I'd handled a recoilless rifle just once in my life. Its shells just bounce off a T-thirty-four. So after a while we *withdrew*. I mean we ran like hell—and we're still running all over Korea, I guess. Wonder what Harry the True and Douglas think about that. Hey, you look terrible. Why are you carrying all that gear?"

"It keeps my mind on my business. You don't look so hot yourself. Neither do your men."

The others had gathered about them now except for the Negro who kept a lookout on the high rock. To Martin's unpracticed eye they were a sorry-looking bunch, incapable of destroying a baby carriage.

Trask twisted his lips. "Don't let their looks fool you. These are MacArthur's own, the palace guard, the cream of Kobe." He glanced at one of the men who carried a barracks bag. "McDowell, close your fly." McDowell put down the barracks bag and stared at him listlessly. "You see what I mean," Trask said to Martin. "He's bucking for a Section Eight. He threw away his rifle. So did Marks. So they have to carry the C rations. Where are you headed?"

"Taejon."

"A nice idea. But where is it? Tordenos lost the goddamn compass. And every one of these Jesus Christing hills looks just like all the others. And except sometimes in the early morning the sun don't travel in any sensible direction. Does old Sam here know the way?"

Li beamed at Trask. He had been learning a bit of English from Martin while teaching him a few words of Korean, and now he astonished Martin by saying, "Christian soldiers." Gesturing to them proudly, he called back to his people in both Korean and English, "Christian soldiers! Christian soldiers!" and the people, smiling, began to get to their feet.

Trask said, "A comedian!" Then he bawled at his men, "Look and act like soldiers for *just one minute,* you—" His outburst of obscenity was the most imaginative Martin ever had heard. When Trask ran out of breath, the Negro on the lookout rock was howling with laughter. "That Rush," Trask said to Martin. "If he wasn't a goddamn nigger, he'd make a goddamn good soldier. Well, we're wasting time. This country will be swarming any time. They're coming down on both sides of us and fanning in. Can old Sam give me the route to Taejon?"

But Li interrupted with a question of his own.

Martin said, "He wants to know if you and your men are hungry. He offers you rice."

"You got a lot?"

"Two small bowls a day for each person for two more days."

Trask looked furious. He swung completely around, his grenades flaring from his hips like a lethal hula skirt. Then he yelled, *"No!"*

Li, beaming and pointing at him, said in Korean to Martin, "Good Christian."

"What's the *matter* with him?" Trask demanded.

"Your reference to Jesus Christ and God convince Li Bum that you're a good Christian."

Trask glared at Li as Rush called down from the rock, "Sergeant Trask, lover, you gonna get us all baptized?"

Ignoring him, Trask said, "All I want is directions."

Li squatted on his heels and drew lines in the dust with a forefinger. A fork, then another, and they would come to a bridge across the Kum River by the following nightfall. Taejon was not far beyond. But he warned Trask to keep a sharp look-out for enemy patrols.

Trask thanked him and told McDowell and Marks to distribute one can of C rations to each person in Li's band. When one of his men protested, Trask told him to do an obscene and impossible thing. "We've got plenty to get us to Taejon." He turned to Martin. "Come on. Forget that crap you're carrying. We've got to *hurry*."

Leave Li and these people who had become his good friends? He would not do it.

Trask was furious with him. "I'm giving you the chance to *make* it with us! Aren't you an *American?*"

"Of course, but these people saved my life. I won't leave them now that we're almost there."

Trask cursed him again, then impatiently sent Rush and another ahead at the double and ordered the rest to get cracking. As they hurried on, he glanced back at Martin and cursed.

Late in the afternoon they heard the distant sound of small-arms fire. It rose to a crescendo, faded, then continued sporadically. Li, talking to himself, quickened the pace.

Night was falling as they trudged into a village which appeared deserted. There was a flash in the mauve shadows of the hills above, and the cough of a rifleshot came down to them. Another answered. Li, greatly agitated, disappeared into a hut, then hurried to another, leaving his people sprawled in the village street.

Martin, resting on his A-frame and eating his can of C rations, gazed up at the darkening hills sadly. He could imagine what had happened: Trask and his men, moving in haste and not taking proper scouting precautions, must have stumbled on an enemy force, taken to the high ground, and been surrounded. Remembering his terror of death in the rice paddy near Yi, Martin knew how the men in the hills must feel.

Li beckoned him to the hut where he had been for some time. Inside it Martin made out the faces of three men, two old and one young, squatting about a low Korean table on which a taper burned. The young man, named Chang Koh, spoke slight, bad English; he had been a soldier—and would be again, he said. A strong patrol of enemy infantrymen, coming back from the Kum, had come face to face with the Americans and pursued them into the hills. Chang had climbed up to see for himself before nightfall. The Americans were in a draw, surrounded on three sides, and did not know there was an easy way out on the upper side—nor did the enemy realize it. When the Americans saw the way out in the morning, it would be too late to escape. But from the upper side Chang could easily make his way into the draw in the darkness. If he called to them in his bad English, however, they would think him an enemy decoy and refuse to follow him out. Chang said, "You—" He pointed at Martin, to himself, and then toward the hills while Li and the two old men nodded approval.

Martin almost said, "Now wait a minute!" He wished to explain that he was not cut out for this sort of work. He was an office man, formerly a clergyman, and was here by sheerest happenstance. Of course, he was a Christian, but he wished Li would understand that the Christian life was not necessarily related to midnight capers in the Korean hills. Was it? It wouldn't matter much if Li held him in everlasting contempt for refusing to try to help the Christian soldiers. But the point was he would have contempt for himself. Perhaps courage was only a fear of being unable to forget one's cowardice later.

Chang said, "We go," and Martin turned numbly toward the door. But Li and Chang had some further embellishment of their scheme. The enemy patrol had left a roadblock of four soldiers beyond the village. Chang and Martin would bring the Americans down well past the roadblock, and they would hurry on all night. Li and his band, anticipating no trouble from the North Koreans, would meet them at the Kum River tomorrow evening.

Chang, taking one end of Martin's staff, led him through the darkness. Soon Martin's eyes adjusted, and he could make out rocks, the steep and rugged slope where they climbed cautiously, quietly. Martin breathed laboredly, probably as much from fear as exertion. After seeming hours they reached a crest where Chang moved even more cautiously. A stone, rolling under Martin's foot, clattered downward, and not far off a nervous finger fired a rifle. Martin flinched at its cannonlike echo. Before long they inched downward through a twisting fissure until Martin sensed they had come out on a promontory. Chang pressed him prone and nudged him.

"Trask!" Martin's voice rose powerfully. "Judson here!"

Bang, bang, bang! Flames flashed, but happily no bullets frightened him. His voice, in fact, seemed to come from down in the draw.

"Prove it!" Trask, the skeptic, sounded not far distant.

Martin thought for a moment, then cried, "If that Rush wasn't a goddamn nigger, he'd make a goddamn good soldier!"

Yee—hee—hee! Rush laughed in the darkness, and the enemy wasted more ammunition.

"I'm talking fancy," Martin called. "You understand why. There's an exit from the theater. You're on the stage. The way is through the balcony. An usher is crawling down to guide you. Trust him."

Bang, bang, bang!

"Read you," Trask replied. "First a little fireworks backstage."

Martin nudged Chang, who slithered away. Soon Trask began a backstage distraction well down the draw. Grenades and yells drew the enemy in that direction. And sooner than Martin had expected, Chang crawled close with another figure behind him. They went up the way they had come, a silent human chain following them while the enemy continued to fire into the draw. . . .

Two had been killed in the running fire fight, and in the draw McDowell had taken a chest wound. Trask had patched him up so that he was able to make it on foot down to the road, where he fainted from loss of blood. Someone said to leave the yellow bastard lay, but Trask said no. They improvised a crude stretcher from two rifles and a barracks bag and took turns by fours carrying the unconscious McDowell along the road.

Trask would not let Martin or Chang take a turn on the stretcher carry. "He's ours to lug," he said. "You two have done enough tonight."

Around two o'clock in the morning, when they paused for one of the frequent changes of bearers, Rush said, "He's dead."

Trask crouched down and put an ear to McDowell's gaping mouth. "Yes, he's dead. We'll take him off the road and leave him out of sight."

All followed the four who carried McDowell into a field, as if dreading separation from the one they had loathed. When they put him down, Rush said, "I knew him away back at Bragg in basic. He was very religious. Didn't talk much about it, but went to chapel every Sunday morning and prayed every night. Too bad somebody can't say a little burial piece over him."

"How about you, Savelson?" Trask asked.

"For Chrissake," Savelson said, "I'm a *Jew*."

"Then say a *Jewish* prayer."

"No!"

"I'll pray," Martin said, taking off his straw headpiece. "Almighty God, in thine infinite wisdom. . . . Ashes to ashes, dust to dust. . . ." He finished the abbreviated service quickly and turned back to the road.

As they hurried on toward the Kum, with Chang leading the way, Trask came up with Martin and said, "You sounded like an old pro chaplain back there."

"I used to be a preacher."

"Why did they throw you out?" Trask asked. "Screwing? Drinking? Gambling?"

"They didn't throw me out. I just got tired and quit."

Trask said, "I'll tell you what's a fact, it took guts for you to pull us out back there. Earlier I sent Rush scouting up that way, but he couldn't find nothing in the dark. Never thought I'd owe my tail to a *preacher*."

"Strayed foundation executive," Martin said.

"*Preacher*," Trask said. "Do you know I've never been to church in my life? Twenty-five years and never once in a church."

"So what are you bragging about?"

"I'll bet it's a record."

"I doubt it," Martin replied.

Trask snorted again. Then he interrogated Martin endlessly. He still was asking questions, while revealing nothing about himself, as gray light grew and Chang led them off the road and up a hillside. Beyond the crest they took cover in tall

cane. Martin, exhausted, ate C rations and began to trample
a bed in the cane as Trask and Chang left to scout the Kum Valley below.

Rush, treading down a bed near Martin's, watched them
disappear into the morning mist and said, "Trask got us out.
You helped, too. We thank ya. Trask won't."

Trask, said Rush, had been born Josef Traschefka of Czech
parents in South Chicago. He had had seven or eight years of
school and become the leader of a youthful gang. Enlistment
in the Army at the age of eighteen had been his means of avoid-
ing prison. Following infantry combat in Italy he had chosen
the good life of the peacetime Army—fat-catting, politicking,
black marketing. "I'll bet Trask got thirty, forty grand—maybe
more—hidden in the smokehouse." He had, inevitably, found
a berth in regimental supply. Martin understood why he was
the ideal soldier: He was filled with pride; he was a proficient
thief, liar, leader.

Rush was still talking about him admiringly when Martin
fell asleep. He was awakened in the afternoon by Trask.

"They have patrols coming in. No heavy stuff yet. We'll
cross the bridge after dark. . . ."

As darkness began to fall, they went down the ridge and
made their way cautiously by moonlight to the bridgehead.
A large crowd milled there, some venturing across the Kum,
but others hesitating.

"Mar-teh!"

Li Bum came to him, smiling in the moonlight, and gripped
his arm in a bony litte hand. Yangseng and many others gathered, all expressing their pleasure by touching him—and
then Trask, as if they were people of great consequence. Chang
returned from making inquiries and said that friendly soldiers
guarding the farther end of the bridge were letting some people
pass on to Taejon but turning others back—no one knew why.

"Let's get cracking." Trask sounded dejected rather than
elated, as Martin had thought he would be. "You gentlemen
of the palace guard"—his tone had lost its authority—"trail

your rifles so the gentlemen over there don't see the silhouettes and blast us. Chang, take a lead and let 'em know who we are. Come on, Judson."

"Wait till the people from Yi are rounded up," Martin told him. "We'll all cross over together."

Lee Bang was so tired she could barely totter under her A-frame, so Martin took the burden from her before they started onto the bridge.

Trask dropped back, calling his name, and when he found him carrying the A-frame, he was angry. "What are you, a Boy Scout or something? Look at that pack! There's even a stool and all sorts of worthless crap. If you're going to carry *hers*, why don't you carry *everybody's*? Why—"

"Joe!" Rush spoke close by. "Leave the pack parson alone! *Get off his back!*"

"Yeah," said Savelson behind them. "Pack parson! That's what he is. The good old pack parson!"

Trask was silent as they trudged on slowly.

There was a growing din, and the throng jammed to a halt short of the farther bridgehead. Then a voice rang out:

"Are there American soldiers on the bridge?"

"Yeah," Trask replied.

"Identify yourselves by name and unit and come through the crowd one at a time."

Trask identified himself, as did the others, and they pressed through the crowd.

The people on the bridge inched forward into the glare of torchlights, where Martin saw American and ROK soldiers. He made out a young American first lieutenant and heard Trask yell, "That's him!"

The lieutenant shoved his way to Martin, who identified himself. When the lieutenant said an MP would guide him to regimental headquarters, Martin replied he would check in with the Army later; he first had to get his people safely to Taejon. The phrase "my people" did not sound strange to Martin, though it might have to the lieutenant, who shrugged and let them pass on. Trask and his men were being sent someplace in another direction from the road to Taejon.

Martin paused to say good-bye to them, but Trask, ignoring his outstretched hand, howled, "Don't you want to get *out?* You goddamn fool!"

Though it is only about seventy-five miles from Taejon to Taegu as an airplane flies, it took Martin, Li, and their band five days to cover the distance along a road jammed with refugees. It seemed that the entire population was fleeing the continuous thud of artillery to the north. Patriarchs of the upper caste wearing tall black hats and city women wearing high-waisted skirts and blouses trudged among the throngs of straw-clad, heavily burdened poor. Many died, and their bodies were left by the wayside, stripped of everything by those who passed, half devoured in darkness by packs of dogs gone wild. More pathetic than the dead were the dying, too weak to go on, moaning, pleading, vomiting beside the road. And most pathetic of all were the gangs of lost children who padded along, stark naked and flecked with lice and flies, a few carrying tatters of clothing, which they had stripped off in a vain effort for relief from the burning heat. These gangs, some gone as wild as the dog packs, moved faster than their elders, swooping from side to side of the road with a weird chittering sound, like that of swallows driven from their nesting places, yet as dangerous as eagles to the knots of aged from whom they wrested food and anything else they fancied. At times the whole conglomerate mass of people stalled to a halt and pitched off the road as sirens sounded and American tanks, trucks, and Jeeps bulled through. At first the roaring machines came from Taegu, but near the end of the journey they clattered from Taejon in the opposite direction, indicating another defeat. But no matter from which direction they came, they did not hesitate to run down the slow or unwary and never paused to aid the injured in their headlong drive. This was not war as idealized by Americans. It was war as described truthfully in Revelation.

On the outskirts of Taegu two MP's, sitting on the hood of an Army truck and watching sharply the horde of passing refugees, stopped Martin. They did not believe him when he identified himself but hustled him into the truck and handcuffed him to a stanchion while Li and the people from Yi gathered about, wailing and protesting in vain. One of the MP's said, "The filthy son of a bitch even threw away his dog tags. . . ."

The stockade for Army deserters was an old compound in Taegu. To Martin, life there was like living in a luxuriant hotel after the rigors of the trek. Though the prisoners were forbidden razors, they were deloused and their beards and heads shaved. Issued half a bar of yellow GI soap, Martin scrubbed himself for half an hour under a shower. The Army slops served them three times a day seemed the most delicious food he had ever tasted. The green fatigues issued him were a delight. For two days and nights he slept most of the time. After his first couple of hours there he ceased protesting that he never had been in the Army, for even his fellow prisoners thought it an amusing dodge. He presumed that eventually he would be put through some kind of processing in which he would convince his inquisitors who he truly was.

At dawn on the third morning they were lined up in the compound, forty-eight angry and frightened men, issued shovels, and marched out into the street under heavy guard after an MP sergeant bawled, "You bastards are going to dig your own graves!"

As they filed out of the compound, Martin heard: "Marteh!" There was Li, hopping along beside him, and there was the entire band from Yi, wailing and crying to him. As the guards shoved the group back, tears started to Martin's eyes at the thought of them camped outside the stockade and waiting for him. The prisoners filed along almost deserted streets at the edge of the city, through noxious dumps, till they came to an area of sandpits. A couple of trucks waited there with empty canvas bags which the prisoners were to fill. As Martin began to work, he saw Yangseng wave to him from the edge of the pit, then disappear.

It was exhausting work in the burning heat of the pit. Some men fainted, and others pretended to; the guards let them lie till they stirred, then prodded them back to work. Travail was curious, Martin thought: The more one endured, the better one was able to endure. Confronted with this labor a month ago, he would soon have fainted, yet now he worked with only mild discomfort.

Trucks came and went with their loads of sandbags. Guards, trucks, and laborers were vague blurred shapes in the yellow glare. Time became only the absence of darkness. Out of the timeless glare (did someone actually say it?) came a rumor: Tonight in the stockade they would be given a choice of going back into the line or staying in the sandpits.

"Judson!"

Martin looked up. The figure dancing toward him was indistinguishable, but his voice and language were familiar. "You" —Trask was howling obscenities at the guards—"what are you holding this man for? He's the *president* of the American Honeywell Foundation! He was on a *State Department* mission! He'll see that every one of you bastards is *busted!*"

Martin found himself in the shadow of a truck. Since the shadow was large, it must be late afternoon. He faced a startled captain, the outraged Joe Trask. Someone tugged at his right hand, and he looked down at Yangseng.

"Didn't you *tell* them who you were?" Trask yelled.

"Of course. But no one believed me."

Trask turned on the captain with profanity. "Don't you *process* your prisoners?" The captain decided to get angry at Trask, but was silenced quickly. "Don't try to pull your rank on me because tomorrow you won't have any rank! . . ."

Out of the whirlwind of Trask's wrath, the embarrassment of the provost marshal's office, the apologies and clumsy helpfulness of guards, Martin finally was spun into the dark and crowded street outside the stockade. Li and the others were there, babbling happily. So, too, was Trask, grasping Martin firmly by an arm and making him feel he merely had exchanged one jailer for another.

"Now *listen,*" Trask told him, "this can't go on forever— you snafuing and me getting you out. I got a Jeep and driver here from the provost marshal. We're going to *Army* headquarters and straighten this out. I'm *personally* putting you on a plane to Japan." When Li insisted on going along, too, Trask consented because he could testify about Martin's identity.

On the way to headquarters Trask said it was by the wildest luck that Yangseng had come across him; apparently the people from Yi had been scouring the city ever since Martin's arrest, searching for someone who might effect his release. Trask and his men had been reassigned at the Kum River. They had fought again—and run again. Now their unit had been placed in reserve, but he knew that wouldn't last long. Taejon had fallen. Taegu would fall next, he said. Before long they would fight—and run. Meanwhile, his unit was resting outside the city, and he had a pass until midnight.

The mood of confusion and tension in the streets of the city extended to Eighth Army Headquarters. Men straining to stem the debacle of the United Nations forces had no time for a wandering civilian. Trask's growing consternation amused Martin, who was beginning to resign himself to his strange fate.

They came, at last, to a harassed public information lieutenant on whom a harassed *Time* correspondent was heaping the wrath of Henry Luce. The young lieutenant simply looked at them with a glazed expression, then turned back to the man from *Time* with sudden abuse.

"Listen, Lieutenant!" Trask yelled, but the lieutenant did not listen, and a man touched Trask on the shoulder and told him not to waste his breath. What was the problem?

The man, Drew Flannigan, was of indeterminate age. His broad face fell into chins; his body sloped into paunch and girth which his dirty suntans barely contained; his expression was serious, perhaps because a smile would display his crooked teeth. Having experienced much war, he had patience with its workings and had transmitted his knowledge of its foolishness through two blunt fingers which seemed to fight a typewriter. The fame his copy had brought him surprised but did not impress him much. He was a sentimentalist but tried to ignore the fact.

Martin did not realize all this at once, of course. It took a while for Flannigan to get through to one, in part because he stammered slightly, in part because he was extraordinarily shy. Since he had learned that nothing in life is simple, he approached each experience with an elaboration of thought that the simpleminded sometimes mistook for obtuseness or ineptness.

Once he understood Martin's problem, he led them out of the public information office to a bungalow nearby, where there was similar chaos. By the light of Coleman lamps men wrote on portable typewriters and argued noisily in a pall of tobacco smoke through which came the reek of sweat. Despite the noise, other men slept on cots which were scattered about the rooms of the bungalow.

Flannigan lowered himself onto one of the cots and hitched around the old World War II issue gas mask container he was wearing. Opening it, he drew out a quart of White Horse, which brought light and hope to Trask's somber eyes. "I've f-filed," Flannigan said. "Time for the evening c-cocktail." He held out the bottle to Martin and Li, who declined, and then to Trask, who gurgled down their share with his own while Flannigan looked at him benignly. Then Flannigan took a hearty swallow himself, recapped the bottle, and put it back in the gas mask container, saying, "All honest fellows here. Nobody'll steal anything except b-booze."

After lighting a cigar, he addressed himself to Martin's problem once more, sounding as if it had not been explained to him already. Trask told him again what had happened, and then

Flannigan asked Martin to describe it. Next, he called over a young Korean translator and heard the story from Li. Suddenly he appeared to lose interest in Martin and talked with Li through the translator about why he and his people had decided to uproot themselves and what they hoped to find when they came to rest. At last, taking out a bit of folded copy paper and a pencil, he carefully printed their names and ages and Martin's address and position in New York. Martin, who remembered having read Flannigan's wire service stories from Europe during the last war in the Upton *Daily Chronicle,* scarcely could believe this was the same moving and sometimes eloquent reporter. He seemed, rather, as slow and fumbling as a cub reporter while he questioned Martin about the Honeywell Foundation and what he had done before working for it.

Suddenly, no longer stammering, he said, "So you want to leave these people from Yi and go home?"

Now Martin stammered. "I—I—No, I don't want to, but I— I don't know what I can do for them. I—I want my wife to know I'm all right—"

Trask started to argue with Martin, but Flannigan silenced him with a look and said, "I can get you off to Tokyo before morning. Any of us here could. We just have you appointed a news courier. You take some copy and negatives and stuff to our offices."

Trask, pleased, said they ought to celebrate Martin's departure with another drink. But Li, to whom the young Korean translated Flannigan's offer, looked so sad that Martin turned his head away.

"What's going to happen to the refugees?" Flannigan sounded as if talking to himself. "They're jamming up by the hundreds of thousands—maybe millions—nobody knows how many. The Army can't help 'em. The UN should, but may never get organized to do it."

A man who had been lying facedown on a cot near Flannigan's spoke. "Maybe the Honeywell Foundation can help."

He rolled over and sat up slowly. Bearded and emaciated, he wore GI fatigues which hung like empty sacks. Smiling wanly at Martin, he asked, "Do you think so?"

"This is Father Francis Reardon," Flannigan said. "We happened on to each other near Taejon about a week ago. He's a Jesuit missionary. He and his people had a long walk from the north, as you did. I wrote a piece about it. Last night, when he came in here, I offered him a chance to ride courier to Tokyo. But he decided to go on to Pusan with his people."

As Father Reardon grasped his hand, Martin wondered if there was no end to the challenge. For that it was. Possibly few but Reardon and Martin would understand. (Maybe Flannigan did, or maybe as a scribe of the human tragicomedy he saw it only as an amusing confrontation of two idealists.) It was not Roman Catholic challenging Protestant, or missionary challenging institutional man. Rather, it was the shared challenge of two men of similar experience who felt, without prideful self-righteousness, that in their travail they had found a profound meeting of East and West, that the spirit of God flowed through them and to them from their suffering people. Did a sincere clergyman basically seek martyrdom? For that was all that appeared to await them on the road to Pusan.

Reardon, standing, was no more impressive physically than he had been seated. He looked as frail as a wren, and his shoulders appeared to have been stooped long over a monastery bench. Yet his voice and blue eyes were spirited. In ancient Rome, Martin thought, he would have gone to the lions while Martin personally would probably have dropped a pinch of incense on an idol to a current god.

"What's in Pusan?" Martin asked him.

Reardon countered with a question of his own in an Irish accent. "How many do your people number?"

"They aren't *my* people. Thirty-six the last I knew."

"Mine number forty-eight," Reardon said. "Let's join forces. I've found a good supply of rice here. Enough for all of us to share."

"What's in Pusan?" Martin repeated.

"Hope," Reardon replied. "The largest port in the country. Rogues, cutthroats, some people who care. Two wise heads are better than one for a start at organization. We can't save everybody, but we can help *some*."

Martin's face must have reflected his decision, for Joe Trask cried, "I'll tell you something, Judson. You're *crazy!* You're the craziest goddamn fool I ever met."

After three weeks had passed, Jane gave up hope that he was alive. She tried to reserve her tears for the hours of darkness after the children were in bed. At first, indeed, she tried not to let them know she was alarmed. But it was impossible to fool Kathy very long about anything.

One evening, when Kathy was saying her prayers and being especially insistent about bringing Daddy home safely and soon ("Let's get *on* with it, Lord, because you shouldn't keep him waiting, he's such a good man and father, to say nothing of how *we* feel . . ."), she suddenly burst into tears and flung her arms about Jane's neck. "Mama, is he *dead?*"

Jane tried to reassure her, but after that she knew Kathy was as uncertain as she. Her own prayers, said silently at all hours of day and night, were as insistent as Kathy's. She knew that Martin would not approve of her beseeching God in this way. Sometimes she imagined she could hear him say, "No point to it, Jane. No asking personal favors in prayer. Just strength to endure and accept God's will."

While Kathy was a great comfort to her, and Abe in his blissful ignorance was a comfort, too, her sense of loneliness sometimes almost overwhelmed her.

Once she had decided Martin was dead and accepted it after a long night of tears, she wished to face up to the future. She felt she needed some sound advice. There seemed no one in the world she could talk to but Tubby.

Phoning him in Boston, she told him what had happened.

"Good heavens, Jane, why haven't you let us know?"

"What could you do, Tubby?"

"Well—"

"What I want is your advice."

"Look," Tubby said. "I have something to attend to in New York I've been putting off. Eunice and I are going to leave the kids with her mother and drive down today."

She was certain he had nothing but concern over her and Marty to bring him to New York. But she never had been so glad to see anyone as when he and Eunice, who was pregnant with their third child, arrived late that afternoon. She found a sitter for the children and went out to dinner with them.

"I have to do something," she told them. "He's missing, not dead, though, I'm certain now—Well, Alex Carpenter says the foundation will pay his salary 'indefinitely.' But I feel I should find a cheaper apartment. I should find someone to help me take care of the children while I prepare myself for a responsible job. Maybe teaching."

"Wait," Tubby said. "Give it awhile, Jane. They say the fisher wives of Aran always attend widowhood. But most of the fishermen always come home. . . ."

Monday, July 30, was a day of humid heat in New York. Despite the weather, Jane took the children to the Bronx Zoo, the place they enjoyed most in the city. When they returned home they had the meal Kathy liked best—frankfurters, baked beans, and potato salad. After supper Kathy read from *Winnie-the-Pooh* to Abe, who did not understand it, while Jane did the dishes and listened to another news broadcast with dread. There seemed to be death and defeat throughout Korea, where the Communists now threatened Taegu and Pusan. Outside, a thunderstorm brewed and broke with dramatic suddenness. The celestial fireworks and heavy rain delighted Kathy and Abe whereas *Winnie* had merely striven to please them. In the midst of the storm, the door buzzer sounded, and old Frank, the apartment doorman, called out that he had a message for Jane.

She opened the door. Frank, who had shared her worry about Martin with sincere sympathy, held out a yellow envelope in a shaking hand. His mouth was open, but he could not speak as Jane tore open the envelope.

AM SAFE WELL LETTER FOLLOWS SOON LOVE MARTY

She burst into tears. After she was sufficiently recovered, she phoned Tubby, who was incoherent with joy. Kathy and Abe stayed up half the night with her, getting hilariously drunk on a deadly concoction Kathy conceived which included cola, chocolate ice cream, raisins, and nutmeg.

On the crowded road from Taegu to Pusan seventy-seven Protestant and Roman Catholic Koreans trudged behind Martin and Father Reardon. As the two walked along together on the first afternoon of the trek, Reardon remarked, "Your man Li Bum doesn't like me."

"He's not my man," Martin replied.

Reardon smiled. "So you're a Baptist. I'm going to call you Martin, and you're going to call me Francis. Martin, what is it you Protestant clergy dislike about us Catholic priests? I don't mean I expect everybody to love me, but I've always wondered. Let's forget the Pope and all the theology. What really is it?"

"Your authority, I think, Francis. Your . . . power."

"Balls," said Father Francis Reardon.

"What?"

"You heard me. A Catholic parish priest has no more power than a Protestant parish clergyman. I know because I had a parish in Brooklyn before I heard the call of the wild and decided I wanted to be a missionary. Sure now, the church is rich —richer than Midas. And Midas it is. Ask any parish priest how much he can get from his diocese. In Brooklyn the bishop invited me to dinner one time and said, 'Father Francis'—at other times I was just Reardon—but he tells me I must build a new school. Very good, your Honor, I says to him—Well, not exactly. But I asked him, How much is coming from the diocese? He grows vague. How much is coming from the parish?

Well, as it turned out, not a bloody cent ever came from the diocese. I raised it all from the parish."

"Bishops," Martin said. "Every Protestant church has several of 'em." He reminisced about the experience that had caused him to leave Central Baptist of Sylvia.

"So you ran to a foundation," Francis said, "as I ran off to the foreign missionary field. And what did you find there?"

"Bishops."

Francis grinned and rested a small hand on Martin's shoulder. "Don't be so discouraging. I'm counting on your foundation to help us with our people when we get to Pusan."

Martin smiled, too. "But I'm counting on the Society of Jesus."

"Ha! Not as long as I'm tied up with a dirty Protestant."

"And ha to you," Martin said. "Not as long as I'm tied up with a dirty cross-back."

"Very discouraging. Is your organization that bad?"

"Not really. It does a great deal of good. On some things it acts swiftly, efficiently. On others it can be as clumsy and bureaucratic as any diocesan idiots you can name."

"We know," Francis said, "that Roman prelates and Dallas hard-shells will never get together in our lifetime. It will be interesting to see what happens."

They and their people reached Pusan in a driving rainstorm. The city, teeming with refugees, was like a muddy ant heap. To its chaos had been added the confusion of the United Nations effort to develop it into the chief supply base for South Korea.

Francis led them to a Jesuit monastery, where he hoped they could find shelter, at least temporarily. Martin and the Koreans huddled in the rain while he was inside for nearly an hour. When he came out, he had exchanged his dirty suntans for a cassock and surplice which he wore under his muddy straw coat.

"No room in the inn," he said. "We'll have to find a manger."

"Cassock and surplice." Martin looked at him accusingly.

"Don't get your Protestant bowels in an uproar," Francis replied. "It will help. Wait and see. I don't know how, but it will help."

Li Bum led the way to a school which was run by his denomination.

"Same story," Martin told Francis when he and Li came out. "This hotel is filled up. They're even sleeping in the corridors. Let's you and I scout the U.S. Army."

They were pressing their way along a crowded street when an Army Jeep braked to a stop and a young captain called, "Can I give you a lift, Father?"

"Sure now," Francis said to Martin, "I see Ireland in that young American face. But where are we going?"

"Let me try this one." Martin stepped toward the Jeep, and Francis followed him. "Captain, this is Bishop Francis Reardon from Washington and I'm his, uh, assistant, Father Martin Judson. Our luggage and papers are at the airport, but supreme headquarters in Tokyo directed us to special services. . . ."

Francis endorsed Martin's story in the aggrieved manner of a bishop who was being treated with indignity. In the chaos of Pusan only implausible stories sounded true. At any rate, their story found belief in the captain and a friend to whom he took them, a major in quartermaster supply who also was a devout Roman Catholic.

"Now would you believe it. . . ." Francis could make his Irish accent very broad when he wished to. "Approved by Washington and Tokyo on a direct pipeline from Rome itself, this noble Catholic plan to aid the refugees. . . . But all balled up!" Francis cried. The endorsements had been sent to General Walker's headquarters in Taegu while they themselves had been unceremoniously dumped in Pusan.

Devout Catholics though the major and captain were, they eagerly wished to unload this problem of the angry bishop and his vociferous assistant.

"We need a place!" Francis cried.

"Don't you understand?" Martin's tone was angry. "A large

place with facilities to house as many as possible and serve food to many more."

The major found them one on the Street of Rising Sun before nightfall. It had been the residence of a wealthy merchant who had fled to Japan in fear of the North Korean forces. It had a fairly large compound surrounded by a gallery; there was a large kitchen, many rooms.

"This will do very well," Francis told the officers. "I give you my blessing. Your names and kindness will go to Rome. You will not be forgotten."

"Yes, bless you both." Martin raised his right hand, as in a benediction.

After the officers had left, Francis said, "Father Judson, the blessing is not offered with all fingers extended. Yours looks like the Nazi salute."

They shared a tiny room—two straw pallets and one tin washbasin—and through the thin walls they could hear the bickering of their followers.

"A roof over their heads isn't enough," Francis said the next morning. "They all must start proselytizing."

"What's that?" Martin pointed to a velvet-wrapped bundle under Francis' arm.

"The sacred vessels, Martin. I was up early and fetched them from the monastery."

"So right off you're turning this place into a sanctified Catholic church."

"*Half* of it," Francis replied cheerfully. "Your people can have whichever half they want. Mine will take the other. I'm offering a mass of thanksgiving for our safe delivery here at nine o'clock this morning. From the east gallery. Li Bum can have a Protestant service from the west gallery at eight or ten or whenever he wants. Mass will be said here once a day, and Li Bum can hold services for twenty-three hours for all I care. Does that suit you?"

"Of course. If I can ever manage to get some command of this language, I'll try to get Li to knock off his proselytizing."

"I'm already working at my people to cut it out. Let's have a
bit of rice and tea and make plans."

Martin suggested that in their sermons both Francis and Li
direct their people to seek jobs on the waterfront. "That's
where the food comes from. That's where we'll have to begin
begging and borrowing."

"Sound." Francis gazed at him thoughtfully. "Your imagina-
tion runs along practical lines. Too bad you never became a
priest. You'd have made archbishop almost overnight."

Francis obtained writing materials from the monastery, and
that afternoon Martin wrote a long letter to Carpenter outlin-
ing plans and offering practical suggestions on how the foundation could help. He had written Jane from Taegu, and he asked
Carpenter to give her a copy of this letter so that she would know
he was well and busy.

By evening Li and one of Francis' men had obtained the use
of two small boats. Francis was dubious about the plan Martin
suggested, but he was willing to try.

The next morning each put out in a boat paddled by a
Korean. Their destination was a freighter anchored offshore
and waiting to unload. By arrangement Martin's boat reached
it first.

"Hey, the watch!" he called. A couple of crewmen looked
over the side curiously. "I'm begging food. My name is Judson,
American civilian, and I'm trying to feed some starving Koreans. I'll take anything you can give me—scraps from your
well-filled plates—anything."

"Ahoy, the master of this vessel," shouted Francis as his
boat came around the ship's bow. He was wearing cassock and
surplice. "I'm Father Francis Reardon of the Society of Jesus,
home port Brooklyn, and I come begging food for starving,
homeless orphans."

"Shove off, Reardon," Martin shouted at him. "I was here
first."

"Shove off yourself, you dirty agnostic," Francis shouted
back at him. "Men," he called to many grinning faces now

leaning overside, "he's not a Catholic. He's not even a Protestant. . . ."

There were cheers and catcalls as the men egged them on.
"Send for cook. . . . Yeee, cookie's even put on his hat!"

A large, hairy man wearing a white chef's cap leaned overside and called in an accent as broad as that Francis had put
on, "Father, what do you need?"

"I was here first!" Martin shouted.

"Dirty agnostic!" Francis yelled.

"Dirty agnostic!" the cook echoed him while the men cheered
and booed.

Soon Francis' boat was laden with rice, flour, cans of Spam,
while Martin sat dejectedly, his head in his hands.

"Hey, agnostic!" A Negro grinned down at him. "They's
plenty of us on this ship. . . ." And before long Martin's boat
was laden, too.

When they reached shore, Francis said, "It's really elementary, isn't it? And I never thought of it."

"Elementary to every parish priest," Martin said. "You have
to sing for your supper."

They did not return from each mission with laden boats.
Sometimes they were rebuffed. Sometimes Francis' request
was granted, sometimes Martin's.

Meanwhile, they organized two daily feedings at the compound, where the lines of hungry refugees grew longer daily.
Since it was impossible to feed all, they faced many problems.
For example, both the Protestant and Catholic Koreans wanted
the payment of conversion in return for a bowl of rice.

"No conversion—no rice," Martin fumed at Francis. "We
could have as many converts as there are bowls of rice. How
can we get across the wrongness of that idea?"

Somehow they managed it. Somehow, too, they worked out
an elaborate system of handing out slips of paper to the waiting
lines and marking each with a symbol in order to cut down
the cheating by those who wanted two portions while others
went without anything.

Flannigan appeared one day late in August and followed them by boat on their daily prowl among the waiting ships.

"You need more than this daily begging," he said.

"The foundation is trying to get something organized," Martin told him. But he felt there was some hesitant, lurking question in Carpenter's letters.

One afternoon a soldier appeared with a note for Martin.

JUDSON:

Have been severely wounded. Like to see you again before I go. This guy will give you a lift if you want to come to the hospital.

TRASK

Martin sprang into the Jeep. As they nudged their way through the jammed streets, he hoped they would reach the hospital in time.

He found Trask in a rec room, hopping about on a bandaged leg and playing Ping-Pong.

"They thought they might have to amputate," he said.

Martin was annoyed. "So you're going to parlay it into a discharge."

Trask shrugged. "You want some lemonade?" He returned to his bed, where he set up a loud moaning. An orderly came, and Trask told him, "Refreshments, Clarence. This is the pack parson I told ya about."

The big glass of iced lemonade was refreshing. It had an interesting flavor, and Martin sipped it again. "Rum?" he asked.

"Bourbon," Trask replied.

"How did you know where to find me?"

"Flannigan told me. He told me about your operation. Sounds patsy to me. Why don't you go big time?"

"We hope to eventually."

"What are you waiting for? These starving kids around here are driving me nutty. Raid a supply base."

Martin looked at him. "Just like that."

"Well, get clever. Get yourself invited to an officers' club. Pal it up with quartermaster personnel."

"And offer them what? My charming companionship?"

Trask frowned. "Jeeze, you can be thick, Judson. Offer 'em salvation. There's a lot of Southern Baptists and Methodists in quartermaster."

Martin tried, but it didn't work.

Late that month a large Army truck ground into the compound one evening. Martin stared with amazement as Trask, smartly uniformed, leaped lightly to the ground.

"I thought you had been discharged."

"Naw. They decided I'm best in quartermaster. I got a base. I mean I'm at a base." His tone grew indignant. "Do you know that line waiting out there is nearly a half mile long? And your people are handing it out by the spoonful. You and Reardon ought to get cracking!"

Martin started to be indignant, too, but Trask said, "I brought you some surplus."

"What is it?"

"Graham crackers."

Martin and Francis gaped when they saw the truck was loaded to its canvas cover with cartons of graham crackers. How had he gotten them?

"Listen, there's a pile of graham crackers at my base the size of a two-story building. There's nothing but graham crackers in Taegu and most of Korea. They're backed up all the way to Ashiya in Japan and on back to Tachikawa Air Base. Only just today the gooney birds stopped flyin' 'em in. Somebody finally caught up with the snafu."

"How could such a thing happen?" Francis asked.

"Father, anything can happen in the Army. But this one is a lulu. Our loyal fighting forces are desperate for three-point-five inch bazooka shells. The code word for bazooka shells is graham crackers. Usually all supply requests are sent in code, except for extreme emergencies, when they're sent clear. This was an extreme emergency, so the request went clear—except that some genius used the code word for bazooka shells. So we got plenty of graham crackers. I'll bring ya another truckload tomorrow."

For several days they were able to feed all the hungry waiting in the long lines. And the Koreans thought graham crackers an extraordinary delicacy.

Joe Trask continued to help them in every way he could. As Francis said, "I get the feeling he *owns* that supply base."

Jane wrote him a revelatory letter in September:

> From the very beginning I've understood what you and Francis Reardon are trying to do. At last I think I've made Alex Carpenter understand, too. Starving is starving, and food is food, and there should be no strings attached to it. Just because the foundation never has attempted a straight relief project is no reason why it should not try. That is the argument I've been pressing with him for some time.
>
> Now, at last, the Honeywell has sprung into action. Sprague leaves today for Japan to expedite the movement of food, clothing, medicines. Probably he has been in touch with you. . . .

Yes, Sprague had cabled that he was on the way.

> Marty, I don't think my goading Carpenter was very effective, but I did my best. What has helped most is the columns Flannigan has written about you and Father Reardon. He made it sound as if the Honeywell was already throwing all its resources into your effort—and this has brought literally hundreds of letters of praise and contributions from all over the country by people who never even had heard of the foundation.
>
> At first Carpenter and the trustees felt very uneasy about the publicity. You know the respectable anonymity in which they've worked for so many years. And then, suddenly, they found they *liked* it. So now they're going full steam ahead in supporting the United Nations relief effort. . . .

Though progress remained slow, they were able to supply food, clothing, and medical treatment for many more persons that fall than were being aided in the early stages of a huge refugee camp set up by the Republic of Korea on the outskirts of Pusan.

Both Roman Catholic and Protestant services, held daily in the compound, were attended by increasing throngs of people. Martin and Francis finally had taught the Korean pastors not to try to *persuade* those who attended that they must accept the Christian faith in return for aid.

"Even Li Bum finally understands," Francis remarked early in December. "We simply are *here,* worshiping. And those many people are *here,* eating and being clothed as much as possible. They understand there's a relationship between the two. But it's implicit—nothing forced. The seeds we sow now, Martin, may flourish years from now."

Francis' health was failing under the constant strain. Joe Trask finally hijacked him to an Army hospital for a physical examination. The doctors wanted to put him to bed, but Francis would not listen to them.

On Christmas Day he officiated at four masses—and then fainted. Martin carried him to his pallet in the little room they still shared, then sent for a doctor.

His heart was "simply worn out," the doctor told Martin. More than a hundred Koreans, weeping and moaning, struggled to carry him by stretcher to the ambulance in the compound. When the ambulance reached the hospital, Francis was dead.

Less than two weeks later Martin was taken violently ill. At the hospital a doctor told him: "Infectious hepatitis. A bad case of it. You're finished in Korea."

 *Five*

IT WAS early May before Martin was able to return to work. On his first day at the Honeywell he was embarrassed to find that he was something of a celebrity. Though he had been away for almost a year, nothing much had basically changed. Partridge still was in a sour mood. Charlie Smith still was arriving late for work because of the doggone Hudson Tubes.

At half past twelve Alex Carpenter took him to lunch at the Century Club. Alex's iced Gibson brought a small lament from him: His wife wanted to go to Arizona for vacation while he wanted to go to Maine, so they would go to Arizona. Then he brightened.

"Martin, may I put in your name for membership in Century?"

He did not really care about it, but he pretended that he did.

"I have some news for you. Larry Sprague is resigning. He's going back to Washington. We're making you head of the Asia department. Your salary is being raised to eighteen thousand."

With growing dismay Martin realized that he did not really care about that either. But he thought, *I owe it to Jane,* and put on, for Alex's benefit, a convincing display of pleasure and enthusiasm.

On Alex's many visits while Martin had been recuperating at home, he never had tired of questioning endlessly about Martin's experiences with Francis in Pusan. Now he resumed it again, asking, in effect, *What was it really like?*

Martin said, "The first day you interviewed me about a job here you expressed a viewpoint about a parish ministry that I'd never thought of before. You said it was such a *housekeeping* job. And it is, of course, in the sense of detail, detail repeated again and again endlessly. Well, that's really what life was for Francis and me in Pusan. . . ."

As Martin talked on, he realized that he rather liked that parish housekeeping work. Maybe it was what he missed since quitting a pastorate. Maybe he missed it even more than preaching.

After a while Alex said, "I never got a very clear picture of what the Jesuits contributed to the effort before everything was merged under UN relief."

"They contributed," Martin said.

"As much as the foundation?"

There it was again, the familiar old story of rivalry between Catholic and Protestant.

"I'll bet they didn't," Alex said, "because they couldn't exercise total control. We ran into the same problem with them a couple of years ago on a project in Latin America. But you handled it very well, Martin. You never let Reardon take over. . . ."

It was depressing. Alex missed the entire point of what Francis and he had been trying to accomplish.

Over coffee Alex thought of something he had forgotten to mention. One of the foundation trustees who was a member of the famed church known as the Cathedral thought it would be a nice idea if Martin spoke there late in September.

Suddenly Martin *was* pleased.

"You don't have to if you don't want to," Alex continued. "You know the head preacher has retired, and they're looking around for a successor. They're taking their time and seeking a variety of Sunday services till they settle on a man. Don't worry, you aren't expected to preach a traditional sermon. Burt put it to me candidly. He thought it would be nice to give the foundation a little plug and have you discuss the subject of Korean relief that many people are interested in at present."

After Martin returned to the office, he phoned Jane, who sounded alarmed and asked, "Are you all *right?*"

"Of course. I just had a bit of interesting news. I'm going to be invited to preach at the Cathedral next month."

"Marty, how *wonderful!*"

But wait, he told himself, that was not the news he had intended to report to her. "I had lunch with Alex Carpenter. He says we're getting a two thousand raise and I'm being put in charge of the Asia department."

"That's really grand."

In her use of superlatives, he recalled, "grand" usually was slightly below "wonderful."

Lance phoned Martin one Friday morning late in August. He and his wife had come up from his church on the Main Line and were staying at the Pierre.

"Marty, I have some alarming news."

"Alarming? What's up?"

"Well—exciting. But somehow alarming to me. I'm preaching at the Cathedral on Sunday. You know they're looking for a new preaching minister, as they call it, and—well, I'm a candidate."

"Lance, congratulations."

"That's the way Esther feels. She knows some people who seem to, uh, carry some weight there. And they tell her my chances are . . . very good. But I'll admit to you I'm a little scared. I'm used to knowing my audience. And they say there's such a great cross section of people there that—Well, my sermon is all prepared, but I'm worried."

Martin, not mentioning that he would speak there in another month himself, tried to encourage him. He invited Esther and him to dinner, but they had an engagement.

"Marty," Lance said before he hung up, "I hope you and Jane can be there on Sunday."

They went gladly.

Whenever Martin went to the Cathedral, he asked an usher to seat him as far forward as possible in the huge church. Yet no matter how far forward he sat, he always felt that the preacher was far removed. He felt the same that Sunday. Gazing up at Lance, wearing his gown with its flaming hood of a Doctor of Divinity, he had a twinge of envy. When he himself stood up there to speak a month thence, he would not be a serious contender for the post because he had quit the ministry. But Lance, with his reputation of being an outstanding preacher, very probably would be chosen the next preaching minister.

Lance had spoken for less than a minute when Martin began to worry about him. The acoustics of the Cathedral were perfect, yet the size of the church impelled Lance to speak too loudly. Seeing his audience so distant from him, he began to gesture too widely. Martin's brow grew damp in sympathy with him. He had fallen into the worst trap a preacher could tumble into: He was overawed by his surroundings. Worse, he was totally unsure of his audience. In his effort to say something to everyone, his message became bland and homogenized. As a result, he said nothing to anyone.

Martin was relieved when the service ended. On the way home by subway he asked Jane what she had thought of Lance's sermon.

She said, "He needs his old Holy Ghost Writer from Upton, P.A."

Tubby telephoned from Boston that afternoon. His voice, heard so soon after Lance's, surprised Martin, and his message was somehow vaguely disturbing. Two weeks thence he was preaching at the Cathedral. Martin insisted that he and Eunice

stay at the apartment. Then he told Tubby they had heard
Lance preach at the Cathedral that very morning.

"Oh?" Tubby sounded crestfallen. "He has the reputation
of being a powerhouse of a preacher. I guess that takes care of
me."

"Don't dash your hopes so fast," Martin replied. "We didn't
hear much power in his house this morning."

After hanging up, he returned to the board game he had
been playing with Kathy. Lance Bishop—Tubby Larsen—
Martin Judson. After so many years there was a disturbing
echo in current events.

The board game was a simple one, with the roll of dice determining the movement of pieces through various hazards to
the goal of winning. But thinking about the Cathedral, Martin moved his piece erroneously.

"Daddy, you can't do that," Kathy told him. "You aren't
beyond the Garden Gate yet, so you can't move into the Vale of
Tears."

Beyond the garden gate.

In the ensuing days he decided on that phrase as the title
of his sermon at the Cathedral. How worthwhile was a religion
practiced safely, snugly, smugly in one's own backyard? One
must go beyond the garden gate into the hazards of the world
to test and, thereby, find faith. And must you necessarily find
a vale of tears? One who had done it was Francis Xavier Reardon
of the Society of Jesus. . . .

The prospect of speaking once more from the pulpit challenged and yet troubled Martin. What did preaching accomplish for any but the one who expressed himself? Oh, those
dull faces! Oh, those difficult Christians! No wonder Saint
Anthony had preferred to preach to the fishes and Saint Francis
to his little brothers the birds.

Soon after Tubby and Eunice arrived at the apartment on
Friday afternoon, Tubby said, "Marty, I'm awful worried
about this coming Sunday."

"We're going out for a walk," Martin told him. "I want to talk to you."

As they walked, Martin described the mistakes Lance had made in his sermon at the Cathedral.

"Now you listen to me, Tubby, and do exactly what I tell you. Your whole attitude—the way you've got to start thinking—is that you don't give a damn about that Cathedral post. You have a mighty good pulpit and reputation in Boston. Why should you care to move? So you're going to give 'em in New York just what you give 'em in Boston. Confidence. A serene manner. Keep your voice down. No fancy gestures. No clever changes of pace. Just concentrate on your message and preach it to Eunice, Jane, and me down toward the front of the church. *Concentrate on your message.*"

"But all of a sudden, Marty, my message is beginning to seem awfully . . . pale."

"What is it?"

"It's a development of thought from the Beatitudes."

"Good."

"But *everybody* preaches on the Beatitudes."

"I said *good*," Martin replied. "The Beatitudes are one of the most fascinating passages in Scripture. It's going to go fine."

And it did. Tubby preached as Martin had urged him to. His spirit, as well as what he said, brought him the rapt attention and respect of the large congregation.

That afternoon, after Tubby and Eunice left for Boston, Martin began to revise his sermon.

It became the story of Francis Xavier Reardon, Jesuit priest, who had gone far beyond the garden gate in Korea, and it would be told to a congregation of Protestants by a close friend who never would use once the first person singular or plural. Because it was a true story of religious faith, it required a text. One came readily to Martin from the Apostle Paul's letter to the Galatians:

"For I through the law died unto the law, that I might live unto God. I have been crucified with Christ; and it is no longer

I that live, but Christ liveth in me. And that life which I now live in the flesh I live in faith, the faith which is in the Son of God, who loved me, and gave himself up for me."

Once it had a text, it could not be merely a lecture. Once it had become informed by the wisdom of the Apostle, it began to be illuminated by God and His Son, in whom both Paul and Reardon had believed. Nevertheless, this would be implicit and inferred, rather than explicit and preached. Martin was simply the narrator, the instrument for the telling. Definitely there would be no appeal for ecumenical bargaining, no cant about the brotherhood of man, for that, too, was implicit in the message. Reardon had been a Roman Catholic, and the church bulletin identified Martin:

"Martin Judson, for many years a Baptist clergyman, is now an executive with the Honeywell Foundation in New York. His work with the foundation took him last year to Korea, where he was associated with Father Francis X. Reardon of the Society of Jesus."

Before the service that Sunday morning he had coffee with the associate and assistant ministers of the Cathedral. Declining to wear clerical robe, he went on wearing a plain dark suit. For a moment he was scared, but then the music of the mighty organ composed him.

His sermon was unlike Tubby's or Lance's. Perhaps some in the congregation did not think it a sermon at all. Nevertheless, he had never had more rapt attention when speaking from a pulpit. And that was all he knew; it was the best any preacher could hope to know.

When he left the pulpit, he was sweating. The speaker at the Cathedral did not mingle with the people but went into a small room. It reminded Martin of an actor's dressing room, making him uncomfortable because it smacked of the theatrical trade, whereas he hoped that preaching was something more than an actor's performance. The associate minister was there, making him think of the producer who came to flatter the star no matter how bad the show had been.

Martin had heard of the associate's executive ability. His role at the Cathedral was like that of the executive officer of a ship: He ran it; he could fulfill any function in it. But Cathedral tradition denied him the high command when the "preaching minister" retired. Did he resent the fact? Did he want it—or did he care? It was impossible to tell, and that was why he was known as the ideal associate.

Jane came in with the children. To Martin's embarrassment there were tears in her eyes. Turning her back to the associate, she silently moved her lips: "The best ever!" Others came in, speaking kindly to him.

Then Alex Carpenter and two of the foundation trustees appeared. Alex looked at him oddly and said, "Martin—well, I'll just be damned. I had no idea you were a great preacher. I didn't know you were running for office here."

All that the old philosopher of Ecclesiastes, who could not possibly have been a preacher, had said about vanity was absolutely true. So Martin reflected later.

Flattered by the praise and attention his sermon brought him, he wished he could preach every Sunday. The congratulations he had received when he became head of the Asia section had meant nothing to him, but now he was pleased when a few people said they had heard he had preached quite a sermon at the Cathedral. He cherished a remark of Carpenter's that several members of the Cathedral who were tired of traditional sermons fancied him for preaching minister, even though he had been out of the ministry for a time.

Vanity was, of course, the wellspring of ambition's murky pools. As the days passed, he found himself increasingly bored with his work at the foundation: too much paper shuffling; too many decisions which should not have to be reached with such tedious formalities; nothing creative about it. Preaching, on the other hand, was satisfyingly creative. Furthermore, and even more important, a preacher lived and worked close to people, whereas a foundation executive seemed to live and work only with programs. Why had he quit the ministry? It would be wonderful if he could return to it with a single vaulting leap that carried him into one of the most prominent pastorates in America.

His wish to race in the Cathedral sweepstakes was whipped onward by a letter he received a couple of days after his sermon. It came from the chairman of trustees of a large church in Fairfield County, Connecticut, who had heard him at the Cathedral and invited him to preach the same sermon at his church. Martin accepted. Certainly he could not be accused of doing it for money, for in both engagements he specified that his honorarium go to Korean relief.

On that Sunday he rented a car, and he and Jane drove to Fairfield County. The community and the church, which was searching for a new minister, reminded them of Sylvia and Central Baptist. After the service they went to dinner at a country club with several members who subjected Martin to a mild, good-natured pulpit flirtation. Were they serious? How did he feel about it? What did Jane think?

He asked her while they were driving home, and she replied, "You want to return to the ministry?"

He hesitated. "I'd like to go to the Cathedral."

"That's like a man who wants to be President but can't be bothered with serving in Congress."

"I've served my time in Congress." Then he frowned. "You're saying I'm thinking of the power and glory of Martin Judson. And you're right. How long does a man stay with anything without becoming bored and a bit corrupted by his own ego? But what do you think of that church?"

"The same as you. It's like Sylvia. But we could be happy there if we accepted things exactly as they are. God must be as interested in the rich of Fairfield County as the poor of Pusan."

"I think you've got it the wrong way around," Martin said. "Are the rich of Fairfield as aware of their own frailty as the poor of Pusan—and therefore as receptive to faith in God? Some are, I'm sure. But I think most feel they've got it made

all by themselves. Why should they want to change anything?
If the weary commuter from Madison Avenue sometimes questions his values, I'll bet he usually tries to drown his doubts on
a New Haven bar car. It's the way his experience has taught
him to act. It's easier than taking his doubts to church."

Jane asked, "Are you tired of the Honeywell?"

"Sort of. But we were talking about Fairfield County.
Would you like to live there?"

"Only if you would. As best I understand you and me, we're
people who want to be involved with the lives of others. Maybe
we want to be helpful. Or maybe we just want to change things
around into idealistic patterns that never can be. Anyway, that's
the way we are."

He touched her hand on the seat and said, yes, that was the
way they were.

She said, "I like New York. That feeling of vital life. But sometimes, when I'm not with you, I get lonely and bored. No real
friends such as we had in Upton and Sylvia. No real . . . *involvement,* except with the children. Those afternoons I spend
at charity work for the church or the hospital—that's for the
birds. And I know you're up at the old Honeywell making pots
of money for us and being bored because you can't feel involved with pushing those papers around. We can't have our
cake and eat it, too. The answer is some sort of compromise. And
I don't think the answer is in dreams of glory about winning
first place at the Cathedral. Even if they offered you that job,
Marty, I'm not sure it's the right place for you."

He decided he would begin putting out feelers toward Fairfield County.

But one did not awaken readily from dreams of glory. The
next day Lance phoned him from Pennsylvania; for the first
time in Martin's memory he sounded hurt, angry, in despair.

"Marty, they've passed me by."

"They?"

"The Cathedral. I can't understand it. They gave every indication that *I was the man.* It seems to me my whole . . . ca-

reer has been aimed at going to that church. I've decided to quit
the ministry and—"

"Hey, wait a minute!" Martin exclaimed. "Slow it down a
bit, Lance. You'd be miserable if you ever quit the ministry."

"Well, *you* aren't," Lance replied. "You seem perfectly
happy to me. And you have a really interesting job. Tell me,
are there any openings at the Honeywell—or any other foundation you could recommend?"

"Nothing at present, Lance. Now you simmer down a bit."

Lance's tone became aggrieved. "You're holding out on me."

"What do you mean?"

"From the rumor I just heard, *you* are the leading contender
for the Cathedral job if you want it. Your sermon wowed 'em."

"Lance, honestly, this is news to me. . . ." And at the same
time he thought elatedly, *Boy, oh, boy!*

After Martin hung up, he started to call Jane, then checked
himself. He would keep the rumor to himself. For she had
said, "Even if they offered you that job, Marty, I'm not sure
it's the right place for you."

The day after Lance's call he received a letter from an official
of Old Fourth Church in New York named Spencer Cook.
Cook, visiting friends in Fairfield County, had heard his sermon
there and wished he would preach at Old Fourth. Well, he
would not preach the same one, for he did not want possible
allies at the Cathedral, who might hear of his preaching again,
to think he was a one sermon man. Yes, he would preach at Old
Fourth—and start preparing a new sermon.

At least he could not be tempted by the pastorate of Old
Fourth, which had been vacant for almost a year. No clergyman
in his right mind would want it. In New York, that graveyard
of preachers, Old Fourth appeared the most dilapidated of
burial plots.

Once it had been renowned as a leading church of its democratic denomination. Around the turn of the century it had
been the pastorate of a famous preacher who lined up the
carriages around three city blocks and even attracted wor-

shipers all the way from Brooklyn. Again, in the days of Calvin Coolidge, its preacher had been a popular fellow who filled the church to overflowing twice on Sundays. But times had changed since then. Even the name of the church's denomination had changed.

The city had not so much grown as fled in many directions, leaving Old Fourth stranded on one of its main arteries. The prosperous residents of the brownstones which once surrounded it had left many years ago; inhabitants of surviving brownstones were a polyglot of roomers and boarders. Not a slum area, it was more like a wasteland where people lingered because they lacked the resources to move. There were many small businesses, prone to misfortune. There were office buildings, too, bleak and deserted on weekends. Thus, Old Fourth was locked in the decaying inner city.

The church itself was of hoary gray stone which aspired to a tall steeple. Within, it was like a huge cavern, encircled on three sides by deep galleries. Paint peeled from its ceiling, which vaulted so high that healing patchwork seemed out of the question. Dark walnut was everywhere, like a forest of somber despair, while elaborate stained-glass windows attested to the wealth and sentiments of members long departed. Adjoining this quaint edifice was a three-story brownstone castle once known as the Sunday-school building, a labyrinth of corridors and rooms which seemed to have been sealed off from human voices; it gave one a ghostly impression, a hint of ectoplasm.

That Sunday Spencer Cook greeted Martin in the dimly lighted keep which once had been the pastor's study. He was middle-aged, cheerful, his manner deliberate and courteous. With him were two members of the board of deacons; though aging men, they were too spry and alert to be artifacts of Old Fourth's vanished civilization. The three rigged Martin up with a small neck microphone and explained where he had to plug in at the pulpit. How the preachers of the days before audio had managed to make themselves heard in the cavernous auditorium was a mystery to all.

Cook, who had been serving as one of various lay ministers of the church after the assistant pastor resigned, went to the platform with Martin to conduct the worship service. The moment Martin stepped onto the platform he had an impulse to flee. In the vast auditorium, which could seat nearly one thousand, about one hundred persons were scattered. They appeared so distant from him that he was not sure he reached them.

Yet he must have. For it was the custom at Old Fourth to invite any who wished to meet the speaker to come forward after the service. Nearly fifty came to shake Martin's hand and speak with him. They were a diversity of people: old, young, middle-aged, a Puerto Rican family, a Negro couple, a Korean woman.

"I wonder where they come from and why," he said to Jane afterward. "That church is such an anachronism in these times —a monstrosity compared to the Cathedral."

A real monstrosity, Jane agreed.

On Monday evening Tubby telephoned from Boston. There was a curious lack of joy in his tone as he said, "Marty, we want you and Jane to know first. They offered me the job by phone this afternoon. . . . I wonder what I'm letting myself in for. . . ."

By ten o'clock in the evening Martin had rationalized his initial disappointment into a kind of relief that his foolish ambition at last had ended. He never had stood a chance of obtaining that job. He would put out feelers toward Fairfield County the very next day.

But he did not. He passed a busy day with a meeting of the foundation trustees, who knocked a program he greatly wished to start in India stone cold dead. Well, various bodies of trustees could not put him on the run forever. His mother's favorite maxim came to mind: Just redouble your effort.

On Wednesday Spencer Cook phoned and said there was something he wanted to discuss. On Friday Martin had lunch with him in the executive dining room of the bank where he was chief trust officer.

"I wonder," Cook said, "if you'd be interested in doing some preaching for us till we find the man we want."

"My job keeps me very busy," Martin said.

"Maybe you have a file of sermons you've preached in the past."

"I've stored filing cabinets in the basement of our apartment house. But I haven't looked into them in—well, it seems like years."

"We pay a hundred a Sunday for a guest preacher."

"I'm not exactly trying to make more money. Can Old Fourth afford that much?"

Cook sighed. "About all Old Fourth has is money. We're heavily endowed."

"Endowments!" Martin grimaced. "They can cause a lot of grief in this life."

"Yes, they can. Especially when they're tied to silly ideas. For instance, we have one large fund which can be used only for the preparation of meals served in the church. The last church supper—free, mind you—was held almost a year ago. Exactly thirty-seven people showed up."

"What do you hope to accomplish there, Mr. Cook?"

"The seemingly impossible. At least a few of us still do. The view of others was expressed by one of our trustees who said, 'Let's just blow up the damn place.' I grew up in Old Fourth. When our kids were coming along, we moved to Westchester. Once they were in college, my wife and I decided to move back to town. There was Old Fourth, where we'd met and married, going to seed. So you can see that some of my motives are sentimental. But there's more to it. Maybe just call it a citizen's moral duty to dig in on some important issue. I never felt that way in Westchester. All I did was gripe about the rising tax rates. But after we came back to New York, both Mary and I got interested in this problem of the decay of the inner city. It's a problem of government—not just municipal, but state and maybe federal, too. Yet it's also a problem for individual citizens—and especially for churches, I think. We want Old Fourth to be a vital force to the people in its area—and thereby make the area more vital, too. We've had a few ideas, but none of them seems to work. All recent ministers have become discouraged and quit. The pastor's salary isn't bad—fifteen thousand and parsonage. Lots of timeservers have been willing to jump at the money. But we don't want any of them. And we haven't been able yet to get an able and ambitious young man because our situation looks so hopeless. I guess the parsonage doesn't encourage a young man and his wife either."

"What's the matter with it?"

"It's an old brownstone around on the side street next door to the church." Cook smiled wanly. "It has twenty-eight rooms."

"Wow! Why not sell it and rent your preacher a decent apartment?"

"Can't be done. It's another gift. There's a provision that if it ever ceases to be used as the parsonage, then *another* trust from the same donor will be withdrawn. And we need the money, even though we don't want the doggone parsonage. A company that wants to put up another office building has offered us plenty for it, but nothing can be done. There are too many office buildings around anyway. Obviously they're destructive to the church. Still, we'd like to offer something to all those office workers that might bring some of them back to the church on Sundays. But nobody has come up with any constructive thoughts."

An idea occurred to Martin. "What sort of dining and recreation facilities does the church have?"

"The best of dining facilities in the basement. We can seat four hundred with a kitchen to match. No recreation facilities. There aren't enough of any age who want to . . . *recreate*."

"That dining fund—or whatever you call it—that you mentioned. Is it large?"

"Ridiculously. About seventy-five thousand and growing bigger. Gift of a senile woman before the Depression. It could almost float a full-time dietitian and small kitchen staff."

"Then why not let it do just that? At least try it for a while. Offer a good luncheon to office workers. Open up some of those musty old rooms upstairs. Reading rooms. Put in some games."

Cook stared at him. "A food handler's license means you're in business. And then you're no longer a tax-exempt organization."

"You wouldn't need a license if you didn't charge. Just a contribution basket."

Cook continued to stare at him. "And every freeloader in Manhattan dropping in a dime for a seventy-five-cent meal."

"I don't think people are quite that bad over a period of time. They shame themselves out of it—or others do. At worst you'd eventually use up that useless fund doing precisely what the donor wished. And meanwhile, you'd move Old Fourth a few steps out of its graveyard."

Cook lifted his coffee cup and set it down again. "Mr. Judson, will you preach for us for a few Sundays?"

"Well," Martin said, "I'll try it a couple of times."

He told Jane about it that evening. "After dinner I'm going down in the basement and bring up some of those sermon files. It might help them out for a couple of weeks. But the situation there is really hopeless. Don't you agree?"

"It sounds so, Marty."

"Imagine a parsonage with twenty-*eight* rooms!"

"Impossible."

"What they need is a young man with lots of get-up-and-go. No seasoned man with any sense would go there."

She looked at him, smiling, and said, "You're absolutely right."

 *Six*

KATHY called it the haunted house. She had read about haunted houses and adored them, but never had seen one till they moved into the parsonage of Old Fourth, in the spring of 1952. It rained the day they moved; Mother said it always did. Skipping school that day, she and Abe explored the adorable haunted house till evening.

From the busy street you could enter by the basement doorway or up a steep flight of stone stairs to the first floor, which was confusing because it really was the second floor. The kitchen was at the rear of the basement, and ridiculously, the dining room was *upstairs* over the kitchen. There was a big pantry off the dining room which was connected with the kitchen downstairs by a marvelous invention called a dumbwaiter. She gave Abe several rides up and down it before he tried to give her one and she got stuck midway and Father and one of the moving men had to rescue her.

Outside the kitchen was a little backyard jungle of spindly trees and weeds and human skulls and stuff hemmed in by a wall. She and Abe got pretty wet exploring that jungle in the rain and hunting snakes and a wildcat they would try to tame in time.

The stairs were wonderful, going up and up, as if to heaven itself. There were two huge living rooms, besides the dining room, on the floor above the basement. On the floor above *that* the rooms were smaller but still pretty big: her own bedroom, and one for Abe, and one for Mother and Father, and two for guests, besides two bathrooms. Mother said the house ended *there*. But it didn't; there were two more floors above, the rooms getting smaller, the top floor having a big corridor which ran the length of the house. It was a perfect runway for her on roller skates and Abe on his tricycle until he crashed into a wall and nearly killed himself.

The next day she had to go to school, where no one believed she lived in a haunted house of twenty-eight rooms. But the day after that, a Saturday, was even better than Thursday. Father introduced Abe and her to Mr. Treadway, the pleasant Negro who was head custodian of Old Fourth, and he let them explore the church. It was a fantastic place, so vast that around ten o'clock she led Abe home and made them peanut butter sandwiches, which she told Mother they would eat on their daylong hike. They played hide-and-seek. Then she found she could walk *all* the way around the galleries on pews, without once touching the floor, by making daring leaps. In the afternoon, when Mr. Treadway came looking for them, they hid behind crates of old hymnals. It took Father to find them.

The house was haunted by life, not ghosts. Something always was happening. Father and Mr. Cook discovered that the "custodial funds" entitled Mother to a helper, so Mrs. Bentley moved into quarters in the basement and took charge of the cooking and cleaning. Then Father brought them a beautiful beagle puppy she named Jefferson. The understanding was that she must walk him morning and evening. While walking Jefferson, she met and fell in love with Adolph Grunmeyer, who, when not in school, carried orders to the office buildings from his father's delicatessen.

Then Mr. Danielson, a man from Yale, became Father's

assistant and moved into quarters on the third floor. He had curly hair and a voice like Sinatra's; naturally she fell out of love with Adolph and into love with him. Soon a kitchenette was installed on the third floor for him, so that he seldom ate with them. It was sad. But before long she found a brighter side: Whenever Mr. Danielson was away, she and the girl-friends who often stayed over night with her could use his kitchenette to cook divine concoctions.

After Mrs. Bentley arrived and began fussing and doing, they had more company than ever. Uncle Tubby, who had a church uptown, and Aunt Eunice came often with the three little monsters who were their sons. So did Mr. Cook and his wife, a jolly woman who became a close friend of Mother's. Another frequent luncheon guest was Mr. Carpenter, who used to be Father's boss and who became one of the first new members Father took into the church.

In their second spring Father took it on himself to clean up the backyard jungle and build a patio where Mother planted flowers. When the weather was good, he liked to prepare his sermons there. He liked to be outdoors so much it was a wonder he was content to live in the city. He bought Grandpa's old farm in Vermont, and early each July they packed themselves into a rented car and their belongings into a U-haul trailer and headed north, not returning till late August. As the summers passed, Kathy realized that Father and Abe liked Vermont much more than Mother and she. It was so *dead* there. When they returned home, Mother always said, "Well, back to Grand Central." She said it cheerfully, and Kathy knew she was glad to be back where things happened.

There was as much life in the church as at home. Father was always thinking up things for people to do. Sometimes his ideas worked and sometimes they didn't, but he never stopped try-ing. His most interesting idea to Kathy was the noon cafeteria luncheon hour for office workers, which went on five days a week for nine months of each year. The church grew gradually.

"Nothing dramatic," Father said, "but at least I can hear it breathing now."

On Kathy's fourteenth birthday she announced an intention to become a minister. But Father and Mother said forget it, the field was overcrowded. Nevertheless, later that year Father let her become a substitute Sunday-school teacher for kids of Abe's age. By her fifteenth birthday she had decided to be a model.

Her wish to be a model lasted only a couple of months until it was drowned by a decision that swept her like a tidal wave: She would be a physician! She harped on it so much that Father finally talked to her seriously about it.

"I don't want to be an *ordinary* doctor," she told him. "I want to be a medical *missionary*. I want to go to the Belgian Congo or someplace and *help* people."

Father said that was okay with him, but she'd better bear down in the science department. Meanwhile, he found ways for her to be of help in the church and neighborhood. She took on a Sunday-school class of youngsters full time; she was a pillar of the young people's society. More satisfying to her was a part-time job at the YWCA local branch working with a couple of women who were trying to tame a wild bunch of girls and didn't know exactly how to go about it. Eventually she enticed a few of the girls to Old Fourth by way of the parsonage.

A couple of school friends needled her about "that do-good kick," saying her father was trying to turn her into a religious prude. They did not understand that Father and Mother and she never sat around and talked about religion. They had grace before meals, she said her private prayers, and no one looked forward to the Second Coming or pondered the plans of God in daily affairs. Over the years, when she had asked Father and Mother questions about such matters as God and the hereafter, they gave her sensible answers, or said they didn't know, or even replied with another question. Her school friends failed to recognize that religion was not a ceremony of piety, but a satisfying way of life.

Abe could not understand why first grade should be so different from kindergarten, where he had had great fun. But in first grade at the public school four blocks from home he found himself, for some curious reason, among enemies.

Fats Goldberg started it. "Preacher's son!" he yelled at Abe the very first day. Abe was pleased that Pop was a preacher. But Fats was mad about it. Abe could not understand.

"Preacher's kid, dirty lid!" Others took up the chant. It took Abe several days to realize that Pop and Fats' father were enemies. Fats' father ran a restaurant a block from Old Fourth, and Pop had become his rival when he put the church in the restaurant business.

In his third week of first grade he was walking to school one morning when Fats, Tony Ruffio, and several other boys jumped him from an alley. He fought gamely, but they were too many for him. They tied him up with rope and left him in the alley, yelling, "Dirty goy, preacher's boy!" After a while a garbage man untied him and helped him to his feet.

He started home, wailing with rage. But soon he stopped crying and turned back to school.

He was nearly an hour late when he walked into his classroom, where Miss Silverstein was writing figures on the blackboard. Picking up a book, he walked to Fats Goldberg's desk, cried, "Fat rat!" and brought the book down on Fats' head with all his strength.

Miss Silverstein tried to arbitrate their dispute with fairness and understanding. But Jim McCoy, who sat behind Abe, offered him greater understanding. Jim explained that Fats was a Jew, meaning a kike, and Tony was an Italian, meaning a wop—and that all kikes and wops were bad people. It was information that Abe accepted gratefully in his feud. . . .

Mom and Pop were badly upset when they got the story from old Silverstein. Abe never had mentioned it himself because he didn't want to be yellow. But old Silverstein squealed on him after he called her a kike.

Pop hadn't realized Fats' father was his enemy. He didn't

know what to do about it. He kept walking around the library and saying Jim was all wrong in his ideas. But Pop did not have to go to school every day and take it from a bunch of rats.

Though the schoolwork came easily to Abe, he hated the place and did not try hard. After Jim moved away, he felt he had no friend. There was no place to play games; Kathy and her school friends had no time for him. Mom finally put him afternoons in something called a play school. The kids there already were friends with one another, so he was wary of them. He did not like it and begged Mom and Pop not to make him go there anymore.

The one thing he enjoyed that winter was building model airplanes with Pop. The first kit Pop brought home was fun, but it was just one to look at. "Gee," Abe said, "couldn't we make one that would *fly?*"

So the very next day Pop brought him a kit from which they fashioned a monoplane of paper and balsa wood, with a long rubber band that you twisted to make the propeller turn.

"Hey," Abe said the evening they finished it. "Where are we going to fly it? It's snowing outside."

"Well now"—Pop thought for a bit—"I have an idea."

They went next door to the church. Pop turned on all the lights in the big auditorium where Henry Warton, the organist, was rehearsing.

"What sad music!" Abe said. "That's no music to fly airplanes to."

"I agree with you, Abe." Pop called to Mr. Warton, "Hey, Henry, could you knock off Bach for a while. Do you know 'Stars and Stripes Forever'?"

Mr. Warton said he did and began to play that wonderful tune while Abe and Pop climbed to the top of the rear balcony.

"Contact!" Pop cried.

"Contact!" Abe cried.

Off into the blue climbed the great airplane while the organ music soared with it and Abe yelled with pleasure.

Abe ran downstairs and brought back the airplane. The

second flight was even better than the first. The plane made a complete circle of the auditorium and came down toward a perfect landing on the pulpit. Mr. Warton was playing the "Stars and Stripes" with both hands and feet and watching the airplane over a shoulder while Abe and Pop cheered when all of them became aware that two women had entered the auditorium.

One of them was old lady Wolff, a real pain. When Abe and Pop went down to get the airplane, she showed right away she didn't like what they were doing.

"*Reverend* Judson." She introduced the other old lady. "I saw the church lighted and brought her in to show her our *sanctuary*. Oh, and this is the preacher's son. . . ."

After they had gone, Abe said, "Pop, I don't want to be called the preacher's son. Don't let them call me that."

"I didn't used to like it either, Abe, when they called me that instead of by my name. But don't pay any attention to it, and after a while they'll get over it."

"I wish you weren't a preacher," Abe said. "I wish you didn't have to work all the time. I wish we could just be together and fly airplanes."

Pop looked at him for a time. Then he called to Mr. Warton, "Music please, maestro!"

As they climbed together to the balcony for another flight, Abe asked, "Pop, what's a *sanctuary?*"

"Well, Abe, maybe it's a place where you can get out of the snow and fly airplanes. . . ."

"We have to enroll him in a private school," Jane told Martin that summer.

"Yes, I guess we do," Martin replied. "Abe has me stymied. He's bright, but he seems to be in perpetual conflict with others—and himself. I try to spend all the time with him I can. Is it possible a minister has less time for his family than other men do?"

Jane smiled. "It's not only possible. It's true."

"On principle I don't like the idea of private schools," Martin said. "I think for a minister to send his children to private schools raises a kind of . . . ethical problem. A basic element of Christianity in this country must be a sense of democracy and—"

"Principle! Basic elements!" Jane was impatient with him. "Marty, the only question is the practical one. Can we afford to send the children to private schools?"

Martin looked startled. "Why, I guess so. Can't we? But there's no point in sending Kathy to private school. She's right at the top of her class in public school, she has friends, and she is perfectly happy."

"There's no reason—yet," Jane said. "But I think there will be advantages of having her transfer to a private school in town her last year or two before college. I even have one picked. Be honest now. You want the children to go to Ivy League colleges, don't you?"

"Yes. But only because I want the children to have the best possible educations."

"I agree, Marty. But how many ministers these days can afford to send their children to Ivy League colleges? And isn't it ironic that most Ivy League colleges began as divinity schools?"

Once Abe was enrolled in private school, Jane began trying harder than ever to save money. Martin's salary then was fifteen thousand, besides free housing in the monstrous parsonage and the services of Mrs. Bentley paid for by the church. Nevertheless, it was not easy.

Once, after a meeting of the women's guild, Mrs. Wolff said to Jane, "Of course, a minister's family gets considerations."

"Considerations?" Jane rapped out. "None that *I* know of in my life as a minister's wife."

There were no considerations from the insurance company when Martin paid the premiums on the fifty thousand of life insurance he carried, and certainly none from Internal Revenue. Jane paid at the same rate at markets and department stores as everyone else. When they occasionally went to the theater, the box office did not offer them a cut rate because Martin was a clergyman. There were no reduced tuitions at the private schools through which Abe progressed unhappily, none at the private school which Kathy attended in her senior year.

Somehow, by working hard at it, Jane managed to save money, however. She and Martin were delighted when Kathy won a scholarship to Wellesley College—not because she was a minister's daughter, but because she was a brilliant student. With the aid of the scholarship, they were able to send her there.

That September morning in 1958 when they put Kathy on a train for Wellesley began gloomily for Martin and Jane. They would miss her so. But the day grew worse. In the afternoon, Spencer Cook, playing golf on a Westchester course, fell dead on the seventeenth green.

His death was not just the passing of a close friend; Spencer had been the most benign and intelligent of those who worked with Martin at Old Fourth. In the preceding year two older, helpful men had died; in August Alex Carpenter, of great aid in the church, had resigned from the Honeywell and retired to Arizona.

After burying Spencer on Friday afternoon Martin came home deeply depressed. He and Jane were eating dinner when he realized that he had not finished preparing his sermon for Sunday; indeed, he scarcely had begun to prepare it in the course of a hectic week. Immediately after dinner he went to the church office, took off his coat and tie, rolled up his shirt sleeves, and put a sheet of paper in his typewriter. (Jane said he went about the preparation of a sermon as if it were an athletic event.)

The theme he had chosen a week previously was one of joy, an optimistic view of life. But Spencer was dead, and joy had gone with him. The theme was impossible now. He could not preach such a sermon on Sunday. He paced around his desk for a time, thinking—or trying to think. But no creative thought came to him. His mind wallowed in a maze of Jell-o.

Turning to the filing cabinets at last, he began to leaf through past sermons. With amazement that mounted into panic, he could not find a single old sermon that would fit the purpose of this coming somber Sunday. How could one who prided himself in his preaching ever have uttered so much drivel?

Soon after midnight Jane phoned from the parsonage and asked, "Are you all right?"

"Yes," he replied irritably. "No. I'm hung up."

"Get a night's rest." Her tone was soothing. "It will work out in the morning. Come home and have a cup of Ovaltine."

"Ovaltine!" Had Washington considered Ovaltine before he crossed the Delaware?

Eventually he went home, and it seemed to him that he did not sleep all night. In the morning the problem was as insoluble as it had been the previous evening.

Toward noon he telephoned Tubby and said, "Well, it finally happened."

"What did?"

"Murder. The total mental block." He went on to explain the hang-up of all hang-ups.

"How about your assistant taking over? Oh, I forgot, you're without one again. Can I send you a boy to fill in?"

"No. I have to go on. Spencer Cook's death, you know. It would look—"

"Yes, I understand." Tubby was deeply concerned. "Shall I go down there, or do you want to come up here?"

"I'll go up there. That's where the supply is. Where do you keep 'em—at the church or at home?"

"At home."

When Martin arrived, Tubby looked at him compassionately and said, "It happened to me once in Thornton."

"Well, it *never* happened to me before," Martin said. "Where are they?"

"In the basement. Do you want some lunch first?"

"No, thanks."

They went to the basement, where Tubby opened a filing cabinet. "Maybe I can make a couple of suggestions." He flipped through the folders. "Try this, Marty. Sit down over there and take a look at it while I keep hunting."

Martin read a couple of pages of the sermon and realized it was not right for now. "No," he said.

Tubby looked around him. "What's wrong with it?"

"Too . . . optimistic. Too—take a look at it yourself."

"Okay. Try this one."

In a moment Tubby looked up from the sermon Martin had been reading and said, "I agree with you. I don't see how I could preach such hogwash. How is that one?"

"*Mmmm,*" Martin said.

"Let me see it. Here, I'll get you another. . . ." In a moment Tubby said with consternation, "This won't do at all." As time passed and he glanced over old sermon after sermon, he became deeply dejected. "Marty, it seems to me I'm the lousiest preacher who ever lived."

Martin tried to encourage him. "No, these really are good, Tubby. They just don't fit the mood that seems appropriate for tomorrow. I'm hungry."

Tubby led the way upstairs to the kitchen, where Martin made himself a thick sandwich of ham, cheese, and tomato and poured himself a glass of milk. As he began wolfing the sandwich at the kitchen table, he asked, "What are you preaching tomorrow?"

Tubby stared at him for a long time and finally rose and went to his study. He returned with a triple-spaced typed script which he placed in front of Martin silently. It began: "There seems to be some contention over whether an Italian or a Scandinavian was the discoverer of America. . . ." And it went on to discuss the role of discoverers, the nature of discovery as related to faith, as well as the secular world.

When Martin had finished reading it, he tapped the script with the back of a hand and said, "That's just about the best sermon I've ever seen. I'm not kidding you. Look it over yourself."

"I don't *want* to." Tubby's tone was peevish. "I don't even want to think about it till I get up in the pulpit tomorrow." Then he resumed staring at Martin. "Does this sermon fit your need?"

"Yes."

"Could we—" Tubby hesitated. "You know. People can't be in two churches at the same time."

"No. It wouldn't be . . . ethical." Martin grimaced. "What I'm doing isn't ethical anyway. But I regret to say, Tubby, the only reason I won't steal it from you is that we might be caught."

"How?"

"Every once in a while the *Times* or the *Tribune* sends a reporter around to cover a sermon. I'm sure they do it more frequently with you than me. They seldom publish anything. I think editors hand out such assignments to make some poor reporter pay penance for something or other. But can you imagine the scandal if two reporters returned from two churches with the same sermon?"

Tubby rubbed his jaw. "I hadn't thought about that." After a while he said, "I wonder what the Freeport Flash is preaching tomorrow out in Chicago."

Martin recalled that Lance, having decided not to take a foundation job, now was packing them in at a leading church; old friends had begun to call him the Bishop of Chicago. "He's as ebullient as ever, I hear, after his nose dive over failing to get this spot."

Tubby said, "Just for the heck of it, let's call him up and ask him."

"Sounds crazy," Martin said. "But this is a crazy day. And I wouldn't mind hearing the Bishop's voice. I'll pay for the call."

"No. I still owe you money for calls I made from that farmer's house when we visited you folks in Vermont last summer. Get on the extension."

From the telephone extension in the hall Martin could see

Tubby at his desk phone. Lance came on like a burst of tropical sunrise. He was delighted to hear their voices. What was cooking? When he learned of Martin's plight, he was both sympathetic and amazed.

"Marty, help yourself to mine. Got a pad and pencil handy? Now listen to this. . . ." Then he began to preach about the great big wonderful world God had created with its golden opportunities for everyone.

Martin stared in at Tubby, who stared back at him and at last pinched his nose between thumb and forefinger and shook his head. It must have been an expensive toll call, for it was impossible to turn the Bishop off once they had turned him on.

"That was the poorest idea of the day," Tubby said after they hung up.

Martin realized he had fooled around long enough. He selected one of Tubby's old sermons, told him it would come out right, and thanked him profusely before he left. On the subway home, however, he knew the sermon was not the right one for him. He had taken it only because he did not want to trouble Tubby further.

When he reached home, Jane followed him into the library. There he closed his eyes, stretched out a hand, turned around twice, and stepped toward the book shelves.

"What are you doing?" she asked.

"Preparing my sermon." Opening his eyes, he saw that his fingers rested on Paul Tillich's *The New Being*. Perhaps he had known where to find it even with his eyes closed.

Selecting one of the twenty-three sermons in the volume, he sat down at the typewriter and began to copy it, changing only a few phrases here and there, tightening his lips firmly as he thought of his arrant piracy. After the crime had been accomplished, Jane asked if he was ready for the dinner already long delayed.

"In a couple of minutes," he said. Then he wrote Dr. Tillich, in care of Harvard University, a full confession of his crime and the circumstances that had led him to commit it. (The gracious reply he received later did not salve his conscience much.)

Nearly a score of people praised the sermon after the Sunday service.

On Monday he began to prepare his next sermon. Setting other matters aside, he toiled at it for three days. Its theme concerned various phases of human responsibility, which he developed elaborately.

The following Sunday, as he began to deliver the sermon, he knew suddenly that he had developed his theme too elaborately. With growing horror he sensed the congregation falling away from him. Old Mrs. Baxter fell asleep. Mr. Phinney began to pick his nose. There were glazed expressions everywhere.

Martin skipped two pages of his text. But he had structured the monster so carefully that the next point made little sense unless one had digested the point which Martin had skipped. He felt like a locomotive engineer whose throttle was stuck at full open, plunging ahead, his passengers flying off in all directions. Now he was entirely alone, talking to himself, in the vast and empty auditorium. Even Jane was glancing about nervously. And the sermon still had eight pages to go.

He never could recover the attention of the four hundred people out there. Or could he? Coming in the text was a phrase about the mighty fortress of faith.

"The mighty fortress of God," he said, and paused. "The mighty fortress of God," he repeated, but no one was paying any attention to him.

Tilting up his head, he sang in his strong baritone, "A mighty fortress is our God, a bulwark never failing."

It had the effect of a bombburst.

"We're accustomed to hearing that phrase in the old hymn which I won't sing for you in its entirety," Martin said. Then he continued to deliver his sermon measuredly.

To the end he had the rapt attention, if not the understand-

ing, of the congregation. Perhaps they thought he might burst
into song again.

Martin fought a sense of depression that fall. He was forty-
three, but sometimes he felt as old as Methuselah.

It was, he knew, the approximate age of the ministerial men-
opause—a time of life that was a crisis point for a clergyman.
He had seen it happen to other ministers—a restiveness, a
wondering whether they were in the right field. And now it
had happened to him.

He felt a creeping erosion in Old Fourth that reflected the
creeping erosion of life in the inner city. Commerce and the
arts gave New York the guise of vitality, but at its heart Martin
found a widespread wish for withdrawal from all the seemingly
insoluble problems of its ghettos, noise, dirt, its pervading
anonymity.

In every possible way he fought the erosion—by preaching
the best that he could, by pursuing personally every person
who showed the slightest interest in Old Fourth, by trying to
keep every member busy in some church job large or small, by
developing programs for young people who came in depress-
ingly few numbers. But sometimes, at the age of forty-three,
it all seemed futile.

That fall Martin had no prospects of finding an able assistant. To make matters worse, his capable secretary, Mrs. Snyder,
retired with her husband to North Carolina. Thus began a
long period of organizational anarchy in which young, not very
bright secretaries came and went.

The first of the secretaries who succeeded Mrs. Snyder was
absent on another of her long, mysterious errands one November afternoon when the phone rang and Martin answered it.

"Pack parson, how are you?"

"Joe Trask!"

He had thought of Joe often in the years since Korea. (Jane
said that from the way Martin talked about him she felt she

knew Joe as well as one of the family.) Joe had written him about leaving the Army after the Korean War and going into business on the West Coast. He had replied to a couple of Martin's letters, but Martin had not heard from him in nearly a year.

"Where are you, Joe?"

"Lower Broadway. Opened my central office here last week. Geraldine—that's my wife—I lost my mind and got married a couple of months ago. We're living. . . ." He gave an address on Park Avenue. "How about you and your wife coming around for dinner?"

Jane and he went a couple of evenings later.

They stepped from the elevator into a large penthouse and saw an archipelago of modern furnishings washed by a creamy sea of carpeting. Joe came to them, smiling warmly, his broad frame tailored expensively.

Geraldine, who awaited them on a long divan, went with the apartment. Or maybe the apartment went with her. Gorgeous by some standards; lacquered, brittle, by Martin's.

The small girl's voice that issued from the woman's body was not reassuring. "You both look younger than I thought you would. You *are* the minister and his wife?"

"Oh, my God, Geraldine," Joe said.

Geraldine came from Los Angeles and had met Joe while working in the business department of a Las Vegas hotel. It was all she said about herself, but unconsciously she revealed much. Martin thought she was not stupid, but a victim of that blankness which comes to a mind insufficiently occupied. Yet she seemed to be kind basically, her darts at Joe being only the defense of a child who had not experienced much but confusion, emptiness, boredom.

Geraldine told them, "You don't know what it's like living with the big operator here. He's gone all the time. Nothing but work, work, work six and seven days a week. And here I am rattling around in this kooky apartment. When we came to New York to live, he promised me everything. But all I got was *nothing*. When I tell him I don't know what to do with myself, he says, 'Why don't you walk the dog? Why don't you go get your hair done?' Since we've been married, he's introduced me to only two people. And they weren't even people, just men who work for him. The first one made a pass at me, as if I'm something cheap—"

"I fired him," Joe said.

"And the second one got drunk and told me what a son of a bitch—excuse me—Joey is."

"I fired him, too," Joe said.

She flared, "That didn't do anything! It was just you shoving people around again like . . . furniture. Why didn't you call up Reverend Judson and his wife last week when we got here? You know nice people, and you don't pay any attention to 'em."

Joe looked embarrassed. "I've been awful busy." He explained that he had gone into the synthetics industry and bought up a failing company which he now was kiting high and planned to use as a lever to—

"Business, business!" Geraldine cried. "What do they care about that? What do *I* care? . . ."

Joe and Geraldine came to the parsonage for dinner about ten days later. At first they were tense, but soon they relaxed. Joe, appreciating the plain life of Old Fourth parsonage, was fascinated by Martin's big library.

Abe, usually silent and withdrawn when guests came to the parsonage, was voluble with Joe. The reason obviously was that Joe treated him seriously, as an equal rather than a child. Abe, knowing that Joe had been a soldier, brought down his collection of pictures of uniformed soldiers, and they pored over it together for a long time.

When they left, Joe borrowed two books from Martin—*The Story of Philosophy* by Will Durant and a theological work that had long been popular, *Our Faith* by H. Emil Brunner.

At the door Martin said, "We'd be happy to have you attend Sunday service if you ever feel like it."

Geraldine said, "I don't think I could do that. You see, I

don't believe in God. I respect people who do, but I don't, and it wouldn't be honest for me to go to church and pretend. The thing I believe in more than anything else is *honesty*."

Joe looked at her blankly. "Yeah, yeah. Just stick with that story, Geraldine. . . ."

On the following Sunday, to Martin's surprise, Joe and Geraldine entered church during the prelude, and an usher led them far forward. Blond Geraldine, wearing a full-length mink as to a table in the Persian Room, created a stir in the congregation. Who was she—Marilyn Monroe, Jayne Mansfield? Joe sat beside her with a pained expression.

Martin's topic that morning was "The Good Old Days." His theme was that when one thinks times past are better, he may be only pining for days when he was more fit to cope with the problems about him. Then he developed the idea into one's religious beliefs.

It was a satisfying preaching experience to observe Joe's expression change from pain to interest as he listened.

After the service Joe gripped his hand, gazed at him intently, and said, "Hey, I *followed* you. How about that?"

They continued to come to church whenever Joe did not make one of his frequent weekend business flights to the West Coast and take Geraldine with him. She stopped wearing mink to church, but Joe made them just as conspicuous by invariably dropping a fifty-dollar bill on the plate to the awe of the ushers.

Their church attendance seemed as much a form of conspicuous consumption as the night they took Jane and Martin to dinner at Le Pavillon and first-row orchestra seats at "My Fair Lady." On the other hand, Joe fell into the habit of coming to the parsonage or the church office at any hour that suited him to borrow a book or, as he put it, "shoot the hooky." Gradually Martin learned what he had accomplished in recent years: taking his stake of ill-gotten Army gains into the jungle of civilian speculation, uncovering a lode of surplus supplies, converting it into credit, expanding credit, wheeling and dealing, doubtless double-crossing and being double-crossed. Now he had emerged onto a promontory of wealth and some power. The whole story was summarized by the name of his company: Trask, Inc. During the years before he moved his base to New York, his occasional relaxation had been to spend a few days at Vegas, presumably enjoying the broads and the booze and the tables. It was there, of course, that he had met and married Geraldine. Why? Well, why any of it? It was the natural direction of his experience, his talents; as well ask why Beethoven chose to compose music or Martin Judson to become a clergyman.

In their conversations Joe seemed to be asking both Martin's approval and disapproval. He liked to argue with Martin about religion, the credibility of God, yet seemed saddened to win every argument—which, of course, he felt he did. After all, a winner like Joe could not bear to break his winning habit.

One Sunday when Joe made a sudden trip to Texas, Martin was surprised to see Geraldine enter church alone. His surprise grew during the sermon when he noticed that she was weeping. Afterward she came to him, taking his hand in both of hers, and saying, "You were wonderful today, Martin." What had he said that was so wonderful? "My feelings have changed. I must talk to you. I want you to tell me what to read in the Bible." Then she attached herself to Jane, who invited her home to dinner.

Later Martin asked Jane, "What's the matter with her?"

"She *says* it's God."

"I beg your pardon?"

Jane looked at him blankly. "She says that listening to you preach has made her believe in God. She has, as they used to say, gotten religion. Or so she says."

He frowned. "I don't—" Then he checked himself from saying he didn't believe it. Who was he to doubt a religious emotion expressed sincerely? "I don't know what to say to her."

Jane continued to look at him blankly. "I imagine just about anything you said would be all right to her."

On Monday Geraldine phoned him at the office and asked urgently that he come at once, there were some things in her

Bible reading she did not understand. He went, disliking his sense of reluctance because he felt it indicated a shirking of duty.

She greeted him warmly and led him to the bar. "No drinks, Martin, but I have the Bible here because the light is good to read by." She had him sit on a stool before the Bible, which was opened on the bar, and pulled another stool close to his. "It's the 'Blesseds' I don't understand." Her long, tinted forefinger nail prodded the words as she read in a child's tone: "Blessed are the poor in spirit: for theirs is the kingdom of heaven."

The Beatitudes, he explained, proclaim God's favor toward those who aspire to live under his rule. The poor in spirit mean those who feel a deep sense of spiritual poverty. The word "comforted" implies strengthening, as well as consolation. Purity of heart is sincerity or singleness of purpose, free from mixed motives; though not the same as chastity, it includes it. The peacemakers are not merely the peaceable, but those who work earnestly to make peace.

As he talked, he became aware that she was leaning against him heavily, as if seeking physical rather than spiritual support. His male senses went on the alert as her left hand closed warmly on his knee and she asked, "Martin, have you ever done anything really bad?"

"Well, of course, I—"

"*I* have. Isn't it possible to do something bad that's good in a way and get it over with and be forgiven?"

He glimpsed her eyes close to his, smelled her perfume, felt her soft, warm flesh against him, and recognized his own carnality. *In this crazy unpremeditated way it can happen to anyone.* Then her premeditated assault on his senses, using God's Word as an instrument, struck him as the most blasphemous crime one could commit.

After he escaped from the apartment, he was more understanding. Over the years he had learned that bored or lonely women of a congregation were likely to fasten on the minister as an object of attachment. Various women members had displayed their fondness for him at various times, though none as flagrantly as Geraldine. Martin knew it had little to do with whether a minister was young or old, handsome or ugly. Certainly it had nothing to do with the nature of true religious faith. But it did have a great deal to do with the fact that many women led bored and lonely lives, that ministers by the very nature of their profession must appear to be tractable men. Such situations would continue to arise as long as there were churches, women members, ministers.

When Martin was almost home, he began to wonder about his own instinctive first reaction to Geraldine's approach. Of course, he had been under control, but now even his instinct seemed implausible.

Jane was in the library writing a letter to Kathy. Finally, she looked at him questioningly as he prowled about, frowning at the shelves of books.

He said, "I've just come from the Trasks' apartment. Geraldine asked me to go over and try to answer some questions. I don't think she's . . . sincere about this—what would you call it? If she asks me there again, I'm going to tell her that both of us have been planning to call on her together."

"Shades of Upton!" Jane said, and resumed writing her letter.

Around midnight in early May Martin and Jane were awakened by the insistent ringing of the doorbell. Jane followed Martin to the head of the stairs, when, in pajamas, he went down and let in Joe. He was howling drunk and brandishing a bottle.

When Martin came upstairs about an hour later, he said, "Geraldine has left him. I think I've convinced him to sleep it off on the sofa."

In the morning Joe was gone. Beside the telephone he had left a hundred-dollar bill and a note which read: "For the calls I made."

"This money is ridiculous," Martin said.

"Don't be so sure," Jane replied. "Wait till the phone bill comes in."

After two weeks passed and they did not hear from Joe, Jane decided he had gone forever. She almost forgot him in her happy anticipation of Kathy's return from college. On the afternoon she was due to arrive home, Martin was working at his sermon on the patio while Jane glanced frequently at the street from the living-room windows. When a taxi drew up, she hurried to the front door and opened it. Joe Trask climbed out of the cab and looked up at her sheepishly.

Jane took him to Martin on the patio, where he told them, "I'm going to stop being such a nuisance, but I want you both to know something. I'm divorcing Geraldine. No alimony either. The people I hired to do the job caught her red-handed with the guy in Vegas. I've been out there. I never felt so free and well-off in all my life. I got rid of that crazy apartment. Got me a sensible one near the office. If you ever see me look at another dame, please knock me on the head."

He went on to say that maybe he was spending too much time at business. "The company made a couple of hundred grand while I was away. You know why? Just because I wasn't there. If I'd been there I'd have done something—the wrong thing—when I should have just sat and waited."

Kathy's voice came to them greeting Mrs. Bentley, and then she came out and threw her arms around Jane and Martin. It had been only three months since Jane had seen her, but in that brief time she felt that Kathy had grown into a mature woman.

"Sergeant Trask!" Kathy exclaimed when Martin introduced her. "I've heard wonderful things about you."

Joe stared at her, then said to Martin, "Please knock me on the head!"

At last Joe said he must go. "But still I haven't said what I came here to. I want all of you—Kathy, Abe, everybody—to be my guests on a trip."

"Where to?" asked Kathy.

"Europe. We'll fly over and back. Take three or four weeks. We'll go to all those places everybody wants to see."

They looked at him with wonder and surprise. Then Jane thought, *Well, strike him on the head.* She said, "That's very kind of you, Joe, but we can't do it."

"Why not?" He looked crestfallen.

"It's too much," Kathy said.

"You mean too much like making you feel indebted or something? No, it isn't, Kathy. I wouldn't be here today if it wasn't for your father. He saved my life."

"And you saved mine," Martin said, "and lots of people go around doing similar things all the time. That doesn't matter, Joe. Kathy's point is that we all feel it's too big a freeloading operation no matter how rich you are. Like Jane, I have to say thanks, but no."

Joe looked so unhappy that Jane felt sorry for him. So did Martin, for he said, "We enjoy your company, so come up to our place in Vermont for a couple of weeks this summer."

"I shouldn't be let near a telephone," Joe said. "It only gets me in trouble."

"We don't have one," Martin replied. "The nearest is at a farmhouse half a mile away, and Mr. Greene gets irritated if you use it too often no matter how much you pay him."

"You'll like it, Joe," Kathy told him. "And just think of all those miles of castles, cathedrals, and museums you won't have to walk through. . . ."

He arrived in Vermont late in July. Kathy was away at the time, visiting a college friend on Cape Cod.

From the moment Joe stepped from his cream-colored convertible and changed into dungarees and a polo shirt he seemed a different person to Jane. His abrasiveness was gone, perhaps with Geraldine, perhaps left behind in the offices of Trask, Inc. He liked the old house, the gentle countryside. His manner, in truth, reflected its gentleness. He no longer tried to monopolize Martin but submitted good-naturedly to Abe's monopolizing him.

His companionship was good for Abe, Jane decided. Beneath her hope that Abe would "find himself" or "settle down" (she always thought about him in such euphemisms) her concern over him grew steadily. At times, when he was sweet and tractable, she would think he really was better, but then, for reasons she never could fathom, he would turn ornery and stubborn. Martin could do nothing with him. Often, indeed, a word from Martin caused Abe to do the opposite. Yet Martin, like herself, could not bear to act against him with the swift, cool authority and violence that possibly was needed. He had come to regard Abe with a quiet watchfulness which, Jane thought, actually was a watchfulness of himself and came from a desperate wish not to repeat the experience of his father and brother.

With Joe, however, Abe acted differently. Joe took him and his young pals, the Greene boys from down the road, riding around the country in his car; they went swimming, fishing, hiking, sometimes with Martin, but more often without him. When Abe acted tough guy or wise guy, Joe told him to cut it out, and he obeyed.

"Sometimes Abe reminds me of myself when I was his age," Joe said once to Jane and Martin when the three were sitting on the porch. "I could be a real mean kid. When I got older, I thought I wouldn't have been so bad if I'd had things like Abe has—good parents, a place to roam and be free the way it is here. I talked about it to him the other day when he was acting up."

"What did he say?" Martin asked.

Joe hesitated. "Something silly, the way kids talk at that age. He said I'd never been a minister's son and had to live in a church where everybody watched and criticized me."

Martin frowned. "My brother felt the same way. So did I, to a degree. But generally I kept my feelings under control. Nathaniel couldn't."

"But people at Old Fourth don't watch and criticize him," Jane said. "We've done everything possible to—"

"Yes, they do—some of them," Martin said. "And he brought it on himself by wanting to be the center of attention. Raising hell is his way of getting center stage. Maybe he'll outgrow it, I don't know."

Jane hoped that Abe was becoming more tractable under Joe's influence. Then, about a week after he arrived, they decided to have a late-afternoon swim and picnic at the lake. Kathy had just returned from the cape, and everyone was in a festive mood. When it came time to drive the half mile to the lake, Abe was missing. But Martin said he'd show up there since he had been delighted by the idea of a picnic. So, wearing swimming suits and loading their picnic things into Joe's car, they left without him.

They were shouting and paddling about in the chill water when a shot rang out and a bullet whined in ricochet somewhere. Abe, wearing swimming trunks and holding a .22 rifle, grinned at them from the shore. He had been begging for a rifle, which they had forbidden him to have. Had he bought one secretly or borrowed it from the Greene boys? Letting out a whoop, he began to reload the single-shot .22.

"Abe," Martin cried, "put down that gun!"

Abe paid no attention as Jane and Kathy shrieked at him. Joe found a footing and sloshed toward shore, calling, "Abe, you heard what the skipper said."

"He's *not* the skipper!" Abe yelled. "If he's the skipper, who are *you?*"

"The skipper's exec. *Drop* it!"

But Abe hugged the rifle to his chest as Joe strode to him. Snatching it from him deftly, Joe whirled the .22 once around his head and flung it spinning far out into the lake. Abe butted and struck at him, yelling angrily, "It cost me six bucks! It cost me six bucks!"

Joe fended him off with one hand and looked inquiringly at Martin coming out of the water. "Skipper, what's the punishment for disobedience?"

Martin stared at Abe grimly. "No picnic supper. Go home!"

Abe, incredulous, cried, "Mom! Mama!"

Jane braced herself. "You heard what Father said."

"Mom!"

"Beat it," Joe told him, and turned to Martin. "We might as well start a fire and haul out that charcoal for the steaks."

After Jane and Martin had gone to bed that night, she agreed with him that Joe had revealed the way they must discipline Abe. It would be hard, she knew, but she was as determined as Martin to try. Now her respect for Joe was unwavering; he possessed a strength that she thought she lacked.

The night before Joe left for New York all of them sat on the porch talking while cicadas shrilled in the darkness and the aurora borealis flickered on the northern horizon.

Joe, who had been talking about something else, brought up the subject suddenly. "Martin, I'd like to join your church. What do I have to do?"

"You know we have what we call open membership. One simply states his belief in God and His Son, Jesus."

"Oh, I believe in that," Joe said. *"Now* I do."

When they went to their room, Jane asked Martin, "But *does* he?"

"We have to take his word for it," Martin said, "though I fear he believes more in the Judson family."

Martin, Tubby, and Lance attended a convention in San Francisco in September. Each had duties which prevented them from getting together for dinner until the night before the closing. At Lance's suggestion they met at the Top of the Mark. Lance ordered a highball, Martin a beer, and Tubby a Coke.

On the second round of drinks Lance began to wax sentimental. His feeling embarrassed Tubby and interested Martin.

"Well, here we are, the Three Musketeers. . . ."

Scarcely. Yet there they were, each in his way a so-called successful clergyman. As Lance talked on, getting a little high, Martin realized he was closer to him than he used to believe he was.

"Preaching," Lance said. "We all think we're great preachers—and maybe we are, though Tubby seems to be the greatest. But is that what does it?"

Tubby's expression was uneasy. "Is that what does what?"

Lance made an odd gesture, as if stirring a cake. "You know — What makes a church work and grow? Is it preaching? I doubt it. My answer is the black book."

"Meaning?" Martin asked.

"I've know a lot of terrific insurance salesmen," Lance said. "The field always has fascinated me."

"Why don't you try it?" Tubby asked.

Lance looked at him, not feeling the barb. He said, "My own career is too interesting. But there's a lot to be learned from insurance salesmen. The most successful one I've ever known had a black book in which he kept a dossier of prospects. He let me look at it once. Darnedest collection of miscellaneous information you ever saw. A lot of odd facts about the prospective clients. No summaries. Just facts. See, this friend of mine did all the summarizing in his mind. On the basis of the facts. He sold—oh, I don't know how much annually. But it was the best tip-off I've ever had in the ministry. Back when we were on the Main Line, before we moved to Chicago, I began keeping a black book of . . . prospects."

Tubby looked revolted, but Martin was fascinated.

Lance said, "Why should we kid ourselves? All of us want to attract as many youngsters as possible into the church. But when we do, what happens? Remember that old song about 'the pig got up and slowly walked away.' That's what happens with youngsters. That's in the nature of . . . things. People move. A church is fixed. So who does a strong church depend on? Middle-aged crocks like us. People who have reached the age of consent. That's where the real prospects lie. Those are the people in my black book. . . ."

On the flight back to New York Tubby mentioned Lance's black book to Martin with some disdain. Martin, far from being disdainful, was absorbed by the idea. One in Tubby's position at the Cathedral could scorn salesmanship. But Martin felt he could not afford to scorn it, and obviously Lance felt the same.

A couple of weeks after his return home he made his first entry in an alphabetized notebook which happened to have a red cover. The prospect was named Michael Jones, and ironically, he was an insurance salesman. Joe Trask sent him to Martin. He had written a group policy for the employees of Joe's company and proposed a small group policy for the salaried employees of Old Fourth: Martin, the assistant minister, the church secretary, the director of music, the custodian, and the assistant custodian. In the course of a long conversation Martin learned as much about Michael Jones as Jones did about the organization of Old Fourth.

He bought an alphabetically indexed notebook that afternoon and made his first entry:

> *Jones, Michael,* 45. Bus.: Insurance broker. Home address: 329 East 61st. Married, one daughter, 14, attending the Hunt School. He a hustler. Heavy smoker. Detests suburban living. Offers good group plan. Minister's son. Lafayette graduate. No present church affiliation. Obviously doesn't attend anywhere. Alerted him to fact no insurance man in membership. Enjoys classical music. Listened to Larry rehearsing Bach on organ with acute ear. Bringing his proposal before board next week.

When Martin brought the proposal before the board, the members were willing to do whatever he wished.

"Well," Martin said, "I suggest we sit on it for a while. It sounds like a good plan to me. But I'd like to see Mr. Jones put himself out a little more for his contract."

Phoning Jones, Martin told him that the board had taken his proposal under advisement. The following Sunday Michael Jones and his wife attended church. And that afternoon Martin made another entry under *Jones, Michael*:

> He a man of deeper feeling than first appears. Eyes moist over anthem. Genuinely liked sermon. Can always tell they

really like it if they look you straight in eye when they say so. Wife, Louise, seems rather withdrawn personality. She gave Jane impression she lonely in N.Y.

Two weeks later he appended further information on *Jones, Michael*:

Surprise, they back for service again. Stayed for after-service coffee and seemed to enjoy. Michael has generous instinct to help serve others. Natural churchman, but wouldn't tell him so—yet. He has contact with Spear Publishers who looking for practicing minister to read manuscript on a religious theme. Me? Michael says so.

Thus it happened that Martin began another entry in his book:

Borrows, Nathan, 38, about. Senior editor with Spear Publishers. Lives in Village with wife and two children either of his or hers from previous marriage. Yale. Denies God. But likes William Buckley. Drinks plenty at lunch. Very lively mind. Would be poor prospect except keeps denying God so vehemently. Agree with Nathan manuscript basically sound but has several inaccuracies. Nathan a frustrated teacher.

Not long afterward Martin made his last entry under *Jones, Michael*:

He got contract and beat it. Says not interested in church membership. That's fishing for you.

But a couple of days later he had another entry for *Borrows, Nathan:*

Nathan told me at lunch this Dec. 12 he likes my criticism of the Burke ms. Told him to send check for $150 for reading to church. Annoyed him. Says he mistrusts any man who lacks profit motive. Big argument. In middle of it asked Nathan to teach boys' Sunday-school class. He so stunned said yes. Let him pay lunch check to show my pure profit motive.

Later:

Margaret Borrows is delightful person.

And the week before Christmas:

Sturtevant, Mr. and Mrs. Richard H., fiftyish, 137 East 36 St. Moved to N.Y. from Seattle last month. He assistant to the president of A. P. Wolf, brokerage firm. Episcopalians. Pleasant, substantial, portly people. She—named Roni—especially portly. Met this Dec. 20 outside Saks Fifth Avenue where I buying Christmas gift for Jane. Sidewalks slippery. Mrs. Sturtevant fell down. I tried to assist her to feet and fell down. Ha-ha. Very funny. No moviemaker would accept this. But Mr. Sturtevant tried to assist and *he* fell down. Ha-ha-ha. Everybody on 5th Ave. laugh & I wish they fall down too. Went into Schrafft's for coffee to salve our injured dignity. Mr. S. quick-tempered. Wants to sue Saks. They much surprised I minister. Same old story: lonely in N.Y. They coming to church on Sunday. Maybe. Some of our best members are former Episcopalians. Maybe. Looks too much of setup to be sure prospects.

On February 14 he made this final entry under *Sturtevant*:

Today took Richard and Roni into membership. He yearns to be member of board.

And a few days later he closed out the *Borrows* dossier thus:

Nathan has quit Spear and going back to New Haven for doctorate. Very sad. Positive he and Margaret about to join the church. See *Cloud*.

If one had leafed to the C's in Martin's book, he would have read:

> *Cloud, William Willow,* 32, field associate, dept. of anthropology, American Museum of Natural History. He a full-blooded Oglala Sioux from South Dakota, educated at Vanderbilt and U. of La. Very intelligent. He writing book for Nathan on religion of Indians of Northern Plains. Nathan introduced me to him today, Feb. 18. William most anti-Christian. Most caustic about Christian missionary effort to Indians. I entered no defense. Hates N.Y. Runs 3 miles in Central Park every morning. He jokingly suggested it time some American Indian do study of Christian religion instead of usual vice versa. Took him seriously. Invited him to begin with Old Fourth.

Later, in May:

> Well, well, well, as Father used to say. William Willow Cloud serious about everything he undertakes. First-rate critic of Christianity. Picks at something in the service every Sunday. Most serious about Suzi Wabara, the pretty Japanese student at Columbia who came into membership in Feb.

And a final entry under *Cloud* in September:

> William has a sense of humor after all. He grinned and told me today, "Lo the poor Indian." He's remaining at Nat'l History Museum and joining church. I'm marrying Suzi and him on Wednesday.

There were many setbacks among the entries. But over the years they traced the slow, steady growth of Old Fourth into a strong church.

❦ *Seven* ❦

NAME: Katherine Judson. Age: twenty-one. Home: New York City. Occupation: junior, Wellesley College, Wellesley, Massachusetts. Affiliation: Student Nonviolent Coordinating Committee.

In the heat and turmoil of the Nashville bus terminal the young, bespectacled black took down the information carefully, then looked Kathy up and down. "Honey, you sure you're twenty-one?"

"I will be in a few days."

He grinned. "So you want to spend your birthday in jail. You doing this to duck your year's finals?"

"I finished them yesterday," Kathy said. "I had to fly to get here on time."

"Plenty of time," the black said. "This bus don't keep much of a schedule. The drivers keep funkin' out. So you're a SNICK." Thus the Student Nonviolent Coordinating Committee was called. "We got five SNICK's, eight CORE's, three SCLC's, seven independents, and not a single N double ACP." He looked around at the next bench. "Suzie Polk over there's a SNICK from Howard. Hey, Suzie!" he yelled above the din at a stout young Negro woman. "Here's an ofay to keep you company."

Suzie Polk treated Kathy coolly. What was SNICK doing at Wellesley? Kathy sometimes had wondered herself. A gang of Nashville white youths, jeering and yelling obscenities at the group planning an integrated bus ride to Montgomery, Alabama, made conversation almost impossible anyway. When a couple of youths began throwing tomatoes, shirt-sleeved sheriff's deputies stepped in front of the gang and said, "Cut it out, boys, now just take it easy." Kathy wanted to tell Suzie that *this* was why she had come here, that they were sisters, that all citizens must have equal rights. But of course, those sentiments, which had seemed convincing on the Wellesley campus, would have sounded banal in the Nashville bus terminal.

"There's Dave Murchison." Suzie pointed to a tall, husky-looking young white man who had just come in carrying an airline flight bag and was being greeted warmly by a couple of the black leaders. "He's one ofay Dr. King trusts. Last year during the Greensboro sit-ins he spent a week in jail."

Kathy found it hard to believe. She thought him sort of handsome in an Ivy League biscuit-cutter way: cropped hair, lean face, deadpan demeanor. He stared at her over the heads of the blacks, then made his way to her.

"I'm Dave Murchison. Who are you?"

"Kathy Judson, New York."

He sat down beside her. "I'm at Union Seminary."

Suddenly he interested her. "My father's a minister in New York."

He looked at her more closely. "Martin Judson?" Yes. "Martin Judson of Old Fourth," he said slowly. "So we have a daughter of the Protestant Establishment with us."

She narrowed her eyelids at him. "What Establishment are you talking about, preacher boy?"

He grinned suddenly. "The New York Protestant Establishment begins at the Cathedral and goes south to Trinity at Wall, then curves through the prettier parts of Long Island and up into Westchester. They wear the sword of liberalism but take care never to join any expedition south of the Mason-Dixon Line."

Father a member of the Protestant Establishment? It was ridiculous. Because he had pulled Old Fourth up by its bootstraps and built it into a strong church, he apparently had become a target for the little preacher boys. Good heavens, Father was a radical! When she had phoned him from Wellesley and asked for money to join the freedom ride, he had not demurred for an instant. "I'll send a check right away, Kathy. Glad you want to act on your convictions. Just do me one favor. If you land in jail and SNICK doesn't have the bail money promptly, send me a wire."

At last they climbed on the bus, and Kathy sat down beside Suzie. David Murchison took the seat across the aisle from Kathy. As the bus rolled through the suburbs of Nashville, he talked endlessly, practically telling her the story of his life.

He had been graduated from the University of Michigan, where he had worked at trying to be a writer. "Only thing wrong with that is I don't have any real talent for it." Then why Union Theological? His answer to her question was vague.

"Well, maybe just to irritate my old man. He's dead and doesn't know it. Dead and buried in Scarsdale. I haven't seen him in three years when I tried to raise some money from him to go to Union. Gosh, it made him mad. He hates Christianity —everything, me included. Says I'm a goddamn Communist."

His father and mother had divorced when he was fifteen, and now she was married to a kooky art dealer and living in Paris. It was his mother who financed him at Union. "She'd like to spoil me. Compensation, I suppose, for walking out on the old bastard in Scarsdale and going off with the art dealer." Did he hate her, too? "No. I sort of like her and feel sorry for her."

There were six white and seventeen black passengers on the bus which sped south through a parched-looking land of yellow clay. The country was as Kathy had expected from her reading about the South. But the atmosphere in the bus was wholly unexpected. In Wellesley and Boston she had heard much about the warm fraternity of the fighters for civil rights, but on this bus there was a restraint amounting to coolness between blacks and whites. Dave, a veteran of the new civil war, was the only white whom the blacks trusted fully.

Early in the afternoon the bus stopped where there was a roadside stand, a dilapidated house above a clay bank, a mangy dog asleep in the dust. An old man began padlocking an outhouse as Kathy walked to the stand where a thin woman with a weathered face stared at her grimly. There was nothing to eat, nothing to drink, the woman cried shrilly.

Dave shared his sandwiches and thermos of iced tea with Kathy, who had not thought to bring food or drink. After they climbed onto the bus, he sat down beside her and at once fell asleep. She marveled at him. When she remembered having read that instant sleep was a capacity possessed by most persons who fought oppressive society, she even began to admire him. In midafternoon the black leader called to him, and he awakened as instantaneously as he had slept.

Following a short conference with Dave, the leader addressed the riders. Montgomery was their destination, but first they must pass through Birmingham. He advised them to segregate themselves by color, remain passive, and not try to leave the bus when it paused at the Birmingham terminal. "But Dave has other ideas. He's going to tell you his, and you're free to act as you please. After all, this is a *freedom* ride."

Dave's voice rose easily, and Kathy realized he must be a persuasive public speaker. "My thought is that the Battle of Montgomery is no more important than the Battle of Birmingham. In fact, the more Southern battlefields the better. I think the police may stop us at the Birmingham city limits and arrest any who refuse to segregate their seats. Personally, this ofay plans to get arrested. They say the Birmingham city jail has nice clean sheets and ice cold drinks." There were jeering cheers. "Is there a black man on this bus willing to go to jail with me?" After a lengthy silence a young CORE man said he would be honored. "Anybody else want to see how the better half lives in a Southern jail?"

Kathy wondered if he was gazing at her. Remembering suddenly a line from one of her childhood prayers—"Let's get on with it, Lord"—she stood up.

Dave smiled at her and called, "Bless thee, Katherine, in the names of Peter, Titus, and Paul. Kathy Judson of New York is looking for a cellmate. Any takers?"

Suzie looked around at her and exclaimed, "Well I'll be! Come sit with me, Kathy."

"You're a pretty dispirited-looking bunch," Dave said. "Let's put some oil in this tired machine. Let's *lubricate* democracy and make freedom hum. Everybody remembers that rascal John Brown. . . ."

As he led them in the well-known song, Kathy thought: *My gosh, an old-time Gospel singing preacher, turned inside out and twisted all around, with different aims and a language part new, part old, but all tuned to strange ears.*

Half an hour later, as they entered Birmingham, the wailing of a police siren made her neck chill. The driver pulled to the side and stopped the bus. Kathy, thinking of what she had heard about Southern police brutality, was scared. Yet she had asked for whatever might happen to her, so there was no reason to William Blake it and think with the poet: "And the bitter groan of a martyr's woe/Is an arrow from the Almighty's bow."

To her surprise, the policeman who stepped onto the bus was young, good-looking. In a courteous tone he said they had entered the city limits of Birmingham. Then he recited the local ordinance on segregation of bus riders and asked them to conform with the law. When Kathy, Dave, and their black seat partners failed to move, the policeman said he would have to take them into custody. Unprotesting, they left the bus with him. Kathy and Suzie rode to police headquarters in the rear seat of one squad car while Dave and his companion rode in another.

At headquarters they pleaded guilty and were booked. After searching through a sheaf of papers, a lieutenant said Dave and his seat companion had criminal records; if they could not post bail of one thousand dollars each, they would be remanded to jail. Dave laughed, and they were led away. Suzie's bail was set at five hundred dollars, and she left with a matron.

"Now look here," the lieutenant said to Kathy. Why should a nice girl like her mess around in things that didn't affect her? It was the most paternal lecture she ever had received. Repent —and go home. She thought of a couple of eloquent remarks but could not bring herself to make them. Instead, she insisted she was guilty, and lacking five hundred dollars' bail, she followed the matron to a reasonably clean cell in the women's block.

A drunken woman yammered down the block, and two cockroaches paraded on the ceiling. After a while Suzie called out her name, and Kathy answered. Having anticipated arrest, Kathy had brought along a paperback edition of *Walden*, which she had started twice in years past but never finished. Now, beginning it again while curled up on her cot, she found herself understanding for the first time why Thoreau went to the pond.

Around six o'clock the matron brought her corned-beef hash, bread, and canned peaches. When she came for the dishes, she lingered for a long time—not to converse, but to lecture. What did Kathy think she was accomplishing? On and on the matron ranted. Didn't she at least want to notify her parents so they could bail her out? No, she had given the lieutenant money for a telegram notifying SNICK headquarters of Suzie's and her arrests, but she was beginning to wonder if the telegram had been sent.

Later in the evening five women who had been on the bus were brought into the block. They said there had been roughing at the bus terminal, and they had been put under something called protective custody. Kathy slept poorly, and the next day she began to understand why the verb "languish" applied to jail. After finishing *Walden,* she started it again and found that the pond had grown stagnant to her.

On the second morning, following a breakfast of bread, powdered eggs, and coffee, she and the six black women riders were taken to the room where they had been arraigned. Two black men riders were brought from their cells and joined them. Kathy inquired about Dave, but the men did not know what had become of him. When the nine were led out and placed by threes in three police cars, she assumed they were being taken to court.

But the cars sped north out of Birmingham along the highway which the freedom riders had followed into the city two days previously. At last Kathy asked, "Where are we going?" Neither of the two policemen in the front seat answered her. It was bewildering and a little frightening, like being caught up in a Kafka creation in which the subject could not relate to the object. She had been arrested and jailed under due process of law, but now the authorities were violating law as flagrantly as the freedom riders. On the police cars raced for what seemed hours.

At last the car began to slow down on a lonely stretch of road fringed by clay banks and pine barrens. When they stopped, one of the policemen spoke for the first time: "Get out!" The woman beside Kathy began to shake and weep. Her terror was infectious, raising unreasonable images of the law gone berserk, of massacre by police guns on the hot and piny clay. Kathy's legs shook as she climbed out.

The policemen stared out at her contemptuously, ignoring the blacks. "This is the state line," one said. "Start walking, and never come back to Alabama."

As they walked north in the heat, cars passed them in both directions. Drivers stared at them curiously, but none stopped. Eventually, Kathy thought, they would reach a town where they could board a bus back to Nashville. It was a sad, a ridiculous ending to her brave protest, her great adventure. Before long the heat began to dissipate her anger into a sullen weariness.

The blaring of a horn behind them warned of some new danger. She looked around at an old outsized limousine such as served airport passengers. Seated beside the black driver was David Murchison, who managed to look at the same time surprised, pleased, sad, and angry. Thus possibly General Nathan Bedford Forrest had looked when surrounded in these parts before issuing his famous order: "We'll charge both ways!" But when Dave climbed out of the swaybacked limousine, his order was: "Hop in! Back to Birmingham!"

Not Bedford Forrest, but Tom Sawyer, Kathy thought. Into jail, out of jail, back to jail again—and like Huck Finn, she wondered to what purpose. "Now wait a minute," she said.

"You've had enough?"

"Not necessarily. I'd just like some explanation of what's being accomplished."

"We've got 'em on the run."

"I'd say they had us on the walk. How did you get out of jail?"

"My outfit raised bail. Reinforcements are pouring in. Our intelligence network is really cracking. We knew the minute you people were run out of town. Both President Kennedy and the Attorney General are trying to get the governor of Alabama on the phone. We're gathering strength at the Birmingham bus terminal. Before long they'll weaken, and we'll bus it on to Montgomery. Climb in!"

After they climbed into the swaybacked limousine and headed back to Birmingham, Kathy asked him, "Have you ever considered an Army career?"

"No dice. I'm a pacifist."

Some pacifist! Like Uncle Tubby, with his medals, or Father, with his Korean adventures. Onward, Christian soldiers, marching on to jail.

More than a score of freedom riders were gathered at the Birmingham bus terminal when they arrived there. Kathy expected momentarily that they would be arrested, but General

Bedford Forrest Murchison proved himself the wiser tactician. They were too numerous now; such a large number of arrests would flood the jail and draw more national attention to Birmingham than the city authorities cared to receive.

Now the police gave them a protective screen against the toughs who wanted to assault them. Now, too, Kathy began to realize that patience was the most important weapon of the resistance fighter. As the hours crept by, she struggled against boredom, fatigue, and—worst of all—a feeling of personal uncleanliness. She would have given almost anything for a shower, a change of clothing, a few quiet moments away from the din— anything, of course, except giving up the effort and going home.

It was a long night on benches which seemed to grow harder as time passed. Their effort to integrate the terminal lunchroom failed when the employees closed it and left. Dave and a white professor from Princeton attempted a sortie out for coffee and food, but they were attacked by a gang of youths and retreated to the terminal somewhat battered. At an early hour of morning, however, a strong force of allies brought them coffee and dry bologna sandwiches.

Wheels were turning in other places, Dave maintained cheerfully. Eventually the governor of Alabama would have to pick up the phone and answer the President of the United States. Eventually something must indeed have happened someplace else, for, about ten o'clock in the morning, they climbed onto a bus and set out for Montgomery.

Ah, Montgomery, first capital of the Old Confederacy, rising from the Alabama River, white columns gleaming through catalpa, sweet gum and magnolia, haunt of Jefferson Davis and the professional auctioneers wearing beaver hats and black tailcoats as they cried, "Niggers is cheap, niggers is cheap . . ." swollen now to one hundred and thirty-four thousand black and white skins, industries capitalized by the North, yet still unreconstructed Confederate. Thus Kathy tried to alleviate her weariness. Thus, too, a black man ahead of her said, "We'll bring those bastards to their knees."

It happened with terrifying suddenness after the bus pulled into the Montgomery terminal. The mob gathered there was much larger, its outraged cries more menacing than the crowds had been in Nashville and Birmingham. Dave led the way off the bus. Kathy, not far behind, saw him suddenly engulfed by several youths. He disappeared, as if the earth had swallowed him. Those behind him began trying to struggle back on, but those still aboard were screaming that the mob was trying to set fire to the bus. Kathy found herself flung into the roaring crowd as by a kind of centrifugal force. She glimpsed a man swing a baseball bat at her and tried to dodge, but someone else shoved her into its arc. There was a numbing pain in her right side, and she went down, struggling for consciousness . . . .

The events that followed always remained vague to her. Somehow she struggled free of the fierce riot and finally was seized by two policemen. When arraigned, the pain in her chest was so severe that she begged for the attention of a doctor. What bail was set she could not remember; neither could she recall whether she gave Father's name and address. She kept asking about Dave, but no one seemed to understand her. And then she found herself in a cell with two Negro women.

Perhaps it was that day, perhaps the next, that a doctor came to her cell. Almost at once he had her carried out on a stretcher and transported by ambulance to a women's ward of a hospital. After a time she was rolled off for X rays, and eventually, at some hour of daylight or darkness, a physician came to her bedside. He was a kindly, competent man named Grey, who talked with her as if she were a close friend. She had four broken ribs and a torn liver, besides cuts and contusions about the head and both arms. Her ribs would heal; so would her liver without surgery if she remained immobile, Dr. Grey believed. She gave him Father's name, and he promised to find out what had happened to Dave.

The next afternoon she awakened from a doze to see Dave standing beside her bed. Both his eyes were blackened, his lip cut, his jaw swollen.

He said something corny: "But you ought to see those other guys." He assumed a John L. Sullivan stance and swung his fists. "Take that, Jeff Davis! Take that, Pierre Beauregard! And you that, Braxton Bragg! Not a scratch on 'em." Incredibly, his eyes filled with tears. Even more incredibly, he leaned over and kissed her gently on the forehead. "Kathy, I'm so sorry about that beautiful face of yours. But the doctor says you're going to be all right." Blinking back his tears, he pulled up a chair and sat down gingerly, wincing. "The greatest indignity came when somebody gave me a tremendous boot in the ass."

"Why aren't you in jail?" she asked.

"Released on bail again. Things are really popping. . . ." Montgomery was under martial law. Martin Luther King, Jr., had arrived from Chicago, and when he tried to address a black mass meeting at a church, there had been an even worse riot than at the bus terminal. Reinforcements for the freedom riders were pouring in from the North, as were federal marshals.

Dave was running on like Tennyson's brook when Kathy saw Father enter the ward with a nurse and come toward her. More gray had come to his hair since the last time she had seen him; he looked frightfully distinguished. For a moment she thought she would cry. Instead, she said, "How did *you* get here? What d'you think this is, a deathbed scene?"

He tried to smile, but his expression was fractured. "First I heard from the police, then the doctor. But when the minister phoned, I thought I'd take an airplane ride."

"What minister?"

Dave thrust out his hand and said, "I'm Dave Murchison. How are ya?"

"*You* called Father? Why?"

"Sort of a fraternal thing. One preacher to another. You know, like, sir, I've got your daughter in trouble."

"Father, he's not even a preacher. He's only a seminary *student*."

Dave shook his head. "But I graduated before I left for here. Didn't I tell you?"

He had said so much about himself that possibly he also had said that.

Dave said, "Mr. Judson, I hope you don't mind my phoning you. I told you Dr. Grey says she'll be okay. But I have to go on, and I don't like to leave her here alone."

He was the most exasperating boy she had ever met. "*You* don't like to leave *me?*" Her voice rose. "Who d'you think you are? The director of a tour of the antebellum South? Where are you going now?"

"New Orleans eventually, we hope. But first to Jackson, Mississippi."

She closed her eyes. "Look, stupid, you're going to run out of bail money. You're already out on bail in Birmingham and Montgomery. I hate to think what they'll do to you in Mississippi. You want to end up in Leavenworth or something?"

Dave grimaced at Father. "Murchison's last ride. Want to come along, Mr. Judson?"

Father smiled. "Theoretically, yes. Practically, no. I have enough problems in New York."

Dave looked him up and down thoughtfully. "We could use you."

"That's what my people tell me in New York. They can use me. So I can't afford to waste time in jail."

Dave started to say something else, then checked himself. "Well, on to Jackson." Leaning over, he kissed Kathy on the forehead again.

"Stop *smooching* me," she said. But then she gave him a light pat on his swollen jaw. "I wish I could go on to Jackson with you. Please take care of yourself, you dope."

He stepped back, looking at her oddly. Then he said one of his typically inane things. "I'll send you a postcard. What's the address?"

But he did not send her a postcard.

After she returned home with Father she read in the *Times* that he and several others had been arrested in Jackson. Sentenced to fines of two hundred dollars or sixty days in jail, they had chosen jail and been sent to a prison farm. Kathy, rather than admiring him, thought Dave was pressing martyrdom too hard. Her enthusiasm for the civil rights movement was unabated, but what did he hope to accomplish by spending sixty days in prison?

To her surprise, Father defended Dave's choice. Probably, he said, it was the decision of the movement, and he could not separate himself from it without abandoning his principles.

When she had recovered from her injuries, she went to Boston and took a summer job with a social welfare agency. It was, alas, pretty boring. She was not allowed to go out on casework but performed office routine and did a little interviewing.

Something happy resulted from her job, however. One Saturday evening in July she went to a party at a fellow worker's apartment and met Dr. Myron Banberg. He was two years out of Harvard Medical and a resident at a Boston hospital. She thought him the handsomest man she ever had met, the most reflective; his cool was extraordinary. While everyone else sounded off interminably, Myron sat quietly, listening, drawing on a pipe, and sipping a glass of beer.

Unlike Dave, Myron did not try to tell her the story of his life. But she found herself telling him the story of her Southern adventures. Actually someone else brought it up, for she was something of a celebrity among her co-workers that summer as a result of having been a freedom rider. Myron questioned her closely about it: her observations, her reactions. At last someone asked him, "Well, Doc, are you making a diagnosis?"

"No," he replied, "I'm just interested in people who involve themselves in—things."

Kathy presumed that he felt involved, too, in the events of these fascinating times, but she could not learn how or in what.

Myron phoned a few days later and asked her for a date.

They drove to Framingham in an old Chevrolet he shared with another hospital resident and had dinner. As at the party, he remained elusive about himself while drawing her out. She told him, among other things, that she had started as a premed but switched to a major in the social sciences.

When he suggested going to a drive-in movie, she wondered, disappointedly, if he thought he could make out with her. They went to a drive-in which was showing, of all things, *Elmer Gantry*. Had someone told him that her father was a clergyman? He did not try to make out with her and sat mesmerized by Burt Lancaster sashaying about on the screen. On their way back to Boston he launched into a serious discussion of the movie, as if it were the latest revelation of Protestantism. And he listened with interest while she explained it was a dated, cornball creation that might be thought revelatory or daring only in backcountry hamlets.

On their next date they went swimming on the north shore. Myron's lean, graceful body held a certain appeal to Kathy. But it was nothing like that exercised by his gentle manner.

He was the only son of orthodox Jews in Toledo, Ohio. How his father earned his living Myron did not explain. Inadvertently he disclosed that he had completed the prescribed undergraduate course at Ohio State in three years. And there must have been great joy in Toledo when he was accepted at Harvard Medical School. His reference to the fact he was a Jew came in an amused account of his bar mitzvah and his parents' consternation at his stumbling over the *brocha* and the longer Torah reading called the haftorah.

Kathy mentioned her respect for the Hebrew faith—then thought she sounded patronizing.

Perhaps Myron thought so, too, for he said, "It doesn't mean anything to me anymore. I've quit it."

"I can understand." She hesitated. "To me personally the stumbling blocks in your faith—your former faith—are its tribalism and legalism. I suppose that's natural for one who's been brought up to seek a proper Christianity."

"What do you mean seek a *proper* Christianity?"

"One that tires to cope intelligently with the secular world as it actually is. Not a Fundamentalist, either as Protestant or Roman Catholic. A Fundamentalist in any faith is completely taken up with tribalism and legalism."

He said, "Your using the word 'proper' is what blocks me. Or maybe you'd say I'm just being legalistic. Doesn't what you call a fundamentalist believe that what he thinks is the only proper faith?"

"Of course. And he has every right to his beliefs as long as he doesn't try to force me to share them. Strike out 'proper' as a subjective adjective."

They continued in this vein for much of the afternoon, not arguing, but nibbling at the fringes of argumentation. Gradually his gentle inquiry made her think she sounded opinionated. In her way, she realized, she sounded as stuck on her own views as Dave Murchison did on his. She did not really know as much as she presumed. Yet Myron seemed to think she did. After a while she realized he was sincerely seeking knowledge from her. There was no question about his intelligence. But there was a great question of whether he knew much about the ways and affairs of the world apart from the study of science and the practice of medicine.

Their courtship, if it could be called that, was a kind of dialogue on human responsibility and kindred matters such as bored Kathy when she attempted the novels of Henry James. Yet courtship it must have been, for in November she wrote home that she was in love with Myron and would like to bring him to New York for a weekend. Mother replied but of course, then ventured to inquire about him.

Kathy, attempting to describe Myron in a letter, found it easier to explain what he was not than what he was. He was a Jew—but not a Jew. He was tremendously skillful—but did not wish to be a surgeon. Internal medicine was his field; next year he would become assistant to a prominent internist in Boston—but he did not really want that either. Kathy, growing somewhat desperate in her effort to describe him, wrote that above all Myron had an open mind, unlike most young men she knew—for example, Dave Murchison, now serving as the campus chaplain of a Wisconsin college, who wrote her when he felt like it, even though she seldom answered his letters.

Mother and Father hit it off fine with Myron that weekend in New York. He heard Father preach on Sunday and found the service interesting. There was nothing objectionable to him in such a Protestant church, he told Kathy on the way back to Boston. At the same time he doubted that he ever could affiliate with any church, probably because his training in science made religious faith impossible for him. Kathy did not mind. She had no wish to try to force him into an uncomfortable mold. She felt, indeed, that her own religious instincts of years past had waned. At Wellesley she attended chapel rarely. Religion, as Father and Mother practiced it, seemed of no significance in her present life. The time might come when religious faith would be as dead to her as it was to Myron.

In March their relationship reached a crisis. Passion had grown with companionship, a passion that both tried to hold in check. But one night in March, when he drove her back to the campus, their passion got out of control, and they narrowly escaped going the limit. Kathy was badly shaken. So, apparently, was he, for she did not hear from him for a week.

Suddenly he appeared at Claflin Hall around five o'clock one evening, and they went for a walk along the shore of Lake Waban. He asked her to marry him, and she said she would. She never had been so happy. She told a classmate, her closest friend who called Myron the dreamboat, and then phoned Mother and Father with the glorious news.

They had a date in Boston for the following Saturday, when she would select a ring. On Friday evening Myron phoned her, sounding deeply distressed. His mother was seriously ill, and he had to fly home at once.

He sent a postcard from Toledo, then phoned her the next Thursday after he returned to Boston and said he would see her late that afternoon. When he came into the lounge at Claflin, he looked so drawn that she asked if he had been ill.

"I think I have been," he said indistinctly. "Let's go for a walk." She inquired about his mother, and he said, "Her troubles are psychosomatic."

When they came to a bench on the shore, he dropped down, buried his hands in his pockets, and gazed with a pained expression at the lake shining in the mellow evening. She asked him what was wrong.

"Plenty. Kathy, I have to ask you a question, and you must promise to think about it and not answer me right away. Could you become a Jew?"

Two thoughts formed simultaneously: Of course she could; of course she could not. She asked, "Your parents?"

"Yes. In their faith they're what you call Fundamentalists. They're unalterably opposed to my marrying a shiksa—you."

The problem, like every other, seemed soluble to Kathy. Throughout her life reason always had prevailed in an unreasonable world. Reaching into her reasoned study of comparative religions, she said, "Judaism tries to discourage converts. If your parents are that deeply religious, I'd always be a shiksa to them no matter what ceremonies I went through."

His head lowered, he said, "My father and mother run a small delicatessen in Toledo. I'm their only child. We lived upstairs over the store. Until I was seventeen, I never got far from the smell of dill. That's why I can't stand to have dill pickles on the table. They spent thousands of dollars—everything they could scrimp and save—on my education. They don't realize that their religion means nothing to me. They only know that I'm a Jew, that they sacrificed everything for me, that I graduated top of my class, that I'm going to be a successful doctor someday. They sit at their table late at night, drinking a glass of tea in the smell of that goddamn dill, and all they think about is me."

Kathy refused to ignore reason: "You mean all they think about is themselves."

"All right!" His tone was angry. "I took a course in psychology, too. Maybe what I really mean is that you can take the boy out of the delicatessen, but you can't take the delicatessen out of the boy."

She tried to contain her sudden sense of anger. "What you really mean is that you're delivering an ultimatum. I must go your way or forget about it."

When he turned his head, his eyes were filled with tears. "I didn't say that. I *love* you, Kathy. I asked you a question. Could you become a Jew? And I asked you not to answer me right away, to think about it."

His tears moistened her own eyes. She never could love anyone as much as him. Still she refused to abandon reason. "Darling, you're trying to tell me that if I became a convert to your parents' faith, they would grudgingly accept me?"

He hesitated, and his hesitation was worse to her than anything that he had yet said. "I think so." Then, "Look, I can't live for the rest of my life feeling I've betrayed their gift of life to me. I merely ask you: Can we try?"

"We? Don't you mean *me*? What about *my* parents? What about their faith and the sacrifices they've made for me?"

"Of course, I've thought about it, Kathy. But from having met them, I don't think it would matter to them. They're . . . liberal. And if you think it would make any difference to them, they'd never have to know."

She stared at him incredulously.

"Look, do you think I care about any of it once we've gone through a wedding in Toledo? I never want to see the inside of a synagogue again. I don't care if my sons go uncircumcised. I only want to do it for the sake of *someone else,* two people who have sacrificed everything to bring me wherever it is I am today. Here's what you do. . . ."

She did not know what to say to him. Perhaps it would not be irrelevant to say that he sounded as if he were recommending an abortionist. But he would not understand what she meant; he would take it as a slur on his parents' faith, rather than a slur on his own lack of integrity. And yet she still loved him.

Getting to her feet, she said, "I have to get back to the dorm. I'll think about it. I'll call you soon."

That night, for the first time in memory, she cried herself to sleep. The next day she cut classes and stayed in her room, loving and hating him. In the afternoon she placed a telephone call home, then canceled it. What could Father or Mother say or do? The decision was hers.

Late that evening she realized she had already made her decision. She wrote Myron a brief note saying that marriage for them was out of the question. Then she mailed it for fear she might vacillate again.

Returning to her room, she did something she had not done since completing a course in comparative religions nearly two years previously. She took out her copy of the Oxford Annotated Bible and began leafing through the New Testament. In the eighth chapter of Romans she found words that comforted her, words Myron would not understand:

"So then, brethren, we are debtors, not to the flesh, to live according to the flesh—for if you live according to the flesh you will die, but if by the Spirit you put to death the deeds of the body you will live. For all who live by the Spirit of God are sons of God. . . ."

She would remember that the next time someone said religious faith no longer was significant to life.

"Help yourself," Abe told them in the summer of 1962, when Pop said they all were going to Europe. "You're wasting your money on me. I want to go to Camp Caldwell on Lake Winnepesaukee."

He had his way. He had learned that he nearly always could have his way if he was adamant.

Mom, Pop, and Kathy sent him cards and letters from England, France, Switzerland, and Italy. It sounded real Dullsville to him. He was having a ball at Camp Caldwell. He took the camp record in swimming the mile. He had swell training in boxing. It was entirely different from the sissy private school in New York, and he could forget all about Old Fourth. People took him for exactly what he was; he no longer was the preacher's son. At Camp Caldwell he felt he was a pretty important person. He made lots of friends, but the best was a tentmate, Jack Fetterman, who attended a military prep school on the Hudson. Abe decided he would go to that military school in the fall.

Early in August Uncle Joe Trask drove up to see him. Uncle Joe took him and Jack and some other guys out for dinner— steaks, milk shakes, the works. Afterward Uncle Joe said he was flying to Italy to meet the folks and come home with them. Would Abe like to leave camp and go with him? Uncle Joe showed him a letter from Pop authorizing the trip.

"No dice," Abe said. "What do I care about all that? I'm having *fun*. . . ." He told him about his determination to go to military school in the fall. Uncle Joe tried to talk him out of it, but Abe had made up his mind.

After they parted, Abe felt that Uncle Joe and he were not as close as they used to be.

As soon as he and the folks came home to New York, he began his campaign to join Jack Fetterman at the military school. They resisted the idea, as he had known they would.

"Junior Sing Sing on the Hudson," Pop called it.

But he worked hard on Mom. "Look," he told her, "I know I'm not doing any good in school. But I *could*. I want to go to West Point or Annapolis. If you'd only give me a chance. . . ."

Pop drove him up the Hudson to the school one beautiful September day.

They talked about this and that. Pop really was all right. Good sense of humor, plenty of cool, never trying to be the cut-up kid like Jack Fetterman's father. But old from worrying about God and Jesus and why doesn't the Sunday school grow faster and where is the next member coming from. Well, that wasn't exactly fair to Pop. He never went around talking about those things. But Abe could feel him *thinking* about them. And he wished Pop would forget them, get a job selling insurance, and no one ever again would point at him as the minister's son.

Wanting to say something nice, he said, "Thanks for sending me to military school."

"You're welcome," Pop said. "Just drop me a line once in a while when you're a major general."

Abe grinned. "I'll even send you a dependency allowance."

"Thanks. We'll probably need it."

Abe still wanted to say something nice to him. "I want to confess something, Pop. I'm the guy who released the white mice into the choir that Sunday last spring."

"I know you are."

Abe was amazed. "How did you know? I was home with a fever."

"You were home because you didn't want to go to church," Pop said. "Before your mother took your temperature, you probably hung your head over the side of the bed. Everybody knows that old dodge."

"But how did you know it was *me*?"

"Nobody else would have *wanted* to do it. Why did you?"

"Those dames in the choir with their silly smirks. They give me a pain. They sit there trying to look like angels. And they aren't. I heard that Sally Struble—"

"Why believe everything you hear? Officers are supposed to be gentlemen. And gentlemen don't repeat gossip about women. So you created a public disturbance. Did you enjoy it?"

"I got a boot out of the screaming as I ran down the hall. I wish I could have been out front to see them jumping around. Pop, did you ever do anything like that when you were young?"

Pop was silent for a while. Then he said, "Once, when my father had a church in Pittsfield, another kid and I— It was during the Sunday evening service— We took all the men's hats from the cloakroom and hid them in the church cellar."

Abe was amazed and delighted. "No kidding? What did your father do?"

"He beat the hell out of me."

Abe rocked back and forth with pleasure. "How did *you* feel?"

"I was mad at him. I made plans to run away from home, but I never did. . . ."

When they reached the school, Abe suddenly was on the verge of tears. Afraid that he couldn't control them, he asked Pop to drive around the grounds before they checked in. When Pop finally turned him over to the authorities, he thought he was okay. But then he had to hurry off without really saying good-bye, for he saw that Pop's eyes were moist.

A constant problem Martin faced at Old Fourth—as do most ministers everywhere—was to find able and willing hands to perform its numerous functions. It began with finding, and keeping, a capable assistant pastor. Martin was without one again that fall. Eight had come and gone during his ministry at Old Fourth. Two had been excellent—and soon had left for pastorates of their own. The others had ranged from mediocre to one Martin had fired because of his insurmountable drinking problem.

Another constant problem was secretarial help. Joe Trask, now chairman of the board at Old Fourth, said it was a universal problem. Joe reasoned that secretaries were like pigeons; they had to be kept in flocks so they could coo and squabble and fly around together and just possibly work a bit. One alone, such as came and went at Old Fourth, languished of loneliness. Jane, a competent typist, often filled in at the church office after one secretary had gone and they were waiting for another to appear.

Every kind of paid help—custodial, a director of music, a carillon player, members of the choir, cooks and busboys for that monstrous responsibility Martin had created in the form of a free cafeteria—presented problems. It seemed that each was merely passing through on his way to some place real or imagined. That year the favored word describing life in New

York and, indeed, most of America was "fluid." Yet in the midst of this fluidity of life, Old Fourth, like numerous institutions, sought to be stable.

The volunteer workers of Old Fourth were almost as fluid as the paid help. The interested young couple who joined the church in October were transferred to Cincinnati in May. When the stalwart couple of thirty years' loyal service reached retirement age they moved to Florida. Though the Sunday school never did flourish as the Sunday schools had in Upton and Sylvia, there always was a shortage of capable teachers.

Nevertheless, the church grew slowly and steadily.

Once, when Tubby asked Martin what he thought were the reasons for its growth, he was at a loss for an answer.

"Well, it's not some one distinguishing thing, like Colonel Birdwell's barber poles."

"I think it's your preaching," Tubby said. "Your reputation—"

"No, I don't think so," Martin replied. "We're having good crowds now. But crowds don't necessarily mean interested members. It's true I try to pin some sort of job on everyone I can, but—"

"Are you still keeping a book of prospects as Lance does?"

"You bet I am. I pursue 'em like the hound of heaven."

Tubby sighed. "Sometimes I envy you that. Getting out hunting and fishing all the time. How is the Sunday school?"

"Only fair to middling. It never will get much better. In our situation in the inner city I haven't been able to make it a neighborhood church. We have to draw from all over."

"Marty, do you ever think you'd like to get out of the city into some quieter spot where you could breathe a little slower?"

"No," Martin said.

Jane, like Martin, enjoyed the stone and steel, the grime, clamor, and nervous excitement of the city. She liked, too, the moments of surcease, as in the stillness of Sunday mornings, when Tim McHugh at the carillon of Old Fourth answered the carillon of St. Andrew's, and the bells of Immaculate Conception volleyed back at both. Best of all were wry moments of consternation, even when the world seemed at peace, as on the Sunday morning when the carillon of Old Fourth failed to answer the carillon of St. Andrew's—and Martin, a spoon of soft-boiled egg suspended, exclaimed, "That crazy Tim McHugh has gone back to the bottle!"

Jane felt her energy was ebbing that winter. She was forty-seven—no longer young, but not as old either as she often felt. Joe observed her fatigue before Martin did.

Joe was Martin's strong right arm at Old Fourth, as Spencer Cook had been before he died. Joe's transformation had been gradual and altogether amazing to Jane. Whether or not he believed in God, he certainly believed in Martin. Whatever his thoughts on the kingdom of heaven, he was eager to bring about the kingdom on earth. For having been a soldier, Joe wanted wars to cease; having been poor, he wanted an end to poverty; having lived with all manner of men, he found none utterly hopeless; having been a superlative cheat, he revered simple honesty. At the same time, however, he adored power for its own sake. As the chairman of the board of Old Fourth, he would have made the church *his*—and Martin's—if Martin had let him. His emotional affiliation with the Judson family was so great that he even had fallen in love with their Vermont countryside; on the shores of the nearby lake he had bought a large tract of land and built a comfortable house, which he enjoyed thoroughly.

Joe prevailed on her to make an appointment with Dr. Jim McKay, the family physician and a member of Old Fourth. One afternoon in January Dr. Jim gave her a thorough examination and found nothing wrong. Blood pressure a little high, that was all.

"Try to get more rest, Jane," he told her. "When you go home today, go to bed and stay there for twenty-four hours."

Leaving the bus at the corner, she rounded Old Fourth onto the side street. It was a raw late afternoon of thaw, of dirty snow patches in empty window boxes, muddy water in the gutters, and a curdled blood-red western sky promising a beautiful evening in Arizona. A man was seated on the top stone step of the parsonage. He was young, rather handsome. Getting to his feet as she started up the steps, he said, "Mrs. Judson?"

"Yes."

"I'm Dave Murchison. There's no one in the church office, and nobody answered the door, so I thought I'd wait."

She suddenly felt confused—an old woman coming from her doctor's and wishing nothing this winter evening but toast, tea, a warm bed. Yet this young man must want something of Martin, which meant something of her. His name was vaguely familiar. She could have jabbered at him about so many names and faces floating through the familiar places of parsonage and church.

However, she said, "Why of *course!* How are you, Mr. Murchison? Come in. Martin should be along any time now. He had hospital calls this afternoon. Sorry you had to wait. Mrs. Bentley"—but he wouldn't know she was the cook—"has the afternoon off." As she searched for her key, she enviously enjoyed a vivid image of Mrs. Bentley munching chocolates in Radio City Music Hall and later betaking herself to Schrafft's for dinner with her cousin from Jersey City.

"How's Kathy?"

"Fine. Well, she had the sniffles when she was home on Sunday. She has a social welfare job and lives with two girls in the Village." Jane finally got the door open. "It's cold and dark as a tomb in here." She snapped on a hall light. "Mr. Murchison, would you like a cup of tea?"

He smiled at her suddenly, and it was the most warming experience of her day. "I surely would, Mrs. Judson."

"Do you know how to make a fire?" Of course he did. She turned on lamps in the living room. "There's all the . . . stuff." She gestured to the fireplace. "Martin brought up wood last evening, but if there isn't enough— I'll start tea."

She was filling the teakettle in the rear pantry when she finally remembered who David Murchison was.

She took tea and cookies into the living room, where he had a fire blazing. He was describing his curious campus ministry to the agnostics of a Wisconsin college when someone unlocked the front door. Jane looked around, expecting to see Martin, and Kathy came in.

"Mom"—her voice was hoarse from a cold—"may I sleep here tonight? I—" She stared at Dave. "Well, hel-*lo!* What are *you* doing here?"

He beamed at her. "Just paying a pastoral call."

"I'll bet!" She stepped to him, hand extended, and there was something in her expression that made Jane think she liked Dave Murchison.

When Martin arrived a few minutes later, he greeted Dave warmly. Soon Jane understood that he had left his campus post in Wisconsin. Again she felt confused. Had he already told her that, and had she failed to listen? Woolgathering during conversation was a growing habit she must curb.

"Why did they fire you?" Kathy asked him.

"They didn't exactly fire me," Dave said. "I resigned"—he smiled— "before they fired me. The trustees and their rubber-stamp president took exception to my . . . philosophy or theology or whatever."

"Trustees!" Martin said. "They remind me of politicians and generals. Always preparing for wars that are past and totally blind to the future."

"Do your trustees give you trouble?" Dave asked.

"No. For the first time in my life I'm trusted by the trustees. A few years back I accomplished one important thing here organizational-wise. We have only one board now. Once trustees are united with deacons or elders in one board, all of 'em have one less thing to quibble about."

Kathy asked Dave what he was doing in New York.

"Hunting employment."

"What sort?" Martin suddenly looked as alert as a beagle on a scent.

"I'm not sure," Dave said hesitantly. "In Wisconsin I realized if I'm going to stay in the ministry at all, I should . . . plunge in and get wet all over. I mean a pastorate. But most of my friends aren't very happy at it. And my experience is . . . poor. I've never conducted a funeral service or a wedding ceremony. I've never even tried to comfort a dying person. I'm not at all sure my preaching is any good and—"

Martin leaned toward him. "I'm without an assistant at present. The starting pay isn't great. Fifty-two hundred. But if you wanted to, you could live in the apartment upstairs. . . . Of course, you'll stay to dinner."

"Of course," Jane said, rising and going downstairs to the kitchen. She was trying to judge whether there was enough left from last night's pot roast when Kathy came down and offered to help her.

"Another assistant living in the house," Kathy said. "That's not going to make life easier for you. And your life seems so . . . stringent. Mother, what reward is there in it?"

Jane turned to the stove. "Kathy, the reward is in meeting the challenges of every day. Not always overcoming them, but just meeting them."

After Dave became assistant pastor in February, Martin asked if there was any church project that especially interested him.

"Have you ever considered surveying the efficacy of the noontime cafeteria for office workers? You said the fund supporting it is almost depleted."

Martin frowned. "It's not designed to be a self-supporting operation. It's aimed at giving the church a role in the community."

Dave knew the project was a source of pride to Martin, for it had brought neighborhood attention to Old Fourth.

"Why are you skeptical about it?" Martin asked.

"Frankly, because it's an out-of-date idea. It reminds me of bread lines in the Depression. It asks no sacrifice of those who benefit from it, and I think events today show that kind of patrimony has few good effects."

Martin suddenly looked amused. "Dave, remember that afternoon you came to the house? What was it I pontificated? Something about generals and politicians preparing for wars that are past. Add preachers to the list. Go to it."

"Well, to begin with, how many of the currently active members of Old Fourth joined the church as a result of the noontime program?"

"Let's check the rolls right now."

Martin's forefinger prodded through the long alphabetical list. Two . . . three . . . four . . . He digressed frequently, recalling why, presumably, this or that one had joined the church. For many members he could offer no specific reason. But *four* over the course of years definitely had joined as a result of the program. Martin looked surprised. "Not many, is it?"

"Let me Sherlock around for a few weeks," Dave said.

Each day he kept a count of those who came for lunch and totaled the daily contributions. He found that only about 20 percent of the people who ate there used the reading and game rooms while only about 3 percent attended the weekly organ recitals. The free religious literature was almost totally ignored.

One day, seeing Lee Sculp, the head custodian, taking some literature to the incinerator, Dave asked him why he was destroying it.

Lee looked embarrassed. "Mr. Judson keeps an eye on that pile. He'd feel right bad if he thought nobody was paying it any mind."

"What do you think of this program, Lee?"

Shrugging, then looking about to make sure no one was near, Lee said, "I guess Mrs. Dwyer has got herself a new Chevrolet out of it."

Dave began sleuthing the activities of Mrs. Dwyer, the dietitian. The average cost of a hot luncheon was eighty-seven cents while the average contribution by each patron was thirty-two cents. Going over the bills submitted by the whole-sale grocer who supplied the kitchen, he thought them far too high. Mrs. Dwyer protested they were not. Then one day, by lucky chance, he happened to see the deliveryman hand Mrs. Dwyer a twenty-dollar bill after she had signed a receipt.

Dave followed the deliveryman outside and said, "I believe the cash to Mrs. Dwyer is the company's weekly contribution to the church."

"Oh, sure." The deliveryman smirked and climbed into his truck.

By chance, too, Dave discovered that the chief cook carried enough home from the kitchen each day to feed her family of three.

Martin looked stunned when Dave gave him a full report on the program. At last he said, "I feel like a bumpkin who has been fleeced. Worse, it makes me feel *old*. The program had a good point when I started it. But it has outlived its usefulness. I should have canned it long ago. Read your report at the board meeting next week, and I'll recommend that we abandon this patsy operation."

The board voted unanimously to cut off the project immedi-ately, and Joe Trask said, "A neat job, Dave. Any time you get tired of being a preacher, you can come to work for me."

After a while Martin said, "A project dead." He sounded sad. "Can we find something to replace it?"

Joe, who had involved himself in a city youth recreational program, suggested something similar for Old Fourth.

"We don't have enough teen-agers, either in the member-ship or the neighborhood, to make it of any significance," Mar-tin said.

"I wish," Dave said, "we could develop interest among peo-ple in their early twenties. The experimental age—or, as they used to say, the courting age."

Martin told Jane, "The Sheik of Chicago is sending me two slave girls."

"I hope they're pretty," Jane replied. "What are you talking about?"

He showed her Lance's letter. Two daughters of people in Lance's church, having graduated from college, had decided to make the well-known migration eastward to New York, where they were taking jobs in the "sub-arts," as Lance put it—television and advertising. Their doting parents, visualizing New York as Sodom on the Subway, were much concerned. They wished their girls could have the protection of "some Christian influence."

"Would much appreciate," Lance wrote, "if you and Jane could interest them in your church. Though must say, life being what it is, suppose you'd do the biggest favor to them by introducing them to a couple of nice boys. 'Twould seem that is the nature of this—and every—age."

Martin said, " 'Twould seem. The Bishop is working his way toward heroic couplets."

Jane said, "There's Horace McIntyre."

"Horace is married to his mama," Martin said. "There's Dave."

"No!"

"Dave's a very attractive young man."

"No! You expect too much of your assistants."

"There's Horace McIntyre," Martin said, "and that's about all. One trouble with Old Fourth is that it's hoary—h-o-a-r-y— with age. Dave had the right idea when he said at the board meeting last week—"

"We'll just wait and meet the girls," Jane said. "I'll invite them to dinner, we can size them up, and—"

"One look at us and they'll take off for Roseland Ballroom," Martin said, "and that's the last you'll ever see of them. End of 'Christian influence.' I sort of hate myself for what I'm going to do, but I'm going to do it anyway."

He phoned Tubby and said, "Judson's date bureau here. Tubby, the Bishop is sending me a couple of chicks. How are you fixed for bantam roosters? I mean it's time we populated the outer islands. . . ."

They were pretty, charming girls. The two young men Tubby sent were delighted to meet them. Tubby showed his usual perspicacity in his selection: Both men lived and worked not far from Old Fourth; they were surplus to the large supply of young males at the Cathedral and were happy to do a favor for a friend of a friend of a friend since it involved pleasant feminine companionship, a good dinner, and drinks—all free. Jane also invited Kathy and Dave, who helped foster a festive atmosphere. Dave was especially helpful in supporting Martin's description of an absolutely fascinating young people's group at Old Fourth—a description that was about 75 percent imagined.

Yet from the imagined there grew the real. Later Martin always traced the beginnings of a strong young people's group at Old Fourth to the evening when they entertained the four youngsters—two from Lance, and two from Tubby. (Doubtless, of course, the group's reputation for having a solid basis of romance was enhanced by the fact that two of the four paired off, then later swapped for the other two, and Martin officiated at the marriages.)

It was, Jane said, a time of romance everywhere. She announced that Dave was in love with Kathy. Well, how did Kathy feel about Dave? Jane was not certain.

She and Martin talked about it one Saturday night when Dave took Kathy out for dinner.

Jane said, "Kathy worries me."

Martin said, "You're always worrying about her. Why now?"

"She never confides in us anymore. I can't tell what she thinks of Dave. And if ever she knew a fine, simply wonderful young man, he is it. He's crazy about her."

"Did he tell you so?"

"Of course not. But can't you tell from the way he looks at her? Like an adoring sheep dog. The way you used to look at me."

"*Used* to? How do I look at you now?"

"More like a preoccupied Great Dane. I wonder if he took her to Carnegie Hall. The Choral Society is there tonight. There's a reading of the Verdi *Requiem*. I could have gotten them tickets from Marjorie Swain. I wonder where he took her to dinner. Do you ever wonder what happened between her and that Jewish doctor she was in love with? All she said was. . . ."

Around eleven o'clock Martin said he was going to bed, and Jane followed him reluctantly. At some dark and silent hour she brought him awake by announcing: "There's the front door!" There, indeed, was the front door closing. She asked what time it was. He did not know or care or think it any of their business. Wide-awake now, he asked if Kathy was spending the night at home.

"I don't *know*. She didn't say."

They heard Dave tread up the stairs and enter his apartment. So Kathy was not spending the night at home. Martin tried to compose himself for sleep, but Jane turned on the bedside light and said, "Marty, it's two *thirty*!"

"So what?" He watched her irately as she paraded aimlessly about the bedroom.

"You'd think she would have come home tonight," Jane said. "Having him take her all the way down to the Village after the concert is thoughtless of her. It's a good thing he doesn't have to preach this morning."

"Jane, he doesn't, but I *do!* This is crazy. Our daughter doesn't live at home, but her boyfriend does. Why should we stay awake for him?"

"I just wish he was her boyfriend. You have to admit it's awfully late for a minister who's going to share a pulpit this morning to—"

Martin groaned and said, "They probably wanted to stay out till the bars closed."

"Marty, what time do the bars close on Sunday morning? After living in New York all these years, I. . . ."

Before the morning service Martin observed that Dave's eyes looked somewhat bloodshot from lack of sleep. And he stumbled twice in the reading, which was from Job. Kathy appeared at church late and sat with Jane. As had become their custom, they had guests for dinner in the early afternoon—Joe, as almost invariably, Kathy, and Dave, too. Martin always offered a drink before dinner and sometimes had one with Joe, who never refused. Dave had declined until that Sunday, when he said he would have a Bloody Mary, and Kathy said she would join him.

"You'll have to mix it yourself," Martin told him. "I'm no good at it. There's vodka in the pantry, I think."

After he had left the room, Jane asked Kathy if she had enjoyed the concert.

"What concert, Mother?"

Jane looked confused. "I somehow had the idea you were going to Carnegie Hall."

"I don't know why you thought so. We were at a couple of places in the Village. One is run by a friend of Dave's. It's called Harry's—a really pleasant little bar. Harry is a Negro—a part-time preacher when he isn't running his bar."

Jane's consternation was apparent. Martin observed that Kathy smiled at her sympathetically, however, rather than lecture her on the changing times. Could Jane and he possibly hope to keep abreast of them?

That evening Jane said to him with a tone of appeal, "Dave is so kind. He will make a good minister, won't he? . . ."

Martin believed he would make the best. And he tried to help him in every possible way.

Dave's most admirable quality was a strong practical sense, a know-how about people and situations that enabled him to get things done. He had no patience with pastoral calling, or what he called "handholding," and Martin tried to teach him to put up with it. His sermons were untraditional, informal in delivery, almost totally contemporary in content. Martin recognized that his theological thought had been shaped by scholars whose work was framed within the changing cultural climate of the world: Barth, Tillich, Whitehead, Bonhoeffer, Bultmann. He also recognized that many of Dave's allusions to the figures of that cultural situation—Camus, Sartre, Kafka, Beckett, Ingmar Bergman—held no significance to most members of the congregation. Sometimes Martin was tempted to try to steer him into shallower waters, but he did not. Eventually Dave would learn how easily a preacher could lose a congregation and, having practical sense, would amend his course accordingly.

Dave's greatest difficulty was understandable, too, for it was the chief problem of most beginning clergymen. Being young, he was instinctively repelled by age. Brimming with life, he did not like to contemplate death. Martin broke him to the hospitals as sternly as a colt to the bit. It was the one duty he would not let him shirk.

Dave's first experience with a case of terminal cancer left him shaken and almost physically ill. After their call, Martin led him out of St. Clare's Hospital into a drugstore on Eighth Avenue for a cup of coffee.

He said, "Dave, you have to accustom yourself to the fact of death—the loneliest of acts. Your most important function as a minister is to try, if you can, to share the loneliness. Isn't that basically what the ministry is about? This lonely life to be shared and filled. You understood and shared the loneliness of Southern blacks. You try to share and fill the lives of lonely kids off the streets. But all that is slight compared to the loneliness of dying."

"I suppose so." Dave lighted a cigarette. "But I wouldn't have known what to say if Mrs. Klassen had asked me, instead of you, about the life hereafter."

"Couldn't you have said to her what I did? That we have been told there is life and so should believe it's true."

"We have been told, Martin, but we have plenty of reason to believe it's not true. Why can't you just say you don't know. Because do you really?"

"Of course not. I *believe*, but I don't know. Maybe if you, with your toughness of mind, were the one dying who had asked the question, I'd have said I don't know. Because it would have made you, with your doubts, feel less lonely to realize that I can't speak with positive authority either. But I didn't lie to Mrs. Klassen or myself this afternoon. I simply asked her to try to affirm the belief with me. I've known her a number of years, and I know that her belief, or her wish to believe, has been with her for a long time. So she was comforted a bit."

Dave said, "I have trouble with prayer."

"So do I—with public prayer. I always have had and always will. Private prayer is another matter. I suppose I do a lot of it, more than I consciously know, because I do a lot of hoping. There's no set formula for the act of trying to comfort—or share—at the end of life. I don't pray with a dying person who does not want me to, just as I don't recite Scripture unless I know it's of comfort. I prayed today because Mrs. Klassen asked me to. It wasn't as hard as it used to be for me because I've learned to pray as if I'm doing it in privacy."

After a while Dave said, "I'll try harder. My trouble begins with an empty feeling in my guts the minute I step inside a hospital. Hospitals are strictly for dying."

"No, they're not. It's merely true that most people die in hospitals these days. They used to die at home. But we think we fixed that along with a lot of other things. Better terminal care and all that. Maybe we did. But maybe we didn't. We keep them alive longer, but are we prolonging life? A hospital is a more lonely place than home. You have a lot of interning to do, Dave. This afternoon you treated Mrs. Klassen's nurse as if she were the angel of death when she's precisely the opposite. Your most helpful contact with a patient is the nurse. Doctors, preachers, family members come and go, but the nurse is constant. . . ."

Martin's deathbed scene. Thus Dave came to think of his insistence on the important role of the clergyman at time of death. His thought was not malicious, for he liked and respected Martin immensely. He simply believed that the clergyman's important role was in *life*. And Martin agreed with him wholeheartedly when he said so. Death, Dave insisted, was a mere footnote to life, and any role of the clergyman at its bed apart from that of simple friend was irrelevant, even presumptuous. No, said Martin, death was the inevitable, dramatic conclusion to the story of life.

Dave felt that religiosity characterized much of the worship service at Old Fourth.

"Frankly, Martin, I find it bores me. It's too long, too filled with words that have become meaningless through endless repetition. Do you ever think so?"

Martin hesitated. "Yes, sometimes. How would you change it?"

"I'm not sure. But I'd tear it apart and experiment with changes. For instance, consider the Elizabethan stage. It's never been beaten for immediacy of dramatic experience. At Old Fourth our stage—the pulpit, choir, and so forth—is too removed from the audience. It's like the wide screen in a movie house. We're away up yonder, and the people are away down there. I'd like to move our stage down toward the pit. I'd like more dialogue and less monologue."

Martin thought for a time, then said, "I don't buy the idea. The people might tolerate it, but I couldn't. I'd become an actor and so self-conscious that I couldn't function."

Around and round they went. They approached many situations differently.

Ruth Salinas, who sang in the choir, consulted Martin about divorcing her husband of sixteen years, Harry. She was thirty-seven, he thirty-nine, and they had two children. According to Ruth, it was completely a case of incompatibility; they could not even agree on breakfast food. She had a responsible office job while Harry was a salesman who was absent from home for long periods. She thought he sometimes slept with a woman in Buffalo and another in Detroit. But that was not the point. What mattered was that they were unhappy together.

Dave did not know that Ruth had consulted Martin before

she made an appointment with him and told her story. After questioning her at length, Dave said, "Since you're set up to take care of the children, I'm all for you. I don't think there's anything more important to one than a sense of freedom. If I were you, I'd divorce him."

Ruth smiled. "I'm glad you see what I mean. When I spoke about it to Mr. Judson, he took the opposite view. He thought I should try to weather things out for a while. . . ."

Dave, troubled, spoke about it immediately to Martin. "I didn't know she'd consulted you first when I gave my advice."

"That's okay," Martin said. "People bent on getting advice keep after it till they hear just what they want to hear. My reason for urging patience was for the sake of the children. They're good kids and crazy about their father—as Harry is about them. I've often recommended divorce in impossible marriages, but never when there are children who love both mother and father. Family doesn't seem to be the sacred institution it once was because fewer people seem to want to work hard at it. But I still think it should—and *can*—be the most stable institution most people ever belong to."

A few nights later Dave took Kathy to a new Off Broadway play about a whore with a heart of gold. It was so boring they left after the first act and went to a café for espresso.

Taking care not to mention names, Dave told her about the different advice he and Martin had offered. "Kathy, I don't think I'll ever make it as a practicing minister. I respect your father's advice in that case. It's why he's truly a successful minister. He expects to *endure* situations himself—and expects others to do the same."

"Well," Kathy said, "isn't that a basic purpose of organized religion?"

"Exactly. And that's why I wonder sometimes whether I should have an active part in it. In this case I now see your father probably is right. But as a generalization for human life I'm not sure about *enduring* as the answer. My instincts go in the direction of personal freedom."

Kathy asked, "What do you mean by personal freedom?"

They talked until one o'clock in the morning.

Dave was in love with her. This love, springing on him at the age of twenty-seven, was not a wonderful, vitalizing experience. It was more like some painful, vitiating disease. The personal cool he cherished was lost in the heat of his longing for her. Much of the time he felt churlish or childish because he could not tell what she thought of him and, fearing the worst, dreaded to find out.

During the first two weeks of July Old Fourth closed its doors so that repairs could be made to the auditorium. Martin and Jane had left for Vermont with Abe when a friend of Dave's, Mac Fuller, invited him to the Jersey shore for the Fourth of July weekend and told him to bring a girlfriend if he wished. Mac, a pastor in Indiana now, and his wife, Meg, were delightful people, Dave told Kathy. He was elated when she agreed to go with him.

They left in his secondhand Volkswagen on the morning of the Fourth, which fell on Thursday that year, and arrived on Long Beach Island about noon. The summer place the Fullers had rented was small and stood bravely alone on a stretch of magnificent beach. On its door was thumbtacked a note which Dave read with surprise.

DAVE—

Meg's mother seriously ill and we have to go Scranton. Be back when we can. You and the girlfriend make yourselves at home.

MAC

Kathy, reading it, said, "The girlfriend! Is that what you call me?"

"No, Kath, that's what Mac calls you."

The cottage consisted of two tiny bedrooms on either side of a small living-dining-kitchen.

"Where do they expect us to sleep?" asked Kathy.

"I don't know. Maybe me on the divan here and you in one of the bedrooms. Maybe you with Meg and me with Mac." He grinned. "Maybe they have their bedroom and we have ours. It wouldn't bother them. When he was at Union, they lived together for a while before they married. Sort of testing it out, you know. They were perfectly candid about it."

"I thought you said he's a Baptist."

"He is. Some of our most advanced theologians these days are Baptists. Guess there's nothing like total immersion to give you new ideas."

"I'm starving." Kathy opened the refrigerator. "Meg's not much of a housekeeper. Some withered-looking franks, jelly, peanut butter. Whoever kept peanut butter in the icebox?"

She served them frankfurters and scrambled eggs. Then they changed into swimsuits and went to the beach, taking along a surfboard which had been propped beside the cottage. Neither had ever surfed, but they made audacious attempts at it.

When they tired at last, they flopped upon the sand. She lay flat on her back, breathing deeply, eyes closed against the blinding glare, dark, wet hair flecked with sand. He sat cross-legged beside her, gazing with a kind of awe, like a Neanderthal who had just built his first fire.

"I love you, Kathy."

He had not intended to say it. And now that he had, he felt frightened. When she did not stir or even open her eyes, however, he repeated it.

"I heard you the first time." Why didn't she open her eyes?

"Do you think you ever could fall in love with me?"

She turned her head and blinked at him then, her expression grave. "I might just do that."

Though he remained motionless, he had a sensation of leaping. "Can I help you in any way?"

"You've been doing a pretty good job of it since you showed up that afternoon last winter."

He said, "That should make me happy, but most of the time

I'm sad about us. Me in your house and you in somebody else's."

Sitting up, she wrapped her arms about her knees. "You cover it well. I'm not happy either. I'm tired of my job and my roommates and all my dates. But I don't know where I want to go or what I want to do instead. I can't go home to live because you're there."

Was that a good or bad sign? Deciding it was good, he said, "I'll move out."

"Mother and Father would miss you. He says you're going to make a great minister some day."

Dave did not want to think about that. He reached out, nearly tipping over, and laid a hand against the curve of her lovely face.

She turned her head, pressing his hand between her chin and shoulder, then sprang to her feet. "I'm full of sand." She shook some on him as she ran toward the surf.

He ran after her. Fast though he was, she was faster. When he lunged at her, a breaking wave smacked him in the face. And she, swimming straight out, glanced back and laughed at him.

When would the Fullers return? Dave hoped not for the entire weekend. If Kathy and he could continue to talk uninterruptedly about everything but her feeling for him, they might suddenly discover that her feeling was deep.

After swimming and sunning some more, they showered and changed into shorts and drove down the island to a store where they bought a steak, charcoal, beer, and other things.

The declining sun wrought its evening change on the beach. All human life but theirs retired to long distances, and a fire began to wink midway of western crimson sky and eastern darkness. The breath of the Atlantic turned cold as it flogged the shore more heavily with blows that seemed to make the cooling sands tremble. At the heart of the crowding darkness Dave's fire glowed cheerfully, giving the good smells of steak and charcoal to the ocean salt. Sprawled close to the fire within a dip of the dunes, they might have been the last people alive. They ate heartily while stars began to blink here and there, and afterward he built up the failing fire.

Like many happenings, theirs did not seem to spring from personal intention. She went to the cottage for a sweater, and when she returned and sat down by the fire again, she shivered suddenly and said she was still cold. He, reaching out, rubbed her back to warm her. She, turning her head, looked at him. Then their arms wound about each other, and they kissed. They were like swimmers going deep, bodies coiling together with the wish never to rise again. At last Kathy's face rose, free of his lips, her voice shaking as she said, "I love you, Dave. I have for some time."

Her trembling was joined to his.

Surely only a moment had passed when she broke free of him, but he realized vaguely that the fire had burned low. Then she disappeared. He put out the fire and blundered to the cottage, so shaken by the recognition she shared his passion that he stumbled over something and did not realize he scraped a knee until much later.

She had turned on all the lights and sat at the little table looking pale and miserable. She said, "I wish the Fullers would come back."

Suddenly he did, too.

"Dave, we can't stay here tonight."

"Then where can we stay?" His voice sounded unlike it ever had to him. He wandered about the room and sank into a chair. "Do you know how to play gin rummy?"

She looked at him as if he were insane, then said, "Yes." They hunted for a deck of cards, and when they could not find one, he said, "You want to drive to Maryland?"

"What's in Maryland?"

"That town—I can't remember its name. You can be married there in an hour or something."

She smiled slowly. "No. That's the nicest thing anybody ever said to me or ever will. But no."

"You want a big church wedding at Old Fourth?"

"No, of course not. Nobody but Mother would want that. We can't live in the parsonage."

"I know that," he said. "I'm going to start hunting a job. I heard of an interesting community project in Buffalo where—"

"No. What you want is a church of your own."

"All you say is no," he said. "Kathy, we shouldn't wait."

Her expression grew grave. "I know that. Isn't it nice we made up our minds a long time ago and have been miserable ever since?"

Doubting that she made sense with that remark, he wished to bring her to some positive thought. "Your father should marry us, Kathy."

"Yes, I'd like him to."

"How long does it take to get a marriage license in Vermont?"

Her lids widened as she stared at him. "I don't know."

"Are you tired?"

"Good Lord, no! This is one night I won't sleep a wink."

"Okay then. It's only ten o'clock. We'll be there for breakfast. . . ."

And they were.

Abe had left for the day, and Martin and Jane were drinking coffee in the kitchen. They were delighted with the news, Jane to the point of tears. After making a couple of phone calls, Martin said they could be married on Monday.

Eight

THE surprising thing to Kathy about Beacon Nondenominational Church was not that it had some hundred and fifty members, but that it existed at all. In February, 1964, when Dave became its pastor, Beacon had survived for eight precarious years in what formerly had been a synagogue on a West Side cross street.

The demise of the synagogue seemed strange, for many Jews lived in the neighborhood. But the rise of a Protestant church there seemed even more strange. Its formation could be traced to a zealous Unitarian, a chemist who had been confined to a mental institution for the two previous years. Whether mad or not, he had possessed a certain genius for interesting some people of the neighborhood in a Protestant church.

Few who lived in the area thought of it as a slum. Yet it came close to being one, for it was highly congested, most of its buildings were deteriorated and unsanitary, and there was much poverty and social disorganization. Puerto Ricans, Cubans, blacks, Italians thronged its streets to the regret of a small hard core of Irish, a surprising colony of French, and a multitude of Jewish shopkeepers. In politics its wards were Tammany. In religion it was Roman Catholic. But human nature being as it is, every generalization about the community had restrictions. Tammany bred Reform Democrats. Roman Catholicism bred skeptics. In the true sense of the word Beacon was a Protestant church, made up of people who protested against various aspects of the human condition.

Kathy was delighted when Dave accepted an invitation to become its pastor. It posed just about every challenge possible in the ministry, except one—that of conformism. Happily, Dave had sidestepped that challenge by declining to become the pastor of a New Jersey suburban church after the trustees wished to assure themselves he was a Republican.

Beacon's governing board was a fairly accurate reflection of its membership: two housewives, two shopkeepers, an Off-Broadway actor who was often unemployed, and seven craft unionists. The union member majority was a no-nonsense bunch. They expected stability, growth, improvement—and to pay their organizer a living wage, so Dave received sixty-five hundred a year and a three-room apartment on the second floor of the two-story building next to the church. They liked him at once, and hired him, because he clearly had a shrewd sense of organization. Their wives liked Kathy at once because she was pregnant—four months so, it happened, when she and Dave moved there.

Father deeply regretted Dave's leaving Old Fourth, yet thought Beacon the sort of challenge he would enjoy himself if young again. Mother understood why Dave should leave, yet thought his and Kathy's choice of Beacon foolish. Though neither Father nor Mother was really old yet, Kathy thought that both sometimes displayed the unpredictability of age. After Dave and she were married, for example, Father had been unable to understand why they wanted to live elsewhere than the parsonage. But Mother, understanding completely, had helped them find an apartment a couple of blocks away. On the other hand, Mother couldn't understand why she kept her job until they moved to Beacon, but Father did.

Some of Kathy's friends were aghast at their choice of Beacon. One was even nasty about it, saying, "Why don't you two join the Peace Corps if you insist on going slumming? What's your insecurity that you can't bear to live with and like your peers?" To which Kathy, for once, did not attempt a retort.

From the start she liked Dave's intent—his style—at Beacon, as did the members. The church, which had had six pastors in the eight years of its existence, consisted of a dreary auditorium with an even drearier basement beneath it. Folding chairs, which served in place of pews, made the auditorium look somewhat like a longshoremen's hiring hall. A gift from the Unitarian benefactor now committed was a Hammond organ, which was played on Sundays by a youngster from Juilliard for practice and enjoyment rather than a fee. The platform, with its lectern and dusty American flag, looked like a podium for Tammany politicians. The lighting was dreadful. In short, Kathy thought, there was nothing about it to suggest that people gathered there to worship God and seek a better Christian way of life.

Dave's first Sunday service was a surprise to Kathy and everyone else. They sang a hymn, and then Dave stepped to the edge of the platform and began to talk informally. His subject was Beacon Church—what it was, and what he hoped it might become. Then he asked for expression from the congregation. People responded with a torrent of suggestions—some thoughtful, others foolish. The discussion lasted well over an hour and was, according to Nick Ricco, a former Roman Catholic who was a member of the board, the best thing that had happened at Beacon in years.

Joe Trask, who skipped Old Fourth to attend Beacon that Sunday, took Kathy and Dave to dinner after church and was enthusiastic about Dave's plans. The next day he sent the church a check for one thousand dollars. Dave, considering it a patronizing gesture, wanted to return it, but Kathy said no. Dave gave the check to the treasurer with the remark it was not to be taken as a sign he was a great fund raiser.

Everyone agreed with Dave and Kathy that somehow the auditorium must be made to seem more like a church. Ideas were discussed, plans drawn, the thought of pews dismissed because the auditorium must fulfill other functions besides that of Sunday services. Evenings and Saturdays, skilled union carpenters, electricians, and plasterers among the members gave of their time, aided by many willing hands. Dave, often assisted by Kathy, wielded a paintbrush day and night.

Surprisingly quickly, the auditorium took on a new look. The old platform was gone, replaced by a sloping stage of modified Elizabethan concept. Paint, curtains, lighting achieved the effects of costly construction which the church could not afford. The volunteers, delighted with their accomplishment, went on to make the basement a place of cheerful rooms.

Meantime, Dave and Kathy began to make changes on the floor below their second-story apartment. Previous pastors had used the front room as a study and left the two rooms behind it vacant. Dave moved his study to the rear room, and they made plans to put the others to good use. To their surprise, they were helped by John O'Hare, the precinct captain. O'Hare, who was intelligent, believed that any helpful gesture toward the people of his precinct was helpful to law and order.

He called on Dave a few days after they moved and asked if it was his Volkswagen which was parked out front. Dave said he had not yet been able to find a place to garage it nearby. O'Hare told him not to bother, to leave it any place in the block day and night.

"Just do one thing, Reverend Murchison. We've chalked circles on all your tires. Keep 'em fresh. The men understand. So do the Black Cats. That's the name of the gang in these blocks. They're young hoodlums, not as bad as lots of gangs in this town, but still no good. They understand those chalk circles. They won't touch your car."

A few mornings later, when Dave went to the street, he found his car resting on its rear axle, the wheels and tires gone. When he went to precinct headquarters and reported the theft, the desk sergeant swore and made a phone call. It definitely was not the work of the Black Cats, he told Dave.

Kathy, standing on the curb, watched Dave put on new wheels. Three youths seated on a doorstep nearby watched him, too. After he had finished the task and started into the house with Kathy, one of the youths called, "Hey, preacher! You forgot something." Stepping to the Volkswagen, he drew circles on its rear tires with a bit of chalk.

Dave smiled at him. "Thanks. Glad you reminded me. It's a cold afternoon, and my wife and I are going to have some coffee. You want some?"

The youths looked suspiciously from him to Kathy, then followed them silently upstairs to the apartment. There Dave said, "I'm Dave Murchison, and this is my wife, Kathy. What are your names?" They told him, and it was the only question he asked them. He talked, with seeming aimlessness, while all drank coffee and ate cookies.

What interested the boys most in the apartment was Kathy's record player. Apparently they did not think much of her records, but they seemed to enjoy pawing through the collection and trying a few. Eventually they left, without thanks for the hospitality. But at the foot of the stairs one looked about the large, empty front room and said, "Hey, Dave, you got space here for a pool table."

The price of one at Abercrombie was out of the question. But Kathy had an idea. "Ask O'Hare about it."

O'Hare looked at Dave blankly across his desk. "Reverend, you think I got a tie-in with the Mafia? You think this precinct is Boys Town? You think you're Spencer Tracy?"

"No," Dave said. "Wrong faith."

O'Hare rubbed his nose and said he'd see what he could do.

The billiard table cost forty-nine dollars. It was installed by four surly men who looked as if they were on parole. They no sooner had gone than the bell rang. The three Black Cats who had come for coffee a few days previously stepped in with four friends. They examined the table carefully, and one asked Dave if he played. It happened that he had wasted much time at billiards when young and was a proficient player.

Drawing lots, Dave and three of the boys played rotation by teams. To their chagrin he was a better player than they. He and his partner won the game and an ensuing play-off.

The next afternoon ten Black Cats appeared with their leader, Studs Gennari, who challenged Dave to a game of three cushion. Though possibly seventeen, Studs talked and acted with the self-assurance of aging Frank Sinatra. He said he would put a buck on the game. But Dave said betting was not allowed on games played there.

Staring at him, Studs said, "Look, preacher, you can't stop us from that. We'll just keep book and pass the bread after we leave."

"You look," Dave told him. "My name isn't preacher. It's Dave Murchison. If you want to pass bread on games, go down to Gino's and pay two bits a string. But you won't do it on games played on this table. And I'll tell you why. Because that's the rule of this house. If you break it, you're banned. Do you still want to play three cushion?"

Continuing to stare at him blankly, Studs picked up a cue and began to chalk it. He was a very good player, but Dave beat him.

Studs said, "How can you shoot pool when there ain't a jukebox to keep your mind on the game?" Then he walked out, and two went with him. But seven stayed.

When Kathy and Dave discussed it later, she said, "Wouldn't a radio do?" But she knew it wouldn't.

O'Hare looked at Dave with wonder after he presented the problem.

"A *free* jukebox, like they rent for Polish weddings, where nobody has to feed the slot? Do you know how much they cost? About three hundred a week. Nobody can get you that, Reverend. If you don't believe me, go see a guy named Tony Maretta. Don't say you talked to me or know the cost. If he asks where you heard about him, say the kids told you. Just tell him what you want and get the answer from the horse's ass." O'Hare gave him the name of a company and an address on Eighth Avenue.

An appointment with Maretta was hard to obtain. But at last Dave managed it. Maretta, a man with vulpine features who spoke a fractured English, gazed at him blankly as Dave explained who he was and what he wanted. A young man who sat beside the large desk answered for Maretta: "Three hundred a week."

Dave shrugged hopelessly, and Maretta asked if he wanted to break the Black Cats.

"Not exactly break them," Dave replied. "Get them off the streets. Take them out of neighborhood hangouts like Gino's and Callahan's. Try to get some of them back in school. Let them see there's a better life than the mindless way they're living. But I guess you don't care anything about that, Mr. Maretta."

"Mindless?" Maretta looked inquiringly at his assistant, who explained the meaning in Italian. Then he turned to Dave again and demanded how he could know what Tony Maretta thought. "The kids send you to me. You can't pay. You go back, and they laugh at you and leave. Tell me more about you. Why are you a Protestant priest?"

Dave told him as best he could.

"Okay. You don't know what Tony Maretta think. Don't never forget that. You get a box for one dollar a month. Put in today. Set not too loud." He looked at his assistant. "A ninety-six. New records every month. Pay the dollar to the guy who change the records."

Dave, feeling stunned, started to thank him profusely, but Maretta cut him short. Getting up and extending a hand, he said, "Good luck, Father."

When Dave went home and described in detail what had happened, Kathy could not quite believe it would turn out as Maretta had said. But it did. Men installed the jukebox that very afternoon, and by five o'clock a score of Black Cats had gathered. For the first time each treated Dave with the utmost respect. They shot pool; they played Ping-pong on the two tables which had been set up in the second room; some even leafed the magazines which Kathy had stacked on a table. A couple lighted cigarettes, but Studs Gennari told them to put them out. Why? "You finks, there ain't no ashtrays in the place." One asked Dave if he smoked, and he replied, "Not in the office." The Office! That's what they decided to call it. Meanwhile, the jukebox never ceased its grinding music.

A few afternoons later, while Dave was making hospital calls and Kathy was working about the apartment, a din of voices rose to her above the thump of the jukebox. By that time a rule had been established for Office hours: from after school till ten o'clock. (When someone had protested that he had quit school, Dave suggested that he try it again.) Now, going downstairs, Kathy confronted a new crisis.

Some of the boys had brought in four girls, and Studs was laying down the law over loud laments and objections. "No chicks! That's the rule!" Someone objected that Dave never had said so. "*No chicks!*" Studs yelled. Then he saw Kathy and said, "Right, Kathy?"

"I suggest," she said, "that the girls come up and visit me."

They followed her upstairs reluctantly, as if expecting punishment. Probably they were fourteen or fifteen, though they succeeded in their efforts to look older. It was difficult to differentiate one from another, and all looked like scores of girls Kathy had seen in the neighborhood. Girls who would be women and possibly had been helped toward their goal already by boys who would be men. Faces and hair created from the contents of bottles, clothing which looked like a product of the plasterer's art. *Oh, sisters,* Kathy thought, *pregnant by seventeen and old by thirty.* She wished she knew some way to communicate with them.

As it turned out, her inspiration was not so bad. She treated them as equals and clued them with the thought their equality was at a high social level by serving tea. Though possibly

none had ever had afternoon tea, all had seen it happen on television and knew from the mythology of the boob tube that only
ladies drank tea in the afternoon. Was she patronizing them?
She hoped not, yet at the same time she wondered why a new
good life need begin with old-fashioned good manners.

She showed them around the apartment. They cared not at
all about the little kitchen, heaven help their future mates. They
were interested, rather, in the bottles on her dressing table and
barely restrained their wish to dive into her closet and examine her wardrobe. While they had tea, she turned on recorded music, which, if not to their taste, at least offered dis-
tracting sounds which, from habit, helped put them at ease.
With such condescending thoughts, Kathy told herself, missionary ladies had confronted God's natural women from
Timor to Timbuktu. But what to do and where to begin?

Dave, who seemed to have taught her nearly everything, had
set a significant example for her with the boys downstairs:
Avoid interrogation, that bench on which as a caseworker she
had built neat little social boxes. And before long the girls began to interrogate her.

"How far along are you?"

"A little over six months."

"What did you think when you found out you were in a family way? . . . Are you hungry all the time when you're pg? . . .
What do you use on your hair to give it that sheen? . . ."

From their talk of pregnancy and grooming began to emerge
clues to their aspirations: to be beautiful and married, to be
admired and secure. Were those aspirations so very different
from Kathy's own?

When they left, they gladly accepted her invitation to return
and bring friends. Yet could her friendship proffered and accepted lead to any significant destination? Or was she only
launched on a long course of helpful hints on homemaking
and aids to beauty?

Almost daily visits by a number of girls were interrupted
in June, when Kathy entered Roosevelt Hospital. There she

was easily delivered of a healthy eight-pound boy whom they called Steven, a name that struck their fancy.

When Mother rather inanely asked why not Martin instead of Steven, Dave said, "Steven, Mother, because on some day far in the future he's sure to get stoned." That amused her, as his put-ons always did.

Lying in her hospital bed the day after her delivery, Kathy pondered Dave's put-ons. She loved him so! And she loved his sense of humor, his kidding that usually veiled some acute observation. Yet had he been straining humor recently over affairs at Beacon? Or was she merely going through that phase called postpartum depression?

Nevertheless, lying there, she worried about his—*their*—ministry at Beacon. Where were they and the church headed? On that humid June day the challenge of Beacon seemed to have lost its bright glow. The trouble was that it often seemed little more than a social organization. Ministry to the less privileged somehow should offer more than greater social privileges. On rare occasions when she tried to talk to Dave about it, he had put her off, as if he himself were uncertain of their direction and did not want to disclose his uncertainty to her.

They had succeeded, for example, in establishing contact with many of the young in the neighborhood. The boys followed Dave now as if he played the irresistible music of the Pied Piper of Hamelin. True, Dave had a program for them. But could he lead them out of their shoddy environment to a better life? None had yet attended Sunday service, which Kathy thought the most important function of Beacon, the significant difference between a church and a social organization. Yet Dave said he would not throw religion at them.

Since becoming the pastor, he had brought six persons into the membership, three of them Negroes, whom the trade and craft families tolerated only because Dave had convinced them that they must. His manner of convincing them had not pleased Kathy, for he had not related tolerance to Christian faith. Rather, he had appealed to their pride and progressiveness, saying that Negroes now were accepted in fashionable midtown churches and in effect asking them didn't they want to be like their economic and social betters. Which, of course, they did. And which had prompted Kathy to say it was regrettable that religion must be caught in the seemingly universal scramble up the hill of economic success.

"Regrettable," Dave had replied, "but true," and then he had quoted doggerel: "The higher up the monkey climbs, the greener grows the grass. The higher up the monkey climbs, the more he shows his ass."

Dave had changed his preaching style in an effort to be understandable to his congregation. He no longer referred to such figures as Camus or Sartre, as he had when he had preached at Old Fourth. His informal manner, his colloquial speech pleased the people, but Kathy wondered sometimes if he almost tossed off his sermons. He virtually abandoned intellectual discourse at Beacon and brought his main efforts to bear on matters such as trying to tame the Black Cats. Perhaps they should start looking for another church right now. But no other church would consider him seriously until he had been pastor of Beacon for at least a year.

Well, it was time she thought of some way to help the girls that might match the program Dave had undertaken with the boys. A few days after she took Steve home from the hospital an idea occurred to her.

The world being a stage and the people players. . . . Beacon having a stage of sorts. . . . The girls having favorite actresses, and each girl acting out some role in almost every waking moment. . . .

Thus, it came about that on Friday nights the girls, led by Kathy, began to act out on the stage of Beacon ideas—the mere suggestions of formal plays—that interested them.

As Kathy said, "We make 'em up as we go along."

By Christmas a score of girls, some of whom never had attended church before, were in the congregation of Beacon each Sunday morning.

One Friday morning in February, 1965, Kathy was talking about her girls at breakfast.

"They're really learning something in this playacting," she said. "They're learning about truth and falsity in thought, speech, manner, movement, the very nature of their own lives. . . ."

And what, Dave wondered, would the harvest be? Would Kathy have any better luck with her girls than he was having with his boys? By that time a number of boys who had been members of the gang once known as the Black Cats were attending church. But Dave doubted that their lives were deeply affected by his sermons. Most attended, he believed, from a sense of loyalty to him, their leader, now that Studs Gennari had been drafted and the Black Cats had become a legend of memory.

After breakfast he went downstairs to his study. For the fourth consecutive week he was having trouble in the preparation of a sermon. His theme for the coming Sunday was difficult, perhaps impossible: What could a citizen of any faith do to help bring peace to the world? The answer, as plain as the nose on Lyndon Johnson's face, was nothing. Then why bring it up in church at all? Why try to talk about the stupid expanding war in Vietnam? Because the church was the institution from which ideas and programs of peace should emanate. One must try. One must undertake seemingly hopeless struggles.

He was pondering how to develop his idea when the front-door trip bell clanged. In a moment he heard the click of billiard balls. It was off-hours for playing billiards, so he went to the front room to investigate.

To his surprise, Abe, wearing his military school uniform, was arched over the table. He completed his shot and looked up at Dave unsmilingly.

"Hi, Abe. What's up?"

"Nothing's up. What's up with you?"

Abe did not like him. Dave did not know why. When he first had gone to Old Fourth, Abe had treated him with indifference. But after he had married Kathy, Abe had begun to treat him with downright hostility. Was it a sibling thing?

"What's up with me is a sermon hang-up."

Abe chalked his cue and made another shot. "Amazing. Your hanging up on anything, I mean. Pop thinks you're perfect. So does Mom. They like you a lot more than they do me."

Was that the reason for Abe's hostility? Dave never had thought of it. Neither had Kathy in her fretting over Abe's attitude.

Dave said, "That's not true, Abe. They're crazy about you. They're nice to me because I married into the family."

"Bullshit," Abe said. "They like you better because you're a nice Christian preacher. And they know I don't dig any of it. You love niggers and peace and all that crap." He grinned tauntingly at Dave. "I'd like a nice long war. Then I could get into it and have some fun."

Dave refused to argue with him. "How come you're home from school?"

"The place has been closed all week. Asian flu or something. They sent everybody home who could walk. I've been staying with a buddy on Long Island. Got a date in Poughkeepsie tonight. Thought I'd say hello to Kathy and then to Mom and Pop." He put away his cue. "See ya. Happy hang-up." He went upstairs to see Kathy.

Dave had still not come to grips with his sermon when it came time for him to leave for Why Club.

The informal organization called Why Club met in a second-rate hotel uptown. Its forty-seven members were young men who presently were or recently had been clergymen. They would have been called extreme radicals by thousands of the American clergy, but among themselves they found significant shades of opinion. Six were rabbis, three were priests from Fordham, and there was one who had left the priesthood in order to marry and now was having trouble in finding satisfactory employment.

When Dave arrived that Friday, a crowd already had gath-

ered in the luncheon room near the impromptu bar where those
who wanted drinks could buy them. Don Quigley, a friend
since Union, who had a pastorate on Long Island, tagged Dave
at once.

"Good news, old buddy. I'm buying you a drink to celebrate." Dave, who had thought he would not have a drink, suddenly changed his mind. "I resigned last Sunday. First of next
month I start in the personnel department at American Can.
Fifteen thousand beginning salary. How about that!" Congratulations, Don, congratulations. "Jean's so happy she doesn't
know which end is up. How can you hope to raise three kids
these days on seven thousand a year? So. . . ." Dave sipped his
scotch and withdrew mentally from Don while continuing to
smile and nod. Was he jealous? He found himself listening to
Rabbi Herb Weinstein, who was haranguing a priest nearby.

"You tell me what kind of God a Jew can believe in after
the death camps of the second war. For at least three thousand
years, Jews have believed that whatever happened to them was
because God wanted it to. When the Babylonians destroyed
Jerusalem in five eighty-six, the Jews said that God is punish-
ing us because we're sinful people. When the Romans destroyed Jerusalem in the year seventy, we Jews said the same
thing. On Saturdays in the synagogue we hear we were exiled
from our land because of our sins. Now then, following through,
don't you have to say that God sent Hitler and God wanted
the death camps? I find that thought absurd and obscene. How
can I any longer believe in a God who controls human destiny
and is actively involved in Jewish history?"

"Well then," the priest asked, "what kind of God do you believe in?"

"It's hard to describe." Herb's tone became vague. "I'm
going in the direction of a more turned-on, mystical God. One
who is a God of earth and nature. A friend of mine, Rabbi
Richard Rubenstein, speaks of God as the holy nothingness,
which is not as peculiar as it sounds. . . ."

Don was saying, "Absolutely nothing but the need to make

a decent living made me do it. Did you see that study of salaries among Presbyterian preachers? Everybody seems to think the Presbyterian is the best-paid denomination. But it turns out the *median* Presbyterian salary is fifty-five hundred a year! Think how many thousands of ministers that puts *below* that figure. Then look at the cost of living index. . . ."

Dave tuned to another conversational station: a Lutheran from Queens who exclaimed, "All this God talk! What was really going on when all the God talk was used correctly, when men spoke of Him from their guts? It wasn't pie in the sky. Was it mystery, fear of dying, loneliness, the need for forgiveness? It wasn't crap. I'm sure of that. But what was really going on, and how was it different from things today? Why—"

"Hey, Dave"—Jerry Granger interposed himself—"have you heard of any decent opening a long way from New York? Not for me. For Joe Foote. His crazy wife has walked out on him again—for the last time, it seems. And his crazy congregation blames *him*, not her. He's got to move."

"No, Jerry, haven't heard of a thing. But if I do. . . ."

They progressed to their tables, where the spirited talk continued. After lunch the chairman introduced Milton Robinson, who had a slum church in Brooklyn which was even more difficult than Beacon. Milt's paper was a discussion of the death of God theme entitled "What Is It, God?" It was a subject Dave had heard discussed often. And there was nothing arresting in the discussion from the floor that followed until Jack Marvin spoke.

"I think," Jack said, "the main problem of the church today is not intellectual but ethical. William Sloane Coffin, Jr., said that recently. I think most people have turned away from the religious community not so much because they don't believe in God as because they're appalled at the way the religious community in this time of prosperity in this country has failed to make common cause with suffering. And when the church and synagogue shape up ethically, when they're really true to their own great ethical imperative, then at that point a lot of people will begin to think the religious community is worth joining. People say to me, How can you be in the church when there are so many hypocrites in it? And I say to them I figure there's room for one more. It's the only answer to that sort of question throughout all history. The only difference between people in the religious community and those outside it is that those of us inside really know we're sick. . . ."

As Dave rode a bus downtown, he thought that Jack Marvin should serve as a pastor to pastors. Heaven knew they needed one. *Or at least I need one.* He continued to mull a remark of Jack's: "The main problem of the church today is not intellectual but ethical." At Beacon he and Kathy had tried to make common cause with suffering, but satisfaction with the effort seemed to diminish steadily. Couldn't one accomplish as much —and even more—in some social effort outside the church? One even could be better paid for it, though not as well as in Don Quigley's wide swing into private enterprise. Maybe, Dave thought, Don's decision had surprised him into silence at today's meeting, where he usually participated vociferously in the discussions, and thus he had listened more carefully to what was said. There was a good sermon in "Common Cause with Suffering," a more fruitful subject than the woeful price of involvement in Vietnam. He would shelve that and begin again. There was something helpful along this line in Paul Tillich's *Biblical Religion and the Search for Ultimate Reality.* He would borrow the book from Martin, whom he had not seen in a couple of weeks.

Leaving the bus, he walked a couple of blocks across town to Old Fourth. When he entered the church office, he paused in surprise, for the woman who looked up at him was unlike any Old Fourth secretary in his experience. Blond, handsome, well groomed, about thirty, she looked as if she should be toiling for an officer of one of those rich advertising agencies rather than performing the Lord's work in a church.

Dave introduced himself and asked if Martin was in.

"He's in Washington, Mr. Murchison, at a National Council

meeting. He won't be back until tomorrow. Mr. Bell"—Martin's present assistant was named John Bell—"is out calling. I'm Martha Frome. May I help you?"

"Well, Miss Frome—"

"Mrs. Frome."

Dave explained that he wanted to borrow the Tillich book and had a pretty good idea of where it was on Martin's study shelves.

Martha Frome smiled. "Maybe it isn't where you think. I've rearranged Mr. Judson's books by subject and alphabetically by author. They were all mixed up."

"Holy smoke, does Martin know? I mean he *knew* where everything was."

Her smile faded. "Will he be annoyed? I—Well, there hasn't been much to do here while he was away. So I just . . . tried to keep myself occupied."

"No," Dave said, "he won't be annoyed. He never gets annoyed about things like that. He'll just be surprised. How long have you been here, Mrs. Frome?"

"I started Monday."

"Why?"

She looked puzzled. "I answered an ad in the *Times*."

He stepped into Martin's study, and she went with him. She was very well formed, he observed, most modernly structured to be serving time in this ancient edifice. Tillich's book was where it should have been in the first place; Martha Frome's reorganization of volumes would have satisfied any librarian. And Martin's desk was neater than Dave had ever seen it.

Since Martin was away, he thought he should ask Jane home for dinner. When he went to the parsonage, she greeted him warmly. Then Abe came down the stairs carrying an athletic bag and said, "Hi again, Rev. You over your hang-up?"

"I'm working at it, Abe."

"Bye, Mom." Abe kissed her on the top of her head.

"Abe"—she clutched him by an arm—"please remember what I told you."

"Okay, Mom." And then he was gone.

She stepped to a living room window and watched till he was out of sight. When she faced Dave, he thought she looked very tired.

At first Jane was reluctant to go home with him. She pointed out it was Friday evening, when both Kathy and he were occupied with the boys' and girls' clubs. (He had forgotten about that.) But then, brightening, she reminded herself that she could sit with Stevie while they were out. Then again, she said that sudden guests, even members of the family, could pose problems. She would phone Kathy. When she did, Kathy urged her to come—and also to remind Dave that he had a wedding rehearsal at six o'clock for a church ceremony he must perform at noon tomorrow. (He had forgotten about that, too.)

"Weddings!" Jane exclaimed. "I think the greatest joy in being a minister's wife is that you have the chance to go to so many weddings. Dave, such *interesting* people are forever getting married." She called down the stairs and told Mrs. Bentley she was going to Kathy's for the evening. "Kathy told me the nice thing you do about your wedding honorariums. You give them to her. That's very sweet. Marty always gives them to me— always has. How did you know about that—and how did he? Do they suggest it to you in the seminary?"

"No, Mother. At least not at mine. I guess it's just . . . instinct."

"Aren't instincts wonderful? You know Marty went down to Washington only on Thursday. But my instincts tell me he's been gone a month. He has an evening panel tonight and was going to fly home afterward, but I told him not to be silly. Get a night's rest and fly home in the morning—Dave, we don't need a cab."

He was chary about taking taxis because they were expensive. But now he flagged one down because Jane was so lovely in the twilight—such a rare and waning kind of lady who should not be subjected to a crowded bus in the rush hour.

"What do you hear from your mother? How is she?"

"Very happy." She was not. She had written him last week from Bern, where the nut she had married was institutionalized with the hope of drying out his liver. Apparently financial problems loomed. "She sent her best to you and Martin." She had not. She thought of no one but herself, and the fact she was a grandmother so shocked her that she did not like to mention it.

When they went into the Office, the jukebox was blaring and the kids playing billiards and Ping-Pong were yelling their heads off. Dave, observing Jane wince at the noise, told them to tone it. They tried to comply, but he knew their restraint would not last long. Upstairs Steve was yelling lustily, too, whether in pleasure or anger even Kathy did not know. When Jane picked him up and began walking him around, he quieted down. Just a little gas on the stomach, she said.

"I hope you don't mind eating early," Kathy said. "But there's the wedding rehearsal at six and the club meetings at seven. Mother, you should have told us Father is away. You could have stayed here."

"Where it's nice and quiet," Dave said.

Jane looked down at Steve on her shoulder. "Doesn't he have a beautifully shaped head? No, Kathy, I'm glad I stayed home. Abe came in last night and left again today."

Kathy paused in setting the table and looked at her searchingly. "What's wrong?"

"Nothing more than usual, I guess. Dave, did you meet Mrs. Frome? Isn't she nice?"

"Very. Kathy, you ought to see your father's new secretary. A wow. Almost as beautiful as Mother."

"Oh, knock it off." Jane smiled at him. "I mean she's intelligent and well bred. I wonder how long we can keep her. She's a divorcée—arrived here from Indianapolis last week and looked in the *Times* for a job. I think she has some kind of sad story. But from talking with her, I know she's the last person who's going to tell it. I'm not sure what her church background is. But I think it's significant that she chose a job with a church —that's the way Marty always advertises the job—instead of taking something else. The salary is eighty-five a week, you know. He says she's very capable and could earn more somewhere else. I just hope she stays awhile."

After they had eaten a meat loaf dinner, Jane volunteered to wash the dishes while they went to the wedding rehearsal in the auditorium. But Kathy said she did not have to attend and urged Jane to go with Dave. She went gladly.

Though nondenominational Beacon was more Unitarian than anything else, most of its members displayed a Roman Catholic fondness for ritual when it came to weddings and funerals. Dave offered a wide variety of wedding ceremonies, ranging from the five-minute legal romp to the pomp and circumstance of a neo-Episcopal ritual. Almost invariably, people wanted the Episcopalian parading and kneeling.

The families of Anthony Flynn and Betty Murch were no exception. As Betty's father put it, "Pastor, we want the whole works." So the works they were getting, with the organist being paid something extra for playing at the rehearsal. *Tum-tum-da-boom!* "Mr. Murch, you're out of step, and we might as well get it right from the start." Two run-throughs finally satisfied friends and families.

As Anthony and Betty knelt for the last time, Dave paused and said, "I want to make an announcement to the entire wedding party. I know that Joe and Julius and some others of you are going to help Tony get into his shirt and tails tomorrow. But Tony here is taking care of his own shoes. That's an order. Remember it."

Afterward someone expressed mystification, but Dave would not explain the reason for his order. When Jane returned to the apartment with him, she said it was going to be a beautiful ceremony, but why the business about the shoes?

"Some of those there already know about it," Dave said, "but I didn't want to put any ideas into the heads of those who don't. There was a disaster at our last High Church ceremony. When the groom knelt, the entire audience saw that someone had painted on the sole of his left shoe the word 'Kick' and on the sole of his right 'Me.' "

"How dreadful!" Jane exclaimed. And then she began to laugh.

He changed into sweat shirt, jeans, and sneakers and walked three blocks to Faller's Gymnasium. More than forty boys, divided into two groups of twelve to fifteen and sixteen and up, already were horsing around in what Mike Faller called his upper gym. Mike rented it to Beacon for five dollars each Friday evening, which some claimed to be the only charitable gesture of his life.

While the evenings were still strenuous for Dave, they were not as rigorous as they used to be. Now he had trained four reliable eighteen-year-olds to aid him in organizing and refereeing. Nevertheless, the boys insisted on his taking part in everything. He must put in a few minutes of each basketball game racing about the floor and blowing his whistle, he must prance about as the referee in at least one round of each boxing match, and he must show the younger boys how it *really* was done on the horses and rings.

Mike Faller dropped by for a few minutes that evening and looked at him critically after he swung off the rings. "Dave, your form ain't what it used to be."

"Mike," he panted, wiping his face with a towel, "I ain't what I used to be. I'm pooped."

"You miss the point," Mike said. "You're supposed to poop *them* out and stay fresh yourself."

By ten o'clock everyone was sufficiently pooped that Dave could call a halt to his self-destruction. A busboy from the Venetian Kitchen rolled in the iced Cokes and pastry which Angelo Caratti supplied in return for five dollars a week and frequent lectures on the extent of his charitableness. Lolling about on the floor, the boys gorged themselves until someone called, "Hey, Dave, remember the Good Man stories you used to tell us? Some of the new kids never heard 'em."

"Yeah," someone else said. "Remember Abie Lincoln?"

"I don't want no school crap," a boy said.

"Well," Dave told him, "maybe that's because you won't *listen* at school." He looked around at a group of former Black Cats and called, "*Who* was Abie Lincoln?"

They answered him in chanting chorus: "A Good Man he who set the black man free."

"Did Abie ever do a dumb thing?"

"Yeah, man, he didn't plan. A school dropout he, poor young Abie."

"Did Abie ever do a bright thing?"

"Yeah, man. He hit the books and fought the crooks."

"What *then?*"

Chorus: "He was the greatest res-i-dent. And he became the greatest Pres-i-dent!"

Someone suggested that they do Good Man John F. Kennedy, and after they had chorused it, Dave said he had thought up a new one the other day—Good Man Marty King He would teach it to them.

O'Hare, who dropped around occasionally, had come in with Chuck Sandren, a former Black Cat, now a probationary patrolman on the city police force. After they had worked out Good Man Marty King, Dave greeted Good Man Sandren and asked him how the traffic went.

Chuck, squatting on his heels beside O'Hare and drinking a Coke, startled him by replying, "Uptown, downtown, side-town, Dave. Heavy enough to make you rave." Then, speaking slowly and sensibly, he gave his testimonial: He was glad that Dave had convinced him it was worthwhile to finish school. He was glad he had become a member of the police department. If he could do it, anybody could.

After they broke up, O'Hare said, "Come on, I'll drive you home, Dave. You're going to catch pneumonia one of these sweaty nights unless you start wearing a thicker jacket." As they climbed in the squad car, he said, "I spotted seven, eight good coming policemen there tonight."

"Is that what I'm doing?" Dave asked him. "Recruiting for the police department? O'Hare, did you know that I've served time?"

"No kidding?" O'Hare looked at him. "I've always felt you had the instinct for crime. What happened?"

Dave was still telling him about his adventures in the South when they pulled up in front of Beacon. "I need a scotch to ward off pneumonia. I'll bet Kathy will, too. Come in and have one with us."

"I'm not one to refuse you," O'Hare said.

When he introduced him to Jane, O'Hare began to display a charm that Dave had not realized he possessed. If O'Hare wasn't careful, he'd end up as a chief inspector with cirrhosis of the liver.

To Dave's surprise, Jane said she would have a little sherry before she went home. Alas, they had none. But O'Hare extolled the virtues of a drop of scotch, and she took one without protest.

"Captain O'Hare"—she raised her glass—"to a gentleman who's a friend to my children. . . ."

O'Hare went on at great length, extolling Dave's work with the boys' club. Jane gazed at Dave as O'Hare turned to Kathy.

She said, "The work with the boys comes easily and naturally to you, doesn't it, Dave?"

Yes, he enjoyed it.

Jane continued to gaze at him thoughtfully. "It's too bad there are so many . . . facets to the work of the ministry. The old, as well as the young. Preaching and—it seems a million things."

"Too many things," Dave said, "for one man to be good at them all. I wish I had Martin's talents."

"You do. You will. It took him a lot of practice. Give it time, Dave."

Realizing that she understood and sympathized with his difficulties in some aspects of the ministry, he suddenly felt closer to her than ever before.

At last she said she must go, and O'Hare replied that she would ride in his personal squad car.

Jane smiled. "That would be wonderful! I've never ridden in one. I'd love to hear the sound of the siren."

"We'll try it," O'Hare said. "It's not my precinct you live in, but I don't think they'll mind."

Kathy and Dave went to the street with them and kissed her good night. The last they saw of her she was talking animatedly to O'Hare, who let his siren growl as they turned the corner.

Martin arrived home around ten o'clock the following morning. Surprised when Mrs. Bentley told him that Jane was still asleep, he went to awaken her and found that she was dead.

✣ *Nine* ✣

O N WEDNESDAY afternoon he stopped at a service station outside Newcomb and bought chains.

"Where you bound?" the serviceman asked.

"Beyond Alden," Martin said.

"You don't need the chains on yet. But there's a big one comin'."

"Feels it." He looked at the gray sky and turned from the bite of the wind which was quartering northeast. "Dropping?"

"Yep. Seven degrees since noon. Steady at thirty-two now."

"Might fall wet."

"Can't tell yet. Might come dry as powder. Those city rubbers won't do you much good up Alden way."

"I've boots and warmer things where I'm bound."

As he drove on, Martin thought it the most satisfying exchange he had had in four days. Friendly enough, but completely anonymous. There was nothing to say, yet people had been trying to say something through all the interminable days and nights since Saturday morning. He had tried to lock in his grief, but a couple of times it had released itself uncontrollably. Now he hoped he had left the heaviest burden of it in New

York, and he did not want it brought to him here in the north country. So he had not told anyone—not even Kathy, Dave, or Joe—where he was going. He simply had said he was getting away for a time.

Probably Abe had guessed his destination. Surprisingly, Abe had been the easiest companion because he had understood the need for silence. (Even Kathy had uttered an inanity or two: "An embolism! Isn't that what took Grandmother?") Except for a couple of outbursts of tears, Abe had kept his grief behind a grimly puckered face. What was he really thinking? Was there, after all, some stoic virtue in that military school training? After the burial yesterday, when Martin drove him back to school, they had maintained their silence all the way. At the school gate he had laid a cheek against Martin's and said, "Take it easy, Pop," then disappeared.

Martin had driven on with tears in his eyes, seeing a sadness in silence as great as the sadness he had found in fumbling efforts at communication. There was something so *Edwardian* about Abe and him, something he did not want, yet a thing he seemed unable to help. He had paused at a diner in a bleak Hudson Valley town and picked at a plate of hash. Then he had checked into a motel and cringed before the blankness of walls in a room which offered no distraction, not even a Gideon Bible. There was no way of telling how little he had slept or eaten recently.

Now, approaching Alden, he believed that the bleak whiteness of hills and valleys under the oppressive gray sky offered something aseptically healing. He should buy supplies in Alden, yet Jane always kept the pantry stocked for what she called emergencies. He did not want to have to answer questions at stores in town, where everyone knew them, and he was not hungry anyway. So he took the cutoff around Alden, wheels churning in the snow a few times before he emerged on the cleared lake road. His circumvention of curious eyes in Alden pleased him somehow. And he was pleased further to see that none of the Greenes gazed out at him curiously as he passed their house. Taking the left fork, he came to his own house with a fugitive's sense of relief.

The practical matters he must attend to were, he thought, a kind of blessing. Stopping the car on the cleared road, he put on the chains, then backed it up the drive until it was hidden by the laurel clumps. If he could, he would have obliterated its tracks in the snow. But he would be discovered soon enough; one could not even pass through this sparsely peopled countryside without being observed.

The key was in its hiding place, and the door screeched open on a familiar room he suddenly dreaded to enter alone. There was a rather pleasant musky odor in the house and a skittering sound of chipmunk claws from the attic. Concentrating on the practical matters, he turned on the electric current, then found that the waterline was frozen. So he would use melted snow. But all the burners of the electric stove were mysteriously dead. Fetching dry wood from the cellar, he enjoyed his careful making of a fire in the big fireplace. An added sense of pleasure came to him when he glanced out a window and saw that snow was beginning to fall lightly.

Going upstairs, he entered his and Jane's bedroom as furtively as a stranger. The cold there seemed almost unbearable. But after rummaging around and finding what he wanted —long johns, woolen shirt and socks, corduroys, a sweater, a fleece-lined parka, an old pair of high laced boots—he stripped to the buff and dressed warmly. Leaving his city clothes crumpled on the bed, like artifacts of some vanished life, he carried a dozen loads from the outdoor woodpile and stacked them near the fire to dry. It was almost dark now, and for the first time in days he was hungry.

The canned goods on the pantry shelves were a treasure trove. There was even a sealed can of coffee, which he could percolate with snow water in the electric pot. He selected a can of beans and one of corned beef, then recalled that the stove was out of order. There used to be an iron grate someplace in the cellar. When he finally found it, he had to wait for the flames to die before he could try to fit it in place. Meanwhile, he went upstairs and dragged down the mattress and pillow from Abe's room along with a couple of blankets. He placed the mattress on the floor before the fire and hoped for a warm, restful night's sleep after he had eaten. Beans—corned beef—coffee. Suddenly, and no doubt irrationally, he wanted bread. Snow was falling heavily now, forming a yellow wall in the glow of lamplight beyond the windows. Nevertheless, he wanted bread.

In his determination to be self-reliant and totally severed from every living person, he decided to make and bake himself a loaf of bread. He had seen yeast and a can of Crisco on a shelf. His mother used to bake bread; Jane had, too, sometimes. Bread contained flour, shortening, water, salt, yeast—maybe something else, he wasn't sure. He found a cookbook in a kitchen drawer, but it was a French cookbook which did not mention a recipe for bread. Yet he was determined to try, because bread was the only thing in the world he wanted to eat now. Bread had to be set in a warm place to rise before baking, he knew. Yeast made it rise. But how much yeast should he put in the paste he was stirring? For good measure, he put in a little baking powder. Gradually his mixture became a lump of dough which filled him with a sense of satisfaction, doubtless childlike and absurd, but still a true satisfaction such as he had not felt since— He got the lump into a bowl, thinking he was dirtying too many dishes, then covered it with a napkin, as he had seen Jane do, and set it near the fire. He kept peeking under the napkin and believed he already could see the dough beginning to change its shape. Then he remembered that he had not brought down the old portable oven from the attic. While flashing his light about up there he saw an old pair of snowshoes which he had used in years past, and he dragged them down with the oven. Examining the gut thongs, he found them very dry and decided to weather the shoes outside in the snow. But first he looked at his dough again.

It had risen enormously, indeed it was beginning to overflow the bowl obscenely. He was going to have a very large loaf of bread. As he started for a tray onto which to place the risen dough, there was a stomping and a muffled shout on the front porch.

"Who's in there?" someone cried.

"Who's out there?" Martin cried back.

"It's me, Jim Whitcomb, Mr. Judson."

Martin groaned and opened the door.

Old Jim, who was the caretaker of Joe Trask's place, stepped in slowly, his fur cap and sheepskin crusted with snow. He gaped from Martin to the disarray of mattress, snowshoes, pots and pans.

"Shut the door!" Martin realized his tone was almost a snarl.

Jim shut it slowly and said, "I seen your lights and—wondered. She's a boomer out there tonight. Bet it's solid snow all the way to Katahdin. Talked to Mr. Trask on the phone a couple o' weeks ago. He said he might be comin' up for some skiin', but he ain't showed. You havin' yourself a little winter vacation? How's Mrs. Judson and the young folk?"

Martin turned away, feeling he might never speak again.

There was a loud pop, a sighing sound, and before his startled eyes his risen dough dwindled into a flat mass. "God *damn* it!" he cried.

Jim Whitcomb fled.

He had just finished his supper of beans, corned beef, and coffee when the electric power failed. Lighting a kerosene lamp, he built up the fire. The wind rushed now with a steady muffled roaring; as Jim had said, she was a boomer. If the storm continued at the same rate, it would take days for the countryside to dig out—a pleasing isolation to contemplate.

Taking a King James Version from a shelf, he read from the Psalms. After a while, still wakeful, he carried his lamp along the rows of books, searching for one that might strike his fancy. Suddenly he found it, a book he had not read in several years, one of the finest books about man and nature ever written, *The Sea and the Jungle* by H. M. Tomlinson.

"Though it is easier, and perhaps far better, not to begin at all. . . ."

The beautiful prose carried him away, back to an age of greater restraint and, therefore, perhaps an age of deeper feeling. He had not thought Tomlinson would take him beyond the stormy Atlantic tonight, but he found himself led on magically into the Amazon country. It was almost midnight when he found himself beginning to nod.

Building up the fire and taking off only his boots, he wrapped himself in the blankets on the mattress. He heard his voice, "Night, Jane," and it did not sound strange, for it seemed that she was there.

He awakened in gray light, talking to her. But she was not there. Confused at first, then alarmed, he finally was deeply depressed. The fire was out, and the house creaked in the cold. According to his wristwatch, it was five minutes past eleven. Springing confusedly to his feet and pulling on his boots, he began to work at a fire. Since the windows were opaque sheets of ice and snow, he opened the door a crack and looked out at a white wasteland, where snow still fell lightly.

Perhaps food would help him overcome his profound depression. But the thought of beans, beef, and coffee rewarmed from last night's mess was revolting. Yet the thought of bread made him ravenous. What ailed him that he had developed this fantastic obsession for something he could not have? He sipped some heated coffee and leafed the pages of Tomlinson. But his midnight joy in isolation had evaporated by noonday.

As he wandered about restlessly, like a prisoner in a cell, he began to plot an escape. There were skis in the attic, but the texture of the snow was better for snowshoes. He would get bread! But he would not slog into town to be tortured by the curious. He would not go the shorter distance over to Joe's and beg bread from yakking Jim Whitcomb and his wife, Nancy. On the other side of the ridge in the hamlet of Bolt's Landing was the best bread ever baked; in summer they often used to drive the four miles around to buy the bread which Miss

Janet Craig made and sold in her tiny general store. But by hiking over the ridge it was only two miles to Bolt's Landing.

He put on an extra sweater under the parka and found fleece-lined gloves, a pair of dark glasses, and a knapsack of Abe's. As he closed the door behind him, he thought it did not really matter if he never returned to this house.

The snow had stopped falling. The air was calm under a bruised gray sky while the winds up there backed and filled and tried to make up their wanton minds what to do next. It was eight above by the porch thermometer. As he had hoped, the dried gut strings of the snowshoes had become resilient after the night in a snowbank. Fitting them on awkwardly, he took a few floundering steps. Perhaps he could not do it at all. But then the rhythm came back to him.

He went up across the meadows where most landmarks had disappeared. Even the brook had been buried deep, but then he heard it, an indistinct trickle, a dark vein somewhere below the pale flesh of snow. When he paused and looked back, panting, the wavering bird tracks of his snowshoes were the only sign of life in a dead world. Taking a sight on the hemlock stand higher up the slope, he tried to straighten his tracks by keeping his gaze fixed on it. An owl used to hang out in those hemlocks, badgered by jays and blackbirds but hanging on grimly to hoot and moan on moonlit nights. What had become of all that life? As if in answer, off west a cannonball of partridge burst into shrapnel and went shredding out of sight.

The going was slower than he had anticipated. It was half past one as he threaded among the dead chestnuts just below the crest. A deer started up, and then another, setting his heart to knocking. They plunged off into the drifts, and he made a detour in order not to frighten them far from their treaded-down feeding hollow. Soon he came out on the crest, where wind lashed his face stingingly. Through thinning clouds, the sunlight was turning white. Putting on the dark glasses and turning his back to the wind, he looked at the way he had climbed. His own house was blocked from view by the hemlock clump, but he saw Joe's big spread beside the curling snow-field of the lake. Then something to the west caught his eye, and he made out a plow churning eastward along the lake road.

It was folly to go on. This wind would crust the southern slopes of the ridge into icy sheets where he would have to break each step of his way. Why not go home? He was beginning to realize that his hike was not motivated by bread alone. When, indeed, had bread alone ever been his total motivation? If that was all he wanted, he could have gone over to Joe's place easily and obtained some from Nancy Whitcomb. Maybe, he thought now, bread was only a kind of symbol of his wish to cross a ridge and communicate with someone. He was not and never would be a solitary. He would go on because he did not want to return to the loneliness of his house.

He had gone only a little way when his shoes skidded on the icy crust and he flipped onto his back. One shoe dangling, the other tilted high, he spun downward dizzily until, by some phenomenon of luck, he jolted to a halt and found himself, one shoe off and the other on, upright and breathless in a vale of blue snow. His mind played back the scene of his fifty-yard descent like a motion-picture film, and he began to laugh. Still laughing, he shoed himself and went on more cautiously.

It was almost three o'clock when he left his snowshoes beside the store door in Bolt's Landing and stepped inside. Miss Janet Craig, a spare woman well along in age, was cutting dried beef on her slicing machine. Without a pause in turning the slicer, she looked at him and said, "Afternoon, Mr. Judson. We've had a bit of snow." What a remarkable woman!

"Uh—yes. I snowshoed over."

"Oh? Well, have a cup of coffee while you catch your breath."

"Thanks, I will. Did you bake this morning?"

"Of course."

"I'll take two loaves, make it three." Stomping his feet and rubbing his numbed hands across his numbed face, he said, "Could you cut me off a couple of slices to have with the coffee, please?"

"Mr. Judson, I've bread of my own going to spare and waste. Set down back by the stove."

While he drank a cup of coffee and ate a delicious ham sandwich, he told her what to put in his knapsack with the bread—two steaks of her home-cured ham, butter, potatoes, carrots. She refused his request for milk and eggs. "You'll break 'em and maybe cut yourself the first time you fall down."

And then, to his complete dismay, he realized he had not brought along his wallet.

But Miss Craig remained imperturbable. "Land sakes, Mr. Judson, if your credit ain't good with me after all these years, then I'll just close shop and ɪetire." When he started out, she told him, "Don't go back over the ridge, Mr. Judson. Go the long way around by road. It's safer, and you might get a lift."

"It's shorter by the ridge," he said. "It's blowing clear and the moon will be up early."

As he started to put on his snowshoes, he thought of something that was only decent. Stepping back inside, he said, "Miss Craig, my wife died on Saturday, and I wanted to . . . get away. I'm . . . batching it over there."

She looked at him, and her underlip quivered before she could tighten it. "I'm awful sorry to hear it, Mr. Judson. Your wife was the finest lady ever came this way." She hesitated. "I reckoned something was amiss when you came in alone. My cousin Hattie Crane used to say nobody ever comes to Bolt's Landing 'less they don't want to go anywhere else."

When he had climbed partway up the southern face of the ridge, he was sorry he had not taken the road. Most of the way he had to carry his showshoes and stamp footholds in the crust. The moon was still low in the east when he glimpsed a movement in the blue shadows to the west. Something—not a man, but an animal; not a deer, but some creature like a wolf or dog—moved again and disappeared.

Only animals were out tonight, he thought. Might not that include himself? His father used to speak of dogs and horses that had gone wild with grief after becoming bereft of some companionship. Had that happened to him? Was there some suicidal instinct in this up hill and down dale through freezing drifts? He shivered—and not just from the cold. Of all the crimes he possibly had committed in his mind at one time or another, he never had committed suicide. "Physician, heal thyself." Perhaps a healing process had begun in Bolt's Landing when he had gone back and spoken to Miss Craig. In a sense she was the first person to whom he had acted decently since Jane died.

Clawing his way up the slope, he winced at this first objective view of himself in several days. What had he been trying to prove with all his death talk all these years? How did he dare try ever again to comfort someone overwhelmed by grief? He had not questioned God's will or His existence when he found Jane dead. He hoped, as he always had, but did not know that there was a life hereafter wherein she and he might be rejoined as recognizable personalities. His faith, though not assailed by doubt, had seemed simply to move aside in his time of grief; it had not offered him the serenity he used to try to make it offer others. Yet that did not mean his faith—or hope—was worthless; rather, it meant that he was guilty of ignoring it in his awful loneliness. *Now* was the time to begin paying it some attention and let it try to help him back from the pit of despair.

At last he tottered onto the crest and sank down, gasping for breath, his eyes watering in the keening wind. *Now* he wanted to get home as fast as he could.

The world north from the ridge was a vast blankness, somewhat, he thought, like the future he faced. But lemon moonlight was beginning to filter across its features. A light winked, and then another. He plunged down through the drifts. There was scarcely any snow crust on this side of the ridge; without snowshoes he could not have gone a dozen yards through the drifts. He sensed rather than saw his route, his memory of this familiar land playing him no tricks; under its great sheath of ice and snow he visualized it in all its October spareness.

As he reached the foot of the steepest slope, he believed he heard someone whistle. He paused, thinking he had been mistaken, but it came again—and then a shout from the general direction of the hemlock stand. He was too cold to whistle in reply, and his attempt at a shout sounded more like a grunt as he slogged on.

Finally, he made out someone waving his arms in the moonlight, and the voice that came to him was unmistakable: "Martin?"

"Yes."

"For Christ's sake, where you been?"

He saved his breath till he was a few yards from Joe. "I went over the ridge for bread."

"You went—Holy Jesus! You—"

"What are you doing here?" Martin asked.

"Looking for *you*. And I busted this. . . ." He sounded like Sergeant Trask used to as he explained he had broken his obscene left ski on a log and had been thrashing around in the obscene snow ever since trying to make his way up or down or someplace.

Martin said, "This isn't good skiing snow."

For some reason Joe found his remark inordinately funny. He laughed and clapped him on the back and said, "Now I know you're o-*kay!*"

Together they hobbled and staggered on down the slope with Joe using his right ski and hooking his left foot onto Martin's right snowshoe. Several times they tripped and fell, each time helping each other up like two clowns who inevitably would fall again.

Electric power had been restored. They turned on lights and

sat recovering their breaths until Joe spoke. "I thought you had come up here. I phoned Jim to ask him to look in on you, but he said he already had." He rubbed his cold face to restore circulation. "I think Jim is getting too old to be responsible. He said something about things here being in a mess. He said you were cussing. Neither he nor I ever heard you cuss. So I decided to come up and see if I could keep you some company. I had to bribe a snowplow man to get me through from Alden. I saw your shoe tracks heading up back. So I went to my place and dressed warm and got skis and started to follow you. Tell me, Martin, were you cussin'?"

Martin got to his feet and started to lay kindling in the fireplace. "Yes, I was! My bread dough exploded."

"Don't bother with a fire," Joe said. "Let's go over to my place."

"I'd rather stay here." Martin looked around at him slowly. "I'd be glad for your company if you want to try frozen bread and ham steak."

Joe grinned. "I sure do. I appreciate your asking me. Martin, you're going to be all right."

If not all right, Martin thought, at least he would be.

One evening in April, when Martin was eating dinner alone in a Child's restaurant on Broadway, he glimpsed a man passing outside in the rain who reminded him of Harold Engel. As the waitress took away his unfinished tomato juice, he remembered what Engel had told him twenty-five years ago in Upton.

"To be a truly effective minister, my young friend, you have to learn the con game."

Probably Engel had meant that one must indulge in some self-deception oneself, as well as con others into the obligations and programs of the organized church. Since Jane's death Martin realized he had become adept at small self-deceptions. It had taken the form of an extreme busyness, an urgent preoccupation with one thing or another from early morning till late at night without regard to the relative importance of the task.

This growing habit was manifest now by the pamphlet opened on the table. It contained the annual report of the city interfaith group of which he was an officer, and though he was thoroughly familiar with it, he kept leafing the pages in an attempt to kid himself he was not bored and lonely sitting there in Child's. Tonight he would attend a meeting of the group. This afternoon he had gone to a meeting at Union, then dropped by to see Tubby, who was ill with a stomach disorder. Declining Eunice's invitation to stay to dinner, he had come downtown by subway and stopped in this Child's before going on to the meeting. Glancing at his watch, he saw he had allowed himself too much time. (He had become a great watch glancer and was forever arriving at appointments too early.)

A woman entered the restaurant. Having the impression she was attractive and not wanting to stare at her, he lowered his gaze to his pamphlet, then looked up surprised, realizing she was Martha Frome. Rising and stepping toward her, he said, "Martha." She turned to him, startled. "If you don't have company, won't you join me?"

She did not say a word until she had sat down at his table and slipped back her raincoat. Then, gazing at him wonderingly, she said, "I somehow never associated you with Child's, Mr. Judson."

"Why not? I can't go to the Copa *every* night. You see . . ." He heard himself reciting the activities of his day, with which she was as familiar as he since she herself had written them on his calendar. Busy, busy, busy Martin Judson. He told the waitress to hold his chicken potpie until Martha was served, then went on at dull length about the afternoon meeting at Union.

After his voice died of boredom with itself, she said, "When I got home from the office, there was a letter from Mr. Trask. Thanks very much, Mr. Judson."

"Thanks? A letter from Joe? Oh. I meant to mention that to you, Martha. You're doing an excellent job."

He had recommended to the board that her salary be in-

creased from eighty-five to one hundred a week, and Joe had
informed her of the raise by letter.

She told him about several telephone calls that had come
that afternoon while he was absent, but he did not pay close
attention. He found himself, as he had many times previously,
wondering about her. How did she live? What did a lone
woman do with herself when not at work?

Before long, without his asking any questions, she disclosed
that a woman friend had come from Indianapolis, found a job,
and they were sharing an apartment. The woman had invited a
man to dinner at the apartment this evening, so Martha had
come to Child's and would find a movie afterward.

Her remark, when she made it, surprised him. "Mr. Judson,
I'm interested that you haven't invited me to join Old Fourth.
Isn't it natural for a church secretary to be a member of the
church?"

"Yes, it is. But not necessary. Everyone would be pleased, of
course. You've been attending services regularly, but, uh, you
don't have to, you know."

She smiled. "You mean, don't disrupt my private life? All
those pot parties I'm always going to? What I liked most when
you interviewed me for the job was that you didn't ask personal
questions. You didn't even ask where I worked in Indianapolis.
I answered your ad for a good reason. I wanted a job as unlike
my last one as I could find." She paused, but he did not ask her
anything. "I was raised an Episcopalian, but I didn't go to
church for years till lately. I find your sermons stimulating
—helpful."

He said, "Episcopalian? Maybe that accounts for something
that impressed me the first day you came to work. I dictated
something involving the phrase 'Father, Son, and Holy Spirit.'
You're the first secretary at Old Fourth in a long time who capitalized Holy Spirit or Holy Ghost. So you must know what
it's all about."

She smiled again. "Not really. What is the Holy Spirit?"

He grimaced. "The few times I've tried to explain it I've

confused both myself and my listeners so thoroughly that I've given up trying. . . ."

He was late for his meeting. It was the first time in weeks he had been late for an appointment.

Toward the end of May Martha felt that she was prepared to make a simple profession of faith and join the church. But on the Friday preceding the Sunday when she would be received into the membership, she told Martin she wanted to discuss a matter with him, and he took her to lunch at a neighborhood restaurant.

Her question came quickly: "Martin, can you really be born anew?" She had been reading things he suggested, and she referred, of course, to the familiar quotation by Jesus in the Book of John: "Verily, I say unto you, except one be born anew, he cannot see the kingdom of God."

She said, "My former husband phoned me last night. He wants us to . . . try it again. I don't want to. . . ."

She had had one year at a small Midwestern college, then had come home and cared for her invalid mother for three years. After her mother died, she had taken a secretarial course and gone to work as a librarian-stenographer for a pharmaceutical manufacturing house. There she met and fell in love with a chemist named Malcolm Scott. They were married after a brief courtship.

"I thought he was perfect. There was only one thing on which we disagreed. I wanted to have children right away. He wanted to wait awhile. Later I thought maybe that was significant. I don't know whether it was or not. But in any case I went along with him on the idea. A little over a year ago he had an offer of a better job in Chicago. It took him awhile to set things up in Chicago. Well"—she made a wry face—"I suppose these stories always are tedious. He met someone else in Chicago, fell in love with her, and asked me for a divorce—all within a very few weeks. I was . . . stunned. After I got the divorce, I came back to my job. But everything was . . . different. People, especially men, treated me differently. I was a divorcée.

Even people I'd known for a long time acted as though I had changed greatly. So I decided to make a new start in New York. And then Mal called last night. Into love, out of love— Big mistake—Martha, let's try it again.' "

"And you say you don't want to."

"Definitely not. So you might wonder why I bothered to bring it up in the first place. I— Well, I hope to join the church on Sunday. But I don't want it to be like joining a bridge club, where the only questions are whether you're socially acceptable and do you know the rules of the game. I've wanted to tell you something about my life because you've been such a kind friend. In a way I don't feel I'm a fit candidate for the kind of religion you practice. That's why I asked if you honestly think one really can be born anew."

"The important thing is," he told her, "you're—what's the word?—coping with your situation. You've made choices and are acting on them. I think that's what Jesus meant by being born anew and thereby seeing the kingdom of God. Do you remember what He said at the end of His discussion of this matter with Nicodemus? He said that everyone who acts evilly—or call it foolishly—hates to face the facts of what he has done because he'll be reproved. And then He makes the point that anyone who faces his folly honestly has 'been wrought in God,' as the old King James Version puts it. In other words, he has been born anew; he has *coped;* he can see the kingdom of God. Basically it's one of the precepts of modern psychology. Analysis, for example, is the way of being born anew. So are various other psychological approaches to full recognition of oneself. No, not everybody can be born anew simply because he won't make the effort to face up to himself. But you can—you *have* in making decisions and starting a new life. . . ."

She was received into the membership with five others on the following Sunday. Martin was somewhat disconcerted when Joe Trask invited her along with them to dinner in an uptown restaurant after church. The reason for his discomfiture was vague: Joe's inviting her smacked somehow of buying a drink for a new member of a club. What about the other five who had just been received into Old Fourth?

But she accepted the invitation graciously and had a good time. Indeed, Joe monopolized her so thoroughly that Martin began to wonder why he had been invited along. Obviously Joe was attracted to her. Well, why not, since she was a very attractive woman? And it seemed to Martin that she was attracted to Joe. Again, why not?

In the following week, when she was momentarily out of the office and he was looking up the answer to a telephone query on her calendar pad, he felt downright startled when he paged to Saturday and found the notation "Dinner Joe Trask 6." Feeling that he was snooping, he hastily turned back the calendar pages and told the phone caller she would have to get the answer to her question from Mrs. Frome personally. Matters between Martha and Joe were no concern of his.

Yet on that Saturday evening at six o'clock, when he sat alone in the big parsonage dining room while Mrs. Bentley served him pork chops with escalloped potatoes (and looked frequently at her wristwatch in anticipation of her previously announced eight o'clock movie rendezvous with Jack Lemmon), Martin found himself wondering where Martha and Joe were having dinner. And what would they do afterward?

He hated to eat dinner alone. At breakfast the *Times* afforded him happy companionship. Lunch usually was a quick glass of milk and sandwich snatched someplace—or possibly ignored. But, oh, those dinners! Abe rarely came home on weekends; no doubt he found the parsonage painfully lonely without Jane there.

Martin loved going to Kathy's and Dave's and horsing around with Stevie, but he confined Kathy's almost constant invitations to one night a week. The numerous dinner invitations from church members, though kindly intended, were becoming a bore, and he was developing evasive maneuvers to avoid them. He always had a good time with Joe, but possibly Joe now had found a more charming dinner companion. Which left him seated alone at the big table in the big parsonage dining room.

The opportunity that came in June was too good to pass. A large church in Denver which had signed a renowned Scots preacher to fill its pulpit for the month of July had been informed that he had died suddenly. One of the assistant ministers, who knew Martin, thought he was the man to fill the pulpit for the month. Would he do it on such short notice? His telephone call brought Martin unmixed joy. At one stroke he could solve or escape from various problems: life in the large and empty parsonage; his reluctance to go to Vermont alone this summer. Also, Abe had signed up for something called a survival camp in Colorado, where he could play Tarzan to his heart's content. Now Martin, constantly feeling neglectful of him, could drive him to Colorado and see him occasionally during the summer; he hoped they would discover new ways to communicate with each other.

Abe, though still under age for a New York State driver's license, prevailed on Martin to let him drive most of the way to Colorado. And their communication was almost totally confined to Abe's interests in baseball, football, sports cars, and girls.

Martin liked Denver and the church where he preached for four Sundays. Though not as prestigious nationally as the Cathedral in New York, it was almost as large in membership and was as skillfully organized. Three assistant ministers left the preaching minister with few responsibilities except his principal one. Martin enjoyed the careful, leisurely preparation of his sermons while living in a comfortable apartment located within a quiet quadrangle of church buildings. The atmosphere was rarefied, like the air of the mile-high city, compared to the humid, sea level din of New York. It set him to thinking of ivied university walls, of teaching the young. He found himself wishing he never had to return to Old Fourth.

But the chance to fulfill his wish took him by great surprise.

He knew that he had preached well in Denver, but he did not think he had been impressive enough to bring about the ensuing result. On the afternoon following his last sermon a church committee invited him to become the preaching minister. He almost accepted on the spot. But then he asked for a month to think it over.

Driving west to the Aspen country, he lingered there and pondered what to do.

The Denver church had offered him twenty-eight thousand a year, while his salary at Old Fourth presently was twenty thousand. Yet now, happily or not, how much money he earned did not matter to him. If Jane had lived—but it would not have made any difference to her either. The difference would have mattered back in Upton or Sylvia when they needed money most. Now she was gone, his needs were simple, Dave supported Kathy, and Abe lacked interest in, though not the capacity for, a college education. Gone all, the money, too.

If he accepted the invitation to Denver, he would become a preaching minister, his job similar to Tubby's at the Cathedral. Practically no more pastoral work. There had been times when he had thought that would be fine. But wouldn't he miss those constant hunting and fishing expeditions for new members?

Another thing: He would simply inherit that thriving Denver church which had been created by others. Old Fourth was thriving now, too, though not as grandly as the Denver church, and it was a being of his and Jane's creation. One had so few thriving children, either of the mind or the flesh, in this life. There came a time, however, when one should let one's child go.

At such a time one inevitably thought of roots in the Latin sense of "radix," meaning straight down, not spreading out. Kathy, Dave, and Steve were in New York, but undoubtedly they would not always be there. Abe now was near New York, but he might end up anyplace. Joe Trask was his closest friend, but he had convinced himself that Joe would marry Martha— and would they then be such close friends? (He also had convinced himself that he would lose the best secretary he had ever had.) There were friends, such as Tubby, in New York, the city that had become home to him—but also the city he had been eager to leave in June. There was his beloved Vermont countryside, yet he had been loath to go there this summer. So what of his roots in the East?

In mid-August he was staying at a lodge not far from Aspen, hiking and reading a lot and fishing some, when Joe appeared one afternoon. Joe's sudden appearances no longer surprised him. Perhaps, he thought later, he would only have been surprised if Joe had failed to appear. For once, Joe was in a somber mood.

They were sitting before a fire after dinner when Martin told him of the Denver offer and said he was considering it seriously.

Joe went to the bar, returned with a double scotch, and said, "This is not my week for happiness."

"What's the matter?"

"Last Monday night I asked Martha to marry me. She said no."

Martin leaned toward him incredulously. "She said *no?*"

"Capital *N*, capital *O*. She likes me but doesn't love me. What's with me and dames? And now you tell me you're thinking of leaving New York."

"Well now," Martin said, "I didn't say I'd made up my mind to move. I just—" And then he wondered if he hadn't made up his mind to stay.

Dave invited Martin to the November meeting of Why Club, and Martin marveled at what he heard there. The subject of the paper was "The Dying Churches of Brooklyn," presented by a young Brooklyn clergyman whose church tottered on the brink of the grave. Recalling the days of Henry Ward Beecher, when Brooklyn was known as the City of Churches, he went on to deplore the failure of organized religion to keep pace with a changing society. The church had done nothing, nothing. *Aieee!* The young men lined up with the speaker at the wailing wall.

Martin did not intend to say anything, but the moderator eventually asked him if he had any thoughts on the subject.

He got to his feet slowly. "I don't like to sound an unpopular note at the wake, Mr. Moderator. Most of you seem to be enjoying the mourning so thoroughly. But I'm guilty of a crime some of you may find unforgivable—a bit of optimism about the church."

In the ensuing murmur of voices he caught a phrase and asked, "Establishment? What is the Protestant Establishment, and why do you call me a member of it?"

Someone said, "Because you have a big, strong church on one of the avenues."

"But it hasn't always been so," Martin said. "What made it grow?"

Someone else said, "Maybe because you're a damn popular preacher."

"Meaning that I tell people only what they want to hear? I do not. I'd be more flattered if you called me a damn good preacher. But if you'll give me a couple of minutes, let's look at this thing called the Protestant Establishment in New York." He named six large churches and their pastors, then discussed the great variety of their philosophies and basic approaches to the religious life.

"One isn't better than another," Martin continued. "He and his church simply are different one from another. Church strength comes from the great variety of people who worship in various ways. Despite the widely discussed disillusionment of Americans, despite the increasing fluidity of our society, church membership and attendance in America are increasing steadily. All of you are familiar with those statistics from the National Council of Churches. I believe the figures. I don't think our society is moving in only one direction."

Someone asked, "How many blacks are members of Old Fourth?"

"Around twenty," Martin replied.

"How many Puerto Ricans?"

"About a dozen."

"What's your total membership?"

"Around twelve hundred."

"Ha! Why such a small proportion?"

A Negro minister called to the inquisitor, "Oh, cut it out, Harry. You know perfectly well that most blacks prefer their own churches, no matter how well they're received in a white church."

Another said, "Martin has given us an interesting rundown on Manhattan churches. But what about Brooklyn? There's only death in Brooklyn."

"I disagree." Martin named several strong churches there.

"But I'm talking about the death of *neighborhood* churches."

"Aren't you really talking about the death of neighborhoods?" Martin replied. "No one ever deplores the death of rural churches, even though they're dying by the hundreds every year. Everyone seems to understand and accept the fact it's because of population shifts. Follow the white Protestant and Jewish population shift from Brooklyn, and it will lead you into places like Nassau County and New Jersey, where churches and synagogues are thriving."

"Then what is there for the city churches?" someone asked.

"I think several of you can answer that. My son-in-law, Dave Murchison, has a very strong program going for young people."

"Hey, Dave," someone else called, "how many new members have you taken in during the past year?"

Dave looked uncomfortable. "Seven."

Martin had not realized Dave had taken in so few.

"Dave," the questioner continued, "are your middle-aged members like mine? Do they ride your tail for spending too much time with the kids?"

"Yes. They call it *wasting* time. Some of them are on my back all the time. It gets tiresome."

Martin had not realized that either.

Another said, "Social action alone won't make a church strong. A lot of us here have found that out. So it's social action *plus* what?"

"I can't offer any suggestion," Dave said.

Martin felt a curious dismay. He understood Dave's skepticism about the efficacy of some aspects of church organizational life. But he had believed Dave was working toward positive answers in his own way.

"Dave, why does your father-in-law's church grow and yours doesn't?"

"Why get personal?" someone asked.

"Why have a Why Club if we don't get personal?"

Dave said, "The answer to the question is that Martin is a much better minister than I am."

"Nonsense!" Martin exclaimed.

"Okay, Martin," Jack Marvin said good-naturedly, "you call it nonsense, but your church has grown. Why? What have you got on the ball—what programs—that have made it click?"

"To begin with," Martin said, "Old Fourth was big. A big physical building. Ugly, yes. A monstrosity. But bigness is a characteristic of our society. People are attracted to it. One problem that Dave has faced is that his church is physically small—"

"Martin," Dave said, "stop defending me. When you went to Old Fourth, it was as big as one of those Kentucky caves—and as empty."

Someone asked, "Do you have a big Sunday school?"

"No. Owing to the nature of our area of the city, we never will. Increasingly there are fewer young children. And maybe someday there will be none—after all have been removed to healthful suburban Valhallas. But increasingly there are fewer old folk, too. And maybe someday there will be none after all have fled to country caves of retirement. Most of our growth has been among the middle-aged."

"Why?" someone asked.

"Personal follow-ups. Most people are lonelier in middle

age than old age." Since no one questioned that, he decided not to mention his book of prospects. Probably they would scorn it anyway.

Dave said, "Martin, you haven't mentioned your strength in people in their twenties. When I was your assistant, that's the age bracket I wanted to bring in. But I never did much with it. Tell them how you did. I'm not sure I know myself."

"Luck," Martin said. "Luck has a lot to do with everything." He tried to say it briefly. Luck in the area of attracting people in their twenties had come to Old Fourth when Lance had sent him two chicks and Tubby two bantams.

"Think of Sunday in New York for young people come to squat here for a while," Martin told them. "A dismal day. You may be a bit hung over from Saturday night. You sleep late. Of course, you wouldn't think of going to church. You read the Times—a two-hour task on Sunday. You can go to a movie or watch TV. But by four o'clock in the afternoon you're probably feeling lost. So we set our Sunday afternoon gathering hour for four o'clock—to run on indefinitely. No closing. And we had to offer programs that were as good as those in various public places. My wife had the inspiration after we entertained some young people at our home. . . ."

He tried to make it very brief and not to bore them.

Jane had remarked on the interest of the young people in a Southern ballad singer who was appearing at a spot in the Village. Martin had found he could obtain the singer's services for a fee of only fifty dollars on a Sunday afternoon. An equivalent amount had paid for a small ad in the Sunday Times. And so it began.

"What interests people?" Martin asked them. "Read the papers and the magazines, and follow your nose. Never mind the generation gaps. There are gaps within gaps. Aged twenty-four often doesn't know what aged twenty is talking about. Each month brings some esoteric little fad, some new personality, some different twist of language. One time I said to a young man,

'You don't know who Allen Tate is?' And he said, 'No, sir. Do you know who Vanessa Redgrave is?' Gaps within gaps. But there are trends of interest, and you try to follow them. . . ."

He did not belabor it. He did not go into the numerous details of his successes—and failures—with the program to attract young people on Sunday afternoons. He mentioned only a few examples.

"Maybe, in one aspect of a minister's job, it's like being the editor of a hep—is that word out of fashion yet?—magazine. I've had bad luck in interesting editors in participating in Old Fourth. But last year one who edits an offbeat magazine joined us. I learned more from him than he'll ever learn from me. He said, 'Just produce what interests *you*. The interest follows. If you try to produce what interests *them*, you're dead.' So, as just one example, I've been interested for a long time—and don't ask me why—in the so-called comedians who work the small-time clubs. They're wise and witty. What keeps them going? What's the nature of humor in America these days? I obtained one for our group for a small fee when he was between engagements. Besides being funny, he had the best *message* ever delivered to our people. He comes back often when he's in town— and he comes back for no fee. If he comes back often enough, I expect he'll join our church."

Comedians, dancers, singers, poets, bankers, anthropologists. . . .

"Mr. Judson." A man rose after Martin had turned himself off and looked at him gravely, accusingly. "What does all this have to do with the Christian life?"

Dave murmured to Martin, "This guy's name is Finley."

"Quite a bit, I think, Mr. Finley," Martin said to him. "If it has anything to do with life it concerns Christianity—or Judaism—or almost any faith you can name."

Finley asked, "Is there any discussion of Christianity in your group?"

"Of course," Martin replied. "It's all being done within a

Christian framework. Every once in a while we even give a Christian minister a crack at interesting us."

"How many of these young people have joined your church?"

"Quite a few. They spill over into the Sunday morning service. They listen to what I have to say with curious or skeptical expressions. They don't *have* to appear in church, but many of them do."

Finley refused to heed suggestions that he sit down. "Mr. Judson, don't you feel like a shill?"

"Meaning salesman?" Martin asked above some jeering of Finley. "Mr. Finley, I consider myself a salesman. I'm not at all ashamed of it. If you are, check up on the Book of Matthew —I think it's the twenty-fifth chapter—where it says, 'Go ye rather to them that sell, and buy for yourselves. . . .'"

When Martin returned to the church office, he told Martha, "It was a fascinating meeting. I'd like to go every month. But I don't think I'll be invited again. They probably see me for what I guess I am—an old crock whose best days are behind him."

"Mr. Judson"—When Martha addressed him thus, it meant that she was taking him to task about something; usually she called him Martin—"Mr. Judson, your senility would not be so noticeable if you didn't keep drawing attention to it."

He retreated into his study. Martha had sounded the way Jane used to. And that seemed unfair somehow because no one should try to sound like Jane.

Martha did a great deal toward keeping the young people's organization thriving. While continuing to put in long hours of office work, she, as much as Martin, recognized the importance of the more complex task. In a sense she was fulfilling the function of a minister of religious education—far-out religious education. Martin, arranging a sizable raise for her in light of her added duties, hoped she would stay at Old Fourth forever.

But then, unexpectedly, he wished she would leave. It happened at Christmas.

He, Abe, Martha, and Joe were invited to Christmas Day

dinner at Kathy's. On the preceding night there was the customary Christmas Eve service in the church. After the service Martha invited Martin and several others to her apartment, where she served refreshments.

Joe, who had been at an office party before attending church and going to Martha's, failed for once to hold his liquor well; he left early after explaining carefully to each, "I'm going now before I make a bigger horse's ass of myself than everybody already knows I am." Others eventually left one by one. By midnight Martin, still nursing his second eggnog, was the only one remaining. Talk, talk, talk— He heard his voice running on. Not wanting to go home, he had some vague and sophomoric idea of staying up all night, of being wakeful all of tomorrow, and collapsing into bed from exhaustion tomorrow evening. Thus, perhaps somewhat like Scrooge, he would try to exorcise the ghost of Christmases past with Jane.

Toward one o'clock he realized that Martha was beginning to look sleepy. Starting to his feet, he said, "I've overstayed. I'm sorry. This past year I've turned into quite an egocentric old coot."

"Martin"—not stirring, Martha looked at him levelly—"do you really think of yourself as an old coot?"

He looked at her levelly, too. "Yes, I do. I'm not feeling sorry for myself or anything like that. But an increasing bit of the time I feel bored—pointless. I'm happy with the accomplishments of the church, but there is no real joy in Mudville anymore."

"Why not?"

Not knowing how to answer her, he said, "Isn't the answer obvious?"

Her gaze fell. "I suppose so." Then she looked up at him again. "Do you know you're a stern, unrelenting taskmaster?"

"No, I didn't know. Do I heap it on you unfairly?"

"Of course not. Only on yourself." She tried to smile, but it emerged as a kind of grimace. "What were your ancestors, Scots Calvinist or something?"

"About eight generations back, I've heard. Since then—well, maybe it's like the Brown man's song about Dartmouth men, maybe the granite of New Hampshire has become the granite of my brain. How am I hard on myself? What would you like me to do—drink up all the booze that's left here and get bagged?"

"Yes, if you felt like it."

"But I don't feel like it. Anything I'm not it's because I don't feel like being it. I guess that sentence parses, or at least you know what I mean."

"Then what do you feel like being? You just said you aren't happy as you are. What would you rather be or do?"

He took a conch shell from the mantel and held it to an ear. He heard no sound; he never had caught the faintest whisper from a conch. He decided not to tell her a story about a horse his father once owned that he called Old Chuck, a faithful, hard-working beast. When Old Chuck grew feeble, his father put him to honorable pasture. But Old Chuck only pined at pasture. He stood all day with his head across the bars gazing morosely at the gelding that had become his father's working companion. Mercifully, or perhaps guiltily, his father asked a neighbor to shoot Old Chuck.

"I really can't answer your question," he told her. "But I know I would not have wanted to do anything except be here this evening. It was a grand party, Martha. Thanks for inviting me."

She went to the door with him after he pulled on his overcoat. "Good night, Martin. Merry Christmas." To his surprise, she kissed him on a cheek.

What happened then was instantaneous and incredible. He smelled her perfume and he not so much saw or felt her loveliness as remembered being aware of it over the course of many months past. His arms were around her, and her straight, firm legs came against his hard as their lips joined in a kiss. Something like a groan or sob escaped him. And then he found himself almost running along the corridor toward the elevator.

In the elevator he found himself trying to forget what had happened while at the same time he tried to remember if she had drawn her arms around him. When he reached the street, he realized he had left his hat in her apartment. He could not go back for it. Yet it would seem the greatest mortification of his life if she brought it to him at Kathy's tomorrow.

The night was cold, and there was a powder of snow on the deserted streets. He wandered around for an hour, his thoughts inchoate. *Jane, I love you so.* Then what was this want of Martha? How long had it been going on, carefully screened by his self-conning tower? When would it end? But at once. *Now.*

He went home at last and found the front door ajar. Abe, preceding him, had vomited on the front stairs. The mess gave off a loathsome stench of gin. He cleaned it up as best he could, hoping Mrs. Bentley would not discover it in the morning but knowing that she would. Then he went up to Abe's room and found him sprawled across his bed, passed out and fully clothed.

Martin moved him into a more comfortable position and covered him with a couple of blankets. As he tucked the blankets around him, Abe muttered, "Mom?"

He went to his own room, tears streaming from his eyes.

Martha was already at Kathy's when Abe and he arrived around noon. He had clapped on a hat he had snatched from the front hall closet, and when Kathy saw it, she laughed and exclaimed, "Father, where did you ever find that old hat?"

Abe, as if seeing him for the first time through the glazed eyes of his hangover, said, "Yeah, Pop, that looks terrible."

Martha merely said, "Hi, Martin," and busied herself with something. She had not brought his hat along.

She acted as if nothing unusual had happened between them, and he tried to act likewise. But how could things ever again be the same?

When he went to the office the day after Christmas, his hat was in its customary place on the rack and Martha was going about her customary secretarial duties. In speech and manner she seemed to be trying to reassure him that things were as always.

But how could they be?

Mrs. Percival was a well-meaning bore in her sixties who was forever being made breathless, baffled, and hurt by the winds of change. Kathy, aware of her since moving to Old Fourth as a child, always had taken great pains to avoid her. Mrs. Percival, in turn, was fond of saying that she and Kathy were lifelong friends.

So Kathy quickly manufactured an excuse when Mrs. Percival telephoned in February and asked her to tea. She had another excuse ready when Mrs. Percival asked her again in March. But there was no refusal possible when she phoned a third time and said, "Kathy, it's absolutely imperative I talk with you as soon as possible. I speak for many people besides myself. It's a matter that concerns your father and the very life of Old Fourth."

Kathy, alarmed, invited her to tea that afternoon. It was an appalling prospect, for Mrs. Percival sometimes took hours to get to, around, and beyond some specific point. As Mother once had observed, "Grace Percival doesn't really know what she thinks till she's heard what she's saying for an endless time." That Wednesday afternoon over tea in Kathy's apartment she demonstrated her great resistance to changes of habit.

After listening for half an hour to her innuendo, insinuation, and insinuendo, Kathy asked her please to make plain what she meant. A few phrases came through the plethora:

"How much we all love your father. . . . How much we all loved your mother. . . . I liked Martha Frome at first. . . . But now that she's set her cap for *our pastor*. . . . The difference in their ages. . . . I'm sure the poor man doesn't know what to do about it. . . . When I told Mr. Trask how many of us feel and suggested the board release her from her job, he was downright rude. . . ."

After Dave came home from pastoral calling, Kathy told him about Mrs. Percival's visit.

He said, "I like Martha."

"So do I."

"I think it would be a swell idea if your father married her."

"So do I," Kathy said.

"What was the old bag driving at? Did she infer they were shacking up together or something?"

Kathy was shocked. "Nobody could ever think that of Father."

"Why not? It can happen. How old is he now?"

"He'll be fifty-one his next birthday."

"I guess it still can happen," Dave said.

Kathy flared, and he agreed that hanky-panky was not in Martin's nature.

His loneliness was apparent, of course, and lately his way of occasionally seeming like a child lost in the woods had more than once brought her to tears. She had lived in parsonages long enough to know that Mrs. Percival's remarks were just congregational gossip. Aging widows always established proprietary interest over the pastor, especially when he was a widower and graying handsome. On reflection Kathy began to think that he was attracted to Martha. And wouldn't it be natural that Martha was attracted to him?

She wondered how to bring up the matter to him. Then, about a week after Mrs. Percival's visit, the opportunity presented itself when he dropped by one rainy afternoon. She made coffee and they chatted about various things while he patty-caked with Stevie.

Her back was to him when she said it: "Father, have you ever thought about marrying again?"

Instantly she felt the room charged with his tension. He was silent, motionless while Stevie urged him on at the wonderful new patty-cake game. At last he said, "Why do you ask that, Kathy?"

She faced him. "Because I think it would be a good idea. It's awful for you rattling around in that big house. We're close by now, but we won't always be. Dave is getting restless and looking around for another church. He feels he'll never really get Beacon off the ground. I'm for moving too. So—"

He tried to divert the conversation to Dave's church hunting, but she brought it back to him.

"I'm serious about my question, Father. I even have a good wife picked for you. Martha."

He lowered Stevie to the floor carefully, his expression drawn tautly. "Why do you say that?"

"Because I think she's a fine woman and you'd be happy together."

"She is a fine woman, Kathy, but that doesn't necessarily mean we'd be happy together. I'm fifty-one, and she's thirty. If I'm still alive when she is my present age, I'll be an old man. Though I'm not old yet, my habit patterns are firmly established. I think everyone tries to live by some mental image of himself, and mine doesn't include being the . . . husband of a beautiful, vital young woman."

Kathy gazed at him. "Then you are attracted to her—sexually?"

"Yes." He returned her gaze bleakly. "It never happened to me before—except with Jane. I'm sure it will pass. I'm sure it's just a kind of middle-aged . . . foolishness."

"You poor dear." Reaching out, she patted him on an arm. "The tension must be terrible for you. And for her, too, because she must sense it and probably feels the same. I know that feeling about Dave came to me all of a sudden, and it was pretty bad till I was sure he felt the same about me. But why do you call it foolishness? I don't think it is."

"What else is it?"

"You just mentioned having a mental image of oneself. I know what yours is. I remember one time when I was talking to Mother about the life you two led. At the time it seemed such a stringent life to me. I asked her what reward there is in it. I never forgot what she said, and now I've come to share her feeling—and yours. She said, 'The reward is in meeting the challenges of every day. Not always overcoming them, but meeting them.' Father, that's fine enough. It's the way everyone feels who's devoted to a life of service for others. But don't you think that feeling of service can be carried too far? It can throw your life out of balance and make you neglect a most important thing—that life is for living. *Your very own life*—not someone else's—is for living. Too much self-abnegation can make you less yourself and, as a result, of less value to others."

He looked at her for a while, then said, "You're good to talk to me this way, Kathy. I'll think about it. I'll give myself some time and . . ."

But the passage of time did not change anything as far as she could tell.

Dave's restlessness at Beacon had finally infected her. The church had a few more members than when they had come there, but it did not give them a feeling of strength and growth. Their chief accomplishment seemed to have been with the young, yet their satisfaction in that dimmed with time. Perhaps a few boys and girls would lead more stable and productive lives as a result of their influence. But somehow, Kathy believed, they had failed to instill a vision of faith and a sense of service such as she herself felt. The world was too much with these children of the West Side, pressing in demandingly, and taking remorselessly. One of many different examples of their disappointment or sorrow came when they heard that Studs Gennari, for whom Dave had had great hopes, had been killed in Vietnam.

Kathy felt as Dave when he said, "I thought we came where the action is when we moved here. But now it seems to me the action is all going off in other directions. I think it's time we went off in some other direction, too."

He began hunting a new job. Following one lead, he was offered a personnel position by a private corporation. But then he decided it was not the kind of employment that would offer him much satisfaction. He looked about for a more satisfying pastorate, but to no avail.

Apparently he was not acceptable for a position that was more appealing to him than any other. A couple of members of Why Club put him on the track of HEART, a privately endowed organization with large financial resources whose purpose was to work in conjunction with municipal, state, and federal government in the rehabilitation of depressed urban areas. He prepared a careful résumé and was interviewed twice, the second time by Joel Steinberg, the executive director of HEART. But he heard nothing more.

In May he was invited to preach at a Presbyterian church on Long Island which was seeking a new minister.

One look at the community where the church was located, and their skepticism about living in the suburbs evaporated. It was a lovely town, an impressive-looking church building. Why, Kathy wondered, had they ever been dubious about living and working in the suburbs? *This* was the direction, if only the church would select Dave. There were practical considerations involved that they could not ignore indefinitely. If they moved there, it meant a raise in salary, a pleasant house with a large yard, an excellent school system for Stevie and the brothers or sisters who came after him. (She had decided there must be two or three more.)

Dave's sermon she thought the best she ever had heard him deliver. The church members they met were friendly, interesting people. She found herself praying that the church would extend a call to Dave.

The *Times* of Thursday, June 9, reported that a group of South Vietnamese officials would arrive at Kennedy International Airport that afternoon for a round of official functions as guests of the United States government. It brought caustic comment from Dave as he scanned the newspaper at the breakfast table, and Kathy seconded his emotion on the subject. Before they had finished breakfast, there was a telephone call from an officer of the Anti-Vietnam War group of which they were members. The group planned to throw up a picket line at Kennedy that afternoon protesting United States military aid to South Vietnam; could they come? Dave said he would be there. Kathy, wanting to go, made three telephone calls in a vain search for a sitter for Steve before she resigned herself to staying home.

Dave, who had gone down to his study, suddenly came bounding up the stairs. "They *want* me!" he cried, thrusting an opened letter at her.

The Long Island church had, indeed, invited Dave to become its minister, offering him nine thousand a year with parsonage and hoping he could begin work there September 1. Kathy felt close to tears as she read the letter twice.

"I'm going downstairs and write a letter of acceptance," Dave said. "And I'll phone Bill Jaquith and give him the good news that I'm resigning on Sunday. It'll make him happy."

Bill Jaquith, the chairman of the board, had become one of Dave's most persistent needlers, complaining that he wasted too much time with the young people and in social action groups.

Dave brought his letter of acceptance upstairs and read it to Kathy. He said he had not been able to reach Jaquith.

"And on Sunday afternoon, Kath, we'll take off for Vermont."

In their growing restiveness at Beacon they had arranged to take their vacation a month early.

"Call your father and tell him the good news."

Kathy glanced at the clock. "Right now, lover, you'd better mail that letter and take off for the picket line at Kennedy."

After he had gone, she telephoned the office at Old Fourth, but to her surprise there was no answer. She called the parsonage, and Mrs. Bentley said she didn't know where Father was.

Around noon she phoned the office again, and Martha, whom she had not seen in several weeks, answered.

"Yes, Kathy." Martha's tone was formal, lacking its customary warmth. "Your father has a burial in Brooklyn and won't be in till afternoon. I'll leave a note you called." She hesitated. "It's odd you should phone, because I was wondering whether to call and say good-bye."

"Good-*bye!*" Kathy exclaimed. "Where are you going?"

"My vacation starts on Monday, and I've decided to begin it early."

"Oh? Where are you going?"

"Job hunting."

"Martha, what on earth are you talking about?"

"I put my resignation on your father's desk half an hour ago. I'm sure you know why. Mrs. Percival says you do."

"What has that old bitch said now?" Kathy cried.

"She—well, she—" Martha's voice trailed off.

"You listen to me, Martha!" Kathy's voice rose. "You take that resignation off my father's desk right now and hustle straight over here. If you don't, I'll grab up Stevie and come over there. Martha, please do as I say."

After a pause Martha said, "All right, I will."

When she arrived she looked wan and took off her white gloves with an agitated movement.

Kathy said, "I'm not usually a noon drinker, but I could stand one today. Join me in a scotch."

"I wouldn't mind. . . . Yes, the resignation is in my purse now. . . . There's no point in repeating everything Mrs. Percival told me last evening. But when you called her an old bitch, I knew you weren't behind her move, as she said you were."

"She's a damn liar, as well as an old bitch." Kathy handed her a scotch and water. "That's not the sort of language my mother ever used, but—"

"But how can any of us ever be like your mother was?" Martha asked. And then she began to cry. Her torrent of tears was the bursting of a month-old dam. At last she regained control of herself and took a stiff drink.

"Then you know." Her voice shook. "I love him. And the tension has become just too much. I have to get out. I have no choice."

"My father can be the biggest stonehead I ever knew," Kathy said. "And there's only one thing that can deal with stone. That's dynamite. Father loves you, if you don't already know it. And I love you both. So does Dave. I know I'm sounding like the little organizer, but this thing is getting pretty silly, and I want you to do what I ask you to, Martha. Don't go back to the office today. Don't show up tomorrow. And on Monday— rather, Sunday afternoon—Dave and I will shoehorn you into the Volkswagen with Stevie and us, and we're leaving for Vermont. You're spending your vacation with us. Father isn't due there till July, but I have a hunch he'll show up early."

Martha protested. Stay at Martin's country home? And what would Dave think? It was a time for them to be together and—

Kathy said, "Dave and I are so much together that we'd have only connubial bliss at an orgy. So that's set."

Martin telephoned about two o'clock. "Kathy, Mrs. Bentley said you called me."

She told him about Dave's acceptance of the Long Island pastorate, and he was elated. "Is he there? Put him on and let me congratulate him. That's wonderful, Kathy!"

When she explained what Dave was doing at Kennedy, he fell silent, then asked in a concerned tone if Dave really must do that at the present moment. She restrained herself from flaring at him. After a long period of questioning and doubt about the wisdom of American intervention in South Vietnam, he finally had come to agree with Dave's and her viewpoint on the matter. Then why didn't he get out and *picket?* It was a pity to see such a basically youthful and brave man as Father become so old and cautious.

He said, "Kathy, a curious thing, Martha didn't show up at the office today. I just phoned her apartment, but there's no answer."

"She was at the office." Kathy crossed her eyes at Martha. "I talked to her when I was trying to reach you. She was going up to Barnard. She's been offered a very good job on the admissions staff there. She said she probably won't be in tomorrow either. From the way things have been going, don't you think that might be for the best?"

"Well now," he said. And then: "But it's completely unlike her just to take off and never say a word about it to me."

"I can understand exactly how she feels," Kathy said. "The way things have been going, Father! What do you expect a woman in love with you to do? I suppose she figures a sudden and complete break is for the best. She's going to Vermont for her vacation with Dave and me. I guess we'll learn her future plans then."

"She never told me about going to Vermont," he said.

"Father, if you'll understand me saying so, I don't see why she needs to explain *anything* to you."

"Well now," he said.

Ten

MARTIN went to the office early on Friday morning. The *Times* was on the doorstep as he went out, and he took it with him.

He had not been so upset in a long time. The previous night he had phoned Martha's apartment twice, and both times her roommate had said she would not be in all evening. Why should she avoid him and act in this incredible way? Phoning Joe, he had told him what had happened. Joe had been as puzzled by her behavior as he, exclaiming, "Dames! Dames! If they keep on improving computers, maybe we can get rid of 'em for good."

Sitting down at his desk, he resumed pondering the questions that had kept him awake in the night. If it was true that Martha loved him, as Kathy maintained, then possibly she was right in leaving abruptly this way. Certainly it was true that he loved Martha. He had admitted that to himself as he prowled about the parsonage last night.

But he would not do anything about it. For it posed seemingly insoluble problems to him as a minister. The problems were not posed simply to *him*. They would confront any minister whose wife had died and who had fallen in love with his secretary—a comely woman twenty years younger than he, and a divorcée! The more a congregation esteemed its minister, the more tightly it tried to possess him. His private life must be a matter of proud public display from the viewpoint of the congregation. If he married Martha, it would create deep resentments, especially among older members of Old Fourth. He must not in any way fracture the strength of the church. He must forget Martha and convince himself that her leaving abruptly was all for the best.

He glanced over the *Times*. As usual, the front-page news was concerned chiefly with mankind's failures; one must turn to the sports pages to read about his successes. A headline caught Martin's attention—VIETNAMESE OFFICIALS ARRIVE FOR OFFICIAL VISIT—PICKETS CLASH WITH POLICE. (They must keep that last line set permanently in type these days.) Remembering suddenly, he read the story swiftly, followed its jump to page five, and what he saw made him utter a groan. There was a four-column photograph of Dave, holding a poster stick like a baseball bat and being wrestled backward onto his prat by two policemen. With its customary accuracy, the *Times* had his name right: The Reverend David Murchison, pastor of Beacon Nondenomination Church in Manhattan. It stood out like twenty-four-point type to Martin. As usual, there were two versions of the scuffle: that of the police, and that of the pickets. There was also a foolish comment by Dave about "the fools in Washington who treat American youth as one huge blood bank." He had not been arrested; he simply was a victim of a nimble photographer.

Martin paced around his desk. He would not call Dave and Kathy. There was no question in his mind about Dave's right to protest; his only concern was the question it might raise in other minds.

Now it was almost nine o'clock, and Martha still had not arrived. As he paced, he began to work up an employer's righteous indignation. What ingratitude after his generous salary raises! Where else could a secretary earn one hundred and thirty-five a week? Yet where else, too, would he find anyone to take her place in the direction of the young people's programs? At precisely nine o'clock he phoned her apartment. There was no answer.

When the phone rang a few minutes later, he sprang to it. The caller was Tubby.

"Tubby, I have it on my calendar to check on you today. How are you feeling?"

"Not so hot. Got back on Wednesday." He sounded depressed. "Marty, I want to ask you a favor. Can you come up and see me sometime today? Any time that's convenient. I'm not going to the office. I'll be home all day."

After Martin hung up, he reflected worriedly on Tubby, who had had bouts of illness for the past several months and ten days ago had gone to Johns Hopkins for a checkup. Oh, this process of growing old.

John Bell came in about ten o'clock and asked where Martha was.

"I'm not sure. I haven't heard from her. Maybe she started her vacation early."

John blinked in surprise. "That's odd. Most unusual of her."

"Most." Martin picked up a letter and frowned at it. . . .

When the phone rang, he answered it and was surprised to hear Abe, who supposedly was working as a lifeguard on the Jersey shore.

"Pop, have you got a couple of minutes to talk with me?"

"Of course. Where are you?"

"In town. I'll be over soon."

He appeared in less than five minutes.

"That was fast," Martin said.

"I was in a phone booth down the street in Bergson's Drugstore. I quit the job in Jersey day before yesterday."

"Oh? Shut the door and sit down." Day before yesterday? Martin checked himself from asking where he had been since.

Abe now was taller than he and more muscular than he ever had been. Within the face of the young athlete there still seemed to exist the slightly snub-nosed face of little Abe Judson. It was this face within a face that strained toward Martin now.

"Pop, I've been thinking about the future. I couldn't get into any of the service academies. I guess I'm just not smart enough."

"Of course you are," Martin said. "You just didn't work hard enough. But now that you've been accepted at—"

"That crummy place!"

Martin did not say anything. It was not an inaccurate description of the college which had accepted him.

"I don't want to go there. I'm *not* going there. Yesterday I joined the Marines."

Martin stared at him incredulously.

"I didn't do it because I'm a gung ho nut. I did it because I think it's right for me. You know how I—well, sort of crap around a lot. Maybe the Marines will knock that out of me. For sure that cruddy college won't."

Martin sank back, badly shaken. "Don't you need—my permission or something?"

"No, Pop, I'm *in*. I leave for boot camp this afternoon. I hope this doesn't hurt you too badly. I've done enough of that. You've done everything for me you can. Now I'm trying to do something for myself."

So join the Marines? Martin thought in despair. Yet at the same time he could understand Abe's motivation.

"I think I follow you." He spoke slowly. "You've rejected higher education—"

"For right now. Maybe I'll get with it later."

"And without education you can't see any interesting job prospects."

"Right!"

"And so—well, how about my taking you to lunch today?"

Abe gazed at him searchingly. Then his eyes suddenly filled with tears. "No thanks, Pop." His voice shook. "I want to say good-bye to Kathy, and it's better this way. Quick."

Martin said something, though he never could remember

what it was. He remembered their shaking hands and Abe's laying his cheek against his for a moment. Then Abe was gone, and he was sitting at his desk again. Stretching his right hand levelly, he saw that it was shaking.

Suddenly he had to get out of the office, and he left without saying a word to John Bell. Standing on the street in the mellow late morning, he remembered Tubby's call. There were times when a pastor needed a pastor. Or maybe this was a time when a man needed *someone*. He flagged down a taxi. . . .

Eunice greeted him distractedly and took him to Tubby, who was hunched in a chair beside an open window of a sun-drenched alcove. His face looked bloated, and there was nothing about him that recalled the Tubby of the past except his clear, blue, strangely innocent eyes. A horror of death struck Martin as he sank into a chair in the alcove.

Tubby said it calmly before long. "Hodgkin's disease, Marty. You know what that means. . . ."

A grave, almost invariably fatal disease marked by chronic enlargement of the lymph nodes and spleen, together with progressive anemia. It seemed that it must have happened to someone other than Tubby, the vigorous and indestructible, who was destined to live to ninety.

"You know how doctors like to sound hopeful. But I don't hold out much myself—and neither does Eunice, despite the cheering things she says. . . ."

What did one say to a friend? What did one clergyman say to another when both for much of their lives had tried to comfort the troubled? Tubby, understanding well the dilemma of the practicing comforter whose every word might be taken as merely professional by the practicing comforter he sought to console, would not let Martin interject a word. After all, old pros knew how banal the lore of their craft could sound.

"The point is I have to resign. I've already missed too many weeks from the pulpit with this illness."

"What will you do?" Martin asked.

Tubby grimaced. "Die, probably. Marty, I know what you

mean. We're fortunate. There's all kinds of insurance, kindness, everything. Eunice and the kids don't have to worry, which is more than you and I could say when we began. I remember a fellow in much my state saying on just about my first involvement with something like this back in Massachusetts— He said, 'All we have is money,' and I thought how lucky he was because that was the only thing I didn't have, and— Well, I still have what I had then. And money, too! How about that? Well, the point is— But before I get to that, tell me what you've been doing this past week—the routine, how's it going?"

Martin did not mention the three really important incidents of recent days involving Martha, Abe, and Dave. Tubby had plenty of trouble of his own. Perhaps the essence of conversation among old pros was that they took care not to mention the really vital problems. He talked a bit about the pastoral routine, knowing that was what Tubby savored and missed.

At last, Tubby said, "To get to my point, I had the key members of the board over here last evening and told them the situation, the fact I have to resign. I said they have to begin to think about my successor. And they unanimously came back with an interesting—and flattering—question. Whom would I suggest? They weren't just being nice. They found out the last time they chose a preaching minister they went through a long and wasteful procedure. Though they do know that for the sake of satisfying the congregation, they have to make a show of something similar again. But they asked me to name precisely *one*. And I named the best preacher in New York and maybe the whole country"— he twisted his lips in a grin—"apart from me, that is. *You*."

Not just now was Martin's first thought. Things were overtaking him too quickly. It always had been so in his experience. One went along for months or years while nothing of much importance happened; then suddenly everything happened at once.

"Are you interested, Marty?"

Of course he was. It would be the unexpected crowning

power and glory of a career that did not seem to have had much of either. *Yes, right now,* he thought. One positive decision now might make other questions fall into perspective.

"Yes, I'm interested."

"Good. I told them you were the *one* not because we've been the closest of friends all these years but because you are the most capable and worthy for the job. They know who you are. Among them they're quite a bunch of bird-dogging G-twos. Most remember the impressive sermon you preached here years ago. They know your record at Old Fourth. They agree the only problem is that you have a New York pastorate and it's a tradition to pick a man from out of the city. Then a couple of the bird dogs mentioned something I didn't know myself. I knew you preached in Denver last summer, but you never told me you received a call there and turned it down. Well, somehow these two bird dogs knew it, and it impressed all the others, almost as if you *were* in Denver and thereby they could invite you here. And some brought up another important matter. Your reputation for being a clever organizer, a first-rate executive. That's very important for us right now. Since I've been ill, some of the staff—one in particular, and you know who I mean—has been throwing his weight around too much. I haven't had the strength to deal with it. But you could easily. It's right down your alley. . . ."

Strangely, at the very moment his ego blossomed under the warm sun of Tubby's praise, Martin vividly recalled Jane's saying years ago when he had lusted for the Cathedral post, "I'm not sure it's the right place for you." She had not said, "I'm not sure you're right for it." What had she meant?

"So you see it's a real challenge, Marty. Your personal life could be very pleasant here. By the way, I saw Dave's picture in the *Times* this morning. Good for him. It reminded me of the time—thirty-five, wasn't it?—when the gang of us picketed the armory in Providence."

Martin told him about Dave's accepting a call to the Long

Island church, and Tubby, leaning toward him suddenly, asked, "When?"

"Yesterday."

"Oh?" They stared at each other.

Martin recalled something he was prone to overlook. In his experience almost every sufferer found a comfort in hearing of another's troubles because it diverted him from his own. "This has turned out to be quite a day for me, Tubby. This morning Abe. . . ."

Of course, Tubby sympathized with him. Yet at the same time he must be thinking of his own problem son and telling himself, "Well, at least he hasn't done *that* yet." Oh, the curious ways of comforting.

Then Martin heard himself talking about Martha. "I think I love her, Tubby. Kathy and Dave feel I should ask her to marry me—to which she might very well say no." He went on to cite his own doubts and objections.

"Marty"—Tubby spoke measuredly—"I know how lonely your life has been for a year and a half now. But Martha *has* been your secretary. And you say she was divorced. And the difference in your ages. Both you and I know, Marty, that there is no bishop in any hierarchical church as ruthless as the congregation of a democratic church."

So there it was: a not so subtle piece of advice from this dearest friend who had totally sublimated his private mind in his working with the public mind.

"You mean?"

"I mean"—Tubby hesitated—"Have you heard that Noel Coward song 'Wait a Bit, Joe'? Not that Mr. Coward is necessarily a font of human wisdom. But he has a point in that song. Why be in a hurry, Marty? If you want the Cathedral post, don't marry her right away. Wait till after you have the job and then —maybe. . . ."

After he left Tubby, he started for the subway. The doors of the Cathedral were open and the organist was playing

Bach's B minor Mass as he passed. The tones from the great organ made him pause and drew him inside where he sat down in a rear pew. Far forward the empty preaching pulpit looked like the loneliest spot in all America.

Yet need it be? Perhaps Tubby had taken his post here too literally. And perhaps he, following Tubby's lead, was considering it too literally also. True, he believed in the vital importance of preaching. But he had worked in the smithy of the church; he knew the anvil, the fire, the hammer. In Upton, Sylvia, Old Fourth he had learned that preaching was only one of the shaping instruments. A minister must live with people, share their troubles and joys. Otherwise, his preaching would become empty. It was as true at the Cathedral as at Old Fourth or any other church. In the ripeness of his experience he could demonstrate that if he took the post in this great church.

Soon he found himself praying. As did not always happen, he consciously recalled a thought of his prayer afterward. *I want this church. But God give me insight, not shrewdness.*

"Are they still there?" Dave asked Kathy.

He knew, of course, that they were. He simply wished she would turn from a front window and say something.

Since nine o'clock that Friday morning a dozen members of Beacon had been parading back and forth on the street bearing signs. Mrs. Aiello, Mrs. Stouffer, Mr. Goldman, who should have been at work. . . . Dave and Kathy had stared at them in utter astonishment. The message of the crudely lettered signs was plain enough. MURCHISON DOES NOT REPRESENT US. Mrs. Jaquith, Walter Berg, and Mrs. Antonelli had worked up a three sign chain message: WE PICKET THE PREACHER—WHO PICKETS OUR SONS IN VIETNAM—WHERE THEY FIGHT FOR FREEDOM. On a couple of turns Walter misplaced himself in line so that the message read: WHO PICKETS OUR SONS IN VIETNAM—WE PICKET THE PREACHER—WHERE THEY FIGHT FOR FREEDOM.

As if the message was not plain enough, Bill Jaquith tried to make it plainer with a brusque telephone call:

"Mr. Murchison, I guess you've looked out your window and seen what's going on. They'll leave as soon as you tell them you'll publicly recant your position on Sunday. We've argued often enough about some of your remarks on the war from the pulpit. But yesterday at Kennedy you went too far."

"Mr. Jaquith, I was acting as an individual, not as a representative of the church."

"Yeah! Try to tell that to the readers of the *Times*. We want a full apology, a—"

"You'll never get it." Dave hung up.

Kathy angrily agreed with Dave. Her moods that morning were as fitful as sunlight on a day of clouds and wind: angry, amused, sorrowful, puzzled.

Now she said, "The crowd of kids is getting bigger."

Hearing them jeering, he went to one of the two front windows, pushed back the screen, and leaned out. Twenty to thirty young people milled on the sidewalk and street, taunting the pickets.

"Jack!" Dave yelled. "Tony! Ron! Lucy! Get off it! Those people have the right to picket." They began to quiet down, looking up at him with wonder. "You heard what I said. Beat it!" A squad car had pulled up, and two policemen, looking baffled, seemed uncertain what to do as Dave called, "All you guys and girls get over on the other side of the street and stay there."

The telephone rang. It seemed not to have stopped ringing all morning. He lifted it and said, "Command Post Beacon."

Kathy said, "Stop being a comedian."

O'Hare said, "This is O'Hare, Dave. You want them run off?"

"Who? The pickets?"

"Who else?"

"No, they're within their rights."

"They're obstructing traffic."

"Thanks, no, O'Hare. The obstruction will get worse when the opposition to the opposition arrives. Mel Meyer phoned

and said a bunch of them are making signs now in the back
of his drugstore. I begged them to knock it off, but they won't
hear to it. These people picketing now are only a minority—"

Kathy said, "A most vociferous minority."

O'Hare said, "If the others show up, we'll have to run everybody off—and maybe some in. You may get your name in the
Times again."

"Please no, O'Hare."

O'Hare grunted and hung up. Stevie began to cry for no discernible reason, and Kathy turned distractedly.

Dave said, "Let's have another cup of coffee and another
council of war."

When they faced each other across the table, he said, "At least
I was lucky on one thing. I never reached Jaquith yesterday
and told him I was resigning."

"Now we can't quit as long as those pickets keep marching,"
Kathy said. "We can't run out under fire."

"Especially till we know where the next paycheck is coming
from."

"Long Island?"

"Kath, the first thing I thought of when I opened the paper
this morning was that the *Times* circulates on Long Island. You
must have thought of it, too."

"Of course I did. I didn't grow up in parsonages for nothing." She made a wry face. "Or did I?"

Dave said slowly, "Those demonstrators out there just about
bring me to the conclusion I don't want to be a minister anyplace."

"You're that angry at them?"

"Not at *them*. They have as much right to demonstrate as I
did at Kennedy yesterday. But I feel they aren't so much protesting against me as against the very ministry itself. What
they're saying in effect is that a minister can't be an individual.
He must always be the figurehead of his church. It's one of the
many things wrong with the organized church as far as I'm concerned. I insist on the right to be an individual. And that's why

I'm fed up with the church—not with God, or my idea of God —but just the plain blasted *church!*"

The door trip bell clanged downstairs, and McGuire, the mailman, shouted, "Mail for the pacifist!"

"Comedian!" Kathy yelled back at him. "Why don't you trade uniforms, you brave little turtle?"

A shouting grew outside, and she went to a window. At the same time the phone rang.

"Mr. Murchison, this is Ray Paulson. . . ." He was chairman of the Long Island pulpit committee. "Under the circumstances. . . ."

"But I was acting as an individual, Mr. Paulson."

"We knew you were a social activist. . . . We're for that, we like it, but. . . . Under the circumstances. . . ."

When he hung up he realized that Kathy had come close and was staring at him gravely. "They turned you down?"

"Yes."

Tears formed in her eyes but did not spill.

"Oh, Kathy, don't." He drew his arms around her.

"I'm not crying," she said. "I'd just hoped that things on Long Island would be . . . different. The crazy thing is I *like* being a minister's wife."

"You want me to try for another church?"

"No. You said a true thing about the ministry. About the importance of being an individual—not a figurehead. That's what is important for us. We have each other and Stevie."

She looked up at him. Her lovely face, so close to his, suddenly made his thoughts and emotions whirl about. He kissed her. She opened her lips to his, her eyes almost closed, and tightened her arms about him. In this crazy noon of shouting pickets and one career fractured while another was yet to be found, they wanted each other. Incredible though it seemed at this particular moment, they must have each other in willful demonstration of their abiding love and passion. No matter what else happened, they—

She released him, breathing quickly, while his arms and lips continued to insist why not in this crazy noon? And then he understood. The telephone was ringing.

"Answer it."

He did.

"Joel Steinberg, Mr. Murchison." At that particular moment the name meant nothing to him. "Of HEART. You remember. . . ."

How could he forget?

Steinberg said, "I wonder if you have any spare time today to drop around to the office. I want to make you an offer."

Dave made an incoherent sound. "Mr. Steinberg, have you read the *Times* this morning?"

"Of course." Steinberg's tone conveyed a smile. "That's why I'm calling you. We liked you—your qualifications. But I wondered—frankly I wondered what your fighting spirit might be since you've been a clergyman for some time. We've had a little difficulty—I mean, well, a lack of guts—with a clergyman who came to work for us. But what happened yesterday convinces me you don't have the same problem. When can you drop around?"

"Right now!" Dave cried.

Kathy watched him go from a window. Several of the pickets acted embarrassed at sight of him. And their discomfiture was not helped by his gay and friendly manner. "Hey there, Walter! . . . Mrs. Aiello, how's Robin? . . ." He passed through their line and hurried toward the subway.

Though Kathy knew she should at least wash the breakfast dishes, she could not bring herself to do anything but prowl restlessly about the apartment and wonder what Dave would learn at HEART.

The next time she went to a window she was astonished to see Abe approaching the pickets. He began to grin, and his face lighted up as he read the signs. She knew his instinct as surely as she always had known when he was headed for devilment as a child. He was going to join the pickets.

Leaning out, she called, "Abe, don't you dare!"

He looked up at her and laughed, then came inside and hurried up the stairs. "And I always thought the ministry was dull!" he cried. "Where's old Dave?"

"Out looking for a job. What are you doing in New York? You're supposed to be—"

"Yeah, but I'm not. Kathy, I dropped by to say good-bye. I joined the Marines yesterday."

Tears, ever close today, suddenly ran down her cheeks.

Abe looked away, so stricken that he might be about to cry himself. "Kathy, *say* something!"

But what? At last she said, "Have you told Father?"

"Yes. He didn't raise hell with me. He took it—the way he takes everything. He asked me to lunch, but I said no. It would be too . . . emotional."

"Abe, why did you do it?"

He told her what he had told Martin.

"I guess I understand, Abe. Anyway, I'll try to. But you should have had lunch with him. Couldn't you spare him more time on this last day?"

"I *want* to. Honest I do, Kathy. But then I get the jimjams when I think back to—well—"

Kathy turned to the phone and dialed the church office number. On that day of surprises none caused her more wonder than Martha's answering the phone.

"I tried to follow your advice," Martha told her. "But I just can't go on in this childish way after he's been so kind. I came in to put everything in order."

"You'll go to Vermont with us?"

"Yes, if you still want me along." Martha said she would tell Martin to phone the moment he came in.

Abe, playing patty-cake on the floor with Stevie, asked why she had called him.

"To ask him over for lunch before you leave."

"Please, Kathy, no last supper. I mean it. It's too . . . sad."

Aware that the noise outside had subsided, she went to a window and saw the pickets departing. O'Hare was across the street, talking persuasively to a few youths who lingered. Glancing up the street, she saw Father striding along.

When he came in, Stevie yelled delightedly at the sight of him while Abe looked around and said, "Hi, Pop. Stevie's getting good at patty-cake. Remember that Indian patty-cake we used to do?"

They rehearsed it slowly at first, then worked into fast time while Stevie yelled and laughed and tried to butt into the game. After a while Abe rose suddenly, his face contorted to hold back tears. "I got to head downtown. Kathy——" He encompassed her in a strong hug and kissed her wetly on a cheek. "Tell Dave to keep the old picket arm in shape." He kissed Steve. "Pop" —Abe hugged him hard and mussed his hair—"take it easy. See all of you on furlough." And then he was gone, rushing down the stairs two at a time.

Martin watched him out of sight. He kept his back turned for some time, and when he looked around, his eyes were damp.

"What a day!" He told her he had visited Tubby, who was critically ill and would have to resign, then had come directly here in the hope of seeing Abe again. "Bad news everywhere. How's Dave?"

Kathy sank into a chair. "Father, I'm afraid you'll find the news bad with Dave, too." She told him of the reactions at Beacon and the Long Island church. "He's gone to see about a job at HEART, a social agency."

"Yes." Martin sat motionlessly, his head lowered, his hands limp. "Yes, I know the organization. It's supposed to be a good one."

Suddenly he looked so tired, so defeated to Kathy that she swung to her feet distractedly. "Coffee." Her voice was unsteady. "I'm going to make coffee. And tuna sandwiches, I guess."

"Kathy." He did not raise his head. "How do you feel about this?"

"I'm sorry things have turned out as they have. But I think he's made the right decision. And I'm all with him."

As she started to make coffee, Dave pounded up the stairs chanting an old song. "You've got to have *heart*—" At sight of Martin his song died. But then he smiled and said, "Let us publish glad tidings."

"What?" Kathy asked. "Tell us."

"On August first we move to Rochester, a city that denies having slums or any social problems. And we're going to scrap with all sorts of people and tear down buildings and move the social landscape around."

"Wonderful!" Kathy said.

"Congratulations, Dave," Martin said, "I mean it if you're sure it's what you want."

"It is what I want," Dave said. "It isn't a wish that happened just this morning. It's been with me for a long time. And while I'm not switching just for money, it will be nice to be making twelve thousand to start. I have neither the desire nor the qualifications to be a good minister. I still believe what I have for many years. But I no longer believe in the church as the means of putting my beliefs into action."

Kathy said, "Father, isn't that just about why you left the church once yourself?"

"Yes. But after I quit an active pastorate, I found myself missing something. It took me awhile to figure out what it was. But finally I did. To me, trying to do social good outside the framework of religious faith is like trying to fly an airplane without an engine. All you can do is glide and hope for a safe landing."

"But look, Martin," Dave said, "I'm taking my beliefs to Rochester with me. I know no greater example in all history than Jesus of Nazareth. He knew what was wrong with the world, and he had a program for trying to set it right. He didn't work within the framework of the organized church of his day. He worked outside it."

"I understand what you mean. But I don't think you understand what I mean. I suppose it's purely subjective. Maybe it has something to do with our ages or changing times. Maybe I— people of my generation and older—are more submissive than your generation. But personally I have a real need for the organization of the church to support what I believe in. And that's taking into account its many glaring flaws and faults. In learning to live with its imperfections, I've learned to live with my own. Well, I didn't mean to carry on so."

"You haven't," Dave said. "I understand better than you realize."

As they started to eat lunch, Father asked if Martha still planned to go to Vermont with them on Monday.

"Yes," Kathy said. "I talked with her awhile ago."

"Talked with her?" He looked perplexed. "Where is she?"

"At the office. She wants to leave everything straight before she goes."

Martha was in the office when Martin returned. He had been eager to see her, but the moment he did, he came under a pall of restraint. How had she fared in her interview? Was she actually going to leave Old Fourth? He could not bring himself to ask her because the questions would be personal, whereas he felt it necessary to be impersonal. For the same reason he would not mention his thoughts about Abe, Dave, the Cathedral.

Her manner was formal when she came into his study about five o'clock and put his schedule for the coming week on his desk. "I almost forgot," she said, "Mrs. Pomfret wants you to call her about going to dinner Tuesday evening."

"I have another engagement."

She looked at him.

"I mean I'll fake an engagement. As a matter of fact, I'm not sure I'll be in town next week. I've been thinking of asking John to take things over." Yet had he thought of it until this very moment? With subdued astonishment, he heard himself going on: "Abe has joined the Marines. Dave is quitting the ministry. I have to decide whether I want to make a try for another pastorate. Too many things on my mind. Joe has been after me to get away with him for a little vacation." Now that, he thought, was the biggest lie he remembered telling in years. But still he went on: "We may go up to his house and fish and loaf next week."

Her surprise showed.

"Kathy tells me you're going to the summer place with them for vacation. That's grand. Think you'll enjoy it. So I may see you up there. Joe's house is just down the road." He held out his hand and knew that his smile was strained. "Have a good time, Martha."

"Thanks." Somehow his strained smile had made its way into her expression as she turned and left quickly.

At half past six he was tilted back in his swivel chair, heels on his desk, smoking a stale cigar which he had found in a drawer. It tasted foul and smelled worse, but he smoked on grimly. Ted Foster, the organist, had arrived early for choir rehearsal and, though he sometimes warmed up with "Tea for Two" or "March on the River Kwai," he now was sending the tones of "Adeste Fideles" reverberating through the church.

When Mrs. Bentley phoned and asked plaintively when he would be home for dinner, he told her, "Put it in the oven. Go to the movies."

No matter how many times he chased his dilemma around the bramble bush, he could not come to grips with it. If he asked Martha to marry him, he believed she might say yes. But if he did not ask her, would it now be because he feared he might hurt his chances of becoming minister of the Cathedral? "Christian, be prudent," advised an old hymn. Prudent about his own career, of course. Socially enlightened though most members of the Cathedral were, some would be displeased by a minister who married his secretary, twenty years younger and a divorcée. Such was an unpleasant aspect of almost every church—and all suspicious human nature. Yet was it any more unpleasant than his own self-seeking prudence?

Lowering his feet to the floor, he phoned Joe. "Do you feel like coming over and eating what's warm in the oven?"

"What *is* in the oven, Martin?"

"I don't know."

"Better not take a chance," Joe said. "Come on to my place. Ring for room service here, and they'll bring you any damn thing *they* feel like."

Martin took a taxi to the apartment hotel where Joe had lived for almost a year. He accepted his offer of a scotch before they risked room service and then told him about Abe and Dave. He did not mention his visit with Tubby, and he did not intend to mention Martha. But after a while he no longer could contain his thoughts about her.

"I told a whopping lie to Martha this afternoon. I said you have been after me to get away for a little vacation. I told her we may go up to your house and fish and loaf next week."

"That sounds like a swell idea to me. But why did you say it?"

"She is going on vacation with Kathy and Dave to my place."

"Oh?" Joe stared at him. "Oh! I've wondered about that for some time. Nothing under the table. I don't mean that. You haven't showed it, but I wondered." He poured himself another scotch. "Martin, what do you think you can say to her in Vermont that you can't say here in New York?"

"Nothing. I want time to think. I don't want to go to my house if she's there. I even kidded myself for a while that I was glad she was going away for a couple of weeks. And now I have to admit that I like the idea of being near her. . . ."

On Monday afternoon they took the downhill curve into Alden. Through the maples Martin glimpsed a dark bulk on the village commons and finally saw a huge canvas tent with a couple of trucks and a trailer parked near it.

"Carnival," Joe said.

"Revival," Martin said. "Look there."

A large poster sign bore the words "I Am the Light of the World." A matching sign proclaimed REVEREND T. T. BONHAM CONDUCTS NIGHTLY SERVICES 8 P.M.

"There hasn't been an evangelist through here in years."

"No sin in Alden," Joe said.

"Plenty of sin. Just not enough people, I thought, to make it worth an evangelist's effort. How did he get so far off the beaten track? Bonham. That name is familiar, but I can't remember—"

Suddenly it came to him. T. T. Bonham and he had carried on that long and wasteful correspondence years ago when he was with the Honeywell. So Bonham finally had come to New England. If not to the main currents of the industrial cities, then to the backwaters. But how had he managed it, and why had he bothered? With a bit of wonder and more amusement Martin thought, *Is T. T. Bonham following me?*

He told Joe about Bonham as they took the road out of town. "Think I'll go down to hear him some evening and learn what he has to say."

The countryside absorbed Martin after they left Alden. A pestilence of caterpillars had begun; he must call George Bunker to spray the red oak he favored in a corner of his yard. The caterpillars, favoring red oaks, too, could strip a tree within a few days. Soon the caterpillars would disappear, and in a few weeks there would be a hatch of moths to plague the window screens at night and cream the lake and dark pools of the streams. The little trout would fatten on the drowned moths, and the otters fatten on the trout. Meanwhile, the warblers, which fancied red oaks for some grubby reason, would begin to drift away once their favorite trees were denuded; thus, before long, the country would be poorer for the lack of their song. But some other interesting species would drift in. Now, riding along the lake road with Joe, he glimpsed the flash of a scarlet tanager. Maybe tanagers were the answer to warblers; until this moment he had not seen one in well over a year.

"There they are," Joe said.

Martin saw them—Kathy, Martha, Dave, and Stevie—distant figures paddling and playing in the waters off the little pebble beach.

By three o'clock he and Joe were out on the lake in separate rowboats. Dave, seeing them from the distant shore, whistled and waved. They waved in reply but did not row over to the beach since they were launched on a hunt for pickerel and largemouth bass.

They rowed north toward the deepest waters. Though the day was warm, there was a layer of moisture in the air that promised changing weather, possibly thunderstorms, by evening. Martin, who had borrowed tackle from Joe, finally shipped his oars, selected a plug, and fell into the pleasing, leisurely rhythm—casting the plug far out, letting it plop into the water, then reeling it in slowly. He made a dozen casts before he felt a twitch. It didn't feel like much, and it wasn't. He hauled in a small bluegill, unhooked it, and tossed it back.

His luck did not improve as the afternoon progressed, and about five o'clock he began rowing back. Joe, following him, signaled that he was emptyhanded, too. Martin did not care about the failure of a catch; what mattered was that he felt relaxed, transported far from the harassments of recent days. As he rowed, he decided to go to the village and hear T. T. Bonham this evening.

He showered and changed into a suit before Nancy Whitcomb served them a hearty dinner. Joe, not wanting to hear T. T. Bonham admonish on the wages of sin, said he would view the situation from the vantage of the television Western, where virtue was bound to conquer sin without so much Bonham bother.

About half past seven Martin drove off in Joe's car. Nearing his own place and seeing Martha, Kathy, and Dave on the porch in the clouding evening light, he turned into the drive. As he walked to the porch, he realized that the restraint he had felt with Martha in New York had evaporated—and as soon as they exchanged greetings, he knew that her sense of restraint had gone, too. Presumably his instinct had been right: A change of scene could bring a change of emotional climate. Yet he was not sure precisely how it had changed. Were they destined to be only good friends—or something more abiding?

On his own front porch he felt like a neighbor who had dropped in from down the road. They talked about neigh-

borly matters such as the plague of caterpillars, the chunks
of chestnut wood which needed sawing, Stevie's surfeit of sunlight and water that had put him to sleep by six o'clock. Then
Martin told them about his experience with Bonham at the
Honeywell Foundation and said he was going to the revival
in Alden.

"I've never been to a revival," Dave said. "I'll go with you.
Kath, if you want to go, too, we can carry Steve. He'll sleep
through anything."

Kathy decided to stay home with Stevie. But Martha, who
never had attended a revival either, said she would go with
them.

The large number of cars parked around the commons surprised Martin, and his surprise grew at sight of a crowd of three
hundred to four hundred people seated on benches under the
big tent suspended from a single large center pole. The flaps
were raised, the interior lighted by arc lamps. On a platform
forward two young men were playing electrical guitars and
singing old hymns set to country music. "Pull, sailor, pull,
sailor, pull for the shore. . . . Brighten the corner where you
are. . . . When the roll is called up yonder, I'll be there. . . ."
The musical marriage of Nashville's Grand Old Opry to Billy
Sunday hymns was redolent of times past more cherished than
this present humid night.

Seated on a bench between Dave and Martha, Martin
glanced around. He could not categorize the audience, which
included persons of all ages from farm and town, as well as
summer residents. Their mood, Martin sensed, was more of
curiosity than piety.

The musical theme became more somber. "This is my Sa-
viour" intoned the guitars and the singers as a tall, spare man
with a great shock of white hair stepped onto the platform. He
wore a white shirt, black trousers and tie; the eyes in the long
face beneath the white hair looked black, too. John Brown, as
Martin imagined the old abolitionist had looked. T. T. Bonham himself.

He took the microphone from the young men, and his voice rose in song more strongly and hauntingly sweeter than theirs. Then, suddenly, the music stopped.

"Who am I?" His voice was like a call from the head of some Southern cove echoing across a hollow. "I am T. T. Bonham. And who are you?" He gestured to the audience, and a few answered with their names. "What say?" He cupped an ear and smiled. "I said I'm T. T. Bonham. Who are you?" More voices answered this time. Who? . . . I . . . You . . . The replies of the audience grew thunderous.

"Who? . . ."

And Martin thought, *Who am I to remain aloofly silent to this altogether sincere man?*

"Who?"

"Martin Judson!"

Martha, shouting her own name at the same time, cast him a gamin grin while Dave looked vaguely uneasy.

"Well, now we know each other." Bonham did a kind of quick two-step about the platform. "I said that I am T. T. Bonham of Ardsley, Tennessee, pastor of the Only True Evangelical Church of God, which now counts members among you after yesterday's opening service. We have had the call from the great Luke: 'Go thou and publish abroad the kingdom of God.'" He looked aloft, apparently his manner of praying. "We got the message, good friend Luke. We have come with glad tidings to New England. . . ."

Bonham went quickly to the Book of Revelation, quoting at length without reading from the Bible—the third angel, in the fourteenth chapter, as Martin recalled—"He also shall drink of the wine of the wrath of God, which is prepared unmixed in the cup of his anger. . . ."

Martin only half listened. Predictably Bonham was summoning his wrathful God. He had heard all this before. It was not his way of approaching God or a way he would recommend to others. Yet it was Bonham's sincere way and therefore worthy of the attention of any who could follow him. Martin tried to concentrate on what Bonham was saying, but his attention kept wandering. Martha, he saw, was listening intently. He was sure he knew her thoughts: It did not matter how you approached God as long as you had an abiding faith that could see you through the joys and sorrows of the present life. Then, glancing at Dave, he observed that his attention was wandering like his own: He was looking out toward pale and distant flashes of lightning which limned the edge of darkness. There came a faint rumble of thunder, and cool air wafted through the tent.

Bonham did not let such celestial attention go unnoticed. "Yes, my good friends, He hears us and answers. As we are told in Zechariah, almost at the very end of the Old Testament, 'And Jehovah shall be seen over them. And His arrow shall go forth as the lightning. And the Lord Jehovah will blow the trumpet, and go with whirlwinds of the south. . . .'" The thunderstorm was, indeed, coming from the south.

But Bonham had a theme, a topic. "The Mean Spirit." Text: Proverbs 22-29. "Seest thou a man diligent in his business? He shall stand before kings. He shall not stand before mean men."

Naturally he flattered his audience by saying he stood now before kings. But, oh, friends, it was not always so. . . . Martin's attention wandered once more to the rising wind, the approaching storm. How many did Bonham hold raptly, and how many were thinking about their open car windows? Then Martin caught something that turned his attention to Bonham quickly.

"A story I have told in all parts of your Yankeeland. Wherever I go, from Maine to Connecticut, I repeat it. I say I was delayed many years in bringing the word of God to you in New England. Why? Because of a man of mean spirit. He was not a Yankee. He was not a Southerner. He was from New York, the Sodom of America. He was supposedly a *Christian,* a man in charge of large funds which were supposed to go to *Christian* purposes. And how did he reply to my request for a little help to bring you the *true* word of God? He refused. . . ."

Both Dave and Martha were looking at Martin in consternation. Yet their amazement could not be as great as his own. His neck had grown chill, not from the rising wind sweeping through the tent, but at the concatenation that had brought Bonham and him together. Why should unfamiliar superstitions suddenly be roused in him? He was here under this big top of his own free will and by the merest chance.

"He was a man of mean spirit," Bonham went on. "All of us who wish to stand before kings have stood before his kind. We know the great anger that sweeps through us at being treated so. . . ."

Yet certainly no greater than the anger sweeping through Martin now.

"I remember that mean man's name. I'll never forget it. I don't know where he is now. I've often wanted to meet him face to face. . . ."

Dave said, "Are you going to let him get away with it?"

Martin was speechless.

Bonham continued, "But if I met him, I would do what I did then. Friends, I *forgave* his meanness of spirit. I *prayed* for him in the hope he someday would acquire the spirit of a king. That is what all of us must do. . . ."

"Are you going to let him get away with it?" Dave repeated.

"Yes."

"Why?"

Now that his anger was under control, it began to dissipate. "Because, Dave, I could break up his service with a public argument. I'm in my own country, and he is not in his. He doesn't have many of these people with him, but he's trying hard. I could laugh him out of town. But why? His message is true and good. I agree with him about meanness—and so do you."

"Then let's get out of here."

"No, I want to speak to him afterward—privately, so that no harm is done to his effort. Maybe each of us can learn something from the other."

"Praise God, I say," Bonham cried. "Praise God. . . ."

Soon there was a crash of thunder, a flash of lightning. A

strong wind tugged at the tent flaps as rain lashed the canvas.

Bonham's expression was ecstatic at the display of celestial allies. "See!" he shouted. "It's like I told you from Revelation. Look out there and see it is just as told in Isaiah. 'And we, how shall we escape? The burden of the wilderness of the sea. As whirlwinds in the south sweep through, it cometh from the wilderness, from a terrible land. . . .' "

"Praise God!" a woman cried hysterically.

Others were shouting incoherently, panicked by the gale of wind, Martin thought, rather than moved by Bonham's fervor. A woman in front of him shrieked and pointed up. In a sudden updraft of wind the canvas top was swelling, the big center pole beginning to bend. There was an explosive crack, like a rifleshot, and Martin glimpsed Bonham's look of complete horror before the tent was plunged into darkness. In the shrieking pandemonium he grasped Martha's arm in one hand and Dave's in the other, shouting at them to sit still. Something crashed close behind them, and he felt that he was smothering.

Joe arrived about eleven o'clock that evening, driving Jim Whitcomb's old car and bringing Nancy along to stay with Stevie.

"The revival tent collapsed in that windstorm," he told Kathy. "Your father called from the hospital in Newcomb. Guess everybody was a bit shaken up. Let's go over there."

Joe spoke so calmly that Kathy kept her alarm under control.

When they reached the small hospital in Newcomb, however, she knew that something was seriously wrong. The lobby was crowded with babbling people. In a corner a man who looked like an Old Testament prophet was braying words to which no one listened. That must be Bonham, the evangelist. Where was Dave? Where were Father and Martha?

Panic grew in Kathy while Joe talked with the desk clerk. Someone said four people had been injured, only one seriously;

the others had been released from the hospital. Then Father, looking pale, appeared and said, "Come in, Kathy." He led the way to an inner room, where Martha sat, her head bowed. When she looked up, Kathy saw that she had been weeping.

"What is it?" she cried. "Where is he?"

"In surgery." Father spoke measuredly. "He's unconscious. They're trying to . . . assess the extent of injury. A piece of the tent pole—or something—struck him on the back of the head."

Tears sprang to Kathy's eyes, and her voice rose hysterically. "Why did he ever go at all? There was no need for it! Why? . . ."

Father looked at her sadly until she brought her emotion under control. "I'm sorry, Father. What can we do? Can't we get him to some better place than this little hospital?"

"No, he can't be moved. We can only . . . wait and learn what the two doctors here say."

Closing her eyes, she prayed for control and acceptance. *Thy will be done. But, oh, please. . . .* When she opened her eyes, she saw Father's head bowed. Then he looked up at her, and she knew that he had been praying, too, though not as selfishly as she.

She said, "I wonder why for such a long time I wanted to be a minister's wife. I only want to be Dave's wife. I thought I had some special strength. But I don't. Father, I'm so scared."

"I'm scared, too, Kathy. Ministers and their wives don't have some special strength that others lack. Maybe they're just a bit more familiar than many others with where to try to find that strength."

Joe came in, and behind him strode the old evangelist, his dark eyes half closed in an expression of anguish.

"I'm the Reverend Bonham. Is this the family? I want to tell you how deeply sorry I am. That tent pole has stood up under— They tell me the young man's name is David Murchison, that his condition is critical. Friends, we know these things are a matter of God's will. Let us pray for strength to accept—"

"Mr. Bonham." Father rose quickly. "We are praying. I must

ask you to wait outside for a while. I'll speak to you in a few minutes."

Joe turned Bonham firmly by an arm and led him away.

"Thanks," Kathy said. "I couldn't stand his sanctimony right now. I wanted to scream at him to get out of here."

"He sincerely means it," Father said.

"I suppose so, but— Oh, Father, I know you're disappointed in Dave for quitting the ministry, but—"

"No, I'm not, Kathy. After our talk at your place on Friday, I saw he's making the right decision. The main thing is that you're with him. You just said it. You want to be Dave's wife— not a minister's wife. So let's believe that you're going to be his wife for a very long time to come. Let's have faith he'll recover. Let's opt for life."

Opt for life! The thought brought strength to Kathy as praying for acceptance of God's will had not.

"Mr. Bonham." Martin followed him out to the hospital porch where he smelled sweet fern and heard cicadas shrilling in the night.

Bonham faced him.

"I'm David Murchison's father-in-law. My name is Martin Judson."

A sighing sound escaped Bonham, and he took a step backward. His voice sounded hoarse when he finally spoke haltingly. "I wish you were anybody else, Mr. Judson. I'm not a vengeful man. I don't feel as deeply about that matter as I sounded in the pulpit. It's just a way I have to . . . make people listen. I don't think God seeks vengeance for *me* because of what *you* did."

"Neither do I," Martin said.

"Do you believe in God at all, Mr. Judson?"

"Of course."

"Who are you? What are you now?"

"A clergyman."

Bonham took a step to the left, then two to the right, as if dodging arrows. He said, "Let us pray together before we talk."

Martin closed his eyes but did not listen to Bonham. He was praying himself.

Bonham shook hands before Martin returned to the inner room.

The senior physician, a man named Craig, had just appeared. His expression was grave, his speech deliberate. David had a fracture of the skull and still was unconscious. But he could not yet determine the extent of trauma. "I know this is of little satisfaction to you people. I can understand if you wonder just how . . . capable we are here in a case like this. If you would like the consultation of a specialist, a neurosurgeon, there's a man in Boston I would recommend. He's expensive, but—"

"Call him," Martin said.

Joe said, "Have him charter a plane to Rutland. I'll meet him there. All expenses will be taken care of. . . ."

The neurosurgeon, Dr. Krauss, arrived from Boston in mid-morning and said he would talk with them at two o'clock that afternoon. Joe had found rooms in a motel nearby, but all of them only dozed fitfully, and from noon on they waited tensely at the hospital.

Krauss, who was about Martin's age, did not try to impress them with kindliness or knowledge. His manner was factual. He cited some medical terms, then, recalling that such phraseology was incomprehensible to them, said, "He has increasing periods of consciousness. That is good. He has speech, sight, hearing, neuro and muscular capacity. And that is wonderful."

Kathy sprang to her feet. "May I see him?"

"In a moment, Mrs. Murchison. For just a little while on this first visit. You're fortunate in having a husband with— well, I call it great life-force. Not just a strong body, mind you. A great life-force is something different. I'll go with you. I'd like you to test his memory. In moments of semiconsciousness he seems to have a vivid memory of Rochester. Something about his work on a clearance project of some sort there."

"Rochester!" Kathy exclaimed. "We haven't even been there yet. I mean that's where we're *going*, not where we've been."

"I see." Krauss smiled. "That's what I mean about his great life-force."

Martin recalled an admonishment from Shakespeare: "Delays have dangerous ends." Nevertheless, he kept finding reasons for delaying his return to New York—and delaying, too, asking Martha to marry him.

He did not want to leave Vermont until Dave had been released from the hospital. Then, one week after the accident, when they brought Dave to Joe's place to complete his recuperation, Martin found other excuses for lingering.

On Tuesday Joe decided after a telephone conversation with his office that he must fly to the West Coast at once. He asked Martin to take him to the Rutland airport and to drive his car back to New York when he was ready to leave.

As he was about to board the small transport, he said, "Martin, don't rush home. Old Fourth has been there a long time. And it'll wait for you forever."

Martin found the remark unsettling as he drove back to the lake. Somehow it was like a reminder and gentle reproof that in his longing for the Cathedral he was being unfaithful to his first true love. Neither Joe nor anyone but Tubby knew of his desire for the post and the fact he had a good chance of obtaining it. There should be someone with whom he could discuss the matter.

When he reached Joe's place, Dave and Kathy were sitting on beach chairs on the dock while Martha played with Stevie in the shallows. Martin sprawled in a chair next to Dave, and after a while he said, "Thinking of you both moving to Rochester makes me wonder whether it's not time I made a move, too."

Dave looked at him oddly. "That's a possibility I never thought of, Martin. It would seem strange to know you were not at Old Fourth, as if the sun failed to rise in the east some morning."

So what was the good of discussion? Who could possibly advise him?

Late that afternoon Tubby phoned. He inquired first about Dave, for he had learned of the accident from John Bell.

"He's fine," Martin said. "We brought him from the hospital yesterday. How about yourself? How are you feeling?"

"Not so hot, Marty." Tubby could not overcome his tone of depression. "The doctor put it to me this morning. I have to resign next Sunday."

"Oh, Tubby!" There was only feeling, no possible words.

Tubby continued slowly, "I've mentioned your name to a couple of people here—important people. They're enthusiastic about you, even though you have a New York church." He hesitated. "Marty, I don't mean to pry, but I think you understand. Have you asked Martha?"

Martin was silent as he stared out a window at Martha and Kathy starting a fire in the outdoor grill. At last he said, "No. No, I haven't, Tubby."

"Well"—he sounded relieved—"I'm meeting with the board Friday evening. I'm going to present your name. . . ."

The next morning Martin asked Martha if she would like to try plug fishing. She never had fished, but she was glad to go with him.

Martha caught the knack at once, casting with extraordinary grace from the stern. Her excitement and delight when she hooked a small pickerel infected him. As time passed, she caught two more. Though he caught nothing, he thought it the best fishing he had enjoyed in years. Or did he mean it was the most enjoyable companionship since—when?

Astonished to find it was after noon and they had been out nearly four hours, he pointed the boat back. As he rowed and gazed at her, he wished they could stay together on the lake for the rest of the day.

"We must do this often," he told her. "You're natural at it. There's good fishing here all summer long."

"But my vacation is nearly over," she said.

"Well—you can always get time off, Martha." He rested on his oars. "And there's next summer." He spoke measuredly. "How would you feel about quitting work by next summer? Our coming here together. I mean, marrying me in the spring?"

She looked away, her eyelids narrowed against the sun glare. At last she spoke measuredly, too. "That's a year off, Martin. And a year is a long time. Too many things happen in the course of it. . . ."

For the rest of the afternoon he felt dazed, confused. What an egotistical ass he was! Subconsciously he had convinced himself that she would marry him whenever he pleased. And now she had told him plainly she would not wait. Momentarily he thought of telling her about his problem over the Cathedral. But she would not understand— no woman would. Perhaps it would be incomprehensible to anyone who loved life deeply.

His perplexity and confusion continued into Thursday. He tried to devote all his attention to Dave, Kathy, and Stevie but found himself gazing constantly at Martha. After all, Dave and Kathy did not need him here. At Joe's insistence they would spend the rest of their vacation at his house, which was more commodious than Martin's. No, they did not need him at all. Then who did?

That Thursday evening he announced he was driving back to New York the next morning. To his surprise he added, "Would you like to come with me, Martha?"

And to his greater surprise she said, "Yes, I'd like to. . . ."

They left early in the morning.

"There's only one route from New York to Vermont," he told her as they passed through Alden. "That's the shortest one. But there are all sorts of ways of going from Vermont to New York. Old—new. Long—short. My idea is to avoid the turnpikes and take the long way."

Their passage south was like a passage backward in time to him.

Rutland. "My father had a church here when I was just a few

years old. I'd forgotten something Mother told me once. When he was here, he had a nibble at a much bigger church in Buffalo but decided to stay in New England. And after a while the churches got smaller."

"Did it really matter?" Martha asked. "I mean about the size of the churches."

"Maybe not. But there's the sense of attainment. It *is* a profession, you know, besides being other things."

Bennington. "One time years ago Kathy got dreadfully carsick here. She couldn't go on, so we stayed at one of those old-fashioned tourist's homes. And I discovered I'd neglected to cash a check before leaving Upton. Fortunately, Jane had some money."

Williamstown. "Williams was my first college choice. But the biggest scholarship money was at Brown. Wonder if my life would have been different if I'd gone to Williams."

They went down the long valleys where the land planed out slowly. Shortly after noon they stopped at an inn in northern Connecticut for lunch.

Martha said, "I'd enjoy a whiskey sour."

"So would I."

While they sipped their drinks, they contemplated an old engraving depicting a busy nineteenth-century inn.

"I like it," Martha said. "Maybe an art critic would say there's too much going on—too busy, busy. But just look at the vitality and life."

Martin, who had had similar thoughts while looking at the engraving, felt the vague surprise of one accustomed to hearing another viewpoint.

Showers came and went in the afternoon. Dark clouds seemed to tilt and the rain blow sideways as they came down the West Side Highway into Manhattan. On their right the Hudson was a smear of angry gray. Then, suddenly, sunlight shafted through the cloud rack, lighting the great tower of the Cathedral ahead and to their left.

There was a turnout for motorists in trouble. Martin swung the car into it and stopped.

"What's wrong?" Martha asked.

He did not say anything. He was looking at the Cathedral tower, which was disappearing rapidly in another rainsquall. Jane and he used to say it rained every time they moved themselves and their belongings from one place to another.

"Nothing's wrong," he said at last. "Say—if you'd marry me *this* summer, we could go back to Vermont *this* summer."

Though the phrasing sounded idiotic, she must have understood what he meant. For in a moment she said, "Martin, go easy. They might not like that at Old Fourth. You've reached the . . . fruition of a wonderful career there. You've . . . created something lasting and fine. I won't do anything to spoil it."

"You can't," he said. "All of us there are friends. We're . . . accepted. It will be fine. I asked you a question, Martha. You haven't answered it."

"Yes," she said.

He stretched his right arm toward her awkwardly, but then a police car drew abreast of them, and a policeman called, "You in trouble, Mac?"

Mac!

"Not that I know of," Martin replied to him. "How do I get to the Cathedral up there?"

"Next turnoff."

The police car moved on, and Martha asked, "Why are you going there?"

"I'm not," Martin said. "I just want us to stop by for a moment and tell the good news to Tubby."